BRITISH CIVIL AIRCRAFT
SINCE 1919

The Tiger Club's Sea Tiger, G-AIVW, in idyllic surroundings at Fritton Decoy, Suffolk, in the summer of 1971. (*A. J. Jackson*)

BRITISH
CIVIL AIRCRAFT

SINCE 1919
VOLUME TWO

A. J. JACKSON

PUTNAM
LONDON

© 1960 A. J. Jackson
New material © 1973 A. J. Jackson
ISBN 0 370 10010 7
Filmset in Photon Times 11 pt. by
Richard Clay (The Chaucer Press), Ltd.,
Bungay, Suffolk
and printed in Great Britain by
Fletcher & Son, Ltd., Norwich
for
Putnam & Company Limited
9 Bow Street, London WC2E 7AL
First Published 1960
Second Edition 1973

Contents

Foreword	7
Chrislea	9, 289 and 385
Cierva	13, 290 and 386
Civilian	27 and 391
Clarke	292
Clutton	293
C.L.W.	292
Coates	382
Comper	30, 294, 382 and 391
Consolidated	352 and 392
Convair	353
Cranwell	295
Cunliffe-Owen	297
Currie	36 and 394
Curtiss	354 and 395
C.W.	382
Darmstadt	356
Dart	297 and 395
de Bolotoff	299
de Bruyne	299
Deekay	300
de Havilland	40, 301, 323, 356, 382 and 395
Desoutter	190 and 495
Dornier	358
Douglas	359 and 497
Druine	303 and 508
Dudley Watt	305
E.A.A.	305
Edgar Percival	195 and 509
Edwards	306
English Electric	306, 325 and 510
Enstrom	363
Ercoupe	364 and 510
Evans	307
Fairchild	364 and 511
Fairchild-Hiller	366
Fairey	199, 307, 326 and 512
Fairtravel	308 and 513
Falconar	309 and 383
Fane	333
Farman	383

F.E.	333
Felixstowe	334 and 513
Fenton	383
Fiat	367
Firth	309
Fleet	367
Focke-Wulf	368
Fokker	368, 383 and 514
Ford	374 and 515
Forney	516
Foster Wikner	205 and 515
Fournier	375 and 516
Fuji	376
Gadfly	310
Gardan	377 and 516
General Aircraft	208, 310, 334 and 517
Globe	378
Glos-Air	314 and 522
Gloster	311 and 335
Gnosspelius	315
Gordon	315
Gosport	342
Gowland	316
Grahame-White	316 and 383
Granger	318
Griffiths	383
Grumman	378
Gunton	383
H2-B1	318
Hafner	319
Halton	319
Handley Page	225, 257, 320, 342, 523 and 538
Handley Page (Reading)	252 and 536
Hanriot	344
Hants and Sussex	322
Hawker	268, 322, 344 and 542
Hawker Siddeley	272, 351 and 543

Appendix A	Other British-built Civil Aircraft	289
Appendix B	Military Types used for Civil Purposes	323
Appendix C	Foreign and Commonwealth Types	352
Appendix D		382
Appendix E	Register of British Civil Aircraft	384
Appendix F	Glider Registrations	552

Foreword

This volume of *British Civil Aircraft* is uniform with the first and continues the history of all transport and light aircraft designed and built in Britain, or imported for civil use under British ownership, since the commencement of civilian flying in 1919. The alphabetical location of an abnormally high concentration of aircraft manufacturers in the A, B and C range, some of whom were among the world's most prolific constructors of civil aircraft, resulted in the termination of the first volume when only the Chilton D.W.1 had been reached. Thereafter companies' names are distributed more evenly through the alphabet so that the present volume, although equal in size, commences with the Chrislea C.H.3 Ace and describes every type right through to the Hawker Siddeley H.S.650 Argosy. In so doing it covers the entire massive output of major British companies such as Cierva, Comper, de Havilland, Desoutter, General Aircraft and Handley Page and in addition to recalling epic flights and famous pilots, also tells the story of the development of rotary winged flight and the single seat sportplane; and describes the advent of the Moth and the founding of the flying club movement; the introduction of cabin comfort; of bold structural explorations; and the building of the classic pre-1939 'giant airliners'.

The small size of Appendix D is a measure of the photographic completeness achieved and every effort has been made to reach a corresponding degree of accuracy in the specifications but the majority of early records were lost, destroyed or fell victim of enemy action, so that many old-time manufacturers lacked full documentation on their more elderly types. Data given in these volumes is therefore the result of careful study and selection since considerable disagreement exists among the various works of reference published in those days.

The author again acknowledges with gratitude the assistance received from many individuals and organisations during the compilation of this second volume. He wishes to thank in particular aviation historian C. H. Barnes; Frank Parker and F. I. V. Walker of the Popular Flying Association: the Airworthiness section of the Civil Aviation Authority; Edgar W. Percival, managing director of Percival Aircraft Ltd., for his invaluable assistance with the story of the E.P.9; the staff of *Lloyds List and Shipping Gazette*; Ann Tilbury, photographic librarian of *Flight International*; David Dorrell, editor of *Air Pictorial*; John W. R. Taylor, editor of *Janes All the World's Aircraft*; L. E. Bradford for an up-dated selection of three view drawings; and photographers Richard Riding, W. L. Lewis and P. J. Bish for their skilled printing.

John Goring has again assisted expertly with the preparation and revision of chapters on transport aircraft; David Roberts has once more double-checked and indexed all factual data; and the marathon task of typing has been completed over a period of years by my wife Marjorie.

Contributions from the personal archives of the following long-term associates has enriched the text and served as a constant check on accuracy: J. A. Bagley,

D. K. Fox and B. Martin, Air-Britain; F. G. Swanborough, editor of *Air Enthusiast*; B. N. Stainer, *Aviation Photo News*; M. J. Vines, Air Portraits; P. M. Jarrett and J. D. Gillies, Royal Aeronautical Society; B. L. King, Gatwick Aviation Society; K. M. Molson, J. R. Ellis and J. Griffin, Canadian Aviation Historical Society; John Hopton and Brian Reed, Aviation Historical Society of Australia; K. Meehan and D. P. Woodhall, Aviation Historical Society of New Zealand; P. J. Birtles, Hawker Siddeley Aviation Ltd., Hatfield; E. C. Clutton; P. R. Duffy; Maj. J. M. Ellingworth; M. D. N. Fisher; W. M. Greenwood; J. S. Havers; M. J. Hooks; Leslie Hunt; J. O. Isaacs; P. R. Keating; Hans Kofoed; T. Leigh; I. MacFarlane; J. McNulty; P. R. March; Ole G. Nordbø; A. W. J. G. Ord-Hume; Bruce Robertson; R. C. Shelley; K. E. Sissons; K. F. Smy; J. W. Underwood; Dr. J. Urmston; and John Stroud, general editor of the Putnam aeronautical series.

Thanks are also extended to Air-Britain for the use of certain material which originated in its publications; to P. W. Moss for data extracted from *Impressments Log*; and to the Photographic Departments of B.E.A.; Dornier-Werke GmbH.; Glos-Air Ltd. and Qantas Airways Ltd.

A. J. J.

Leigh-on-Sea,
August 1972

The prototype G-AKFD was typical of all production Super Ace aircraft.

Chrislea CH.3 Ace and Skyjeep

The prototype four seat Ace Series 1 G-AHLG, designed by R. C. Christophorides and built at Heston by the Chrislea Aircraft Co. Ltd., made its first flight in September 1946 piloted by R. S. Stedman. It was a high wing cabin monoplane with fabric-covered welded steel tube fuselage, fitted with a tricycle undercarriage and powered by a 125 h.p. Lycoming flat four air-cooled engine. This unusual layout excited little comment in face of the tremendous interest shown in its unique control system for although the flying controls were themselves conventional, their mode of operation was altered in an attempt to evolve a more 'natural' system. Stick and rudder bar were not fitted, all control being effected by a single wheel mounted on a column protruding from the dashboard on a universal joint. Lateral movement of the wheel operated the ailerons in the normal way, but climbing and diving were achieved by moving wheel and column up and down, rudder being applied by a sideways movement. Early flight trials proved the single rudder inadequate, and within three weeks the prototype was flying with twin units, making its first public appearance over the Business Man's Air Display at White Waltham on 28 September.

In the following year Heston closed and the firm moved to Exeter, where the Chrislea CH.3 Series 2 Super Ace G-AKFD was built, its first flight being made by R. S. Stedman in February 1948. Unlike the earlier model, the wing and tailplane were internally of metal construction, the fins and rudders were smaller and rounder and the engine was a Gipsy Major 10. The aircraft still retained the patent control and the original's characteristic foolproof stability in all three axes but following a tour of the flying clubs with handling trials by the instructors and other experienced pilots, the 'natural' control came in for a great deal of adverse criticism. The firm then bowed to the inevitable, and G-AKFD and all subsequent aircraft were sold with rudder bars fitted.

Two Super Aces G-AKUX and 'UY were exhibited at the S.B.A.C. Show at Farnborough in September 1948, after which two were sold in Southern Rhodesia

9

and gave demonstrations at Almaza, Cairo, en route. Two others were shipped to Buenos Aires on delivery to the Argentine aircraft importers Casa Iturrat, another to a private owner at Kuala Lumpur and one each to Pakistan and Switzerland.

Sales resistance to the control system and to the operating costs of an aircraft needing 145 h.p. resulted in only six being sold on the home market. Inevitably a reduction in planned production and other internal economies followed, and the managing director and chief designer, Mr. R. C. Christophorides, left the firm. G-AKUV was sent to Cambridge, where Mrs. R. Morrow-Tait and her navigator named it 'Thursday's Child' in readiness for a proposed flight round the world but following a landing accident in which the Super Ace was considerably damaged, the flight was made in a Proctor 4 G-AJMU, and its predecessor languished for three years until rebuilt and used privately by Mr. J. Chapman. Two years later it was damaged beyond repair at Thruxton and replaced by G-AKVB which met a similar end in a field at Rettenden, Essex soon after its sale to E. F. Thurston at Stapleford in May 1955. Two others had short private careers before being banished to distant places. The first, G-AKVA, was successively owned by the Suffolk Trust Co. Ltd. at Fairoaks, Autowork (Winchester) Ltd. at Eastleigh and W. A. Eley at Denham before going to the Gold Coast in 1954. Its sister aircraft, G-AKVD, fitted with enlarged fins and rudders with trim tabs, first sold to Autocars (Worcester) Ltd. for instruction at the Hereford Aviation Centre, later became the property of P. F. de Mulder at Brough before being sold in Japan in 1953.

Further concessions were made to tradition in August 1949, when a late production airframe, G-AKVS, was fitted with conventional joystick and rudder bar control, tail wheel undercarriage and a Cirrus Major 3 engine to become the prototype CH.3 Series 4 Skyjeep. Although normally a four seater with appreciably more leg room than the Super Ace, it was provided with removable top decking to the rear fuselage, enabling it to be used as a single seat freighter or to carry a stretcher case with attendant. The first flight was made by D. Lowry at Exeter on 21 November 1949, R. S. Stedman having resigned in the previous year. In the next season's King's Cup Race at Wolverhampton on 17 June 1950, with the same pilot, it lapped the course at an average speed of 119·5 m.p.h., going on to win the Goodyear Trophy at 116 m.p.h. Four other airframes were then

G-AHLG, the prototype Ace, in its original form at Heston in September 1946.
(*Aeroplane*)

The non-standard Super Ace G-AKVD was fitted with enlarged vertical tail surfaces and rudder trim tabs. (*W. K. Kilsby*)

The Skyjeep prototype at its first public appearance, the Royal Aeronautical Society's garden party at White Waltham, 14 May 1950. (*A. J. Jackson*)

completed as Skyjeeps, one each being exported to Australia and Uruguay. The former was re-engined with a 200 h.p. Gipsy Six in 1957. The prototype, G-AKVS, was exported to France in 1952, a year when the assets of the Chrislea concern were acquired by C. E. Harper Aircraft Ltd. and all partly constructed aircraft, comprising seven Super Aces and two Skyjeeps, were scrapped.

SPECIFICATION

Manufacturers: Chrislea Aircraft Ltd., Heston Airport, Hounslow, Middlesex. Transferred to Exeter Airport, Clyst Honiton, Devon, April 1947.
Power Plants: (CH.3 Series 1) One 125 h.p. Lycoming O-290-3.
               (CH.3 Series 2) One 145 h.p. de Havilland Gipsy Major 10.
               (CH.3 Series 4) One 155 h.p. Blackburn Cirrus Major 3.

	CH.3 Series 1	CH.3 Series 2	CH.3 Series 4
Span	34 ft. 0 in.	36 ft. 0 in.	36 ft. 0 in.
Length	21 ft. 0 in.	21 ft. 6 in.	22 ft. $2\frac{1}{2}$ in.
Height	7 ft. 9 in.	7 ft. $7\frac{1}{2}$ in.	7 ft. 0 in.
Wing area	167 sq. ft.	177 sq. ft.	177 sq. ft.
Tare weight	1,040 lb.	1,350 lb.	1,623 lb.
All-up weight	1,950 lb.	2,350 lb.	2,550 lb.
Cruising speed	116 m.p.h.	112 m.p.h.	113 m.p.h.
Initial climb	720 ft./min.	750 ft./min.	550 ft./min.
Range	290 miles	400 miles	500 miles

Production: (a) CH.3 Super Ace

Twenty-eight aircraft comprising (c/n 102) VP-YGI/VP-KGY; (103) VP-YGM; (128) ZK-ASI; (129) ZK-ASJ/VH-BAE; (130–131) ZK-ASK and 'SL construction abandoned; (132) VH-BRO; and the British registered machines listed in Appendix E.

(b) CH.4 Skyjeep

Five British registered aircraft listed in Appendix E.

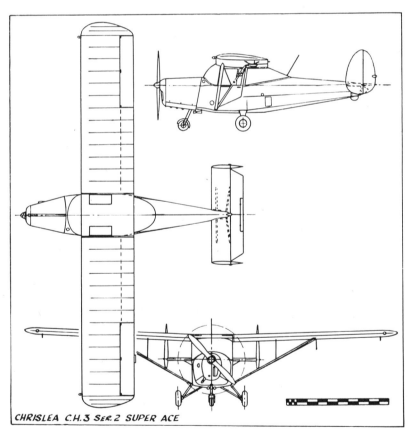

CHRISLEA C.H.3 SER.2 SUPER ACE

The Avro 587 or Cierva C.8R, flying over the C.8V at their public demonstration at Hamble in 1927. (*Topical Press*)

Cierva Autogiros C.6D to C.25

Don Juan de la Cierva, Spanish inventor of the first practical rotating wing, non-stalling aircraft, brought his C.6A machine to England in 1925 at the invitation of H. E. Wimperis, Director of Scientific Research at the Air Ministry. It was basically an Avro 504K, without mainplanes, fitted instead with a four bladed rotor, mounted on a steel tube pylon. This rotor was not engine driven, but was kept in motion purely by the forward speed of the machine, a characteristic which gave rise to the name Autogiro. The C.6A was demonstrated at Farnborough by F. T. Courtney on 10 October 1925, and its performance led the Air Ministry to order two similar machines from A. V. Roe and Co. Ltd. The second of these was the civil Avro 575 or Cierva C.6D, G-EBTW, powered by a 130 h.p. Clerget rotary. Like the earlier model it was built from Avro 504K components and its four rotor blades were hinged at the roots to allow movement in a vertical plane, orthodox aeroplane control surfaces being fitted, with the ailerons mounted on outriggers. The aircraft was historically important as the first two seat Autogiro, and its maiden flight was made by F. T. Courtney at Hamble on 29 July 1926. On the following day Cierva himself became the first passenger to fly in a rotating wing aircraft and the German expert Ernst Udet also flew in G-EBTW at Tempelhof, Berlin, on 5 September 1926.

Development was slow, minor crashes were numerous but each was painstakingly investigated, and as a result of an accident to the Air Ministry sponsored C.6C J8068, G-EBTW was rebuilt in 1927 as the C.8R with tapered rotor blades incorporating drag hinges to decrease the risk of fatigue failure at the roots. Stub wings were also fitted to partly unload the rotor in forward flight. Later in the same year the Avro 552 slave aircraft G-EAPR was converted into the Avro 586 or Cierva C.8V. It was test flown by H. J. Hinkler, who also made the world's first cross-country flight in a civil Autogiro by flying from Hamble to Croydon and back on 20 October 1927. Apart from its water-cooled 180 h.p. Wolseley Viper engine, it was identical with the C.8R. It is interesting to note that in 1930 the same aircraft was acquired by L. G. Anderson, who took it to Hanworth and reconverted it into an Avro 552, G-ABGO, for banner towing. The pylon pick-up points on the top longerons were in evidence to the end of its days.

Experimental flying with Autogiros in 1926–27 saw the beginning of a long association between the Cierva Autogiro Co. Ltd., formed on 24 March 1926 and A. V. Roe and Co. Ltd., who built the machines in their Hamble works. A further prototype, the C.8L Mk. I, was ordered by the Air Ministry later in 1927, this time based on the Lynx engined Avro 504N and fitted with a four bladed rotor having tubular steel spars, spruce ribs and fabric covering. A civil equivalent, the C.8L Mk. II G-EBYY, was also built to the order of Air Commodore J. G. Weir, chairman of the Cierva Company, without whose financial backing most of the development work would have been impossible. Hinkler flew it for the first time early in May 1928, and on the 20th it started in the King's Cup Race, flown by the newly appointed Cierva test pilot, A. H. Rawson. After a forced landing at Caldecote, near Nuneaton, through fuel shortage, he was compelled to retire from the race. A comprehensive 3,000 mile tour was made by the same pilot later in the month during which all the principal flying clubs, civil and Service aerodromes were visited. On 18 September 1928 Cierva, carrying the editor of *L'Aéronautique* as passenger, flew it from Croydon to Le Bourget, and thus G-EBYY became the first rotating wing aircraft to cross the Channel. After local demonstration, Cierva and Rawson left Le Bourget on 4 October 1928 and flew it to Berlin via Brussels, returning on 13 October, via Amsterdam. It has remained ever since in the Musée de l'Air at Chalais-Meudon near Paris, except for a brief appearance at the Brussels Aero Show in 1950.

A licence to build the Autogiro in France was obtained by Weymann-Lepère, and it is probable that the C.8L Mk. II was handed over to that concern for

The Parnall Gyroplane, powered by a 120 h.p. Airdisco engine, was the C.11 in the Cierva series. (*Royal Aeronautical Society*)

14

The cross-Channel Cierva C.8L Mk. II during its tour of the British Isles, August 1926.
(*Royal Aeronautical Society*)

The Cirrus engined C.17 Mk.I at Hamble in October 1928.

experimental use prior to the appearance of the French-built C.18. This was a large two seater powered by one 195 h.p. Salmson A.C.7 radial and a British specimen G-AAIH registered to the Cierva Company in June 1929 is believed to have been taken to the U.S.A. by Loel Guinness three months later.

The majority of early Autogiros were Avro built, including the experimental C.9 and C.12, which had wooden Avian IIIA fuselages, but George Parnall and Company were entrusted with the construction of the C.10 and C.11. The airframes were designed by Harold Bolas, and the second of these, G-EBQG, was fitted with a 120 h.p. Airdisco and registered as a Parnall Gyroplane. Cierva tested it at Yate in 1928, but it turned over on take-off and was taken by road to Hamble for reconstruction. A simple pyramid-type pylon was then fitted, with engine driven rotor starting incorporated but after tests it ended its days with Air Service Training Ltd., Hamble, as an instructional airframe. Experiments with the C.9 landplane and the C.12 on floats led to another Avian derivative, the C.17 Mk. I, G-AABP, with 90 h.p. Cirrus III, first flown by Cierva on 23 October 1928. This model was underpowered, and although one Mk. II version, G-AAGJ, with the 100 h.p. Avro Alpha radial, was completed, both C.17s followed 'QG into the A.S.T. workshops in 1931. The airframe of G-AAGJ was reconstructed as the Alpha engined Avian II G-ADEO by A.S.T. engineers in 1935.

Although originally intended as C.17 Mk. IIs, the next three airframes, G-AAGK, 'GL and 'HM, were in fact an entirely new Cierva design, the C.19 Mk. I. The short, rotund fuselage was a fabric covered welded tubular steel structure fitted with a four bladed rotor mounted on ball bearings and a wide chord fixed wing with turned-up tips. The wide track, long travel undercarriage was fitted with Bendix brakes, and the 80 h.p. Genet II engine was mounted uncowled, although G-AAHM was fitted with a totally enclosed long chord cowling for exhibition at the Olympia Aero Show of July 1929.

The rotors of all Autogiros previous to the C.19 Mk. I were started manually by hauling on a rope wound round the blade roots. G-AAHM was therefore an important exhibit at Olympia, as it was the first mark of Autogiro with automatic starting, and therefore suitable for private ownership or club use. This Autogiro was fitted with a box-like biplane tail unit with twin rudders, so that by locking both elevators and tailplanes in a near vertical position, the slipstream was deflected upwards and thus started the rotor.

Three C.19 Mk. II Autogiros with partly cowled 100 h.p. Genet Major I radials and four bladed 30 ft. rotors were then built, the first, G-AAKY, being sent to the U.S.A. At the Cleveland Air Races in August 1929 it made the first public demonstration of such an aircraft in America, and was then sold to the newly formed Pitcairn Autogiro Company at Willow Grove, Pennsylvania. G-AALA, last of the three, was the machine in which at Heston on 7 January 1930 A. H. Rawson carried Sir Sefton Brancker, who thus became the first D.C.A. to experience rotary winged flight. A modified version, the C.19 Mk. IIA G-AAUA, with long travel undercarriage, increased tankage and rotor head modifications was demonstrated at Hamble in May 1930. In the following August Cierva completed 300 hours of Continental touring in it, and made many landings in wild, windy and inaccessible spots in his native Spain.

The large Cierva C.18 G-AAIH built in France by Weymann-Lepère in 1929.

16

Cierva C.19 Mk.II G-AAKZ making its demonstration flight at Heston on 28 May 1931.
(*Aeroplane*)

SPECIFICATION

Manufacturers: A. V. Roe and Co. Ltd., Hamble, Southampton.
Power Plants: (C.8L Mk. II) One 180 h.p. Armstrong Siddeley Lynx.
  (C.17 Mk. I) One 90 h.p. A.D.C. Cirrus III.
  (C.18)   One 195 h.p. Salmson A.C.7.
  (C.19 Mk. I) One 80 h.p. Armstrong Siddeley Genet II.
  (C.19 Mk. II) One 105 h.p. Armstrong Siddeley Genet Major I.

	C.8L Mk. II	C.17 Mk. I	C.19 Mk. I	C.19 Mk. II
Rotor diameter	39 ft. 8 in.	33 ft. 3¼ in.	30 ft. 0 in.	30 ft. 0 in.
Length	36 ft. 0 in.	28 ft. 9 in.	18 ft. 0 in.	18 ft. 0 in.
Height	14 ft. 9 in.	11 ft. 1 in.	10 ft. 0 in.	10 ft. 0 in.
Tare weight	1,650 lb.	970 lb.	750 lb.	850 lb.
All-up weight	2,470 lb	1,455 lb.	1,300 lb.	1,400 lb.
Maximum speed	100 m.p.h.	90 m.p.h.	95 m.p.h.	95 m.p.h.
Cruising speed	85 m.p.h.	70 m.p.h.	80 m.p.h.	70 m.p.h.
Initial climb	500 ft./min.	500 ft./min.	500 ft./min.	500 ft./min.
Range	255 miles	210 miles	280 miles	300 miles
Rotor speed	115 r.p.m.	130 r.p.m.	—	—

As Autogiro experience increased, skilled pilots perfected a slow landing technique at a high angle of attack with tail wheel touching first. To prevent damage to the rudders, the lower edges were sloped sharply upwards in a new C.19 Mk. III version, the rotor of which was also 5 ft. greater in diameter. G-AALA was modified to this standard to be flown by R. A. C. Brie in Barnard's Flying Display in 1931, and six others, G-AAYN–'YP, G-ABCK–'CM, were also built. G-AAYO and G-ABCM were sold to the Air Council in 1930, one appearing in the comic event at the Hendon R.A.F. Display in 1932 as K1696, while G-AAYP flew the Autogiro's first race when R. A. C. Brie carried off second prize in the Skegness Air Race at 93 m.p.h. on 14 May 1932. G-ABCK was sold to the North Island Safety Flying Association in December 1930 and despatched to Wellington, New Zealand, by sea. After a crash at Oamaru in 1932, lack of spares resulted in its shipment back to Hanworth, which in that year had become the headquarters of the Cierva Company.

Slipstream deflection was not an entirely satisfactory method of rotor starting, and when the Pitcairn Autogiro Company produced a reliable clutch and engine-drive mechanism, it was incorporated in the C.19 Mk. IV of 1932. The redundant box tail was replaced by a monoplane unit and a 34 ft. cantilever three bladed rotor was fitted for the first time. The prototype Mk. IV, G-AAHM, a converted Mk. I, carried out many novel demonstrations, but was wrecked on take-off after landing in the arena at White City Stadium on 29 September 1932. Interest was such that at least 15 were built at Hamble, the production models G-ABFZ–'GB, 'UC–'UH and 'XD–'XI carrying the designation C.19 Mk. IVP. J. N. Young left Hanworth in the first of these on 25 April 1932 in an attempt to fly to the Cape, arriving in Tunis from Catania on 19 May. In the following year it returned to join G-ABGB in Sir Alan Cobham's National Aviation Day Displays, the latter also going on the South African Tour at the end of the year. G-ABXG was sold to J. A. McMullen, then aged 69, who had learned to fly Autogiros under H. A. Marsh at the Autogiro Flying School at Hanworth, and others went to Singapore, Germany, Sweden, Australia, Japan and Spain.

Having achieved some measure of success in applying the Autogiro principle to

A Cierva C.19 Mk.IVP with monoplane tail and cantilever rotor, the engine driven starting shaft for which can be seen ahead of the pylon. (*Flight Photo 12104*)

The de Havilland-built Cierva C.24 cabin Autogiro. (*Flight Photo 11002*)

Señor de la Cierva running up the Comper Autogiro G-ABTO at Hooton in March 1932. (*P. T. Capon*)

the conventional open cockpit two seater, Cierva commissioned two other types. Orders were placed with de Havilland Aircraft Co. Ltd. for a cabin two seater designated C.24 and with the Comper Aircraft Co. Ltd. for a sporting single seater known as the C.25. The 120 h.p. Gipsy III powered C.24, built at Stag Lane, Edgware, employed the C.19 Mk. IV rotor and was test flown by Cierva in September 1931. No more flights took place until the dorsal fin and a two bladed rotor were fitted in the following month, in which form it was granted a C. of A. in the following April.

A. H. Rawson first flew the Hooton-built C.25 early in 1933, after which it was flown south by Flt. Lt. Nicholas Comper for demonstrations at Heston and Hanworth on 27 April 1933. It obviously owed much to the Comper Swift not only in appearance but also in the high performance imparted by the 85 h.p. Pobjoy R radial.

19

SPECIFICATION

Manufacturers: A. V. Roe and Co. Ltd., Hamble, Southampton; de Havilland Aircraft Co. Ltd., Stag Lane, Edgware; Comper Aircraft Co. Ltd., Hooton, Cheshire.

Power Plants:

(C.19 Mk. III)	One 105 h.p. Armstrong Siddeley Genet Major I.
(C.19 Mk. IVP)	One 105 h.p. Armstrong Siddeley Genet Major I.
(C.24)	One 120 h.p. de Havilland Gipsy III.
(C.25)	One 85 h.p. Pobjoy R.

	C.19 Mk. III	C.19 Mk. IVP	C.24
Rotor diameter	35 ft. 0 in.	34 ft. 0 in.	34 ft. 0 in.
Length	18 ft. 3 in.	18 ft. 3 in.	—
Height	10 ft. 3 in.	10 ft. 3 in.	—
Tare weight	960 lb.	975 lb.	1,280 lb.
All-up weight	1,400 lb.	1,450 lb.	1,800 lb.
Maximum speed	95 m.p.h.	102 m.p.h.	115 m.p.h.
Cruising speed	75 m.p.h.	90 m.p.h.	100 m.p.h.
Initial climb	500 ft./min.	630 ft./min.	—
Range	300 miles	250 miles	350 miles
Rotor speed	125 r.p.m.	180 r.p.m.	200 r.p.m.

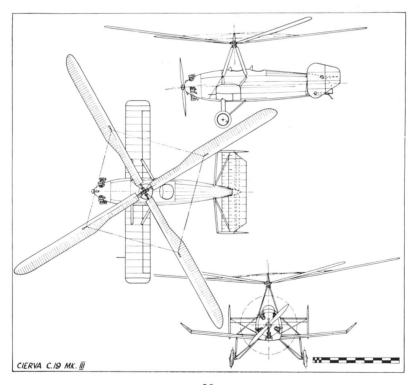

CIERVA C.19 MK. III

A standard Cierva C.30A showing the undercarriage fitted to production models. (*Flight Photo 14516*)

Cierva C.30A

When it became possible to start the rotor by means of the engine through a reliable shaft and clutch, and a satisfactory cantilever rotor had been built, the Autogiro at last became a practical non-stalling aircraft. During near-vertical landings at forward speeds of the order of 10 m.p.h. the aeroplane type controls of the C.19 were almost totally ineffective, resulting in a number of accidents and wrecked rotors through lack of lateral control on the final approach. Cierva then commissioned the Avro Company to modify a C.19 Mk. IV to a single seater without stub wing, ailerons, rudder or elevator, but fitted with a tilting rotor head. A control column hanging from this enabled the pilot to tilt the rotor in any direction, whereupon the machine would climb, descend or go into a turn, at the same time automatically assuming the correct angle of bank. Control was thus finally divorced from forward speed, full control being available until the moment of touch down. This experimental direct-control Autogiro, G-ABXP, was fitted with the usual 100 h.p. five cylinder Genet Major I and designated the C.19 Mk. V. It flew a great deal at Hanworth and was later fitted with a small fixed tailplane and two bladed rotor.

When Air Service Training Ltd. occupied Hamble in 1932 the Avro factory closed and National Flying Services Ltd. were therefore commissioned to erect the next version, G-ACFI, a two seater known as the C.30 which used the same system of direct control. It was fitted with a 37 ft. rotor with faired hub mounted on a tripod type pylon, the undercarriage was also simplified and rotor torque was balanced by a large tailplane with turned-up tips and having reverse aerofoil section on the port side. The fuselage was converted from a standard C.19 type by Airwork Ltd. at Heston, the Mollart Engineering Company built the hub and clutch, and the rotor was entrusted to Oddie, Bradbury and Cull Ltd. of Eastleigh. Cierva personally demonstrated the machine in public at Hanworth on 27 April 1933 after making the first flight earlier in the month.

G-ACKA, the prototype of an improved model known as the C.30P, built by Airwork Ltd. at Heston later in the year, was powered by a 140 h.p. seven cylinder Genet Major IA radial and had a four-legged pylon, folding rotor blades and additional radius rods in the undercarriage. Three other C.30Ps—G-ACIM, 'IN and 'IO—were built by A. V. Roe and Co. Ltd. at their Manchester works, the P indicating pre-production; whereas in the case of the C.19 Mk. IVP it signified full production status.

In 1934 Avros acquired a licence to build the C.30 at Manchester, the production model with wide track, parallel undercarriage being designated the C.30A, civil and export production amounting to 66 aircraft, all distributed through the Cierva base at Hanworth. Construction also took place in France where 25 were built by Lioré et Olivier as the Le.O. C.301 (175 h.p. Salmson 9NE) and in Germany where Focke-Wulf built 40 (Siemens engine). Twelve acquired by the R.A.F. for Army Co-operation evaluation in 1934 were allotted airframe and engine names Rota I and Civet I, Specification 16/35 being written round this combination in 1935 at the same time as it received the belated type number Avro 671.

The experimental direct control Cierva C.19 Mk.V in the interim condition with tailplane and three-bladed rotor.

The pylon and undercarriage of the C.30 differed from all other models. (*Aeroplane*)

22

The second of the three Avro-built C.30P Autogiros, showing the modified undercarriage, pylon and folding rotor.

The first production C.30A, G-ACUI, delivered to Hanworth in July 1934 and sold to the Marquis of Dufferin and Ava at Heston in 1935, was forerunner of many used privately which included J. G. Weir's G-ACWR and A. Q. Cooper's G-ADBJ. Others were used for instruction: G-ACUT by Airwork Ltd. of Heston; 'UU by Air Service Training Ltd., Hamble; 'XW by the Lancashire Aero Club, Woodford; 'WZ by the Redhill Flying Club, joined in 1936 by Mrs. Bruce's 'VX; and 'XP by the Bristol and Wessex Aeroplane Club, Whitchurch. The National Aviation Day Displays were enlivened by the antics of G-ACYH in 1935 and '36, in which year the former Airwork 'UT joined C. W. A. Scott's Flying Display. 'YH was used by Aerial Sites Ltd. for advertising in 1938, and passed into the hands of Capt. H. R. Starkey-Howe at Hanworth in 1939 as a replacement for his veteran C.19 Mk. IVP G-ABFZ. Open cockpits were, however, no longer fashionable, while contemporary cabin light aircraft also had the added attraction of lower fuel consumption. Thus in the course of time at least 16 British registered C.30As were sold abroad in Holland, France, Germany, Switzerland, Poland, Italy and Australia, so that by 1939 the only major user was the Autogiro Flying Club at Hanworth with G-ACUI, 'WM, 'WO, 'WP, 'WR and 'WS.

Direct exports in 1934 included PP-TAF to Brasiltrad Ltda.; VT-AFF to Prince Ghanshyain Singhji; and VT-AFQ and 'FS to Tata Airlines, Bombay.

A certain amount of development work had been done on a side-by-side two seat cabin Autogiro built by Westland Aircraft Ltd. to the design of G. Lepère. Power was supplied by a 90 h.p. Niagara III radial in an enclosed cowling. The prototype, G-ACYI, known as the Westland CL.20 and first flown at Hanworth by H. A. Marsh on 4 February 1935, was not proceeded with because the Cierva Company was by that time engaged on a more important line of research as a result of experiments which had taken place at Hanworth in 1933 with the C.30 G-ACFI fitted with a special rotor head enabling a direct take-off without forward run. By 1936 Cierva had perfected this Autodynamic head, which allowed the rotor to be speeded up beyond its take-off revolutions with the blades at zero incidence, and then suddenly to go into positive pitch, creating sufficient excess lift to leap some 20 ft. into the air. This device, together with a long travel undercarriage, was fitted to the C.30A G-ACWF for demonstrations on Hounslow Heath by H. A. Marsh on 23 July 1936 alongside the Weir W.3. The latter was one of four small direct-control Autogiros built by G. and J. Weir Ltd. at Glasgow, all of which flew under B conditions as W-1 to W-4 and did not go beyond the experimental stage or achieve full civil status. The W.1 was also allotted the Cierva design number C.28.

On 9 December 1936 Cierva was killed at Croydon in the take-off crash of the K.L.M. Douglas DC-2 PH-AKL, with the result that Autogiro development gradually came to an end. Nine production aircraft of the final C.40 version, erected at Hanworth in 1938 by the British Aircraft Manufacturing Co. Ltd. from major assemblies built by Oddie, Bradbury and Cull Ltd., were side-by-side two seaters designed by Dr. J. A. J. Bennett, with wooden semi-monocoque fuselages having an internal metal structure carrying the pylon and undercarriage. They were fitted with 175 h.p. Salmson radials, and an improved Autodynamic head was fitted to the rotor, which, unlike that of the experimental G-ACWF, was free of vibration. It was found necessary, however, to re-introduce a normal rudder. Seven C.40s were delivered to the R.A.F. and the remaining two became civil as G-AFDP and 'DR, the former being lost in France in June 1940.

Most of the surviving Cierva C.30As were impressed for R.A.F. use in 1939–40, many seeing service with No.529 Squadron at Crazies Hill, Henley-on-Thames. At the end of hostilities the 12 survivors were offered for civilian purchase at Kemble, three proving to be from the batch of Rotas K4230–39 supplied to the R.A.F. in 1935 and the rest former denizens of Hanworth. The majority of these machines were bought up by the Cierva Autogiro Co. Ltd. and overhauled at Eastleigh, but Southern Aircraft (Gatwick) Ltd. acquired two. V1186, which had once been G-ACWO was eventually sold as spares for the former K4233, which they registered G-AHUC for export to Sweden. The Fairey Aviation Co. Ltd. also had two which were put into commission as G-AHMI and 'MJ in 1946 along with the restored G-ACXW, as a means of gaining rotary wing experience during the building of the prototype Fairey Gyrodyne helicopter. All

The Westland CL.20 outside the Cierva hangar at Hanworth in May 1935.

One of the two civil Cierva C.40s making a vertical take-off on Hounslow Heath in 1939.

were short-lived, and in dereliction were familiar at White Waltham and at the Sea Scouts headquarters at Heston until 'MJ was rescued by the Shuttleworth Trust in 1954. Longest lived was G-AHTZ, formerly G-ACUI of the Autogiro Flying Club, which, as HM581, was disposed of to Essex Aero Ltd. and civilianized at Gravesend in 1946. It was then sold to the Birmingham firm of Rota Towels Ltd., who maintained it in serviceable condition at Elmdon until it was burned out in an accident on 4 March 1958. Also at Elmdon was the one-time A.S.T. machine G-ACUU, which was overhauled by the Cierva Company and sold to G. S. Baker, by whom it was exhibited at the Fifty Years of Flying Exhibition at Hendon in July 1951.

Six of these historically important aircraft are preserved for posterity, R.A.F. Rotas K4234 and K4239 (flown postwar as G-AHMJ and G-AIOC) by the Shuttleworth Trust, Old Warden; the export C.30As SE-AEA and SE-AFI (originally delivered as LN-BAD), on show in the Stockholm Technical Museum and the Dutch National Air Museum, Schiphol respectively; VH-USR hangared by the Royal Aero Club of N.S.W. at Bankstown, Sydney; AP507, (formerly G-ACWP), at the Science Museum, London, and LV-FBL in Buenos Aires.

SPECIFICATION

Manufacturers: (C.30A) A. V. Roe and Co. Ltd., Newton Heath, Manchester.

(CL.20) Westland Aircraft Ltd., Yeovil, Somerset.

(C.40) British Aircraft Manufacturing Co. Ltd., Hanworth Air Park, Feltham, Middlesex.

Power Plants: (C.30A) One 140 h.p. Armstrong Siddeley Genet Major IA.

(CL.20) One 90 h.p. Pobjoy Niagara III.

(C.40) One 175-h.p. Salmson 9NG.

	C.30A	CL.20	C.40
Rotor diameter	37 ft. 0in.	32 ft. 0 in.	40 ft. 0 in.
Length	19 ft 8½ in.	20 ft. 3 in.	—
Height	11 ft. 1 in.	10 ft. 3 in.	—
Tare weight	1,220 lb	840 lb.	1,350 lb.
All-up weight	1,800 lb.	1,400 lb.	1,950 lb.
Maximum speed	110 m.p.h.	106 m.p.h.	120 m.p.h.
Cruising speed	95 m.p.h.	—	100 m.p.h.
Initial climb	700 ft./min.	—	—
Range	285 miles	—	200 miles

Production: (a) Cierva C.30A

Thirty-seven British registered aircraft listed in Appendix E and the following for export: (Avro c/n 734) VR-HCT; (735) LN-BAD/SE-AFI; (738) PP-TAF; (739) OK-ATS; (740) SE-AEA; (741) VT-AFF; (742) VT-AFS; (748) VT-AFQ; (750) Danish Army M.1/SE-AKW; (756) EA-SCA; (757) EA-SCB; (777) LY-LAS; (779) Russia; (781–782) Spanish Air Force 41–2 and 41–3; (792) VH-USR; (800–804) French Air Ministry; (808) China; (809) OE-TAX; (818) Belgian Air Force; (819) Danish Army M.2; (1029–1030) Yugoslav Air Force; (1031–1032) Argentina.

(b) Avro 671 Rota I

Ten (later 12), ordered by the Air Ministry February 1934 and delivered between August 1934 and May 1935: K4230–K4239, followed by K4296 (floatplane) and K4775.

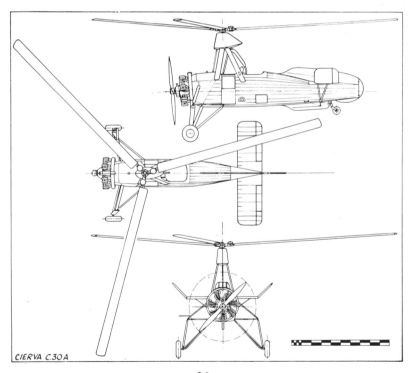

CIERVA C.30A

26

Despite the size of the Genet Major engine, the Coupé Mk.II was noted for its exceptionally fine field of vision. (*Flight Photo 9939*)

Civilian Coupé

The Civilian Aircraft Co. Ltd. was formed at Burton-on-Trent in 1928 by Harold D. Boultbee, who left Handley Page Ltd. to become managing director and chief designer to the new company. Its sole product was the Civilian C.A.C. Mk. I Coupé, a two seat light aeroplane in the traditional strut braced, high wing configuration. It was of mixed wood and metal construction with the occupants in slightly staggered seats which gave side-by-side convenience without too wide a fuselage. The engine was a 75 h.p. A.B.C. Hornet air-cooled flat four and the prototype first flew in July 1929. Coming as it did in the very heyday of the wire braced two seat biplane, it was considered a unique aeroplane indeed, being designed essentially for robust utility with plywood covering throughout, all controls push-rod operated, and fitted with wheel brakes and folding wings.

The prototype G-AAIL was available at Heston for demonstration flights during Olympia Aero Show week in July 1929 and made its public debut at the Garden Party there on 20 July. Eighteen months of experimental flying were necessary to cure a number of teething troubles, modifications being made chiefly to the engine mounting to overcome excessive vibration. The machine was then sold to private owner T. E. Richardson at Hedon, the municipal airport of Hull, where the Civilian Aircraft Company's factory had been established on the southern perimeter.

Two more Coupés, G-ABFI and 'FJ, were built there in 1930, but were improved models powered by the 100 h.p. Genet Major I radial and known as the Mk. II. They made their first public appearance together in the Heston–Cramlington Race on 30 May 1931 and experienced a foretaste of the ill fortune which was to dog the type out of existence. Among a large number of competitors I. W. Mackenzie flew G-ABFI into seventh place at 119·4 m.p.h., but G. A. Pennington forced landed 'FJ en route through fuel shortage. The same aircraft were entered for the Hanworth–Blackpool Race on 8 July 1931 but both had engine trouble and both forced landed. Tommy Rose in 'FI had an argument with a horse and a hedge and went over on his back at Iver, Bucks., while L. S. Dawson in 'FJ went up on his nose at Sandbach, Cheshire.

27

The Hornet engined prototype Civilian Coupé at Heston in July 1929. (*Flight Photo 7447*)

Flt. Lt. V. S. Bowling, a serving R.A.F. officer, bought 'FJ with the intention of racing it for the 1931 King's Cup Race but repairs were not completed in time and he was a non-starter. Meanwhile two more Coupé IIs, G-ABNT and 'PW, had been constructed at Hedon, and in the first of these Flt. Lt. Bowling came tenth in the Heston–Cardiff Race on 19 September, but at a mere 89 m.p.h.

The last Civilian Coupé, G-ABPW, built to foreign order, was ferried to a firm of aerial photographers in Germany by S. B. Cliff who left via Heston on 14 October 1932. On arrival it was appropriately re-registered D-EPAN and remained in use until after the outbreak of the 1939–45 war. In the following year the Hornet powered prototype was sold in Ireland but suffered damage landing at Stranraer while being flown home by the new owner, James Gilmour, a civilian engineer employed by the I.F.S. Army Air Corps. He rebuilt it at Baldonnel in 1934 with a Genet II engine as EI-AAV and the machine survived until cancelled in January 1949 following the death of the owner in North Africa.

G-ABFI was sold to a Dutch radio company, Stadtverkeer Eindhoven, and re-registered PH-BBC but no more Coupés were ordered and the Civilian Aircraft Co. Ltd. was forced to close down. Harold Boultbee then joined Pobjoy Airmotors and Aircraft Ltd. at Rochester where he later designed the Pobjoy Pirate cabin monoplane. The one remaining airworthy Coupé, G-ABNT, acquired by S. B. Cliff early in 1933, was based first at Woodley and later at the former Bristol civil aerodrome, Whitchurch. Before the year was out it was disposed of to Mr. G. O. Rees, then of Cardiff, who flew it from the sands along the South Wales coast until 1939 when it was dismantled and stored. In 1961 it was still in storage at Carmarthen and when examined by Harold Boultbee, all the plywood covering and glued joints were as good as ever.

The fate of the unregistered fourth airframe remains a mystery, nothing having been heard of it since the Hedon factory closed down in 1933, but is possibly the second, new and incomplete, Coupé which Mr. Rees also stored as a source of spares for G-ABNT.

SPECIFICATION

Manufacturers: Civilian Aircraft Co. Ltd., 27 Moor Street, Burton-on-Trent, Staffs. Works at Hull Municipal Airport, Hedon, East Yorks.

Power Plants: (Mk. I) One 75 h.p. A.B.C. Hornet.
                 (Mk. II) One 100 h.p. Armstrong Siddeley Genet Major I.

Dimensions: Span, 35 ft. 6⅜ in. Length, 19 ft. 4 in. Height, 6 ft. 3 in. Wing area, 167·8 sq. ft.

	Coupé Mk. I	Coupé Mk. II
Tare weight	918 lb.	985 lb.
All-up weight	1,500 lb.	1,500 lb.
Maximum speed	102 m.p.h.	110 m.p.h.
Cruising speed	85 m.p.h.	96 m.p.h.
Initial climb	550 ft./min.	810 ft./min.
Ceiling	12,000 ft.	16,000 ft.
Range	360 miles	300 miles

Production: One Coupé Mk. I only: (c/n 1) G-AAIL. Five Coupé Mk. II: (c/n 0.2.1) G-ABFI; (0.2.2) G-ABFJ; (0.2.3) G-ABNT; (0.2.4) unregistered; (0.2.5) G-ABPW. See also Appendix E.

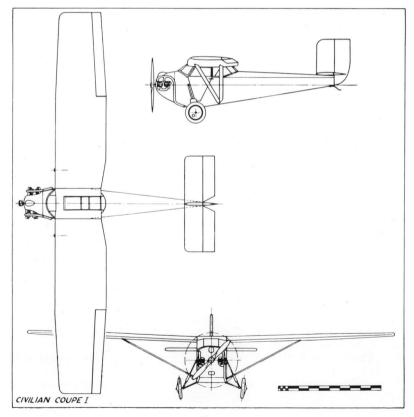

CIVILIAN COUPE I

The prototype Swift with the horizontally opposed Scorpion engine. (*Aeroplane*)

Comper C.L.A.7 Swift

Flt. Lt. Nicholas Comper began his career with the Aircraft Manufacturing Co. Ltd., but left to join the R.A.F., where he designed the C.L.A. aircraft (described in Appendix A) for the Cranwell Light Aeroplane Club. On leaving the Service he founded the Comper Aircraft Co. Ltd. with works at Hooton, and there built the C.L.A.7 Swift. Clearly evolved from the C.L.A.3, it was a diminutive and dainty single seat sporting aircraft of wooden construction, fabric covered except for the plywood rear decking, which formed the locker. The engine was a 35 h.p. A.B.C. Scorpion, the wings folded and the shock absorbing gear of the under-carriage was housed inside the front fuselage. The prototype G-AARX made its first public appearance at Brooklands on 17 May 1930 flown by Sydney St. Barbe.

Seven more Swifts were built in 1930, all fitted with the 50 h.p. Salmson A.D. 9 radial, but meanwhile D. R. Pobjoy had opened a works at Hooton alongside Comper's for the production of the seven-cylinder Pobjoy geared radial. The seventh Swift, G-AAZF, fitted with the prototype Pobjoy P engine and entered by Gerard Fane in the 1930 King's Cup Race, was a non-starter, but for the 1931 race was fitted with the first production 75 h.p. Pobjoy R, which, with only five and a half hours' previous running, brought Sqn. Ldr. (later Air Marshal) J. M. Robb into sixth place at 118·3 m.p.h. Comper then flew it on a 2,500-mile European sales tour to Italy, after which it was decided to standardize the Pobjoy, and most of the 1930 batch were eventually re-engined, at the same time acquiring modified vertical tail surfaces. Two were registered in Argentina as R222 and R232, and the first of these made the record 18,000 ft. crossing of the Andes from Mendoza to Valparaiso in 1 hr. 50 min. on 9 March 1932. It was flown by C. H. A. Taylor of Aerofotos, the Comper agents who acquired two more later in the year. The fifth Swift, G-AAZD, first owned by A. H. Youngman, spent 1934 in Egypt where, as SU-AAJ, it was entered for the Oases Rally by Mohamed Husak but was forced to land in the desert and was a non-starter. The last of the 1930 Swifts, which went to New Zealand as ZK-ACG 'Kitten', was fitted in later years with a dorsal fin and the Salmson A.D.9 engine from a defunct B.A. Swallow.

Nine Swifts with Pobjoy R engines were built at Hooton in 1931, one of which went to a private owner in Tanganyika as VR-TAF. It was a vintage year in which Swifts made two long distance flights, and home aerodromes became increasingly familiar with the soft whine of Pobjoys turning the big geared propellers of the sprightly Swifts. Lt. C. Byas, R.N., bought G-ABNH and fitted it with an

The third 1930 production Swift, with Salmson radial and original fin and rudder. (*Aeroplane*)

Comper Swift CH-351 (Pobjoy R), delivered to Dr. Tschudi at Dübendorf, Switzerland in June 1933, was registered to Flugmotor Studien Ges. in 1936 as HB-EXO. (*Willi Erni*)

31

Alban Ali's 'Scarlet Angel' VT-ADO awaiting collection at Hooton in August 1932.

additional tank to increase the range to 600 miles for a flight home to Cape Town but although he intended to make a leisurely trip, his time of 10 days for the 7,320 miles was a near record. C. A. Butler (later the founder of Butler Air Transport Ltd., Sydney) ordered a long range Swift G-ABRE, which was cleared for a maximum take-off weight of 1,160 lb. In it he made a record flight from Lympne to Darwin, Australia, reached on 9 November 1931 in a time of 9 days 2 hours 20 minutes. He subsequently toured Australia, completing 22,967 miles in eight weeks before it was shipped back to England and sold to Victor Smith for his attempt on Amy Mollison's Cape record. After leaving Croydon on 15 December 1932 Smith forced landed near St. Malo and abandoned the flight. G-ABPE, third of the 1931 Swifts, had an equally colourful career, belonging originally to Flt. Lt. Christopher Clarkson and sold abroad in February 1933. No more was heard of it until early in 1935, when it appeared in Kuala Lumpur, Malaya, as 'Vital Spark' flown by Dr. (Miss) Enid Robertson. Flg. Off. F. B. Chapman brought it back to England along with the temporary Egyptian G-AAZD, and in March 1936 sold it to Flt. Lt. D. W. Atcherley, who kept it first at Andover, and in 1938, at Lee-on-Solent. In 1941–42, when its owner was C.O. of No. 25 (Fighter) Squadron at Wittering, 'PE was painted in night fighter black with roundels and code ZK, but without registration. It was often flown at night and had long range tanks fitted for the purpose, but at the end of 1943 it was disposed of to E. A. Boulter at Sywell. After a post war overhaul at Heston for its last owner, A. B. Golay, in 1946, it crashed at St. Albans in April 1947.

The seventh 1931 aircraft, registered in Ireland as EI-AAL on 12 February 1932, left Baldonnel for Ceylon via Heston a week later piloted by M. G. A. Scally who was killed when it crashed near Marseilles on the 21st.

The year 1932 saw Swift production at its peak, no less than 12 being sold, many destined to achieve almost legendary reputations in the world of sporting flying. The climax to eight years of rebuilding, begun by Sqn. Ldr. Banner at Farnborough and completed at Tangmere by the enthusiastic Gp. Capt. J. A. Kent, came on 29 December 1956, when a post war C. of A. was at last reissued to G-ABTC, first of the 1932 batch, which R.C.A.F. officer J. F. Reed had stored in Wiltshire during the war. Two contemporaries also survived. G-ABUS, originally in the green, red and gold of Shell Mex, was re-engined with a 90 h.p. Pobjoy Niagara III and did a vast amount of post war competition flying in the hands of A. L. Cole and David Ogilvy, the latter gaining second place in the 1956 Goodyear Trophy Race at 126 m.p.h.

Swifts were entered for every King's Cup Race from 1930 until 1937, and for the majority of the minor classics also. G-ABUU, restored by John Pothecary at Christchurch in 1962, was a veteran of these events. Mark Lacayo flew it in the 1932 King's Cup Race, it was second in 1933 at 126·89 m.p.h. flown by E. C. T. Edwards, third in that year's Newcastle Race at 130 m.p.h. at the hands of G. H. Stainforth and fourth in the Folkestone Trophy Race at 126 m.p.h., piloted by Duncan Davies. It was sold in 1939 to Miss Constance Leathart, who gave it to No. 131 (Tyneside) Sqn. A.T.C. at the outbreak of war. In 1950 it was found stored at its birthplace, Hooton, and went to Speeton where Desmond Heaton flew it again in 1954.

Quite the most extraordinary life story was that of the ninth of the batch, which started life in August 1932 as the famous VT-ADO 'Scarlet Angel'. Alban Ali, a tea planter of Silchar, Assam, attempted to fly it from Calcutta to Heston and found time to compete in the Viceroy's Cup Race at Delhi on the way, making second fastest time for the 699 mile course at 124 m.p.h. R. O. Shuttleworth flew Swift G-ABWE out from England for the event, but forced landed with a broken oil feed in the main street of a village during the race. After an eventful flight, 'Scarlet Angel's' Pobjoy gave up the task of running when full of sand and a final forced landing was made at Abu Sueir in Egypt, whence it was crated home, sold to and rebuilt by G. B. S. Errington as G-ACTF. After the war 'TF was resurrected by Airspeed test pilot R. E. Clear, who flew it into fifth place in the 1950 *Daily Express* Race to establish an F.A.I. Class Record at the phenomenal speed, for an aged Swift, of 141 m.p.h. and it was still active at Baginton in the hands of E. M. Woodhams in 1972. EC-AAT, last of the 1932 Swifts, was certificated in the name of the Spanish aircraft designer J. Rein Loring on 13 January 1933 and painted up with the words 'Visit Spain' and 'Madrid–Manila' for a projected flight to the Far East.

Such was the interest in air racing in 1932 that two Gipsy engined Swifts were ordered. The first, G-ABWW, fitted with a 130 h.p. Gipsy Major, was painted in

The Gipsy Major Swift G-ABWW after S. T. Lowe's 1938 modifications. (*A. J. Jackson*)

Guards colours and flown by Flt. Lt. (later Sir Edward) Fielden on behalf of the Prince of Wales, while the second, with 120 h.p. Gipsy III, was the property of the British Air Navigation Co. Ltd. of Heston and flown by their chief pilot, A. J. Styran. After a neck-and-neck race for the 1932 King's Cup, both failed to cross the line properly, but Fielden scrambled to re-cross and came second at 155·74 m.p.h. On 28 May 1933, 'WW was flown by Comper in the Coupe Deutsch de la Meurth Race at Etampes at an average speed of 148·8 m.p.h., but was hopelessly outclassed by the French racers. 'WH passed into the hands of W. L. Hope, who fitted it with a Fox Moth sliding hood for the 1933 King's Cup Race, in which 'WW was flown by G. H. Stainforth and a third and final Gipsy III Swift G-ACBY by F. R. Walker. This actually belonged to R. O. Shuttleworth and had just returned from Delhi, where, piloted by G. G. Stead, it had competed against 'WE and the 'Scarlet Angel' in the Viceroy's Cup Race, making fastest time of 153 m.p.h.

Pre-war air racing and the Swift were synonymous; six faced the starter for the 1933 Folkestone Trophy and seven, including the Gipsies, for the King's Cup. The latter were again unlucky, Walker ran out of fuel and 'BY was destroyed in the crash, while the others were eliminated after making fastest times in their heats. A month later, however, H. H. Leech averaged 166·25 m.p.h. in 'WW to come fifth in the Brooklands–Newcastle Race. In 1934 'WH was in the United States, where it was raced at Cleveland as NC27K, and 'WW was sold to A. H. Cook, who was eliminated in the King's Cup heats after averaging 163 m.p.h. In July 1935 'WH came back to Croydon and eventually went to Australia, where it lasted until 18 December 1950, when owner, E. A. Sarau, crashed on the fairway of Great Lakes Golf Course, Sydney. G-ABWW was later acquired by S. T. Lowe, who fitted a hinged racing windscreen and a fairing between the wing bracing struts. After this grooming he flew it to victory in the Isle of Man Race at 159·5 m.p.h. Its last owner, H. O. Winters, kept it at Gravesend, but all trace of it was lost after he gave it to the Tonbridge A.T.C. in 1943. G-ABWH, on the other hand, was rebuilt by E. R. Burnett-Read at Adelaide in 1963 and was still flying as VH-ACG in 1972.

The final batch of Swifts was built in 1933, many going to buyers in Switzerland, France, Italy, Kenya and India, although Henshaw's G-ACGL had a long private life, ending with P. G. Leeson at Braunstone in 1939. Another, G-ACML, flown a great deal by Flt. Lt. Pope, C.F.I. of A.S.T., Hamble, was sold in Belgium by Philip de Walden Avery in 1935. In June 1934 a single Swift, the forty-first and final machine, was built at Heston for a French customer, after which the name of the company was changed to Heston Aircraft Ltd. and the Comper directors resigned.

SPECIFICATION

Manufacturers: Comper Aircraft Ltd., Hooton Park Aerodrome, Wirral, Cheshire— transferred to Heston Aerodrome, Hounslow, Middlesex, in 1933.

Power Plants: One 40 h.p. A.B.C. Scorpion II.
One 50 h.p. British Salmson A.D. 9.
One 75 h.p. Pobjoy R.
One 120 h.p. de Havilland Gipsy III.
One 130 h.p. de Havilland Gipsy Major.

	Scorpion	Salmson	Pobjoy	Gipsy
Span	24 ft. 0 in.	24 ft. 0 in.	24 ft. 0 in.	24 ft. 0 in.
Length	17 ft. 8½ in.	17 ft. 8½ in.	17 ft. 8½ in.	18 ft. 4 in.
Height	5 ft. 3½ in.	5 ft. 3½ in.	5 ft. 3½ in.	5 ft. 3½ in.
Wing area	90 sq. ft.	90 sq. ft.	90 sq. ft.	90 sq. ft.
Tare weight	470 lb.	515 lb.	540 lb.	610 lb.
All-up weight	730 lb.	780 lb.	985 lb.	1,130 lb.
Maximum speed	100 m.p.h.	115 m.p.h.	140 m.p.h.	165 m.p.h.
Cruising speed	85 m.p.h.	100 m.p.h.	120 m.p.h.	140 m.p.h.
Initial climb	500 ft./min.	600 ft./min.	1,400 ft./min.	1,400 ft./min.
Ceiling	14,000 ft.	15,000 ft.	22,000 ft.	20,000 ft.
Range	360 miles	300 miles	380 miles	400 miles

Production: (a) Standard Swifts

One prototype and 41 production aircraft including British registered machines listed in Appendix E and the following for export: (c/n S.30/4) R232/LV-YEA; (S.30/8) ZK-ACG; (S.31/7) EI-AAL; (S.31/9) Aerofotos, Buenos Aires; (S.32/3) VT-ADF; (S.32/6) Aerofotos, Buenos Aires; (S.32/9) VT-ADO/G-ACTF; (S.32/11) untraced; (S.32/12) EC-AAT; (S.33/1) CH-351/HB-EXO; (S.33/4) CH-352/HB-OXE/F-ANHO; (S.33/7) I-RASN; (S.33/8) VP-KAV; (S.33/9) I-REBO; (S.33/11) VT-AEY; (41) F-ANEY.

(b) Gipsy Swifts

Three aircraft (c/n GS.31/1 to 31/3) G-ABWW, G-ABWH and G-ACBY.

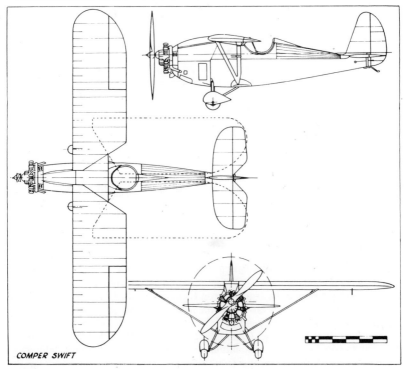

COMPER SWIFT

Super Wot G-AVEY (Pobjoy R radial) took four years to build and first flew at Halfpenny
Green in pre-1939 U.S. Navy colours on 10 January 1971. (*Keith Sedgwick*)

Currie Wot

The Wot was a wood and fabric aerobatic single seater, with plywood fuselage,
designed by J. R. Currie, himself a pilot and lecturer at the College of
Aeronautical Engineering, Chelsea. Two examples, G-AFCG and G-AFDS, built
by Cinque Ports Aviation Ltd. at Lympne in 1937, shared a single 40 h.p.
Aeronca-J.A.P. J-99 two-cylinder engine (salvaged from a wrecked Aeronca C-3,
G-ADZZ) but differed in detail and were known as the Wot 1 and Wot 2
respectively. Both were destroyed in a German air raid on Lympne in May 1940
but after the war J. R. Currie, then chief engineer at the Hampshire Aeroplane
Club, Eastleigh, was persuaded to produce original drawings from which two
more Wots, financed by V. H. Bellamy, were built at the Club by J. O. Isaacs.

The first, G-APNT, first flown with an Aeronca-J.A.P. by V. H. Bellamy on
11 September 1958, was quickly re-engined with a four-cylinder, in-line inverted
60 h.p. Walter Mikron II and also trial-mounted on wooden floats. The J.A.P.
engine was refitted before delivery to Yeovil on 31 March 1959 but on 18 January
1960 it returned by road and flew again at Eastleigh with a 55 h.p. Lycoming flat
four on 11 March prior to re-delivery to Yeovil on 29 May as 'Airy Mouse',
famed personal mount of Westland test pilot H. J. Penrose.

The second machine, G-APWT, first flown on 20 October 1959, had increased
fin and rudder area and the same Mikron II engine that had flown in G-APNT. An
11 gallon fuel tank was installed and the nose shortened by 10 in. to correct the
c.g. position with the heavier engine. In this form it was dubbed 'Hot Wot' but was
rechristened 'Wet Wot' when tested unsuccessfully on the Hamble River with the
original float undercarriage a month later. It was then fitted experimentally with a
60 h.p. Rover 1S.60 gas turbine from a naval auxiliary power unit and was first

flown with this engine by V. H. Bellamy on 26 January 1960 as the 'Jet Wot'. Later it received a 65 h.p. Mikron III ('Hotter Wot') as mount for Flt. Lt. H. R. Lane in the Lockheed International Aerobatic Competition at Baginton, 8–9 July 1960. In November that year it became flying test bed for the 70 h.p. Rover TP.60/1 single stage, axial flow turbine but eventually reverted to Mikron power for delivery to R. W. Mills for the M.P.M. Flying Group, Elstree in January 1962.

Several home-built Wots appeared in later years, the first, G-ARZW, built over a two-year period at Botley, Hants. with Mikron III by Dr. J. H. B. Urmston, made its maiden flight at Eastleigh on 18 April 1963. It was based subsequently at a private strip at King's Somborne, Hants. Wots G-APWT and G-ARZW both made cross-channel flights piloted respectively by A. J. Butcher and Dr. Urmston. The latter also bought the design rights but eventually sold them to Phoenix Aircraft Ltd.

Other noteworthy Wots included G-ASBA with 55 h.p. Lycoming, streamlined headrest and superior finish, built at Baldock, Herts. by Albert Etheridge; 'Super Wot' G-AVEY with Pobjoy R radial by K. Sedgwick at Wolverhampton; and N11QB completed without stagger or top wing dihedral by W. R. Bullock and flown with 26 h.p. Volkswagen engine at Lakesville, Minnesota in 1971.

The most sensational Wots were six, G-AVOT to 'OY, built by Slingsby Sailplanes Ltd. at Kirkbymoorside, Yorks. in 1967 with changes in external profile so as to resemble ·83 scale S.E.5A replicas under the designation Slingsby Type 56. They were powered by 115 h.p. Lycoming engines with $2\frac{1}{2}$ in. plastic rainwater pipes as dummy exhausts and the first machine, G-AVOT, was first flown by Derek Piggott from Welburn airfield alongside Slingsby's factory on 20 June 1967. This and two others were ferried to Casement Aerodrome, Dublin via Squires Gate in a flying time of four hours by Lorne Welch, John Oxborough and Henryck Doktor on June 27; and the remaining three by Oxborough, Doktor and Derek Goddard on 30 June. On arrival they were registered to Shillelagh Productions Inc. as EI-ARH to 'RM, and equipped with dummy guns initially for the film 'Darlin' Lili'.

The original Wot 1, G-AFCG, with Cinque Ports Flying Club crest, at Lympne in December 1937. The diagonal centre section struts were reversed on all later Wots.
(*Aeroplane*)

Top to bottom: Wot G-APWT with Rover gas turbine engine at Eastleigh, November 1960 (*Flight Photo 41393S*); G-ASBA with 55 h.p. Lycoming flat four (*Aviation Photo News*); Slingsby Type 56 Wot/S.E.5A replica EI-ARM at Kirkbymoorside in June 1967 prior to delivery to Ireland as G-AVOY. (*Norman Ellison*)

These replicas were flown again in August 1969 during the filming of 'I Shot Down Richthofen, I Think', after which EI-ARI and 'RJ were crated for sea and road transport to Aksaray, 300 miles S.E. of Ankara, Turkey where Derek Piggott, L. J. Benjamin and Charles Boddington flew 1914–18 war sequences for the film 'Dubious Patriot'. The aircraft were then shipped back to Ireland.

SPECIFICATION

Manufacturers: Cinque Ports Aviation Ltd., Lympne Aerodrome, Kent; The Hampshire Aeroplane Club Ltd., Eastleigh Aerodrome, Hants.; Slingsby Sailplanes Ltd., Kirkbymoorside, Yorks.; Dr. J. H. B. Urmston t/a Botley Aircraft; also home constructors.

Power Plants: One 40 h.p. Aeronca-J.A.P. J-99.
One 55 h.p. Lycoming.
One 60 h.p. Walter Mikron II or 65 h.p. Mikron III.
One 70 h.p. Rover TP.60/1 gas turbine.
One 115 h.p. Lycoming O-235-C2A.

* Dimensions: Span 22 ft. 1 in. Length 18 ft. 3$\frac{1}{2}$ in.
Height 6 ft. 9 in. Wing area 140 sq. ft.

* Weights: Tare weight 550 lb. All-up weight 900 lb.

* Performance: Maximum speed 95 m.p.h. Cruise 80 m.p.h.
Initial climb 600 ft./min. Range 240 miles.
*G-ARZW with 65 h.p. Walter Mikron III.

Production: Two pre-war and various post-war machines detailed in Appendix E.

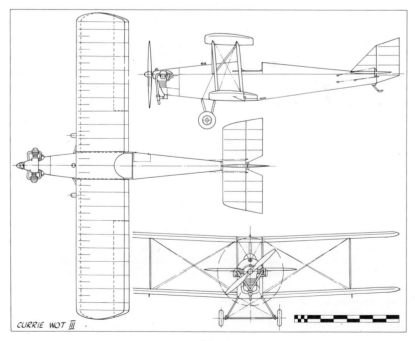

CURRIE WOT III

The veteran D.H.4 three seater G-AUBZ of Queensland and Northern Territory Aerial Services Ltd. at Longreach in 1922. A cabin top was added later.

De Havilland D.H.4 and Variants

Capt. Geoffrey de Havilland built the first D.H.4 two seat day bomber at Hendon in August 1916 and by the end of the First World War many hundreds had seen operational service. The D.H.4 was a conventional two bay biplane of wire braced, fabric covered, wooden construction powered by a variety of engines in the 200–300 h.p. range. After the war a considerable number were reconditioned at Croydon by the Aircraft Disposal Co. Ltd. and flown out to the air forces of Spain and Belgium in temporary civil markings, G-EAXE, 'XF and 'XN in particular, making fast times of about 1 hr. 50 min. between Croydon and Brussels in June–July 1921. Four were supplied to the pioneer Belgian airline SNETA for Brussels–Croydon and other services; twelve forming part of an Imperial gift were used for forestry patrol and survey work in Canada; and two were shipped to Australia for C. J. de Garis. Flown by F. S. Briggs, the first of these, G-AUCM, made the first-ever Melbourne–Perth, Perth–Sydney and Brisbane–Melbourne flights 1920–21, and in 1924 was named 'Scrub Bird' for the Adelaide–Sydney mail service of Australian Aerial Services Ltd. The other, G-AUBZ, won the first Australian Aerial Derby at 142 m.p.h. on 28 December 1920 piloted by R. J. Parer and in 1922 flew the first QANTAS air mail between Charleville and Cloncurry. In 1928 it was sold to Matthews Aviation Ltd. and remodelled with cabin top and D.H.50 centre section tank as VH-UBZ 'Spirit of Melbourne'.

Large numbers of American-built DH-4s with 400 h.p. Liberty 12 engines, converted for carrying the United States mail, were still in use in 1927.

Three main types of civil conversion were carried out on the demilitarized airframe, two of which made their public debut in the Aerial Derby Race at Hendon on 21 June 1919. Both were owned by Aircraft Transport and Travel Ltd., founded by George Holt Thomas to operate a pioneer air service with machines built by the Aircraft Manufacturing Co. Ltd. ('Airco'—later the de Havilland Aircraft Co. Ltd.). Their first entrant, K-142, powered by a 375 h.p.

40

Rolls-Royce Eagle VIII water-cooled engine, merely had the Scarff ring removed to form a conventional cockpit. The other, K-141, with a 450 h.p. Napier Lion, had the lower wing clipped at the first bay and the top wing overhang supported by inclined struts in the same manner as the B.A.T. Bantam K-125, with which it was competing. The rear cockpit was faired over, and with the heavy uncowled Lion and chin radiator on a shortened front fuselage it was scarcely recognizable as a D.H.4 derivative. It was therefore known as the D.H.4 racer, or D.H.4R. Ingenuity was rewarded when Capt. Gerald Gathergood made the two circuits of London in 1 hour 2 minutes to win the race at an average speed of 129·3 m.p.h. and set up a world's record for speed in a closed circuit. Marcus D. Manton, flying the standard D.H.4 came third at an average speed of 117·39 m.p.h. A very creditable performance by two machines which left the ground for the first time on the morning of the race!

The most important version of the D.H.4. was the D.H.4A which seated two passengers face-to-face in a glazed cabin behind the pilot. In 1918 at least five were used by No. 2 (Communication) Squadron R.A.F. for daily courier services between Kenley and Buc, near Paris, and in July 1919 four new D.H.4s on Airco's Hendon production line were similarly converted as G-EAHF, 'HG, 'JC and 'JD for Aircraft Transport and Travel Ltd. Two others, O-BARI and O-BATO, were also supplied to SNETA.

H. J. Saint flew G-EAHG to Amsterdam in August 1919 as an exhibit at the First Air Traffic Exhibition and on 25 August E. H. Lawford piloted G-EAJC on the first British commercial passenger service from Hounslow to Le Bourget, but without subsidy or mail contracts the fare was 20 guineas. The D.H.4s were based at Hendon and flew to Hounslow before going on service but after only four months the first two had been lost in crashes. When the new aerodrome was opened at Plough Lane, Croydon, on 28 March 1920, the survivors started from there and also flew on the new route to Schiphol, Amsterdam, which opened on 17 May 1920. The low subsidized fares of foreign airlines eventually forced A.T. & T. to close down, 'JC and 'JD were therefore scrapped after the firm ceased operations on 17 December 1920.

The equipment of Handley Page Transport was naturally the H.P. O/400

One of the forestry patrol D.H.4s used in Canada 1920–1924.

converted bomber, but the D.H.4A G-EAVL was used for charter work and on the Cricklewood–Schiphol service. With the aid of a favourable gale on 4 December 1920 it also created a record, piloted by Lt. Vaughan-Fowler, by reaching Paris with two passengers in 1 hour 48 minutes. Handley Pages were also forced to close down in February 1921, but re-opened their services on 21 March, following the adoption of a hastily drawn up subsidy scheme. A new D.H.4A G-EAWH was acquired for the Paris service, and for six weeks Major E. L. Foot flew 'VL on the Schiphol run until it crashed in the April.

The D.H.4's career in scheduled service ended when SNETA suffered major crashes at Folkestone and Croydon in January–February 1921 and most of its remaining D.H.4 and 4A fleet was destroyed in a hangar fire at Brussels on 27 September 1921.

The shipping firm of S. Instone and Co. Ltd. also acquired a special D.H.4, G-EAMU, with two seat open rear cockpit and engaged Capt. F. L. Barnard as pilot, intending to use it for the fast carriage of ship's papers. A brand new aircraft, it flew for the first time on 12 October 1919 and appropriately named 'City of Cardiff' left Hounslow for Cardiff later in the day. The next day it made its first trip from Hounslow to Le Bourget. In February 1920 'MU was fully converted to D.H.4A standard by A. V. Roe and Co. Ltd. at Hamble, and with the

D.H.4A G-EAJC in which E. H. Lawford flew the first British commercial passenger service from Hounslow Heath to Le Bourget on 25 August 1919.

A D.H.4A of the Belgian airline SNETA about to leave Croydon for Brussels in 1921.
(*H. C. Rayner, O.B.E.*)

K-141, the Lion engined single seat D.H.4R was capable of 150 m.p.h.

introduction of subsidies, went into service on the London–Paris route of the new Instone Air Line as the 'City of York'. At the end of the year it was relegated to charter work to the North and to Ireland, but on 8–9 September 1922 made history by winning the very first King's Cup Race, when Capt. F. L. Barnard flew it from Croydon to Renfrew and back at an average speed of 123 m.p.h. It then survived to be handed over to Imperial Airways Ltd. at its formation on 1 April 1924, afterwards being broken up at Croydon.

SPECIFICATION

Manufacturers: The Aircraft Manufacturing Co. Ltd., Hendon, London, N.W. (R.A.F. serials prefixed A and F). Waring and Gillow Ltd., Cambridge Road, Hammersmith, London, W.6. (R.A.F. serials prefixed H.)

Power Plants: (D.H.4 and 4A) One 375 h.p. Rolls-Royce Eagle VIII.

(D.H.4R)a   One 450 h.p. Napier Lion.

	D.H.4	D.H.4A	D.H.4R
Span	42 ft. $4\frac{5}{8}$ in.	42 ft. $4\frac{5}{8}$ in.	42 ft. $4\frac{5}{8}$ in.
Length	30 ft. 6 in.	30 ft. 6 in.	28 ft. 1 in.
Height	11 ft. 0 in.	11 ft. 0 in.	11 ft. 0 in.
Wing area	434 sq. ft.	434 sq. ft.	—
Tare weight	2,387 lb.	2,600 lb.	2,490 lb.
All-up weight	3,472 lb.	3,720 lb.	3,191 lb.
Maximum speed	143 m.p.h.	121 m.p.h.	150 m.p.h.
Initial climb	1,300 ft./min.	—	—
Ceiling	23,500 ft.	—	—
Range	$3\frac{3}{4}$ hours	—	—

Civil conversions: (a) D.H.4

Three British registered aircraft detailed in Appendix E and six for de Garis and SNETA (with former R.A.F. serials): F2682/G-AUBZ; F2691/G-AUCM; H5915/O-BAIN; H5925/O-BABI; H5931/O-BALO; H5936/O-BADO.

(b) D.H.4A

At least F2663, F2664 'H.M.A.P. Lady Iris', F2665, F2681 and F5764 used by No. 2 (Communication) Squadron; seven British civil aircraft listed in Appendix E; and the following for SNETA: H5928/O-BARI; H5929/O-BATO.

(c) D.H.4s ferried to the Belgian Air Force 1921

Nineteen temporarily registered to the Aircraft Disposal Co. Ltd. and cancelled in two batches, 15 on 13.10.21 and four on 28.11.21: F2686/G-EAXD; F2697/G-EAXE; H5934/G-EAXF; A7988/G-EAXH; F2698/G-EAXI; F5794/G-EAXJ; F2678/G-EAXN; F2680/G-EAXO; F5774/G-EAXP; F2675/G-EAYE; F5779/G-EAYF; H5902/G-EAYG; F2684/G-EAYH; F2693/G-EAYI; F2677/G-EAYJ; F2689/G-EAYR; H5898/G-EAYS; F5797/G-EAYV; H5896/G-EAYX.

(d) D.H.4s. ferried to the Spanish Air Force 1921

At least 37 with temporary civil markings: M-MHAC; M-MHDE to M-MHEN.

(e) In Canada

Twelve used for Canadian Air Board Civil Operations: F2705/G-CYBO; F2709/G-CYBU; F2710/G-CYBV; F2672/G-CYBW; F2713/G-CYCW; F2673/G-CYDB; F2711/G-CYDK; F2712/G-CYDL; F2706/G-CYDM; F2708/G-CYDN; F2714/G-CYEC; F2707/G-CYEM.

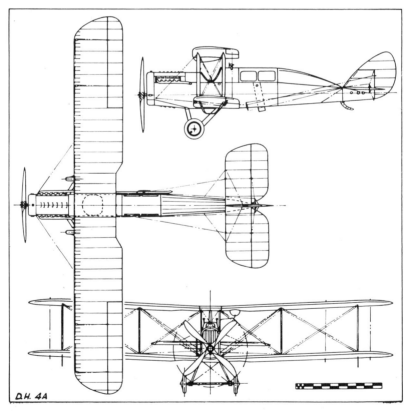

D.H. 4A

44

K-100 with prototype rudder, racing at Hendon 1919. It was the first aeroplane ever to carry British civil markings. (*Flight*)

De Havilland D.H.6

Over 2,000 D.H.6 primary trainers were built by the Aircraft Manufacturing Co. Ltd. and seven main sub-contractors during 1917–18. For a brief period it was the standard trainer of the R.F.C., and for ease of maintenance and repair was built with an eye to structural simplicity rather than beauty of line. It was a rugged two bay biplane of primitive aspect, seating instructor and pupil in tandem in a single cockpit. Although of orthodox wire braced wooden construction with fabric covering, the sides of the front fuselage were plywood covered and the 90 h.p. R.A.F. 1A vee-eight air-cooled motor was bolted to the top longerons without any pretence at cowlings. A small number were fitted with Curtiss OX-5 water-cooled engines with a radiator which somewhat improved the frontal appearance.

When civil flying began after the war, over 50 D.H.6s or 'Clutching Hands'—a soubriquet deriving from their heavily cambered wings—were sold for civil purposes. The first of these was notable for being the first aeroplane in the United Kingdom, and probably in the entire world, to receive civil markings. As K-100, first of the temporary British series, it was flown a great deal at the Hendon race meetings by Capt. Gathergood and others during the summer of 1919. It was a unique aircraft fitted with one of the horn balanced rudders of typical D.H. shape taken from one of the prototypes, instead of the standard straight sided production type. In March 1920 Marconi's Wireless Telegraph Co. Ltd. bought it for experimental R/T work, after which it became well known at Croydon, where, as G-EAAB, it was flown continuously by H. 'Jerry' Shaw until written off in a crash in November 1921.

The strength, the ample spares backing and the unbelievably safe flying characteristics of the D.H.6 made it an obvious choice for instruction. G-EALS and 'LT were operated by the Cambridge School of Flying at Hardwicke Aerodrome during the summer of 1919 and two others, G-EAGE and 'GF, were in use during the same period at Hendon with the Grahame-White Aviation Co. Ltd. It was more widely used, however, for joy flights, chiefly in the north, Lancashire being

45

the main hunting ground of the itinerant D.H.6, while the beaches of the neighbouring North Wales coast also served as landing grounds for the Manchester Aviation Company's aircraft. The career of International's D.H.6 G-EARB was typical of many. This was a former R.F.C. trainer, B5533, built by Harland and Wolff, first flown as a civil machine on 15 March 1920. At the beginning of the season L. J. Rimmer flew it to Bidston, Cheshire, where it completed 10 hours' pleasure flying. Later it made a two hour flight to the Isle of Man, where a further 12 hours' flying was completed at Douglas by the end of June. It then rounded off the year's activities by being blown over in a gale.

Although initially they earned a considerable amount of easy money, the post-war slump of 1920 forced many of these companies out of business and most of the D.H.6s were short-lived. A few were acquired, however, by a select band of pioneer private owners. Grahame-White's G-EAGF was sold to the Hon. Elsie Mackay in October 1921; Leatherhead's OX-5 powered G-EANU was acquired by J. V. Yates at Croydon in May 1922; A. B. Ford operated G-EAOT in 1920–21; Dr. E. D. Whitehead Reid was active at Bekesbourne, Canterbury, with G-EAPW in 1920; P. A. A. Boss had G-EAQQ; and H. B. Elwell of Blackpool successively owned G-EAQY, 'RL and 'VR during the period 1922–25. One example was dismantled at Sherburn-in-Elmet and rebuilt as G-EAWG, a monoplane with a 150 h.p. Bentley B.R.1 rotary and an Alula parasol wing as described in Appendix A. Another, G-EAWD, had wings of lesser camber and was the private mount of Capt. Geoffrey de Havilland, who, in the cold and wet, bravely completed the course to finish last in the Croydon Handicap Race on 17 September 1921.

From the ruins of early ambition there emerged a new and more lasting phase in the history of the civil D.H.6. After the Director of Research, Air Ministry, had finally approved their modification as three seaters, they were permitted to carry a second fare paying passenger at an all-up weight of 2,380 lb. In Lancashire, S. N. Giroux acquired the hangars at Hesketh Park, Southport, and used the beach as his aerodrome, at the same time buying up the aircraft of the International and Golden Eagle concerns. He began operations in 1921 as the Giro Aviation Co. with G-EARC, 'RJ, 'RK, 'RM and 'VG, and in 1964 still offered pleasure flights

Capt. Jackson of the Midland Aviation Service Ltd. with G-EARR, the company's joy-riding D.H.6, at Retford, Notts. in the summer of 1921. (*R. C. Shelley*)

The Leatherhead Motor Company's OX-5 engined D.H.6 G-EANU at Croydon 1919, where it was flown by W. G. Chapman. (*C. A. Nepean Bishop*)

in vintage Fox Moths from the same pitch. In 1925 a new D.H.6 G-EBEB was built at Hesketh, probably by cannibalization of earlier machines, and was joined in May 1929 by G-EBWG bought from R. J. Bunning, an itinerant joyrider. These were named 'Maysbus' and 'Silver Wings' respectively, and became famous on Southport Sands, giving thousands of holidaymakers their baptism of the air until replaced by Avros 548s in 1933.

The critical 1921–22 seasons found the Martin Aviation Co. Ltd., another new D.H.6 operator, doing good business with the three seaters G-EAWT, 'WU and 'WV in the Isle of Wight. These machines, which were fitted with 80 h.p. Renault motors, became a familiar sight in all parts of the island and were well patronized, although 'WU was written off in a minor landing accident on 31 March 1922. Giro and Martin were virtually the last users of the D.H.6 as a commercial aircraft, although F. J. V. Holmes of Berkshire Aviation Tours converted G-EBPN and 'VS at Witney in 1926 He toured the Midlands with them for a couple of years until they were sold in April 1928 to British Flying and Motor Services Ltd. at Maylands Aerodrome.

In 1919 the Aircraft Disposal Co. Ltd. sold several D.H.6s in Spain where one, M-AAAB, registered to Hispano-Britannica S.A., Madrid, is believed to have acted as prototype of 60 built under licence at Guadalajara from 1921 onwards. Three were used by P. O. Flygkompani for joyriding in Sweden 1919–21 and one was privately owned in Belgium in 1924. Greatest overseas D.H.6 activity was in Australia where six were collected from Point Cook airfield in 1920 by Capt. P. G. Taylor, Capt. S. G. Brearley and others for pioneer pleasure flight ventures in N.S.W. and Victoria while a seventh, G-AUEA, was built from spares by C. D. Pratt at Geelong, Vic. At least one remodelled D.H.6 offered for sale in the U.S.A. by Chamberlain Aircraft Inc., New Jersey, had a 150 h.p. Benz and others were re-engined with 110 h.p. Clerget rotaries as late as 1929.

SPECIFICATION

Manufacturers: The Aircraft Manufacturing Co. Ltd., Hendon, London, N.W.9; and other contractors.

Power Plants: One 90 h.p. R.A.F. 1A.
One 90 h.p. Curtiss OX-5.
One 80 h.p. Renault.

Dimensions: Span, 35 ft. 11 in. Length, 27 ft. $3\frac{1}{2}$ in. Height, 10 ft. $9\frac{1}{2}$ in. Wing area, 436·3 sq. ft.

| | R.A.F. 1A | | Curtiss OX-5 | Renault |
	2 seater	3 seater	2 seater	3 seater
Tare weight	1,460 lb.	1,670 lb.	1,539 lb.	1,360 lb.
All-up weight	2,000 lb.	2,380 lb.	1,926 lb.	1,900 lb.
Maximum speed	66 m.p.h.	—	75 m.p.h.	—
Initial climb	225 ft./min.	—	185 ft./min.	—
Ceiling	—	—	6,100 ft.	—
Duration	$2\frac{3}{4}$ hours	$2\frac{3}{4}$ hours	$2\frac{3}{4}$ hours	$3\frac{1}{2}$ hours

Civil conversions:

Fifty-two British registered D.H.6s listed in Appendix E and at least the following overseas: (c/n 3204*) G-AUBH; (642*) G-AUBO; C9374/G-AUBW; C1972/G-AUDO; (3858*) G-AUDS; (3202*) G-AUDW; (2) G-AUEA; F3368/O-BAQQ; M-AAAB; M-AAEE; N-XAAA; NC22264; NC4066; NC4124.

* As documented (G-AUBH and 'BO believed ex B2802 and B2803)

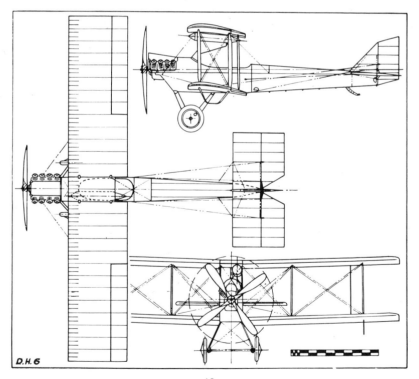

D.H.6

The Puma engined D.H.9 G-EBKV was converted into a three seater by the Aircraft Disposal Co. Ltd. in 1925. (*Flight Photo 3748*)

De Havilland D.H.9 and Variants

Capt. Geoffrey de Havilland designed the D.H.9 for the Aircraft Manufacturing Co. Ltd. in 1916 as a successor to the D.H.4. The prototype, actually a converted D.H.4, first flew at Hendon in June 1917, and although the flying surfaces and tail unit were identical with those of the earlier type, the fuselage was of an entirely new design. The pilot no longer sat in jeopardy between the engine and the fuel tanks, but next to and in easy communication with the gunner and the nose was of a better streamlined shape with the radiator retracting into the underside of the fuselage. The D.H.9 was built in large numbers but its operational life in 1918 was brief and unhappy due to the poor serviceability record of the B.H.P. six-cylinder engine, even when de-rated from 300 to 230 h.p.

The demilitarised D.H.9 was used extensively by air transport concerns in the years immediately following the 1914–18 war and in order to exploit the full load carrying capacity of this cheap and rugged aircraft, extensive modifications were devised by the Aircraft Manufacturing Co. Ltd., the de Havilland Aircraft Co. Ltd. and later by the Aircraft Disposal Co. Ltd. Pioneer air services between London, Paris and Amsterdam operated by Aircraft Transport and Travel Ltd. in 1919–20 employed sixteen D.H.9s, eight of which were newly erected by the infant de Havilland Aircraft Co. Ltd. at Stag Lane Aerodrome, Edgware, Middlesex and the remainder surplus Government stock stripped of military equipment. Some were fitted with the B.H.P. engine and others with the Siddeley Puma. One of them, C6054, was the first aircraft to make a flight other than for military or experimental purposes in this country, and for this it was allotted, but did not carry, the first permanent British registration marking G-EAAA. Its commercial life was confined to the early hours of the morning of 1 May 1919 because bad weather delayed its departure from Hendon from midnight until it took off at 4.30 a.m. with news-papers for Bournemouth, piloted by Capt. H. J. Saint. Thick mist was en-countered and an hour later the machine was wrecked on Portsdown Hill, north of Portsmouth.

Some of the Amsterdam services were flown under contract to K.L.M., the Royal Dutch Air Line, which at that time had no aircraft of its own, but when Aircraft Transport and Travel Ltd. closed down, four of its D.H.9s were taken over by K.L.M. to fly in competition with ten machines of the same type flown over the same route by the Handley Page Transport Co. Ltd. At least five D.H.9s also operated between Croydon or Cricklewood and Brussels in 1920–21, often flying in groups of two or three on the services of the Belgian airline SNETA. Another of the former A.T. & T. D.H.9s, G-EAQP, went to Newfoundland in 1922 to join the Aerial Survey Company founded by F. S. Cotton for seal and fishery spotting and for taxi work during the Labrador gold rush.

The earliest civil conversions merely involved the removal of the Scarff ring, bomb racks and other armament but by the end of 1919 nearly all D.H.9s flying on Continental services had been equipped to carry a second passenger in front of the pilot. In this form it was known as the D.H.9B but late in 1921 the de Havilland company further increased the load carrying capacity by a rearward extension of the back cockpit to accommodate light freight or a third passenger. The designation D.H.9C was coined to cover this version and at least 12 were erected at Stag Lane in 1922–23, the first two of which left Croydon on 23 September 1921 piloted by A. J. (later Sir Alan) Cobham, F. J. Ortweiler and C. D. Barnard on delivery to the Cia Española del Trafico Aéreo for a subsidised air mail service started in January 1922 between Seville and Larache in Spanish Morocco. Three British pilots, F. W. Hatchett, Sidney St. Barbe and C. F. Wolley Dod were employed initially, and the 9Cs gave quite extraordinary service for nearly seven years. F. W. Hatchett remained with the company and in 1929 was still flying over the original route in the surviving 9C M-AAGA which he had personally maintained through the years and considerably modified to suit chang-ing conditions. All the pilot's controls and instrumentation were redesigned

The Aircraft Transport & Travel D.H.9B G-EAGX 'Ancuba' taxying at Hendon in 1919.

50

A fully converted D.H.9C of the de Havilland Aeroplane Hire Service. (*Flight Photo 2077*)

and moved into the rear cockpit and the front fuselage was widened to accommodate two passengers and mail and covered with a low cabin roof of local manufacture.

Eight D.H.9Cs based at Stag Lane formed the fleet of the de Havilland Aeroplane Hire Service in 1922. They flew hundreds of hours to all parts of Europe and the British Isles at a charge of £8 per hour, mainly on hire to film and newspaper companies.

All passengers carried in D.H.9s wore helmet, goggles and flying clothing provided by the operator and in winter they were issued with hot water bottles. To improve the hard lot of passengers, the de Havilland Aircraft Co. Ltd. devised a further modification converting the rear cockpit into a cabin for two passengers face to face. A light wood and fabric roof hinged about the port upper longeron for ease of entry and although at first the windows remained unglazed, hinged wind deflectors were fitted at the front end to make conversation possible. At this stage it was felt advisable to compensate for the aft movement of the centre of gravity and the wings were given 8 inches of sweep back measured at the outer interplane strut. In this form it was still known as the D.H.9C, the first completed being the khaki drab G-EAYT in which A. J. Cobham made several long distance charter flights to North Africa and the Near East. Its short life ended in the sea when fog overtook it while landing at Venice Lido in October 1922. For the carriage of light freight or for the convenience of cameramen, the cabin top was frequently removed altogether and many of the Hire Service D.H.9Cs flew permanently in this condition. Some 150,000 miles were flown in 1922–23, in the course of which the earliest recorded crop spraying sortie was made in Kent in June 1922. When pensioned off in 1924, D.H.9C G-EAYU was sold with several military D.H.9s to the Hedjaz Government but unfortunately the ground crew fused some bombs incorrectly and 'YU and its Russian pilot were blown to pieces before reaching the rebel tribesmen.

Two new Stag Lane-built D.H.9Cs, G-AUED and 'EF, supplied to QANTAS for the 385 mile Charleville–Cloncurry route, which opened on 3 November 1922, were joined in February 1927 by G-AUFM built entirely by QANTAS at

O-BELG, a D.H.9 fitted with D.H.4A cabin top and underwing luggage containers by the Belgian concern SNETA.

Longreach with D.H.9 fuselage, D.H.50 mainplanes and controls, and the pilot's cockpit behind the cabin. A considerably more elaborate cabin conversion was made in Brussels by the Belgian concern SNETA which equipped two of their D.H.9s with the cabin tops and Triplex sliding windows removed from their defunct D.H.4As. Additional luggage space was provided under the fuselage and also in special containers under the lower mainplane just outboard of the undercarriage. These aircraft were acquired by Flg. Off. Nevill Vintcent and J. S. Newall in 1927 and flew to Stag Lane for modernisation which included the fitting of nose radiators and centre section fuel tanks of the type then in production for D.H.50s, an undercarriage incorporating the new D.H. system of rubber-in-compression and Dunlop car tyres to reduce puncture risk. Leaving Stag Lane on 9 January 1928 they made a leisurely flight to India, arriving at Karachi on 26 April to commence a tour of the sub-continent during which 5,000 passengers were given flights and the foundations of Indian air transport were laid.

The Aircraft Disposal Co. Ltd. at Croydon was responsible for the civil conversion of a very considerable number of D.H.9s but worked independently of the manufacturers and produced its own series of modifications. These inevitably began with the simplest type of demilitarised two seaters, some examples of which took part in long distance flights, notably F1287/G-EAQM in which R. J. Parer and J. C. McIntosh left Hounslow on 8 January 1920 and reached Darwin in 206 days in a very patched-up condition to complete the first England–Australia flight by a single engined aeroplane. It was repaired after a considerable crash on the last leg of the flight and after 50 years in store was reconditioned 1971–72 for display at Ray Parer's old school at Bathurst N.S.W. The first flight from England to South Africa, begun by a Vickers Vimy, was completed by Sir Pierre van Ryneveld and Sir Quintin Brand in D.H.9 H5648 'Voortrekker'.

Discarded Imperial Gift D.H.9s served on scheduled services in the Dominions for many years and in New Zealand three each were loaned to the N.Z. Flying School, Auckland (F1252, H5546, H5641); the Canterbury Aviation Co., Christchurch; and the N.Z. Aero Transport Co., Timaru. On 4 April 1922 Canterbury's D.H.9 D3136/G-NZAH completed the first flight ever made between Gisborne and Auckland and the New Zealand Aero Transport D.H.9 D3139/G-NZAM later became the first aircraft to make the direct flight from Invercargill to Auckland.

By 1922 nearly all the important long distance flights had been accomplished and only the round-the-world flight had not yet been attempted. An expedition for this purpose was therefore organised by Major W. T. Blake who planned to fly the overland stages between London–Calcutta and Vancouver–Montreal with three D.H.9s. Although the second machine, G-EBDL, piloted by Capt. Norman Macmillan, succeeded in reaching India where it was purchased by a Calcutta newspaper magnate and presented to the University of Benares, the flight was abandoned. D.H.9 G-EBDF, already positioned at Vancouver, was therefore sold to the Laurentide Air Service in Ottawa and converted into a D.H.9C.

The Disposals Company favoured neither the double rear cockpit nor the cabin top and their conversions were fitted mainly with four individual cockpits one behind the other. Entry to the rearmost pair was simplified by hinging the decking along the port side, a device incorporated in most of the aircraft overhauled at Croydon during more than ten years. Over 60 four seat D.H.9s of this type were supplied to Rumania by May 1922 and four to the Danish firm Det Danske Luftfartselskab A/S whose first service with land aircraft was opened on 15 September 1920 when D.H.9 T-DOGH flew from Copenhagen to Hamburg. When the route closed on 31 October the four machines had carried 83 passengers and 1,160 kg of mail. On 17 April 1923 the route was reopened with three surviving D.H.9s, 311 scheduled services being completed before the last flight of the season on 17 October 1923. One of these aircraft was kept airworthy for pleasure flying until 1930 by the cannibalisation of the other two.

In 1924 two two-seat Puma Nines were shipped to the British and Egyptian Tea Co. Ltd., one of which was test flown at Rochester with Short wooden main and tail floats. Undercarriages of this type were fitted to D.H.9s used

One of the D.H.9 floatplanes with which the Air Survey Co. Ltd. mapped the River Irrawaddy in 1924.

The D.H.9 G-EBEZ modified to single-seater and fitted with a Napier Lion engine for the 1923 King's Cup Race. (*Leonard Bridgman*)

by the Air Survey Co. Ltd. during the Irrawaddy, Sarawak and Indian surveys in 1924–25, and for a number supplied to Bolivia. The first of these, AM-1, was erected and test flown by J. R. 'Joe' King at Riberalta on the Rio Beni in 1925.

After 1924 the A.D.C. company no longer fitted a cockpit ahead of the pilot and later conversions such as G-EBJW and 'JX, supplied to Northern Air Lines for a short lived Stranraer–Belfast service, were three seaters fitted with the 300 h.p. A.D.C. Nimbus, Major Halford's re-design of the 230 h.p. Siddeley Puma. Thus after 10 years and two modifications, the designed power of the original B.H.P. engine was at last achieved. The Nimbus was also fitted to two special D.H.9s G-EBPE and 'PF erected at Stag Lane in 1926 for an aerial survey of Northern Rhodesia by the Aircraft Operating Co. Ltd. They were equipped as two seaters having a camera position under the tail and twin metal floats 21 ft. 9 in. long of the type built by Short Bros. for Sir Alan Cobham's D.H.50J. After transportation through the jungle on Ford trucks and erection by local labour they operated from the Zambesi River, 'PF alone successfully photographing 52,000 square miles of the Copper Belt.

Conversions to full swept wing D.H.9C standard by outside firms was confined to G-AUEU by H. C. Miller at Albert Park Aerodrome, Adelaide, S.A.; H4890/G-EBDG by the Manchester Aviation Co. Ltd. at Alexandra Park and H5886/G-EBIG by Berkshire Aviation Tours Ltd. at Monkmoor Aerodrome, Shrewsbury. Both the latter served with Northern Air Lines on the abortive Stranraer–Belfast service in 1925 and afterwards as joyriding machines at Barton until 1930.

In common with most open cockpit types the D.H.9 occasionally appeared as a single seat racer as in the 1922 King's Cup Race when G-EAAC, G-EBEN and 'EP came third, fourth and tenth respectively. In the following year the de Havilland Hire Service machine G-EBEZ was fitted temporarily with a 450 h.p. Napier Lion with which it came second at 144·7 m.p.h. piloted by Cobham, and

54

in 1927 W. G. R. Hinchliffe reached fourth place at 123·6 m.p.h. in a special single seater G-EBKO with A.D.C. Nimbus engine. The most spectacular result was achieved by the standard two seater VH-UHT in which H. C. Miller won the £1,000 first prize in the handicap section of the 2,200 mile Western Australia Centenary Air Race from Sydney to Perth in September 1929.

In 1934, when the type was nearly at the end of its career, Aerial Sites Ltd. of Hanworth employed G-AACP for banner towing and Sir Alan Cobham used 'CR for early flight refuelling experiments at Ford, Sussex. For this purpose the hinged decking to the rear cockpits was entirely removed to provide maximum working space.

Just after the 1914–18 war four civilian flying schools were given contracts for the annual training of R.A.F. Reservists and the de Havilland School of Flying began this training at Stag Lane on 1 April 1923, using Avro 548s, Hire Service D.H.9s and pilots who included A. J. Cobham, W. L. Hope, H. S. Broad, V. N. Dickinson and others. By the end of 1924 the D.H.9Cs had all been pensioned off and replaced by standard Puma-engined D.H.9s equipped as two seat advanced trainers including the ancient G-EAAC which de Havillands kept in flying trim in order to find out just how long an aeroplane would last in normal usage.

The school flourished until 1926, in which year the Avro 548 primary trainers gave place to Cirrus Moths and the veteran D.H.9s, including G-EAAC, were modernized and redesignated D.H.9J, the ultimate variant. The lengthy nose was cut right back to accommodate the heavier 385 h.p. Armstrong Siddeley Jaguar 14-cylinder two row radial engine, the V-strut undercarriages with their bungee shock absorbers were replaced by the new D.H. rubber-in-compression unit, and the original aileron circuit was modified to incorporate the patent D.H. differential aileron system. The school colours were also revised, and the D.H.9Js were among the smartest aeroplanes of their day, with red fuselages and struts, and gold flying surfaces.

D.H.9J G-EBGT, c/n 82, of the de Havilland School of Flying showing the 385 h.p. Armstrong Siddeley Jaguar III radial and rubber-in-compression undercarriage.
(*John Cope*)

The powerful Jaguar engines, purchased secondhand from Imperial Airways Ltd., had previously been installed in A.W. Argosy Is and many of them had flown more than 4,000 hr. Others were in seized-up condition but after overhaul gave sterling service in the D.H.9Js.

Two D.H.9Js G-EBOQ and 'OR were newly converted for the Armstrong Whitworth Reserve School in 1926 but were replaced by three new specimens in 1929. These were G-AARR–'RT, one of which, 'RS, was also used as a flying testbed for the Armstrong Siddeley Serval IV engine. When Air Service Training Ltd. was formed in 1931, they moved south to Hamble, where 'RS crashed in 1934, and the others continued in daily use until 1936. Later specimens included G-EBTN, built at Stag Lane in 1927 as a replacement for G-EBLH, which crashed at White Waltham on 12 May 1927. A further example, G-AASC, flew in 1929 after the elderly G-EBHV retired. The last D.H.9J, however, did not appear until the autumn of 1931, not long before the type was withdrawn from service. This machine, G-ABPG, powered by a Jaguar IVC, was built as an exercise by the students of the de Havilland Technical School. It went into normal Flying School use and was probably the only purely civil D.H.9 airframe of non-military origin ever constructed and in common with all D.H.9J aircraft converted after 1925, had a plywood covered front fuselage.

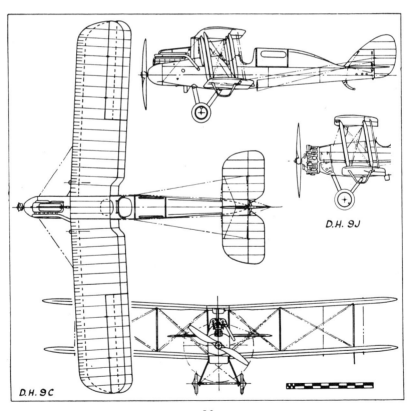

D.H. 9J

D.H. 9C

SPECIFICATION

Manufacturers: The Aircraft Manufacturing Co. Ltd., Hendon, London, N.W.9 and sub-contractors.

Conversions by: The Aircraft Manufacturing Co. Ltd.; The de Havilland Aircraft Co. Ltd.; Handley Page Ltd.; The Aircraft Disposal Co. Ltd.; Northern Air Lines; Berkshire Aviation Tours Ltd.; Queensland and Northern Territory Aerial Services Ltd.; Miller Aviation Ltd.; and SNETA.

Power Plants: One 230 h.p. B.H.P.
One 240 h.p. Siddeley Puma.
One 300 h.p. A.D.C. Nimbus.
One 385 h.p. Armstrong Siddeley Jaguar III.
One 450 h.p. Napier Lion.

Dimensions: Span, 42 ft. $4\frac{5}{8}$ in. Length, 30 ft. 6 in. (D.H.9J) 28 ft. 9 in. Height, 11 ft. 2 in. Wing area, 434 sq. ft.

Weights and Performance:

	D.H.9 Puma	D.H.9 Lion	D.H.9C Puma	D.H.9J Jaguar
Tare weight	2,230 lb.	2,544 lb.	2,600 lb.	2,375 lb.
All-up weight	3,900 lb.	3,667 lb.	3,300 lb.	3,900 lb.
Maximum speed	110 m.p.h.	144 m.p.h.	115 m.p.h.*	—
Initial climb	650 ft./min.	1,800 ft./min.	600 ft./min.	—
Ceiling	15,500 ft.	24,500 ft.	19,000 ft.	—
Duration/Range	4 hours	$3\frac{1}{2}$ hours	500 miles	—

* Cruising speed, 95 m.p.h.

Civil conversions: (a) D.H.9

Thirty-seven British registered machines listed in Appendix E and the following exported or converted overseas (with former military serial if recorded): D3180/G-IAAB; G-IAAG; H9129/G-IAAP; E611/G-IAAQ; D5686/G-IAAS; A6-5/G-AUEG; A6-4/G-AUEH; G-AUFB; H9340/G-AUFS; G-AUHT; D3017/A6-11/VH-UMB; A6-21/VH-UML; A6-19/VH-UMM; A6-9/VH-UMT; H9274/T-DOBC; H9359/T-DOGH/OY-DIC; H5521/T-DODF; H5636/G-NZAD; H5627/G-NZAE; D3136/G-NZAH; D3139/G-NZAM; H5672/G-NZAQ; O-BATE; F1148/O-BEAU; F1221/O-BLAC; F1293/O-BIEN.

(b) D.H.9B

Twenty British registered aircraft listed in Appendix E.

(c) D.H.9C

Ten British registered examples listed in Appendix E and the following exported by the de Havilland company: (c/n 11) M-AAAG; (12) M-AAGA; (13) M-AGAA; (86) G-AUED; (87) G-AUEF. Also G-AUEU and G-AUKI converted in Australia and G-AUFM built by QANTAS.

(d) D.H.9J

Fourteen British registered aircraft listed in Appendix E.

Rex Stocken in the Eagle engined D.H.9A at Croydon on 8 June 1922.
(*Leonard Bridgman*)

De Havilland D.H.9A

Contrary to general belief, the D.H.9A was not a conversion of the D.H.9, but an entirely different type of aeroplane. Its wings were of greater chord and span, the fuselage employed different methods of construction and the radiator was positioned in the nose, as in the D.H.4. This extensive redesign was carried out by the Westland Aircraft Works at Yeovil in 1918, and the vast majority of production aircraft were powered by the American 400 h.p. eight-cylinder Liberty engine. There were 13 British civil D.H.9As, but only three had this engine, the remainder being non-standard.

The first six, fitted with closely cowled 450 h.p. Napier Lion 12-cylinder engines cooled by underslung radiators, were actually R.A.F. machines registered to the British Government as G-EAOF–'OK in October 1919 and loaned to Aircraft Transport and Travel Ltd. for the carriage of mail to the Army of Occupation on the Rhine. This service, begun by the R.A.F. on 17 December 1918 with standard D.H.9s, was handed over to A.T. & T. as a going concern on 15 August 1919. The difficult sector over the Ardennes and into Cologne called for the machines of higher performance and load carrying capacity and thus, for the last winter of the service, a Lion engined fleet of 9As was provided, G-EAOH returning to the R.A.F. in April 1920 and the rest in the following June.

Encouraged by the performance of the Lion powered D.H.4R, the Aircraft Manufacturing Co. Ltd. built a similarly powered sesquiplane using D.H.9A components and designated the D.H.9R. In it Capt. Gathergood made a fast trip to Amsterdam in 2 hours 10 minutes when visiting the First Air Traffic Exhibition in July 1919 and while there won a closed circuit race at 145 m.p.h. On 15 November 1919 the same pilot broke several British speed records at Hendon, raising the closed-circuit record to 149·43 m.p.h.

The other six D.H.9As were all surplus military stock civilianised at Croydon by the Aircraft Disposal Co. Ltd. for demonstration or overseas delivery. The first, G-EAXC, converted in 1922, won the Club Handicap Race at the Croydon Easter Meeting 1922, flown by the A.D.C. test pilot Rex Stocken. On 22 May he also flew 'XC in the race for the Coupe Lamblin over the course Le Bourget–Brussels–Croydon–Le Bourget and made fastest time. A second demonstration conversion G-EBCG appeared in April 1922, fitted with a 350 h.p. Rolls-Royce Eagle VIII engine for participation in the Croydon Whitsun Races but cooling trouble resulted in the replacement of the nose radiator by smaller side radiators in time for the first King's Cup Race, which started at Croydon on 8 September 1922. It was piloted in this event by H. H. Perry but forced landed at Northolt with ignition trouble.

This type of Eagle conversion was originally carried out on the military demonstrator G-EBAN, which was fitted with Lamblin radiators between the undercarriage legs and despatched to Madrid in February 1922 to take part in the Spanish trials, its performance resulting in an order for a batch of similar machines. The remaining three civil D.H.9As consisted of G-EBAC and 'LC,

One of the six A. T. & T. Lion engined D.H.9A mailplanes.

Capt. Gerald Gathergood with the D.H.9R at Amsterdam in July 1919. (*Photo courtesy of Firth Vickers Stainless Steels Ltd.*)

59

G-CYAJ, the Canadian Air Board D.H.9A in which Flt. Lt. C. W. Cudemore flew the Regina–Medicine Hat section of the first trans-Canada air mail on 11 October 1920. (*R.C.A.F. Photo*)

The removal of the radiator on A.D.C. Eagle conversions gave the D.H.9A a more streamlined appearance.

Liberty powered, flown overseas in 1922 and 1927 respectively, and G-EBGX fitted with a Napier Lion in 1923.

Australia and Canada received D.H.9As in 1920 as part of the Imperial Gift but after modification by the Whitehead Aviation Company all 11 Canadian D.H.9As were handed over to the Air Board Civil Operations Branch for forestry patrol and survey work alongside the D.H.4s. Between 11–17 October 1920 three of them took part in the first trans-Canada flight, each covering one leg of the Winnipeg–Vancouver section, piloted respectively by Flt. Lts. J. B. Home-Hay, C. W. Cudemore (G-CYAJ) and G. Thompson (G-CYBF). In 1922 six were at Camp Borden and the remainder were on photographic survey work on wheel or ski undercarriages at Rockliffe but the majority were destroyed in a hangar fire at Camp Borden on 16 October 1923.

SPECIFICATION

Manufacturers: The Aircraft Manufacturing Co. Ltd., Hendon, London, N.W.9. and other contractors.

Power Plants: One 400 h.p. Liberty.
                     One 350 h.p. Rolls-Royce Eagle VIII.
                     One 450 h.p. Napier Lion.

Dimensions: Span, 45 ft. $11\frac{3}{8}$ in. Length, 30 ft. 3 in. Height, 11 ft. 4 in. Wing area,
                     486·73 sq. ft.

	Liberty	Eagle VIII	Lion
Tare weight	2,800 lb.	2,705 lb.	2,557 lb.
All-up weight	4,645 lb.	4,815 lb.	4,660 lb.
Speed at 10,000 ft.	114·5 m.p.h.	110·5 m.p.h.	134 m.p.h.
Initial climb	725 ft./min.	600 ft./min.	1,000 ft./min.
Ceiling	18,000 ft.	14,000 ft.	21,300 ft.
Duration	$5\frac{1}{4}$ hours	$3\frac{1}{2}$ hours	—

Civil conversions:

Twelve British registered aircraft listed in Appendix E with one D.H.9R racer and the following used in Canada (quoting former R.A.F. serial): E1000/G-CYAD; E998/G-CYAJ; E994/G-CYAK; E996/G-CYAN; E1002/G-CYAO; E997/G-CYAZ; E995/G-CYBF; E992/G-CYBI; E993/G-CYBN; E1001/G-CYCG; E999/G-CYDO.

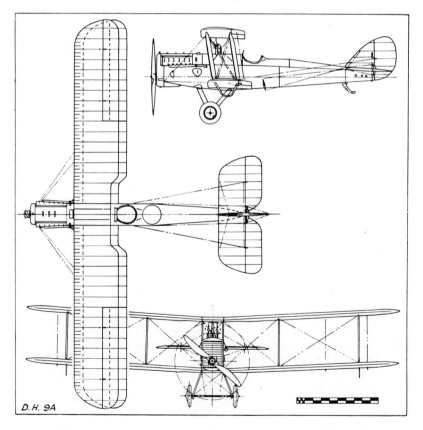

D.H. 9A

One of the Lion engined D.H.16s of Aircraft Transport and Travel Ltd. at Croydon in 1920. (*Flight Photo 895*)

De Havilland D.H.16

The D.H.16 was a cabin version of the war surplus D.H.9A, built for the Hounslow–Paris service of Aircraft Transport and Travel Ltd. in 1919. Conversions were carried out by the Aircraft Manufacturing Co. Ltd., who widened the rear fuselage to accommodate four passengers in facing pairs in a glazed cabin. Power was supplied by an Eagle VIII engine, and the D.H.16 was thus a larger yet more economical relative of the D.H.4A. The prototype, K-130, went into service in May 1919, two and a half months before the first D.H.4A, and was exhibited at the First Air Traffic Exhibition at Amsterdam in the following July. As G-EACT, and piloted by Capt. C. Patteson, the same aircraft flew the 12.30 p.m. service to Paris, on 25 August, inaugural day of the London–Paris air route. By June 1920 nine D.H.16s had been constructed, one of which, G-EAQG, was sold to the River Plate Aviation Co. Ltd. for a highly successful Buenos Aires–Montevideo cross-river ferry.

The last three D.H.16s to be built, G-EAQS, 'RU and 'SW, were fitted with the more powerful Napier Lion engine. Although considered trickier to handle, they set up a high standard of reliability, and during one week in the summer of 1920 'QS made seven return trips between Croydon and Paris in six consecutive days, making fastest time of the week in each direction. It was the Eagle-powered G-EALU, however, which H. 'Jerry' Shaw had the honour of piloting on the first K.L.M. flight ever scheduled between Croydon and Amsterdam. This took place in extremely bad weather on 17 May 1920 with two passengers and freight in a flight time of 135 minutes. The early K.L.M. services were thereafter all flown by A.T. & T.

For reasons already outlined, the firm was forced to shut down in December 1920, when its aircraft, including seven surviving D.H.16s, went into storage in a Bessoneau hangar at Croydon. The D.H.9s were sold to K.L.M., and many ways were suggested for finding useful employment for the 16s. An air service to Le Touquet, Deauville and Dieppe was proposed, but their fate was finally sealed when the Casino authorities refused to subsidize it.

During the summer of 1922 the D.H. Hire Service secured the early morning newspaper contract to Ostend. The D.H.9C aircraft were based at Lympne to avoid the habitual low cloud in the Caterham Valley, and after delivering the papers, brought back casual passengers. So popular was the service that the best of the stored D.H.16s were pressed into use, the two selected being G-EALM and 'PT, which after overhaul at Stag Lane went straight on service. Four passengers were now brought back on each trip—good business at £3 a head. On 10 January 1923 the engine in G-EALM failed while on test flight near Stag Lane, the machine stalled on a turn and R. E. Keyes and a mechanic were killed. The survivor, G-EAPT, continued in service until scrapped in the following July, and when those at Croydon met the same fate, the type became extinct.

SPECIFICATION

Manufacturers: The Aircraft Manufacturing Co. Ltd., Hendon, London, N.W.9.
Power Plants: One 320 h.p. Rolls-Royce Eagle VIII.
              One 450 h.p. Napier Lion.
Dimensions: Span 46 ft. $5\frac{7}{8}$ in. Length, 31 ft. 9 in. Height, 11 ft. 4 in. Wing area, 490 sq. ft.
Weights: Tare weight, 3,155 lb. All-up weight, 4,750 lb.
Performance: Maximum speed, 136 m.p.h. Initial climb, 1,000 ft./min. Range, 350 miles.
Production: Nine British owned aircraft listed in Appendix E.

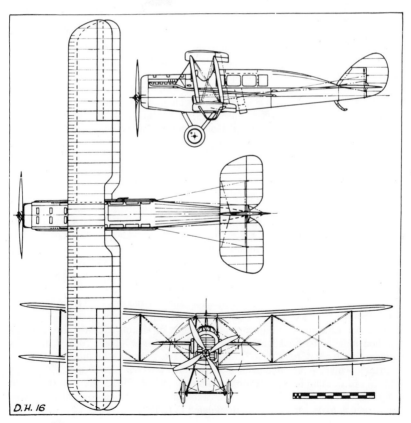

D.H. 16

The prototype D.H.18 at Hounslow in September 1919. (*Flight Photo 545*)

De Havilland D.H.18

This was the first Airco machine specifically designed for airline work. It was a single engined two bay biplane of wire braced, wooden construction with the front fuselage plywood covered. The prototype, G-EARI, was allotted the de Havilland constructor's number one, built at the beginning of 1920 and test flown by F. T. Courtney. After evaluation and certification, it went into service on 8 September 1919, on loan to Aircraft Transport and Travel Ltd. Eight passengers were accommodated in a large cabin amidships, with the pilot in an open cockpit behind—a fashion set by the F.K.26. The engine was the famous Lion, which gave it the impressive top speed, for those days, of 125 m.p.h. It was wrecked after a comparatively short life when Cyril Holmes forced landed with engine trouble in some back gardens in Wallington, just after take-off from Croydon on 16 August 1920. Two others, G-EARO and 'UF, designated D.H.18A, begun by Airco at Hendon, were the first aircraft completed at Stag Lane by its successor, de Havilland Aircraft Co. Ltd., and were fitted with improved engine mountings, undercarriages and control cable fairleads.

When subsidized air services commenced in March 1921, the Air Council was empowered to purchase a limited number of up-to-date commercial aircraft and to lease them to approved firms. The ex A.T. & T. D.H.18As were purchased in this way, and after plywood coverings had been fitted to their top centre sections they were handed over to the Instone Air Line. A fourth machine, G-EAWO, was then built to Air Council order and also assumed the blue Instone livery. By September 1921 'RO had flown more miles on the Paris, Brussels and Cologne routes than any other aeroplane but its C. of A. was not renewed and it retired from service in November 1921. As G-EAUF had been lost in a crash in the previous June, the Instone Air Line found itself so severely short of aircraft that the Air Council supplied it with the final machines, G-EAWW and 'WX. The former made its maiden trip from Croydon to Paris on 18 December 1921 piloted by F. T. Courtney while 'WX, fitted with a Leitner-Watts three bladed metal airscrew, went to Martlesham for type testing in January 1922 before delivery to Instone at Croydon a month later. Their fuselages were entirely plywood covered with built-in emergency exits and they were designated D.H.18B.

Meanwhile Daimler Hire Ltd. had successfully applied for recognition as an 'approved firm' and commenced a Croydon–Paris service on 2 April 1922. Pending the delivery of its new D.H.34s, the Air Council transferred the D.H.18A G-EAWO to the new company. Having completed 600 hours' flying in Instone service it was overhauled, fitted with new mainplanes and repainted in Daimler red. Piloted by R. E. Duke on 4 April 1922—two days after the firm began operations—it collided head on with Farman Goliath F-GEAD in bad visibility at Grandvilliers, Northern France where both crashed and were burned out. In the same month 'WX was loaned to Handley Page Ltd. to alleviate its fleet shortage and after this the two remaining aircraft, 'RO and 'WW, were used almost exclusively on the Brussels route.

When declared obsolete in 1923, 'RO had flown 90,000 miles without mishap and together with 'WW returned to the manufacturers for partial reconditioning for test purposes. On 16 April 1924 G-EARO was flown from Stag Lane to the R.A.E. Farnborough where, from July 1924 to July 1926, it was used for testing

The Instone Air Line's veteran D.H.18A G-EARO, c/n 2, at Croydon in 1922. The stringers of the fabric covered fuselage are clearly visible. (*L. T. Mason*)

The sixth and last machine of the type was G-EAWX, a D.H.18B with plywood-covered fuselage.

fuel consumption, cabin silencing, and a drift sight for aerial photography. On 7 July 1927 it was flown to Biggin Hill and the return flight to Farnborough on 10 November is believed to have been its last. The other machine, D.H.18B G-EAWW, was the subject of an experiment carried out at Felixstowe on 2 May 1924 to determine the time taken for an aircraft to sink after a forced landing at sea. With the cowlings removed and the cabin sealed, it took off from Martlesham piloted by Sqn. Ldr. C. A. Rea who shortly afterwards put it gently into the water where it floated for 25 minutes, enabling a salvage crew to recover the Lion engine.

SPECIFICATION

Manufacturers: The Aircraft Manufacturing Co. Ltd., Hendon, London, N.W.9. Reconstituted as the de Havilland Aircraft Co. Ltd., 25 September 1920.

Power Plant: One 450 h.p. Napier Lion.

Dimensions: Span, 51 ft. 3 in. Length, 39 ft. 0 in. Height, 13 ft. 0 in. Wing area, 621 sq. ft.

Weights: (D.H.18A) Tare weight, 4,040 lb. All-up weight, 6,516 lb.
(D.H.18B) Tare weight, 4,310 lb. All-up weight, 7,116 lb.

Performance: Maximum speed, 125 m.p.h. Cruising speed, 100 m.p.h. Initial climb, 660 ft./min. Ceiling, 16,000 ft. Range, 400 miles.

Production: Six aircraft (c/n 1 to 6) listed in Appendix E.

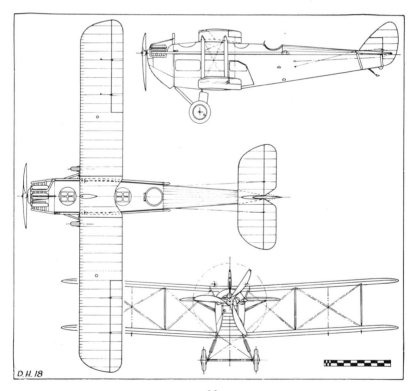

D.H.18

The prototype D.H.34, G-EBBQ, at Stag Lane in March 1922 ready for delivery to Daimler Hire Ltd. at Croydon.

De Havilland D.H.34

By 1921 the purely civil D.H.18s had been in service long enough for the economics of air transport to begin to be understood. It was evident that if commercial aviation were to pay its way, more payload would have to be carried per horsepower and at a higher speed. The de Havilland Aircraft Co. Ltd. therefore built the 10 passenger D.H.29, the first large high performance cantilever monoplane to fly in the United Kingdom. Plans were also drawn up for the D.H.32, an eight seat biplane of similar appearance to the D.H.18, but fitted with the lower powered and more economical Eagle VIII engine.

With the expansion of cross-Channel services under the permanent subsidy scheme, however, the need for new commercial types became urgent. Development work on the D.H.29 was therefore dropped in favour of the well proven biplane but certain of its features were introduced into the D.H.32 design to create the now famous D.H.34. The fuselage was a wooden structure, plywood covered for strength and ease of maintenance and almost identical in appearance to that of the D.H.29. The Napier Lion was retained but the cockpit, seating two pilots instead of one, was positioned ahead of, instead of behind, the wings. Petrol was carried in streamlined tanks under the top mainplane, well clear of the fuselage and the ailerons were differentially operated, a system first flown on the D.H.29, and subsequently embodied on all later de Havilland types. The cabin seated nine passengers in wicker chairs and was fitted with a door large enough to permit the carriage of a spare engine if necessary. Inertia starting was introduced, and marked the end of primitive propeller swinging on commercial aeroplanes.

Two D.H.34s were ordered by Daimler Hire Ltd. the first of which, the prototype G-EBBQ resplendent in the firm's all-red colour scheme, made its first flight at Stag Lane on 26 March 1922 piloted by A. J. Cobham. It was the first of an initial batch of nine aircraft, seven of which were to Air Council order. 'BQ was delivered to the owners at Croydon on 31 March and after the Daimler pilots had obtained their D.H.34 endorsements, W. G. R. Hinchliffe made the inaugural flight to Paris on 2 April 1922. Some of the Air Council's machines were leased to the Instone Air Line, and the first, G-EBBR, painted in blue and silver, went into service on the same day as the prototype. Piloted by F. L. Barnard, it carried a full load to Paris in 2 hours 40 minutes. Unfortunately 'BQ turned over during a forced landing at Berck a fortnight later, leaving its newly delivered sister ship, 'BS, to carry on during its reconstruction at Stag Lane. During April–May 1922 the second Instone machine G-EBBT 'City of New York' and the third Daimler G-EBBU were delivered but after a ground collision at Croydon a few weeks later, the latter also went back to Stag Lane, leaving 'BS again to carry on alone. This stalwart flew 8,000 trouble free miles during the season, a foretaste of the enormous mileage the D.H.34 fleets were to log successfully in the next few years.

The 'City of New York' inaugurated a new Croydon–Brussels service of the Instone Air Line on 7 May 1922, and later in the year the Director of Civil Aviation decided to prevent unneccessary competition for the small amount of traffic by means of route allocation. The Paris route went to Handley Page Ltd., the Brussels and Cologne route to the Instone Air Line and a new Berlin route to Daimler Hire Ltd. Thereafter the Instone D.H.34s flew only on their allotted service, and on 15 September 1922 W. G. R. Hinchliffe opened the new Daimler service to Berlin by carrying Maj. G. Woods Humphery and Col. F. Searle in the faithful G-EBBS. Disagreement between the British and German Governments eventually forced the termination of this route at Amsterdam. Traffic increases then resulted in the lease of G-EBBW to Instones as the 'City of Chicago' and G-EBBY to Daimlers, leaving the Air Council with one D.H.34 in hand. This was G-EBBX, which subsequently went into service with Daimlers as a replacement for G-EBBU, which crashed at Berck on 3 November 1922. The seventh production aircraft, built to the order of the Russian airline Dobrolet, received its C. of A. on 16 June 1922 and was exported without markings.

Having two machines which were their own property, Daimlers were in a position to operate routes other than those approved under the subsidy arrangements. This led to the extension of the Croydon–Amsterdam route inland as far as Manchester. This once-daily service was well patronized after the inaugural flight by the evergreen G-EBBS on 23 October 1922. Diversions were also made to Castle Bromwich for the British Industries Fair in March–April 1923 but on 14 September 1923 'BS was destroyed through stalling near the ground while attempting a forced landing at Ivinghoe Beacon, Bucks. The pilots G. E. Pratt and L. G. Robinson and three passengers were killed and the accident was attributed to the high stalling speed of 63 m.p.h. which made forced landings extremely difficult. The opportunity was taken therefore to equip Daimler's G-EBBX, at that time under repair at Stag Lane after a forced landing in the sea off Ostend, with mainplanes of greater area as a D.H.34B.

At the end of 1922 de Havillands built two more D.H.34s, G-EBCX and 'CY, which proved to be the last of the type. The first was handed over to Daimler Hire Ltd. but 'CY was not used commercially and may not have been completed. Thus, when Imperial Airways Ltd. was formed on 1 April 1924 by a merger of existing operators, it inherited six D.H.34s—G-EBBT, 'BV, 'BW, 'BX, 'BY and 'CX— which continued in service on the Brussels and Amsterdam routes until retired in 1926. The sole exception was G-EBBX, which crashed and burned immediately after take-off from Croydon on 24 December 1924 despite its modification, Capt.

D. A. Stewart and his seven passengers being killed in an attempted forced landing in similar circumstances to those in which 'BS met its fate. G-EBBT, rebuilt after an accident near Kenley on 11 February 1924, first flew as a D.H.34B on 12 June 1925 piloted by H. S. Broad and the last of these conversions, G-EBBY, was rigged as a three bay biplane and first flew in this form on 7 September that year.

SPECIFICATION

Manufacturers: The de Havilland Aircraft Co. Ltd., Stag Lane Aerodrome, Edgware, Middlesex.

Power Plant: One 450 h.p. Napier Lion.

Dimensions: Span, 51 ft. 4 in. (D.H.34B) 54 ft. 4 in. Length, 39 ft. 0 in. Wing area, 590 sq. ft. (D.H.34B) 637 sq. ft.

Weights: Tare wt., 4,574 lb. (D.H.34B) 4,674 lb. A.U.W., 7,200 lb.

Performance: Cruising speed, 105 m.p.h. Range, 365 miles.

Production: Twelve aircraft (c/n 27–36 and 40–41) comprising one (c/n 33) for Dobrolet, Russia and 11 for British operators.

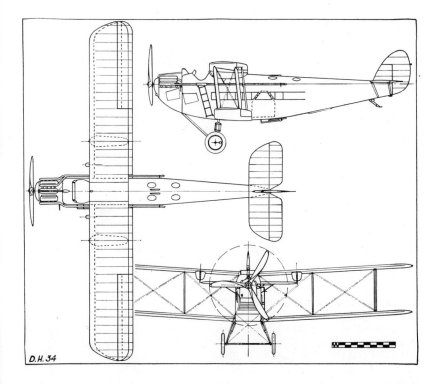

D.H.34

The D.H.50A G-AUEI in which F. S. Briggs flew the inaugural Adelaide–Sydney service for Larkin on 18 November 1924.

De Havilland D.H.50

The D.H.50 was a four seater designed in the light of operational experience gained by the de Havilland Hire Service with the D.H.9C. It was a two bay biplane with plywood covered fuselage seating the pilot in an open cockpit behind a small cabin and thus can be regarded as a scaled-down version of the D.H.18B. Using the same engine as the 9C—a 230 h.p. Siddeley Puma—the new type not only carried one more passenger but had also a higher cruising speed. The prototype, G-EBFN, made its first flight at Stag Lane in August 1923 and four days later was flown to Gothenburg by A. J. Cobham, manager of the Hire Service. Competing against all the well known contemporary European manufacturers, he gained 999 points out of a possible 1,000 to win first prize in the International Air Traffic Competitions. A year later, on 12 August 1924, Cobham won the King's Cup Race in the same aircraft, averaging 106 m.p.h.

The second D.H.50 became the most famous of all contemporary British civil aircraft. This was G-EBFO in which Cobham made the long distance flights which earned him a knighthood. Fitted experimentally with automatic full-span camber-changing flaps, it flew to the Prague Aero Exhibition on 30 May 1924 but the flaps were later removed and the aircraft sold to Imperial Airways Ltd. After a flight to Rangoon, undertaken by Cobham to enable Sir Sefton Brancker, the Director of Civil Aviation, to attend a conference, 'FO returned to Stag Lane to be prepared for a survey flight to the Cape. The extra power needed for taking off from high altitude aerodromes in Africa was obtained by replacing the water-cooled Puma by a 385 h.p. Armstrong Siddeley Jaguar air-cooled radial motor. With additional cabin fuel tanks and carrying A. B. Elliott as engineer and a ciné photographer B. W. G. Emmott, the D.H.50 started from Croydon on 16 November 1925. The 16,000 mile flight was a masterpiece of sound organisation and Cape Town was reached on 17 February 1926. The D.H.50 landed at Croydon on 13 March after an even more rapid return flight and preparations were immediately put in hand for a similar survey flight to Australia. As much of this route lay over water, the aircraft was fitted with twin metal floats by Short Bros. Ltd. at Rochester and the flight started from the Medway in the early hours of 30 June 1926. The return flight to Melbourne was made with such apparent ease that it caused a sensation but cost the life of Cobham's talented engineer A. B. Elliott, killed by a Bedouin's stray bullet when flying over the desert between Baghdad and Basra on 5 July. When 'FO returned to make its historic landing on the Thames at Westminster on 1 October, its Empire flights totalled 62,000 miles but in 1929 a Nimbus engine was fitted and this historic aircraft was shipped to West Australian Airways Ltd.

The third D.H.50, G-EBFP, was a familiar sight at Croydon for eight years, first in Imperial Airways blue and later in silver and black. In the hands of the charter section manager, Capt. G. P. Olley, and others, it was in daily use for private hire and scheduled service relief until disposed of to the Iraq Petroleum Transport Co. Ltd. in 1932. Its final year of service was spent in ferrying the company's personnel from Haifa to the pumping stations along the desert pipeline. A companion aircraft, G-EBKZ, added to the Imperial Airways fleet in 1925, was a production model known as D.H.50A with slightly longer cabin, centre section struts more splayed out, additional radiator area and the undercarriage set slightly farther forward. Fourteen D.H.50As were built at Stag Lane, 9 being to Australian order, the first of which, G-AUAB, was built in 1924 along with a D.H.37 and two D.H.53s for the Controller of Civil Aviation. Seventeen years later, in November 1942, it was fitted with a Pratt & Whitney Wasp C and impressed for war service. The second QANTAS aircraft G-EBIW/G-AUER gave many years of faithful service as the first flying doctor machine, first named 'Hermes' and later 'Victory'.

Three D.H.50As were also shipped to West Australian Airways Ltd. for the Wyndham–Perth–Adelaide service, and three to the Larkin sponsored Australian Aerial Services Ltd. for the mail run between Adelaide and Sydney. Other Antipodean D.H.50As were A8-1 for the Governor General of Australia, G-AUAY for the Australian Government and c/n 135 for R.N.Z.A.F. survey work. G-AUAY was later re-engined with a 420 h.p. Bristol Jupiter VI radial and impressed into the R.A.A.F. in 1940, while the R.N.Z.A.F. aircraft was sold to Holdens Air Transport, New Guinea in 1933 as VH-UQX.

Finding the serviceability record of its original D.H.50 so impressive, QANTAS obtained a manufacturing licence for the D.H.50A, G-AUFA 'Iris', which first flew on 8 August 1926, being the first of seven built at Longreach to

Alan Cobham in the D.H.50J G-EBFO during final adjustments on the eve of his Cape flight, November 1925. (*Flight Photo 3338*)

D.H.50J G-EBOP 'Pelican' with 420 h.p. Bristol Jupiter IV radial at Rochester on 15 November 1926. (*Flight Photo 4173*)

replace the veteran D.H.4 and the D.H.9Cs. Three were fitted with Puma engines but four had Jupiter VI radials to improve climb and cruising speed. They were known as D.H.50Js even though this designation had already been given to Cobham's Jaguar engined long distance machine.

Concurrently with QANTAS production, Larkin built a single Puma D.H.50A under licence and West Australian Airways Ltd. built three more, completing their first aircraft in November 1926 and two others in the following year. One Jupiter engined D.H.50J was also built at Stag Lane to the order of the North Sea Aerial and General Transport Co. Ltd. and equipped with Fairey-Reid metal airscrew, additional D.H.9A-type fuel tanks and Short twin metal floats for a pioneer mail service along the Nile between Khartoum and Kisumu. Christened 'Pelican' at Rochester on 15 November 1926, it was shipped to the Sudan and Capt. T. A. Gladstone flew the inaugural service in the following month.

The last British registered D.H.50A, G-EBQI, built for Air Taxis Ltd. in 1927, was the only D.H.50A fitted with the original D.H.50 type radiator. Sir Philip Richardson bought it in 1929 and kept it at Brooklands but later sold it to Northern Air Lines Ltd. but the major part of its career was spent as a taxi aircraft after its return to the Brooklands School of Flying Ltd. in 1930.

SPECIFICATION

Manufacturers: The de Havilland Aircraft Co. Ltd., Stag Lane Aerodrome, Edgware, Middlesex and under licence by SABCA, Brussels and Aero, Prague.

Power Plants: One 230 h.p. Siddeley Puma or 300 h.p. A.D.C. Nimbus.
One 385 h.p. Armstrong Siddeley Jaguar III.
One 420 h.p. Bristol Jupiter IV or 450 h.p. Jupiter VI.
One 450 h.p. Pratt & Whitney Wasp C.

Dimensions: Span, 42 ft. 9 in. Length, 29 ft. 9 in. (D.H.50J) 28 ft. 9 in.
Height, 11 ft. 0 in. Wing area, 434 sq. ft.

Weights: (Puma) Tare weight, 2,413 lb. All-up weight, 4,200 lb.
(Jupiter) Tare weight, 2,336 lb. All-up weight, 4,200 lb.

Performance: (Puma) Maximum speed, 109 m.p.h. Cruising speed, 95 m.p.h.
Initial climb, 605 ft./min. Range, 375 miles.
(Jupiter) Maximum speed, 132 m.p.h. Cruising speed, 110 m.p.h.
Initial climb, 1,250 ft./min. Range, 240 miles.

Production: (a) By de Havilland at Stag Lane

Seventeen aircraft comprising eight British registered and the following for export: (c/n 106) G-AUAB; (127) G-AUEL; (128) G-AUEM; (129) G-AUEI; (130) G-AUEJ; (131) G-AUEK; (134) R.A.A.F. A8-1; (135) R.N.Z.A.F. 135; (137) G-AUAY.

(b) D.H.50As built by QANTAS at Longreach

Four aircraft: (c/n 1) G-AUFA; (2) G-AUFW; (3) G-AUGD; (6) G-AUJS.

(c) D.H.50Js built by QANTAS at Longreach

Three aircraft: (c/n 4) G-AUHE; (5) G-AUHI; (7) VH-ULG.

(d) D.H.50As built by West Australian Airways Ltd. at Perth

Three aircraft: (c/n 1) G-AUFD; (2) G-AUFE; (3) G-AUFN.

(e) D.H.50A built by the Larkin Aircraft Supply Co. at Melbourne

One aircraft only: (c/n 1) VH-UMN.

(f) D.H.50As built by SABCA at Brussels 1925

Three aircraft: O-BAHV, O-BAHW, O-BAHX.

(g) D.H.50As with 240 h.p. Walter W-4s built by Aero at Prague 1926

Seven aircraft: (c/n 1/1 to 1/7) L-BALA to L-BALG (later OK-ALA to 'LG).

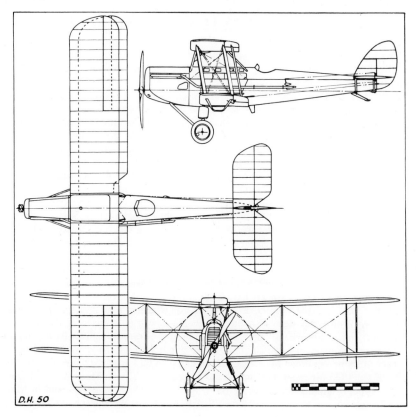

D.H. 50

73

Flg. Off. G. E. F. Boyes flying the Scorpion engined Humming Bird at Lympne on 31 July 1925. (*Flight*)

De Havilland D.H.53 Humming Bird

The first light aeroplane designed by the de Havilland Aircraft Co. Ltd. was the little D.H.53 low wing, single seat monoplane built for the *Daily Mail* trials at Lympne in October 1923 and following the firm's usual practice, the fuselage was built of spruce longerons and cross struts covered with plywood. The two spar wings were fabric covered and thickened at the points where V struts braced it to the top longerons. Two identical prototypes named 'Humming Bird' and 'Sylvia II' (actually G-EBHX and 'HZ respectively) were flown in the competitions by the D.H. test pilot H. S. Broad and Major H. Hemming and although neither won a prize, Broad's loops and rolls, never before performed on a light aircraft, gave rise to the opinion that they were the most practical aircraft present. Major Hemming covered 59·3 miles to the gallon in the consumption tests, but the 750 c.c. Douglas motor cycle engines with which they were fitted were a constant source of trouble.

Early in 1924 a production batch of 12 machines laid down at Stag Lane were named Humming Birds, after the prototype, becoming the first civil aircraft of de Havilland manufacture to receive a type name. Eight of these were to Air Ministry order for evaluation as R.A.F. primary trainers, three went to Australia, one to the Aero concern in Prague which was building D.H.50As under licence, and almost a year later a thirteenth machine was built to a Russian order. The production aircraft were powered by 26 h.p. Blackburne Tomtit inverted V, two-cylinder engines, and had the new D.H. rubber-in-compression rear undercarriage legs. The two prototypes were also fitted with the new legs in place of the original bungee shock absorbers, and 'HX acquired a Tomtit engine. Rechristened 'L'Oiseau Mouche', it came eighth at 67·35 m.p.h. in the 1924 Grosvenor Trophy Race at Lympne piloted by A. J. Cobham and also took part with varying success in all the 1925 air races, in which it was joined by G-EBHZ. This was the second prototype, originally the property of A. S. Butler, which had been sold in May 1925, less engine, to a group of seven R.A.F. officers at Eastchurch. As the Seven

Aero Club they had fitted it with a 35 h.p. A.B.C. Scorpion engine, but the engine was wrecked through lack of oil while racing at Lympne on 1 August 1925 and the machine was eventually sold.

The first six D.H.53s for the R.A.F. were numbered J7268–J7273 and all made their public debut together in the race between the Air Ministry Directorates at the 1925 Hendon R.A.F. Display. J7272 also took part in that year's Lord Mayor's Show—on a trailer. The remaining two, J7325 and '26, were earmarked for experimental hooking and unhooking from the airship R-33 (G-FAAG) and on 4 December 1925 Sqn. Ldr. R. A. de Haga Haig was dropped from the airship in J7325 (fitted with the rudder from J7326), successfully re-engaged the trapeze and was safely hauled in. The second special D.H.53 also had the pick-up superstructure fitted, but was powered by a 32 h.p. Bristol Cherub.

Although initially no production machines had been sold for private use in the United Kingdom, when the R.A.F. struck its D.H.53s off charge in 1927 all eight became civil aeroplanes. A leading share in their subsequent activities was taken by the Royal Aircraft Establishment Aero Club at Farnborough, where P. G. N. Peters and his colleagues made several airworthy. The club owned G-EBRW in 1929 after it had spent two years with Fred Gough at the Norfolk and Norwich Club, G-EBXN from 1928 to 1932 and G-EBQP in 1927–28. The last mentioned had been the Cherub engined J7326 during its airship career, and retained this engine during its civil life which began when Flg. Off. Mackenzie Richards came third in the Nottingham Air Race on August Bank Holiday 1927, and finished when an unlicenced pilot stalled it from 60 ft. and was killed at Hamble on 21 July 1934. The actual machine which had made the hooking-on experiment was acquired in a crashed condition in April 1928 by K. V. Wright, also of Farnborough, by whom it was rebuilt and sold to Capt. A. V. C. Douglas at Bekesbourne in 1929.

Others became G-EBRJ, kept at Brooklands by the Tellus Super Vacuum Cleaner Co. Ltd., R. P. Cooper's G-EBRA (sold abroad by D.H.s in 1928) and R. W. H. Knight's G-EBRK. In 1972 the only surviving specimen of the type was the prototype, G-EBHX, preserved at Old Warden by the Shuttleworth Trust. This was owned for many years by F. J. V. Holmes of Berkshire Aviation Tours, and finally by E. W. Kennett at Walmer. Longest lived among the others were G-EBRW, owned in 1933 by R. L. Burnett at Broxbourne, and the Cherub engined G-EBXN, the seventh and last owner of which, as late as 1938, was E. D. Ward at

VH-UAC, first of the Australian D.H.53s, with cut-back front fuselage to accommodate the 35 h.p. A.B.C. Scorpion engine. (*B. Van Sickle*)

G-EBRW with the Tomtit inverted engine, taking part in the comic event at the Woodley Flying Meeting on 5 April 1930. (*Flight Photo 8510*)

Hooton. 'XN was undoubtedly the most flown of all the Humming Birds and was a familiar sight anywhere between Squires Gate and Hamble in its day. It was burned eventually in the grandstand fire at Hooton Park Racecourse on 8 July 1940.

When it retired in 1930, G-EBRJ was hung from the roof of the Phillips and Powis hangar at Woodley but its ultimate fate, and those of G-EBHZ, 'RK, 'RW, 'TT and 'XM are shrouded in mystery. One at least was in the possession of R. J. Coley and Co. Ltd., scrap merchants of Hounslow, in February 1937 and is thought to have been the machine rebuilt at Brooklands by students of the College of Aeronautical Engineering and flown by Capt. Duncan Davis in July 1936. It is evident that three of the six lived on for one became the R.A.E. Scarab (otherwise the P.B. Scarab) built at Farnborough 1930–32 under the direction of Messrs. Peters and Brewer of the R.A.E. Aero Club; another was re-registered G-ABPS to J. K. Lawrence at Cramlington, Newcastle, in September 1931 (but never appeared as such); and a third donated major components to the Clarke Cheetah G-AAJK.

The first two Australian Humming Birds were delivered to the Civil Aviation Department in time for the light aeroplane competitions held at Essendon, Melbourne, at the end of 1924 in which one was flown by Capt. E. J. Jones. The same one was also flown in the Australian Aerial Derby at Richmond, Sydney, by Sqn. Ldr. Anderson on 8 January 1925. Later, as G-AUAC and 'AD, the two machines enjoyed long careers and were used by the Aero Club of New South Wales. By the early 1930s the first had been fitted with an A.B.C. Scorpion and re-registered VH-UAC and in 1937 was acquired by J. Bowen for shipment to Samoa where it appeared in the 1946 Victory Parade towed behind a truck.

The purpose of the third Australian machine, c/n 118, is obscure for it appears in neither civil nor R.A.A.F. records but in 1937 was acquired in wrecked condition by Dr. R. J. Coto who rebuilt it from data, spruce and fabric mailed to him by de Havillands. He fitted a 40 h.p. Aeronca engine, named it 'Icarus', and with a 17 gallon fuel tank behind the cockpit, startled the world in May 1937 by flying 1,950 miles from Wyndham to Perth W.A. in $6\frac{1}{2}$ days in an airborne time of 30 hr. 5 min. This is thought to be the D.H.53 which was to be seen in the Perth Technical College annexe in 1972.

A D.H.53 replica, CF-OVE, built at Calgary, Alberta, Canada by aircraft engineer S. N. Green and powered by a 40 h.p. Continental A-40, made its first flight on 7 May 1967 piloted by G. Fryer.

SPECIFICATION

Manufacturers: The de Havilland Aircraft Co. Ltd., Stag Lane Aerodrome, Edgware, Middlesex.

Power Plants: One 750 c.c. Douglas.
One 698 c.c. (26 h.p.) Blackburne Tomtit.
One 32 h.p. Bristol Cherub III.

Dimensions: Span, 30 ft. 1 in. Length, 19 ft. 8 in. Height, 7 ft. 3 in. Wing area, 125 sq. ft.

Weights: Tare weight, 326 lb. All-up weight, 565 lb.

Performance: Maximum speed, 73 m.p.h. Cruising speed, 60 m.p.h. Initial climb, 225 ft./min. Ceiling, 15,000 ft. Range, 150 miles.

Production: Fifteen aircraft comprising ten British registered and the following for export: (c/n 103) G-AUAC; (104) G-AUAD; (117) Czechoslovakia; (118) Australia; (151) Russia.

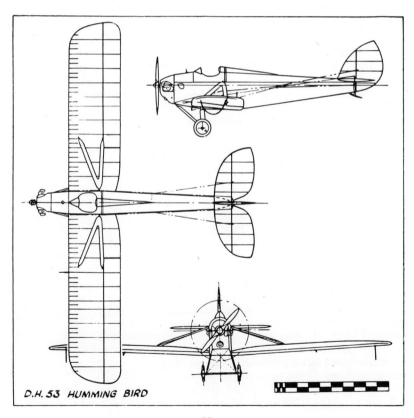

D.H. 53 HUMMING BIRD

D.H.60X Moth (A.D.C. Cirrus II) G-EBSP of the Phillips and Powis School of Flying, dropping a parachutist over Woodley in October 1932. (*Fox*)

De Havilland D.H.60 Moth

The sixtieth de Havilland design resulted from the realization that the fragile, underpowered ultra lights of the 1923–24 Lympne Trials would not be the club aeroplanes of the future. A much more robust two seat biplane was built which would be capable of withstanding the wear and tear of instructional flying, and Major F. B. Halford of the Aircraft Disposal Co. Ltd. was called in to design a special four-cylinder air-cooled engine for it, known as the A.D.C. Cirrus I. This used existing A.D.C. parts and was actually one half of an Airdisco eight-cylinder V-type engine, giving 60 h.p. for a weight of only 290 lb.

The famous Moth prototype G-EBKT, which made its first flight at Stag Lane on 22 February 1925 piloted by Capt. Geoffrey de Havilland, was of standard wooden construction with plywood covered fuselage, fabric covered surfaces, folding wings and differential ailerons on the lower wings. Its simple lines and extraordinary performance on low power set a revolutionary, yet instantly popular fashion in light aeroplane configuration which was to last for several decades. Sir Samuel Hoare, the Secretary of State for Air, became interested, with the result that the Air Ministry initially subsidized five flying clubs and equipped them with Moths. The first of these, G-EBLR, delivered to the Lancashire Aero Club by A. J. Cobham on 21 July 1925 had a life of only two years but G-EBLV, which he ferried to the same owners on 29 August, was still preserved in flying condition by Hawker Siddeley Aviation Ltd., Hatfield in 1972 as the oldest surviving Moth. A similar aircraft, G-CAUA, reconditioned at Downsview by de Havilland Canada Ltd., was presented to the Canadian National Aviation Museum on 10 May 1963 by Carl F. Burke, its owner since 1933. Another, G-CAPA, was still flying in the U.S.A. as N1510V in 1972 and a fourth, VH-UAU, was on exhibition in the Museum of Applied Arts and Sciences, Sydney, Australia.

Later in 1925 G-EBLI and 'LU were delivered to the London Aeroplane

Club, 'LX and 'LY to the Newcastle Aero Club, 'LT and 'LW to the Midland Aero Club and 'LS to the Yorkshire Aeroplane Club. It was a memorable summer during which the Moth founded the flying club movement in the United Kingdom.

Although first flown with an unbalanced rudder, the prototype was fitted with the horn balanced type common to production models in time for the 1925 King's Cup Race in which it was flown by A. J. Cobham, who made a simultaneous 6 a.m. take-off from Croydon with 'KU, the second prototype, flown by the designer but both made forced landings north of London because of fog. By the end of the year G. B. H. Mundy and Wg. Cdr. A. Wynn had become the first Moth owners with G-EBME and 'MF respectively while others were exported to Australia, Chile, Japan and Ireland. An exhibition machine, c/n 273, became the first Moth seaplane when H. S. Broad flew it from the Medway at Rochester in November 1926 fitted with the all-metal, twin float undercarriage originally fitted to the Short Mussel. Sir Alan Cobham shipped this machine to the U.S.A., flew the last few miles from Sandy Hook and landed in New York Harbour prior to a comprehensive demonstration tour with wheeled undercarriage.

Even in 1926 Moths made up two-thirds of visiting aircraft at air meetings and by 1929 the Hampshire, Cinque Ports, Scottish, Nottingham, Norfolk & Norwich, Northamptonshire and Bristol & Wessex Clubs had come into being, together with the Brooklands and Phillips and Powis Schools of Flying. All of these were Moth equipped. One Moth, G-EBOU, was fitted with a 75 h.p. Genet I radial as competitor No. 2 in the 1926 Lympne Trials. It met with no success, but was flown in several club races by Sempill, d'Arcy Greig and others until sold to Flg. Off. F. O. Soden at the end of 1927. After a brief aerobatic career it was sold in Germany as D-1651.

Public imagination in the late 1920s was fired by the many racing successes and record breaking long distance flights achieved by these machines. To the man-in-the-street every small aeroplane became a 'Moth', just as every large aeroplane in the 1914–18 war had been a 'Handley Page'. This chapter in the Moth's career began in May 1925 when A. J. Cobham flew the prototype 1,000 miles from Croydon to Zürich and back in a day. In the following year H. S. Broad won the King's Cup Race in G-EBMO at an average speed of 90·5 m.p.h. This machine

De Havilland's chief engineer James Norman standing by the prototype Moth at Stag Lane in 1925. Note the unbalanced rudder.

was fitted with the new 85 h.p. Cirrus II engine and during the November and December was flown to India by T. Neville Stack in company with B. S. Leete in 'KU. The next King's Cup also went to a Moth—G-EBME, specially modified by W. L. Hope of Air Taxis Ltd., who averaged 92·8 m.p.h. with a Cirrus I engine. In another sphere it also became supreme when Lady Bailey took G-EBQH to 17,283 ft. over Stag Lane on 5 July 1927 to establish a new light aeroplane altitude record. A sister machine, G-EBPP, shipped to Australia in 1928, broke the Perth-to-Melbourne record piloted by Major Hereward de Havilland.

The three unsuccessful Moths, G-EBQH, 'RT and 'SK, in the 1927 King's Cup Race were of the first of an improved type, having considerable internal modifications and Cirrus II engines on lowered mountings. In the original model the Cirrus was bolted high on the top longerons but now the thrust line was lowered to improve streamlining by bringing the cylinder heads into line with the fuselage decking. The new designation was D.H.60X (X for experimental), but this was quickly dropped in favour of Cirrus II Moth.

One of these was G-EBSO 'Dorys', in which Lt. R. R. Bentley made two return trips from Croydon to Cape Town in 1927–29, thus winning the A.F.C. and the Britannia Trophy. Lady Bailey, well known as a private owner, left Croydon in G-EBSF on 9 March 1928, but wrote it off at Tabora on 8 April, thereafter completing a successful solo flight of 18,000 miles to, from and around South Africa in a replacement Cirrus II Moth G-EBTG. Lt. Cdr. H. C. Macdonald slipped away unobtrusively in G-EBVX at the same time as Lady Bailey and made a totally unpublicised flight to Baghdad with only eight hours' solo in his log book. Several British-owned Moths were based overseas, G-EBSR with the Johannesburg Light Plane Club, 'SQ and 'UL at Nairobi with Mrs. Carberry and Cdr. L. M. Robinson respectively, floatplanes 'UJ and 'UK with the Royal Singapore Flying Club and G-EBTI in Johore with A. L. Birch. Another floatplane, 'XU, left London in the s.s. *Andorra* on 6 June 1928 en route to Brazil, where it completed a 450 square mile aerial survey of Rio de Janeiro.

Six R.A.F. Genet I Moths, J8816–J8821, performed formation aerobatics at the Hendon R.A.F. Display on 2 July 1927 flown by C.F.S. instructors d'Arcy

D.H.60X Moth seaplane K-SALF, c/n 447, taking off from Rochester in September 1927 prior to delivery to Aero O/Y, Helsinki. (*Flight Photo 5178*)

Flg. Off. F. O. Soden flying the Genet Moth G-EBOU in 1928.

Greig, Stainforth, R. L. R. Atcherley, Waghorn, Beilby and Smart, and one of these, J8818, was later flown by the Director of Civil Aviation, Sir Sefton Brancker, as G-EDCA. In 1928 this was replaced by a Cirrus Moth with the same markings.

A Cirrus Moth with U.S.N. serial 7564, issued to the U.S. Naval Attaché in London and based at Stag Lane to replace his ancient DH-4B, remained in use until disposed of to the Midland Aero Club as G-AADB at the end of 1928. Considerable shipments were made also to South Africa, India, Singapore, Canada, Argentina, Italy and the U.S.A., as shown in the accompanying production list, and licences were also granted for construction to take place in Australia by the General Aircraft Co. Ltd., Sydney and in Finland by the Government Aircraft Factory.

The 1928 Moth was a further improvement, powered by the new 90 h.p. Cirrus III engine and identified by its split axle (or 'X') undercarriage. Machines of this type bore the permanent designation D.H.60X Moth, and by the end of the year 403 Moths of all types had been built, of which 137 were of British registry. One of them, G-EBXG, was acquired by Handley Page Ltd. for experimental fitment of automatic slots and another, 'ZC, reached an altitude of 18,800 ft. at Croydon on 4 October 1928 piloted by Lady Heath. After the delivery of G-AABL to the London Aeroplane Club in September 1928 the D.H.60X largely went out of production in favour of newer models, but a few were later constructed to special order. These included G-AADJ and 'DK for the Singapore Club in 1929 and a batch of 26 for the clubs of National Flying Services Ltd. in 1930. The D.H.60X Moth also gave faithful service in remote areas. G-EBZL was flown to Kano, Nigeria, by G. R. Boyd Carpenter, and G-EBZZ to the Gold Coast by Capt. R. L. Rattray. Both returned in 1930 and joined sister machines which continued in club and private use right up to the outbreak of the 1939–45 war, the principal users in 1939 being the Yapton and Portsmouth Aero Clubs. Several modified to take the 105 h.p. Cirrus Hermes I engine included the famous G-EBSO, the A.D.C. demonstrator 'UF, the Singapore floatplanes and R. O. Shuttleworth's G-EBWD. The last mentioned was still airworthy in 1972, maintained by the Shuttleworth Trust at Old Warden.

SPECIFICATION

Manufacturers: The de Havilland Aircraft Co. Ltd., Stag Lane Aerodrome, Edgware, Middlesex; and under licence in Australia and Finland.

Power Plants: One 60 h.p. A.D.C. Cirrus I.
One 75 h.p. Armstrong Siddeley Genet I.
One 85 h.p. A.D.C. Cirrus II.
One 90 h.p. A.D.C. Cirrus III.
One 105 h.p. A.D.C. Cirrus Hermes I.

Dimensions: Span, 30 ft. 0 in. Length, 23 ft. $8\frac{1}{2}$ in. Length (Genet), 24 ft. 3 in. Height, 8 ft. $9\frac{1}{2}$ in. Wing area, 243 sq. ft.

	D.H.60 Moth	Genet Moth	Cirrus II Moth	D.H.60X Moth
Tare weight	770 lb.	810 lb.	855 lb.	955 lb.
All-up weight	1,240 lb.	1,550 lb.	1,550 lb.	1,750 lb.
Maximum speed	91 m.p.h.	101 m.p.h.	95 m.p.h.	98·5 m.p.h.
Cruising speed	80 m.p.h.	85 m.p.h.	85 m.p.h.	85 m.p.h.
Initial climb	430 ft./min.	590 ft./min.	650 ft./min.	570 ft./min.
Ceiling	13,000 ft.	16,000 ft.	17,000 ft.	14,600 ft.
Range	320 miles	410 miles	430 miles	290 miles

Production: (a) Cirrus I Moths
Thirty registered in Britain and the following for export or the Royal Air Force: (c/n 192) G-AUAE; (196) Chile; (199) A7-1; (200) A7-2; (233) J8030; (241) G-AUAJ; (242) G-AUAK; (243) G-AUAF; (244) G-AUAG; (245) G-AUAH; (246) G-AUAL; (247) J8031; (248) J8032; (264–267) Irish Air Corps 23–26; (273) U.S. demonstrator, later G-CAIL; (274) Japan; (275) G-AUFU; (351) G-AUFR; (352) G-AUFL.

(b) Cirrus II Moths
Twenty registered in Britain and the following for export or to the R.A.F.: (c/n 354) G-AUGH; (356) untraced; (362) G-UAAA; (363) G-AUFT; (364) G-AUAM; (365) G-AUAP; (366) G-AUAR; (367) G-AUAS; (368) G-AUAT; (369) G-AUAV; (372) U.S.N. 7564; (374) Germany as G-W101; (377) G-CAHK; (379) J8818: (380) J8816; (381) J8817; (382) J8821; (383) J8820; (384) J8819; (390) Argentine.

(c) D.H.60X Moths
One hundred and twenty-two registered in Britain initially and the following for export or the R.A.F.: (c/n 400–403) G-CAOU to 'OX; (406) G-AUHF; (407–408) Australia; (409) G-CAHS; (411) Australia; (412) G-AUHB; (424) G-AUGO; (425) G-AUGX/VH-UGX, later G-ACXF; (426) G-AUHA; (433) D-1238; (434) G-CAIG; (435) G-UAAB; (439) G-UAAE; (440) G-UAAF; (442) G-UAAG; (445) Germany; (447) K-SALF; (448) G-CAKA; (449) G-CAKB; (453) G-AUGM; (454) G-CAKC; (455) G-CAKD; (456) G-CYYX; (457) G-CYYW; (458) G-CAKE; (459) G-CAKF; (460–461) R.C.A.F. 27–28; (462) G-CAKG; (463) G-CAKH; (464) G-AUHD; (465) G-AUHG; (466) G-AUHJ; (468) I-RUSP; (470) I-GINO; (472) G-CAKI; (473) G-CAKJ; (477) C-PAAA; (479) G-UAAI; (480–482) S-AABM to 'BO; (484) G-CATH; (485) G-CYYS; (486) G-CYYR; (487) G-CYYQ; (488) G-CYYL; (489) G-CYYK; (490) G-CYYJ; (491) G-CYYP; (492) G-CYYO; (493) G-CYYN; (494) G-CYYM; (495) G-CYYI; (496) G-CYYH; (497) M-CACC; (498) M-CCAA; (499) M-CCCA; (500) G-NZAT; (502) G-UAAL; (503) G-CAYG; (504–508) G-CAOY to 'PC; (510–528) J9103–J9121; (529) G-EDCA; (530) G-CYXI; (531–533) Argentine; (534) Northern Rhodesia; (535) G-CAJW;

(536) P-BABL; (540) VH-UAQ; (541) Australia; (542) VH-UAN; (543–544) Australia; (545) VH-UPU; (546) Australia; (547) NC5359; (549–551) Australia; (554) G-CAJV; (555) G-CANS; (559) I-BUBI; (560) G-CAJU; (561) Argentine; (562–565) G-CAKK to 'KN; (567–582) G-CAKO to 'LD; (585) I-BIBL; (586) Argentine; (587) G-UAAX; (588) G-UAAN; (589) I-SIDE; (591) G-NZAU; (595) G-CANA; (596) Australia; (597) VH-UQC; (598) VH-UPX; (599) VH-UPK; (600–603) Australia: (604–606) G-AUGS to 'GU; (607) G-UAAW; (608) VP-YAA; (610) G-CARV; (611) G-CARW; (612) G-CATK; (613) VH-UAO; (614) VH-UAU; (616) NC7106; (617) G-CATG; (618) G-CATI; (619) G-CAJY; (620) G-CAJZ; (621) G-CATZ; (622) G-CATJ; (623) G-CATF; (624) M-CDDA; (625) G-UAAP; (628) G-CAUC; (629) G-CAUN; (630) G-CAUA; (631) G-CAUB; (632) G-CAVI; (633) G-CARZ; (634) G-CAUO; (635) G-CARX; (636) G-CARY; (637) G-CAUE; (638) G-CAUQ; (639) G-CAUD; (640) G-CARU; (641) R.C.A.F. 55; (642) G-CAUP; (645–646) R.C.A.F. 56 and 57; (651–671) Chile G.1 to G.21; (673–675) Chile G.22 to G.24; (677) C. Cooper; (680) R.C.A.F. 58; (688–690) G-CAVF to 'VH; (692) I-ABEB; (693) I-ABEC; (696) G-CAUM; (698) G-UABD; (701) G-UABC.

(d) Licence construction

At least nine by the General Aircraft Co. Ltd., Sydney including (c/n 1, 2, 3, 6, 9) VH-UFV, 'GE, 'GJ, 'GL, 'MK; twenty-two aircraft built 1929–30 by the Finnish Government Aircraft Factory (c/n 1–22) Finnish Air Force MO-91 to MO-112 of which (c/n 8–10) were sold for civil use as K-SILD, OH-ILB and OH-ILC. Two others were reworked by Veljekset Karhumäki as (c/n 1–2) OH-VKD and 'KE.

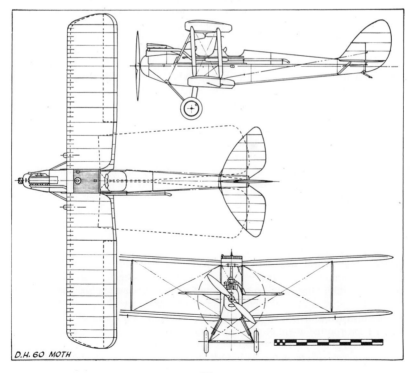

D.H. 60 MOTH

One of the red and black Brooklands School of Flying Gipsy Moths, G-AABJ, fitted for night operation and blind flying. (*Flight Photo 11512*)

De Havilland D.H.60G Gipsy Moth

In 1927 the de Havilland Company commenced the manufacture of the now almost legendary Gipsy motor. Designed by Major F. B. Halford, the first experimental engines, rated at 135 h.p., were handmade by D.H. engineers S. T. Weedon and Mitchell for installation in the record breaking D.H.71 Tiger Moth monoplane but production engines were derated to 85 h.p. for club and private use and named Gipsy I, the first being fitted to the firm's trial installation Moth G-EBQH. Thus engined, the Moth became the D.H.60G Gipsy Moth and sales technique demanded that it should make its public debut in the 1928 King's Cup Race, consequently three of the 14 competing Moths were Gipsy powered. These were G-EBQH, 'YK and 'YZ flown by A. S. Butler, H. S. Broad and W. L. Hope, the last handsomely winning his second King's Cup at an average round-Britain speed of 105 m.p.h. Although many earlier models were subsequently fitted with Gipsy engines, 'YZ, with constructor's number 801, was the first production Gipsy Moth but had a straight axle undercarriage for racing.

Initial racing success was followed by a skilfully arranged proving and publicity programme. On 25 July 1928 Capt. Geoffrey de Havilland reached the record altitude of 21,000 ft. in his private machine G-AAAA, and during 16–17 August, H. S. Broad made an unofficial 24 hours' endurance record over Stag Lane in G-EBWV. A. S. Butler, chairman of the company, completed the hat trick on 7 December by breaking the 100 km. closed circuit record in G-AACL, completing the course from Stag Lane to Twyford, Berks. and back at 119·84 m.p.h. The Gipsy's final ordeal was designed to prove its reliability and to increase the between-overhauls life of the engine. One of the firm's earlier Moths, G-EBTD, was fitted with a Gipsy I taken at random from the production line and sealed by the A.I.D. Between 29 December 1928 and 24 September 1929 the D.H. Reserve School instructors flew it for 600 hours, equivalent to a distance of 51,000 miles. Apart from routine attention the Gipsy ran untouched, and at the end of the test the overhaul and replacement cost was a mere £7 2s. 11d.

These events made immense impact on the aviation world and whereas the earlier models had sold in dozens, the Gipsy Moth was built in hundreds. Large numbers were shipped to Australia, six (VT-AAA, 'AB, 'AE —'AH) equipped Indian flying clubs and five (ZS-ABH —'BL), shipped to South Africa in 1929, formed the initial fleet of Union Airways Ltd. Licences were also granted for production by Morane-Saulnier in France; de Havilland Aircraft Pty. Ltd. and the Larkin Aircraft Supply Co. Ltd. in Australia; and the Moth Aircraft Corporation in the U.S.A., but against a background of solidly efficient yet often unspectacular service with flying clubs, private owners and taxi firms, it also carved for itself a racing and long distance record breaking career.

The fourth production Gipsy Moth was the long range G-AAAH which W. L. Hope of Air Taxis Ltd. acquired for a rapid flight to Kisumu and back in September 1928, the month in which the Vicomte de Sibour left Stag Lane for a world tour in G-EBZR. Encouraged by H. S. Broad's 24 hour record, Lt. Cdr. H. C. MacDonald D.S.C. shipped G-EBWV to Newfoundland for an Atlantic flight and took off for England on 17 October 1928 with fuel for 25 hours but after being seen by a ship 600 miles out, was never heard of again.

The Gipsy Moth will be associated for ever with the Australia route for soon afterwards Amy Johnson used the long range G-AAAH, named 'Jason', for the historic flight which began at Croydon on 5 May 1930 and reached Darwin on 24 May. Although she failed to beat Bert Hinkler's record, it was the first England–Australia flight by a woman. The first male Gipsy Moth flight over the route was made by Francis Chichester in G-AAKK 'Madame Elijah'. He arrived at Darwin on 25 January 1930, five weeks after leaving Croydon, shipped it from Sydney to New Zealand and a year later fitted floats for his all-time epic of navigation in finding and landing at the microscopic Norfolk and Lord Howe Islands during his flight back to Australia. This famous aeroplane was eventually wrecked at Katsuura, Japan, on 14 August 1931.

Prince Jean Ghica of Rumania, who attempted an overland long distance record in single seat Gipsy Moth CV-TUR, left Bicester for Istanbul on 9 July 1930 but crashed in Central Bulgaria next morning. Another Moth, G-ABEN, which made a leisurely flight to Australia October–December 1930 flown by Flt. Lt. C. W. Hill, returned as VH-UPV piloted by Mrs. H. Bonney April–June 1933. First to break the record however was VH-UFT flown from Wyndham to Pevensey Bay by J. A. Mollison in 8 days 19 hours 23 minutes in July 1931. This machine eventually toured with National Aviation Day displays as G-ABUB.

Maurice Jackaman's Coupé Moth 'Peridot III'. (*Flight Photo 6799*)

VH-UGX 'Edith', a Gipsy conversion of an early D.H.60X, left Darwin for England on 6 June 1932 piloted by J. N. Weir who was taken ill and abandoned the flight at Karachi on 3 July. Two years later, with a 120 h.p. Gipsy II, this machine was flown to England in 74 days by D. L. Rawnsley who arrived at Lympne on 22 April 1934 and later re-registered it as G-ACXF.

Others penetrated to the remotest parts of the earth. John Grierson flew G-AAJP 'Rouge et Noir' to Lahore in 1930, to Baghdad in 1931, to Moscow in 1932 and on floats from Brough to Iceland in 1933; G-EBZY, shipped out by N. S. Chalmers, was the first light aircraft in Fiji; and an R.A.A.F. Gipsy Moth seaplane, A7-55, located the missing Antarctic explorer Lincoln Ellsworth on 15 January 1936.

The Gipsy Moth was now in large scale production at Stag Lane and a number of variants appeared. Capt. Geoffrey de Havilland's personal G-AAAA was fitted with a coupé top and in October 1928 the first coupé Moths 'DX, 'EE and 'GE were supplied to A. C. M. Jackaman, Lady Bailey and Loel Guinness. It was not a popular innovation, and all subsequently reverted to standard. A special coupé Moth, G-AAIM, with Cirrus Hermes I was also used by Shell Mex and B.P. Ltd. in 1929 while two others with interchangeable float and ski undercarriages were supplied to the British Arctic Air Route Expedition for survey work along the Greenland coast in 1930. The Norwegian registered N-40 was used for whale spotting in the Antarctic; ZK-ABK and 'BL were supplied to Union Airways Ltd. and five (MW-113 to MW-117) were ferried to Spain.

Other variants of note were two Moth amphibians G-AADV (Gipsy I) and G-AAVC (Hermes I) fitted with Short all-metal central floats with retractable wheels for J. Scott-Taggart and the Hon. A. E. Guinness respectively 1929–30. A Gipsy Moth was also employed at Hanworth in 1935 as test bed for the prototype 85 h.p. General Aircraft V.4 inverted engine.

The wooden Gipsy Moth continued in production until 1934, the British-built total of 595 including G-ABTS and G-ACAM built by de Havilland Technical School students as constructional exercises. The final production machine,

A Hermes engined Moth with Short amphibian undercarriage, owned by the Hon. A. E. Guinness in 1930. One similar machine with Gipsy I engine, G-AADV, also existed, flown in the previous year by John Scott-Taggart. (*Aeroplane*)

J. N. Weir flying the long range, single seat Gipsy Moth VH-UGX 'Edith' in which he left
Darwin for England on 6 June 1932. It became G-ACXF in 1934. (*Shell*)

HB-OFI, returned from Switzerland in May 1939 for instructional use by Malling
Aviation Ltd. as G-AFTG and during the 1939–45 war was one of many im-
pressed for R.A.F. use. Sister aircraft HB-OBA, which survived to be flown
home as G-ATBL by Edward Eves in 1965, was later completely refurbished by
C. C. Lovell at Netheravon but G-ABJJ, which did considerable post-war flying,
was sold in Canada in 1962 as CF-AAA. Others flying in 1972 included J. F. W.
Reid's Tarrant Rushton-based G-AAWO; Dr. Ian Hay's immaculate G-ABYA at
Redhill (damaged in a crash near Biggin Hill on 21 May 1972); ZK-ADT at
Wairoa, New Zealand; and VH-AFN flown at Glendale, California, as N168G.
Several were also to be seen in Australian museums and Amy Johnson's im-
mortal G-AAAH 'Jason' was on permanent display at the Science Museum,
London.

SPECIFICATION

Manufacturers: The de Havilland Aircraft Co. Ltd., Stag Lane Aerodrome, Edgware,
Middlesex; and under licence in Australia, France and the U.S.A.
Power Plants: One 100 h.p. de Havilland Gipsy I.
One 105 h.p. Cirrus Hermes I.
One 120 h.p. de Havilland Gipsy II.
Dimensions: Span, 30 ft. 0 in. Length, 23 ft. 11 in. Height, 8 ft. $9\frac{1}{2}$ in. Wing area,
243 sq. ft.
Weights: Tare weight, 920 lb. All-up weight, 1,650 lb.
Performance: Maximum speed, 102 m.p.h. Cruising speed, 85 m.p.h. Initial climb,
500 ft./min. Range, 320 miles.

Production: (a) At Stag Lane
595 aircraft including a large number registered in Britain and the following for export:
(c/n 812) Argentine; (813) G-CAVK; (818) Argentine; (819–824) G-AUID to 'IH, 'IJ;
(828) Chile; (830) S.A.A.F.; (832) CH-205/HB-ULO; (833–838) G-AUGV, 'GW, 'IA,
'JU, 'JW, 'JX; (840) Sarawak; (842) G-UABA; (843) G-CALE; (846–849) G-AUJV, 'LA,
'IB, 'IC; (850–857) VT-AAA to 'AH; (858–863) G-CAVJ, 'VW, 'UR, CF-CAK,
G-CAVU, CF-ADS; (864) Argentine; (866–869) G-NZAW to 'AZ; (870–873)

Danish Navy Gipsy Moth serial 148 (c/n 899) on skis in 1929.

R.N.Z.A.F. 870–873; (875–880) G-AUHN to 'HS; (881) Canada; (882) CF-AAD; (883) Australia; (884) CF-AAC; (885) NC9720; (886) NC9718; (888) ZK-AAA; (890) T-DMOT/OY-DUF; (891–898) G-AUIO to 'IS, VH-UMV, G-AUKG, 'LC; (899–900) Danish Navy 148, 149; (901–906) Danish Army S.100 to S.105; (907–908) VT-AAI, 'AJ; (909–910) G-CAPH, CF-AQF; (911–912) two U.S.A.; (913) NC9733; (914–915) G-NZEA, 'EB; (918) O-BAJW; (920) CH-208/EC-AQQ; (922) ZK-AAO; (923) Mexico; (924) U.S.A.; (925–926) NC9970, NC9971; (927–929) G-NZEC, 'ED, 'EF; (930–969) Chilean Govt. G.25 to G.64; (971) untraced; (972–977) G-AUKN, 'KL, 'KF, R.A.A.F., G-AULQ, 'LR; (978–980) NC491E, NC490E, NC492E; (982–987) G-AUJH, 'JI, 'JK to 'JN; (992) K-SATA; (995) R.N.Z.A.F. 995; (996) VT-AAR/G-AULB.

(1000) EI-AAC; (1001) C-PMAA; (1004) VP-KAC; (1013–1016) MW-113 to MW-116; (1018) Germany; (1020) Argentine; (1023–1026) Shanghai; (1029) Spain; (1031) D-1644/D-EONA; (1032) CH-235; (1033–1036, 1038–1039) Shanghai; (1041) Australia; (1044) NC493E; (1046) PK-SAD; (1057) Argentine; (1060) G-AULT; (1061) G-UAAE; (1063–1064) NC605E, NC606E; (1065–1066) G-AUKU, 'KV; (1069–1074) G-AUKO, 'KM, R.A.A.F., G-AULE, 'KX, 'LJ; (1075) MW-118; (1076) M-CHAA; (1077) SP-TUR; (1078) I-AANC; (1086) MW-121; (1088) VH-UMA; (1098) MW-117; (1102) ZK-AAR; (1107) ZS-ABH; (1109) SP-ADX; (1111) ZK-AAS; (1112–1121) Shanghai; (1122) VT-AAU; (1124–1125) ZS-ABI, 'BJ; (1128) G-AULD; (1131–1132) ZK-AAU, 'AT; (1133) MW-122; (1136) untraced; (1138) VT-AAX; (1141) Shanghai; (1143) ZS-ABK; (1144) Shanghai; (1145) ZS-ABL; (1147) ZS-ABM; (1148) D-1724; (1155) VT-ABB; (1156–1158) Shanghai; (1161) VT-AAZ; (1163) Germany; (1181–1183) Jugoslavia; (1185) ZK-AAV; (1188) F-AJMC; (1189) Jugoslavia; (1190) ZS-ABP; (1191–1194) Portuguese Air Force; (1195) C-PMAB; (1196) VT-ABC; (1197) ZK-AAW.

(1202) ZK-AAX; (1204–1206) Shanghai; (1207) ZK-AAZ; (1208) VP-YAJ; (1210–1211) Shanghai; (1212–1214) CV-HAR, 'OR, 'AZ; (1217) ZK-ABB; (1218) MW-128; (1219–1220) Shanghai; (1221) ZK-AAF; (1222) A-78; (1223–1224) MW-129, MW-130; (1225) Argentine; (1226–1227) VT-ABE, 'BF; (1240) F-AJNZ; (1242–1243) Shanghai; (1249–1250) ZK-ABH, 'BP; (1269) CV-TUR; (1274) VH-UPF; (1283) Caribbean A/W seaplane; (1293) MW-134; (1295) airframe to D.H. Servicing Dept.; (1297) CH-216/HB-OFI.

(1801) VT-ACG; (1803) South Africa; (1805) CV-TUR replacement a/c; (1806) ZK-ABQ; (1810) OO-ADG; (1815) South Africa; (1818) SP-AEU; (1821) India; (1823)

CH-217/HB-OKI; (1829) CS-AAC; (1832) Argentine; (1833) untraced; (1834) OO-ANG; (1835) CH-277/HB-OKE; (1836) VT-ACL; (1843) CH-220; (1844) ZS-ACO; (1847) OO-ARG; (1849) ZS-ADB; (1855) CH-279; (1858) Malaya; (1861) South Africa; (1864) CH-320/HB-OPI; (1872–1873) CH-321/HB-OPU, CH-322; (1875–1876) OO-AMM, 'ML; (1878) CH-325/HB-AFO; (1880) CH-324/HB-UKI; (1881) F-ALRR; (1882) CV-ASP; (1886) VT-ADC; (1887) OO-AMR; (1888) ZS-ACW; (1889) CH-329/HB-OLE; (1890) CH-341/HB-OTI; (1892) CH-330; (1895) ZS-ACY; (1909–1910) ZK-ADA, 'DB; (1911) VP-KAS; (1912) CH-350/HB-OLO; (1913) VP-KAX; (1914) SU-ABF; (1916) EC-TTA; (1917) CH-353/HB-OBA; (1918) EC-UAU; (1919) CH-357/HB-UBA; (1920) HB-UKI; (1922–1923) VT-AFE, 'FG; (1925–1926) ZK-AGU, 'GV; (1927) HB-OFI.

(b) By Morane-Saulnier
(c/n 1–10) F-AJOE, 'OC, 'QD, 'QC, 'RT, untraced, F-AJRL, 'QG, 'OQ, 'QH; (11–20) F-AJOD, 'RP, 'NY, 'OF, 'OG, 'OH, 'OI, 'RS, 'OJ, 'OK; (21–30) F-AJOL, 'RO, 'OM, 'RN, 'QI, untraced, F-AJON, 'OO, 'RF, 'OP; (31–40) F-AJRM, 'UJ, 'UE, 'UF, 'VN, two untraced, F-AJVP, untraced, F-ALCB.

(c) By the Moth Aircraft Corporation
(c/n 1A–1R) NC9797, NC809E, NC810E, NC811E, NC830E, NC831E, untraced, NC318H, NC319H, NC320H, NC372H, NC373H, untraced, NC825H to NC829H.

(d) By the Larkin Aircraft Supply Co. Ltd.
Thirty-two aircraft built for the Australian Government in 1929, including A7-25 and (c/u 1) VH-UQN; (2) VH-UPG; (3) VH-UKY; (7) VH-ULH; (8) VH-UMS.

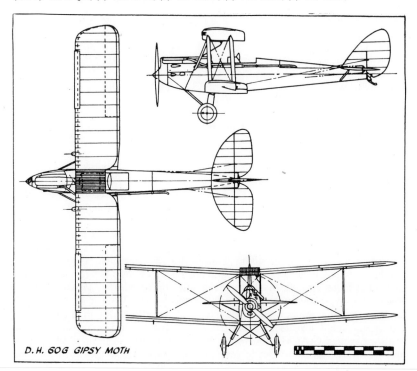

D.H. 60G GIPSY MOTH

Four Moth Majors acquired by the Austrian Aero Club in 1936 for training military pilots.
(*Aeroplane*)

De Havilland D.H.60GIII Moth Major

The year 1931 saw an important advance in light aero engine design when several well proven power units were persuaded to run upside down. De Havillands inverted their 120 h.p. Gipsy II engine and renamed it the Gipsy III, which when fitted to the wooden Moth airframe, created a new variant known as the D.H.60GIII Moth. Without the familiar cylinder block in front of him, the pilot's view was very much improved, and it was also possible to improve streamlining by cowling the engine to conform to the lines of the fuselage. The prototype, G-ABUI, which appeared in March 1932, was followed by a special high performance single seater with an experimental 133 h.p. Gipsy IIIA engine. This was G-ABVW, flown into fifth place in the 1932 King's Cup Race by H. S. Broad at the astonishing average speed for a Moth of 131·34 m.p.h. In July 1932 a standard Gipsy III was fitted and the machine sold to Amy Johnson, who named it 'Jason 4'. Following her marriage to J. A. Mollison on 29 July 1932 she flew it from Stag Lane to Renfrew for her Scottish honeymoon, after which it was sold to Lawrence Lipton. The Gipsy IIIA eventually went into production as the 130 h.p. Gipsy Major, one of which powered the Hon. R. Westenra's single seat Moth G-ACCW for the 1933 King's Cup Race, in which it averaged 118·55 m.p.h. These special Moths were entered for the majority of the 1933–34 air races, but only Lipton had success. He was third in the 1933 Folkestone Trophy Race, third in the 1934 King's Cup Race, second in the Yorkshire Trophy Race and won the Brooklands–Cramlington race at an average speed of 124·02 m.p.h.

The main role of the D.H.60GIII Moth lay not in racing but in the club and private sphere. Of the 57 built, 30 were registered to British private owners and to the Ipswich, Midland, London Transport, Leicestershire, Hull, Scottish, Edinburgh and Cinque Ports clubs and ten fuselages were diverted for R.A.F. Queen Bee target aircraft. Many were later sold abroad, the first, G-ABWT, being flown from Woodley to Nairobi as VP-KAR by H. W. Sear in May 1932. Lipton's special machine went to the Netherlands as PH-ART in August 1937, and others found owners in Austria, Sweden, India and Sourabaya. The final British machine, G-ACMY, owned by Sir Malcolm Campbell in 1934, went to Italy as I-RAFF in the following year. With the exception of the Scottish Flying

Club's G-ABZT and the Edinburgh Club's G-ACGD, which were involved in serious crashes in the Isle of Islay and on Broad Law, Peebleshire, respectively in 1936, the rest gave stalwart service until impressed in 1940.

Commencing with the fifty-eighth airframe in February 1934, the Gipsy Major engine was fitted as standard. The machine then paradoxically retained the designation D.H.60GIII, but now for the first time bore the type name Moth Major. Precise identification was possible only by inspecting the fins of No. 1 cylinder through the air intake because Gipsy Major fins tapered towards the crankcase, Gipsy III fins did not. The prototype, G-ACNP, nominally registered to Peter de Havilland, was sold abroad in the following month, after which the type continued in production until May 1935 when 96 had been built. As before, ten fuselages were diverted to the Queen Bee contract and large numbers were shipped abroad. Notable long distance flights were also made by Senor Carlos Bleck who left Lisbon in D.H.60GIII CS-AAI on 19 February 1934 and flew 6,600 miles to Goa, Portuguese India, in 14 days; by Miss Freda Thompson who flew Moth Major G-ACUC from Lympne to Darwin between 28 September and 10 November 1934; and by Maj. Stephenson who covered the 6,300 miles from Calcutta to Leeming, Yorks. in VT-AFP, 30 April to 28 May 1936. In June 1939 he flew the same machine from New Delhi to Ceylon and back.

Twenty-seven Moth Majors were to British order, the principal user being the Midland Aero Club which purchased G-ACNR, 'OG, 'OH and 'OI through Brian Lewis & Co. Ltd. in May 1934, trading in its four elderly Cirrus Moths in part exchange. These included the historic G-EBLT, originally provided under the Air Ministry subsidy scheme in 1925. A fifth Moth Major, G-ACTW, was purchased in the September, but 'OH was lost in a fatal air collision with a Hawker Hart of No. 605 Squadron over Castle Bromwich on 9 December 1934. Seventeen of the British-owned specimens were later sold in Singapore, Australia, Southern Rhodesia, India, Austria and elsewhere. The rest saw service with the Hampshire, Edinburgh, Bristol, Portsmouth, Tollerton and London Transport clubs and with several private owners.

Another, G-ACUR, owned by that great sportswoman the Duchess of Bedford and based at Woburn Abbey, figured in one of aviation's saddest mysteries. In 1929–30 the Duchess had made several record breaking trips to India and Africa with C. D. Barnard in the Fokker F. VIIA 'Spider', and in 1934 Sydney St. Barbe

D.H.60GIII Moth G-ACCW and Desoutter I G-AAPZ at Hatfield for the start of the 1933 King's Cup Race. (*Flight Photo 13434*)

taught her to fly and she later received instruction from her personal pilot Flt. Lt. R. C. Preston. On 23 March 1937 at the age of 72, she took off solo in 'UR and was never heard of again, the aircraft being presumed lost at sea after the interplane struts were washed ashore at Great Yarmouth on 2 April.

Total production, excluding G-AABK, VH-UMO and other early Moths re-engined with Gipsy IIIs and Gipsy Majors, amounted to 154 aircraft including G-ADIO built by D.H. Technical School students, but the only example to survive the 1939–45 war was G-ADHE which bore the initials of its original owner, H. E. Evans, who used it for business trips between Heston and India. After 11 years of postwar flying at Denham it finally came to grief on 22 March 1958.

SPECIFICATION

Manufacturers: The de Havilland Aircraft Co. Ltd., Stag Lane Aerodrome, Edgware, Middlesex.

Power Plants: One 120 h.p. de Havilland Gipsy III.

One 130 h.p. de Havilland Gipsy Major.

Dimensions: Span, 30 ft. 0 in. Length, 23 ft. 11 in. Height, 8 ft. $9\frac{1}{2}$ in. Wing area, 243 sq. ft.

Weights: (Gipsy III) Tare weight, 1,005 lb. All-up weight, 1,750 lb.

(Gipsy Major) Tare weight, 1,040 lb. All-up weight, 1,750 lb.

Performance: (Gipsy III) Maximum speed, 108·5 m.p.h. Cruising speed, 92 m.p.h. Initial climb, 780 ft./min. Ceiling, 18,750 ft. Range, 320 miles.

(Gipsy Major) Maximum speed, 112·5 m.p.h. Cruising speed, 96 m.p.h. Initial climb, 892 ft./min. Ceiling, 20,000 ft. Range, 300 miles.

Production: (a) D.H.60GIII Moths

Thirty British registered aircraft and the following for export: (c/n 5001) SU-ABC; (5002) SU-ABB; (5006) OO-GUT; (5009) VT-ADP; (5010) OO-GUY; (5013) India; (5018) SE-ADN; (5019) VP-KAU; (5021) ZS-ADF; (5024) SE-ADO; (5028) untraced; (5031) RY-LAL; (5032) EI-AAU; (5040) PH-AJI; (5041) CH-359/HB-OKA; (5043) PP-TEG; (5052) VH-URL; (5053) CS-AAI; (5054) VT-AFA; (5056) VP-NAC.

(b) D.H.60GIII Moth Major

Twenty-seven British registered aircraft and the following for export: (c/n 5059–5060) Argentine; (5063) Penang; (5064) VR-SAB; (5065) VR-SAC; (5066) OY-DAH; (5069) CH-369/HB-UXO; (5074) Czechoslovakia; (5075) EC-XAA; (5076) EC-AXX; (5078) CH-348/HB-UPE; (5081) SX-AAA; (5083) untraced; (5085) VH-URR; (5086) VH-URS; (5092) VT-AFL; (5093) HB-UBO; (5094) HB-UTI; (5096) VT-AFP; (5098) EC-YAY; (5101–5112) EC-W28 to EC-W39; (5114) ZK-ADK; (5115) ZK-ADL; (5117) VR-SAK; (5118) ZK-ADM; (5119) ZK-ADN; (5120) ZK-ADO; (5121) ZK-ADP; (5123) VP-YAV; (5124) VP-YAW; (5125) OE-TAM; (5126) OE-TEM; (5129) OE-TIM; (5130) OE-TOM; (5131) OY-DIK; (5132) SE-AGF; (5133) VR-HCU; (5138) OY-DAK; (5139) EC-W47; (5140) VT-AGK; (5141) Spanish Navy; (5142) VT-AGL; (5146) OE-TUM; (5148) OE-TAE; (5149) OE-TEE; (5150) OE-TIE; (5151) OE-TOE; (5152) OE-TUE.

(c) D.H.60GIII Moth Major built by the D.H. Technical School

One aircraft only: (c/n 2263) G-ADIO.

Alan S. Butler leaving Heston in his special Gipsy II D.H.60M during the 1930 Round Europe touring competition. (*Flight Photo 9199*)

De Havilland D.H.60M Moth

A metal fuselaged Gipsy Moth, known as the D.H.60M and identified by a number of prominent stringers under the fabric, was introduced for overseas customers in 1928 and the prototype, G-AAAR, went to Canada at the end of that year as G-CAVX for evaluation on floats and skis by the R.C.A.F. which placed an initial order for 50. Ninety others were shipped to de Havilland Aircraft of Canada Ltd. to meet orders by the Ontario Provincial Air Service and the flying clubs, some being fitted with locally made coupé tops. One aircraft, CF-ADC, was shipped back to England by J. H. Hibert who flew it from Heston to Darwin between 12 October and 6 December 1932 but after a crash at Cloncurry it was sold on the spot and became VH-UQV.

The D.H.60M was sold in large numbers for military and civil use all over the world and was built under licence by D.H. Canada, the Moth Aircraft Corporation in the U.S.A. and by the Norwegian Army Aircraft Factory. A considerable number were delivered to the R.A.F. and over 60 were sold in the U.K. to the de Havilland School of Flying, National Flying Services Ltd., the Brooklands School of Flying Ltd., the Northamptonshire Aero Club, the oil companies and other owners between 1928 and 1930. D.H.60M Moths were owned by the Prince of Wales and Duke of Gloucester, who flew G-AALG and G-ABDB accompanied by E. H. Fielden, D. Don and other Royal safety pilots.

Inevitably the type was selected for attacks on the Australia record, the first to do so being E. L. Hook and J. Matthews, who left Lympne in G-AAWV on 20 June 1930, but Hook died after they crashed at Tomas, Burma, on 3 July. Another, G-AASA, piloted by Oscar Garden, left on 17 October and made Wyndham in 18 days, but a third, G-ABHY, broke the record. This long range single seater had the new 120 h.p. Gipsy II motor and, flown by C. W. A. Scott, completed the 10,500 miles in 9 days 4 hours 11 minutes. The same pilot repeated the performance in the opposite direction in another D.H.60M, VH-UQA, between 26 May and 5 June 1931. During its stay in England it toured the country with the owner's air display, becoming G-ACOA in the process. In the following season the pair again lowered the record by arriving at Darwin on 28 April 1932, 8 days 20 hours 47 minutes out from Lympne. In contrast, Richard Allen took nearly seven weeks to complete the journey in G-AAUS during the August and

September, and in the following year Jean Batten, last of the Moth brigade, appeared on the scene. She broke the women's record at her third attempt by arriving at Darwin in G-AARB on 28 May 1934 in a time of just under 15 days. A very abnormal D.H.60M, G-AAXG with Gipsy II engine, was built for A. S. Butler to fly in the 1930 Round Europe Touring Competition. Ease of access to the coupé front cockpit was made possible by eliminating the main centre section struts, and after the event the aircraft was sold to a prominent French owner, Edouard Bret, as F-AJZB. On its return in 1933 the machine went by sea to New Zealand where it was still flying as ZK-AEJ in 1972.

The ultimate development was the D.H.60T Moth Trainer of 1931 which was essentially a D.H.60M modified for all kinds of military training. For ease of parachute escape from the front seat both flying wires were anchored to the front root end fittings of the lower wing and the exhaust was taken forward and downward, useful recognition features which identified the Moth Trainer as the transitional type between the Gipsy Moth and the Tiger Moth.

Four of the initial batch of six, G-ABKM to 'KS, were supplied to the Swedish Air Force for ab initio, gunnery and bombing training in June 1931 and other small batches equipped the Egyptian, Iraqi and Brazilian Air Forces, but after the introduction of the Tiger Moth, production of metal fuselaged Gipsy Moths virtually ceased.

SPECIFICATION

Manufacturers: The de Havilland Aircraft Co. Ltd., Stag Lane Aerodrome, Edgware, Middlesex.

The de Havilland Aircraft Pty. Ltd., Bankstown, Sydney, N.S.W.

Some airframes assembled by de Havilland Aircraft of Canada Ltd., Downsview Airport, Toronto.

Haerens Flyvemaskinefabric, Kjeller, Norway.

Power Plants: One 90 h.p. A.D.C. Cirrus III.

One 100 h.p. de Havilland Gipsy I.

One 120 h.p. de Havilland Gipsy II.

Dimensions: Span 30 ft. 0 in. Length 23 ft. 11 in. Height 8 ft. 9½ in. Wing area 243 sq. ft.

Weights: Tare weight 962 lb. All-up weight 1,750 lb.

Performance: Maximum speed 105 m.p.h. Cruising speed 85 m.p.h. Initial climb 700 ft./min. Range 320 miles.

Production: (a) D.H.60M Moths at Stag Lane and Hatfield

A large number of British registered aircraft and the following for export: (341) NC9731; (711) G-AUKC; (712) Australia; (713) R.C.A.F.66; (714) 64/CF-CFX; (715) 65/CF-CFN; (716) 67/CF-CFR; (717) 68/CF-AVF; (718) 69; (719) 70/CF-CFM; (720) 71; (721) 72/CF-CFS; (722) 74/CF-CGC; (723) 73; (724) 75/CF-CFZ; (725–728) 76–79; (729) CF-CAA; (730) CF-CAB; (731) CF-CAH; (732) CF-CAD; (733) CF-CAE; (734) 80/CF-CEU; (735–737) 81–83; (738) 84/CF-CEL; (739) 85/CF-CDO; (740–745) 102–107; (746) 86/CF-CDP; (747) 87/CF-CEH; (748) 88; (749) 89/CF-CEI; (750) 90/CF-CEJ; (751) 91/CF-CEK; (752) CF-CAC; (753) CF-CAF; (754) CF-CAG; (755) CF-CAI; (756) G-CYXH; (757) G-CYXE/CF-CEG; (758) G-CYXG/CF-APC; (759) G-CYXF; (760) G-CYYY/CF-CEC; (761) G-CAJW/CF-OAA; (762) CF-OAC; (763) G-CAOU*; (764) CF-AAF; (765) CF-OAD; (766) CF-CAP; (767) CF-AAB; (768)

---

* Replacement for D.H.60X c/n 400.

CF-AAG; (769) CF-AAH; (770) CF-AAE; (771) CF-ADH; (772) CF-ADF; (773) CF-CAL; (774) CF-CAM; (775) CF-CAN.

(776) CF-CAO; (777) CF-ADG; (778) CF-ADJ; (779) CF-ADA; (780) CF-ADV; (781) CF-ADI; (782) CF-ADB; (783) CF-ADC; (784) CF-ADD; (785) CF-ADE; (786–787) R.C.A.F. 118–119; (788) 120/CF-CFW; (789–790) 121–122; (791) CF-ADK; (792) CF-AAI; (793) CF-AAJ; (794) CF-CAV; (795) CF-ADL; (796) CF-ADM; (797) CF-ADQ; (798) CF-ADR; (799) CF-ADN; (800) CF-ADO.

(1300) CF-ADY; (1301) CF-ADX; (1302) CF-AAA; (1303) CF-CAS; (1304) CF-ADP; (1305) CF-CAT; (1306) CF-CAU; (1307) CF-CAW; (1308) CF-CAX; (1309) G-CYWY/R.C.A.F. 212/CF-CCX; (1310) CF-AFB; (1311) CF-CBG; (1312) U.S. Embassy, later VT-ABV; (1313) CF-ADZ; (1314) CF-ADU; (1315) CF-ADT; (1316) CF-ADW; (1317) CF-AGD; (1318) CF-CBE; (1319) CF-CBF; (1320) CF-AGC; (1321) G-CYWW/CF-APB; (1322) G-CYWV/CF-APA; (1323) CF-AGF; (1324) CF-AGG; (1325) CF-AGE; (1326) CF-ABG/CF-CBH; (1327) CF-AGH; (1328) CF-AGI; (1329–1330) untraced; (1331) CF-AGM; (1333) SE-ABY; (1334) R.C.A.F. 117/CF-CCY; (1335) Peru; (1337) U.S. Embassy; (1339) N-42; (1340) untraced; (1341) CF-APM; (1342) untraced; (1343) CF-AGK; (1344) G-CYYR/CF-CEB; (1345–1348) untraced; (1349) CF-AGJ; (1350) untraced.

(1351) CF-AGL; (1353) CF-AGN; (1354–1361) R.A.A.F.; (1364) G-AULW; (1366) G-AULY; (1367) South Africa; (1368) VH-UNF; (1370) VH-UOA; (1371) VH-UMZ; (1372) VH-UMJ; (1373) N-35; (1375) VT-AAY; (1376) VH-UMU; (1377) VH-UMD; (1378) Colombia; (1379) VH-UMO; (1381) OO-AKM; (1382–1392) R.A.F.; (1393) VT-ABA; (1397) D-1737/D-ETER/PH-ASU; (1398) VH-UNE; (1399) VH-UMR; (1400) VH-UNX; (1401) VH-UOZ; (1403) VH-ULM; (1404) VH-ULN; (1405) VH-ULO; (1406) VH-ULP; (1407) VH-UNP; (1408) VH-UNB; (1415) Argentine; (1418) VH-UNL; (1419) VH-UNN; (1420) VT-ABM; (1421) VT-ABO; (1422) VH-UND; (1423) VT-ABP; (1425) Colombia.

(1426) VP-KAF; (1427) MW-124; (1428) MW-125; (1429) Argentine; (1431) VH-UNI; (1432) China; (1435) Norwegian 101; (1436) Norwegian 103; (1437) CH-251/HB-UXE; (1442) Norwegian 105; (1443) F-AJKT; (1444) VH-UNU; (1445) Danish S-106/OY-DOH; (1446) Danish S-107/OY-DEH; (1447) ZK-ABF; (1448) ZK-ABE; (1449) ZK-ABA; (1450–1459) R.A.F.; (1461) Argentine; (1463) F-AJLV;

Brazilian military D.H.60T Moth Trainer, civilianised as PP-TZE for the Santos Aero Club, showing the revised flying wire anchorage and forward facing exhaust. Another, PP-TYF, was re-engined with a 120 h.p. Walter Major.

(1464) VH-UNQ; (1465) F-AJLX; (1466) VT-ABR; (1468) F-AJLQ; (1469) ZS-ABT; (1470) VT-ABL; (1471) VT-ABK; (1473) D-1800; (1475) airframe to Morane-Saulnier.

(1478) VH-UOI; (1479) CH-253; (1481) Argentine; (1483) VH-UOQ; (1484) VH-UOR; (1487) ZK-ABT; (1488) ZK-ABS; (1489) CF-CBK; (1490) CF-ABL; (1491) VT-ABQ; (1492) CF-CBM; (1494) VH-UOK; (1496) VH-UVO; (1497) CF-CBP; (1498) CF-CBO; (1499) CF-CBN; (1500–1529) R.A.F.; (1530) VH-UOT; (1531) China; (1532) VT-ABH; (1533) VT-ABI; (1534) N-20/LN-ABI; (1536–1537) Colombia; (1541) MW-131; (1543) untraced; (1544) D-1869; (1545) SP-ADY; (1548) D-1921; (1550) Argentine; (1551) VT-ACE; (1554) ZK-ACD; (1558) VH-UPD; (1559) Bandoeng; (1560) R.N.Z.A.F.1560/ZK-AEB; (1561) ZK-ACE; (1562) ZK-ACF; (1563) ZK-ACH; (1564) ZK-ACI; (1565) VH-UQY; (1566) VH-UQA; (1567–1569) R.N.Z.A.F. 1567– 1569.

(1570–1579) China; (1580–1662) R.A.F.; (1663) Argentine; (1664–1668) China; (1669) VP-KAI; (1670) China; (1671) SE-ACN; (1673) Argentine; (1674) D.H. test airframe; (1675–1679) Iraqi Air Force Nos. 1–5; (1681) J9107*; (1682–1684) Danish Navy 145–147; (1686) Swedish Air Force; (1687) PK-SAF; (1688–1692) China; (1693) Argentine; (1694–1697) China; (1699) China; (1707–1708) China; (1709) Austrian A-78; (1710) China; (1713) VT-ABX; (1714–1716) China; (1717) Belgian Air Force; (1723) China; (1776–1779) Iraqi Air Force; (1780–1793) China; (1795) VT-ACK; (1797) VT-ACM; (3027) VT-ACN; (3029) SE-ADC; (3034) VT-ADL; (3035) VT-ADS; (3048) VT-ADR; (3049) ZK-ACZ; (3053) SU-ABB†; (3054) VT-AEI; (3055) VT-AET; (3056) VT-AFC.

(b) Assembled in Canada

(c/n DHC.101) R.C.A.F. 157/CF-CGA; (102) 158/CF-CFV; (103) 159; (104) 160/CF-CFO; (105–106) 161–162; (107–109) 151–153; (110) 154/CF-CCD/CF-CFT; (111) 155/CF-CFU; (112) 156; (113) 163; (114) 164/CF-CFK; (115) 165/CF-CFY; (116) 166/CF-CFP; (117) 167/CF-CFQ; (118) 168; (119) CF-ALV; (120) CF-OAE; (121) CF-OAG; (122) CF-OAF; (123) CF-CBY; (124) CF-CBX; (125) CF-AGR; (126) CF-AGP; (127) CF-AGX; (128) CF-CBQ; (129) CF-CDA; (130) untraced; (131) CF-CDC; (132) CF-APN; (133) R.C.A.F. 223/CF-CGB; (134) CF-OAO; (135) CF-AGZ.

(c) Built by the Moth Aircraft Corporation

(c/n 2A–23A) NC894E. NC300H–NC302H, NC857H, and 17 exported; (41–100) NC229K–NC237K, NC556K–NC566K, NC961H–NC970H, NC55M–NC64M, NC580M–NC589M, NC131M–NC140M; (101–150) NC900M–NC919M, NC922M– NC941M, NC215V–NC222V, NC969K, NC970K; (151–179) NC713M–NC717M, NC572N–NC578N, NC583N, NC966K, NC590N–NC595N, NC603V–NC605V, NC597N, NC613V–NC617V.

(d) Built by the Norwegian Army Aircraft Factory

Ten aircraft in 1931, odd serials only in the Norwegian Army range 107–125.

(e) D.H.60T Moth Trainers

Seven British registered aircraft and the following exported: (c/n 1718–1722) Swedish Air Force Fv.5108 to Fv.5112; (1731) China; (1734–1738) Egyptian Air Force E-105, E-104, E-103, E-102, E-101; (1799) E-106; (3000–3014) Brazilian Army; (3015– 3026) Brazilian Navy Al-5 to Al-16; (3030) Brazilian Navy; (3031–3032) Iraqi Air Force 13–14; (3036–3047) Brazilian Navy; (3050–3052) Iraqi Air Force 25–27.

* Replacing R.A.F. Moth c/n 514.   † Replacing D.H.60GIII c/n 5002.

Sir Alan Cobham leaving Stag Lane in May 1929 in the Jaguar engined Giant Moth 'Youth of Britain' at the start of his campaign for municipal airports. (*Aeroplane*)

De Havilland D.H.61 Giant Moth

In August 1927 the de Havilland Company announced that a large single engined biplane was under construction to suit colonial requirements. It proved to be typically D.H. in appearance, and flight trials by Hubert Broad took place at Stag Lane in December 1927. As in the D.H.50, the pilot sat in an open cockpit behind the cabin and surveyed the occupants thereof through a peephole in the dashboard. This layout was first used by the company in the old D.H.18, and in later years was incorporated in the Fox Moth design. The D.H.61 was of robust wooden construction, and the plywood covered fuselage of large cross-section permitted a cabin affording a high degree of comfort for six passengers. The two bay, equal span, fabric covered wings could be folded to save hangar space.

G-EBTL, the prototype, was fitted with a Bristol Jupiter VI motor and christened 'Canberra', which for a time was also the type name until changed to Giant Moth in 1929. This aeroplane, as its name suggested, was shipped to Australia and flight tested at Melbourne on 2 March 1928. Renamed 'Old Gold' it was used successively by the MacRobertson Miller Aviation Co. Ltd., West Australian Airways Ltd. and Guinea Airways Ltd.

Ten Giant Moths were built, mainly with 500 h.p. Jupiter XIs and two, G-CAJT and 'PG, were flown at Rochester on Short metal floats by H. S. Broad in June 1928 and delivered to Western Canada Airways Ltd. and the Ontario Provincial Air Service for conveying fire fighting squads to the scene of forest fires. The last D.H.61, G-CARD, was shipped to London Air Transport Ltd., Ontario, in 1929 but was never used and its components were probably used in the Canadian-built, Hornet engined CF-OAK first flown in June 1932.

Three D.H61s were used on air mail services in Australia, G-AUHW (also named 'Canberra') by Larkin's Australian Aerial Services Ltd. and G-AUJB 'Apollo' and G-AUJC 'Diana' by QANTAS.

Production included two to British order, the first of which was the red-and-silver G-AAAN acquired by the *Daily Mail* in August 1928, and named 'Geraldine'. Fitted with a Jupiter XI motor, it was used as a rapid means of news gathering, a motor cycle being carried on which the photographer could hasten from the aerodrome to the scene of interest. On the return flight the negatives were developed in the dark room installed in the cabin and the story typed on a folding desk. G-AAAN was so employed for about 18 months, visiting all parts of the British Isles and Europe, and was the very first aeroplane ever to be passed A.1. at Lloyds. In February 1930 it was sold to National Flying Services Ltd., and spent its last two years in that company's orange and black colours on joyriding and taxi work at Hedon, Hull. In 1932 it was sold to Holden Air Transport Ltd. in New Guinea, replacing the crashed D.H.37 VH-UAA and joining the former Larkin D.H.61 G-AUHW on goldfield freight runs.

The final British example was 'Youth of Britain', registered G-AAEV in February 1929 to the Alan Cobham Aviation Co. and flown by Sir Alan on a five months' propaganda tour from May to October in that year. Unlike its six seat Jupiter engined forebears, it was fitted with a Jaguar VIC engine, and being intended for short haul work was furnished as a 10 seater. During the 21 weeks of the tour all the important towns and cities of the British Isles were visited in an attempt to convince local worthies of the necessity for municipal aerodromes. Some 3,500 mayors and members of corporations were taken for flights, and thanks to the generosity of Sir Charles Wakefield 10,000 schoolchildren were given free trips, while some 2,500 other joyride flights were made.

The tour ended at Stag Lane on 7 October 1929 and on 10 December Cobham set out for Africa to deliver the aircraft to Imperial Airways Ltd. to whom it had been sold. After an uneventful flight it was handed over to an Imperial crew at Salisbury, Southern Rhodesia, on 7 January 1930, only to be completely wrecked in a crash at Broken Hill a fortnight later.

The second production Giant Moth, G-CAJT, with Bristol Jupiter XI, being launched at Rochester in June 1928. (*Flight Photo 5847*)

SPECIFICATION

Manufacturers: The de Havilland Aircraft Co. Ltd., Stag Lane Aerodrome, Edgware, Middlesex; de Havilland Aircraft of Canada Ltd., Toronto.

Power Plants: One 500 h.p. Bristol Jupiter XI.
One 500 h.p. Armstrong Siddeley Jaguar VIC.
One 525 h.p. Pratt & Whitney Hornet.

Dimensions: Span, 52 ft 0 in. Length, 39 ft 0 in. Height, 12 ft. 0 in. Wing area, 613 sq. ft.

Weights: Tare weight, 3,650 lb. All-up weight, 7,000 lb.

Performance: Maximum speed, 132 m.p.h. Cruising speed, 110 m.p.h. Initial climb, 900 ft./min. Ceiling, 18,000 ft. Range, 650 miles.

Production:

Ten aircraft comprising three of British registry and the following for export: (c/n 328) G-CAJT; (329) G-CAPG; (330) G-AUHW; (333) G-AUJC; (334) G-AUJB; (336) G-CARD believed used in the construction of CF-OAK (c/n DHC.141).

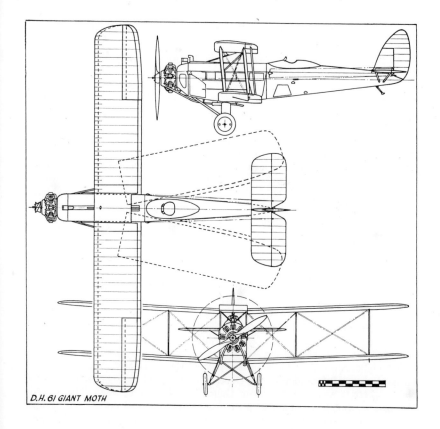

D.H. 61 GIANT MOTH

The open cockpit prototype Hercules on an early test flight near Stag Lane, without ailerons on the upper mainplane. (*Flight Photo 4164*)

De Havilland D.H.66 Hercules

In 1925 an agreement was reached with the Air Ministry whereby Imperial Airways Ltd. were to open a regular fortnightly passenger, freight and air mail service between Cairo and Karachi. They were to relieve the R.A.F. of the responsibility of running the existing desert air mail and were to receive a subsidy of £500,000 annually for five years. Imperial Airways then drew up a specification for a passenger aircraft with at least two engines to minimize the risk of forced landings in inhospitable desert areas and with ample reserves of power for tropical operation. Construction of a fleet of five was entrusted to the de Havilland Aircraft Co. Ltd., which produced a large two bay biplane powered by three Bristol Jupiter radials. The mainplanes were of normal two spar wooden construction but the usual D.H. all-wood, plywood covered fuselage gave place to a fabric covered metal structure more suited to tropical conditions. Two pilots sat in an open cockpit in the nose, while the wireless operator and seven passengers were accommodated in a spacious cabin, which also provided 465 cu. ft. of mail space. An aft baggage compartment was of 155 cu. ft. capacity and, like the cabin, was a large plywood-sided box fitted within the main metal structure.

In June 1926 the type name was chosen by means of a competition in the *Meccano Magazine*, won by E. F. Hope-Jones of Eton College, who suggested Hercules. H. S. Broad took G-EBMW, the prototype, on its first flight at Stag Lane on 30 September 1926, and after acceptance trials and some crew training at Croydon, it left for Cairo on 18 December 1920. The desert air route was inaugurated by the flight of the Air Minister, Sir Samuel Hoare, and Lady Maud Hoare right through to India in the second Hercules 'MX. Piloted by F. L. Barnard, they left Croydon on 27 December 1926 and on 8 January arrived in Delhi, where it was named 'City of Delhi' by Lady Irwin, wife of the Viceroy. The first eastbound commercial flight was made in the prototype, now named 'City of Cairo', by Capt. Wolley Dod, who took off from Heliopolis Airport, Cairo, on 12 January 1927, but for the first two years the service terminated at Basra.

100

The Hercules contract was completed with the delivery of G-EBNA 'City of Teheran' at Heliopolis in March 1927, after which the fleet settled down to earn a name for utter reliability. West Australian Airways Ltd., operators of D.H.50s over difficult country of a similar nature, also ordered four Hercules aircraft in 1929. They were similar to the originals, except for the enclosed pilot's cabin and the tail wheel (later removed). The first of the new type was tested by H. G. Brackley at Stag Lane in March 1929, and the first Perth–Adelaide service was flown by G-AUJO 'City of Perth' on 2 June.

Imperial Airways then ordered G-AAJH 'City of Basra', commissioned in June 1929 but in the following September 'MZ stalled on approach to Jask at night and was destroyed by fire, Capt. Woodbridge and two passengers being killed. A replacement, G-AARY, was then built and delivered at Croydon on 27 January 1930 as the 'City of Karachi' but Hercules G-EBNA was damaged beyond repair at Gaza a month later and G-AUJR was purchased in Australia to replace it in service, becoming G-ABCP 'City of Jodhpur' in July 1930.

In 1931 two experimental air mail flights were despatched to Australia but the prototype Hercules, G-EBMW, which left for the Far East with the first load, ran short of fuel in appalling weather and was wrecked in a forced landing in rock-strewn grassland 10 miles from Koepang on 19 April 1931. The mail was quickly retrieved by Kingsford Smith, and flown to Darwin in the Fokker mono-plane 'Southern Cross'. Once more West Australian Airways provided the re-placement, this one becoming Imperial's final Hercules G-ABMT 'City of Cape Town', the choice of name underlining the forthcoming southward extension of the Empire Air Route. The survey flight for this was carried out by H. G. Brackley and Capt. J. Alger in 'RY with its name repainted in Afrikaans as 'Stad van Karachi' for the occasion. Their arrival in Cape Town on 22 December 1931 paved the way for regular services in 1932. South African associations were further strengthened when Sir Alan Cobham hired 'MT in October 1932 as the 'giant airliner' for his air pageant. It proved the mainstay of an otherwise unlucky South African tour, rejoining Imperial Airways in March 1933 to ply its usual routes until sold to the South African Air Force along with G-EBMX and G-AAJH. G-ABCP was damaged beyond repair when taking off from soft ground

G-AARY arriving at Cape Town at the conclusion of the 1931 African air route survey. The pilots' cabin common to D.H.66s built in 1929, was later fitted to those built in 1926.
(*New York Times*)

at Salisbury, Southern Rhodesia on 23 November 1935, the last D.H.66s in civil use being the first two Australians, by then VH-UJO and 'JP, used by Stephens Aviation Ltd. between Lae and Wau in New Guinea.

SPECIFICATION

Manufacturers: The de Havilland Aircraft Co. Ltd., Stag Lane Aerodrome, Edgware, Middlesex.

Power Plants: Three 420 h.p. Bristol Jupiter VI.

Dimensions: Span, 79 ft. 6 in. Length, 55 ft. 6 in. Height, 18 ft. 3 in. Wing area, 1,547 sq. ft.

Weights: Tare weight, 9,060 lb. All-up weight, 15,600 lb.

Performance: Maximum speed, 128 m.p.h. Cruising speed, 110 m.p.h. Initial climb, 765 ft./min. Ceiling, 13,000 ft.

Production: Eleven aircraft comprising seven of British registry and the following for Australia: (c/n 344) G-AUJO; (345) G-AUJP; (346) G-AUJQ; (347) G-AUJR.

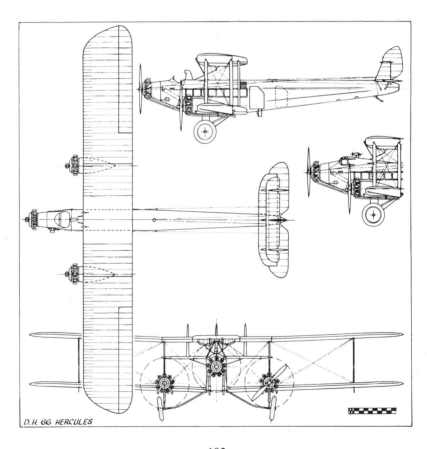

D.H. 66 HERCULES

The prototype Hawk Moth G-EBVV with 198 h.p. de Havilland Ghost Vee-8 engine.
(*Aeroplane*)

De Havilland D.H.75 Hawk Moth

In 1928 Maj. Halford reversed the birth process of the Cirrus I by mating two Gipsy I engines on a common crankcase. Known as the D.H. Ghost the new engine was similar to the old wartime Renault but gave over twice the power at a much lower weight and was developed for the new D.H.75 Hawk Moth four seat cabin monoplane which combined a fabric covered steel tube fuselage with a wooden wing.

H. S. Broad flew the prototype, G-EBVV, for the first time at Stag Lane on 7 December 1928 but it was underpowered and the performance was disappointing. Subsequent Hawk Moths were therefore built with mainplanes of increased span, 16 in. greater chord and 240 h.p. Armstrong Siddeley Lynx engines which gave them a much more useful performance. They were designated D.H.75A and were known briefly as the Moth Six, emphasising their relationship with the Puss Moth, then coming on the market as the Moth Three.

One D.H.75A was exhibited without markings at the 1929 Olympia Aero Show and the first one, G-AAFW, was demonstrated in Canada in December of the same year. Trials with this machine on skis and with the sister aircraft G-AAFX on Short floats at Rochester led, in 1930, to an order for three machines with interchangeable undercarriages for the Canadian Government. First of these, appropriately re-registered CF-CCA and based at Ottawa for the personal use of the Controller of Civil Aviation, was the former G-AAFW but, having no doors on the port side, was not permitted to fly as a seaplane. The others, G-CYVL and 'VM, intended for Government civil operations, had doors on both sides and Hamilton adjustable pitch metal airscrews. Both were cleared for float operation after tests at Rockcliffe by D.H.C. test pilot Leigh Capreol on 4 October 1930 but payload was limited and they flew thereafter only on wheels or skis. Several undercarriage failures occurred and 'VL crashed during acceptance tests as a landplane at Longueil, Quebec, in 1931.

The first D.H.75A Hawk Moth (Lynx engine) on skis in Canada, December 1929.

The unregistered D.H.75B Hawk Moth, c/n 394, with 300 h.p. Wright Whirlwind R-975.
(*Flight Photo 8451*)

G-AAFX went to de Havilland Aircraft Pty. Ltd. as Australian demonstrator and on 3 June 1930 Amy Johnson flew it from Brisbane to Sydney after her Moth G-AAAH 'Jason' had come to grief. Later Hart Aircraft Services of Melbourne used it for taxi work until Tasmanian Airways bought it in February 1934. After a forced landing at Brighton, Tasmania, on 10 January 1935 it was rebuilt with a Wright Whirlwind J-5 and flew with a series of owners until January 1943 when an Armstrong Siddeley Cheetah IX was fitted by the final operator, Connellan Airways Ltd., Alice Springs.

VH-UOY was delivered to Aircraft Pty. Ltd. for its Toowoomba–Maryborough services but in 1931 went on charter to the goldmining centre of Cracow. The fifth production aircraft, G-AAUZ, certificated in June 1930, was H.R.H. Prince George's entry for the King's Cup Race in which it was flown from Hanworth to Cramlington and back by Flt. Lt. E. H. Fielden and came seventh at an average speed of 126·2 m.p.h. In 1932 it was acquired by Air Taxis Ltd. and thereafter flew from Stag Lane in their traditional red colour scheme until stored in 1936 prior to eventual sale abroad.

Competition from American types such as the Ryan B-1 Brougham killed the Hawk Moth within a year, despite an attempt to recapture the market by fitting one machine with a 300 h.p. Wright Whirlwind in May 1930 under the designation D.H.75B. Production therefore ceased at the eighth aircraft.

SPECIFICATION

Manufacturer: The de Havilland Aircraft Co. Ltd., Stag Lane Aerodrome, Edgware, Middlesex.

Power Plants: (D.H.75) One 198 h.p. de Havilland Ghost
(D.H.75A) One 240 h.p. Armstrong Siddeley Lynx VIA
One 300 h.p. Wright Whirlwind J-5
One 350 h.p. Armstrong Siddeley Cheetah IX
(D.H.75B) One 300 h.p. Wright Whirlwind R-975

Dimensions: Span, 47 ft. 0 in. Length, 28 ft. 10 in. Height, 9 ft. 4 in. Wing Area, 334 sq. ft.

Weights: Tare weight, 2,380 lb. All-up weight, 3,650 lb.

Performance: Maximum speed, 127 m.p.h. Cruising speed, 105 m.p.h. Initial climb, 710 ft./min. Range, 560 miles.

Note: The data given above refers to the D.H.75A Lynx engined landplane.

Production: Eight complete and two incomplete aircraft:
D.H.75: (c/n 327) G-EBVV. D.H.75A: (343) G-AAFW; (348) G-AAFX; (705) G-AAUZ; (706) VH-UOY; (707) G-CYVL; (708) G-CYVM; (709) not completed. D.H.75B: (394) unregistered; (395) not completed.

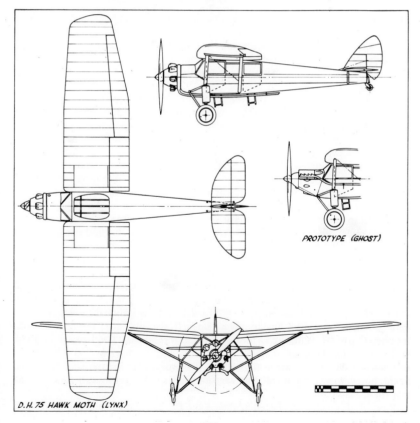

PROTOTYPE (GHOST)

D.H. 75 HAWK MOTH (LYNX)

105

Puss Moth CV-AAI (c/n 2199) at Stag Lane in August 1931, ready for delivery to the Archduke Anton of Hapsburg. (*Flight Photo 10172*)

De Havilland D.H.80A Puss Moth

By the end of 1928 the new generation of light biplanes had fostered a flourishing private flying movement and as their enthusiasm mounted and they ventured farther afield, private owners demanded cabin comfort and an end to traditional flying clothing for themselves and their ladies. Thus was born the unnamed D.H.80 strut braced, high wing monoplane E-1/G-AAHZ, c/n 396, which made its first flight at Stag Lane on 9 September 1929. Traditional methods of wooden construction were employed, the fuselage being plywood covered and seating two in tandem, each occupant having his own compartment and his own door on the starboard side. The opportunity was also seized of incorporating improvements which were to become permanent features of D.H. types to follow. The mainplane was made in two halves and shoulder mounted to avoid the undesirable airflow disturbances associated with conventional centre sections. A standard Gipsy II was also persuaded by modification to run inverted, thus removing the cylinder heads from the pilot's line of vision and allowing an excellent view over a smooth cowling.

Interest in this almost revolutionary design was such that large scale production began at once, the first machine, G-AATC, flying in March 1930 but it was not seen much in this country, being shipped to Australia, where it flew as VH-UON until sent to New Zealand as ZK-ADU. The production model was known as the D.H.80A Puss Moth and differed internally from the prototype as, for the first time, a de Havilland light aeroplane boasted a welded steel tube, fabric covered fuselage. This had no partition, the two occupants sitting in tandem in staggered seats which permitted the aircraft to be used as an occasional three-seater and detail refinements to the upside down Gipsy II also produced the now familiar inverted Gipsy III. With such a 'clean' design it was necessary to steepen the glide, and to this end the wide undercarriage shock absorber fairings could be turned through 90 degrees to form air brakes. The wooden prototype was not flown again, but with wings and rear fuselage sawn off, spent several years as an engine test rig at Stag Lane.

Puss Moth production lasted at Stag Lane for just three years, the 259th and last aircraft G-ACFE, supplied to W. L. Hope in March 1933, departing for France as F-AMYR a year later. Almost 50 per cent. were exported, mainly for passenger and mail services, taxi and survey work but on 13 October 1930 VH-UPC crashed in Western Australia, first of nine accidents which marred the early career of this aeroplane. On 5 May 1931 Lt. Cdr. Glen Kidston and Capt. T. A. Gladstone were killed when ZS-ACC crashed in the Drakensberg Mts. and another South African crew was lost at Sir Lowry's Pass on 13 November in the crash of ZS-ACD which R. F. Caspareuthus had delivered from Stag Lane to Germiston in the record time of 78 hours, 5–13 October 1930. Then on 21 May 1932 the ski-equipped Puss Moth G-CYUT crashed at Ottawa and test pilot A. L. James, who survived, was able to describe the circumstances which led up to the failure of the port mainplane. Unfortunately Bruce Bossom and his two passengers were killed when G-ABDH crashed near Hindhead, Surrey, on 27 July; pilot R. Virtue, Capt. Les Holden and Dr. G. R. Hamilton lost their lives when VH-UPM of New England Airways crashed at Byron Bay, N.S.W., on 18 September; J. F. Fowler's G-ABFU was destroyed at Grenoble, France, on 29 October; H. J. 'Bert' Hinkler was killed when crossing the Alps in CF-APK en route to Australia on 7 January 1933, and HS-PAA of the Aerial Transport Co. of Siam Ltd. dived into the ground between Khonkaen and Udorn on 23 June.

Investigations by the N.P.L. and R.A.E., flight tests at Martlesham with the Air Ministry Puss Moth K1824 and its destruction in static tests at Farnborough in October 1932, showed that in certain circumstances, when flying at high speed in turbulence, wing failure could occur. Flutter tests with mass balanced ailerons were made by H. S. Broad in G-AAVA in January 1931, and modifications eventually included a small strut from the forward wing strut to the rear wing root fitting. A much larger rudder was also substituted, final tests with which were made at the R.A.E. in December 1932 using D.H.'s experimental Puss Moth E-8 which had an additional 18 in. of mainplane sweepback. This aircraft reverted to standard for sale as G-ACYT in 1934 by which time the Puss Moth's early misfortunes had been forgotten and it had become one of the world's outstanding aeroplanes with many great flights to its credit.

CF-APK, the British-built Puss Moth in which Hinkler met his death, became the first Canadian registered aeroplane to land in Great Britain under its own

The unnamed D.H.80 G-AAHZ (c/n 396) forerunner of the Puss Moth, showing the flat sided wooden fuselage, the absence of doors on the port side and the pronounced dihedral.
(*Flight Photo 7803*)

The Puss Moth floatplane on the Welsh Harp, Hendon, in September 1930. Like all early models it had no small jury strut to the rear wing root fitting. (*Aeroplane*)

power when it touched down at Hanworth from Madrid on 7 December 1931 at the end of a solo trip that included the first nonstop flight from New York to Jamaica, the first British air crossing of the Caribbean Sea, the first British flight from Jamaica to Venezuela and a 22 hour South Atlantic crossing from Natal to Bathurst. Sqn. Ldr. C. S. Wynne-Eaton's attempt to cross the North Atlantic in a similar long range single seater, G-AAXI, ended when the aircraft was destroyed by fire when taking off from Lester Field, Newfoundland on 6 July 1930.

Early in 1931 Nevill Vintcent flew the sixth production aircraft G-AAXJ to Ceylon, which had not previously seen an aeroplane, and on 15 October 1932 J. R. D. Tata flew the first air mails over the 1,330 mile Karachi–Bombay–Madras route in VT-ADN. At home the Prince of Wales bought G-ABBS, 'FV, 'NN and 'RR which were decorated successively in the red and blue of the Guards, and Amy Johnson was presented with G-AAZV 'Jason II' in recognition of her solo Moth flight to Australia. Accompanied by C. S. Humphreys she used it for a rapid flight to Tokyo in 8 days 22 hours 35 minutes, leaving Lympne on 26 July 1931, reaching Moscow the first day and arriving in the Japanese capital on 6 August. The third production machine, G-AAVB, was fitted temporarily with Short floats, enabling it to be flown 1,040 miles nonstop from the Welsh Harp, Hendon, to the Stockholm Aero Show by Col. the Master of Sempill in 12 hours on 4 September 1930. He returned via Norway and Scotland on the 22nd and later toured the entire British coast. Senor Carlos Bleck, who had flown a Cirrus Moth to West Africa, repeated the performance in the 100th production Puss Moth, covering 11,500 miles in the course of a return trip from Lisbon to Loanda early in 1931. His route crossed that of Mrs. Wilson and S. F. Mostert, at that time engaged on a flight from Kenya to England via West Africa and the Canary Islands in the first of three Wilson Airways Puss Moths, VP-KAH. Their flying time was 80 hours 40 minutes. Carl Nauer was less fortunate in that area and disappeared off the mouth of the Congo River in CH-326 on 6 August 1933 while attempting a Cape Town–Europe record.

In the U.S.A. Frenchman H. A. Darren and two friends flew from Newark Airport to San Francisco in 1934 in G-ABEL which belonged originally to Lady Hay Drummond Hay, crossing the Rockies with three up and luggage at 12,000 ft. Later that year the Master of Sempill flew from England to Australia in his personal G-ABJU to attend the Centenary celebrations.

The first Puss Moth flight to Australia was made by F. R. Matthews who left Croydon in G-ABDW on 16 September 1930 and reached Darwin in a leisurely 4 weeks 4 days. Together with C. D. Pratt's VH-ABU, this aircraft was used at Sydney by Marshall Airways Ltd. as VH-UQB and flew for many years with locally devised strengthening in the form of an additional pair of wing struts. Quite the most remarkable flights over this route were made by C. J. Melrose in the Australian registered Puss Moth VH-UQO. After flying 8,000 miles round Australia in the record time of 5 days 11 hours in August 1934, he flew it from Darwin to Croydon in 8 days 9 hours in order to compete in the MacRobertson Race to Melbourne. Leaving Mildenhall on 20 October he averaged 103 m.p.h. to come third in the handicap section.

The Cape record also suffered at the hands of Puss Moth pilots. Leaving Lympne in G-ABEH 'Good Hope' on 31 October 1931, Peggy Salaman and Gordon Store lowered the record to 6 days 6 hours 40 minutes, but the greatest Puss Moth epics were those of Jim and Amy Mollison. The former left Lympne in his special long range single seater G-ABKG on 24 March 1932 and, flying via the Sahara and the west coast of Africa, reached the Cape in 4 days 17 hours 19 minutes. A second special Puss Moth G-ABXY, 'The Heart's Content', was then built, having extra windows in the rear cabin enabling the pilot to sit behind a huge 160 gallon fuel tank which gave a range of 3,600 miles. Taking off from the natural runway afforded by Portmarnock Strand, Dublin, on 18 August 1932, he made the first solo east–west Atlantic crossing and landed at Pennfield Ridge, New Brunswick, 31 hours 20 minutes later. It was then Amy's turn and, flying a new Gipsy Major powered machine G-ACAB 'Desert Cloud', she not only lowered her husband's Cape record by 10 hours 26 minutes, but also broke that for the homeward journey. The supreme Puss Moth performance came, however, when 'The Heart's Content', again piloted by Mollison, left Lympne on 6 February 1933 on a successful flight to Natal in Brazil. He thus became the first man to fly from England to South America and the first to make a solo east–west crossing of the South Atlantic. This historic aircraft, the first to cross both the North and South Atlantic Ocean, was then sold to H. L. Brook, but was unfortunately damaged beyond repair in a forced landing at Genholac, France, on 28 March 1934 after leaving Lympne in an attempt on the Australia record.

The most important non-standard Puss Moth was W. D. Macpherson's G-ABMD which was considerably modified by Airwork Ltd., Heston and fitted

G-ABMD, the red and white competition Puss Moth at Heston in 1934. (*Aeroplane*)

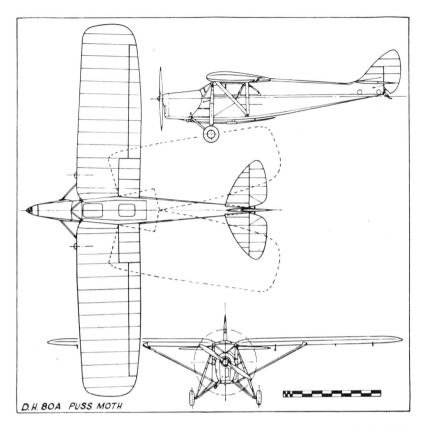

D.H. 80A PUSS MOTH

with a 147 h.p. Gipsy Major high compression engine for participation in the 1934 Warsaw International Touring Competition. Dr. Lachmann of Handley Page Ltd., James Martin of Martin-Baker Ltd. and Herr Hoeffner joined forces to design full span slots and wing flaps inboard of the ailerons which were rigged to droop 10 degrees in flight and in conjunction with a Fairey adjustable pitch airscrew, reduced the minimum flying speed to 35 m.p.h. Extra rear windows of the type fitted to 'The Heart's Content' were also provided to improve rearward vision.

The Puss Moth was comfortable and easy to fly, features which endeared it to every pilot, five of those impressed by the R.A.F. in 1939 having been with their original owners for over eight years. They were Maj. A. A. Nathan's G-AAYC, G. W. Garnett's G-AAZW, the Master of Sempill's G-ABJU (kept on a private strip at the Lizard), Will Hay's G-ABLR and H. C. D. Hayter's G-ABUX.

After wartime service as A.T.A. taxi aircraft, several reappeared in 1946 to fly again in civil guise. These included G-ABDF, 'EH, 'KZ, 'RR and 'YP. By 1973 only a handful remained, including several in Australia; ZK-AJN grounded in New Zealand; four in the U.S.A.; G-AAZP with the Hawker Siddeley Club, Chester; G-ABLS restored at Southampton in 1968 by C. C. Lovell; G-AEOA reconstructed at Botley by Dr. J. H. B. Urmston in the same year; and Father McGillivray's CF-PEI in Canada. This was formerly the Tiger Club's Redhill-based G-AHLO, built in 1931 and serialled 8877 for the U.S. Naval Air Attaché in London. It was impressed for A.T.A. use as HM534 in 1942 and finally became a British civil aircraft in 1946 at the age of 15 years.

SPECIFICATION

Manufacturers: The de Havilland Aircraft Co. Ltd., Stag Lane Aerodrome, Edgware, Middlesex.
Power Plants: One 120 h.p. de Havilland Gipsy III.
One 130 h.p. de Havilland Gipsy Major.
Dimensions: Span, 36 ft. 9 in. Length, 25 ft. 0 in. Height, 7 ft. 0 in. Wing area, 222 sq. ft.
Weights: Tare weight, 1,265 lb. All-up weight, 2,050 lb.
Performance: Maximum speed, 128 m.p.h. Cruising speed, 108 m.p.h. Initial climb, 630 ft./min. Ceiling, 17,500 ft. Range, 300 miles.

Production: (a) de Havilland D.H.80 prototype
One aircraft only: (c/n 396) E-1/G-AAHZ

(b) de Havilland D.H.80A Puss Moth

Two hundred and fifty-nine aircraft including 143 registered in Britain and the following mainly for export: (c/n 2004) CF-AGO; (2008) ZS-ACA; (2015) CF-AGQ; (2016) CF-AGS; (2017) CF-AGU; (2018) CF-AGT; (2019) CF-AGV; (2021) VH-UPC; (2022) VH-UPA; (2023) VH-UPN; (2032) VT-ABJ; (2039) CF-AGW; (2044) K1824; (2046) ZK-ABG; (2048) CF-AGY; (2049) CF-APK; (2050) CH-261; (2052) VH-UPM; (2053) VH-UPJ; (2054) ZK-ABR; (2056) VT-ABZ; (2058) ZS-ACC; (2060) ZS-ACB; (2062) CH-260; (2064) MW-135; (2065) ZS-ACF; (2066) VH-USV; (2067) VH-UQK; (2068) D-1943; (2069) D-1944; (2078–2079) Australia; (2080) VT-ACA; (2082) D-1948; (2084) VH-UPO; (2085) VH-UPQ; (2086–2087) Australia; (2088) VH-UQL; (2089) VH-UQO; (2092) VT-ACB; (2093) VT-ACC; (2094–2095) Australia; (2096) VT-ABG; (2097) OK-ATF; (2098) VT-ACD; (2099) VT-ACF, later VT-ADU; (2100) Portugal; (2102) OK-ATG; (2103) ZS-ACE; (2107) ZK-ACB; (2108) Argentina; (2110) ZS-ACD; (2111) VT-ACI; (2112) Argentina; (2114) I-FOGL; (2118) VP-KAK; (2119) VT-ACH; (2124) VT-ABU; (2126) ZS-ACG; (2128) J-BAWA; (2129–2130) Argentina; (2131) ZS-ACH; (2133) J-BAXA; (2138) CH-270; (2142) UN-SAA; (2146) D-2030; (2148) YI-ABB; (2151) CH-271; (2152) ZS-ACP; (2153) VP-KAM; (2165) ZS-ACR; (2169) ZS-ACS; (2171) HS-PAA; (2175) HS-PAB; (2177) ZS-BBC; (2179) HS-PAC; (2180) HS-PAD; (2181) ZS-ACT; (2182) CH-274; (2183) CH-276; (2184) UN-PAX; (2186) I-FOLO; (2187) 8877/G-AHLO; (2188) U.S. Embassy/G-ABNF; (2192) CH-273; (2193–2194) China; (2195) ZS-ACV; (2197) ZS-ACU; (2198) VP-YAH; (2199) CV-AAI; (2202) ZS-ADK; (2204) ZK-ACX; (2205) VT-ABW; (2206) CH-303; (2208) ZS-ACX; (2210) OO-AMN; (2211) CH-326; (2212) untraced; (2214) PH-MAG; (2215) Argentina; (2221) J-BBAA; (2222) J-BBBA; (2224–2226) Iraqi Air Force; (2227) D-2235; (2230) India; (2231) E-8; (2235) CR-MAE; (2237) Japan; (2239) Japan; (2242–2245) Japan; (2248–2257) Japan; (2258) PH-ATB.

(c) Built by de Havilland Aircraft of Canada Ltd.

Twenty-five aircraft: (c/n DHC.201) R.C.A.F. 169; (202) 170; (203) 171/CF-CCI; (204) 172/CF-CCF; (205) 173; (206) 174; (207) 175/CF-CCL; (208) 176; (209) 177/CF-CCJ; (210) 178/CF-CCK; (211) 179; (212) 180/CF-CDN; (213) 181/CF-CCM; (214) G-CYUR; (215) G-CYUS; (216) G-CYUT; (217) G-CYUU; (218) untraced; (219) CF-IOL; (220) CF-APD; (221) CF-APE; (222) untraced; (223) CF-AVA; (224) CF-AVB; (225) CF-AVC.

The Auckland Gliding Club's Tiger Moth tug ZK-AIA, still flying in 1970, was Hatfield-built in 1938 as ZK-AGI and served with the R.N.Z.A.F. as NZ721. (*K. Meehan*)

De Havilland D.H.82A Tiger Moth

The summer of 1931 saw the birth of the Tiger Moth, probably the greatest biplane trainer of all time, destined to find a place in aviation history alongside the historic Avro 504K. Stag Lane had that year seen the Gipsy Moth reach its ultimate variant, the D.H.60T trainer, and from Puss Moth experience knew the advantages to be gained by the use of inverted engines. Inevitably the D.H.60T acquired the Gipsy III, and to improve the instructor's escape route still further, the centre section struts were all moved forward of the front cockpit. The mainplanes were then given sweep-back in order to maintain the C. of G. position. The new type was dubbed the D.H.60T Tiger Moth, and for a short period the T changed in meaning from Trainer to Tiger Moth. Two, E-5/G-ABNJ and G-ABPH, were tested at Martlesham in September 1931, the second having increased dihedral on the lower wing and increased sweepback which led to a change in type number to D.H.82, the first aircraft to bear it being G-ABRC, first flown at Stag Lane under B conditions as E-6 on 26 October 1931.

Large scale production which began at Stag Lane and later continued at Hatfield for the R.A.F. and foreign governments, included civilian Tiger Moths for use at the Elementary and Reserve Flying Schools. These were to replace antique equipment and later, under the Expansion Scheme, to equip and augment new and existing Schools. The Bristol Aeroplane Co. Ltd. operated theirs in black and orange at Filton and Yatesbury; the de Havilland School of Flying in red and silver at Hatfield (later at Panshanger) and White Waltham; the Brooklands School of Flying Ltd. in red and black at Sywell; the Phillips and Powis School of Flying Ltd. in red and silver at Woodley; Reid and Sigrist Ltd. in cream and brown at Desford; Airwork Ltd. in white and green at Perth, and Scottish Aviation Ltd. in orange and silver at Prestwick.

Few machines could be spared for normal civilian purposes, although the National Aviation Day displays used G-ABRC, 'UL, G-ACEZ and 'FA for aerobatics and joyrides, the Scottish Motor Traction Co. Ltd. and C. W. A. Scott's Air Display using G-ACDY and G-ADWG for a similar purpose.

G-ACEZ survived the war. With a spike fitted on its wing tip, Geoffrey Tyson used it to bring the crowd to its toes as he picked up a handkerchief off the ground. In this machine he celebrated the twenty-fifth anniversary of Blériot's cross-Channel flight on 25 July 1934 by repeating the performance upside down. Three others, G-ACBN, 'EH and 'YN, were registered for ferrying to Spain, Poland and Palestine respectively, and 'JA was the demonstrator exhibited at the Geneva Aero Show in May 1934. It was afterwards flown in the King's Cup Race by Peter de Havilland.

After 1937 it became possible to earmark part of the production for the clubs, and the tired Gipsy and Cirrus Moths were at last replaced at London, Newcastle, Castle Bromwich, Brooklands, Cardiff, Liverpool and York, while one Tiger Moth was added to each of the R.A.F., Leicestershire, Cinque Ports, South Staffs. and Coventry Clubs. The Scottish and Luton Clubs had two each and the Straight Corporation distributed G-AFSP–'SU among the Thanet, Ipswich, Exeter, Plymouth and Weston Aero Clubs. They were all standard aircraft, including G-ACPS, built for the London Aeroplane Club by the de Havilland Technical School. The majority of these machines were fitted with Gipsy Major engines and plywood decking to the rear fuselage, and bore the now-familiar designation D.H.82A.

A pre-production D.H.60T Tiger Moth G-ABPH flying near Stag Lane in July 1931. It was eventually sold to the Portuguese Government. (*Flight Photo 10605*)

Orders were also accepted from clubs and private owners in Australia, Egypt, Greece, Holland, India, Lithuania, Mozambique, New Zealand, Southern Rhodesia and Switzerland, the largest customer being France which bought 17. In 1937 an order was placed with de Havilland Aircraft of Canada Ltd. for 25 Tiger Moths for the R.C.A.F. and a year later the firm was asked to supply 200 fuselages to the parent company but it is evident that not all of these reached England. By the outbreak of war 1,150 had been built at Hatfield, 227 at Toronto, one at Wellington, New Zealand, and three for the London Aeroplane Club by the de Havilland Technical School.

The majority of British and Commonwealth civil Tiger Moths were impressed into their respective air forces in 1939, London Aeroplane Club aircraft being shipped to the R.N.Z.A.F. and most of the Bristol Reserve School fleet to a civilian school in India, while in 1940 about 30 more were also exported to India, South Africa and elsewhere.

113

In 1941 all Hatfield factory space was required for the Mosquito, and Tiger Moth production was transferred to the assembly line of Morris Motors Ltd. at Cowley, Oxford, so that total output to 15 August 1945 rose to approximately 7,290 aircraft. De Havilland built 795 at Hatfield, Morris 3,216 at Cowley and the overseas companies contributed the remainder. Large numbers of Australian-built Tiger Moths were shipped to Southern Rhodesia and South Africa for use under the Commonwealth Air Training Plan which also operated in Canada where the Tiger was redesigned and adapted to local conditions by de Havilland Aircraft of Canada Ltd. and fitted with a 125 h.p. Menasco Pirate D.4 engine.

When hostilities ceased a number of redundant Tiger Moths were put up for civilian disposal and these bore the brunt of club and private flying in the immediate postwar period but in 1947, when the R.A.F. released its entire stocks, the trickle became a flood so that during a single month in 1954 no less than 103 were ferried from the R.A.F. to Croydon alone. This also occurred on a smaller scale in other parts of the world, and, at a time when there were virtually no new light aeroplanes, the Tiger Moth took on a new lease of life.

It symbolised the very spirit of sporting flying and in Britain its chief advocates were members of the Tiger Club who flew from Croydon and later Redhill. These dedicated enthusiasts, recruited by founder Norman Jones, kept the biplane age very much alive by enlivening flying meetings with formation flying, aerobatics, glider towing and parachute dropping in their gaily painted Tigers, pride of the fleet being G-ACDC restored to the colours in which it was delivered new to the D.H. School of Flying in 1933. They also possessed a number of special lightweight single seaters converted by Rollason Aircraft and Engines Ltd., the first of which, G-APDZ, was named 'The Bishop' after their veteran performer C. A. Nepean Bishop, and for some years operated the only British registered floatplane, Tiger Moth G-AIVW, from Lee-on-Solent. The formation of an American Tiger Club during the 1960s produced a number of keen exponents of 'two hole' flying in the States some of whom redecorated their expensively imported Tiger Moths in R.A.F. wartime colours.

Cabin conversions were many and varied, ranging from the standard fitments of the Canadian D.H.82Cs to 'one-off' designs such as the coupé top fitted to G-AIZF by H. M. Woodhams at Baginton in 1950, the simple Taxi Tiger

Australian-built Tiger Moth VH-BRM with Commonwealth Wackett canopy.

Martin Barraclough flying the Tiger Club's single seater G-ANZZ 'Archbishop'.
(*John Blake*)

The Dutch National Flying School's Ypenburg-based Tiger Moth PH-UDE with elongated fin, was first civilianised at Croydon in 1947 as G-AJXJ.

canopy devised by Rollasons for the front cockpit of G-AOXS (and later flown on C. M. Roberts' G-AHVU), a more elaborate version fitted to G-ANSA by Personal Plane Services, White Waltham, and the Commonwealth Wackett canopies used in Australia.

The Tiger Moth will be chiefly remembered commercially as the aircraft which established agricultural aviation as an essential industry. Large numbers were used for top dressing in New Zealand, Australia, the U.K. and elsewhere, or in the alternative role of crop spraying with perforated pipes under the wings or rotary atomisers on the lower mainplanes. One Australian-built Tiger Moth, ZK-AJO, which flew 6,500 hours in New Zealand with James Aviation Ltd. and dropped the incredible total of 6,000 tons of fertiliser, is permanently preserved by the company.

A number were converted into four seat Thruxton Jackaroos (q.v.) by the Wiltshire School of Flying but even more imaginative reconstructions were later undertaken for war films, three Tiger Moths being converted at Croydon in 1961 by Film Aviation Services Ltd. for use in Jordan during the filming of 'Lawrence of Arabia' in which T7438 became a replica Fokker D.VII and two others, R5146/G-ANNF and T6945/G-ANLC, Rumpler C Vs. At a later date Personal Plane Services Ltd. built a Pfalz replica G-ATIF; Charles Boddington a B.E.2c replica G-AWYI at Sywell; and Slingsby Sailplanes Ltd. two Rumpler C IVs G-AXAL and 'AM at Kirkbymoorside, all from Tiger Moth components.

SPECIFICATION

Manufacturers: The de Havilland Aircraft Co. Ltd., Stag Lane Aerodrome, Edgware, Middlesex. Works transferred to Hatfield Aerodrome, Herts. in 1934; Morris Motors Ltd., Cowley, Oxford; The de Havilland Aircraft Pty. Ltd., Bankstown, Sydney, Australia; de Havilland Aircraft of Canada Ltd., Downsview, Toronto; de Havilland Aircraft of New Zealand Ltd., Wellington; and in Portugal, Norway and Sweden.

Power Plants: (D.H.82) One 120 h.p. de Havilland Gipsy III.
(D.H.82A) One 130 h.p. de Havilland Gipsy Major.
One 145 h.p. de Havilland Gipsy Major 1C.
(D.H.82C) One 145 h.p. de Havilland Gipsy Major 1C.
One 125 h.p. Menasco Pirate D.4.

Dimensions: Span, 29 ft. 4 in. Length, 23 ft. 11 in. Height, 8 ft. $9\frac{1}{2}$ in. Wing area, 239 sq. ft.

Weights: (D.H.82) Tare weight, 1,075 lb. All-up weight, 1,825 lb.
(D.H.82A) Tare weight, 1,115 lb. All-up weight, 1,825 lb.

Performance: (D.H.82) Maximum speed, 109·5 m.p.h. Cruising speed, 85 m.p.h. Initial climb, 700 ft./min. Ceiling, 17,000 ft. Range, 300 miles.
(D.H.82A) Maximum speed, 109 m.p.h. Cruising speed, 90 m.p.h. Initial climb, 673 ft./min.. Ceiling, 18,000 ft. Range, 300 miles.

British production: (a) D.H.82 Tiger Moth
Seventeen British civil aircraft, large batches for the R.A.F. and foreign air forces, and the following civilian exports: (c/n 3100) VR-HAR; (3112) SE-ADE; (3113) SE-ADF; (3114) SE-ADG; (3115) SE-ADH; (3142) D-2357.

(b) D.H.82A Tiger Moth
Quantity production for the R.A.F. (civilianised in large numbers post-1945), foreign air forces, British civil operators and the following civilian exports: (c/n 3190) PH-AJG; (3222)´ Austrian A-78; (3289) OA-CCH; (3320) VH-UTD; (3336) OY-DOK; (3358) VT-AGQ; (3359) VT-AGR; (3462) VT-AHD; (3463) VT-AHE; (3478) CF-CBR; (3479) CF-CBT; (3480) CF-CBU; (3481) CF-CBS; (3493) LY-LAT; (3494) OE-DAX; (3502) VT-AHL; (3507) VP-YBG; (3508) VH-UVZ; (3515) VH-UXC; (3519) VP-YBH; (3520) VT-AIF; (3522) ZS-AIN; (3523) ZS-AIO; (3524) OE-DIK; (3525) ZS-AIL; (3526) ZS-AIM; (3527) OE-DAF; (3528) ZS-AIP; (3529) ZS-AIR; (3532) VP-CAB; (3537) VR-RAM; (3542) LY-LAM; (3591) VR-RAN; (3592) VR-RAO; (3593) VH-UYJ; (3597) SU-ABX; (3598) VH-UYK; (3600) VH-UYL; (3601) VT-AIS; (3603) VP-YBO; (3604) ZS-AJA; (3608) SU-ABY; (3621) VH-UYR; (3622) VH-UYP; (3623) VH-UYQ; (3626) ZS-AMN; (3629) ZK-AFN; (3630) ZK-AFO; (3632) VH-UZT; (3634) ZS-AMZ; (3635)

VH-UZV; (3638) ZK-AFY; (3639) ZK-AFZ; (3640) ZK-AGA; (3641) ZK-AFU; (3642)
ZK-AFV; (3643) ZK-AFW; (3644) ZK-AFX; (3650) CS-AAA; (3654) ZK-AGE; (3655)
F-AQJU; (3656) F-AQJV; (3657) F-AQJX; (3658) F-AQJY; (3659) F-AQJZ; (3661)
VT-AJU; (3663) ZS-ANU; (3665) F-AQNF; (3666) F-AQNG; (3667) F-AQNH; (3668)
F-AQNI; (3669) F-AQNJ; (3670) VH-AAE; (3671) ZK-AGF; (3672) ZS-ANV; (3677)
F-AQOS; (3678) VP-RAG; (3680) ZK-AFP; (3685) F-AQOZ; (3686) F-AQOQ; (3687)
F-AQOV; (3688) F-AQOX; (3689) VH-AAI; (3690) VH-AAJ; (3691) F-AQOY; (3692)
F-ARAR; (3693) ZK-AGG; (3696) ZK-AGH; (3697) ZK-AGI; (3701) VP-YBW; (3702)
HB-OKU; (3703) VH-ABM; (3704) VH-AAR; (3705) ZK-AGL; (3721) SX-AAK;
(3723) VH-AAP; (3746) VH-AAK; (3750) VP-CAE; (3769) ZS-APF; (3771) ZS-APE;
(3789) ZK-AHA; (3792) VT-AKS; (3795) ZK-AGZ; (3832) ZK-AHB; (3833)
ZK-AGW; (3834) ZK-AGX; (3835) ZK-AGY; (3880) VT-AKW; (3935) ZK-AHF;
(3936) ZK-AHG; (82052) ZK-AHH; (82143) ZS-API; (82144) ZS-ARG; (82230)
ZK-AHO; (82231) ZK-AHM; (82232) ZK-AHR; (82348) VH-ADH; (82349)
VH-ADI; (82447) VP-TAC; (82448) VP-TAD; (82576) VT-ALL; (82577) VT-ALB;
(82578) VT-ALC; (82579) VT-ALD; (82580) VT-ALE; (82581) VT-ALF; (82582)
VT-ALG; (82583) VT-ALH; (82874) XY-AAB; (82875) XY-AAC; (83571) VT-AMI;
(83572) VT-AMJ; (83573) VT-AMK; (83599) VT-AML; (83600) VT-AMM; (83601)
VT-AMN; (83627–83633) VT-AMO to VT-AMV; (83654–83660) VT-AMW to
VT-ANC; (83701–83705) VT-AND to VT-ANH; (83746) VT-ANI.

     (c) D.H.82A Tiger Moths built by the de Havilland Technical School
Three aircraft only: (c/n 1993) G-ACPS; (2262) G-ADGO; (2264) G-AEVB.

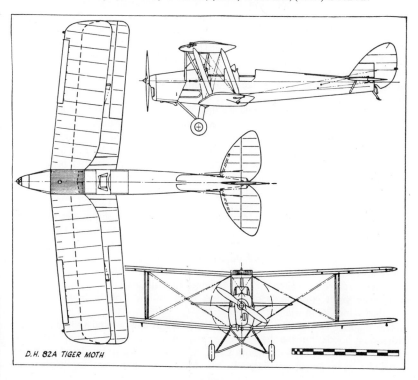

D.H. 82A TIGER MOTH

Neil Williams flying the Tiger Club's famous Fox Moth G-ACEJ near Redhill in 1967. (*John Blake*)

De Havilland D.H.83 Fox Moth

The Fox Moth was produced early in 1932 to the designs of A. E. Hagg, whose aim was a light transport aeroplane of outstanding performance and economy. His success was unquestionable, low initial cost being ensured by the use of Tiger Moth undercarriage, engine mounting, tail unit and mainplanes. The only new major component was the wooden, plywood covered fuselage which had an open cockpit for the pilot and a small cabin forward. Its performance was astonishing, and on short pleasure flights, for which it was ideally suited, it would carry pilot and four passengers on the mere 120 h.p. of one Gipsy III engine. Even on longer flights up to the maximum range of 360 miles, it would carry pilot and three passengers.

G-ABUO, the prototype, made its first flight in March 1932, and was then shipped to Canada for evaluation on floats and skis by Canadian Airways Ltd. It later became CF-API, and its performance was such that the Fox Moth was put into production at de Havilland's Toronto factory. A total of 98 Fox Moths was built at Stag Lane, 46 initially of British registry. The yellow first production machine, G-ABUP, had a short career with British Hospitals Air Pageants Ltd., and G-ABVI and 'VK commenced operations in June 1932 on the Clacton–Maylands–Ramsgate scheduled service of Hillmans Airways Ltd.

In its first summer the Fox Moth distinguished itself as the mount in which W. L. Hope won his third King's Cup. His machine, G-ABUT, was powered by a 130 h.p. Gipsy IIIA (later Gipsy Major) engine and had a sliding cockpit canopy. Fuel was carried in the cabin, and, devoid of the drag and turbulence created by the centre section tank, baffled the handicappers to win the race at 124·13 m.p.h. It was afterwards sold to Surrey Flying Services Ltd. at Croydon, where, during the next seven years, thousands of joyriders paid 5s. for a flight in the suitably inscribed King's Cup winner.

The majority of later Fox Moths had Gipsy Major engines and about one-third had sliding hoods, but the designation remained unchanged. An early purchaser was the Prince of Wales, for whom G-ACAJ was changed to the double suffixed G-ACDD as a Royal privilege. It was little used, and went to Belgium as

118

OO-ENC at the end of 1933, the new owner, Guy Hansez, using it for a fast return flight to the Congo before returning it to the makers in 1935. G-ACGB, L. Ingram's well known G-ACID and Henri Deterding's G-ACIY were among the few private Fox Moths, the majority being used commercially. Scottish air transport, previously non-existent, was inaugurated with them in 1933. The Scottish Motor Traction Co. Ltd. acquired eight, G-ACDZ–'EE, 'EI and 'EJ, and Midland and Scottish Air Ferries Ltd. had four, G-ACBZ, 'CB, 'CT and 'CU. They were all based at Renfrew, and ran scheduled services, with intermittent pleasure flights, to remote and often unprepared fields near towns in the Highlands and Islands. When S.M.T. bought Dragons and M. & S.A.F. closed down in the following year, the fleets dispersed, some continuing in service with West of Scotland Air Services. One, G-ACEB, went south to inaugurate the air ferry from Southend to Rochester. Two others, G-ACCB and 'EJ, went to Southport where, a quarter of a century later, 'EJ was still joyriding on the sands, before becoming flagship of the Tiger Club vintage flight at Redhill in 1967.

Other operators were National Aviation Day Displays with G-ACEX 'Youth of Ireland' and 'EY 'Youth of Newfoundland' and Blackpool and West Coast Air Services Ltd. of Squires Gate had G-ACFC 'Progress I' and 'FF 'Progress II'. The latter pair eventually passed to Olley Air Service Ltd. at Croydon, and thence to the controlling interest, Great Western and Southern Air Lines Ltd. C. W. A. Scott's Air Display used G-ACCF and, for a short period in 1935, G-ACGN and 'KZ also. In that year the ex Cobham machines 'EX and 'EY became the first aircraft of the newly established Provincial Airways Ltd. Renamed 'Mercury' and 'Jupiter' respectively, they inaugurated the company's route between Croydon, Portsmouth, Christchurch, Exeter and Plymouth. Two others, G-ACCA and 'IG, were used for six years on the Portsmouth–Ryde ferry of the Portsmouth, Southsea and Isle of Wight Aviation Ltd., while on the island itself, 'EA was the resident pleasure flight machine at Sandown.

After the 1932 King's Cup success, spectacular Fox Moth flights were few. In February 1933 Lord Clydesdale flew G-ACCS from Heston to India, where it was employed as a taxi for the British Everest Flight Expedition. Painted yellow overall, G-ACRU spent three years on survey work in the Falklands and Antarctica, returning to Heston in July 1937. Another yellow Fox Moth—on floats—was John Grierson's G-ACRK, in which he left Rochester on 20 July 1934 and, after an outstanding flight via Iceland and the Greenland Ice Cap,

Canadian-built D.H.83C Fox Moth ZK-AQB, c/n FM.49, showing the elevator trim tab modification and enlarged Plexiglas hood. (*K. Meehan*)

The Fox Moth floatplane G-ACRK in which John Grierson flew to New York in 1934. A wheeled undercarriage was fitted at Ottawa.

reached Ottawa on 30 August. Fox Moth G-ACSW, the ninety-second built, put up the final sporting performance when it was raced for the 1934 King's Cup by H. F. Broadbent but came eighth at 121·03 m.p.h. It was later sold in India where VT-ADZ and 'FI flew on Tata's Bombay–Karachi route and VT-AFB on the Indian National Airways service between Karachi and Lahore. Fox Moth seaplane VT-AFZ was operated in Burma by the Irrawaddy Flotilla Co. Ltd. and two others, VO-ABC and 'DE were used by Imperial Airways Ltd. when it took over the Newfoundland air mail service in 1935.

Five Fox Moths were used as navigational trainers by the Brazilian Navy; four others, SU-ABA, 'BG and VP-YAD, 'AK were used on local services in Egypt and Southern Rhodesia; and Victor Holyman opened the 108 mile Launceston–Flinders Island route with 'Miss Currie' in 1932. Others were used for the Flying Doctor Service and for the goldfield service in New Guinea. A Spanish machine, registered EC-AEI, originally a floatplane registered EC-VVA in April 1934, later served the Spanish Air Force as 30-147.

A copy known as the Chidorigo, registered J-BBJI and powered by a 150 h.p. radial, was used by the Japan Aerial Transport Co. for taxi work alongside four British-built machines.

During the 1939–45 war Fox Moths in Britain were camouflaged and impressed, three for Air Transport Auxiliary, three for a radar trials unit at Christchurch and one each to the Royal Navy and the Blackburn company as hacks. Elsewhere they flew in civil colours until the end of their useful lives, and a few still survived in 1972.

In 1946 de Havilland Aircraft of Canada Ltd. commenced production of an all-Canadian D.H.83C version with 145 h.p. Gipsy Major 1C and sold 52 in Canada, Southern Rhodesia, India and Pakistan, one of which, AP-ABO, landed at Southend on 24 September 1955 after an unpublicised ferry flight from Karachi, later becoming the Squires Gate-based joyride machine G-AOJH.

SPECIFICATION

Manufacturers: The de Havilland Aircraft Co. Ltd., Stag Lane Aerodrome, Edgware, Middlesex; and de Havilland Aircraft of Canada Ltd., Toronto.

Power Plants: One 120 h.p. de Havilland Gipsy III.
One 130 h.p. de Havilland Gipsy Major.
One 145 h.p. de Havilland Gipsy Major 1C.
Dimensions: Span, 30 ft. 10½ in. Length, 25 ft. 9 in. Height, 8 ft. 9½ in. Wing area, 261·4 sq. ft.
Weights: Tare weight, 1,100 lb. All-up weight, 2,070 lb.
Performance: (Gipsy Major) Maximum speed, 113 m.p.h. Cruising speed, 96 m.p.h. Initial climb, 492 ft./min. Ceiling, 12,700 ft. Range, 360 miles.

Production:

Ninety-eight aircraft comprising 46 initially of British registry and the following for export: (c/n 4003) EI-AAP; (4010) VH-UQM; (4011) CF-ATV; (4013) Japan; (4016) Japan; (4019) VH-UQS; (4020) VH-UQP; (4021) VH-UQQ; (4023) ZS-ADH; (4024) SU-ABG; (4025) ZK-ADC; (4027–4031) Brazilian Navy; (4032) VT-ADZ; (4034) VP-YAD; (4035) VP-YAK; (4037) CF-APF; (4038) CF-APG; (4039) D-3408; (4043) VT-AEA; (4045) VT-AEB; (4049) CF-ATX; (4050) CF-APH; (4051) VH-UQU; (4052) CF-APO; (4061) Austrian A-129; (4066) EC-AVA; (4070) Eagle Oil; (4071) VT-AEJ; (4073–4076) EC-W19 to EC-W22; (4078) VT-AEM; (4079) Japan; (4080) Japan; (4081) VT-AEN; (4082) VT-AEQ; (4084) VH-URI; (4085) ZK-ADH; (4086) VT-AFB; (4087) EC-W23/EC-VVA/EC-AEI; (4088) VT-AFI; (4092) VT-AFZ; (4093) VO-ABC; (4094) VO-ADE; (4095) CF-AVE; (4096) VH-USL; (4097) ZK-ADI.

Also two aircraft (c/n DHA.5) VH-UZS and (DHA.6) VH-AAA/VH-GAS in Australia and 54 (c/n FM.1 to FM.54) in Canada less (FM.53) ZK-ARQ not completed.

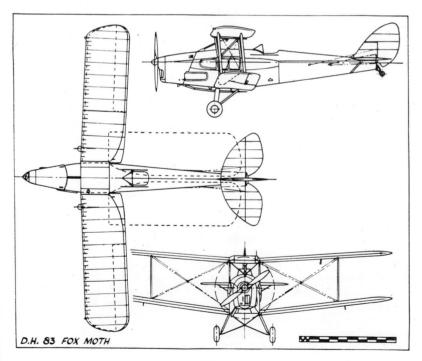

D.H. 83 FOX MOTH

121

Railway Air Services' G-ADDI 'City of Cardiff' in 1935 showing the framed windows and faired undercarriage of the Mk.2. This aircraft was well known in the 1960s as the Chrisair joyriding machine. (*E. J. Riding*)

De Havilland D.H.84 Dragon

Realizing that the built-in economies of the Fox Moth were largely responsible for the success of his cut-price internal services, Edward Hillman asked de Havillands for a twin engined equivalent with which to open a Paris service. A. E. Hagg thereupon produced the Dragon, a two bay biplane of high aspect ratio, employing the well proven D.H. plywood covered fuselage and powered by Gipsy Major engines. The nose compartment, reached via the cabin, accommodated one pilot, and for ease of storage the wings were made to fold outboard of the engine nacelles. The prototype, E-9, made its first flight at Stag Lane on 12 November 1932, and in Hillman's blue-and-white livery was delivered to Maylands as G-ACAN in the following month and the rest of the order, comprising G-ACAO, 'AP and 'BW, was delivered in time for the service to open in April 1933. The Dragons cruised at 109 m.p.h., carrying six passengers with 45 lb. of luggage each, for an hourly petrol consumption of only 13 gallons and permitted a typical Hillman fare structure which ensured the popularity of the service and necessitated the acquisition of G-ACEU and 'EV in the May.

What it lacked in beauty of line, the Dragon amply made up in revenue earning ability and attracted wide interest. Midland and Scottish Air Ferries Ltd. took delivery of two, G-ACCZ and 'DL, for services from Renfrew to Belfast, Liverpool and Dublin; and the Scottish Motor Traction Co. Ltd. three, G-ACDM, 'DN and 'ET. The first ambulance service to the Western Isles was also inaugurated. Hubert Broad flew G-ACFG in the 1933 King's Cup, but although he averaged 132·7 m.p.h., came last. This was the machine with which George Nicholson later founded Northern and Scottish Airways Ltd. and which, in company with G-ACJS and 'JT, plied between Renfrew, Campbeltown, Islay and the Outer Hebrides. Farther north Aberdeen Airways Ltd. operated from Dyce with G-ACRH, G-ADFI and the ex Hillman prototype. Highland Airways Ltd., based at Inverness, inaugurated a service between Dyce and Orkney with G-ACIT on 7 May 1934, their fleet later including G-ACCE, 'ET and 'GK.

Overseas orders included D.H.84M military Dragons with gun rings and dorsal fins for the Iraq, Danish and Portuguese Air Forces, one ferried to Automobiles Fernandez of Barcelona as EC-W14 (later EC-TAT), and three shipped to Canada. The first of these, CF-APJ, bought by Canadian Airways Ltd. in 1933, carried the mail between Moncton, N.B. and Charlottetown, P.E.I. for ten years. Other examples were G-ACKC and 'KD which replaced the ancient D.H.50 on the pipeline patrol of the Iraq Petroleum Transport Co. Ltd.; ZS-AEF, 'EG and 'EH erected at Baragwanath for African Air Transport Ltd.; VT-AEK and 'EL which left Heston on delivery to Indian National Airways Ltd. on 2 November 1933; G-ACIE/OK-ATO used for executive travel by the Bata Shoe Company in Czechoslovakia; SU-ABH, 'BI and 'BJ flown to Egypt for the extension of the routes of Misr Airwork, and VP-KAW and 'BA acquired by Wilson Airways Ltd., Nairobi.

VH-URF and 'RG were used for survey work by the Western Mining Corporation in the Kalgoorlie goldfields and three others, VH-URW–'RY, flew the 2,252 mile Perth–Daly Waters route of the MacRobertson-Miller Aviation Co. Ltd. In New Zealand ZK-ADS and 'ER commenced a four times daily Napier–Gisborne service on 15 April 1935. CF-AVD, one of the several used in Canada, was fitted with metal floats and the D.H.84M dorsal fin.

A few Dragons were privately owned; W. L. Everard had G-ACEK 'Leicestershire Vixen II'; F-ANES was used for this purpose in Morocco; M. Jean Germain and family of Algiers circumnavigated Africa in 27 days in F-AMTN, 'TR and 'UZ; and the Prince of Wales acquired a V.I.P. four seater G-ACGG.

Jim and Amy Mollison's special Dragon G-ACCV 'Seafarer' was equipped with cabin fuel tanks and strengthened undercarriage for an attempt on the world's long distance record. While taxying out at Croydon on 8 June 1933 to take off for New York, starting point of their intended nonstop flight to Baghdad, the under-

Dragon 1 ZS-AEH, supplied to Stewart & Lloyd of South Africa Ltd. in 1933 (and later used by the Aircraft Operating Company for survey work), after impressment by the South African Air Force in 1940. (*S.A.A.F.*)

The historic transatlantic Dragon 2 G-ACJM 'Seafarer II'. (*New York Times*)

carriage collapsed, but after repairs they successfully got away from Pendine Sands, South Wales on 22 July. Thirty-nine hours later they arrived over Bridgeport, Connecticut, but through fatigue and darkness landed down wind and turned over. Engines and special tanks were salvaged and built into a successor, G-ACJM 'Seafarer II', shipped to Canada in the following September through the generosity of Lord Wakefield. After three unsuccessful take off attempts at the maximum permissible weight of 7,334 lb. at Wasaga Beach, Ontario on 3 October, the Baghdad flight was abandoned and the aircraft sold to would-be record breakers J. R. Ayling and L. Reid. Renamed 'Trail of the Caribou' it took off successfully on 8 August 1934 but excessive fuel consumption resulted in a landing at Heston 30 hours 50 minutes later at the end of the first nonstop flight from the Canadian mainland to Britain.

Commencing with the sixty-third aircraft, G-ACMO for Jersey Airways Ltd., an improved version known as the Dragon 2 came off the production line with individually framed windows and faired-in undercarriage struts. First of the new model to fly was the sixty-seventh aircraft G-ACKU, built for W. L. Everard in

CF-AVD, c/n 6086, showing the framed windows of the Dragon 2 and the twin float undercarriage designed by de Havilland Aircraft of Canada Ltd.

Australian-built Dragon ZK-AXI (formerly A34-68 and VH-AEF) which the Auckland Flying School, New Zealand, presented to the local Transport Museum in 1967. (*K. Meehan*)

November 1933 and flown to victory in the Oases Circuit Race in Egypt by W. D. Macpherson a month later. Seventy Dragons used on British internal airlines included thirty-one Mk. 2s operated principally by Jersey Airways Ltd. and Railway Air Services.

The former ran a high density tourist shuttle between Heston and the Jersey beaches with aptly named aircraft, while R.A.S. Ltd. operated over the Liverpool–Birmingham–Cardiff–Plymouth and Birmingham–Bristol–Isle of Wight network. Important over-water routes with 10 seat Dragons were Portsmouth–Ryde by P.S. and I.O.W. Aviation Ltd. with G-ACRF; Squires Gate–Ronaldsway by Blackpool and West Coast Air Services Ltd. with G-ADCP and 'CR; Weston-super-Mare–Cardiff by Western Airways Ltd. with G-ACAO, 'JT, 'MJ, 'PX and G-AECZ; and Lands End–Scilly Islands by Channel Air Ferries Ltd. with G-ACPY and G-ADDI. The last was one of the few civil routes maintained after the outbreak of war, 'PY being shot down by a German fighter near the Scillies on 3 June 1941. At the outbreak of the 1939–45 war most of the 20 surviving British registered Dragons were impressed into the R.A.F. although a few continued, fully camouflaged, in civil use. These included G-ACIT, delivered to Southend on 19 September 1971 to be kept airworthy for the Historic Aircraft Museum, and G-ADDI flown to Rotterdam on 21 February 1971 as N34DH for shipment to Irwin Perlitch at Morgan Hill, California. The former Western Airways G-AECZ also survived and went to Ireland as EI-AFK in 1950 after a short post-war career with Air Taxis Ltd. at Croydon.

During the 1939–45 war 87 Dragons were built as navigation trainers for the R.A.A.F. at Bankstown, Sydney, where the first, A34-12, first flew on 29 September 1942. After the war 46 became civil including one shipped to New Zealand as ZK-AXI, and VH-BDS intended for joyriding at Butlin's camps in the U.K. as G-AJKF but never imported.

SPECIFICATION

Manufacturers: The de Havilland Aircraft Co. Ltd., Stag Lane Aerodrome, Edgware, Middlesex. Works transferred to Hatfield Aerodrome, Herts. in 1934.
Power Plants: Two 130 h.p. de Havilland Gipsy Major.

Dimensions: Span, 47 ft. 4 in. Length, 34 ft. 6 in. Height, 10 ft. 1 in. Wing area, 376 sq. ft.

Weights: (Mk. 1) Tare weight, 2,300 lb. All-up weight, 4,200 lb.

(Mk. 2) Tare weight, 2,336 lb. All-up weight, 4,500 lb.

Performance: (Mk. 1) Maximum speed, 128 m.p.h. Cruising speed, 109 m.p.h. Initial climb, 612 ft./min. Ceiling, 12,500 ft. Range, 460 miles.

(Mk. 2) Maximum speed, 134 m.p.h. Cruising speed, 114 m.p.h. Initial climb, 565 ft./min. Ceiling, 14,500 ft. Range, 545 miles.

Production:

One hundred and fifteen at Stag Lane and Hatfield, 66 initially of British registry and the following for export: (c/n 6003–6008) Iraq Air Force Nos. 16 to 21; (6012–6013) Iraq Air Force Nos. 22 and 23; (6020) EC-W14/EC-TAT; (6024) CF-APJ; (6026) ZS-AEF; (6028) SU-ABH; (6029) VH-URE; (6030) ZS-AEG; (6031) SU-ABI; (6037) VH-URD; (6044) YI-AAC; (6045) VH-URF; (6046) VH-URG; (6047) VP-KAW; (6048) VT-AEL; (6050) VT-AEK; (6051) SU-ABJ; (6054) ZS-AEH; (6057) F-AMTR; (6059) VP-KBA; (6060–6061) Danish Army Air Force S.21 and S.22; (6064) F-AMUZ; (6065) VT-AES; (6068) VH-URO; (6074) VH-USA; (6080–6082) VH-URW to VH-URY; (6083) F-ANES; (6085) PP-SPC; (6086) CF-AVD; (6088–6089) VH-URU and VH-URV; (6090) ZK-AER; (6091) ZK-ADS; (6093) CF-AVI; (6101) OE-FKD; (6102) VH-UVB; (6104) VH-UTX; (6111) Portuguese Air Force; (6113–6114) Portuguese Air Force.

Also 87 by de Havilland Aircraft Pty. Ltd., Sydney (c/n 2001–2087) initially to the R.A.A.F. as A34-12 to A34-98.

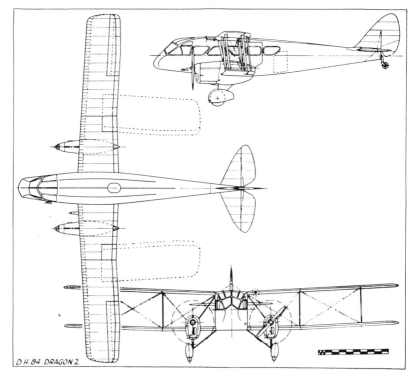

D.H.84 DRAGON 2

126

H. F. Broadbent's Australia–England Leopard Moth VH-AHB re-registered G-AFDV for a private owner at Redhill in 1938. (*W. K. Kilsby*)

De Havilland D.H.85 Leopard Moth

This was primarily a Gipsy Major powered private owner's machine, produced in 1933 as a successor to the Puss Moth. The welded steel construction of the earlier type was abandoned in favour of a spruce-and-plywood fuselage which was not only cheaper to build but improved the gross to tare weight ratio sufficiently to enable the Leopard Moth to be designed as a three seater. The pilot sat in front, with the passengers side by side in the rear, but the aircraft was also easily distinguishable externally from its older relative. Not only did the swept-back leading edge give a tapered wing, but the shock absorber legs were carried to pick-up points below the front windscreen instead of to the top longerons. The prototype made its first flight with Class B marking E-1 at Stag Lane on 27 May 1933 and only a fortnight later, on 8 July, as G-ACHD, it made fastest time in the final to win the King's Cup Race at Hatfield, piloted by Capt. Geoffrey de Havilland at an average speed of 139·51 m.p.h. Two others, 'HB and 'HC, also competed, flown by Mrs. A. S. Butler and A. J. 'Bill' Styran. Both qualified for the final and came third and sixth respectively.

No better form of publicity could have been devised and Leopard Moth production continued at Stag Lane and later at Hatfield, for three years. During this time 132 were built, 71 of which eventually went into service in the United Kingdom. Many prominent private owners bought them, notably Nigel Norman, founder of Heston Airport, whose registration G-ACNN (in chromium plated letters used on shop fronts) included his initials. W. Lindsay Everard's 'KM was of course named 'The Leicestershire Fox III', Alex Henshaw bought 'LO, Sir Philip Sassoon 'LW and Wg. Cdr. F. O. Soden G-ADAP. Bernard Rubin and Ken Waller flew 'LX to Australia in 15 days in March–April 1934 to survey the route for the MacRobertson Race and succeeded in breaking the record for the return journey by arriving at Lympne on 1 May in a time of 8 days 12 hours. Several Leopard Moths remained with the same owners throughout their useful lives, including Sir Pyers Mostyn's 'KK, Nigel Norman's 'NN, Capt. G. de Havilland's 'KP, F. Matusch's 'LL, Mrs. B. Urquhart's 'OO, A. S. Butler's 'UO, C. A. MacDonald's G-ADAA

and H. R. A. Kidston's G-AEFR. They were very well liked, and the same
security of tenure was enjoyed by National Benzole Ltd.'s yellow G-ACMA,
Morris Motors Ltd.'s 'TG and the Cinque Ports Flying Club's 'PG. The prototype remained in the possession of the manufacturers, and in 1935 was flown
as the D.H.85A with a 200 h.p. Gipsy Six engine driving a constant speed
airscrew.

M. Christian Moench, president of the French Aéro Club de l'Est, who had
taken delivery of Leopard Moth F-AMXA in March 1934, later flew it from
Marseilles to Madagascar in seven days. On 10 October of that year a red
machine without markings landed at Heston to clear Customs for Paris on delivery to Portugal, piloted by Lt. Humberto del Cruz with the well known Carlos
Bleck as passenger. This aircraft, c/n 7083, was fitted with extra fuel tanks in the
cabin and left Lisbon with the same crew on 25 October to visit all the Portuguese
possessions overseas and arrived at Dili, Timor on 7 November. The flight was
sponsored by the Lisbon daily paper *O Seculo* and the Leopard Moth completed
the journey of 43,495 miles by crossing Africa to visit the Cape Verde Islands
before returning home to be handed over to the Portuguese Air Force. The last
great Leopard Moth flight ended at Lympne on 3 May 1937 when H. F. 'Jimmy'
Broadbent landed in VH-AHB, only 6 days 8 hours 25 minutes after leaving
Darwin. The special cabin fuel tank giving a 1,500 mile range was later removed
at Hanworth and the aircraft sold to veteran Redhill private owner Sam Harris as
G-AFDV.

Forty-four British Leopard Moths were impressed at the outbreak of the 1939–
45 war for communications duties in camouflage with the R.A.F. and A.T.A.
Several of those in India formed part of the Delhi Communications Flight, and
others were 'called up' in Southern Rhodesia, South Africa and elsewhere. Very
few survived to re-enter civilian life but in 1946 G-ACRW and 'TJ reappeared
briefly before sale to Norway and Switzerland, while G-ACLL, 'MA and 'MN
owned respectively by British Midland Airways Ltd., and two private owners at
Baginton, were still airworthy a quarter of a century later.

YI-ABI which arrived by air from Iraq in September 1946 and had, as a new
machine, been exported to an Egyptian owner as SU-ABM 12 years before,
became G-AIYS in March 1947 after overhaul at Hanworth. In later years it
forr..ed part of the Surrey Flying Club fleet at Croydon and in the early 1960s
gave hundreds of joy flights when in service with Chrisair.

A handful of these veterans also flew postwar in Australia (VH-UUE, 'UL,
VH-AJN and VH-BAH), India (VT-AHO and 'KH), Kenya (VP-KER and 'FM)
and Switzerland (HB-ABA, 'LI and HB-OTA), the last of which arrived at Biggin
Hill on 23 May 1965 for registration in Britain as G-ATFU.

SPECIFICATION

Manufacturers: The de Havilland Aircraft Co. Ltd., Stag Lane Aerodrome, Edgware,
Middlesex. Works transferred to Hatfield Aerodrome, Herts. in 1934.

Power Plant: One 130 h.p. de Havilland Gipsy Major.

Dimensions: Span, 37 ft. 6 in. Length, 24 ft. 6 in. Height, 8 ft. 9 in. Wing area,
206 sq. ft.

Weights: Tare weight, 1,405 lb. All-up weight, 2,225 lb.

Performance: Maximum speed, 137 m.p.h. Cruising speed, 119 m.p.h. Initial climb,
625 ft./min. Ceiling, 21,500 ft. Range, 715 miles.

Production:

One hundred and thirty-two aircraft, 66 initially of British registry and the following for export: (c/n 7004) ZS-AEE; (7005) ZS-AEJ/VP-KFM; (7007) CH-366/HB-OTA, later G-ATFU; (7010) Japan; (7015) VT-AEP; (7017) CH-367/HB-ORU/F-AQRU; (7018) F-AMUP; (7019) ZS-AEK/VP-YCH; (7020) ZS-AEP; (7021) VH-URK/VH-AJN; (7022) CH-388/HB-ARI; (7029) F-AMXN; (7030) F-AMXR; (7031) OO-NAD; (7034) F-AMXS; (7035) F-AMXP; (7037) F-AMXO/PH-VYG/PH-NCP; (7039) Argentine; (7041) F-AMYT; (7043) F-AMXQ/PH-HJP/PH-SCH; (7045) CH-368/HB-OXO; (7047) EC-5E; (7053) F-ANBS; (7055) VP-KBE; (7059) CH-290/HB-ALI; (7063) China; (7069) F-AMYS; (7072) D-EGYV; (7078) VP-YAT/SR22; (7083) Portugal; (7084) VH-USK; (7085) VT-AGB; (7086) VH-USM; (7088) OO-APS; (7089) SU-ABM/YI-ABI; (7092) OO-AVD; (7094) PH-FDK; (7089) ZS-AFI/VP-KCO; (7096) OO-JFC; (7097) HB-ABA; (7098) PH-JUH; (7099) ZS-AET; (7101) VP-YAY; (7102) VT-AGG; (7105) HB-OKO; (7107) VP-KBP; (7108) EC-W49; (7109) VH-UUE; (7110) VH-UUG; (7111) VH-UUL; (7112) South Africa; (7113) VP-KBV/I-NENO; (7114) VP-KBX; (7115) VP-YAZ/VP-RBR; (7116) ZS-AHA/VP-KER; (7118) VH-UVD/VH-AAG; (7119) VT-AHA; (7120) VH-AHB; (7121) VT-AHG; (7122) F-AOUH; (7123) VT-AHK; (7124) VT-AHH; (7126) VH-UVF; (7127) HB-XAM; (7129) South Africa; (7130) VT-AIL.

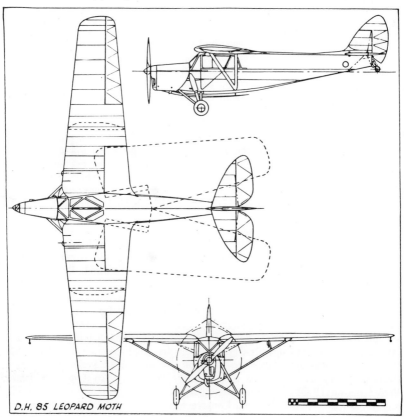

D.H. 85 LEOPARD MOTH

129

Jersey Airways Ltd.'s D.H.86 G-ACZN 'St. Catherine's Bay'

De Havilland D.H.86

The unnamed D.H.86 was designed and built in four months to a specification issued in 1933 by the Australian Government who required a high performance mail and passenger aircraft embodying multi-engined safety for use by QANTAS on the Singapore–Australia section of the proposed Empire Air Route. The prototype, E-2/G-ACPL, fitted with four Gipsy Six engines, which were themselves only just through their Air Ministry Type Test, was first flown by Hubert Broad at Stag Lane on 14 January 1934. After Martlesham trials the C. of A. was issued on 30 January, one day before the time limit set by the Australian authorities. Constructionally the D.H.86 followed de Havilland practice but with a difference. As usual, the fuselage was a plywood box, but this time the spruce longerons and stringers were on the outside, the whole being fabric covered. Accommodation was for a maximum of 10 passengers with a single pilot in the extreme nose and a second crew member behind him on the starboard side.

After exhaustive flight testing, the prototype was fully furnished and painted in the livery of Railway Air Services Ltd. Two others, G-ACVY 'Mercury' and 'VZ 'Jupiter', were also delivered to Railway Air Services, and from 21 August operated the new trunk route between Croydon, Castle Bromwich, Barton, Belfast and Renfrew.

Although the performance of the D.H.86 was well above the stipulated minimum, the Imperial Airways/QANTAS joint order called for a captain and first officer side by side. The prototype therefore returned to Stag Lane and reappeared in August 1934 with an elongated two seat nose, repainted in full Imperial Airways colours and named 'Delphinus'. The first production aircraft, VH-URN 'Miss Hobart' was then shipped to Holyman Airways for the Melbourne–Hobart route but Victor Holyman and 10 passengers were lost when it vanished in the Bass Strait on 19 October, a tragedy closely followed by the crash of VH-USG, one of the six for QANTAS, near Longreach on 15 November. This necessitated the reallocation of the Imperial Airways G-ACWE to QANTAS as VH-UUA 'Adelaide'. After the loss of Holyman's second D.H.86 VH-URT 'Loina' off Flinders Island on 2 October 1935, VH-USW 'Lepena' and VH-UUB 'Loila' were delivered as replacements.

Jersey Airways Ltd. replaced its Dragons with six D.H.86s on the Heston–Eastleigh–Channel Islands service and three dark blue, unnamed examples flew the Stapleford–Paris route of Hillmans Airways Ltd. Four D.H.86s also super-seded Dragons on Misr Airwork's services between Cairo, Alexandria, Assiut, Baghdad, Cyprus and Haifa, while late in 1935 three were shipped to New Zealand. They were assembled at Wigram, and given the names of local birds for use by Union Airways of New Zealand Ltd. on a passenger and mail service between Palmerston North, Blenheim, Christchurch and Dunedin inaugurated on 16 January 1936. By the time it ceased on 25 September 1939 the three D.H.86s had flown 1,373,000 miles and were afterwards absorbed by the R.N.Z.A.F.

Late in 1935 the D.H.86A was introduced having pneumatic undercarriage legs, larger brakes and tail wheel, metal rudder and a steeper windscreen. Gipsy Six I engines were standard but one aircraft, E-2, was tested at Martlesham with Series II engines and v.p. airscrews before delivery to Misr Airwork Ltd. as SU-ABV.

During 1936 Imperial Airways Ltd. put the first D.H.86A G-ADFF 'Dione' and eleven others into service on their European network and on the Khartoum–Accra route opened by 'Daedalus' on 13 February 1936. On 23 March 'Dorado' inaugurated the Penang–Saigon–Hong Kong shuttle on which 'Dardanus' was shot up by a Jap fighter near Wai Chao in 1939. Also in 1936 the Hillman D.H.86s were taken over by British Airways Ltd. to supplement its fleet of four D.H.86As on unsubsidised day passenger and night mail services between Gatwick and the Continent; and two 18 seaters, G-ADVJ and 'VK, maintained the Isle of Man ferry of Blackpool and West Coast Air Services Ltd. G-ADVJ subsequently became 'Eire', the first four engined aircraft owned by Aer Lingus, which in 1938 acquired another, 'Sasana', from Imperial Airways Ltd. to enable daily schedules to be flown between Dublin, the Isle of Man and Speke, or Bristol and Croydon. After the loss of British Airways' G-ADYF in September 1936,

The single pilot type D.H.86 'Mercury' of Railway Air Services Ltd. at Croydon in 1934.

'YH was the subject of a Martlesham report criticising rudder and aileron control which led to the attachment of large auxiliary fins to the end of the tailplane. In this form the aircraft was known as the D.H.86B, to which standard all existing D.H.86As were then modified.

The final developmental stage was the construction of ten production D.H.86Bs having tailplanes with increased chord at the tips and higher gearing in the aileron circuit. The first of these, G-AENR, tested at Martlesham in February 1937, was followed by 'Venus' for Railway Air Services Ltd. and 'Silver Star' flown on the Woolsington–Stavanger service of Allied Airways Ltd. in 1938, on the Weston–Cardiff ferry of Western Airways Ltd. in the following year and in 1940 as an ambulance of the Finnish Naval Coastguard Service. Four were sold to the Turkish State Airline (Devlet Hava Yollari) for its Istanbul–Ankara–Izmir and Ankara–Adana routes, while the last three built were shipped to Australia for the 3,000 mile service operated by W. R. Carpenter and Co. Ltd. between Sydney and Rabaul, New Britain, via Townsville and Thursday Island.

D.H.86B G-AETM 'Silver Star' awaiting delivery to Allied Airways (Gandar Dower) Ltd., June 1937. (*Flight Photo 16790*)

Sixty-two of these aircraft were built, 44 being of British registry, but with the approach of the 1939–45 war the D.H.86 fleets began to disperse. G-ACYF and G-ADEA were sold in Singapore and eventually saw ambulance service in the Western Desert with the Royal Australian Air Force as A31-2 and A31-7 respectively. G-ADEC and 'YE went to Uruguay, 'UH to Eire and 'YC, 'YG and 'YJ to the R.A.F. as flying classrooms. The Western Airways machine 'TM was sold in Finland, where it was destroyed during the war as OH-IPA. The old D.H.86s 'Mercury' and G-ACZP, and 86Bs G-ADYH and 'ENR, were camouflaged and continued to operate the skeleton internal services of National Air Communications during the war. Many were impressed for ferrying supplies to the armies in France, where 'Neptune' and 'Venus' were lost in action in June 1940. One, G-AEJM, survived as a Royal Air Force V.I.P. transport X9441 named 'The Cathedral' for several years.

Several of these aged four engined biplanes reappeared post 1945, including 'Mercury', then in its twelfth year, and the former Imperial Airways 'Dido', which came back to England after spending the war years in Egypt as SU-ACR. Another

No.24 Squadron D.H.86B L7596, formerly G-ADYJ, during a Ministerial visit to Swordfish squadrons in Malta in 1938.

Misr Airlines D.H.86B, SU-ABV, was bought by Peacock Air Charter of Alexandria as G-AJNB in 1947. Others saw post-war service with Skytravel Ltd. of Speke and Bond and Union Air Services of Gatwick, one of which, 'YH, was flown out to Australia in 1948 and thence to the Indonesian rebels. After capture by the Dutch at Manguwo on 12 December 1948 it was scrapped at Bandoeng. The last airworthy example was the one-time Jersey D.H.86 G-ACZP overhauled by V. H. Bellamy at the Hampshire Aeroplane Club only to be damaged beyond repair when the undercarriage collapsed at Madrid on 21 September 1958.

SPECIFICATION

Manufacturers: The de Havilland Aircraft Co. Ltd., Hatfield Aerodrome, Herts.
Power Plants: Four 200 h.p. de Havilland Gipsy Six series I.
Four 205 h.p. de Havilland Gipsy Six series II.
Dimensions: Span 64 ft. 6 in. Length 46 ft. 1 in.* Height 13 ft. 0 in. Wing area 641 sq. ft.

* Single pilot type D.H.86, 43 ft. 11 in.

Weights and Performances:

	Prototype	D.H.86*	D.H.86A Gipsy Six I	D.H.86A Gipsy Six II	D.H.86B
Tare weight	5,637 lb.†	6,303 lb.	6,140 lb.‡	7,228 lb.	6,489 lb.
All-up weight	9,200 lb.	10,000 lb.	10,250 lb.	11,000 lb.	10,250 lb.
Maximum speed	170 m.p.h.	170 m.p.h.	166 m.p.h.	150 m.p.h.	166 m.p.h.
Cruising speed	145 m.p.h.	145 m.p.h.	142 m.p.h.	135 m.p.h.	142 m.p.h.
Initial climb	1,140 ft./min.	1,200 ft./min.	925 ft./min.	1,100 ft./min.	925 ft./min.
Ceiling	—	20,500 ft.	17,400 ft.	18,000 ft.	17,400 ft.
Range	450 miles	760 miles	760 miles	748 miles	800 miles

* Two pilot type.   † Single pilot production type 5,520 lb.
‡ 6,730 lb. when modified to D.H.86B.

Production: (a) Single pilot type

Three aircraft only: (c/n 2300) G-ACPL; (2302) G-ACVY; (2303) G-ACVZ.

(b) Two crew type

Twenty-nine aircraft, 15 British registered and the following for export: (c/n 2301) VH-URN; (2307–2311) VH-USC to VH-USG; (2312) VH-URT; (2315) VH-USW; (2320) SU-ABN; (2326) VH-UUB; (2329) SU-ABO; (2330) ZK-AEF; (2331) ZK-AEG; (2332) ZK-AEH.

(c) D.H.86A (converted to D.H.86B in 1937)

Twenty aircraft, mainly British registered but the following for Misr Airwork Ltd., Cairo: (c/n 2342) SU-ABV 'Al Mahroussa', later G-AJNB.

(d) Production D.H.86B

Ten aircraft, seven British registered and the following for W. R. Carpenter Ltd.: (c/n 2359–2361) VH-UYU, VH-UYV and VH-UYW.

Note: Parts of Union Airways D.H.86s ZK-AEF, 'EG and 'EH, impressed 9.39 as NZ552 to NZ554, were used to construct a new 'NZ553' which became civil in 1945 as ZK-AHW.

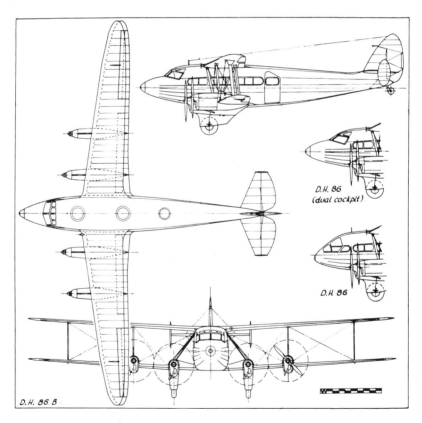

D.H. 86
(dual cockpit)

D.H. 86

D.H. 86.B

W. Lindsay Everard's D.H.87A Hornet Moth 'The Leicestershire Foxhound II'.
(Aeroplane)

De Havilland D.H.87 Hornet Moth

The D.H.87 Hornet Moth originated as an experimental one-off design built in 1934 for full scale research into the most suitable type of biplane replacement for the Gipsy Moth. It was a side-by-side, two seat, Gipsy Major powered aircraft, the front end of which was reminiscent of the Leopard Moth. The fabric covered rear fuselage was built on D.H.86 lines with the stringers and longerons outside the plywood box and the similarity was carried further with the fitting of tapered wings with rounded tips. E-6, the prototype, first flew at Hatfield on 9 May 1934 and, in accordance with usual practice, flew in the King's Cup Race as G-ACTA on 13 July piloted by Capt. Geoffrey de Havilland but was eliminated in the heats after averaging 127 m.p.h. Two other Hornet Moths, E-1/G-ADIR and 'IS, then joined the prototype in a flight testing and modification programme which lasted a year and eradicated many teething troubles before large scale production began. The most noticeable result was the fitting of new mainplanes with an even more pronounced taper, thus changing the designation to D.H.87A.

The first production batch left the factory in August 1935, and when the last appeared three years later, 165 had been constructed, including 84 for British use. Early in 1936, however, the second production Hornet Moth G-ADIS suddenly appeared with new mainplanes featuring only the slightest of tapers and almost square ends. It then became known as the D.H.87B. The exact point at which the wide chord mainplanes were embodied at manufacture is uncertain, but O. R. Guard's G-ADOT, the sixty-eighth machine, was certainly built as a D.H.87A. Owners were invited to trade-in the original mainplanes, and eventually only five British examples retained their pointed wings. They were the prototype, flown on D.H. communications as a camouflaged civil aeroplane along with D.H.87B G-ADUR during the 1939–45 war, Geoffrey Linnell's G-ADJZ, Lady Loch's 'KA, W. D. Macpherson's 'KI and F-ARAX, a French machine re-imported by Airwork Ltd. as G-AFHX in June 1938.

Spectacular record breaking successes were not for the Hornet Moth, which enjoyed its brief pre-war career only in the private, club and executive fields. A. S. Butler had G-ADKU, W. Lindsay Everard's 'LY was called 'The Leicestershire Foxhound II', Shell Mex and B.P. Ltd. had three, the Fairey Aviation Co. Ltd.

kept 'ND at Harmondsworth, C. B. Mills of circus fame owned 'MS, and Lord Londonderry 'MR (to quote but a few). One, G-AFED, was kept in the Sudan.

The Hornet Moth soon shared the wide popularity of all the de Havilland types and the company's factories in the Dominions assembled the following quantities—South Africa 17, Canada 11, Australia 7 and India 4; at the same time others were delivered by air and sea to Austria, Belgium, Denmark, Egypt, Eire, France, Greece, Hong Kong, Java, Kenya, Northern and Southern Rhodesia, Singapore, Spain, Sweden and Switzerland. D.H. Aircraft of Canada Ltd. was entrusted with the design of an undercarriage with Fairchild floats and one Hornet Moth seaplane, CF-AYJ, became the personal aircraft of P. C. Garrett, managing director of the firm. Four others were supplied to the British Air Ministry for evaluation as seaplane trainers and after extensive tests at the M.A.E.E., Felixstowe, were restored to wheels and despatched to Lee-on-Solent in June 1939. Two of them survived the war to reappear in 1946 at White Waltham where, stripped of camouflage they were reconditioned before joining the fleet of the West London Aero Club as G-AHBL and 'BM.

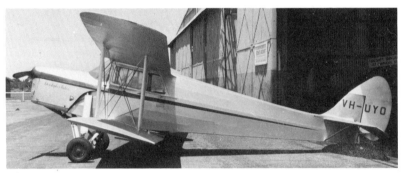

Miss Freda Thompson's 1937 wide chord wing D.H.87B Hornet Moth VH-UYO 'Christopher Robin' at Essendon, Melbourne in 1953.

The vast majority of British registered Hornet Moths were relatively new in 1939 and being ripe for impressment, were snapped up rapidly by the R.A.F. as communications aircraft and for the calibration of early radar installations. OY-DOK, which had been delivered to C. Thielst at Kastrup in March 1936, succeeded in escaping from German occupied Denmark on 21 June 1941 flown by Lts. Kjeld Petersen and Thomas Sneum of the Danish Naval Air Service. On arrival in Britain it too was impressed and served with No. 24 Squadron, Hendon as HM498 until wrecked in collision with Avro Tutor K4811 at Bicester on 25 March 1942.

G-ADMO, impressed as AV969, went briefly to Denmark postwar as OY-DTI; and G-AMZO, delivered initially to the Malayan Aero Club in 1935 as VR-RAI, also went to Denmark later as OY-DEZ and thence to Sweden as SE-ALD, coming under British ownership for the first time in 1954. Two decades later, when vintage biplanes were much sought after on the western side of the Atlantic, G-AEET was acquired by George Neal of de Havilland Canada, Toronto, as CF-EEJ; and G-ADNB, a one-time Tiger Club machine, was repainted at White Waltham in 1971 as N36DH to show its year of construction, and then shipped to the U.S.A.

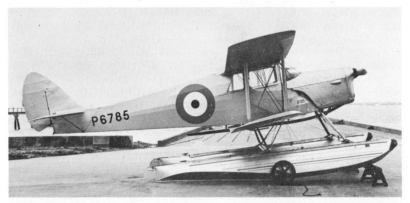

Hornet Moth seaplane P6785 at Felixstowe in 1937. (*Imperial War Museum MH.2858*)

SPECIFICATION

Manufacturers: The de Havilland Aircraft Co. Ltd., Hatfield Aerodrome, Herts.
Some airframes assembled by de Havilland Aircraft of Canada Ltd., Downsview Airport, Toronto.

Power Plants: One 130 h.p. de Havilland Gipsy Major 1 or 1F.
One 145 h.p. de Havilland Gipsy Major 1C (in Canada).

	D.H.87	D.H.87A	D.H.87B Landplane	D.H.87B Seaplane
Span	30 ft. 7 in.	32 ft. 7 in.	31 ft. 11 in.	31 ft. 11 in.
Length	24 ft. 11½ in.	24 ft. 11½ in.	24 ft. 11½ in.	26 ft. 6 in.
Height	6 ft. 7 in.	6 ft. 7 in.	6 ft. 7 in.	9 ft. 6 in.
Wing area	220½ sq. ft.	220½ sq. ft.	244½ sq. ft.	244½ sq. ft.
Tare weight	1,170 lb.	1,192 lb.	1,241 lb.	1,405 lb.
All-up weight	1,800 lb.	1,925 lb.	1,950 lb.*	2,000 lb.
Maximum speed	117 m.p.h.	131 m.p.h.	124 m.p.h.	115 m.p.h.
Cruising speed	—	111 m.p.h.	105 m.p.h.	95 m.p.h.
Initial climb	680 ft./min.	800 ft./min.	690 ft./min.	675 ft./min.
Ceiling	—	17,800 ft.	14,800 ft.	—
Range	—	640 miles	620 miles	500 miles

* Later increased to 2,000 lb.

Production: (a) Prototype
One aircraft only: (c/n 1997) E-6/G-ACTA

(b) Production Hornet Moths
One hundred and sixty-four aircraft comprising 84 initially of British registry and the following for export: (c/n 8009) CF-AVH; (8010) VT-AGE; (8011) VT-AGF, later VT-AJX; (8013) ZS-AFR; (8015) VP-YBA; (8017) VP-KBM/ZS-AMD; (8021) HB-OFE; (8022) OE-DKS; (8023) VH-UTE; (8024) OO-ROB/F-BECS; (8025)

137

SE-AEK; (8026) VP-RAD/VP-YBX; (8028) HB-UIM; (8030) CF-BFH; (8031) CF-AYG; (8034) CS-AAS/VP-KBR; (8036) VH-UUD; (8038) HB-OBE/F-AQBY; (8039) EC-W51; (8040) VP-RAI/SE-ALD, later G-AMZO; (8041) VH-UUW; (8043) EC-W52/EC-BBF; (8047) ZS-AFY; (8048) ZS-AFZ; (8049) EC-W53; (8050) HB-OMI/F-APXN; (8052) CF-BBE; (8053) CF-BFG; (8055) HB-OBI/F-AQOT; (8056) F-AONI; (8057) SU-ABT; (8058) F-AQMM; (8059) ZS-AHF; (8060) ZS-AHG; (8061) CF-AYI/P6788; (8062) CF-AYJ; (8063) HB-OFA/F-AQIX; (8065) OY-DOK; (8070) VR-SAN; (8075) VP-YBE; (8077) VH-UVV; (8078) VH-UUX; (8079) EC-W55; (8083) EC-W56; (8088) ZS-AHP/VP-YIX; (8090) OO-RDK; (8094) OE-DKK/HB-UBD; (8095) PK-WDR; (8099) CR-AAA; (8103) ZS-AHU/VP-YBF; (8104) CR-AAC; (8107) EI-ABL, later G-AFRE/VP-AAC; (8110) VH-UXO; (8111) VH-UYO; (8113) ZS-AKA; (8115) OY-DIL; (8117) ZS-AKG/VP-YIW; (8118) ZS-AKF; (8119) F-APZA; (8120) EI-ABO; (8121) ZS-ALA; (8123) ZS-AKH; (8124) F-AQZV; (8125) VT-AIU; (8126) CF-BFJ/P6785, later G-AHBL; (8127) CF-BFK/RCAF.5600/CF-DIP; (8128) VT-AIT; (8129) VR-HCW; (8130) F-AQBZ; (8134) CF-BFI/P6787; (8135) CF-BFN/P6786, later G-AHBM; (8136) SE-AGE; (8139) VH-UYX; (8142) ZS-ANN; (8143) VP-YBS/CR-ABG; (8144) F-AQJR; (8147) F-AQJS/LR-AAQ; (8148) ZS-AOT/VP-KEP; (8151) F-ARAQ; (8152) OY-DON/SE-ALE; (8153) OY-DUN; (8159) SX-AAI; (8161) ZS-AOA; (8163) ZS-APD.

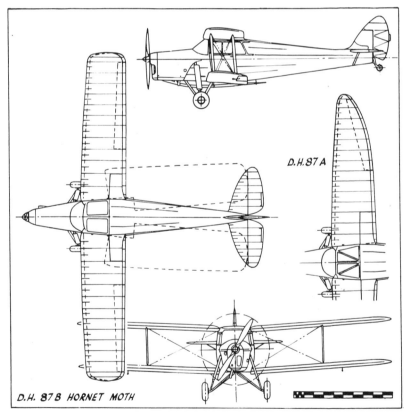

D.H.87 A

D.H. 87 B HORNET MOTH

The historic D.H.88 Comet 'Grosvenor House', winner of the 1934 MacRobertson Race to Australia.

De Havilland D.H.88 Comet

In 1933, when Sir Macpherson Robertson put up the prize money for the Victorian Centenary air race from England to Melbourne, existing aircraft with the necessary performance were all American. The Comet was born solely of the de Havilland Company's patriotic determination to counter this threat and to build a winner, even at a financial loss to themselves. Their willingness to build a 200 m.p.h. racer was therefore advertised with the proviso that orders must be placed by February 1934—a mere nine months before the race. Three were ordered almost at once, by Jim and Amy Mollison, Bernard Rubin and A. O. Edwards, managing director of Grosvenor House Hotel. De Havillands were as good as their word, and the first Comet E-1/G-ACSP was flown at Hatfield by H. S. Broad on 8 September 1934—six weeks before the start of the race. It was a small low-wing, cantilever monoplane of all-wood construction, having a very thin section wing planked with laminations of spruce strip and the two crew members sat in tandem behind three large fuel tanks which gave an ultimate range of 2,925 miles at 220 m.p.h. Power was supplied by two special high compression Gipsy Six R engines giving 230 h.p. each at take-off. They drove Ratier two position airscrews which automatically changed to coarse pitch when, at 150 m.p.h., the disc on the spinner was pushed back to release their internal air pressure, the airscrews being returned to fine pitch with a bicycle pump before each flight. Other notable contributions to success were the split flaps and manually retracted undercarriage—then considered novel features.

The three Comets were painted in distinctive colours, the Mollisons' G-ACSP 'Black Magic' was black and gold; Bernard Rubin's green and nameless G-ACSR was flown by Owen Cathcart-Jones and Ken Waller, while G-ACSS, flown by C. W. A. Scott and Tom Campbell Black, was resplendent in red and white and named 'Grosvenor House'.

The race started from Mildenhall at dawn on 20 October 1934, and the story of its progress will live for ever. The Mollison and Scott and Black Comets both made Baghdad nonstop, but 'SR became lost and forced landed in Persia. It finally overtook 'SP at Allahabad, where the Mollisons had retired with engine trouble. Meanwhile Scott and Black were beyond Singapore with the K.L.M.

Douglas DC-2 in hot pursuit, but only after superhuman efforts to overcome mechanical faults and fatigue did they arrive first at Melbourne to win the speed prize in a time of 70 hours 54 minutes. Cathcart-Jones and Waller arrived fourth, but immediately collected newsreels and photographs of the winners and set off again for England. They arrived at Lympne $13\frac{1}{2}$ days after leaving Mildenhall to create an out-and-home record. On 20 December the same aircraft, suitably named 'Reine Astrid', left Evere, Brussels, piloted by Ken Waller and Maurice Franchomme, to carry the Christmas mail to Leopoldville in the Congo, arriving back on the 28th.

It was then sold to the French Government as F-ANPY and lowered the Croydon–Le Bourget record to 52 minutes during delivery by H. S. Broad on 5 July 1935. In the course of experimental work for a projected South Atlantic mail service, Jean Mermoz made Paris–Casablanca and Paris–Algiers high speed proving flights in this machine in the following August and September, and later a fourth Comet, F-ANPZ, with mail compartment in the nose, was also constructed for the French Government.

The Portuguese Government had similar mail carrying ideas and acquired 'Black Magic' for a projected proving flight from Lisbon to Rio de Janeiro. Renamed 'Salazar', it was ferried from Hatfield to Lisbon on 25 February 1935 by Senor Carlos Bleck and Lt. Costa Macedo who covered the 1,010 miles nonstop in 6 hours 5 minutes. A return trip was made in the following September and in 1937 Macedo again brought the aircraft back to Hatfield for overhaul and made an outstanding return flight to Lisbon in 5 hours 17 minutes in July of that year.

A fifth and final Comet named 'Boomerang' was built to the order of Cyril Nicholson who planned a series of attempts on the major long distance records. Piloted by Tom Campbell Black and J. C. McArthur it made a record Hatfield–Cairo nonstop flight of 2,240 miles in 11 hours 18 minutes on 8 August 1935 during the first stage of an attempt on the Cape record. This was abandoned through oil trouble and the machine returned nonstop in 12 hours 15 minutes and established a new out-and-home record to Cairo. Although entered in the King's Cup Race of 7 September 1935 'Boomerang' was a non-starter and left a fortnight later for a second attempt on the Cape record but airscrew trouble over the Sudan on 22 September compelled the crew to abandon the aircraft by parachute.

'Grosvenor House' went to Martlesham for R.A.F. trials in 1935 and as K5084 was a memorable feature of the 1936 Hendon Display but was subsequently damaged when landing with a full load and disposed of as scrap. F. E. Tasker then acquired it, and Essex Aero Ltd. rebuilt it at Gravesend with Gipsy Six series II engines driving D.H. variable pitch airscrews. In pale blue, and named 'The Orphan', G-ACSS was flown into fourth place in the 1937 Marseilles–Damascus–Paris race by Flg. Off. A. E. Clouston and George Nelson.

Bearing a third name, 'The Burberry', the veteran aircraft left Croydon on 14 November 1937 piloted by Clouston and Mrs. Kirby Green, who succeeded in lowering the out-and-home Cape record to 15 days 17 hours. Carrying its final name 'Australian Anniversary', it left Gravesend on 6 February 1938, but broke no records after the undercarriage collapsed in Cyprus. The last historic flight by 'SS was perhaps its greatest. Flown by Clouston and Victor Ricketts, it took off from Gravesend on 15 March 1938, reached Sydney in 80 hours 56 minutes, crossed the Tasman Sea to Blenheim, New Zealand in $7\frac{1}{2}$ hours, stopped overnight and returned to Croydon on 26 March. The 26,450 miles had been covered in 10 days 21 hours 22 minutes to create a record which still stands. The Comet then returned to Gravesend, where it remained under tarpaulins until rediscovered in 1951. The D.H. Technical School then restored it to its original 'MacRobertson' condition for display at the Festival of Britain Exhibition, after which it was preserved by the makers at Leavesden until handed over to the Shuttleworth Trust on 30 October 1965.

SPECIFICATION

Manufacturers: The de Havilland Aircraft Co. Ltd., Hatfield Aerodrome, Herts.

Power Plants: Two 230 h.p. de Havilland Gipsy Six R.
Two 205 h.p. de Havilland Gipsy Six series II.

Dimensions: Span, 44 ft 0 in. Length, 29 ft. 0 in. Height, 10 ft. 0 in. Wing area, 212·5 sq. ft.

Weights: Tare weight, 2,840 lb. All-up weight, 5,320 lb.

Performance: Maximum speed, 237 m.p.h. Cruising speed, 220 m.p.h. Initial climb, 900 ft./min. Ceiling, 19,000 ft. Range, 2,925 miles.

Production:

Five aircraft only: (c/n 1994) G-ACSP; (1995) G-ACSR; (1996) G-ACSS; (1999, later changed to 2260) F-ANPZ; (2261) G-ADEF.

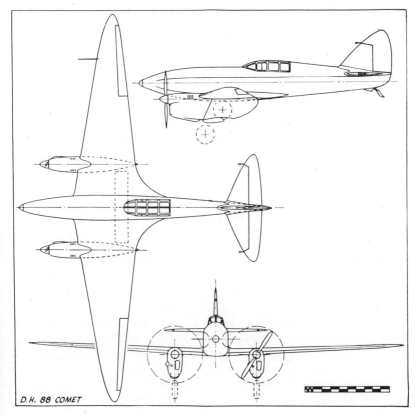

D.H. 88 COMET

G-AFEZ 'R.M.A. Lord Shaftesbury', an Islander Class Rapide of British European Airways leaving the coast of Jersey, 1956. (*B.E.A.*)

De Havilland D.H.89 Dragon Rapide

Designs for a faster and more comfortable Dragon commenced late in 1933, resulting in a scaled down, twin engined version of the high performance D.H.86, employing the same type of fuselage construction, tapered mainplanes, nacelles and trousered undercarriage. Designated D.H.89 Dragon Six and powered by two Gipsy Six engines, this grand old biplane was a mainstay of world commercial aviation for so long that, although renamed Dragon Rapide in its production form, it became known everywhere simply as the Rapide. During the ten years it was in production, 728 were built and it is true to say that no real replacement was found until the Britten-Norman Islander of 1967.

The prototype, E-4, first flown at Stag Lane by H. S. Broad on 17 April 1934 and sold direct to the Ostschweiz Aero Ges. at St. Gallen as CH-287, was still joyriding at Zürich nearly 30 years later. The next aircraft, G-ACPM, built for Hillmans Airways Ltd., made its public debut in the King's Cup Race at Hatfield on 13 July 1934, when H. S. Broad averaged 158 m.p.h. until intense hail near Peterborough forced a retirement with damaged airscrews and leading edges. Together with 'PN and 'PO it flew on Hillman's Paris and Belfast routes but on 2 October 1934 hit the sea and disintegrated 4 miles off Folkestone with the loss of seven lives. The fifth aircraft 'PP, in full Railway Air Services colours, boldly named 'City of Bristol' and exhibited at the 1935 R.Ae.S. Garden Party at Harmondsworth, was the first of a fleet of eight which plied between Croydon, Speke, Renfrew and Belfast and in the summer between Speke, Whitchurch, Eastleigh and Shoreham, each aircraft being named as under:

G-ACPP	'City of Bristol'	G-AEAL	'Star of Yorkshire'
G-ACPR	'City of Birmingham'	G-AEAM	'Star of Ulster'
G-AEAJ	'Star of Lancashire'	G-AEBW	'Star of Renfrew'
G-AEAK	'Star of Mona'	G-AEBX	'Star of Scotia'

Production mounted rapidly but from 1936, commencing G-AEOV, small trailing edge flaps were built into the lower plane outboard of the nacelles and the designation amended to D.H.89A. In 1935 an armed D.H.89, K4772 with dorsal fin, was an unsuccessful contender for the Anson contract but three others were supplied to Iran and two to Lithuania as well as a standard Rapide, K5070, as a VIP transport for No. 24 Squadron, Hendon, to join the King's Flight G-ADDD. Others were delivered to the R.A.F. and R.A.A.F. as radio trainers and ZK-ACO 'Tainui' finished fifth in the MacRobertson Race to Australia piloted by J. D. Hewitt and C. E. Kay.

Deliveries were made to K.L.M., Ala Littoria, the Asiatic Petroleum Co. Ltd. in New Guinea and the Maharajah of Jammu (VT-AHB). CF-AEO, first of several for Canadian Airways and Quebec Airways, was fitted with floats and the long dorsal fin of the military D.H.89M. As one of the world's most widely used transports, the Rapide also flew in the colours of Alpar; Aer Lingus; Transports du Proche Orient, Paris; the Turkish, Persian, Rumanian and Jugoslavian State airlines; the Chinese ambulance service; P.L.U.N.A. in Uruguay; Wilson Airways Ltd. in Kenya; Rhodesia and Nyasaland Airways Ltd.; Union Airways of New Zealand; Wearnes Air Services Ltd. in Singapore; Indian National Airways Ltd.; and transport companies in Australia, Finland, Portuguese East Africa and South Africa. The last civil delivery before the outbreak of war in 1939 was the 205th aircraft, VT-ALO, for Tata Airlines Ltd., Bombay.

British owned Rapides ranged far over Europe and the Near East in the service of charter firms such as Olley Air Service Ltd., whose G-ACYR piloted by Capt. Bebb was General Franco's personal transport at the time of the civil war of 1936. Rapides were also used as flying classrooms at the Shoreham and Perth air navigation schools of Airwork Ltd. and others patrolled the desert pipelines of the Iraq Petroleum Transport Co. Ltd. In May–June 1940 nine were lost while ferrying supplies to the British forces in France, after which the majority were impressed for duty with Air Transport Auxiliary and the air forces and navies of Britain and the Commonwealth. Fourteen were camouflaged to continue in a

VT-ARK, one of four Dominies (HG650 to HG653), operated by Air India in the autumn of 1943 prior to their impressment as MA963 to MA966. (*B.O.A.C.*)

civil capacity with blanked off windows on essential services in Scotland, and a number of others performed similar duties in New Guinea, India and New Zealand.

To supplement impressments, production was stepped up at Hatfield and the Rapide took on a new lease of life as the D.H.89B Dominie Mk. 1 navigation and radio trainer and Mk. 2 communications aircraft, the former externally identified by the roof-mounted direction finding loop. North Eastern Airways' G-AFEP and Wrightways' G-AFEZ were impressed into the Fleet Air Arm which, between 1940 and 1945, also took delivery of 63 Dominie Mks. 1 and 2. Remaining production was for the R.A.F., A.T.A. and U.S.A.A.F. units in Britain, but one was released to the Anglo Iranian Oil Co. Ltd. as G-AGFU, one to Canada as CF-BNG and five to Scottish Airways Ltd. for increased priority traffic to the Hebrides and Shetlands.

Vast numbers of surplus Dominies were put up for disposal after the war and soon became a familiar sight with civilian marks roughly daubed on top of camouflage. Small firms carried out their own civil conversions but the de Havilland Repair Unit at Witney was responsible for a considerable proportion, including G-AJGS and 'KS built from spares with constructor's numbers W.1001 and W.1002 in 1947. Many pre-war machines were also demobilized, and in the postwar period it is true to say that British-owned Rapides flew in almost every country of the world. At home the Rapide contingent grew bigger than ever as ex military machines encouraged new enterprise in the charter, club and private spheres. Internal accommodation varied according to their function, either with pilot, radio operator and six passengers or pilot and eight passengers. Marks II and III, created to cover these cabin layouts were ignored in practice and never used. One of the largest fleets operated over the Scottish, Scilly and Channel

Canadian Rapide CF-AYE on Fairchild floats and fitted with compensatory dorsal fin.
(*B. Van Sickle*)

Islands routes of British European Airways, which in 1950 grouped the survivors into the 'Islander' class with individual names as under:

G-AFEZ	'Lord Shaftesbury'	G-AHKS	'Robert Louis Stevenson'
G-AFRK	'Rudyard Kipling'	G-AHKT	'Lord Tennyson'
G-AGPH	'Sir Henry Havelock'	G-AHKU	'Cecil John Rhodes'
G-AGSH	'James Keir Hardie'	*G-AHKV	'Sir James Outram'
G-AGSK	'Lord Kitchener'	†G-AHLL	'Sir Henry Lawrence'
G-AGUP	'Sir Robert Peel'	*G-AHXW	'John Nicholson'
G-AGUR	'Lord Roberts'	G-AHXX	'Islander'
G-AGUU	'Sir Colin Campbell'	G-AJXB	'William Gilbert Grace'
G-AGUV	'General Gordon'	G-AKZB	'Lord Baden Powell'

* Name not painted on aircraft.
† Name transferred to G-AJCL following accident at St. Just 21.2.59.

By 1958 sales abroad and casualties had reduced serviceable British-owned Rapides to 81 including those used in the industry by Armstrong Whitworth, Martin-Baker, Blackburn, Hawker, Vickers, Westland, Short and Saro; on charter work and scheduled services from Jersey to the Orkneys, with L. H. Riddell's Yeadon-based G-AHGD as the only active private specimen. Others were employed in the Near East by the Arab Contracting and Trading Co. Ltd. and by Bahamas Helicopters (U.K.) Ltd. on the oil prospecting contract in North Africa. Only two of the original unflapped D.H.89s remained, G-AEMH of East Anglian Flying Services Ltd., Southend, and the Armstrong Whitworth communications aircraft G-AEML, both of which had been impressed during the war. Surplus R.A.F. Gipsy Queen 3 engines were fitted to most aircraft but in 1953 Flightways Ltd. of Eastleigh produced the prototype Rapide Mk. 4, G-AHGF, by replacing them with Gipsy Queen 2s driving constant speed airscrews. This aircraft was sold to K. G. R. Broomfield of Gisborne, New Zealand, as ZK-BFK. Subsequently a considerable number of such conversions took place to improve take-off from indifferent or high altitude overseas aerodromes. The de Havilland Company fitted manually operated variable pitch airscrews to the Gipsy Queen 3s of one of their communications Rapides, G-AHKA, which then became the sole example of a Rapide 5, sold in French Guiana as F-OAQL in 1954.

Finally in 1958 the Fairey company developed their X5 fixed pitch metal airscrews to improve performance of standard Rapides, the first so fitted being G-APBM, modified at Croydon by Air Couriers (Transport) Ltd. as the prototype Rapide Mk. 6.

In 1967, after standing 20 years in a hangar at Dyce, Rapides G-ADAH and G-AJGS were taken by road to Booker where 'GS flew again in February 1968. Two years later it was sold to Fritz Ludington of Miami, Florida and left Halfpenny Green on 28 August 1970 piloted by E. Wein and C. D. Downes who delivered it via Iceland, Greenland and Labrador in 77 hr. 44 min. of almost continuous instrument flying.

SPECIFICATION

Manufacturers: The de Havilland Aircraft Co. Ltd., Hatfield Aerodrome, Herts.
Brush Coachworks Ltd., Loughborough, Leicestershire.
The de Havilland Repair Unit, Witney Aerodrome, Oxford.

Power Plants:	(D.H.89 and D.H.89M)	Two 200 h.p. de Havilland Gipsy Six
	(D.H.89A Mks. 1, 2, 3 and 6)	Two 200 h.p. de Havilland Gipsy Queen 3
	(D.H.89A Mk. 4)	Two 200 h.p. de Havilland Gipsy Queen 2
	(D.H.89A Mk. 5)	Two 200 h.p. de Havilland Gipsy Queen 3 M.V.P.

Dimensions: Span 48 ft. 0 in. Length 34 ft. 6 in. Height 10 ft. 3 in. Wing area 336 sq. ft.

Weights: Tare weight, 3,230 lb. All-up weight, 5,500 lb. (Mk. 4) All-up weight, 6,000 lb.

Performance: Maximum speed, 157 m.p.h. Cruising speed, 132 m.p.h. Initial climb, 867 ft./min. Ceiling, 19,500 ft. Range, 578 miles.

(Mk. 4) Maximum speed, 150 m.p.h. Cruising speed, 140 m.p.h. Initial climb, 1,200 ft./min. Ceiling, 16,000 ft. Range, 520 miles.

Production: (a) Hatfield-built Dragon Rapides

Large numbers registered in Britain and the following for export or the R.A.F.: (c/n 6250) E-4/CH-287/HB-ARA/HB-APA; (6256) ZS-AES/VP-YBZ; (6259) ZK-ACO/VH-UUO; (6260) I-DRAG; (6262) EC-W27; (6265) VH-UVS; (6267) K5070/VP-KCK; (6270) A3-1/VH-UFF; (6271) K4772; (6273) OO-JFN; (6279) CF-AEO; (6285) VP-YAU; (6292) PH-AKV; (6294) PH-AKW; (6295) CF-AVJ; (6296) PH-AKU; (6298) SU-ABP; (6299) SU-ABQ; (6302) SU-ABR; (6303) SU-ABS; (6304) CF-AYE; (6305) ZK-AED; (6306) ZK-AEE; (6307) CF-BBC; (6308) VT-AHB; (6313) SU-ABU; (6314) VH-UVG; (6318) VH-UVI; (6319) VH-UVT; (6321–6323) Iran D.H.89Ms; (6329) YR-DRA; (6330) YR-DRI; (6331) YR-DRO; (6333) CX-ABU; (6334) ZK-AEC; (6338) YR-DNC; (6343) ZK-AEW; (6346) VH-UXT; (6347) OH-BLA; (6348–6349) Lithuanian D.H.89Ms; (6351) YL-ABC; (6352) YL-ABD; (6354) CF-BBG; (6357) VP-KCG; (6358) VP-YBJ; (6359) VP-YBK; (6360) VR-SAV; (6361) CR-AAD; (6362) CR-AAE; (6364) VR-SAW; (6365) VH-UXZ; (6366) VP-KCJ; (6370) CF-BBH; (6371) CF-BFM/CX-ABI; (6373) CF-BFL; (6374) CF-BFP; (6375) CF-BND; (6376) CF-BNE; (6378) VT-AIZ; (6379) VT-AJA; (6380) ZS-AKT/OO-CJU; (6381) VT-AJB; (6382) F-AQIL; (6383) F-AQIM; (6384) VH-UZY; (6385) China; (6387) ZS-AME/VP-KHJ/ZS-DFL; (6388–6392) China; (6393) F-AQIN; (6394) VP-KCL; (6395) F-AQJH; (6396) F-AQJI; (6397) CR-AAM; (6398) CR-AAN; (6401) OH-BLB; (6403) F-AQOH; (6404) VP-YBT; (6407) F-AQOI; (6411) ZS-AOM; (6412) VP-YBU; (6413) VP-KCR; (6414) YI-ZWA; (6415) YI-HDA; (6416) YI-FYA; (6420) F-ARII; (6421) P1764; (6422) P1765; (6423) ZK-AGT; (6424) F-ARIJ; (6425) F-ARIK; (6427) F-ARIL; (6428) F-ARIM; (6437) HB-AME/HB-APE; (6438) HB-AMU/HB-APU; (6439) CR-AAT; (6440) CR-AAU; (6444) China; (6446–6448) R2485–R2487; (6449) PP-LAA; (6451) CR-LAV; (6452) CR-LAU; (6453) CR-LAT; (6454) VT-ALO; (6455–6456) P9588–P9589.

Note: For c/n 6400 see D.H.92 Dolphin.

(b) Hatfield-built Dominies

One hundred and eighty-five aircraft, all but three for the R.A.F.: (c/n 6457–6461) R5921–R5925; (6462) experimental aircraft; (6463–6471) R5926–R5934; (6472) CF-BNG; (6473–6492) R9545–R9564; (6493–6527) X7320–X7354; (6528–6577) X7368–X7417; (6578–6583) X7437–X7442; (6584) G-AGDM; (6585–6598) X7443–X7456; (6599–6642) X7482–X7525.

(c) Loughborough-built Dominies

Three hundred and forty-six aircraft for the R.A.F.: (6643–6673) HG644–HG674;

(6674–6717) HG689–HG732; (6718–6767) NF847–NF896; (6768–6800) NR669–NR701; (6801–6844) NR713–NR756; (6845–6891) NR769–NR815; (6892–6917) NR828–NR853; (6918–6950) RL936–RL968; (6951–6957) RL980–RL986; (6958–6978) TX300–TX320; (6979–6983) TX326–TX330 contract cancelled; (6984–6988) TX336–TX339 and TX361 contract cancelled.

(d) Witney conversions

Ninety-five aircraft in the constructor's number range 6884–6978, many of British registry and the following for export: (c/n 6890) PH-RAA; (6891) PH-RAB; (6893) PH-RAC; (6894) LR-AAE; (6895) PH-RAD; (6896) LR-AAF; (6897) YI-ABD; (6898) YI-ABE; (6899–6901) CS-ADI to CS-ADK; (6904) CR-LBN; (6905) CR-LBO; (6906) YI-ABF; (6907) YI-ABG; (6909) YI-ABH; (6914) ZS-ATV; (6915) ZS-ATW; (6919) SE-APH; (6920) PP-AIA; (6921) PP-AID; (6922) PP-AIB; (6923) PP-AIC; (6924) VP-YDF; (6925) VP-YDE; (6927) PP-OMB; (6928) CF-DIM; (6929) VH-BKR; (6933) conversion abandoned; (6938) Canada; (6939) conversion abandoned; (6947) VT-AVW; (6953) VT-AVX; (6954) TJ-AAA; (6955) TJ-AAB; (6956) OY-DZY; (6957) VT-AXG; (6958) TJ-AAC; (6959) TJ-AAD; (6960) PP-OMC; (6961) TJ-AAE; (6969) ZS-AXS; (6970) PP-AIE; (6971) PP-AIF; (6972) PP-AIG; (6973) OB-RAA; (6974) OB-RAB; (6975) OB-RAC; (6976) OB-RAD; (6977) OB-RAE; (6978) OB-RAG.

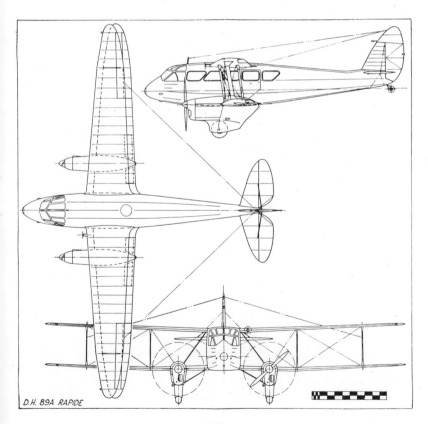

D.H. 89A RAPIDE

Lord Beaverbrook's Dragonfly at Croydon in 1936.

De Havilland D.H.90 Dragonfly

Outwardly a scaled down Rapide, the Dragonfly luxury tourer differed a good deal structurally from its famous forebear. The familiar spruce-and-plywood box structure gave place to a monocoque shell of pre-formed ply stiffened with light spruce stringers. Very stout spars in the lower centre section permitted the elimination of all diagonal bracing struts and wires from the inner wing bay, resulting in improved performance and easier access to the cabin. It also allowed the use of a clean cantilever undercarriage built integral with Rapide-type nacelles housing twin Gipsy Major engines. One passenger sat next to the pilot, one in a single seat directly behind and two others on a double seat in the rear of the cabin.

The maiden flight of the prototype, E-2/G-ADNA took place at Hatfield on 12 August 1935 and a second aircraft G-AEBU, powered by Gipsy Major IIs with provision for v.p. airscrews, flew as the D.H.90A demonstrator in February 1936. It was the first of 66 production aircraft built in the 7500 constructor's number sequence and as was to be expected, the prototype was on the starting line of the King's Cup Race at Hatfield on 10 July 1936 and in the two days' racing piloted by Capt. Geoffrey de Havilland and his son Geoffrey, averaged 143·75 m.p.h. and came eighth.

The Dragonfly achieved maximum performance on low power by the use of new constructional methods, but at £2,650, initial sales on the British market were restricted to 21. Prominent owners of the day such as Sir Philip Sassoon, Lord Beaverbrook, Loel Guinness, and Lt. Col. E. T. Peel bought them, and Sir W. Lindsay Everard named his G-ADXM 'Leicestershire Vixen II'. The London Aeroplane Club acquired G-AECW for which the dual instruction charge was £5 10s. per hour and 'WZ was used as a navigation trainer by Air Service Training Ltd., Hamble.

The second production aircraft YI-HMK, specially furnished as the markings suggest, for the personal use of King Feisal of Iraq, was later joined by YI-OSD. Wealthy French owners Baron L. de Armella, Baron Jules de Koenigswater, Jacques Duprey and Gustav Wolf took delivery of F-AOZC, 'YK, F-APAX and 'DE respectively in 1936–7 while others were supplied to QANTAS; Wearnes Air Services Ltd., Singapore; Rhodesia and Nyasaland Airways; P.L.U.N.A.,

Uruguay; Divisão dos Transportes Aéreos (DTA) in Angola; Linile Aeriene Române Exploatate cu Statul (L.A.R.E.S.), Rumania; Misr Airwork Ltd., Egypt; Ala Littoria, Italy; the Turkish State Airline; and the Swedish (local type number Tp.3) and Danish Air Forces. Others were built for private ownership and taxi work in Argentina, Belgium, Holland, India, Italy, Kenya, New Zealand, Nigeria and South Africa. As usual, de Havilland Aircraft of Canada Ltd. was responsible for conversion to Fairchild floats and CF-BFF was equipped in this way for Gold Belt Air Services Ltd. The Royal Canadian Mounted Police used four Dragonflies CF-MPA–'PD to combat rum running off Nova Scotia.

Within a year there came a marked drift away from private ownership and into the export market or the charter business. Together with G-AEDH, the prototype carried on taxi work and pleasure flights with the Straight Corporation; 'FN went to Air Commerce Ltd., 'DV to Birkett Air Services Ltd.; both of Heston, and the bright red 'SW to Air Taxis Ltd. To replace and supplement the weary Dragons on the Army Co-operation contract, the Hon. Mrs. Victor Bruce built up the only Dragonfly fleet ever formed. Six in number, these were initially operated at Croydon by Air Dispatch Ltd. and Anglo-European Airways Ltd. until evacuated to Cardiff Airport, Splott, in 1939. They included 'CX, based at Croydon by International Air Freight Ltd. after its return from a year with Air Services of India Ltd. as VT-AKC; 'DJ bought from A. J. D. Jamieson, 'DK from Mutual Finance Ltd., G-AFRF brought back from France, where it had been sold to

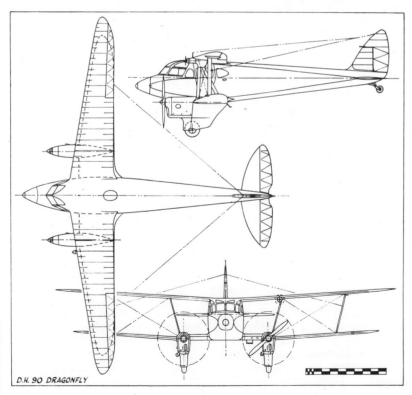

D.H. 90 DRAGONFLY

Baron L. de Armella as F-AOZC in 1936; G-AFTF from de Havillands in Australia, whence it has been exported new as VH-UXA, and G-AFRI originally sold in 1936 to Jacques Duprey in France as F-APAX.

Excluding 'CW, which flew on D.H. affairs as a civil aeroplane throughout the 1939–45 war, fourteen Dragonflies were impressed for war service, several going to the industry on communications duties. An example was Air Service Training's 'WZ, which was handed over to Shorts at Rochester as DJ716, and restored post-war to Silver City Airways Ltd., who fitted it with Gipsy Major 1D engines as a D.H.90A. In January 1947 the Dragonfly SU-ABW also returned. It had been exported to Misr Airwork Ltd. in Egypt 10 years before, and after overhaul by Southern Aircraft (Gatwick) Ltd. was used privately as G-AIYJ by C. G. M. Alington until withdrawn from use in 1948. The only other British registered Dragonfly had a complex foreign history starting in September 1936, when it was sold to Gustav Wolf in France as F-APDE. After roaming the Continent in Belgian, Spanish and French Colonial ownership for two decades, it arrived in Jersey from Toussus-le-Noble as F-OAMS in August 1954. It was dismantled and conveyed in a Bristol Freighter to Eastleigh where it was rebuilt and flew again in March 1959 as G-ANYK with Gipsy Major 10s and also designated D.H.90A.

By 1972 two Dragonflies alone survived, A. G. Mechin's ZS-CTR, formerly D.E.T.A.'s CR-AAB, at Rand Airport, Johannesburg; and G-AEDT 'Endeavour', sold to Adastra Airways Ltd. in Australia in 1938 as VH-AAD, which Charles Masefield and Lord Trefgarne delivered to the Tallmantz collection at Santa-Ana, California via the North Atlantic route in August 1964 after first flying it from Sydney to Shoreham for overhaul in December 1963.

SPECIFICATION

Manufacturers: The de Havilland Aircraft Co. Ltd., Hatfield Aerodrome, Herts.
Power Plants: Two 130 h.p. de Havilland Gipsy Major.
Dimensions: Span, 43 ft. 0 in. Length, 31 ft. 8 in. Height, 9 ft. 2 in.
Wing area, 256 sq. ft.
Weights: Tare weight, 2,500 lb. All-up weight, 4,000 lb.
Performance: Maximum speed, 144 m.p.h. Cruising speed, 125 m.p.h.
Initial climb, 875 ft./min. Ceiling, 18,100 ft. Range, 625 miles.

Production:

Sixty-seven aircraft, twenty-one initially registered in Britain and the following for export: (c/n 7502) YI-HMK; (7506) CF-AYF; (7512) VP-YAX; (7513) VH-UXB; (7519) F-AOZC, later G-AFRF; (7520) VP-YBB; (7521) F-AOYK; (7522) CF-BBD/CF-MPC/R.C.A.F.7628/CF-BXU; (7523) ZS-AHV; (7525) YI-OSD; (7526) CR-AAB/ZS-CTR; (7527) VT-AHW; (7528) VP-KCA; (7529) F-APDE/OO-PET/F-OAMS, later G-ANYK; (7530) CF-MPA/R.C.A.F.7626; (7531) CF-MPB/R.C.A.F.7627/CF-BZA; (7532) CX-AAR; (7533) VH-UXA, later G-AFTF; (7534) CX-AAS; (7535) South Africa; (7536) F-APAX, later G-AFRI; (7537) Shell Mex, Argentine; (7538) CF-MPD/CF-BPD; (7539) PH-KOK/PH-ATK; (7540) VT-AHY; (7541) I-DRAG; (7542) F-APFK; (7543) R.C.A.F.7623/CF-BFF; (7545) VT-AIE; (7546) VH-UXS; (7547) YR-FLY; (7548) YR-FLO; (7549) YR-FLU; (7550) Swedish Air Force 3-6; (7551) Danish Army Air Force S.23; (7552) S.24; (7553) SU-ABW, later G-AIYJ; (7557) R.C.A.F.7624/CF-BXV; (7558) R.C.A.F.7625; (7560) ZK-AFB; (7561) OO-JFN; (7562) VH-UTJ; (7563) Shell Mex, Argentine; (7564) ZS-ANM; (7565) VR-NAA; (7566) ZK-AGP.

After modifications to the tail surfaces the prototype Albatross flew with full civil markings.
(*Aeroplane*)

De Havilland D.H.91 Albatross

The Albatross was designed by A. E. Hagg in 1936 to an Air Ministry specification calling for two transatlantic mailplanes but when R. G. Waight took the prototype E-2/G-AEVV into the air for the first time at Hatfield on 20 May 1937, it was seen to bear no family resemblance to previous de Havilland types. On the power of four new and untried 525 h.p. Gipsy Twelve inverted V-type engines, it had a cruising range of more than 3,000 miles at a speed of over 200 m.p.h. This amazing performance was only achieved by aerodynamic refinement, the Albatross being one of the most beautiful aeroplanes ever built. It was an all-wood cantilever monoplane having a long, tapering fuselage of circular cross section built of laminations of cedar ply with a balsa wood layer between. The one-piece mainplane was built as in the Comet, around a stress-bearing box spar with spruce planking applied diagonally in two layers. Wheel wells were constructed ahead of the main spar to take the large inward-retracting undercarriage, operation of which was by means of a 5 h.p. electric motor. The four engines, driving D.H. constant speed airscrews, were encased in close fitting circular section nacelles culminating in perfectly matched spinners. Cooling was unorthodox but efficient, air being led to the back of the engines from intakes in the leading edge of the wing. The cantilever tail unit was fitted with twin strutted fins carrying horn balanced rudders. In early flight trials, however, this arrangement proved unsatisfactory and the tailplane was redesigned with the fins mounted as end plates and with new unbalanced rudders fitted with trim tabs. Trouble was also experienced with undercarriage retraction, resulting in a belly landing at Hatfield on 31 March 1938.

A second prototype, E-5/G-AEVW, was also completed and flown, but when undergoing overload take-off tests on 27 August 1938 the rear fuselage broke in two during the final stages of the third landing run. It reappeared in a few weeks with the new and reinforced fuselage, which later became standard on the production model built for Imperial Airways Ltd. Apart from tankage considerations, there were minor differences between the mail and passenger versions, the latter having extra windows and slotted flaps in place of the split type.

Deliveries commenced in October 1938 with G-AFDI, which, as 'Frobisher', became flagship of a new 'F' class which carried 22 passengers and four crew. Apart from an accidental undercarriage retraction on 'DI, the five aircraft of the type were trouble free and settled down to fast competitive schedules on the Croydon–Paris, Brussels and Zürich routes. An experimental Christmas mail was also flown to Cairo in the December, and after lowering the Croydon–Paris record, the type gained further laurels when 'DJ 'Falcon' arrived in Brussels 48 minutes after leaving Croydon on 10 January 1939. Imperial Airways crews also carried out experimental flights with the two long range mailplanes G-AEVV and 'VW, which had been added to the 'F' class as 'Faraday' and 'Franklin'.

At the outbreak of war in 1939 the Albatross fleet was evacuated first to Bramcote and then to Whitchurch, Bristol, whence they operated the Lisbon and Shannon shuttle services. 'Fortuna' left for Karachi on 30 August 1939 with 11 senior Army officers, rejoining the fleet after a rapid turn-round. The two long range machines were impressed in September 1940 and went into service with No. 271 (Transport) Squadron on a third shuttle service, between this country and Iceland. In the confusion of the period, the serial numbers K8618 and K8619 allotted by the Air Ministry during the design stage were overlooked, and they operated as AX903 and AX904 instead. Both retained the names bestowed by Imperial Airways, and both ended their careers in destructive crashes at Reykjavik.

The passenger fleet also suffered two casualties, the first when 'Fingal' forced landed with a fractured fuel pipe at Pucklechurch, Glos., and collided with a farmhouse in October 1940. Its remains were acquired by C. J. Packer and for several years were stacked on the flat roof of his garage at Burton, Wilts. Two months after the loss of 'Fingal', the flagship was destroyed by fire in an air raid on

The prototype D.H.91 Albatross mailplane E-2/G-AEVV, in its initial form with tall inset fins and rudders. (*Aeroplane*)

'Fortuna', a passenger version Albatross, in Imperial Airways colours at Croydon, 1939. (*B.O.A.C.*)

Whitchurch. The three survivors carried on unobtrusively until July 1943, when 'Fortuna' crashed at Shannon. It was the beginning of the end, and with spares almost non-existent, 'Fiona' and 'Falcon' were broken up in the following autumn.

SPECIFICATION

Manufacturers: The de Havilland Aircraft Co. Ltd., Hatfield Aerodrome, Herts.

Power Plants: Four 525 h.p. de Havilland Gipsy Twelve series I.

Dimensions: Span, 105 ft. 0 in. Length, 71 ft. 6 in. Height, 22 ft. 3 in. Wing area, 1,078 sq. ft.

Weights: (Mail) Tare weight, 20,860 lb. All-up weight, 32,500 lb.

(Passenger) Tare weight, 21,230 lb. All-up weight, 29,500 lb.

Performance: (Mail) Maximum speed, 222 m.p.h. Cruising speed, 204 m.p.h. Initial climb, 550 ft./min. Ceiling, 15,100 ft. Range, 3,300 miles.

(Passenger) Maximum speed, 225 m.p.h. Cruising speed, 210 m.p.h. Initial climb, 710 ft./min. Ceiling, 17,900 ft. Range, 1,040 miles.

Production:

Seven aircraft comprising two long range mailplanes (c/n 6800–6801) G-AEVV and G-AEVW; and five passenger carriers (c/n 6802–6806) G-AFDI to G-AFDM.

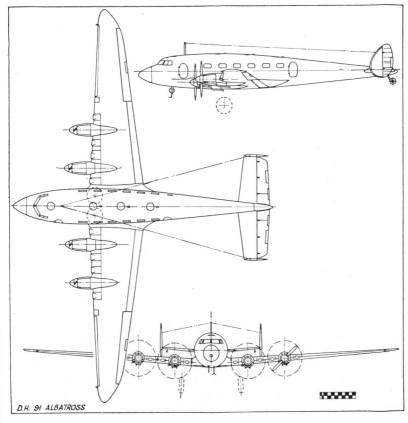

D.H. 91 ALBATROSS

An early production Moth Minor in R.A.F. Flying Club colours, 1939.

De Havilland D.H.94 Moth Minor

A low-wing successor to the Moth, more easily built, devoid of rigging problems and capable of an equal performance on lower power, had attracted the attention of the de Havilland Company for many years. As early as 1930 designs had been considered for such an aircraft, and the unregistered D.H.81 Swallow Moth (c/n 1992) made its first flight at Stag Lane on 24 August 1931. This was a two seat, open cockpit, low-wing cantilever monoplane powered by a special 82 h.p. Gipsy IV engine, later modified as the D.H.81A with thicker wing and enclosed cockpit, but then shelved because the factory was fully engaged in producing biplane Moths.

Five years elapsed, but Capt. Geoffrey (later Sir Geoffrey) de Havilland person-ally kept the idea alive and was instrumental in developing it as the Moth Minor with 90 h.p. Gipsy Minor engine. He made the first flight in the prototype, later G-AFRD, at Hatfield on 22 June 1937, and thereafter did most of the test flying. The airframe employed the well proven spruce and plywood box structure of the earliest wooden Moths married to a high efficiency mainplane, built on similar lines to that of the Comet and Albatross, with box spars and plywood covering. The cantilever undercarriage was anchored to the front spar of the centre section, to which were also hinged the outer panels of the folding wing. Unlike its famous progenitors, the Moth Minor was flown from the front seat and was provided with a large perforated air brake under the centre section.

By June 1939 production in the Hatfield '94 shop' had already reached eight aeroplanes a week, mainly in a constructor's number series commencing 94001 but including nine special aircraft commencing 9400. They were priced at £575 ex works and to initiate the sales drive one Moth Minor was despatched to each of the Australian, Canadian, Indian and South African companies while British flying clubs, eager for modern equipment, ordered it in considerable numbers. A few were acquired by private owners including Lord Londonderry with G-AFNE, and following the Paris and Brussels Aero Shows of 1938–39, by owners in Switzerland, Holland, Portugal, Egypt, Singapore and New Zealand. G-AFPB was used executively by the British Aviation Insurance Group.

Over 100 Moth Minors had been built by September 1939 but early in 1940 production was abandoned because all the Hatfield factory space was required for the war effort. All the Moth Minor drawings, jigs and tools, along with stocks of finished and unfinished airframes were then shipped to Australia where construction was completed in the Bankstown factory of de Havilland Aircraft Pty. Ltd. At least 40 were supplied to the R.A.A.F., many surviving to become civil aeroplanes for the first time after the war. Thirty-two already delivered to British owners were impressed for R.A.F. duty and Lt. Kent's G-AFPJ, caught at Almaza, Cairo was almost certainly procured by the U.S.A.A.F. and flown as 42-94128 'Sand Fly'.

The nine Moth Minors in the 9400 series included several with hinged coupé tops, the first of which flew in the summer of 1938. Three others were despatched to de Havilland Aircraft of India Ltd. at Karachi on 21 September 1940 and one of these was supplied originally to the Maharajah of Jaipur as VT-AMG. Another, VT-AMF, ex G-AFSD, was sold in January 1941 as VP-CAG to C. A. S. Booth in Ceylon where in July of the following year it was impressed by the Admiralty as NP490 and shipped to Mombasa on a carrier.

One of the Moth Minor Coupés flying on war-time communications. (*Aeroplane*)

At home the de Havilland Company modified two anonymous Moth Minors (c/n 94101 and 94102) into experimental long range and tricycle variants respectively, the latter flying under B conditions as E-0226. They also camouflaged the open model G-AFTH and the coupé 'OJ, which both continued on civil communications until 1942. After the war 'OJ was acquired by the London Aeroplane Club and raced with vigour by Pat Fillingham in the *Daily Express* and South Coast Races of 1950, in which he averaged 137·5 and 135·5 m.p.h. respectively.

In 1972 several Moth Minors were still flying in New Zealand and the type was well represented in Britain by cabin models G-AFNG and 'OJ; open cockpit versions G-AFOJ and 'OZ, with G-AFOB under reconstruction by R. E. Ogden at Woodley. Also airworthy was airframe 94095 (G-AFUV), shipped to the R.A.A.F. 1940 as A21-30, civilianised 1945 as VH-AFQ, and shipped to Robert Diemert in Manitoba 1968 to become CF-AOO.

SPECIFICATION

Manufacturers: The de Havilland Aircraft Co. Ltd., Hatfield Aerodrome, Herts.
Power Plant: One 90 h.p. de Havilland Gipsy Minor.
Dimensions: Span, 36 ft. 7 in. Length, 24 ft. 5 in. Height, 6 ft. 4 in. Wing area, 162 sq. ft.
Weights: Tare weight, 983 lb. All-up weight, 1,550 lb.
Performance: Maximum speed, 118 m.p.h. Cruising speed, 100 m.p.h. Initial climb, 620 ft./min. Ceiling, 16,500 ft. Range, 300 miles.

Production: (a) Hatfield-built open cockpit models

Forty-four British registered machines and the following for export or test: (c/n 94002) VH-AAM; (94003) CF-BFQ; (94004) VT-ALI; (94005) ZS-ARE; (94006) crashed on test; (94011) ZS-ARF; (94017) VR-SBE; (94020) HB-OMU; (94025) CS-ABS; (94028) VH-ADA; (94036) PH-ATX; (94037) VR-SBF; (94046) ZK-AHL; (94049) VH-ACO; (94051) SU-ACE; (94054) SU-ACG; (94062) SU-ACI; (94069) SU-ACJ; (94101) Long range cabin conversion; (94102) E-0226.

(b) Completed in Australia

Nineteen already allotted British registrations and the following extra airframes: (94060) A21-4/VH-AFT; (94061) NZ591/ZK-AKL†; (94071) NZ592/ZK-AJX; (94073) VH-ADC/PK-BFC; (94075) VH-AGT*; (94076) VH-AMI*; (94077) VH-ADB; (94078) R.A.A.F.; (94079) A21-3/VH-BKI; (94080) VT-ALJ*; (94081) R.A.A.F.; (94085) R.A.A.F.; (94087) VH-AHT*; (94088) VH-AFV*; (94090–94) R.A.A.F.; (94096) R.A.A.F.; (94097) A21-24/VH-AHK; (94098–94099) R.A.A.F.

* Previous R.A.A.F. serials not known.   † Converted to cabin model.

(c) Hatfield-built cabin models

Nine British registered aircraft listed in Appendix E.

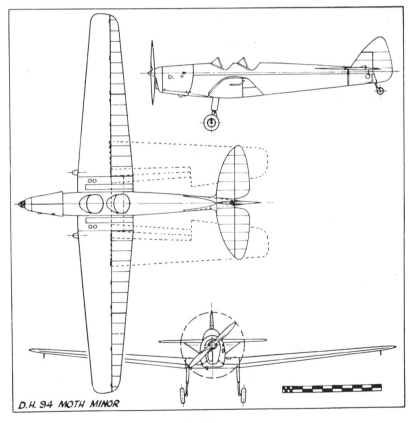

D.H. 94 MOTH MINOR

The prototype Flamingo G-AFUE outbound to Jersey in June 1939.
(*Flight Photo 17504S*)

De Havilland D.H.95 Flamingo

This twin engined medium range transport, designed by R. E. Bishop, was unique as the first aircraft of all-metal, stressed skin construction to be built by the de Havilland Aircraft Co. Ltd. It was an up-to-date design with split trailing edge flaps and hydraulically retracted undercarriage, but defied both the general trend towards four engines and the American insistence on low wings. Ample power reserves were ensured by using Perseus XIIc sleeve valve radials giving 890 h.p. each at take-off and the high-wing layout permitted very low ground clearance, with extreme ease of entry and loading. The flight deck housed a crew of three and passenger accommodation varied between 12 and 17, according to the range. The prototype made its first flight without markings at Hatfield on 28 December 1938 piloted by the company's chief test pilot, Geoffrey de Havilland Jr. A third, central, fin was later fitted but flight trials proved the adequacy of the original tail surfaces and it was removed and in May 1939 the aircraft was registered G-AFUE and loaned to Guernsey & Jersey Airways Ltd. for proving flights between Heston, Eastleigh, Jersey and Guernsey.

The Flamingo also attracted Air Ministry interest as a possible troop transport and 40 twenty-two seaters, R2510–R2529 and R2550–R2569, to be known as Hertfordshires were ordered as well as three Flamingoes, R2764–R2766, two for communications duties with No. 24 Squadron, Hendon, and one for the King's Flight, Benson. Only one Hertfordshire, R2510, was actually built but the Flamingo order was increased to six by the purchase of the prototype, Guernsey Airways' intended first machine G-AFUF, and one which had been laid down for the Egyptian Government. All flew in wartime camouflage and during the invasion scare in 1940, the King's Flight Flamingo was temporarily registered G-AGCC in case the Royal Family should be compelled to leave the British Isles but in February 1941 it was transferred to No. 24 Squadron as R2766 and named 'Lady of Glamis' in 1942.

The fifth Flamingo, E-16/G-AGAZ, and all subsequent aircraft, were powered by 930 h.p. Perseus XVI engines including seven delivered to the British Overseas

Airways Corporation at Bramcote. As the 'K' Class they were named after Kings of England and then despatched to the Near East, where for several years they were the backbone of wartime local services between Addis Ababa, Aden, Asmara, Jedda, Cairo, Lydda, Adana and Teheran. The eleventh aircraft, G-AFYH, intended for B.O.A.C., was requisitioned for the Royal Navy and went to No. 782 (Transport) Squadron, Donibristle on 30 November 1940 as BT312 'Merlin VI' (later 'Merlin 27') for communications with the Orkneys, Shetlands and Northern Ireland. Its replacement was the 20th and last airframe, originally intended for Egypt, which had been allotted R.A.F. serial BK822, not used because the aircraft was delivered instead to B.O.A.C. as G-AGBY 'King William' in 1941. Construction of the 16th to 19th machines R2511–R2514 was abandoned when the Hertfordshire contract was cut back to one aircraft.

B.O.A.C. Flamingoes G-AFYI 'King Henry' and 'YE 'King Arthur' were lost in crashes at Adana, Turkey, and Asmara, Eritrea, 1942–43 and a third, 'YG 'King Harold', was damaged beyond repair after the undercarriage collapsed on take-off from Addis Ababa in November 1942. By 1944 shortage of spares grounded the remaining five which were then shipped back and stored at Croydon, Redhill and Witney. The Royal Navy's BT312, which ground looped when landing at Gatwick on 19 August 1945, was acquired by Southern Aircraft (Gatwick)

The second B.O.A.C. Flamingo, G-AFYF 'King Alfred', at Bramcote in August 1940 ready for delivery to Cairo. The A.W.27 G-ADSR 'Ensign' is in the background. (*Aeroplane*)

The King's Flight Flamingo R2766/G-AGCC at Hatfield in August 1940. (*Flight Photo 17905S*)

Ltd., overhauled and delivered to British Air Transport Ltd. at Redhill as G-AFYH on 25 May 1947 but after a few charter flights it was relegated to a hangar until broken up when Redhill closed down in May 1954. G-AFYF, 'YK and 'YL, acquired by B.A.T. in March 1948, were to have been reworked by Tiltman Langley Laboratories Ltd. at Redhill but the scheme fell through and they too were scrapped.

SPECIFICATION

Manufacturers: The de Havilland Aircraft Co. Ltd., Hatfield Aerodrome, Herts.

Power Plants: Two 890 h.p. Bristol Perseus XIIc.

Two 930 h.p. Bristol Perseus XVI.

Dimensions: Span, 70 ft. 0 in. Length, 51 ft. 7 in. Height, 15 ft. 3 in. Wing area, 639 sq. ft.

Weights: Tare weight, 11,325 lb. All-up weight, 17,600 lb.

Performance: Maximum speed, 239 m.p.h. Cruising speed, 184 m.p.h. Initial climb, 1,470 ft./min. Ceiling, 20,900 ft. Range, 1,210 miles.

Production:

Twenty aircraft laid down, comprising 13 initially civil registered, the following for No. 24 Squadron, R.A.F.: (c/n 95003) R2764, crashed near Great Ouseburn, Yorks. 30.4.42; (95004) E-10/R2765 'Lady of Hendon', w.f.u. 1944; (95006) R2510, crashed at Mill Hill, near Hendon 23.10.40; and (95016–95019) R2511–R2514, not completed.

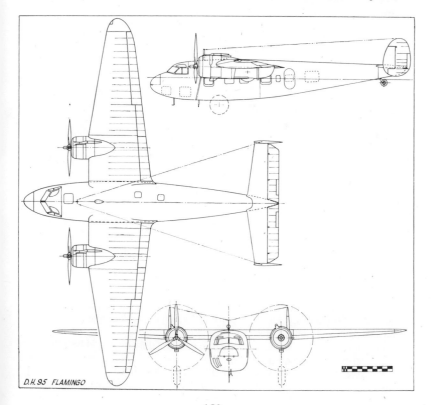

D.H.95 FLAMINGO

The first civil Mosquito at Hatfield in 1943, awaiting delivery to B.O.A.C.

De Havilland D.H.98 Mosquito

The immortal Mosquito, designed by R. E. Bishop and his team, was the smallest two seat bomber which could be built around two Merlin engines. Its mainplane used the form of stressed skin wooden construction first devised for the Comet racer, and the fuselage was a laminated wooden monocoque structure in pure Albatross tradition. It was unarmed, the radiators were buried in the wings, and with retractable undercarriage was a clean and worthy descendant of the mighty Comet. Geoffrey de Havilland Jr. took the prototype into the air for the first time on 25 November 1940 and, as expected, no contemporary fighter could catch it. A total of 7,781 was built during the 1939–45 war, a small number of which eventually earned their living as civil machines.

In 1943 one Mosquito 4 and six Mosquito 6 aircraft were converted at Hatfield and Bramcote respectively and handed over to B.O.A.C. for service on the diplomatically important route between Leuchars in Scotland and neutral Sweden. Mail, with newspapers and magazines to counter enemy propaganda, were the chief loads, while urgently required ball bearings were brought back in the bomb bays. This service, previously flown at night with Lockheed Lodestars, was operated in daylight high above the concentrated German anti-aircraft defences in the Skaggerak. After Capt. Gilbert Rae was shot up by a Focke-Wulf Fw 190 on his way back from Stockholm and forced to make a belly landing in Sweden, the route was flown only at night. On several occasions, important passengers were carried—locked in the bomb bay with a supply of refreshments, reading material and oxygen. The service continued until the end of the European war, three additional Mosquitos G-AGKO–'KR, converted for civil use at Croydon, being added to the fleet in 1944 to replace losses. Most of these were due to crashes in disabled aircraft or to accidents in bad visibility in the vicinity of Leuchars, the exception being G-AGKR, posted missing after leaving Gothenburg on 29 August 1944. The five historic survivors were flown to Croydon in August 1945, three proceeding to Marshall's at Cambridge for reduction to produce and two to meet a similar fate at No. 71 M.U., Slough.

A more unsuitable aircraft for private or commercial flying would be difficult to visualize, yet several achieved civil status for a variety of unusual reasons. Two Mosquito P.R. Mk. 16s, G-AIRT and 'RU, were acquired by Grp. Cpt. G. L. Cheshire, V.C. in October 1946, and after overhaul were stored, the first at

Cambridge, the other at Abingdon. In May 1948 both were sold to a dealer, but on 5 July 1948 a ferry pilot collected 'RT ostensibly to take it to Exeter, and on 16 July 'RU was collected for a flight from Abingdon to nearby Thame. Neither arrived, but were flown instead direct to Nice, en route to the Israeli Air Force.

Another pair of Mosquitos, P.R. Mk. 34s G-AJZE and 'ZF, were owned by the Ministry of Supply and consequently had careers of a more scientific nature. They were fitted out and based at Cranfield on loan to the British European Airways Gust Research Unit formed there in March 1948. For some two years they flew all over Europe, from Scandinavia to Lisbon, investigating clear-air turbulence in readiness for the operation of the new Vickers Viscounts at heights above 20,000 ft. At the conclusion of the research programme in 1949 they were flown to Waterbeach, eventually rejoining the R.A.F. after overhaul at Cambridge in May 1951.

A Mosquito Mk. 36 G-ALFL, powered by Merlin 114A motors and also Ministry of Supply owned, appeared for a few months at the end of 1948, but its *raison d'être* was never disclosed. After returning to the R.A.F., it languished at Hawarden until broken up at the end of 1953. Flight Refuelling Ltd. was the only other British Mosquito operator, having two Mk. 19s, G-ALGU and 'GV,

One of the gust research Mosquito P.R. Mk.34s at Cranfield in 1948. (*B.E.A.*)

acquired in 1949 for use as fast photographic aircraft capable of covering jet fighter refuelling operations. The first was overhauled at Tarrant Rushton, and was in commission during 1949–50, thereafter going to the scrap heap along with its less fortunate companion. Six others, G-AOCI–'CN, purchased by R. A. Short, were flown from Naval Air Station Lossiemouth to Thruxton in 1956, and, after a lengthy period in the open, three were sold to the Israeli Air Force and went to Hurn for pre-delivery overhaul. In 1959 a 4,500 mile South Atlantic flight by Miss Roberta Cowell in B.Mk.35 G-AOSS, made ready at Burnaston by Derby Aviation Ltd., (who also prepared EC-WKH for Spain) was abandoned through lack of suitable engines.

No further Mosquitos were allotted British civil markings until July 1963 when three T.T.Mk.35s were ferried from No. 3 A.A.C.U., Exeter to Bovingdon as G-ASKA, 'KB and 'KC to feature, with ever changing serials, in the film *633 Squadron*. The last, actually TA719, owned by the Skyfame Museum, crash landed at Staverton on 27 July 1964 and was replaced by RS709/G-ASKA until this was sold to Col. E. A. Jurist for the Confederate Air Force, U.S.A. and went to Booker for overhaul in September 1970.

CF-HMK, one of Spartan Air Services' fleet of photographic survey Mosquitos, was a conversion of VR974 built as a B.Mk.35.

A fourth Exeter Mosquito, a T.Mk.3, sold to Hawker Siddeley Aviation Ltd. as G-ASKH, was maintained in airworthy condition at Hawarden as RR299 and flew at most major air displays as well as in the film *Mosquito Story*. The last example, T.T.Mk.35 TA635, acquired by the City of Liverpool for exhibition at Speke, was also used for film work until taken to Salisbury Hall, near Hatfield, for preservation with the prototype Mosquito W4050 in October 1970.

Among numerous Mosquitos flown in civil markings abroad was P.R.Mk.4 DK310, forced down at Belpmoos, Switzerland on 24 August 1942 and afterwards loaned to Swissair as HB-IMO for mail carrying until 1945. Several were raced in the U.S.A. in the immediate postwar years including N4928V, NX66422, N98691, N37878 'Wooden Wonder' and N66313 (Capital Airways, Nashville, Tennessee) which came 5th in the Bendix Trophy Race at Cleveland, Ohio on 5 September 1948.

Nine surplus R.C.A.F. Mosquitos in China National Aviation Corporation civil markings were used at Montreal in 1948 to train pilots for 100 others shipped to China; and two surplus R.A.A.F. P.R.Mk.41s, VH-WAD and VH-KLG, were entered for the 1953 London–Christchurch (N.Z.) Air Race. The first was a non-starter; Sqn. Ldr. A. J. R. Oates was compelled to ditch VH-KLG off the south Burma coast; and six registered ZK-BCT to 'CY were scrapped unconverted at Palmerston North, New Zealand, except ZK-BCV which was sold in the U.S.A. as N9909F.

A series of P.R.Mk.34 aircraft were converted at Hatfield for aerial mapping 1955–56, N9911F, N9869F and N9870F being ferried by the North Atlantic route to Fotogrametric Engineers Inc., Los Angeles and others which included N9868F and N9910F to the IREX Survey Co. for oil prospecting in Tripoli. CF-FZG, CF-GKK and 'GL were used by Kenting Aviation on similar tasks in Canada, but by far the largest fleet was that of Ottawa-based Spartan Air Services Ltd. which acquired 15 P.R.Mk.35s CF-HMK to 'MT (including 'MQ) and CF-IMA to 'ME 1954–57, five of which were cannibalised at Hurn to provide spares for ten prepared by Derby Aviation Ltd., Burnaston which completed high altitude photographic surveys in Kenya, Canada, U.S.A., Mexico, Colombia, British Guiana, Argentina and the Dominican Republic. Two left behind are believed to have become LV-HHN and XB-TOX, the latter still an exhibit at Mexico City Airport in 1970.

SPECIFICATION

Manufacturers: The de Havilland Aircraft Co. Ltd., Hatfield Aerodrome, Herts. and sub-
contractors.

Power Plants: (Mk. 4) Two 1,250 h.p. Rolls-Royce Merlin 21.
(Mk. 6) Two 1,635 h.p. Rolls-Royce Merlin 25.
(Mk. 16) Two 1,680 h.p. Rolls-Royce Merlin 76 or 77.
(Mk. 34) Two 1,710 h.p. Rolls-Royce Merlin 113 or 114.
(Mk. 35) Two 1,710 h.p. Rolls-Royce Merlin 113 or 114.

Dimensions: Span, 54 ft. 2 in. Length, 40 ft. $9\frac{1}{2}$ in. Height, 15 ft. 3 in. Wing area,
435 sq. ft.

	Mosquito 4 and 6	Mosquito 16	Mosquito 34	Mosquito 35
Tare weight	17,500 lb.	14,600 lb.	16,631 lb.	15,600 lb.
All-up weight	20,870 lb.	23,000 lb.	25,500 lb.	25,200 lb.
Maximum speed	380 m.p.h.	415 m.p.h.	425 m.p.h.	422 m.p.h.
Cruising speed	300 m.p.h.	310 m.p.h.	315 m.p.h.	310 m.p.h.
Initial climb	1,700 ft./min.	2,000 ft./min.	1,500 ft./min.	1,400 ft./min.
Ceiling	28,800 ft.	40,000 ft.	36,000 ft.	34,000 ft.
Range	1,500 miles	1,370 miles	3,500 miles	1,750 miles

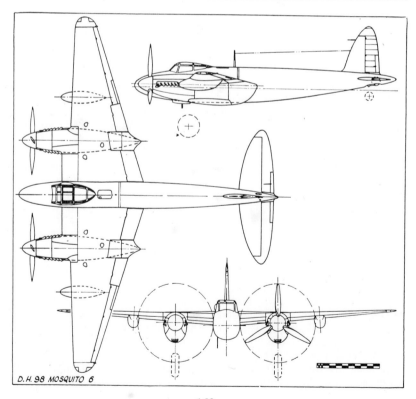

D.H. 98 MOSQUITO 6

163

A 1957 production Dove 6 used by Smiths Industries Ltd., Staverton, for demonstration and research for more than 13 years.

De Havilland D.H.104 Dove

A replacement for the Rapide was the obvious choice of design for the first post war product of the de Havilland Company, which lost no time in producing the now familiar Dove. Like the veteran to be replaced, it was twin engined and normally carried eight passengers, but there the similarity ended. The Dove, which conformed to the Brabazon Committee's specification 5B, was an all-metal, low-wing, cantilever monoplane having a semi-monocoque fuselage, provision for two pilots in the nose and pneumatically retracted tricycle undercarriage. The prototype, G-AGPJ, made its first flight at Hatfield only six weeks after the end of hostilities—on 25 September 1945—the twenty-fifth anniversary of the founding of the company. Power was supplied by two of the new D.H. Gipsy Queen 71 six-cylinder, in-line, supercharged, air-cooled engines driving three bladed D.H. hydromatic feathering and reversible pitch airscrews. It was thus the first aircraft built entirely by the de Havilland organization and the first British transport to employ braking airscrews. After trials at Farnborough, where it made its public debut on 29 October 1945, it was sent back to Hatfield for the fitting of a large dorsal fin to improve control during asymmetric flying. Further modification was necessary, and in the following May 'PJ flew with the now familiar curved fin before being handed over to the Ministry of Supply. Its final employment in M.O.S. service was on tyre research with the Dunlop Rubber Co. Ltd. at Baginton, in R.A.F. colours as WJ310. This important prototype, forerunner of over 500 production models was sold eventually to the Portuguese Government as CR-CAC after overhaul at Exeter in 1954.

Although the Dove was immeasurably superior to the Rapide in range, cruising speed and single motor performance, its high initial cost was beyond the resources of most struggling charter firms. Operating costs were also 50 per cent. greater than those of the biplane, and it got away to an unlucky start when both the second prototype and the third production machine were destroyed in fatal crashes. The first, G-AGUC, on loan from the Ministry of Supply to the B.O.A.C. Development Flight at Hurn, crashed four miles from base on 14 August 1946. The other, G-AHRA, crashed in bad weather at New Milton, Hants., with the loss of three lives, on 13 March 1947. Nevertheless the Dove went into large scale production, first at Hatfield and later at Hawarden, near Chester. The majority of Doves made a valuable contribution to the export drive, but a number were also used commercially by British concerns. Early deliveries in 1946–47 included G-AHRJ, G-AIIX, 'IY and G-AJOS to Sudan Airways Ltd., Khartoum; and G-AHRI, 'YX, G-AICY, G-AJHX, 'JF, G-AKJP and G-ALBF to supplement the Rapides on desert communications of the Iraq Petroleum Transport Co. Ltd. Four of the Iraq Doves were still in service with the same owner 24 years later. CF-DJH was unique among early production Doves, having flown at Toronto in 1947 with a twin float undercarriage.

The first Dove to go into commission with a home-based charter firm was the fifth production machine, G-AHRB, which received its C. of A. on 7 October 1946. Owned by Skyways Ltd., named 'Sky Maid' and based at Dunsfold, it gave Croydon a foretaste of its long future association with the Dove. The years 1949 and 1950 found it at New Delhi on charter to the United Kingdom High Commission, history being made on 9 December 1949, when Capt. Balnave flew it from Patna, high into the Himalayas, to Katmandu. There it became the first British aircraft to land and to be inspected by the King of Nepal. Its wanderings, typical of many hard-worked Doves, took it in May 1951 to Lagos, where as VR-NAJ it commenced six years' airline service with the West African Airways Corporation. Other early Dove users were Hunting, Olley and Morton Air Services Ltd. of Croydon, Cambrian Air Services Ltd., Cardiff, and B.O.A.C. The last employed G-AJPR and G-AKCF for crew training while the Flying Unit of the Board of Trade and its predecessors used a varying fleet for aircrew licence testing and for calibrating airfield radio aid systems, the 1970 fleet comprising Dove 6s G-AJLV, G-ALFT, 'FU, 'VS, G-ANAP, 'OV, 'UT, 'UU and 'UW.

The 15th production Dove 1, CF-DJH, operating on floats over Toronto, Canada in 1947.

In 1948 a six seat executive version known as the Dove 2 was introduced, one of the first being G-AKSV, purchased by Vickers-Armstrongs (Aircraft) Ltd. and demonstrated at that year's Farnborough S.B.A.C. Show. Other executive Dove 2s also found British employment, including G-ALMR with the English Electric Co. Ltd. at Warton, G-AKYS with David Brown and Sons (Huddersfield) Ltd., G-AKSW with the Enfield Rolling Mills Ltd., G-ALCU with Staffordshire Potteries Ltd., G-AJOT with Short Bros. and Harland Ltd., G-ALVD with the Dunlop Rubber Co. Ltd., G-AMDD with Shell, G-APCZ with Ind, Coope and Allsop Ltd. and G-ANMJ with Ferranti Ltd. at Turnhouse.

Apart from the fitting of an asymmetrical elevator to eliminate buffeting, air-frame modifications were few, and it was the development of the Gipsy Queen series of engines which has led to the production of the major Dove variants. In its production form with fuel injection, this engine, known as the Gipsy Queen 70, giving 330 h.p. at take-off, was fitted to the second prototype G-AGUC and all subsequent aircraft. In its developed form as the Gipsy Queen 70-3 it became the standard power-plant of the Dove 1 passenger aircraft and the Dove 2 executive version. In 1952 an improved model, the 340 h.p. Gipsy Queen 70-4, amended Dove designations to Dove 1B and 2B respectively. A year later the introduction and installation of the 380 h.p. Gipsy Queen 70 Mk. 2 not only amended them still further to Dove 5 and 6, but permitted an increase in the all-up weight to 8,800 lb. and gave a 20 per cent. increase in payload over a 500 mile stage as compared with the Series 1.

Dove 3 was a projected high altitude survey model but Dove 4 was a military communications version, 39 of which (VP952–VP981, WB530–WB535, WF984, XA879 and XA880) were supplied to the R.A.F. as Devon C.Mk.1s in 1948 and others to overseas air forces. Thirteen more (XJ319–XJ324, XJ347–XJ350 and XK895–XK897) were delivered to the Fleet Air Arm as Sea Devon C.Mk.20s in 1955–1956. In five instances R.A.F. Devons were sent to foreign capitals such as Teheran and Buenos Aires and registered as civil Dove 4s for the temporary use of the various Air Attachés.

Final variants were the Dove 7 and 8 with 400 h.p. Gipsy Queen 70-3 engines and Heron-type cockpit canopy, operating at an increased all-up weight of 8,950 lb., a special variant for the U.S. market being designated Dove 8A and marketed as the Dove Custom 600. A single Mk.5X, G-AJGT, delivered new in July 1947 as a Dove 1 to the Bata Shoe Co. Ltd. for touring its European factories, was used later as an engine testbed by the de Havilland Engine Co. Ltd., and in 1972 was in service with Rolls-Royce (1971) Ltd. at Filton as a Dove 7XC alongside their Mk.8XC G-AMZY.

The majority of earlier Doves were fitted with improved engines during over-haul and upgraded to higher marks, secondhand Doves finding a ready sale for many years in all parts of the world. Some former exports also returned to the home market, these including G-AHRB, G-ANVU, G-AOBZ, 'CE, 'ZW and G-APAG which East Anglian Flying Services Ltd. (later Channel Airways Ltd.) acquired from the West African Airways Corporation 1954–1957. In 1971 Channel's G-ANVU was the only Dove still flying on U.K. scheduled services, although others previously operated by the larger companies had included British Eagle's Dove 5 G-AROI 'Eaglet'; British Midland Airways' Dove 5 G-AROH; Transmeridian Air Cargo's Dove 6 G-AOFI; and Morton Air Services Ltd. which disposed of its last three, G-AMYO, G-ANAN and G-AOYC in 1969 after nearly 20 years as a Dove operator.

Over 50 Doves of all marks were on the British register in 1972 among which were Mk.1Bs G-AKSS and G-AMKS used for many years by Fairey Surveys Ltd. and joined by Dove 6 G-AWFM in 1969; Dove 8 G-ARHX of Hunting Surveys Ltd.; as well as Dove 6 G-AMXW and Dove 5 G-APSO, flying classrooms of the College of Aeronautics, Cranfield. Charter operators included Fairflight Charters Ltd., Biggin Hill with G-ARFZ, 'OH and 'OI.

Among the Dove 8s the National Coal Board's G-ARUM; British Insulated Callender Cables' G-ARYM; and IEAF.803, which was ferried to Ethiopia as G-ASYR and presented to Emperor Haile Selassie at Addis Ababa by H.M. The Queen on 5 February 1965, were typical of the many Doves of all marks used for executive flying all over the world. G-ASPA operated by Fortes (Publicity Services) Ltd., formerly served Dowty Group Services Ltd., Staverton but was replaced by the 542nd and final production Dove, G-AVHV, delivered on 20 September 1967 but tragically destroyed on 9 April 1970 when it crashed into houses when landing at Wolverhampton. Components of the penultimate Dove, Mk.8 G-AVVF, were sent from Chester to Baginton by road for erection late in 1967 and a production run of nearly 25 years ended when it was delivered to Martin-Baker Ltd. in February 1968.

The Dowty Group's Dove 8 G-ASPA at Staverton in 1964 showing the higher cockpit canopy which identified Doves Mks.7 and 8.

Two Dove conversions which originated in the U.S.A. enjoyed only limited success. The first, intended for the executive market and offered by Riley Aeronautics Corp. as the Riley Turbo Exec 400, featured two 400 h.p. Lycoming piston engines in place of the Gipsy Queens, better flight deck, restyled cabin and swept fin, the prototype, N1472V, being demonstrated in Britain in 1965. At least 17 conversions were completed in the U.S.A. including the European-based F-BGOA and N477PM; and others were undertaken by McAlpine Aviation Ltd. at Luton which included demonstrator G-ASUW, G-ARDH for David Brown Industries Ltd., G-ASUV (later 5N-AGF) for Bristow Helicopters Ltd. and F-BORJ for Roger Beldon, Le Bourget, but only the last had the swept fin.

A more ambitious third-level conversion, conceived by Carstedt-Air Inc., first flown in the U.S.A. on 18 December 1966 and known as the Carstedt CJ-600A Jet Liner, featured an 87 inch fuselage stretch allowing up to 18 passengers to be carried on the power of two Garrett TEP-331 propeller-turbine engines. Four such conversions, N4921V–N4923V and N1563V (originally CC-CAD to 'CF

Formerly Dove 6 OY-ADG, N880JG was one of five swept-fin Riley conversions made in the U.S.A. for third-level services out of Honolulu by Sky Tours Hawaii Inc. (*Aviation Photo News*)

and G-ANJC) were in service with Apache Airlines alongside two Riley Doves in 1969. A CJ-600 conversion of the former Morton Air Services Dove 1B G-AKJR, begun by Channel Airways Ltd. at Southend, was abandoned at an early stage.

SPECIFICATION

Manufacturers: The de Havilland Aircraft Co. Ltd., Hatfield Aerodrome, Herts. and Hawarden Aerodrome, Chester.

Power Plants: (Dove 1 and 2)   Two 330 h.p. de Havilland Gipsy Queen 70-3.
(Dove 1B and 2B) Two 340 h.p. de Havilland Gipsy Queen 70-4.
(Dove 5 and 6)   Two 380 h.p. de Havilland Gipsy Queen 70-2.
(Dove 7 and 8)   Two 400 h.p. de Havilland Gipsy Queen 70-3.
(Riley)   Two 400 h.p. Lycoming IO-720-AIA.

Dimensions: Span 57 ft. 0 in. Length 39 ft. 4 in. Height 13 ft. 4 in. Wing area 335 sq. ft.

	Dove 1 & 2	Dove 1B & 2B Devon and Sea Devon	Dove 5 & 6	Dove 7 & 8
Tare weight	5,650 lb.	5,650 lb.*	5,725 lb.	6,580 lb.
All-up weight	8,500 lb.	8,500 lb.	8,800 lb.†	8,950 lb.
Maximum speed	201 m.p.h.	210 m.p.h.	210 m.p.h.	235 m.p.h.
Cruising speed	165 m.p.h.	179 m.p.h.	179 m.p.h.	162 m.p.h.
Initial climb	850 ft./min.	750 ft./min.	920 ft./min.	1,420 ft./min.
Ceiling	20,000 ft.	20,000 ft.	20,000 ft.	21,700 ft.
Range	1,000 miles	1,000 miles	1,070 miles	1,175 miles

* Devon 5,780 lb.   † Dove 6B 8,500 lb.

Production: (a) Dove Mks. 1 to 6

Two prototypes (c/n 04000/P.1) G-AGPJ and (04000/P.2) G-AGUC followed by five hundred and forty-two production aircraft including a large number of British registered examples and the following for the R.A.F. or export: (c/n 04001) CF-BNU; (04002)

VH-AQO; (04006) VP-YES; (04007) VP-YER; (04009) ZS-BCB; (04011) OO-AWD; (04012) VH-AQP; (04013) OO-AWE; (04014) OO-CBM; (04015) CF-DJH; (04017) VP-YET; (04020) VP-YEU; (04021) ZS-AVZ; (04022) VT-CEH; (04024) ZS-AVH; (04025) PP-RUC; (04027) LV-XWH; (04030) CF-DJI; (04032) YI-MYOB; (04035) LV-XWU; (04038) LV-XWI; (04039) LV-XWO; (04040) CF-DJO; (04042) LV-XWL; (04044) VR-NAB; (04045) LV-XWM; (04046) LV-XWN; (04047) LV-XWJ; (04048) VP952; (04049) VR-NAG; (04050) ZK-AQV; (04052) Iraq 270; (04055) VR-TAN; (04060) EP-ACF; (04061) EP-ACG; (04062) EP-ACH; (04065) VT-COW; (04066–04070) LV-XWP to 'WT; (04072) YI-ABJ; (04073) VP954; (04074) Indian HW201; (04075) Indian HW202; (04076) Swedish 46001; (04077) VT-CQA; (04078) Indian HW203; (04079) ZS-BCC; (04080) Belgian Congo CGG; (04081) Indian HW204; (04082) VR-NAP; (04083) OO-CFD; (04085) ZS-BVN; (04086) VP-YEV; (04087) ZS-BTM; (04088) VP959; (04089) Iraq 265; (04090) Egyptian SU-Z-900; (04091) VH-AZY; (04092) VT-CKE; (04093–04095) LV-XWV to 'WX; (04096) VR-NAY; (04097) YI-ABK; (04098) VR-NET; (04099) VT-CSO; (04100) Egyptian SU-Z-901; (04101) VR-NEW; (04102) Egyptian SU-Z-902; (04103) OO-CFE; (04104) VT-CQY; (04105) Iraq 266; (04106) CS-TAB; (04107) CS-TAC; (04108) LV-XWY; (04109) LV-XWZ; (04110) LV-XXD; (04111) LV-XZP; (04112) Egyptian SU-Z-903; (04113) YI-ABL; (04114) VR-NIB; (04115) LV-XZO; (04117) VP-KDE; (04118) VP-KDF; (04119) VP-KDG; (04120) VP-KEJ; (04123) Iraq 267; (04124) Egyptian SU-Z-904; (04127) VR-NIL; (04128) VR-NIT; (04129) Egyptian SU-Z-905; (04130) LV-XXE; (04131) LV-XZR; (04132) VP-YHU; (04133) Iraq 268; (04134) VT-CTX; (04136–04139) LV-XZS to 'ZV; (04140) Pakistan P1300; (04141) Iraq 269; (04142–04145) LV-XZW to 'ZZ; (04146) LV-YAD; (04147) CR-ACI; (04148) CR-ACJ; (04149) LV-YAE; (04150) LV-YAM; (04151) VT-CTG; (04153) LV-YAG; (04154) VP-YHV; (04155) LV-YAH; (04156) LV-YAI; (04157) CR-ACL; (04158) CR-ACM; (04159) Indian HW516; (04160) Indian HW517; (04162) Indian HW525; (04163) Indian HW515; (04164) Indian HW518; (04165) LV-YAJ; (04167) VT-CVA; (04169) R.N.Z.A.F. NZ1802; (04171) Indian HW526; (04172) Indian HW519; (04173) VP953; (04174) VR-NIX; (04175) XY-ABN; (04176) XY-ABO; (04177) Indian HW520; (04178) LV-YAL; (04179) LV-YAF; (04180) LV-YAO; (04182) VP956; (04183) XY-ABP; (04184) XY-ABQ; (04185) Indian HW521; (04186) Indian HW522; (04187–04194) LV-YAP to 'AW; (04195) XY-ABR; (04196) XY-ABS; (04197) LV-YBN; (04198) LV-YBO; (04200) LV-YBQ; (04201) VP955; (04202) LV-YBR; (04203) LV-YAX; (04204) LV-YBS; (04205) VP981; (04207) VR-NOB; (04208) VP957; (04209) VP958; (04210–04213) VP960–VP963;

The Carstedt CJ-600A Jet Liner conversion N4922V, one of five used by Apache Airlines Inc. for commuter services radiating from Phoenix, Arizona. It was formerly a Dove 2 delivered to Chile in 1950 as CC-CAE. (*Neil A. Macdougall*)

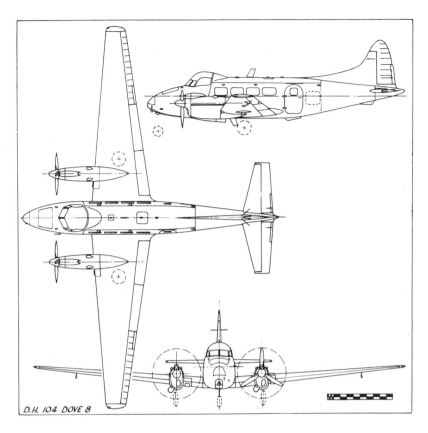

D.H. 104 DOVE 8

(04214) LV-YBU; (04215–04217) LV-YBG to 'BI; (04218) VP966; (04219) VT-DBG;
(04220–04224) VP967–VP971; (04225) LV-YAY; (04226) LV-YAZ; (04227) VP972;
(04228) VP974; (04229) VP973; (04230–04232) LV-YBD to 'BF; (04235) S.A.A.F.101;
(04237) LV-YBJ; (04238) LV-YBL; (04239) LV-YBM; (04240) S.A.A.F.102; (04241)
S.A.A.F.103; (04242) LV-YBP; (04243) S.A.A.F.104; (04244) Indian HW524; (04245)
Indian HW523; (04246) S.A.A.F.105; (04247) S.A.A.F.106; (04248) LV-YBT; (04249)
Indian HW527; (04250) S.A.A.F.107; (04251) Indian HW528; (04252) Belgian Congo
CGG replacement; (04253) Indian HW529; (04254) Indian HW530; (04255) VP975;
(04256) S.A.A.F.108; (04257–04263) VP964, VP965, VP976–VP980; (04264) WB530;
(04265) S.A.A.F.109; (04266) WB531; (04267) WB532; (04268) CC-CLE; (04269–
04271) WB533–WB535; (04272) CC-CLN; (04273) CC-CLW; (04274) CC-CLX;
(04275) CC-CLY; (04276) CC-CLZ; (04278) CR-ADC; (04279) CR-ADD; (04280)
CC-CAA; (04281) CF-GQH; (04282–04286) CC-CAB to 'AF; (04287) WF984;
(04288) TJ-ACC; (04289) TJ-ACD; (04293) N4952N; (04294) NZ1803; (04295)
NZ1804; (04297) N80013; (04298) CF-GQQ; (04299) Lebanon LR-M-110; (04301)
G-5-18/N4953N; (04302) N4261C; (04303) N4954N; (04304) Lebanon LR-M-109;
(04305) N4955N; (04306) G-5-16/N4262C; (04307) N4956N; (04308) N4271C;
(04309) N4957N; (04310) N4263C; (04311) N4959N; (04312) NZ1805; (04313)
F-BFVL; (04314) N4958N; (04315) N4264C; (04316) N4960N; (04317) N4270C;

(04318) NZ1810; (04319) NZ1806; (04320) N4265C; (04321) NZ1811; (04322) NZ1812; (04323) NZ1807; (04324) NZ1808; (04325) N4980N; (04326) N4962N; (04327) CF-GYR; (04330) N4979N; (04332) N4964N; (04333) N4965N; (04334) PT-AMP; (04335) CF-GYQ; (04337) N4267C; (04338) F-OAKG; (04339) N4966N; (04340) N4967N; (04341) N4268C; (04342) N4968N; (04343) N4269C; (04344) F-BGOA; (04345) CF-GCU; (04346) N4969N; (04347) N4970N; (04348) N4274C; (04349) N1516V; (04350) N4971N; (04351) N4272C; (04352) N4972N; (04353) N4273C; (04354) N1517V; (04355) N1536V; (04356) CF-GBE; (04357) N4276C; (04358) N4275C; (04359) N4277C; (04360) N1558V; (04361) N1538V; (04362) N1539V; (04363) N1541V; (04364) N1542V; (04365) N1571V; (04366) N4278C; (04367) Belgian Congo D.14; (04368) Irish 176; (04369) N1572V; (04370) N1573V; (04371) N1564V; (04372) N1574V; (04373) CR-AGT; (04374) XA879; (04376) N4279C; (04377) CF-ODI; (04378) N1575V; (04379) N4280C; (04380) N1576V; (04381) N1577V; (04382) N4281C; (04383) N1578V; (04384) N1579V; (04385) CF-GBW; (04387) CF-EYL; (04388) N4282C; (04389) N1559V; (04390) CF-EYM; (04391) N4283C; (04392) N1561V; (04393) N1562V; (04395) YV-O-CVF2; (04396–04399) NZ1813–NZ1816; (04402) XB-SUU; (04403–04405) NZ1817–NZ1819; (04411–04413) NZ1820–NZ1822; (04415) XB-TAN/XJ321; (04416) XB-TEZ; (04417–04419) NZ1823–NZ1825; (04423) YU-ABO; (04424–04428) NZ1826–NZ1830; (04432) YU-ABN; (04434) VP-RCV; (04436) XA880; (04442) Belgian Congo D.15; (04443) Belgian Congo D.16; (04447) Belgian Congo D.17; (04452) OY-FAL; (04453) XJ350; (04456) YV-P-AEQ; (04459) ZS-MTD; (04462) HB-LAS; (04463) Ceylon CS401; (04464) Ceylon CS402; (04465) YV-P-AEO; (04466) I-SNAM; (04467) YV-P-BAP; (04469) I-TONY (04472–04474) XK895–XK897; (04480) OH-IOA; (04481) PH-IOG; (04483) PH-IOH; (04484) PH-IOL; (04485) PH-IOM; (04486) PH-ION; (04488) OE-VBM; (04489) Ceylon CS403; (04491) OY-ADG; (04492) YV-P-AEA; (04493) PH-ILI; (04494) PH-IOB; (04495) I-ANIC; (04496) HB-LAP; (04497) Ceylon CS404; (04498) XM223; (04499) VH-DHH; (04500) OE-FAC; (04501) Ceylon CS405; (04502) Ceylon CS406; (04503) Irish 188; (04506) Belgian Congo D.21; (04507) Belgian Congo D.22; (04508) VH-DHK; (04510) G-5-12/PH-FST.

(b) Dove Mk.7* and Mk.8

(04521–04523) Malaysia FM1051–FM1053*; (04524) Egyptian 906; (04527) D-IFSC; (04530) Irish 194; (04531) D-IFSA; (04534) CN-MBA; (04535) CN-MBB; (04539) Jordan 120; (04540) Jordan 121.

N 4914V 'City of Riverside', one of sixteen Dove 2Bs operated by C-Air Inc. (a Carstedt associate) on third-level commuter routes out of Los Angeles in 1969.
(*Aviation Photo News*)

171

Mexicana's second Comet 4C, G-AOVV/XA-NAS, on a test flight near Hatfield, December 1959

De Havilland D.H.106 Comet

Preliminary design work on the Brabazon Committee's Type IV jet transport was begun by de Havillands in 1944 because they felt a complete breakaway from piston engined tradition was urgent if the wartime lead in transport aircraft were to be wrested from the Americans. The calculated performance of their proposed D.H.106 interested the British Overseas Airways Corporation, who recommended its development, and in December 1945 agreed to purchase 10. Several configurations were investigated by chief designer R. E. Bishop and his team, including one with twin booms and three Goblin turbojets. A short fuselage, swept-wing tailless type was also considered, but rejected in the light of experience with D.H.108 single seat tailless research aircraft during 1946. It would have been neither practical nor economical for passenger work, and the Comet, as it had been named in December 1947, was built on more orthodox lines.

The prototype, G-5-1, later G-ALVG, made a first flight of 31 minutes at Hatfield on 27 July 1949, piloted by the firm's chief test pilot, John Cunningham, with a crew of four. Of all-metal construction, its circular section fuselage would accommodate 36 passengers. Four crew were situated on a flight deck in the nose, the exact shape of which had been determined with extreme care after flight trials with a suitably modified Horsa glider towed by a Halifax. Its thin, mildly swept wing, with generous flap area, incorporated design features which ensured good slow flying characteristics in spite of sensational performance at the other end of the speed range. Lockheed Servodyne hydraulically assisted power controls were also employed. Four Ghost 50 turbojets, newly through their civil type test, were mounted close to the fuselage, and, without airscrew clearance problems, the outward retracting undercarriage was unusually short. The aircraft was publicly demonstrated at the 1949 S.B.A.C. Show before commencing flight trials which were principally concerned with fuel consumption measurements and involved a series of fast overseas flights. The first of these, made by John Cunningham on 25 October 1949, was a return flight to Castel Benito, Libya, at an average speed of 448 m.p.h. Then came a $5\frac{1}{2}$ hour endurance test round the British Isles, followed on 21 February 1950 by the first pressurization flight, the maximum cabin altitude being 8,000 ft. when flying at 40,000 ft. For the first of a new class of transports, its relatively trouble-free trials were remarkable, and in 11 months it completed 324 hours flying. To build up hours to good purpose, out and home inter-capital records were set up early in 1950 between London and Rome, Copenhagen and Cairo, all at an average speed in excess of 420 m.p.h. The Cairo record was established while carrying 11 technicians to the tropical trials at Khartoum and the high altitude take-off tests at Nairobi.

A year to the day after the prototype's first flight, John Cunningham and Peter Buggé took the second Comet, G-5-2, into the air at Hatfield and it was delivered to the B.O.A.C. Comet Unit at Hurn as G-ALZK on 2 April 1951 for a 500 hour crew training and route proving programme. Attention was focussed on fuel consumption and techniques of holding and descent, 12 long distance flights being made to Johannesburg, Delhi and Singapore.

Production aircraft appeared in rapid succession, commencing with the first flight of G-ALYP in January 1951 and ending with the delivery of G-ALYZ in September 1952, all in full B.O.A.C. blue, white and gold livery, but unnamed. Their multi-wheel bogie undercarriage units retracted snugly into the mainplane, whereas considerable bulges had been necessary to house the large single wheels of the prototypes. Simulated passenger schedules with freight began on the South African route in January 1952, the first C. of A. being issued to G-ALYS on 22 January, and on 2 May 1952 G-ALYP took-off on the first scheduled service to Johannesburg. It was the world's first pure jet flight with fare-paying passengers and a fortnight later the training programme begun on the Far East route culminated on 3 April 1953 in the opening of a day-and-a-half scheduled service between London and Tokyo, a distance of 10,200 miles.

The Comet 1s operated at 89 per cent. load factors, cut flying times by over 50 per cent. and created considerable consternation among airline magnates in America and elsewhere. When, therefore, on 23 May 1952, Queen Elizabeth the Queen Mother, Princess Margaret, Sir Geoffrey and Lady de Havilland and others made a 4 hour Royal request flight around Europe, the Comet reached unprecedented heights of fame and popularity. In the following year the same Royal passengers flew in G-ALYW, Capt. A. P. W. Cane, to attend the Rhodes Cen-

The prototype Comet at Farnborough in 1952, showing the large single wheels.
(*A. J. Jackson*)

tenary celebrations at Salisbury, Southern Rhodesia. A first set-back came, however, in October 1952, when G-ALYZ, Capt. R. E. H. Foote, was damaged beyond repair on take-off from Rome. None of the 42 occupants was injured, and the nose section subsequently became an office at London Airport. Its replacement was CF-CUM, one of two built for Canadian Pacific Airlines, the first to be ordered by an overseas customer, but redundant after the loss of sister aircraft CF-CUN 'Empress of Hawaii' in a take-off disaster at Karachi while on its delivery flight on 3 March 1953. This was a Mk.1A fitted for water-methanol injection and tankage for 6,906 gallons and it went into B.O.A.C. service as G-ANAV on 12 August. Other orders for Comet 1As were received from the R.C.A.F. which took delivery of 5301 and 5302 and flew them until retirement in 1964; and three each for Air France (F-BGNX to 'NZ) and Union Aéromaritime de Transport (F-BGSA to 'SC).

Comet 1XB N373S, formerly CF-SVR and R.C.A.F. 5301, at Hamilton, Ontario on 18 July 1967 on the eve of delivery to Dallas Airmotive, Miami. (*J. McNulty*)

On 2 May 1953 G-ALYV, Capt. M. W. Haddon, left Calcutta for Delhi but while climbing to cruising altitude was inexplicably destroyed with the loss of 43 lives. This accident was repeated twice more in almost exact detail, first on 10 January 1954, when G-ALYP, Capt. A. Gibson D.F.C., plunged from 26,000 ft. into the sea near Elba with the loss of 35 lives, just after taking-off from Rome. The other came on 8 April when G-ALYY, Capt. W. K. Mostert, crashed off Stromboli with 21 occupants, also after take-off from Rome. The fleet was promptly grounded and its Cs. of A. withdrawn, but expert ground exmination failed to reveal any mechanical defects. Then followed a public inquiry backed by an accident investigation, the magnitude of which had never previously been known in any country. As a result of fully instrumented flight trials with G-ANAV, the pressure testing to destruction of G-ALYU in a huge water tank at Farnborough and a microscopic examination of the salvaged wreck of 'YP, reassembled at Farnborough, the cause of failure was accurately pin-pointed. Structural failure of the pressure cabin had occurred at one corner of the rear ADF window. It was the end of the Comet 1, but the lessons it had taught were embodied in later marks.

Although stage lengths over the Empire routes suited the Comet 1, its range

G-AMXA, first of the Comet 2 production.

was insufficient for transatlantic operations, more power and more fuel being needed. Plans were therefore drawn up for the stretched Comet 2 with Avon 502 axial flow jet engines and fuel capacity increased by 1,000 gallons. For test purposes a Comet 1 airframe G-ALYT had been fitted with Avon 502s while retaining standard tankage, and as the Comet 2X, first flew at Hatfield on 16 February 1952. Tropical trials took place in May 1953, and the London–Cairo time was lowered en route. Twelve 44-seat Comet 2s were then ordered by B.O.A.C. for the South Atlantic route, the first of which, G-AMXA, made its maiden flight on 27 August 1953 and appeared at the S.B.A.C. Show a month later. In January 1954 its long range characteristics were handsomely demonstrated when John Cunningham flew it 3,064 miles nonstop from London to Khartoum in $6\frac{1}{2}$ hours for tropical trials. In the light of the Comet 1 disasters, fuselage pressure shells of all production Comet 2s were rebuilt with a heavier gauge skin and rounded openings but trials with this mark showed that although its range was adequate for the South Atlantic route it was still not suitable for the difficult North Atlantic crossing. With four exceptions the Comet 2s were therefore delivered to No. 216 Squadron, R.A.F. Transport Command which used them in Service markings on trooping flights between Lyneham and Australia until April 1967.

Their successor, the stretched Comet 3 G-ANLO, with Avon 523 motors, extra tankage in large wing nacelles and a maximum accommodation for 78 passengers, was flown by Messrs. Cunningham and Buggé for the first time on 19 July 1954. In its developed form as the Comet 4 with Avon 524s and greater fuel capacity, it met B.O.A.C. North Atlantic requirements, and 19 registered G-APDA–'DT were ordered for delivery in 1959. As part of the development programme, John Cunningham and Peter Buggé flew round the world in the Comet 3, leaving Hatfield on 2 December 1955 and arriving home on the 28th via Australia, New Zealand, Fiji, Vancouver and Dorval. While in Australia they lowered the Perth–Sydney record to 4 hours 6 minutes at an average speed of 501 m.p.h.

While awaiting delivery of its Comet 4s, the first of which, G-APDA, made its first flight at Hatfield on 27 April 1958, two modified Comet 2s were handed over to B.O.A.C. for route proving trials. This pair, G-AMXD and 'XK, designated Comet 2E and owned respectively by the Ministry of Supply and the Corporation, were fitted with Avon 524s in the outboard nacelles and Avon 504s inboard. With these, Avon experience was built up by the Comet Unit on simulated services between London, Beirut and Calcutta in 1957. In May 1958 they were used on the first route proving trials over the North Atlantic and in September G-APDB was loaned to B.O.A.C. for crew training and the first, 'DA, was engaged on route proving trials prior to certification and entry into the North Atlantic service. On 14 September John Cunningham and crew startled the world by covering the 7,925 miles from Hong Kong to Hatfield in one day in a flying time of 16 hours 16 minutes at an average speed of 487 m.p.h. Three days later it lowered the London–Gander record to 5 hours 47 minutes. The first two Comet 4s for B.O.A.C., G-APDB and 'DC, were delivered on 30 September 1958 and on 4 October the latter flew westbound in 10 hr. 22 min. and the former eastbound in the record time of 6 hr. 11 min. to inaugurate the long-awaited world's first North Atlantic scheduled jet service. Other Comet 4 customers were Aerolineas Argentinas which ordered six (delivered 1959–60) and East African Airways which took delivery of VP-KPJ and 'PK in 1960 and a third, VP-KRL, in 1962.

In July 1956 the U.S. operator Capital Airlines ordered four Comet 4s and 4As, the latter designed to operate shorter stages at lower altitudes and featuring stretched fuselages, wings being 7 ft. shorter in span but without the pinion fuel tanks of the Comet 4. This order was eventually cancelled but 14 aircraft were built as Comet 4Bs for B.E.A. with fuselages lengthened by 38 inches and seating 99 passengers.

G-ANLO, fully painted in B.E.A. livery as 'R.M.A. William Brooks' and with span reduced to simulate the Comet 4B, was demonstrated under designation Comet 3B at the S.B.A.C. Show in September 1958. B.E.A.'s first aircraft of the type, G-APMA, was delivered on 9 November and scheduled services were inaugurated on 1 April 1960 with the departure of G-APMB from Tel Aviv for London. The Greek airline Olympic Airways also ordered four Comet 4Bs which were registered initially as SX-DAK and 'AL and G-APZM and G-ARDI for pooled operations with B.E.A. during which the latter's G-ARJL also appeared in Olympic livery in February 1964.

Inevitably the Comet 4B stretched fuselage was mated to the Comet 4 long range wing to create the final variant, the 4C, announced in December 1957. The first, XB-NAR for Mexicana, which first flew on 31 October 1959, was temporarily registered G-AOVU for C. of A. and development flying. XB-NAS and 'AT were delivered during 1960 and all three flew 'Golden Aztec' international services linking Mexico City with the U.S.A. and the Caribbean Islands. Other Comet 4C orders came from Misrair (later United Arab Airlines) which ordered nine (SU-ALC to 'LE, 'LL, 'LM, 'MV, 'MW, 'NC and 'NI) delivered 1960–64, the final aircraft (replacing SU-ALD lost at sea between Bangkok and Bombay on 28 July 1963) being the last civil Comet built. Middle East Airlines received four (OD-ADQ to 'DT) but did not take up its fifth option. This aircraft was exhibited at the September 1961 S.B.A.C. Show in M.E.A. livery as G-AROV before going to Aerolineas Argentinas in 1962 as LV-AIB. The gap caused by the loss of three M.E.A. Comet 4Cs in the Israeli attack on Beirut airport on 28 December 1968 was filled by leasing two Comet 4Cs, 9K-ACA and 'CE, which Kuwait Airways had received in 1963–64, together with B.O.A.C. Comet 4 G-APDG leased to Kuwait as 9K-ACI in 1966.

The tail end of the Comet 4C production line included ST-AAW and 'AX for Sudan Airways (the former temporarily G-ASDZ for demonstration in Khartoum); a luxurious V.I.P. model for King Ibn Saud of Saudi Arabia, SA-R-7, which first flew on 29 March 1962 but crashed in the Alps between Nice and

Production Comet 4 G-APDR, c/n 6418, for B.O.A.C. with standard fuselage and long range wing.

VP-KPJ, c/n 6431, first Comet 4 for East African Airways.

Production Comet 4B G-APYC, c/n 6437, for Olympic Airways with stretched fuselage and standard wing.

Production Comet 4C SU-ALE, c/n 6434, for United Arab Airlines with stretched fuselage and long range wing.

177

G-AYVS, formerly Kuwait Airways' 9K-ACE, one of a number of Comet 4Cs purchased by Dan-Air Services Ltd. from overseas operators in 1971. (*Aviation Photo News*)

Geneva on 30 March 1963; XR395–XR399 for No. 216 Squadron, R.A.F., Lyneham; XS235 which the R.A.E., Farnborough, equipped with highly sophisticated radio aids for world wide navigational research which took it over the South Pole; and two machines which were flown from Chester to Woodford for conversion into prototypes of the H.S.801 Nimrod.

Few Comets reached the secondhand market although several acquired military marks for trial and development work for Decca/Dectra, Smiths Autoland, and long range radio aids. Another XM823 (ex F-BGNZ and G-APAS), was used for many years by Hawker Siddeley Dynamics.

Six of B.O.A.C.'s Comet 4s, redundant after the last scheduled service, flown by G-APDM from Auckland to Heathrow on 24 November 1965, were leased to Malaysia-Singapore Airlines; two others to M.E.A.; two to Mexicana; two to Aerovias Ecuatorianas; and one to Kuwait Airways. The Ministry of Technology purchased G-APDF as XV814 in 1967 and Dan-Air Services Ltd. progressively acquired 12 others (G-APDA to 'DE, G-APDJ to 'DP) 1966–69 for inclusive tour work, losing 'DN in the mountains near Barcelona on 3 July 1970. Rundown of the B.E.A./Olympic fleet followed, seven (G-APMD, 'MF, 'MG, G-ARGM, 'JK, 'JL and 'JN) being transferred to the inclusive tour subsidiary, B.E.A. Airtours, in 1970 and five (G-APMB, 'YC, 'YD, 'ZM and G-ARDI) to Channel Airways Ltd., Stansted.

SPECIFICATION

Manufacturers: The de Havilland Aircraft Co. Ltd., Hatfield Aerodrome, Herts. and Hawarden Aerodrome, Chester.

Power Plants:	(Comet 1)	Four 4,450 lb. s.t. de Havilland Ghost 50 Mk. 1.
	(Comet 1A)	Four 5,000 lb. s.t. de Havilland Ghost 50 Mk. 2.
	(Comet 2)	Four 6,500 lb. s.t. Rolls-Royce Avon 503.
	(Comet 3)	Four 10,000 lb. s.t. Rolls-Royce Avon 523.
	(Comet 4 and 4B)	Four 10,500 lb. s.t. Rolls-Royce Avon 524.
	(Comet 4C)	Four 10,500 lb. s.t. Rolls-Royce Avon 525B.

	Comet 1	Comet 2	Comet 4	Comet 4B	Comet 4C
Span	115 ft.	115 ft.	115 ft.	107 ft. 10 in.	114 ft. 10 in.
Length	93 ft. 0 in.	96 ft. 0 in.	111 ft. 6 in.	118 ft. 0 in.	118 ft. 0 in.
Height	28 ft. 4 in.	28 ft. 4 in.	28 ft. 6 in.	28 ft. 6 in.	28 ft. 6 in.
Wing area	2,015 sq. ft.	2,015 sq. ft.	2,121 sq. ft.	2,059 sq. ft.	2,121 sq. ft.
Tare weight	—	—	72,595 lb.	73,816 lb.	—
All-up weight	105,000 lb.	120,000 lb.	160,000 lb.	152,500 lb.	162,000 lb.
Cruising speed	490 m.p.h.	490 m.p.h.	503 m.p.h.	532 m.p.h.	503 m.p.h.
Cruising altitude	35,000 ft.	40,000 ft.	42,000 ft.	23,500 ft.	39,000 ft.
Maximum stage with capacity payload	1,750 miles	2,100 miles	3,225 miles	2,300 miles	2,650 miles
Passengers	36–44*	36–44*	60–76*	84–99*	72–101*

* Lower figure represents first class, higher represents alternative tourist seating.

Production: (a) Comet 1
Eleven British registered aircraft.

(b) Comet 1A and 1XB* (Hatfield or Chester* built)
Ten export aircraft: (c/n 06013) CF-CUM; (06014) CF-CUN; (06015) F-BGSA; (06016) F-BGSB; (06017)* R.C.A.F. 5301/CF-SVR/N373S; (06018)* R.C.A.F. 5302; (06019) F-BGSC; (06020–06022) F-BGNX to 'NZ.

(c) Comet 2
Twelve British registered aircraft and the following for the R.A.F. or not completed: (c/n 06034) XK698; (06035) XK699; (06036) static test airframe; (06037) XK715; (06038–06040) scrapped before completion; (06045) XK716; (06046–06049) scrapped before completion.

(d) Comet 3
One British registered aircraft, G-ANLO, only.

(e) Comet 4 (Hatfield or Chester* built)
Nineteen British registered aircraft and the following for test or export: (c/n 6402) tank test airframe; (6408) LV-PLM/LV-AHN; (6410) LV-PLN/LV-AHO; (6411) LV-PLP/LV-AHP; (6430) LV-POY/LV-AHR; (6431)* VP-KPJ/5X-AAO; (6432)* LV-POZ/LV-AHS; (6433)* VP-KPK/5H-AAF; (6434)* LV-PPA/LV-AHU.

(f) Comet 4B
Eighteen British registered aircraft

(g) Comet 4C (Hatfield or Chester* built)
Five British registered aircraft and the following for export or the R.A.F.: (c/n 6439)* SU-ALC; (6441)* SU-ALD; (6444)* SU-ALE; (6445) OD-ADR; (6446)* OD-ADQ; (6448)* OD-ADS; (6450)* OD-ADT; (6454)* SU-ALL; (6458)* SU-ALM; (6461) SA-R-7; (6462)* SU-AMV; (6463) ST-AAX; (6464) SU-AMW; (6465) 9K-ACA; (6466) SU-ANC; (6467–6471) XR395–XR399; (6472) VP-KRL/5Y-AAA; (6473) XS235; (6474) 9K-ACE; (6475) SU-ANI.

(h) Comet 4C converted to H.S.801 Nimrod prototypes
Two aircraft only: (c/n 6476) XV147; (6477) XV148.

The prototype Heron, G-ALZL, in Japan Air Lines markings for demonstration at the 1952 Farnborough S.B.A.C. Show.

De Havilland D.H.114 Heron

When the Dove appeared as the post war Rapide replacement, de Havillands already had in mind a four engined version which would be the modern counterpart of the feeder line D.H.86B. As the market for such a type did not then exist, the idea was shelved until 1949, when W. A. Tamblin began the detailed designs. When the prototype Heron, G-ALZL, first flew at Hatfield in the hands of Geoffrey Pike on 10 May 1950 its close relationship to the Dove was evident. Designed as a simple and economical vehicle for operators using small fields, it was devoid of complicated hydraulics and its undercarriage was fixed and featured a faired and castoring nose wheel. The engines were ungeared, unsupercharged Gipsy Queen 30s, driving two bladed variable pitch airscrews. The prototype was built largely from actual Dove components, with Dove nose and tail units joined by lengthened Dove keel, roof and side members. The outer wing panels were also Dove units. Two pilots and a maximum of 17 passengers could be carried, although the normal complement was 15.

After 180 hours of test flying the prototype left for tropical trials at Khartoum and Nairobi, and in the following May was handed over to the Sales Department, in the course of whose demonstrations it appeared in many colour schemes, including those of Morton, B.E.A.C. and Japan Air Lines. In 1954 it was leased to Braathens for three weeks as LN-BDH.

In April 1952 the first production aircraft, ZK-AYV, left on its long delivery flight to New Zealand National Airways, but only seven Herons were Hatfield built before production was transferred to Chester. The last of the seven was G-AMTS, the prototype Heron 2 with retractable undercarriage which made its first flight on 14 December 1952. Without undercarriage drag, it was 20 m.p.h. faster than the Heron 1 and more economical on fuel. Production of Gipsy Queen 30 Mk.2 engined Heron 1B and 2B basic variants then continued at Chester, mainly to foreign order including Mk.1Bs for Braathens (4); U.T.A. (9); Garuda Indonesian Airways (14); P.L.U.N.A. (4); and New Zealand National Airways Corp. (4). Purchasers of Mk.2Bs included Turkish Airlines (7) and Indian Airlines (8); as well as eight Mk.2s for the West African Airways Corporation. Two Mk.1Bs for Butler Air Transport Ltd. were ferried to Australia as G-AMUK and G-ANFE; and three for Japan Air Lines were flown to Tokyo as

G-ANAX, 'FF and 'FG. Before delivery in July 1955, Bahamas Airways' Mk.2 VP-BAO made a 35,000 mile South American sales tour under British registry as G-ANOL and carried H.R.H. Princess Margaret during her visit to the West Indies.

The first Heron 1B to go into British service was the seventeenth production aircraft, G-AMYU, which made its inaugural flight from Gatwick to Jersey in the colours of Jersey Airlines Ltd. on 9 May 1953. It was later joined on the company's network to Guernsey, Exeter, Eastleigh, Hurn, Gatwick, Manchester, Paris and Bilbao by Mk. 1 G-ALZL, the Mk. 1Bs G-ANLN, 'SZ and 'WZ and the Mk. 2Bs G-AORG and 'RH. Two Mk. 1Bs G-ANXA and 'XB went into service with British European Airways in February 1955 to replace the Rapides on the Scottish ambulance runs and to operate scheduled services between Renfrew–Tiree–Barra, their short take-off characteristics making them ideal for operation from the small beach airstrip on Barra. They were joined later by G-AOFY, delivered on 12 April 1956, but Capt. T. M. Calderwood and his crew were killed when trying to land it at Port Ellen, Islay, to pick up a sick woman during a gale at 1.46 a.m. on 28 September 1957. Another operator of Herons on scheduled services was Cambrian Airways Ltd., which flew between Cardiff, Jersey, Bristol, Manchester, Belfast, Southampton and Paris with Heron 1B G-ANCI and Heron 2Bs G-AOGO, 'GU and 'RJ. Dragon Airways Ltd., formerly operating from Speke with Heron 1B G-ANCI and the first 17 seat Mk. 2s G-ANYJ and G-AODY, was absorbed by Silver City Airways Ltd. in 1957 and the Heron 2s sold to Braathens as LN-SUB and 'UA respectively, displacing LN-PSG and LN-SUD which returned to Silver City for use by Manx Airlines as G-AOZM and 'ZN.

'R.M.A. Sister Jean Kennedy', a Heron 1B used on the Scottish services of British European Airways. (*B.E.A.*)

Production modifications were few but wide chord rudders were fitted to all marks in 1955 and D.H. fully feathering airscrews became an optional extra amending the designation to Heron 2D, the first, G-ANCJ, being demonstrated at the 1955 Farnborough S.B.A.C. Show. Heron 2Ds were ordered by Aviacion y Comercio to which EC-ANJ, 'NX to 'NZ, 'OA to 'OC and 'OF were delivered in 1957 and Ghana Airways which received 9G-AAA and 'AB in 1958 followed by a V.I.P. machine, 501, for the Ghana Air Force. Special executive models were designated Heron 2C and 2E and some aircraft were 'upgraded' to better standards during overhaul.

181

Aviaco's first Heron 2D, EC-ANJ, on a pre-delivery flight near Hatfield, May 1957. It crashed into the sea south of Barcelona on 14 April 1958.

In its executive role the Heron found a small but ready market and among those still serving their original owners in 1972 were Vickers-Armstrongs' Mk. 1B G-ANNO and Mk. 2B G-AOGW (1954–56); Shell's Mk. 2D G-ANUO (1955); Rolls-Royce's Mk. 2D G-AOTI (1956) and Ferranti's Mk. 2E G-APMV (1958). Foreign civil and military customers included Prince Talal al Saud of Saudi Arabia to whom Mk. 2 SA-R5 'The Blue Arrow' was delivered in 1954; the Royal Iraqi Air Force which purchased Mk. 2Cs '393' and RF-5 (the latter as personal transport of King Feisal II); the Sultan of Morocco who acquired Mk. 2D CN-MAA 'La Tourterelle', first flown as G-AOZX; and the Belgian Force Publique Aérienne to which Mk. 2 'GGG' was delivered 1954.

The Queen's Flight received Heron C.3 (Mk. 2B) XH375 in 1955, Heron C.4s (Mk. 2Ds) XM295 and XM296 in 1958 and XM391 in 1961. The Mk. 2 prototype, G-AMTS, also temporarily joined the Flight in 1956 as XL961 for H.R.H. Princess Margaret's African Tour. One other military Heron, Mk. 2B XG603, was built for the Joint Services Mission in Washington but the Royal Navy also acquired Mk. 2s XR441 to XR445 from secondhand sources and some were still in use at Lee-on-Solent as Sea Herons in 1972.

An early purchaser of used Herons was Gulf Aviation Ltd. which acquired G-AMUK, G-ANFE, G-APJS, G-APKV and 'KW 1955–59 for scheduled services centred on Bahrein, although G-APJS, (formerly the first production Heron ZK-AYV, crashed in Southern Italy on 19 February 1958 while en route to Leavesden for pre-service modifications. When the B.U.A. group was formed in 1960, eight Herons belonging to constituent companies were transferred to Morton Air Services Ltd. whose Mk. 1B G-AOXL flew the last airline service out of Croydon on the evening of its closure, 30 September 1959. Four Aviacion y Comercio Heron 2Ds were also purchased by Morton in 1964 as G-ASUZ, and 'VA to 'VC, two of which were ferried to Fiji Airways. Emerald Airways Ltd. used G-ALZL, G-ANCI, G-AOZN and G-APRK on short-lived services to Northern Ireland 1965–66 but a more recent operator was Channel Airways Ltd., Southend, which acquired G-AMUK, G-ANCI, G-AOZM, G-APKV, G-APKW and G-AXFH during 1969, G-APKW being flown with Air England titling. Scheduled services were flown through Norwich where a new company, Progressive Airways Ltd. was formed in November 1970 with G-AODY and G-AYLH 'City of Norwich', both purchased in Denmark.

Heron Mk. 2C XB-ZIP, ferried to the Banco Nacional de Mexico in October 1957 as G-APHW, was later re-engined with Lycomings and was forerunner of similar conversions to the Riley Heron made in Florida by Riley Aeronautics Corporation who improved payload and cruising speed still further by fitting turbo-supercharged Lycoming IO-540-G1A5 engines. Aircraft so modified were known in America as the Riley Heron (or Turbo-Liner), examples being Pony Express Airlines' N19D; Virgin Islands Airways' N782R; Wright Airlines' N506W to N510W; Puerto Rico International Airlines' N4789C and N12517 (part, in 1971, of an 18-strong Heron fleet); Apache Airlines' N12333; King Airlines' N14146; Royalair's CF-RAB (formerly TC-HER and N484R; later Fleet Airlines' N138FA, joining N844FA); and Shell's Venezuelan based YV-P-AEB. A similar conversion was also made at Baginton by Executive Air Engineering Ltd. in 1969 to the former East African D.C.A. machine 5Y-KVC.

A more ambitious venture was undertaken by Saunders Aircraft Ltd. of Dorval, Montreal, who replaced the four Gipsy Queens by two 715 e.s.h.p. United Aircraft PT-6A-27 propeller turbines, lengthened the fuselage by 8 ft. 6 in. to accommodate 24 passengers and enlarged the fin and rudder. Their first conversion was the former B.J.S.M. Heron 2B XG603 which made its first flight at Dorval as CF-YBM-X on 28 May 1969. Design responsibility was undertaken in Britain by Aviation Traders (Engineering) Ltd. and on 4 November 1968 two

Riley Heron N19D (Lycoming engines) of Pony Express Airlines was formerly G-AOXZ and Bahamas Airways VP-BAN. It later served with Trans-Isle Airways. (*Aviation Photo News*)

CF-XOK, the 24 passenger ST-27 conversion of the former Queen's Flight Heron XM295 (two PT-6A-27 propeller turbines), at Southend during European demonstrations in June 1971. (*Tony Leigh*)

former Queen's Flight aircraft XH375 and XM295 arrived at their Southend base with Class B markings G41-1-68 and G41-2-68, the former leaving for Saunders on 9 February 1969 as CF-YAP. The latter, temporarily OY-DHE, left on 23 May as CF-XOK and subsequently became the second ST-27. Early in 1972 the R.A.F.'s penultimate Heron, XR391, and the Kuwaiti 9K-BAA (once G-APXG) were ferried westbound via Prestwick as CF-CNT and 'NX respectively, also to become ST-27s.

In 1972, twenty years after its first flight, the prototype Heron was still in service with Cimber Air in Denmark as OY-DGS, and the 148th and final production machine, completed in 1963 and stored until 1966, was in service as Hawker Siddeley's Hatfield-based 'hack' G-AVTU.

SPECIFICATION

Manufacturers: The de Havilland Aircraft Co. Ltd., Hatfield Aerodrome, Herts. and Hawarden Aerodrome, Chester.

Power Plants: (Prototype) Four 250 h.p. de Havilland Gipsy Queen 30.

Four 330 h.p. de Havilland Gipsy Queen 30-3.

Four 340 h.p. de Havilland Gipsy Queen 30-4.

(All production marks).

Four 250 h.p. de Havilland Gipsy Queen 30 Mk. 2.

(XB-ZIP) Four 340 h.p. Lycoming GSO-480-B1A6.

(ST-27) Two 715 e.s.h.p. United Aircraft PT-6A-27.

Dimensions: Span 71 ft. 6 in. Length 48 ft. 6 in. Height 15 ft. 7 in. Wing area 499 sq. ft.

	Mks. 1 and 2	Mks. 1B, 2B, 2C	Mks. 2D, 2E, 3 and 4
Tare weight	7,960 lb.	7,985 lb.	8,150 lb.
All-up weight	13,000 lb.*	13,000 lb.†	13,500 lb.
Cruising speed	160 m.p.h.	165 m.p.h.	183 m.p.h.
Initial climb	1,200 ft./min.	1,060 ft./min.	1,140 ft./min.
Ceiling	18,500 ft.	18,500 ft.	18,500 ft.
Range	805 miles	805 miles	915 miles

* Prototype 12,500 lb. † Heron 2C 13,150 lb.

Production: (a) Hatfield-built Heron 1s

One prototype and six production aircraft: (c/n 10903) G-ALZL; (14001) ZK-AYV; (14002) 'LN-PSG; (14003) PP-SLF; (14004) PP-SLG; (14005) LN-SUD; (14006) G-AMUK.

(b) Chester-built Heron 1s

Forty-five aircraft including 14 British registered and the following 'for export: (c/n 14008) F-BGOH; (14010) F-BGOI; (14011) ZK-BBM; (14012) ZK-BBN; (14013) F-BGOJ; (14014) PK-GHA; (14015) PK-GHB; (14016) PK-GHC; (14018) PK-GHD; (14019) CX-AOR; (14020) PK-GHE; (14021) F-BGXU; (14022) PK-GHG; (14023) PK-GHH; (14025) CX-AOS; (14026) PK-GHI; (14027) PK-GHK; (14028) PK-GHL; (14029) PK-GHM; (14030) PK-GHN; (14031) PK-GHO; (14032) PK-GHP; (14033) ZK-BBO; (14038) F-OANR; (14039) F-OANS; (14040) F-OAPM; (14041) F-OAPN; (14042) F-OAPO; (14045) CX-AOU; (14046) CX-AOV.

184

(c) Chester-built Heron 2s

The Hatfield-built prototype, G-AMTS, followed by 97 production machines, many British registered and the following for export or the R.A.F.: (c/n 14050) SA-R5; (14051) ZS-DIG; (14054) LN-NPI; (14055) GGG; (14056) TC-HAK; (14057) TC-HAN; (14058) XG603; (14059) XH375; (14060) TC-HAT; (14061) TC-HER; (14063) TC-HIZ; (14064) TC-HAS; (14065) VT-DHD; (14066) TC-HUN; (14067) VT-DHE; (14068) VT-DHF; (14069) VT-DHG; (14070) VT-DHH; (14071) VT-DHI; (14072) VR-NAQ; (14073) VT-DHK; (14075) VT-DHJ; (14076) VR-NAV; (14077) VR-NAW; (14078) ZS-DLO; (14079) CR-IAA; (14083) VR-NCB; (14084) CR-IAB; (14085) S.A.A.F. 120; (14086) VR-NCC; (14087) S.A.A.F. 121; (14088) VP-BAP; (14090) VR-NCD; (14091) VR-NCE; (14092) VR-NCF; (14093) LN-SUF; (14103) LN-BDS; (14105) Iraq 393; (14106) Iraq RF-5; (14108) Luftwaffe CA+001; (14110) VP-KVC; (14111) VH-ASH; (14113) EC-ANJ; (14114) I-BKET; (14115) EC-ANX; (14116) EC-ANY; (14117) EC-ANZ; (14119) N3999A; (14120) EC-AOA; (14121) EC-AOB; (14122) EC-AOC; (14123) EC-AOF; (14124) Luftwaffe CA+002; (14126) Jordan H.105; (14127) Jordan H.106; (14129) XM295; (14130) XM296; (14131) YV-P-AEB; (14133) 9G-AAA; (14134) 9G-AAB; (14135) Ceylon CR801; (14136) Ceylon CR802; (14138) Ceylon CR803; (14139) CR804; (14141) XR391; (14142) Ghana 501; (14144) Malaysian Air Force FM1054; (14145) Malaysian FM1055; (14146) 5N-ABH; (14147) OY-AFO.

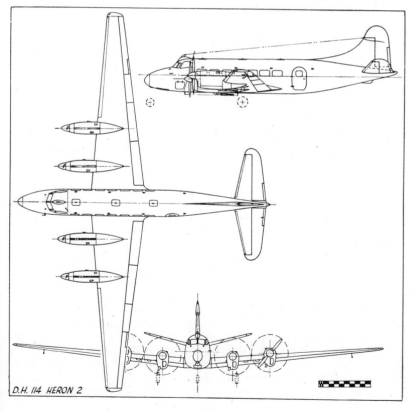

D.H. 114 HERON 2

185

A Chipmunk 21 of Air Service Training Ltd., flying near Hamble in 1952

De Havilland D.H.C.1 Chipmunk

This low-wing trainer, intended as a Tiger Moth replacement, was the first aircraft wholly designed and built by de Havilland Aircraft of Canada Ltd. and was of stressed skin construction with fabric covered flying surfaces, powered by a Gipsy Major 1C and seating instructor and pupil in tandem under a sliding canopy. There was no doubting its parentage since the rear fuselage and tail unit were almost perfect metal replicas of the Mosquito and the prototype, CF-DIO-X, flew for the first time at Toronto on 22 May 1946 piloted by W. P. I. Fillingham, chief production test pilot of the Hatfield company.

Pressure of U.S. military contracts brought Canadian Chipmunk production temporarily to an end at the 157th aircraft (sixty more were delivered to the R.C.A.F. in 1956) but the 10th and 11th were shipped to Hatfield and there equipped with British radio, blind flying panels and Gipsy Major 10 engines. Registered G-AJVD and G-AKDN, they went to Boscombe Down for Service trials in November 1948, in which month the prototype also arrived to become G-AKEV. After minor undercarriage and elevator modifications the type was adopted as the new standard R.A.F. and R.A.F.V.R. ab initio trainer under designation Chipmunk T. Mk. 10. Large scale production, begun at Hatfield, was later transferred to Chester and the appearance of the first British-built aircraft, WB549, at the 1949 S.B.A.C. Show led to additional orders from 14 foreign air forces.

One other Canadian machine was imported, erected at Witney and put into instructional use by Loxham's Flying Services Ltd. at Squires Gate as G-AKCS in November 1947 but the firm closed and in 1950 it was sold to the New South Wales Aero Club as VH-AFR. The trials aircraft 'VD and 'DN were handed over to the London Aeroplane Club at Panshanger, where they gave yeoman service for eight years and in the latter machine J. N. Somers averaged 139 m.p.h. to win the Osram Cup in the 1956 National Air Races at Yeadon. For a number of years no

British-built aircraft were diverted to civil usage, but the one hundredth production machine, G-ALWB, became de Havilland's T. Mk. 10 demonstrator. It was often raced by W. P. I. Fillingham, who won the 1951 Goodyear Trophy Race at 142 m.p.h.

Essentially an expensive precision instrument for the perfection of all branches of practical airmanship, it appealed neither financially to the clubs nor sociably to the private owner with the result that, at that time, in civil form as the Chipmunk 21, it was used only by the Ministry of Transport and Civil Aviation which maintained G-AMMA and G-ANWB at Southend for licence testing duties, and by Air Service Training Ltd. which, from 1952, operated a fleet of six, G-AMUC to 'UH, at Hamble. Three others, G-AMLC, G-ANAG and 'OW, appeared in 1954, but were purely for delivery to Australia, Japan and South America respectively, and Chipmunk production ceased in 1955 at the one thousand and fourteenth aircraft. Modifications were few, the chief in 1952, when spinning characteristics were improved by fitting a wide chord rudder cut away at the bottom to allow maximum elevator movement.

The Turbo Chipmunk G-ATTS with Rover TP-90 gas turbine engine flying past at the Farnborough S.B.A.C. Show, September 1966. (*W. L. Lewis*)

Large numbers of Service Chipmunk T.Mk.10s were put up for civilian disposal in 1956 following the closure of all Reserve Schools and the switch to all-jet instruction, many being acquired by clubs and private owners eager for modern equipment at secondhand prices. They appeared all over the country with roughly daubed ferrying marks but unfortunately failed to meet A.R.B. airworthiness requirements, the fuel venting system particularly being considered unsatisfactory. After certain essential modifications, the problem was overcome by creating a new mark, the Chipmunk 22, the 'prototype' being G-AOJO, formerly WB665, which gained its C. of A. on 25 May 1956. Conversion was by the Airways Aero Club which eventually owned 10 and supplied a similar number to the Lufthansa Pilot School at Bremen. Modifications were, however, costly so that many club and privately owned Chipmunks were completed very slowly but difficulties were eventually overcome and a number were sold in Finland, Australia and elsewhere to supplement a small number of civil machines exported new from Chester.

Further modification to Chipmunk 22A by fitting mainplanes with 12 gallon fuel tanks in place of the old T. Mk. 10 wings with 9 gallon tanks followed, the

Art Scholl's much modified Super Chipmunk N13Y at Hullavington for the World Aerobatic Championships, July 1970. (*J. M. G. Gradidge*)

first of this variant being the cleaned-up, red and white G-AOTM raced by P. G. Masefield in 1961 with a one-piece clear view canopy of the type also fitted to G-APOY when this was modernised in 1963. Real racing honours did not come to the 'Chippie' however until a Surrey and Kent Flying Club team comprising G-AOTG, G-APPK and 'TS fought its way to the final of the 1966 King's Cup Race, won by club instructor John Miles at Rochester at an average speed of 135 m.p.h.

Also in 1966 Hants and Sussex Aviation Ltd., Portsmouth, modified G-ATTS in collaboration with Mr. Vivian Bellamy, as flying test bed for the 118 s.h.p. Rover TP-90 gas turbine and flew it at that year's S.B.A.C. Show. Over 100 hr. of development flying were completed before it reverted to standard for sale in the U.S.A.

The final British variant, the Chipmunk 23, was a single seat crop spraying version devised by de Havillands in 1958 with built-in wing tip slots and raised pilot position as on the Piper Pawnee. The prototype, G-APMN, formerly WB680, crashed after a life of only five weeks while under evaluation by Fison-Airwork Ltd. but was replaced by G-APOS in time for demonstrations at the 1958 S.B.A.C. Show. Orders did not materialise but in the 1960s 'OS was acquired by Farm Aviation Ltd. of Rush Green, Herts., who later converted three more to Mk. 23 standard for their own use. VH-SJD, first of several similar Australian conversions known as the Sasin SA-29 Spraymaster, flew at Bankstown in 1965 where a year or so later Aerostructures Pty. Ltd. also flew their reworked Sundowner sport version, VH-CXZ, with metal wing covering, clear view canopy, wing tip tanks and 180 h.p. Lycoming O-360 engine. A similar conversion of standard Chipmunk G-AOSU, undertaken at Staverton 1968–70, was not completed but a Canadian-built machine, CF-CYT-X, c/n 192, converted for aerobatics by J. P. Huneault, first flew at Quebec on 16 July 1969 with a 210 h.p. Continental IO-360-C fuel injection flat six which imparted a maximum cruise speed of 160 m.p.h. and initial rate of climb of 2,400 ft./min.

An even more powerful Lycoming, the 260 h.p. GO-435, was fitted to Super Chipmunk N13Y as Art Scholl's United States entry in the 1968 World Aerobatic Championships at Magdeburg. He brought this machine to

Hullavington for the 1970 contest but with clipped, symmetrical section wings, no dihedral, retractable undercarriage and enlarged, angular rudder, it was scarcely recognisable as a Chipmunk.

SPECIFICATION

Manufacturers: The de Havilland Aircraft Co. Ltd., Hatfield Aerodrome, Herts. and Hawarden Aerodrome, Chester.

Power Plant: One 145 h.p. de Havilland Gipsy Major 10 Mk. 2.

Dimensions: Span, 34 ft. 4 in. Length, 25 ft. 8 in. Height, 7 ft. 1 in. Wing area, 172·5 sq. ft.

Weights: Tare weight, 1,425 lb. All-up weight, 2,014 lb.

Performance: Maximum speed, 138 m.p.h. Cruising speed, 119 m.p.h. Initial climb, 840 ft./min. Ceiling, 16,700 ft. Range, 280 miles.

Production:

One thousand and fourteen aircraft, the majority for foreign air forces and the R.A.F. (many civil later), but also the following civil exports: (c/n C1/0153) VH-AKW; (C1/0383) VH-AMB; (C1/0408) VR-TBE; (C1/0453) VH-ROG; (C1/0997) PK-AAO; (C1/0998) PK-AAP; (C1/0999) PK-AAQ; (C1/1001) PK-AAS; (C1/1002) PK-AAT; (C1/1014) PK-AAR.

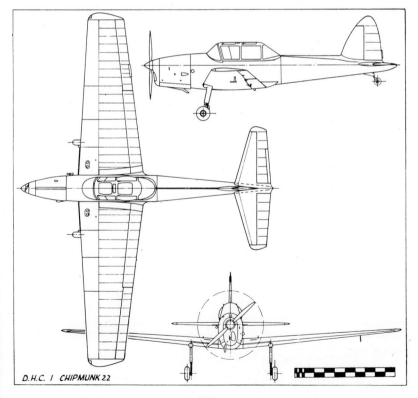

D.H.C. I CHIPMUNK 22

One of the two standard Desoutter Is operated by the British Red Cross Society in 1931.
(*Flight*)

Desoutter Monoplanes

Marcel Desoutter re-entered aviation in 1929 to form a company for manufacturing Frederick Koolhoven's Cirrus III powered F.K.41 three seat, high-wing monoplane under licence. It was of wooden construction with plywood fuselage and fabric covered wing, the second to be built, G-AAGC being flown to Croydon where, in April 1929, the Desoutter Aircraft Company's chief engineer, G. H. Handasyde, remodelled the engine cowlings and lowered the high-set tailplane to the thrust line. In this form it was exhibited without markings as the Desoutter Dolphin at the Olympia Aero Show, London, of July 1929 and a month later the third Dutch-built F.K.41 visited Croydon with these modifications. It was registered to Desoutters as G-AALI but carried these markings only for one flight from Rotterdam to Croydon on 28 August 1929 and returned to the Koolhoven factory next day for export to Australia where it reverted to the high-set tailplane and acquired a heavy duty undercarriage.

During the month of August 1933 G-AAGC, which had been sold to John Williamson* of the Air Taxi Co., Cape Town in 1930 as ZS-ADX, made a remarkable yet unpublicised search over primitive country for Carl Nauer, missing in Puss Moth CH-326 while attempting to lower the Cape–England record via the west coast of Africa. Accompanied by Carel Birkby, Williamson flew more than 5,000 miles from Cape Town via Mossamedes to Boma and back via Leopoldville, Broken Hill, Bulawayo and Johannesburg.

The name Dolphin was not used again, and the machines built at Croydon, in part of the former A.D.C. factory, were fitted with Hermes I engines and known simply as Desoutters. National Flying Services Ltd. placed a large order and eventually received 19, which in black and bright orange soon became a familiar sight at their nation-wide chain of flying clubs, where they were used for instruction, pleasure flights and taxi work. The fleet dwindled rapidly, 'NC crashed on

* Former owner of Boulton and Paul P.9 G-EASJ/G-UAAM/ZS-AAM.

Leith Hill; two were sold to AERA in Antwerp; 'PP went joyriding at the Cape piloted by J. R. King; and 'PY was sold to C. B. Wilson, specialist in press charters, who flew it 5,500 miles from Croydon to Baghdad and back in an airborne time of 62 hours in June 1930.

When N.F.S. ceased operations in 1933, G-AAPT was sold to Rollason Aircraft Services Ltd. at Croydon, where it was fitted with a Gipsy I engine and long exhaust pipe. G-AAPU was sold to Aero Research Ltd., Duxford, and 'NE toured with the National Aviation Day displays.

The first non-N.F.S. Desoutter, G-AATI, left Croydon for New Zealand on 9 February 1930, piloted by H. L. Piper and C. E. Kay, who, with skill and courage, completed their journey to Sydney on 23 March and shipped the Desoutter to New Zealand, where it continued in use for nearly 20 years. Its days ended with Blackmore's Air Services Ltd., taking tourists to view the volcanic wonders of Rotorua, where it was damaged beyond repair in a crash landing in 1950. There were only four other early Desoutters in British employ: G-AATF with Air Taxis Ltd., G-AAWT which Vivian Holman demonstrated for Cirrus Aero Engines Ltd. and two suitably decorated ambulances. These were G-ABMW and 'RN, owned by the British Red Cross Society, the first based at Croydon and the other at Woodford. When the Society closed its aviation department, they became taxi aircraft with Imperial Airways and the Lanchashire Aero Club respectively. The remaining three aircraft of the initial production run were sold for taxi work abroad, R-187 to Ferrand and Rayson Ltd., Buenos Aires; and ZK-ABX and 'BY to Bryant House Airways and G. A. Nicholls respectively in New Zealand. ZK-ABX was later mispainted as ZK-AVX and crashed at Rotorua in September 1931.

In 1930 an improved version, the Desoutter II, was built with a Gipsy III engine, redesigned ailerons and tail surfaces and fitted with wheel brakes. The prototype, G-AAZI, first flew in June 1930, after which the earlier model automatically became the Desoutter I. Of the seven British registered Desoutter IIs, the prototype alone saw lengthy service and became well known at Croydon in Rollason's blue. After a period with R. O. Shuttleworth at Old Warden in 1938, it was impressed and finally scrapped at Twinwood, Bedford, in July 1944.

The first imported Koolhoven F.K.41, G-AAGC, at Croydon after its delivery flight from Rotterdam on 22 April 1929.

Miss Winifred Spooner and Flg. Off. E. C. T. Edwards acquired G-ABCU for an attempt on the Cape record but after a nonstop flight to Rome, were forced down in the Mediterranean. The wreck was salvaged by the Italian Air Force, dumped at the Naples Aero Club and eventually shipped back to Heston where it was burned in May 1931. Personal Flying Services' G-ABFO was also lost and its pilot, Maj. I. N. C. Clarke, killed when it struck a hill near Stranraer in fog in May of the following year.

G-ABDZ, sold through University Motors Ltd. to Count J. de Wenckheim and delivered via Croydon–Cologne on 29 August 1930, visited Hatfield some years later in Hungarian marks as HA-AAA. G-ABIG went to the Northern Aviation Co. Ltd. for joyriding and charter work in Northern Rhodesia.

Desoutter production totalled 41, including twelve Mk. IIs, six of which were for export. EI-AAD spent a year in Ireland with Iona National Air Taxis before being flown from Heston to Sydney in six weeks by Australians H. Jenkins and

Desoutter I G-AAWT at Croydon in 1930 while in use by Cirrus Aero Engines Ltd. as testbed for their new 115 h.p. Hermes IV inverted engine.

Lt. Michael Hansen (in beret) at Mildenhall in October 1934 with his Australia Race Desoutter II OY-DOD. (*Aeroplane*)

192

Desoutter II G-ABDZ at Croydon in August 1930 before leaving for Cologne en route to Budapest where it was registered to Count J. de Wenckheim as H-MAAA.

H. Jeffrey as G-ABOM January–February 1932. It flew on the Tasmania–King Island service of Tasmanian Aerial Services as VH-UEE 'Miss Flinders' and was still airworthy as VH-BQE more than 30 years later, subsequently being preserved at Launceston Airport as VH-UEE. VH-UPR and 'PS were shipped to Hart Aircraft Services, Melbourne; ZK-ACA to Dominion Air Lines, New Zealand; VT-ADB to Rai Sahib Gopaldas, first Punjabi private owner. OY-DOD, delivered to Det Danske Luftfartselskab in June 1931, was flown in the Mildenhall–Sydney MacRobertson Race in October 1934 by Lt. Hansen who completed the course in a flying time of 129 hr. 47 min., came 7th in the handicap section and took-off to return to Denmark on 13 November.

The non-standard Desoutter Mk. Is were G-AAWT in which Cirrus Aero Engines Ltd. fitted their new inverted Hermes IV before it went to the Dutch East Indies in 1933; G-AANB re-engined with a Gipsy III by Warden Aviation Ltd.; and G-AAPZ which had been assembled by N.F.S. at Hanworth using components supplied by Desoutters. This was the Hermes II powered machine in which E. D. Ayre averaged 115·89 m.p.h. and almost won the 1933 King's Cup, being overtaken in the very last seconds. It was acquired by R. O. Shuttleworth in 1935 and later fitted with Mk. II tail surfaces modified windscreen and Menasco C-4 Pirate engine. It first flew in this condition at Woodley on 17 January 1938 in the hands of R. O. Shuttleworth and G. H. Miles and flew in camouflage at Barton during the 1939–45 war. After exhibition at Hendon in July 1951 it was stored at Old Warden until loaned to the Torbay Aircraft Museum in 1971.

Four Desoutters impressed in 1941 for communications work in the aircraft industry were G-AANB as HM508 for Helliwells Ltd., Walsall; G-AATK as HH980 for Saunders-Roe Ltd., Cowes; G-AAZI as HM507 for Percival Aircraft Ltd.; and G-ABMW as HM560 for Vickers-Armstrongs Ltd. A fifth, G-AAPS, was used by the R.A.F. at Turnhouse and Tempsford as ES946.

SPECIFICATION

Manufacturers: The Desoutter Aircraft Co. Ltd., Croydon Aerodrome, Surrey.
Power Plants: (Mk. I) One 105 h.p. Cirrus Hermes I.
                 One 115 h.p. Cirrus Hermes II.
             (Mk. II) One 120 h.p. de Havilland Gipsy III.

	Desoutter I	Desoutter II
Span	36 ft. 0 in.	35 ft. 8½ in.
Length	27 ft. 0 in.	26 ft. 0 in.
Height	7 ft. 0 in.	7 ft. 0 in.
Wing area	190 sq. ft.	183 sq. ft.
Tare weight	1,100 lb.	1,180 lb.
All-up weight	1,900 lb.	1,900 lb.
Maximum speed	115 m.p.h.	125 m.p.h.
Cruising speed	97 m.p.h.	100 m.p.h.
Initial climb	700 ft./min.	1,000 ft./min.
Ceiling	18,000 ft.	17,000 ft.
Range	400 miles	500 miles

Production: (a) Desoutter I

Twenty-eight aircraft comprising 24 British registered and the following for export: (c/n 7) R-187; (17) ZK-ABY; (21) ZK-ABX. Airframe c/n 26 was used in the reconstruction of (c/n 24) G-AANE.

(b) Desoutter II

Thirteen aircraft comprising six British registered and the following for export: (c/n 30) EI-AAD; (31) untraced; (35) VH-UPR; (36) ZK-ACA; (37) VH-UPS; (40) OY-DOD; (41) VT-ADB.

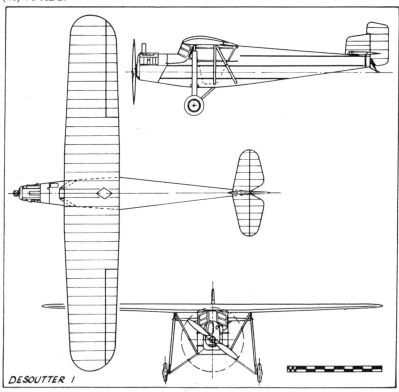

DESOUTTER I

G-APIA, first of two Edgar Percival E.P.9 aircraft delivered by air to Skyspread Ltd. in Australia, October 1957. (*R. A. Cole*)

Edgar Percival E.P.9

Edgar W. Percival, Australian-born designer, builder and pilot of the world famous Percival Gull series, re-entered the British aircraft industry in 1954. He formed Edgar Percival Aircraft Ltd. and established a factory at Stapleford Aerodrome, Essex, where he constructed a private-venture single engined aircraft which he had designed. This was known as the Edgar Percival E.P.9, based upon ideas he confirmed during a tour of New Zealand and Australia in 1953–54. He piloted the prototype, G-AOFU, on its maiden flight on 21 December 1955 and also did all the test and development flying for type certification, the addition of a dorsal fin being the only modification found necessary.

The unusual pod-and-boom fuselage configuration was dictated both by agricultural and aerodynamic considerations, permitting an extra deep front fuselage capable of carrying a ton of fertiliser in a special hopper, discharging through a 20 in. square hole in the floor. Pilot and one passenger sat high in the front with the perfect view so necessary for low-level flying and the cabin accommodated four more passengers, or three stretcher cases with an attendant, or a variety of rural loads, the side and rear clam-shell doors being large enough to take standard wool and straw bales, 45 gallon oil drums or small livestock.

By November 1956 some 20 production aircraft had been completed or were in an advanced stage of construction, several being sold in the Commonwealth and one to the French concern S.A. Fenwick. Edgar Percival also demonstrated an E.P.9 to the Army Air Corps at Middle Wallop and at Sandhurst as a result of which an order was received for two E.P.9s which were delivered to the Army Air Corps in military marks.

The majority of E.P.9s demonstrated their remarkable versatility while operating overseas in British civil markings. In March 1957 the third production aircraft, G-AOZY, was delivered to the German concern Ernst Lund K.G. for spraying fruit crops, insecticide from the 170 gallon tank being distributed through orifices in underwing booms to spray a swathe 90 ft. wide at 100 m.p.h. It was destroyed in a flying accident while spraying near Wunsdorf a couple of months later and was replaced by the seventh production aircraft, G-APBF, which in May 1957 had completed a demonstration tour of Sweden.

The next aircraft, G-APAD, which left the works in April 1957, was fitted with four seats in the cabin, crated and shipped to Australia, where it was demonstrated for six weeks by B. J. Snook. Following this tour, orders were received for four E.P.9s, which all completed the 14,000 mile delivery flight to Australia without incident. First of these, G-APBR, originally shown at the Paris Aero Show in June 1957 was acquired, together with G-APFY, by Super Spread Aviation (Pty.) Ltd. of Melbourne. Carrying miscellaneous freight, including a racing car engine in each, they were flown out by Messrs. Miller and Tadgell in September 1957. A month later, the second pair, the all red G-APIA and 'IB, left Croydon piloted by Messrs. Oates and Whiteman en route to Skyspread Ltd. of Sydney. Three others, G-APCR, 'CS and 'CT, left Croydon in September 1957 on delivery to Bahamas Helicopters (U.K.) Ltd. for light freighting and communications duties in connection with the oil drilling contract in Libya. British domestic use of the E.P.9 was confined to two aircraft, mainly because of import restrictions on American engines for installation in British-owned machines. The prototype, acquired by L. Marmol of Air Ads Ltd., Stapleford, in June 1957 was employed intensively in its primary role as a crop sprayer and G-APLP, was temporarily employed for a similar purpose by the Bembridge, I.O.W. firm, Crop Culture (Aerial) Ltd.

As well as aircraft delivered abroad in British marks, six initially registered overseas were ZK-BDP sent to New Zealand in May 1957 for agricultural work with the Manawatu A.T.D. Co. Ltd. (crashed at Palmerston North on 19 February 1958); G-43-2 shipped to Canada in the following July for N.W. Industries Ltd., Edmonton, Alberta (flown on floats as CF-NWI); G-43-1 shipped to Proctor Rural Services and registered in Australia as VH-PRS (later VH-BOG, crashed at Glen Innes, N.S.W. 10 April 1962); ZS-CHZ which left Croydon on 28 December 1957 flown by B. J. Snook on delivery to Lush Products (Pty.) Ltd. in South Africa; F-BIEG for Fenwick Aviation, Toussus in April 1958; and VH-TCA supplied to the Tasmanian Aero Club in the same month.

G-AOZO appeared at most major air displays during 1957, and in April 1958 was flown to Ostersund, Sweden, by L. Marmol for demonstration on skis to the

XM819, second of two Edgar Percival E.P.9s supplied to the British Army for evaluation in March 1958. (*K. M. Elliott*)

The second Skyspread E.P.9, VH-FBZ, formerly G-APIB, re-engined in Australia with a 375 h.p. Armstrong Siddeley Cheetah 10 radial.

military authorities. Later in that year Edgar Percival, who owned 80 per cent of the equity of Edgar Percival Aircraft Ltd., was approached with an offer by Samlesbury Engineering Ltd. and decided to sell his shareholding to them, together with his rights to the design for the United States, Canada and Mexico, of which he was the sole owner. Included in the sale were G-AOZO, G-APLP, and 20 E.P.9s in process of manufacture—five completely assembled, five ready for assembly and the remainder completed in component form. These were transferred to Squires Gate where the company, renamed the Lancashire Aircraft Co. Ltd., completed G-APWX and 'WZ with 295 h.p. Lycoming engines and three bladed airscrews under the revised designation Lancashire Prospector E.P.9. Sales drives included demonstrations by G-AOZO and G-APWX at Vienna in March 1960, and an African tour by 'WX flown by the Earl of Bective.

Early in 1960 production was transferred to Samlesbury where five more Prospectors were erected, including VH-SSR for Super Spread Aviation Pty. Ltd. Production ceased at the 47th airframe, completed as G-ARDG with a 375 h.p. Armstrong Siddeley Cheetah 10 radial. This was the sole factory-built Prospector Series 2 although Skyspread's VH-FBZ had been so converted at Sydney in 1959. Last Prospector to fly was G-47-1, later G-ARLE, which was sent to Stansted in July 1961 along with one remaining unfinished airframe (c/n 45), G-APWX and G-ARDG, en route to a permanent base at Lympne where they were joined by G-AOZO and G-APWZ.

The Army evaluation E.P.9s, XM797 and XM819, were eventually declared surplus and flew from Middle Wallop to Staverton on 26 October 1961 for civilianisation by Steels (Aviation) Ltd. as G-ARTU and 'TV. At the Biggin Air Fair in May 1963 G-APXW was presented as a freighter and 'WX as a six seater, in which form it ended its days as Skyways' hack and joyrider until sold in the U.S.A. in 1968.

SPECIFICATION

Manufacturers: Edgar Percival Aircraft Ltd., Stapleford Aerodrome, Essex (up to airframe c/n 41). The remainder by the Lancashire Aircraft Co. Ltd., Squires Gate and Samlesbury Aerodromes, Lancs.

Power Plants: (E.P.9)   One 270 h.p. Lycoming GO-480-B1.B.
(Prospector) One 295 h.p. Lycoming GO-480-G1.A6.
One 375 h.p. Armstrong Siddeley Cheetah 10.

Dimensions: Span, 43 ft. 6 in. Length, 29 ft. 6 in. Height, 8 ft. 9 in. Wing area, 227·6 sq. ft.

| | E.P.9 | | Prospector | |
	Normal	Agricultural	Normal	Agricultural
Tare weight	2,010 lb.	2,010 lb.	2,072 lb.	2,072 lb.
All-up weight	3,550 lb.	4,140 lb.	3,700 lb.	4,320 lb.
Maximum speed	146 m.p.h.	144 m.p.h.	146 m.p.h.	144 m.p.h.
Cruising speed	128 m.p.h.	120 m.p.h.	128 m.p.h.	126 m.p.h.
Initial climb	1,120 ft./min.	960 ft./min.	960 ft./min.	600 ft./min.
Ceiling	17,500 ft.	—	14,000 ft.	—
Range	580 miles	—	580 miles	—

Production: (a) Stapleford E.P.9s

Twenty-one aircraft comprising 13 registered in Britain and the following for the R.A.F. or export: (c/n 22) ZK-BDP; (30) G-43-2/CF-NWI; (31) G-43-1/VH-PRS; (36) ZS-CHZ; (37) F-BIEG; (38) XM797, later G-ARTU; (39) XM819, later G-ARTV; (40) VH-TCA.

(b) Squires Gate and Samlesbury Prospectors

Seven aircraft comprising five British registered, one unfinished airframe (c/n 45), and (46) VH-SSR.

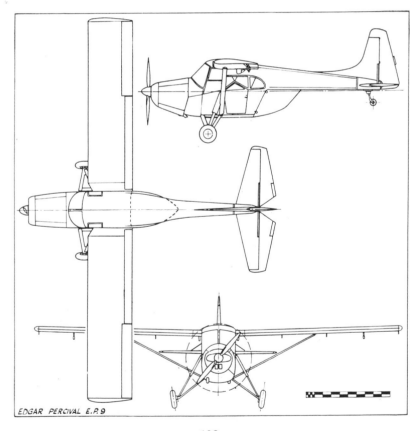

EDGAR PERCIVAL E.P.9

198

One of Col. G. L. P. Henderson's Fairey IIIC aircraft on skis in Sweden, 1920.
(*Fairey Aviation Co. Ltd.*)

Fairey III to IIIF

The remarkable series of Fairey III variants which spanned two decades stemmed from the two experimental two seat patrol seaplanes built by the Fairey Company in 1917. These bore constructor's numbers F.127 and F.128, and in the easy manner of the period became known as the Fairey F.127 and Fairey F.128 respectively, their Admiralty serial numbers N9 and N10 being used as an alternative nomenclature. The F.127, intended for shipboard operation, was a sesquiplane powered by a 190 h.p. Rolls-Royce Falcon I water-cooled engine, and after trials at Hamble and the Isle of Grain, carried out early catapult trials on H.M.S. *Slinger*. In 1919 it was repurchased from the Admiralty by the manufacturers and demilitarised as a civil aircraft with the temporary marking K-103, subsequently flying as Fairey III G-EAAJ. It was modified with equal span wings and Maori engine, and commencing on 3 May, Sidney Pickles made a few flights in it from Blackfriars to the Thanet towns, landings being made in and around the Medway estuary to deliver the *Evening News*.

In May 1920 this veteran was sold to the Norwegian Navy who disposed of it to a coal mining company at Svalbard in August 1927. It was never used and after storage at Gardermoen was acquired by A.S. Norsk Flyveselskap of Bergen but during a test flight by pilot Bjarne Nielson on 12 June 1928, was written off when it struck driftwood following a forced landing on the River Vorma.

The fuselage and tail unit of the second experimental aeroplane, the Fairey F.128, N10, were identical with those of the F.127 but it had equal span folding wings, Fairey patent camber gear, a larger fin, a 260 h.p. Maori engine and side radiators. A more formal designation—Fairey III—was then bestowed upon it, but at the end of 1917 it became a landplane with the radiator placed in the conventional position behind the airscrew. In this form it was known as the Fairey IIIA, and in 1919 was bought back by the makers to become a civil aeroplane, G-EALQ. Later it was modified as a single seat seaplane for entry in the Schneider Trophy Race held at Bournemouth on 10 September 1919. The wing span was reduced from 46 to 28 ft. and a 450 h.p. Napier Lion installed with side radiators, the designation reverting once more to Fairey III. Piloted by Lt. Col. Vincent Nicholl, D.S.O., 'LQ was the only entry to return to moorings under its own power but fog eventually caused the event to be declared void. A year later, on 17 September 1920, the same pilot arrived at Martlesham flying the same machine greatly modified for the Air Ministry's commercial amphibian competition. Standard 46 ft. folding wings had been replaced, a cockpit for two passengers side by side was provided behind the pilot and manually retractable, narrow track wheels were fitted between the floats. Although it performed creditably, making slow speed runs at 47·25 m.p.h. and completing various sea trials at Felixstowe, no prize was awarded owing to its failure to take off after the 24 hours mooring test on 26–27 September. Its useful life came to an end in 1922 after a period on communications duties between Hamble and the Isle of Grain.

Fifty Fairey IIIA naval floatplanes, powered by 260 h.p. Sunbeam Maori engines, built in 1918, saw little service and were put up for disposal. One of these, N2876, was acquired by the Navarro Aviation Company as G-EADZ but proposals to use it as a landplane for joyriding came to nought. Lt. Col. G. L. P. Henderson then converted it to Fairey IIIC standard under a new registration, G-EAMY, by fitting a 360 h.p. Rolls-Royce Eagle VIII engine before shipment to Sweden in company with the second prototype Fairey IIIC, G-EAPV, formerly N2255. The latter made three trans-Baltic proving flights between Stockholm and Helsinki with passengers and newspapers during the summer of 1920, afterwards doing pleasure flying for the P.O. Flygkompani at Barkaby. Both machines operated on skis during the winter and were modified to carry a passenger beside the pilot and four others in the rear cockpit. Unfortunately 'MY crashed in an inaccessible forest of 50 ft. trees due to the breakage of a rudder control cable.

A Fairey IIIC, N9256, was taken from the production line in 1919, fitted with sliding cockpit canopies and extra tanks and shipped to Newfoundland in March 1920 as G-EARS for a nonstop transatlantic flight. The attempt was never made and the aircraft remained in its crate until shipped to Montreal for erection by Canadian Vickers, becoming G-CYCF for the Halifax–Winnipeg leg of a joint Civil Operations Branch/Canadian Air Force attempt to win the William Dennis £5,000 prize for the first Halifax–Victoria flight. During tests at Montreal in September 1920 'CF would not take-off from the St. Lawrence with full fuel load, nevertheless Sqn. Ldr. B. Hobbs started from Halifax on 7 October with Wg. Cdr.

The famous Fairey III N9/K-103/G-EAAJ moored at Eidsvold in 1928 as N-20 and still wearing the Norwegian flag, souvenir of its naval service. (*Ole G. Nordbø*)

The Fairey III amphibian taxying at Martlesham during the Air Ministry Competitions, September 1920. (*Flight Photo 893*)

R. Leckie as passenger but the flight ended in a forced landing a few hours later near St. John, New Brunswick, the aircraft being seriously damaged. It was then shipped back to Faireys at Hamble where it flew again as G-EARS with standard cockpits in June 1921 before sale abroad by the Aircraft Disposal Co. Ltd.

In June 1922 a Fairey IIIC from the same batch was civilianised in India by the makers as G-EBDI for the Calcutta–Vancouver section of Major W. T. Blake's proposed World Flight and on 19 August 1922, piloted by Capt. Norman Macmillan and carrying cameraman Geoffrey Malins, it became the first seaplane to take off from the Hooghly, course being set for Akyab in Burma. An air lock in the fuel system caused a forced landing in a gale near the island of Lukhidia Char in the Bay of Bengal, and eventually 'DI turned turtle with a waterlogged float. Its crew were rescued after six gruelling days afloat on the wreckage, which sank following an attempt to tow it to Chittagong.

The Fairey IIID powered by a 450 h.p. Napier Lion engine and fitted with redesigned fuselage and tail unit had a much improved performance and was in production for the R.A.F. and Fleet Air Arm from 1920 until 1925. One machine, G-EBKE, powered by a 360 h.p. Rolls-Royce Eagle IX, was built to the order of Real Daylight Balata Estates Ltd. for ambulance duties in British Guiana with the rear fuselage decking fitted with portholes and hinging upwards in two sections to admit a stretcher case. After acceptance trials at Hamble in October

The so-called 'Atlantic IIIC' G-CYCF, formerly G-EARS, at Canadian Vickers' yard, Montreal on 27 September 1920. (*via K. M. Molson*)

201

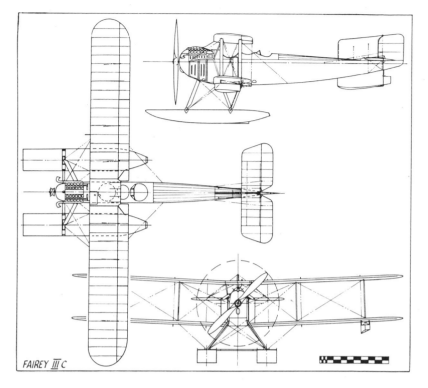

FAIREY III C

1924, it was shipped to Georgetown, where Capt. G. N. Trace flew it regularly for some years, to and from the mining areas 200 miles up-river.

The tropics also claimed the only other British civil Fairey IIID. In December 1926 the North Sea Aerial and General Transport Co. Ltd. inaugurated a mail and passenger service along the Nile between Khartoum and Kisumu with the D.H.50J seaplane G-EBOP 'Pelican'. After only a few flights it struck floating wreckage when taking off, sank and became a total loss. The Air Council thereupon loaned the company a Lion engined Fairey IIID, S1076, converted into a four seater as G-EBPZ at Aboukir. Its first service ex Khartoum was flown by Capt. Boyle on 8 February 1927 and it was in this aircraft that the Director of Civil Aviation, Sir Sefton Brancker, and two other passengers were marooned on Lake Victoria a few weeks later when altitude and midday heat combined to make take off impossible. On 13 March 1927 the IIID's undercarriage failed after four unsuccessful take-off attempts and it sank in Lake Victoria, later to be damaged beyond repair during salvage operations.

By this time the IIID had been replaced in the R.A.F. by the three seat Fairey IIIF. Thus in September 1928 the manufacturers commissioned a standard IIIF, G-AABY, as a civil demonstrator which figured largely in the proceedings at Heston during the Olympia Aero Show of July 1929. On 30 July 1930 it was flown to Brussels by C. R. McMullin, demonstrated to the Belgian Air Force and later flown to Tatoi, Athens, via Vienna and Belgrade, arriving on 1 August. During similar demonstration to the Greeks, it was towed to Phaleron Bay and fitted with floats and at a later date the performance was repeated for the military authorities in China, where it met with an accident. In September 1934 'BY reappeared as an entry in the handicap section of the MacRobertson Race to Australia and was rebuilt at North Weald. Starting from Mildenhall on 20 October 1934 piloted by Flg. Off. C. G. Davies and Lt. Com. C. N. Hill, it suffered many vicissitudes, landed south of Paris for fuel and again in Cyprus with minor troubles and eventually retired from the race. It reached Australia under its own power and eked out the remainder of its useful life in the New Guinea goldfields.

Last civil specimens of a noble line were two Fairey IIIFs, G-AASK and 'TT, fitted with Jaguar VIC air-cooled radials which were used by the Air Survey Co. Ltd. for mapping the Sudan, 'SK completing its delivery flight to Juba on 23 January 1930. The second IIIF, 'TT, also flown out, left Croydon on 9 February 1930 piloted by R. C. Kemp who made the distance in easy stages, arriving at Juba on 22 February 1930. Although 'TT crashed in October 1930, 'SK had a long and useful career and became an important aeroplane in the annals of aerial photography until withdrawn from use at the end of 1934.

Sole example of a British civil Fairey IIIF with Lion engine, G-AABY at Mildenhall prior to the race to Australia 1934.

The first of two special Jaguar engined Fairey IIIF survey aircraft.

SPECIFICATION

Manufacturers: The Fairey Aviation Co. Ltd., Hayes, Middlesex, and Hamble Aerodrome, near Southampton, Hants.

Power Plants: (Fairey III) One 450 h.p. Napier Lion.
(Fairey IIIA) One 260 h.p. Sunbeam Maori II.
(Fairey IIIC) One 360 h.p. Rolls-Royce Eagle VIII.
(Fairey IIID) One 360 h.p. Rolls-Royce Eagle IX.
One 450 h.p. Napier Lion.
(Fairey IIIF) One 450 h.p. Napier Lion XI civil.
One 490 h.p. Armstrong Siddeley Jaguar VIC.

	Fairey III (Lion) Seaplane	Fairey III Amphibian	Fairey IIIA Landplane
Span	28 ft. 0 in.	46 ft. $1\frac{1}{4}$ in.	46 ft. 2 in.
Length	—	34 ft. 4 in.	31 ft. 0 in.
Height	—	12 ft. 0 in.	10 ft. 8 in.
Wing area	—	488 sq. ft.	476 sq. ft.
Tare weight	—	3,771 lb.	2,532 lb. ⎫(1)
All-up weight	5,000 lb.	5,250 lb.	3,698 lb. ⎬
Maximum speed	—	118 m.p.h.	109·5 m.p.h.
Cruising speed	—	82 m.p.h.	—
Initial climb	—	—	750 ft./min.
Ceiling	—	—	15,000 ft.
Duration	—	—	$4\frac{1}{2}$ hours

	Fairey IIIC Seaplane	Fairey IIID (Lion) Seaplane	Fairey IIIF (Lion) Landplane
Span	46 ft. $1\frac{1}{4}$ in.	46 ft. $1\frac{1}{4}$ in.	45 ft. 9 in.
Length	36 ft. 0 in.	36 ft. 0 in.	36 ft. $8\frac{5}{8}$ in.
Height	12 ft. $1\frac{3}{4}$ in.	13 ft. 0 in.	14 ft. $2\frac{3}{8}$ in.
Wing area	476 sq. ft.	500 sq. ft.	438·5 sq. ft.
Tare weight	3,549 lb. ⎫(2)	—	3,890 lb. ⎫(3)
All-up weight	5,050 lb. ⎬	—	5,900 lb. ⎬
Maximum speed	101 m.p.h.	117 m.p.h.	120 m.p.h.
Cruising speed	—	—	—
Initial climb	600 ft./min.	800 ft./min.	900 ft./min.
Ceiling	9,100 ft.	19,500 ft.	—
Range/Duration	5 hours	530 miles	400 miles

(1) G-EADZ, (2) G-EARS, (3) G-AABY, take-off, Australia Race.

Civil conversions:

Two Fairey III G-EAAJ and 'LQ; one Fairey IIIA G-EADZ not proceeded with; four Fairey IIIC G-EAMY, 'PV, 'RS and G-EBDI; two Fairey IIID G-EBKE and 'PZ; one Fairey IIIF (Lion) G-AABY; two Fairey IIIF (Jaguar) G-AASK and 'TT.

The first production Wicko G.M.1 at Whitchurch, September 1938, after delivery to the Bristol and Wessex Aeroplane Club. (*W. K. Kilsby*)

Foster Wikner Wicko

The Wicko two seat, high-wing monoplane originated in 1936 as an attempt by Geoffrey N. Wikner to produce a cabin aircraft at approximately half the price of contemporary light aeroplanes. Mr. Wikner, an Australian, built his first aircraft in 1931. This was the Wicko Sports Monoplane, a single seat, high-wing cabin type powered by a 60 h.p. Anzani air-cooled radial. Two years later he built an open cockpit variant known as the Wicko Lion, and both aeroplanes bore a remarkable resemblance to the later British-built Wickos. His third aircraft, the Wicko Wizard VH-UPW, reminiscent of the D.H.71 Tiger Moth, was a two seat, low-wing monoplane.

Encouraged by the success of his first designs, Mr. Wikner left Australia for England in May 1934 with well defined ideas on the construction of cheap and efficient aircraft. He enlisted the support of Messrs. V. Foster and J. F. Lusty and formed the Foster Wikner Aircraft Co. Ltd., construction commencing in a corner of Lusty's furniture factory in Colin Street, Bromley-by-Bow. Low initial cost was achieved by fitting a standard Ford V.8 water-cooled engine in place of the more costly aero engine. When fitted with a Pobjoy reduction gear, the Ford V.8 was known as the Wicko F power unit and gave 85 h.p. at 1,500 r.p.m., an aerodynamically clean nose being obtained by fitting a Gallay radiator under the fuselage. The latter was a simple plywood box with a two spar, fabric covered mainplane of Clark YH section attached directly to the top longerons and braced by parallel tubular steel struts. On completion in September 1936, the prototype, G-AENU, known as the Wicko F.W.1, was taken by road to Hillman's Aerodrome at Stapleford, Essex, where its designer completed the initial test flying.

Although the estimated performance was realised, the 450 lb. dead weight of the motor inevitably resulted in an excessive take-off run and poor rate of climb. The aircraft was consequently rebuilt as the Wicko F.W.2 with the Ford V.8 and its attendant plumbing replaced by a 90 h.p. Cirrus Minor I engine. Tare weight was cut from 1,170 lb. to 938 lb., but the price went up from £425 to £650. The Wicko appeared at several flying meetings during the 1937 season, and in the same year the firm took over premises at Eastleigh. There the second aircraft

The unflapped prototype Wicko F.W.1 G-AENU showing the underslung radiator and pointed nose. (*Flight Photo 13636S*)

G-AEZZ was completed in time for the King's Cup Race of 10 September 1937, in which it was flown, and forced landed north of Skegness, by Flt. Lt. H. R. A. Edwards. In common with all subsequent Wickos, 'ZZ had a plywood covered wing, split trailing edge flaps and full dual control, but was specially fitted with a 150 h.p. Cirrus Major engine for the race. With this motor it was allotted the type number F.W.3. A Gipsy Major engine was installed in 1938, after which the aeroplane was sold to the Cardiff Aeroplane Club.

Nine production aircraft were built, all powered by Gipsy Majors and designated G.M.1, one of which went to New Zealand as ZK-AGN, those built to British order being G-AFAZ for the Bristol and Wessex Aeroplane Club, G-AFJB for the Midland Aero Club and G-AFKU for F. L. Dean of Cardiff. G-AFKS, 'KK and 'VK were demonstrators, the first of which, operated by Nash Aircraft Sales Ltd., was at one time experimentally fitted with skis. Two others had also been completed before the outbreak of war brought an enterprise of great merit to a premature halt. Rolls-Royce Ltd., Hucknall, bought G-AFJB for communications duties in 1939 but like most Wickos it was eventually impressed into the R.A.F. with the Service type name Warferry.

ZK-AGN flew with the Hawkes Bay and Middle Districts Aero Clubs in New Zealand until it too was impressed and served with the R.N.Z.A.F. as NZ580 until it crashed near Johnsonville on 26 November 1942. In Britain only G-AFJB and the 11th and last aircraft, HM497, survived military service. Both reverted to the designer in October 1945 and 'JB was then sold to Miss Philippa Bennett, late of A.T.A., who used it for charter work at Eastleigh. The unused tenth aircraft, stored during the war, was unearthed in 1946 and cannibalised to service HM497, which became G-AGPE to join Miss Bennett's charter activities. Although 'JB forced landed in bad visibility on Walney Island on 8 September 1946, fell over an 80 ft. cliff and landed upside down in the sea, the occupants were unhurt and the aircraft survived to pass into the hands of M. J. Dible at Denham in 1955. In 1965, its flying days over, G-AFJB was recamouflaged as DR613, its wartime impressment condition, by Messrs. K. Woolley and R. F. Bass for preservation at Berkeswell Forge, Warwickshire.

SPECIFICATION

Manufacturers: The Foster Wikner Aircraft Co. Ltd., Southampton Airport, Eastleigh, Hants.

Power Plants: (F.W.1) One 85 h.p. Wicko F modified Ford V.8.
(F.W.2) One 90 h.p. Blackburn Cirrus Minor I.
(F.W.3) One 150 h.p. Blackburn Cirrus Major.
(G.M.1) One 130 h.p. de Havilland Gipsy Major.

Dimensions: Span, 34 ft. 6 in. Length, 23 ft. 3 in. Height, 6 ft. 7 in. Wing area, 153 sq. ft.

	Wicko F.W.1	Wicko F.W.2	Wicko G.M.1
Tare weight	1,170 lb.	938 lb.	1,255 lb.
All-up weight	1,700 lb.	1,500 lb.	2,000 lb.
Maximum speed	115 m.p.h.	120 m.p.h.	140 m.p.h.
Cruising speed	98·5 m.p.h.	103 m.p.h.	120 m.p.h.
Initial climb	—	—	800 ft./min.
Ceiling	10,000 ft.	15,000 ft.	20,000 ft.
Range	250 miles	450 miles	480 miles

Production:

Eleven aircraft comprising eight British registered at manufacture and three others: (c/n 3) ZK-AGN; (10) unfinished airframe; (11) HM497 (later G-AGPE).

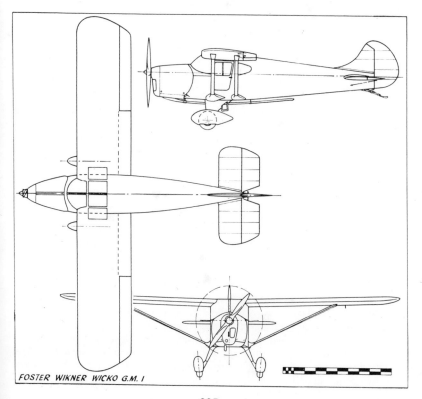

FOSTER WIKNER WICKO G.M. I

G-ABUZ, prototype ST-4, flying in 1932 with experimental bulged fin. (*Flight*)

General Aircraft Monospars ST-3 to ST-12

In the 1920s the cantilever monoplane was not only viewed with a superstitious distrust dating back to the 1914–18 war but most attempts at construction, using contemporary materials, had resulted in excessive structural weight. A typical example was the metal covered wing of the three engined Inflexible monoplane built 1925–27 by Wm. Beardmore and Co. Ltd. under licence from the German Rohrbach concern. H. J. Stieger, a Swiss-born engineer working on the Inflexible, brought new thinking to the subject of strength/weight ratios of cantilever wings and invented the 'Monospar' system of construction. As the name suggested, his immensely strong metal wing was built round a single duralumin Warren girder spar capable of resisting bending and braced by a pyramidal system of tie rods to take the torsional loads. An experimental wing designated ST-1, fabric covered in the manner of all subsequent Monospar wings, was then built to Air Ministry order, exhibited at the Olympia Aero Show of July 1929 and later subjected to strength tests.

When Beardmore closed down its aviation interests, H. J. Stieger joined forces with F. F. Crocombe, Sqn. Ldr. Rollo de Haga Haig, A. E. L. Chorlton and C. W. Hayward to form the Monospar Wing Co. Ltd. A second Air Ministry order was then received, this time for the ST-2, a wing large enough for, and eventually flight tested on, the Ministry's Fokker F.VIIB/3m J7986. Work also proceeded on an experimental, twin engined, three seat, low-wing, cabin monoplane designated the Monospar ST-3. Like the Fokker wing, the ST-3 G-AARP was built at Brockworth by the Gloster Aircraft Co. Ltd. with the Gloster works designation S.S.1 (Stieger Salmson One) and first flew in 1931. Monospar principles also featured in the fuselage construction, the main frames being anchored to a diamond section Warren girder keel member. Power was supplied by two 50 h.p. Salmson radials with which the aircraft completed more than 1,000 hours of manufacturer's and Martlesham trials. These included officially observed terminal velocity dives up to 178 m.p.h. and single engined take-offs. Much of the development flying was done by Sqn. Ldr. de Haga Haig, who gave a convincing and almost aerobatic demonstration to members of both Houses of Parliament at Hanworth in June 1931.

Success with the ST-3 prompted the formation of a new company, General Aircraft Ltd., to exploit the Monospar company's patents, one of the former Aircraft Disposal Company hangars at Croydon being acquired for the construction of a Pobjoy powered four seat ST-4. The prototype, G-ABUZ, made its first flight in May 1932, piloted by the company's test pilot H. M. Schofield, its many novel features including engine starting from the cockpit by cable-operated manual inertia starters. A great deal of its unusually high performance was obtained by a reduction in interference drag, achieved by thinning the mainplane inboard of the engines, the top main spar member continuing through the cabin. The latter was of mixed dural and steel tube riveted construction, and the rear fuselage retained the Monospar features of the ST-3. Orders for five production aircraft G-ABVN to 'VS were placed during the construction of the prototype, and later in 1932 they were delivered to Portsmouth, Southsea and I.O.W. Aviation Ltd.; the Maharajah of Patiala; A. C. M. Jackaman, Heston; Capt. O. E. Armstrong, Baldonnel; and a Swiss customer respectively. Capt. Armstrong's ST-4 flew as EI-AAQ but returned to the United Kingdom as G-ABVS after a few months. G-ABVN, first flown on the Ryde ferry was privately owned at the outbreak of war but no trace of it was found until 1954 when its wingless fuselage came to light among derelict aircraft at Bankstown Aerodrome, Sydney.

A batch of 24 improved ST-4 Mk. IIs followed, externally identifiable by a nose landing light similar to that which had first been fitted experimentally to G-ABVP. Deliveries took place throughout 1933, commencing with G-ACCO for Geoffrey Ambler at Yeadon and including VT-ADW for the Jodhpur Flying Club; CH-356 for Jules Borvin; J-BBDA for flights between Osaka and Manchuria by the Japanese Asahi Newspaper Co.; SE-ADS for the Swedish polar pilot Gosta Andree; one unregistered for the Italian Government; and two for the Brazilian airline VASP.

The Duchess of Bedford's G-ACKT, the last ST-4 delivered in 1933, was short lived and Flt. Lt. Allen, personal pilot to the Duchess, was killed when it struck high tension cables in poor light and crashed 4 miles from base at Woburn Park.

The prototype ST-3 at the time of its first flight at Brockworth in 1931.

The prototype ST-6 G-ACGI with undercarriage retracted and showing the redesigned nacelles. (*Aeroplane*)

One of the batch, G-ACCP, first delivered to the Hon. A. E. Guinness, was later sold to the Cambridge Aero Club and in 1939 was flying a regular service between Barnstaple and Lundy Island in the colours of Lundy and Atlantic Coast Air Lines Ltd. Another, G-ACEW 'Inverness', purchased by Highland Airways Ltd., was flown by E. E. Fresson on the first Inverness–Kirkwall service on 8 May 1933. Two others, G-ACJE and 'JF, were operated by International Airlines Ltd., a newly formed company which inaugurated its Western Air Express between Croydon, Portsmouth, Southampton and Plymouth on 25 August 1933 but went out of business after a few weeks.

The sale of six ST-4 Mk. II aircraft direct to foreign buyers led to too optimistic a view of the order book and, in turn, to over-production, and several unsold machines stood in the hangar for two years. The last of these Niagara powered machines were acquired by Commercial Air Hire Ltd. in June 1935 and registered G-ADIK, 'JP and 'LM for charter work and occasional trips on the Inner Circle Air Line between Croydon and Heston. Their commercial lives ended a year later when two crashed and the survivor, 'JP, was sold to R. K. Dundas Ltd.

During 1933 technical development went on apace and resulted in the appearance of the ST-6. This was basically an ST-4 but had a manually retracted undercarriage, new engine cowlings and a redesigned nose contour giving enough cabin space to accommodate an occasional fifth passenger. It was the second British commercial aeroplane ever to fly with a retractable undercarriage, being antedated by only a few weeks by the Airspeed Courier, and the allotted markings G-ACGI were a fortuitous reminder of its designer's graduation from the City and Guilds (Engineering) College. With a top speed of nearly 140 m.p.h. it was a favourite in the 1933 King's Cup Race, in which, piloted by H. M. Schofield, it carried H. J. Stieger as passenger, but hopes were dashed when it ran out of fuel and retired. Only three other ST-6s existed, G-ACIC built with Pobjoy Niagaras for R. E. Gardner, and special conversions of G. H. Ambler's G-ACCO and R. G. Cazalet's G-ACHU. The prototype ended its peacetime career joyriding at Ipswich six years later; 'IC was similarly employed by the Romford Flying Club at Maylands; and 'HU was acquired by L. W. Hamp and based at Wolverhampton.

The Croydon factory closed down at the end of 1933 but in 1934 the company was reorganised financially and larger and better equipped factory premises were obtained at Hanworth. Here a fresh start was made with the construction of a developed Monospar, the General Aircraft ST-10 first flown as T-5, and later as G-ACTS. This was structurally similar to the earlier models but fuel was carried under the cabin floor and dual controls of the throw-over spectacle type were provided. The engines were the new 90 h.p. Pobjoy Niagaras which imparted a performance sufficiently impressive for H. M. Schofield to secure a runaway win in the King's Cup Race of 13–14 July 1934 at an average speed of 134·16 m.p.h. The design skill of H. J. Stieger, who rode as passenger, in giving a better streamline shape to the fuselage in spite of increasing its frontal area by 2 sq. ft., and in altering the fore-and-aft attitude of the machine in flight, gave an additional 10 m.p.h. which defeated the handicappers. A. C. M. Jackaman flying his ST-4 G-ABVP 'Peridot V' was eliminated in the heats after averaging 118 m.p.h. and Charles Gardner, who flew his brother's ST-6 G-ACIC into the semi-final at 131·5 m.p.h., suffering a similar fate.

Strangely, the remarkable ST-10 did not go into production, and the prototype passed into the hands of Portsmouth, Southsea and Isle of Wight Aviation Ltd., for service on the Ryde Ferry and the company's route to Heston. The only other, VH-UST, was destroyed in an air collision with Gipsy Moth VH-UFV over Mascot, Sydney, on 19 November 1939.

More success greeted the Gipsy Major powered variants, two examples of the retractable undercarriage ST-11 being built for Australia (VH-UAZ for the D.C.A. and VH-USN for Eastern Air Transport), and ten fixed undercarriage ST-12s, four of which appeared in British markings. The first, G-ADBN, went briefly to the well known Swiss pilot Robert Fretz at Altenrhein as HB-AIR in 1935 before going to Stockholm for a year with Peter and Niels Jensen. It then returned to become an air taxi with Air Dispatch Ltd., Cardiff and two others, G-ADDY and G-ADDZ, were flown during 1935–36 by racing motorist R. J. B. Seaman

The King's Cup winning ST-10 at Hatfield on the day of its victory, 14 July 1934.
(*Flight Photo 10591S*)

ST-12 G-ADBN flying near Hanworth prior to delivery to Sweden in 1935.
(*Flight Photo 11253S*)

VH-UAZ, first of the two retractable undercarriage ST-11s to be built, standing outside the works at Croydon, September 1934. (*Aeroplane*)

and the manufacturers as private and demonstration aircraft respectively. The fourth and last British ST-12, G-ADLL, was fitted with 145 h.p. Gipsy Major high compression engines to the special order of Owen G. E. Marshal Roberts of Hamble who flew a very good race for the 1935 King's Cup, coming 12th at 166·86 m.p.h. before taking the all-gold ST-12 on a world tour and going as far afield as California. It eventually returned, bedecked with the flags of countries visited, and continued in service with the same owner until impressed for war service with the other surviving ST-12, G-ADBN, and the ST-10, G-ACTS. They were all scrapped in 1943 and the sole memorial in Britain to the early pre-production Monospars in those days was the skeleton of the ST-4 G-ACJF, up-ended against the fuel pyramid at Heston until it was destroyed in the gale of 16 March 1947.

The six export ST-12s were VH-UTH and 'TK for New England Airways (the latter burned in a hangar fire at Mackay, on 1 July 1938); VH-UTM and 'TZ for the Monospar agents (the latter crashed at Alice Springs, N.T., on 6 September 1935); one ferried to the Ministerio Hacienda, Spain, as EC-W43; and F-AODV which went to France in 1935 and was still flying 20 years later.

VH-UTH also survived and on 22 August 1961 left Darwin to fly back to the land of its birth piloted by Dr. John Morris and Bruce Harrison. The 26 year old aircraft covered the 12,000 miles in a flying time of 120 hours with only minor unserviceabilities and arrived at Lympne on 30 November. It flew a little at Redhill and Biggin Hill but during storage at Panshanger, Croydon and Booker, gradually fell into disrepair and in 1968 its engineless airframe was handed over to the Newark Air Museum.

SPECIFICATION

Manufacturers: (ST-3)   The Gloster Aircraft Co. Ltd., Hucclecote Aerodrome, Gloucester.

(ST-4 and ST-6) General Aircraft Ltd., Croydon Aerodrome, Surrey.

(ST-10 to ST-12) General Aircraft Ltd., Hanworth Air Park, Feltham, Middlesex.

Power Plants: (ST-3) Two 50 h.p. British Salmson A.D.9.

(ST-4) Two 85 h.p. Pobjoy R.

(ST-6) Two 85 h.p. Pobjoy R.
          Two 90 h.p. Pobjoy Niagara I.

(ST-10) Two 90 h.p. Pobjoy Niagara I.

(ST-11) Two 130 h.p. de Havilland Gipsy Major.

(ST-12) Two 130 h.p. de Havilland Gipsy Major.

	ST-3	ST-4	ST-6	ST-10	ST-12
Span	38 ft. 0 in.	40 ft. 2 in.	40 ft. 2 in.	40 ft. 2 in.	40 ft. 2 in.
Length	21 ft. 11½ in.	26 ft. 4 in.	26 ft. 4 in.	26 ft. 4 in.	26 ft. 4 in.
Height	9 ft. 0in.	7 ft. 0 in.	7 ft. 0 in.	7 ft. 10 in.	7 ft. 10 in.
Wing area	183 sq. ft.	219 sq. ft.	219 sq. ft.	217 sq. ft.	217 sq. ft.
Tare weight	1,057 lb.	1,480 lb.	1,500 lb.	1,470 lb.	1,840 lb.
All-up weight	1,800 lb.	2,550 lb.	2,600 lb.	2,750 lb.	2,875 lb.
Maximum speed	110 m.p.h.	130 m.p.h.	135 m.p.h.	142 m.p.h.	158 m.p.h.
Cruising speed	95 m.p.h.	115 m.p.h.	120 m.p.h.	130 m.p.h.	142 m.p.h.
Initial climb	950 ft./min.	850 ft./min.	850 ft./min.	900 ft./min.	1,233 ft./min.
Ceiling	18,000 ft.	18,000 ft.	18,000 ft.	18,000 ft.	21,000 ft.
Range	—	540 miles	550 miles	585 miles	410 miles

Production: (a) ST-3
  One aircraft only: (c/n S.S.1) G-AARP.

(b) ST-4 Mk. I

Seven aircraft comprising six British registered and (c/n 7) VT-ADV for the Maharajah Sahib Baladin.

(c) ST-4 Mk. II

Twenty-two aircraft comprising 14 British registered and the following for export: (c/n 9) VT-ADW; (13) CH-356; (16) J-BBDA; (22) Italian Government; (23) SE-ADS; (24) PP-SPA 'VASP I', to T.A.I. do Brasil 9.43 as PP-LAE; (25) PP-SPB 'VASP II', to Empreza Nacional de Fotografia Aerea 12.45 as PP-MFD; (31) untraced.

(d) ST-6

Three aircraft only: (c/n 14) G-ACGI; (18) G-ACHU converted from a production ST-4 Mk. II; (20) G-ACIC.

(e) ST-10 and ST-11

Two ST-10 only: (c/n 32) G-ACTS; (34) VH-UST. Two ST-11 only: (c/n 33) VH-UAZ; (37) VH-USN.

(f) ST-12

Ten aircraft comprising four British registered and the following for export: (c/n 36) VH-UTH; (38) VH-UTK; (41) VH-UTM; (42) VH-UTZ; (43) EC-W43; (44) F-AODV.

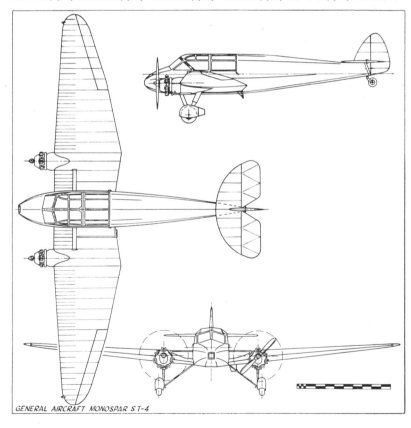

GENERAL AIRCRAFT MONOSPAR ST-4

214

J. W. Adamson's Monospar ST-25 Universal flying near Hanworth prior to delivery in May 1936.

General Aircraft Monospar ST-25

The year 1935 saw not only the Silver Jubilee of King George V but also H. J. Stieger's departure from General Aircraft Ltd. Thus Monospar development became the responsibility of F. F. Crocombe as chief designer, with D. L. Hollis Williams as chief engineer and E. C. Gordon England as managing director and at Hanworth on 19 June of that memorable year, their last basic design made its first public bow in the presence of Lady Shelmerdine, wife of the D.C.A. Substantially the same as an ST-10, it was fitted with a folding seat for an occasional fifth passenger. Additional cabin windows were therefore necessary and the radio receiver and homing device was standard fitment. To mark the 25th anniversary of the reign of King George V, type numbers 19–24 were omitted and the new aircraft received both the designation ST-25 and the type name Jubilee. The prototype, G-ADIV, in standard black and yellow and powered by two Niagara II engines, was sold to Radio Transmission Equipment Ltd. for the further development of its specialised radio but met a watery end in Wigtown Bay a year later. Unlike most small contemporary aircraft, the list price included all instruments, night flying and other primary equipment. The popularity of this idea was such that when production ceased in 1939, 57 had been delivered, all but 19 registered in the United Kingdom, these including a number ferried abroad.

During 1935–36 Air Commerce Ltd. of Heston employed the fifth ST-25 Jubilee, G-ADLT, on various domestic and continental charters, while at Hanworth G-ADPI became the executive aircraft of the Mobiloil concern under the ownership of Hubert Holliday. The largest 'fleet', three strong, was acquired in 1935 by Crilly Airways Ltd., their aircraft G-ADPK–'PM, being -based at Braunstone, Leicester, for the company's scheduled internal air services to Sywell,

Tollerton, Mousehold, Speke and Whitchurch. When the firm was absorbed by British Airways in 1936, two of the ST-25s were sold to Portsmouth, Southsea and Isle of Wight Aviation Ltd. to join the ST-10. The third, 'PM, went to Stanley Park, Blackpool, to end its days in private ownership with H. S. Ashworth. The last Jubilee model, G-AEAT, was acquired by Aerial Sites Ltd. of Hanworth, stripped of furnishings and flown at night for advertising purposes with underwing neon tubes fed from banks of accumulators in the cabin.

In 1936 an improved version known as the ST-25 De Luxe made its appearance, powered by Niagara III engines with Rotax electric starters. Controllable trimming tabs were used for the first time on rudder and elevators, and directional stability was improved by increasing the fin area and thereby endowing the new model with its sole recognition feature. The prototype, G-AEDY, made its appearance in March 1936, and once more the R.T.E. homing receiver was standard

The prototype Monospar ST-25 Jubilee on the occasion of its public presentation, 19 June 1935. (*Flight Photo 14891*)

K8307, first of two ST-25 Jubilee aircraft supplied to the R.A.E. Farnborough for radio equipment trials in April 1936 (*Flight Photo 12552S*)

G-AEDY, sole example of the Monospar ST-25 De Luxe, showing the enlarged fin. (*Flight*)

The ST-10 prototype, G-ACTS, in use at Hanworth in 1936 as test vehicle for the twin tail unit built for the ST-25 Universals. (*via R. P. Howard*)

fitment. Although publicity was given to five basic versions, in fact only one other, the ambulance, was built. The first aircraft of this type, G-AEGX, which had an all-white colour scheme, Red Cross insignia and the appropriate name 'Florence Nightingale', was provided with a large door in the starboard side to admit a stretcher, with a seat for an attendant situated to port. The De Luxe and the ambulance made their first public appearances together at the Hatfield S.B.A.C. Show of 28 June 1936, thereafter becoming well known at demonstrations in all parts of the British Isles.

Sales abroad included VH-UUV, 'VJ and 'VM to Australia where 'UV was named 'Boyana' for service with Adelaide Airways Ltd. and 'VM was re-exported to the Canterbury Aero Club in New Zealand, becoming ZK-AET. Two also went to Rumania, YR-NIC for Prince Nicholas and an ambulance, YR-SAN for the Ministria Aeronautica Romana S.A.

The autumn of 1936 found the design staff still not satisfied with directional control with one engine stopped and the ST-10 G-ACTS was used as a test vehicle for a new twin rudder tail unit. Tests with this and G-AEDY, similarly modified, proved eminently satisfactory and no further modifications took place, 26 twin finned production models, designated ST-25 Universal, being sold. Two of the first to appear, standard model G-AESS and ambulance G-AEVN, were exhibited at the garden party of the Royal Aeronautical Society at Heathrow on 9 May 1937. Several other ambulance versions were built, all for export.

Models embodying the large starboard hatch but without ambulance interiors were known as Freighters, five of which were handed over to Eastern Canada Air Lines Ltd. by Lady Shelmerdine at a naming ceremony at Hanworth on 28 September 1936 as under:

CF-BAH	'City of Halifax'	CF-BAK	'City of Charlottetown'
CF-BAI	'City of Moncton'	CF-BAO	'City of Sydney'
CF-BAJ	'City of Saint John'		

This pioneering attempt to start a Moncton, New Brunswick-based airline in the bleak Maritime Provinces in winter without route licences, postal contracts or navigation aids, was foredoomed to failure and after only two months CF-BAJ was seriously damaged nosing-over in snow at Moncton on 2 February 1937; and on 4 March both CF-BAK and 'AO were wrecked during precautionary landings in deteriorating visibility and snow at Saint John N.B. and Windsor N.S. respectively.

Other ST-25 Universal exports were CF-AZW delivered to Maritime Airline Ltd., Saint John N.B., in June 1936; YR-NIO to Prince Nicholas of Rumania; ambulance G-AEYF to Zone Redningskorpset, Copenhagen as OY-DAZ; and two Freighters G-AFBM and 'BN to the Turkish Government for parachute training which left Hanworth on 2 October 1937, one with the ferry marking TC-TK4.

A standard ST-25 Jubilee G-ADWI was fitted experimentally with 90 h.p. Cirrus Minor 1 in-line engines in 1936 and flew as T-6 with the designation G.A.L.26. It was the first new type to fly after H. J. Stieger left the company and the last to employ his Monospar wing.

T42, the experimental ST-25 Universal with tricycle undercarriage, at Hanworth in 1937. It was acquired by the R.A.F. with modified gear in 1938 as N1531.

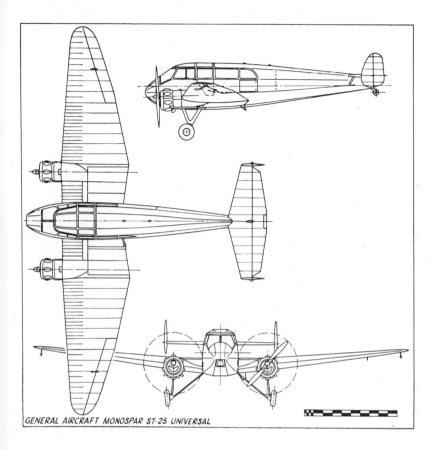

GENERAL AIRCRAFT MONOSPAR ST-25 UNIVERSAL

In 1937 the ST-25 Universal G-AEJB went to Aden to inaugurate the services of Arabian Airways, afterwards becoming the executive aircraft of a local firm. The Cinque Ports Flying Club at Lympne operated G-AEJV until the club's manager W. E. Davies and three passengers were killed when it crashed in 1938; Lord Londonderry visited all parts of Europe in his private Universal G-AEPG J. A. M. Henderson raced G-AEPA at the Lympne International Meeting of 28 August 1937; and G-AEGY went to Clifton Aerodrome, York, for use by J. W. Adamson, well known after the war as the operator of Oldstead Aircraft. A trek to the north was undertaken in 1938 by 'PA, which joined H. S. Ashworth's G-ADPM at Stanley Park Aerodrome, Blackpool; by 'DY, christened 'Alcaeus', which went into service with Utility Airways Ltd., Hooton; and by G-ADYN acquired by Williams and Co. of Squires Gate. All three ended their days giving pleasure flights.

When war was declared in 1939, all Monospars fell quickly into the impressment net, but none survived to fly again in peace, although one Universal and one Jubilee later succeeded in functioning for the first time as British civil aeroplanes. CF-BAH, Eastern Canada Air Lines' 'City of Halifax', delivered in 1936, returned in December 1941 to become G-AGDN and in camouflage with yellow undersides, flew throughout the war on communications work for General Aircraft Ltd. It passed to Geoffrey Alington in 1945 but was later scrapped. The other, an equally unusual Monospar, was overhauled by Southern Aircraft (Gatwick) Ltd. in 1946, sold to E. I. H. Ward and later to N. L. Hayman of Fairoaks as G-AHBK. Second of two Jubilees delivered to the R.A.E. for radio development in 1936, it started life as K8308, and although for 10 years a military aeroplane, it flew in civil colours for only twelve months. Following a successful forced landing on Barnsley Wold, near Cirencester, in June 1947, the owner had the misfortune to collide with the only large tree in the vicinity and 'BK was consequently destroyed by fire, its engineless skeleton remaining a feature of the countryside for several years afterwards.

Last airworthy Monospar in the world was ZK-AFF, purchased at Hanworth as G-AEJW by Piet van Asch in July 1936 and used for aerial photography by New Zealand Aerial Mapping Ltd. until 1943. It was then stored at Bridge Pa aerodrome, Hastings, until overhauled and flown again on 11 April 1968. It left for Blenheim in South Island on the same day to attend the 40th Anniversary celebrations of the Marlborough Aero Club and was still immaculately airworthy in 1972.

SPECIFICATION

Manufacturers: General Aircraft Ltd., Hanworth Air Park, Feltham, Middlesex.
Power Plants: (Jubilee)   Two 90 h.p. Pobjoy Niagara II.
              (De Luxe) Two 95 h.p. Pobjoy Niagara III.
              (Universal) Two 95 h.p. Pobjoy Niagara III.
              (G.A.L.26) Two 90 h.p. Blackburn Cirrus Minor 1.
Dimensions: Span, 40 ft. 2 in. Height, 7 ft. 10 in. Wing Area, 217 sq. ft.

	Jubilee	De Luxe	Universal
Length	26 ft. 4 in.	26 ft. 4 in.	25 ft. 4 in.
Tare weight	1,680 lb.	1,758 lb.	1,818 lb.
All-up weight	2,875 lb.	2,875 lb.	2,875 lb.
Maximum speed	142 m.p.h.	135 m.p.h.	131 m.p.h.
Cruising speed	130 m.p.h.	123 m.p.h.	115 m.p.h.
Initial climb	800 ft./min.	700 ft./min.	710 ft./min.
Ceiling	16,000 ft.	12,000 ft.	15,300 ft.
Range	585 miles	496 miles	419 miles

Production: (a) Monospar ST-25 Jubilee
Thirty aircraft, mainly British registered but the following for export or the R.A.F.: (c/n 48) VH-UUV; (60) VH-UVJ; (65) YR-NIC; (66) YR-SAN; (68) untraced; (69) VH-UVM/ZK-AET/NZ584; (70) K8307; (71) K8308.

(b) Monospar ST-25 Universal
Twenty-nine aircraft, mainly British registered but the following for export or the R.A.F.: (c/n 74) L4671; (76) L4672; (81) CF-AZW; (85) YR-NIO; (86) CF-BAO; (89) CF-BAH; (90) CF-BAI; (91) CF-BAJ; (92) CF-BAK; also one tricycle experimental, T42, c/n not traced, later to the R.A.F. as N1531.

D. L. Hollis Williams flying the first production G.A.L.42 Cygnet II near Hanworth in July 1939.

General Aircraft G.A.L.42 Cygnet

The stressed skin, all-metal, two seat Cygnet side-by-side cabin tourer, initially known as the Cygnet Minor, was designed and built in 1936 by C. R. Chronander and J. I. Waddington, who formed C. W. Aircraft for the purpose. It was an attempt to create a light aircraft more durable and more easily produced in quantity than the usual strut and longeron, plywood and fabric types, and was the first light aeroplane built in the United Kingdom with metal skin on both wing and fuselage. The prototype, G-AEMA, powered by a 90 h.p. Cirrus Minor and built in the firm's workshop at Slough, was noteworthy for its extremely slim semi-monocoque rear fuselage and single, metal-clad fin and unbalanced rudder. It was also fitted with a split trailing edge flap running right under the fuselage, a tailwheel undercarriage and front windscreen panels which raked sharply forward to encourage rapid removal of raindrops by the slipstream.

The prototype was completed in time for exhibition without markings at the Royal Aeronautical Society's Garden Party at Heathrow on 9 May 1937, and made its first flight at Hanworth later in the month. Public demonstration then took place at the Hatfield S.B.A.C. Show of 27–28 June with A. G. M. Wynne Eaton at the controls. Modifications, involving the installation of a Gipsy Major and a rounded windscreen and the removal of the under-fuselage section of the flap, were then carried out in readiness for the King's Cup Race of 10–11 September. Redesignated Cygnet Major, it was flown round the Hatfield–Dublin–Hatfield course by Charles Hughesdon and came 13th at an average speed of 141·3 m.p.h. Flight trials of the revised version continued at Hanworth until March 1938, when the C. W. concern foundered. No orders had been received, and additionally a great deal of money had gone into the twin engined C. W. Swan project, for which a provisional registration G-AERO had been reserved but not taken up. The Cygnet designs were then sold to General Aircraft Ltd. and the prototype appeared at the R.Ae.S. Garden Party at Heathrow on 8 May 1938 bearing the name of its new proprietors. Again piloted by Hughesdon, it competed for the King's Cup, but at an advanced stage of the race and when a very probable winner, retired at Barton through oil starvation.

General Aircraft Ltd. fitted G-AEMA with twin fins and rudders during the autumn of 1938 to obtain increased elevator efficiency, the first of a series of modifications leading to an aircraft which would be viceless and easy to fly. Logically therefore a tricycle undercarriage was added early in 1939, after which the firm went ahead with the construction of the G.A.L.42 Cygnet II prototype G-AFVR. Structurally identical with Chronander and Waddington's much modified prototype, it incorporated the final features necessary for its designed role. It was powered by a 150 h.p. Cirrus Major and the wings were given increased dihedral, large sliding doors were fitted, and the strutted main undercarriage legs of the rebuilt prototype gave place to cantilever General Aircraft oleo units. It was now virtually a foolproof aeroplane, as D. L. Hollis Williams, the chief engineer and test pilot demonstrated convincingly and amusingly in the few brief months before the outbreak of war. Plans for the construction of an extremely large batch of Cygnet IIs were perforce abandoned, but ten production machines are said to have been completed 1939–41 including three for South America which remain untraced although two of the British registered Cygnets eventually went there.

The original C.W. Cygnet with raked windscreen. (*Flight*)

The Cygnet prototype at Hanworth in November 1938 in the interim condition with twin fins and rudders and tail wheel undercarriage.

222

Unlike those of production aircraft, the main undercarriage legs of the prototype in tricycle form were strutted.

One aircraft, G-AGAX, non-standard with straight instead of curved runners for the sliding roof, served the makers as a camouflaged civil communications machine throughout the war, while five others and the G.A.L.45 Owlet G-AGBK, were impressed to familiarise R.A.F. Boston squadrons with tricycle techniques.

In 1946, when the four survivors came up for civilian disposal at Kemble, 'VR, G-AGAU and 'BN were sold to Newman Aircraft Ltd. at Panshanger and 'BA to R. L. Whyham at Squires Gate. Although the last languished untouched until melted down by scrap metal dealers at Kirby, Lancs., 11 years later, the others became well known private aeroplanes. G-AGAU was re-engined with a Gipsy Major, afterwards being flown without success by Flt. Lt. R. Harding in the Folkestone Trophy Race at Lympne on 30 August 1947 and by James Mollison in the Norton Griffiths Race at Elmdon on 29 August 1949. It was at that time owned by Denham Air Services and carried the name 'Dumbo'. During a bombing competition at a Cowes air display in 1949, 'Dumbo' was flown into the ground and destroyed, the wreck afterwards being sold to a local scrap dealer. The wartime communications machine G-AGAX, successively owned by Sir Mark Norman and L. V. D. Scorah, was reconditioned at Ringway in 1955, only to meet an untimely end on the Yorkshire Moors soon afterwards.

T. F. W. Gunton, who had owned and flown his West Raynham-based Cygnet II prototype, G-AFVR, for more than 20 years, was killed when it crashed at Woerth, Northern France on 26 August 1969, leaving Biggin Hill's highly polished G-AGBN as the sole remaining example.

SPECIFICATION

Manufacturers: (C.W. Cygnet)   C. W. Aircraft, Slough Trading Estate, Slough, Bucks.

(G.A.L.42 Cygnet II)   General Aircraft Ltd., Hanworth Air Park, Feltham, Middlesex.

Power Plants: (Cygnet Minor) One 90 h.p. Blackburn Cirrus Minor.

(Cygnet Major) One 130 h.p. de Havilland Gipsy Major.

(Cygnet II)   One 150 h.p. Blackburn Cirrus Major II.

223

	Cygnet Minor	Cygnet Major	Cygnet II
Span	34 ft. 6 in.	34 ft. 6 in.	34 ft. 6in.
Length	24 ft. 3 in.	24 ft. 3 in.	23 ft. 3 in.
Height	6 ft. 0 in.	5 ft. 10 in.	7 ft. 0 in.
Wing area	165 sq. ft.	165 sq. ft.	179 sq. ft.
Tare weight	1,050 lb.	1,200 lb.	1,475 lb.
All-up weight	1,600 lb.	1,900 lb.	2,200 lb.
Maximum speed	125 m.p.h.	150 m.p.h.	135 m.p.h.
Cruising speed	105 m.p.h.	128 m.p.h.	115 m.p.h.
Initial climb	750 ft./min.	850 ft./min.	800 ft./min.
Ceiling	20,000 ft.	17,000 ft.	14,000 ft.
Range	500 miles	650 miles	445 miles

Production:
Ten aircraft, seven British registered and three (c/n 111, 115 and 116) untraced.

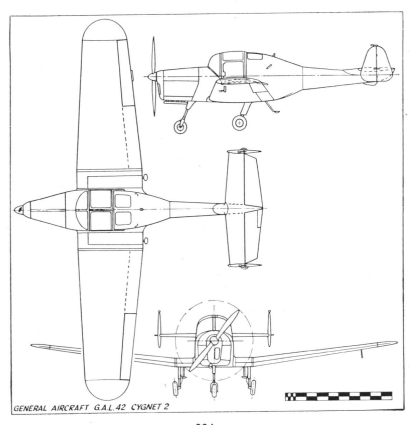

GENERAL AIRCRAFT G.A.L.42 CYGNET 2

The Handley Page O/10 G-EASY. All civil 'Handleys' carried their conversion number on the extreme end of the fuselage. (*Handley Page Ltd.*)

Handley Page O/400

Although the distinction of being G-EAAA, the first British civil aeroplane, fell to a de Havilland D.H.9, that of receiving the first British Certificate of Airworthiness went to a Handley Page O/400. Over 400 of these twin Eagle VIII engined heavy bombers were built during 1918–19 and, retrospectively allotted type number H.P.12, made useful interim civil transports. In spite of their 100 ft. wing span and general immensity, they were structurally simple, the fuselage being a braced box girder of spruce longerons and cross struts, fabric covered, as were the wooden, folding wings.

C. of A. No. 1 was issued on 1 May 1919 to Handley Page O/400 F5414, which on that day became G-EAAF in company with three others, certificated as G-EAAE, 'AG and 'AW respectively. They were the first of 43 civil conversions, six of which were exported to the Chinese Government. Thirty-four were of British registry, all were owned by the manufacturers, and none ever suffered a change of ownership. Scheduled services and charter flying were undertaken by a subsidiary concern, Handley Page Transport Ltd. under the management of George Woods Humphery with Lt. Col. W. F. Sholto Douglas (later Lord Douglas of Kirtleside, chairman of B.E.A.) as chief pilot. He carried 10 passengers from Cricklewood to Alexandra Park Aerodrome, Manchester, on 1 May 1919 in D8350, not yet painted up as G-EAAE and on 5 May took-off to fly north with a 1,500 lb. load of newspapers, which were dropped over Carlisle, Dundee, Aberdeen (where Major Ord-Lees, the 'Guardian Angel' demonstrator, left the aircraft by parachute) and Montrose, a landing being made at Edinburgh. The passengers sat in hastily fitted wicker chairs in a draughty fuselage without soundproofing or windows, only the fortunate, but helmeted, occupants of the front and rear gunners' cockpits being able to view the countryside.

Within three months, however, Handley Page Ltd. produced the O/7 version, fitted with a properly appointed and windowed cabin for 14 passengers, the chief external recognition features being the engine nacelles, lengthened rearward to accommodate the fuel tanks which had been banished from the fuselage to increase cabin space. Nacelle struts were modified and the oil tanks were repositioned under the upper mainplane. The first O/7 bore no markings other than its conversion number HP-1, but was, in fact, K-162. The first civil O/400 was also converted to O/7 standard and repainted as G-5414 flew to Amsterdam for exhibition at the First Air Traffic Exhibition of August 1919. A fortnight later, on 2 September, the company inaugurated its thrice weekly service to Paris when Major E. L. Foot carried seven passengers in G-EAAE from Cricklewood to Le Bourget.

On 22 September the first Brussels service was flown by G-5417 (actually G-EAAW), Customs clearance taking place at Hounslow Heath until Customs were made available at Cricklewood on 18 February 1920, but all services were transferred to Croydon from 27 May 1921. The 'Handleys' were equipped with the first Marconi airborne R/T and their pilots—G. P. Olley, A. S. Wilcockson, F. Dismore, H. H. Perry, W. Rogers, R. Vaughan-Fowler, W. L. Hope, H. G. Brackley, E. L. Foot and R. H. McIntosh—laid true foundations for the air transport industry of today. In the first nine months nearly 1,500 passengers and 40 tons of freight were carried in nine O/400s and the H.P.O/7 G-EAAF. The

One of the seven seat Handley Page O/400s converted for use on the Continental services. These had short nacelles and only four windows.

original four O/400s were then joined by 'KF, 'KG and 'LX–'LZ, nil-hour machines built by the Metropolitan Wagon Co. Ltd. at Birmingham in the previous year. All had furnished cabins for seven passengers but the fuel tanks remained in the fuselage. Short nacelles were therefore retained, and they continued to be styled O/400s.

A windowless O/400, G-EAKE with seats for 10 passengers, was flown to Copenhagen in August 1919 by two R.A.F. officers, one of whom was the Norwegian Tryggve Gran, who became famous on 30 July 1914 by making the first flight across the North Sea, in a Blériot monoplane. His O/400 was unlucky, suffering an accident near Lillisand, Norway on 6 September 1919, followed by a rebuild and a second crash, this time beyond repair, near Stockholm in the following June. An equally unlucky giant was G-EAMC, the *Daily Telegraph* entry for the £10,000 *Daily Mail* prize for the first flight from Cairo to the Cape. With Maj. H. G. Brackley as pilot and Capt. Frederick Tymms navigating, the machine left Cricklewood on 25 January 1920, picked up the sponsor's corre-

The first Handley Page O/7, K-162/G-EAGN (conversion number HP-1), flagship of the Chinese Government's six-strong air mail fleet.

spondent Major C. C. Turner at Cairo on 20 February and set off southward. Five days later the flight ended 6 miles north of El Shereik, Sudan, G-EAMC being damaged beyond repair in a crosswind forced landing with jammed controls following severe tail flutter.

An awakening to the possibilities of air transport was at this time taking place overseas, China already possessing at least six Handley Page O/7s, the first of which, formerly K-162, first flew after erection at Pekin on 6 December 1919. A first experimental Tientsin–Pekin air mail service was flown in May 1920 but one aircraft, used for bombing rebels, caught fire in the air and crashed. Also in December 1919 a standard O/400, G-EAMD, was fitted with a long range tank on top of the fuselage and flown to Warsaw by E. D. C. Hearne on delivery to the Polish Government, and in the following year the Handley Page Indo Burmese Transport Co. Ltd. was formed to operate seven aircraft, commencing G-IAAA, in India (together with an eighth, G-IAAC, on behalf of an Indian rajah). A single O/7, G-EANV, was also flown in South Africa in 1920 by Maj. McIntyre who made advertising sorties around Cape Town with 'Commando Brandy' painted on wings and fuselage in large letters but the aircraft's own individual name was 'Pioneer'.

An unregistered example, HP-17, was damaged in a forced landing at Durango, near Bilbao, while en route to Lisbon but after repair was towed through the town by oxen and flown out of a larger field by R. H. McIntosh. Another, believed HP-29, was flown in the Argentine by C. E. Wilmot as demonstrator for the abortive Buenos Aires–Pernambuco air mail scheme.

The company's passenger and freight services were augmented in 1920 by the route to Amsterdam, and two further variants of the O/7 were devised. The first, known as the O/11, carried mixed traffic, two passengers in the bow cockpit, three in a cabin in the rear fuselage and freight in a large hold amidships. Three machines of this type, G-EASL–'SN, were in use until their Cs. of A. expired in March 1921 and it was in one of these that R. H. McIntosh inaugurated the company's internal service to Castle Bromwich on 22 December 1920. The freighters were joined later by a fleet of nine aircraft G-EASX, 'SY, 'TG–'TN, fitted for the carriage of 12 passengers and designated the O/10, all of which were in daily service between Croydon and the Continent by August 1920.

The *Daily Express* had earlier announced a prize of £10,000 for the first flight to India and back, one of the several entries being a special long range O/400 G-EASO, named 'Old Carthusian II', fitted with Napier Lions, and therefore unique. Although machine and crew, Maj. A. Stuart MacLaren and Capt. J. A. Barton, were in readiness at Croydon on 14 May 1920, strained relations with the Arabs compelled R.A.F. Middle East Command to forbid flights east of Cairo. The competition was therefore abandoned and G-EASO dismantled.

The end of 1920 was a black period for the embryo air transport industry and particularly for Handley Pages. On 14 December 1920, the O/7 G-EAMA was lost in a disastrous crash at Golders Green, in which the pilot Robert Bager and three others were killed after striking a tree on take off. By the end of the month, intense competition from government subsidised French airlines had compelled the abandonment of most British services. Handley Pages fought the inevitable until February 1921, when they too ceased operations, one of the O/10s flying the final service. Following a Government enquiry under the leadership of Lord Londonderry, then the Under Secretary of State for Air, operations were resumed on 21 March 1921, with a subsidised reduction in the Paris fares to the French level of six guineas single and £12 return. Freight did not bear a subsidy and in the following month the company's three O/11 freighters were scrapped.

The transfer of Handley Page operations to Croydon on 27 May 1921 saw the end of Cricklewood as an air terminal but it remained the maintenance base, necessitating daily positioning flights. Some difficulty was experienced in taking off from Croydon, with full load, and an aircraft was despatched to Martlesham for weighing, after which the all-up weight was reduced from 13,000 to 12,050 lb. by removing all wireless gear, limiting the passengers to 10 and the maximum fuel and oil load to 180 and 12 gallons respectively. Thereafter they gave no trouble but by 1922 the new Handley Page W8bs were coming into service, and Croydon

The Napier Lion engines of the India flight O/400 being run up at Cricklewood before departure to Croydon.

The Jupiter installation of G-EATK, with cowlings removed to show the disposition of the fuel tanks in the rear of the nacelle. (*Bristol Photo*)

saw the war-time veterans no more. Last to go to the breaker's yard was G-EATH, which, as late as May 1923, inaugurated a thrice-weekly route from Paris to Basle and Zürich. Although based at Le Bourget it occasionally came to Croydon on Saturday afternoons, and after maintenance left again on Monday mornings. In the following September it made its last flight, from Zürich to London in the day—surely no mean feat for an O/10. It was then picketed behind the hangars to fall into dereliction, a sad fate for the last of a worthy line.

During their service careers, two O/10s were the subject of interesting modifications. During the development of the new Handley Page W8 in 1920, interest in 'hands off' flight quickened to the point where an early automatic pilot, the Aveline Stabiliser, was invented. The prototype was fitted in G-EATN, and during the French Government's Competition in January 1921, was repeatedly flown 'hands off' by H. G. Brackley for periods of over an hour. On 8 January the device brought 'TN from Lympne to London through bad weather, but engine trouble caused a forced landing in a fog-free field at Gravesend. G-EATK was flown to Filton during the winter of 1921, where, in collaboration with the Bristol Aeroplane Co. Ltd., the Eagles were replaced by Jupiter radials in newly designed mountings. A net reduction of 900 lb. was thereby effected in the tare weight and G. P. Olley, who did the test flying, recorded an appreciable increase in rate of climb and top speed, but with the new Handley Page W8bs in the offing, the proposal to re-engine the whole fleet was shelved.

SPECIFICATION

Manufacturers: Handley Page Ltd., Cricklewood, London, N.W.2; The Metropolitan Wagon Co. Ltd., Birmingham; The Birmingham Carriage Co. Ltd., Birmingham.

Power Plants: Two 360 h.p. Rolls-Royce Eagle VIII.
Two 436 h.p. Bristol Jupiter IV.
Two 450 h.p. Napier Lion II.

Dimensions: Span, 100 ft. 0 in. Length, 62 ft. 10¼ in. Height, 22 ft. 0 in. Wing area, 1,648 sq. ft.

Weights: Tare weight (Eagle VIII), 8,326 lb. (Jupiter IV), 7,526 lb.

All-up weight (Eagle VIII), 12,050 lb. (Jupiter IV), 12,050 lb.

Performance: (Eagle VIII)   Maximum speed, 97·5 m.p.h. Ceiling, 8,500 ft. Duration 7½ hours.

(Jupiter IV)   Initial climb, 500 ft./min.

Civil conversions: Forty-three aircraft (conversion numbers HP-1 to HP-43):

(a) Handley Page O/400

Eighteen aircraft comprising sixteen British registered, including (HP-15) at first allotted to O/400 C9713 for conversion to Handley Page W4 prototype and two others: (HP-17) flown to Spain and back by R. H. McIntosh 1921; (HP-29) believed to the Argentine.

(b) Handley Page O/7

Twelve aircraft comprising five British registered and the following for export: (HP-2 to HP-6) China; (HP-8) G-IAAA*; (HP-9) G-IAAB*.

(c) Handley Page O/10

Ten British registered aircraft (HP-34 to HP-43) commencing G-EASX.

(d) Handley Page O/11

Three British registered aircraft (HP-30 to HP-33) commencing G-EASL.

* Markings later carried by D.H.9 aircraft.

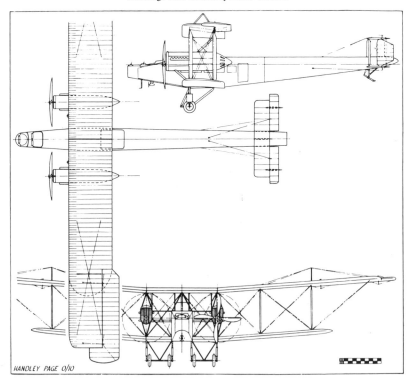

HANDLEY PAGE O/10

230

The prototype Handley Page W8 in its original competition form with fuel tanks in elongated nacelles.

Handley Page W8, W9 and W10

As soon as Handley Page Transport Ltd. was fairly launched with its fleet of converted O/400s, work began at Cricklewood on the construction of the firm's first purely civil transport. It accommodated two pilots in an open cockpit forward of a roomy, well glazed cabin for 15 passengers. Although embodying the well proven wood and fabric construction of its predecessors, it was cleaner aerodynamically, of lower structural weight and fitted with two Napier Lions, 450 h.p. units renowned for their unequalled power/weight ratio. First intimation of the existence of the prototype, G-EAPJ, was when news was released of its first flight at Cricklewood on 4 December 1919. It was then flown to Le Bourget for exhibition at the Paris Aero Show, 19 December 1919 to 4 January 1920.

It was obviously an outstanding aeroplane and on 4 May 1920 Capt. (later Professor, of Pterodactyl fame) G. R. T. Hill set up a British Class C.5 record by climbing the machine to 14,000 ft. while carrying a useful load of 3,690 lb. The exact designation of this important aeroplane is complex, being known during its lifetime as the Handley Page W8 with constructor's number W8-1. It also carried on the rear fuselage a factory number HP-15 in the series reserved for converted O/400s, reminder that it had started life as an earlier transport project, the experimental W4 rebuild of O/400 C9713, first flown by W. Sholto Douglas on 22 August 1919 and in later years retrospectively allotted type number H.P.18.

After exhibition at the Olympia Aero Show, London, in July 1920, it was flown to Martlesham by H. G. Brackley on 3 August for participation in the Air Ministry's heavy commercial aeroplane competition. Not only was there no comparable aeroplane for comfort and appearance but it was also supreme in the reliability and handling tests, achieving 118·5 m.p.h., fastest speed of any machine present, to win the highest award of £7,500. In obedience to an Air Ministry ruling, the seating capacity was later reduced to 12, although it had once carried 27, and fuel tanks were removed from the engine nacelles to reduce fire risk, and refitted above the top mainplane. Development flying continued until 21 October 1921, when H. H. Perry flew it on the first W8 service to Paris in 2 hours 5 minutes. A number of trips were made during which it established a record of

1 hour 44 minutes but it was eventually wrecked at Poix, N. France, on 10 July 1922 when a leaking tank starved the port engine of fuel, necessitating a quick downwind forced landing. G-EAPJ fell into a sunken road and broke its back but Capt. A. S. Wilcockson and Flight Engineer A. P. Hunt were only slightly hurt. A projected successor, the W8a G-EAVJ, was never built.

In June 1921 the Air Ministry announced a three year plan for assisting the airlines and was empowered by the Treasury to authorise the construction of a limited number of aircraft for lease to approved firms. Three Handley Page W8b 12 seaters were therefore ordered, which were similar in appearance to the W8. Still known as the H.P.18, they were powered by uncowled Rolls-Royce Eagle VIIIs and consequently more economical to run. In April 1922 the first W8b G-EBBG 'Bombay' went to Martlesham for official trials and on 16 May was renamed 'Princess Mary' at Croydon by the new D.C.A., Sir Sefton Brancker, 'BH at the same time receiving its baptism as 'Prince George'. The third machine 'BI, delivered in the June, became 'Prince Henry' and all three maintained the Paris and Brussels services of the company until absorbed into Imperial Airways Ltd. on 1 April 1924. Although their habits did not change for many years, the W8bs were repainted in the blue and silver of the new owners, returning to the original silver and black when the company's policy changed in 1927.

The only other Cricklewood-built W8b, O-BAHK, built for the Belgian airline SABENA and delivered in 1924, was followed in the same year by three others, O-BAHJ, 'HL and 'HM, built by SABCA under licence in Belgium. All saw service initially on SABENA's Amsterdam–Rotterdam–Brussels–Basle route and were re-registered as OO-AHJ to 'HM in 1929.

In an attempt to reduce the possibility of accidents through engine failure, the H.P.26 or W8e was developed with one 360 h.p. Rolls-Royce Eagle IX in the nose and two 240 h.p. Siddeley Pumas in outboard nacelles. The first of the type was sold to the Belgian airline SABENA and registered O-BAHG in 1924. During the next two years ten others, commencing O-BAHN, were constructed by SABCA for SABENA's Kinshasa–Elizabethville trunk route in the Belgian Congo, O-BAHO 'Princesse Marie-José' being flown out by Capt. E. Thieffry early in 1925 and the rest shipped in crates.

A slightly modified version, the W8f Hamilton, with cabin heating provided by exhaust muffs, was completed for Imperial Airways Ltd. on 15 June 1924, and

'Princess Mary', first of the three Handley Page W8b passenger aircraft.

232

O-BAHG, SABENA's Cricklewood-built Handley Page W8e Hamilton prototype.

made its first flight at Cricklewood five days later. This flew for several years on the Continental routes as G-EBIX 'City of Washington', its maiden flight to Paris taking place on 3 November 1924.

At Cricklewood the three engined theme led to the W9 Hampstead, a similar aircraft with a bigger power reserve and higher cruising speed, flown by a crew of two and carrying 14 passengers in wicker chairs in a warmed cabin. Only the prototype, G-EBLE, was built, water-cooling being dispensed with in favour of three 385 h.p. Armstrong Siddeley Jaguar IV radials. First flown on 1 October 1925, named 'City of New York' and carrying Mr. (later Sir Frederick) Handley Page among the passengers, it was delivered to Imperial Airways at Croydon by W. G. R. Hinchliffe on 19 October, entered scheduled service on 3 November and on 10 March 1926, lowered the London–Paris record to 86 minutes. In April 1926 its Jaguars were replaced by Bristol Jupiters for 250 hours endurance flying under airline conditions, total cost of the replacement parts needed by the three engines at the end of this period amounted to only 35 shillings! The Jupiters were then retained until its retirement from the Imperial Airways fleet.

The change from Jaguars to Jupiters in the W9 is most important historically because it settled the choice of engine for the D.H.66 and H.P.42 fleets. This had remained in the balance since Cobham's flight to the Cape in the Jaguar engined D.H.50 G-EBFO and Minchin's to Cairo in the Jupiter engined Bloodhound G-EBGG had cancelled each other out and shown both engines to be equally reliable under tropical conditions. The choice had then to be made on a basis of maintenance cost, and here the Jupiter (with fewer parts) scored heavily on overhaul, strip and reassembly time. Many people had their first flights in the Hampstead at the Bournemouth and Hamble air pageants but on 27 June it was seriously damaged when Leslie Minchin forced landed, without injury to the nine passengers, in a small field near Biggin Hill.

In March 1929 G-EBLE was dismantled and sent by sea to Port Moresby, New Guinea, where it was erected by local labour under the direction of Capt. G. I. Thompson who then flew it to Lae on delivery to its new owner, the Ellyou Goldfield Development Corporation for operation by New Guinea Goldfields Ltd. as VH-ULK. Capt. Thompson flew regular $1\frac{1}{2}$ ton loads over the treacherous, cloud enveloped mountains between Wau and Salamaua for nearly nine months in

233

Handley Page W9 Hampstead G-EBLE 'City of New York' flying with Jupiter engines at the Bournemouth Easter Meeting 1927. (*Flight*)

The Imperial Airways Handley Page W10 'City of Pretoria' (*Flight Photo 3517*)

the old 'Handley' until, inevitably, he flew into trees on a mountainside at an altitude of 8,000 ft. in bad visibility. The Hampstead was a total loss but he and mechanic McMurtree were rescued unhurt after five days in the wreck, sheltering from tropical rain.

A twin Lion development for 16 passengers, known as the H.P.30 or W10 also appeared in 1925, four aircraft being delivered to Imperial Airways Ltd. These were G-EBMM, 'MR, 'MS and 'MT, allotted City Class names and commissioned on 30 March 1926, which flew on all the regular routes, supplementing earlier brethren, from which they differed by virtue of their rectilineal fins and rudders. The Hamilton G-EBIX was also fitted with this type of tail assembly, and in 1929 lost its central engine and reappeared as the lone W8g with two Eagle IXs.

Although in the 1920s more passenger miles were flown on cross-Channel services by the Handley Page W8 and its offspring than by any other type, they were involved in several serious accidents. With the exception of the Hampstead, none could maintain height with one engine stopped. Thus the comparatively new W10 'City of London' was lost when one engine failed over the Channel on 21 October 1926, Capt. F. Dismore and his 10 passengers being rescued by a trawler. 'City of Ottawa', outward bound for Zürich on 17 June 1929, was less fortunate. An engine failed in mid-Channel, compelling Capt. R. P. D. Brailli to land in the sea 3 miles off Dungeness, the drowning of four of the 11 passengers bringing to an end an unblemished record of 3,900,000 injury-free passenger-miles. 'Princess Mary' was damaged beyond repair in a forced landing at Abbeville while flying from Paris to Croydon on 15 February 1928, but the final accident to the W8g 'City of Washington' was a disaster. Motor stoppage in bad visibility led to its destruction at Neufchatel near Boulogne on 30 October 1930, Capt. J. J. 'Paddy' Flynn being critically injured and three passengers killed. Later, in an attempt to improve single engine performance, the W10 G-EBMR was temporarily fitted with Rolls-Royce F.XI engines.

With the introduction of the Handley Page H.P.42s in 1931, the aged W series retired from airline service. 'Prince Henry' was hired by E. B. Fielden of Aviation Tours Ltd. to be flown by him with the National Aviation Day Displays during 1932 and the surviving W10s G-EBMM and 'MR were sold to Sir Alan Cobham for a similar purpose in 1933. In the following year 'MM, renamed 'Youth of New Zealand', was converted into a tanker for refuelling Sir Alan's Airspeed Courier G-ABXN at the start of the attempted nonstop flight to India on 24 September 1934, while G-EBMR stood by in Malta to refuel him over the Mediterranean. As soon as the Courier had been fuelled over the Isle of Wight, 'MM landed at Ford, where the tanks were removed and in the afternoon left for Whitley to rejoin the Air Display. Near Aston Clinton, failure of a tailplane bracing bolt caused major

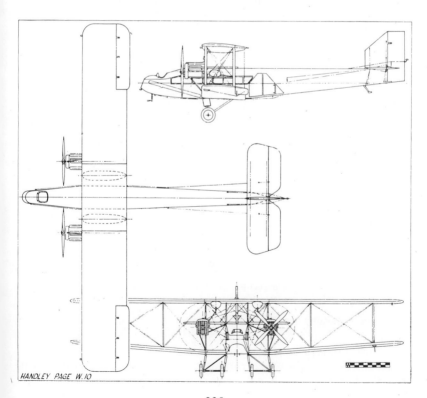

HANDLEY PAGE W.10

structural failure and 'MM crashed and burned, with the loss of Capt. C. H. Bremridge and crew. This incident sealed the fate of a single W8e built by SABCA as O-BAHJ in 1924, and later converted to W8b standard with two Eagle VIIIs as OO-AHJ, which British Hospitals Air Pageants Ltd. bought from SABENA in December 1932. It lay dismantled at Ford during 1933–34 awaiting overhaul for joyriding as G-ACDO but when G-EBMM crashed and 'MR was sold for scrap in Malta, the embryo G-ACDO suffered the same fate.

SPECIFICATION

Manufacturers: Handley Page Ltd., Cricklewood, London, N.W.2.
SABCA, Haren Airport, Brussels, Belgium.
Power Plants: (W8) Two 450 h.p. Napier Lion.
(W8b) Two 360 h.p. Rolls-Royce Eagle VIII.
(W8f) One 360 h.p. Rolls-Royce Eagle IX and two 240 h.p. Siddeley Puma.
(W8g) Two 360 h.p. Rolls-Royce Eagle IX.
(W9) Three 385 h.p. Armstrong Siddeley Jaguar IV.
Three 420 h.p. Bristol Jupiter VI.
(W10) Two 450 h.p. Napier Lion.
Two 480 h.p. Rolls-Royce F.XI.

	W8	W8b	W8f Hamilton	W9 Hampstead	W10
Span	75 ft. 0 in.	75 ft. 0 in.	75 ft. 2 in.	79 ft. 0 in.	75 ft. 0 in.
Length	60 ft. 3 in.	60 ft. 1 in.	60 ft. 1½ in.	60 ft. 4 in.	58 ft. 4 in.
Height	17 ft. 0 in.	17 ft. 0 in.	17 ft. 0 in.	16 ft. 9 in.	17 ft. 0 in.
Wing area	1,450 sq. ft.	1,456 sq. ft.	1,456 sq. ft.	1,563 sq. ft.	1,456 sq. ft.
Tare weight	—	7,700 lb.	8,600 lb.	8,364 lb.	—
All-up weight	12,250 lb.	12,000 lb.	13,000 lb.	14,500 lb.	13,780 lb.
Passengers	12	14	12	14	16
Maximum speed	115 m.p.h.	104 m.p.h.	103 m.p.h.	114 m.p.h.	100 m.p.h.
Cruising speed	90 m.p.h.	90 m.p.h.	85 m.p.h.	95 m.p.h.	—
Initial climb	600 ft./min.	550 ft./min.	—	900 ft./min.	700 ft./min.
Ceiling	18,000 ft.	10,600 ft.	13,000 ft.	13,500 ft.	11,000 ft.
Range	500 miles	—	—	400 miles	—

Production: (a) Handley Page H.P.18 and H.P.26 (W8 to W8f)
At Cricklewood: One W8 (c/n W8-1) G-EAPJ; four W8b (W8-2) G-EBBG; (W8-3) G-EBBH; (W8-4) G-EBBI; (W8-5) O-BAHK; one W8e (W8-6) O-BAGH; one W8f (W8-7) G-EBIX.

By SABCA: Three W8e (c/n 1) O-BAHJ; (2) O-BAHL; (3) O-BAHM; ten W8f (c/n not recorded) O-BAHN to O-BAHU, O-BAHY and O-BAHZ.

(b) Handley Page H.P.27 (W9) Hampstead
One aircraft only: (c/n W9-1) G-EBLE, later VH-ULK.

(c) Handley Page H.P.30 (W10)
Four aircraft only: (c/n W10-1) G-EBMM; (W10-2) G-EBMR; (W10-3) G-EBMS; (W10-4) G-EBMT.

236

The prototype Handley Page H.P.42, G-AAGX, on an early test flight near Radlett in November 1930 with nose-mounted test gear including a crude 'artificial horizon'.

Handley Page H.P.42

The H.P.42 was designed specifically for use by Imperial Airways Ltd. on the European and eastern sections of the Empire air routes. A cabin mock-up was exhibited at the Olympia Aero Show of July 1929 and when Sqn. Ldr. T. H. England and Major J. L. B. H. Cordes took the prototype, G-AAGX, on its maiden flight at Radlett in November 1930, it was seen to be an extremely large biplane in true Handley Page tradition. Although of all-metal construction, with the major part of the fuselage covered with corrugated duralumin plating, all flying surfaces and the rear fuselage were fabric covered. Large automatic slots were fitted to wings braced by Warren girder struts in place of wires, and the biplane tail was fitted with triple fins and rudders. Passenger convenience and comfort had been the designer's watchwords, and the H.P.42 was renowned in its day for setting new standards in furnishing, quietness and cuisine. The inboard lower mainplanes swept sharply upward to take the main spars over, instead of through, the cabin and the noisy fuselage section adjacent to the engines was occupied by toilets and baggage hold, the passenger cabins being situated fore and aft. Captain and First Officer occupied a glazed compartment high in the nose.

Four geared and moderately supercharged Bristol Jupiter engines were mounted close together to simplify asymmetrical flying in the event of engine failure, and a Bristol gas starter was carried in the port side of the fuselage. A simple device on the throttle quadrant prevented the upper engines being opened up first, thus making it impossible to nose over and emulate the ill-fated Tarrant Tabor. The H.P.42 proceeded majestically and economically along the air routes in the unhurried certainty that its humble 95 m.p.h. could better any surface transport and at the same time put its passengers completely at ease with its ability to carry them in Pullman comfort and, in an emergency, to land slowly in a confined space. Its appearance brought much ribald criticism but its unparalleled record of service, safety and revenue earning, eventually compelled respect and finally affection.

Including the prototype, total production consisted of four aircraft of each of two versions. Those based at Cairo for the Cairo–Karachi and Cairo–Kisumu sections of the India and South Africa routes were known as the H.P.42E or Eastern model. Initially six, and later 12, passengers were carried in the forward cabin and 12 in the rear, 500 cu. ft. of space being available amidships for the carriage of luggage and mail. The four Croydon-based H.P.42W or Western models were externally identical, but carried 18 passengers forward and 20 in the rear, baggage space being reduced to 250 cu. ft. In post-war years when these aircraft were but a memory, the designation H.P.45 was applied to the Western model, but this was not reflected in their constructor's numbers, and was not used during their flying lives.

The prototype was completed to H.P.42E standard, named 'Hannibal' and made its first public appearance at a garden party given at Hanworth on 6 June 1931, for members of both Houses of Parliament and three days later it made the first of a series of proving flights to Paris, carrying its first fare-paying passenger on the 11th. These flights continued until 8 August, when a piece of flying metal damaged three airscrews, resulting in a masterly forced landing by Capt. F. Dismore in a field at Tudeley, near Tonbridge. The tail was torn off by telephone wires, but repairs were quickly effected at Croydon and it afterwards left for Cairo to join 'Hadrian', which had made a brief appearance at the Household Brigade Flying Club meeting at Heston on 22 July 1931 before proceeding eastward.

'Hanno', first of the H.P.42E models to be delivered, left Croydon on 9 November piloted by Capt. E. S. Alcock and H. G. Brackley to inaugurate the Empire route to South Africa but while under the command of Capt. H. J. Horsey

'Horatius', second Handley Page H.P.42W, undergoing a pre-flight check at Croydon in the 1930s.

at Galilee on 17 November 1932, 'Hannibal' suffered damage in a gale, repairs taking six months, after which it gave eight years of unbroken service. 'Horsa' left the factory in September 1931 together with 'Heracles', first of the H.P.42Ws. The remaining three, which appeared at Croydon in rapid succession, thereafter became familiar and regular features of the Kent and Sussex skies for many years. 'Heracles' was flown to Hanworth by Capt. W. Rogers on 19 June 1932, to give flights at the garden party of the Royal Aeronautical Society but when leaving, the port wheel sank through a drainage culvert under the aerodrome surface, and for some weeks Middlesex also boasted the silhouette of an H.P.42. Thus, like its Eastern brother, the first Western model became hors de combat right at the beginning of a long and meritorious career. Five years later, on 23 July 1937, 'Heracles' completed its millionth mile on the Paris, Cologne and Zürich routes and by 11 September 1938, seventh anniversary of its first scheduled flight, it had flown $1\frac{1}{4}$ million miles and carried 95,000 passengers.

Utilisation figures for the other H.P.42Ws were equally startling, figures which their Eastern brethren equalled in their own sphere but with different load analyses. 'Helena' was the aircraft chosen to fly to Paris on 20 January 1932 with the first through air mail to Cape Town and 'Hengist' performed a similar function with the first through Australian air mail on 8 December 1934. Soon afterwards 'Hengist' went east after conversion to H.P.42E but was burned out in a hangar fire at Karachi in May 1937. In that year 'Hanno' returned home and was converted to H.P.42W to replace 'Hengist' on European services.

All continued in service until, on 1 September 1939, with war imminent, the Croydon-based machines were evacuated to Whitchurch. Operating from Whitchurch and Exeter, they were used mainly for ferrying war supplies to France. On 7 November 1939 'Horatius' arrived from the Continent to find Exeter enveloped by a storm, forced landed down wind on the golf links at Tiverton, Devon, collided with trees and was written off. It was the beginning of the end of a fleet whose names had been household words for a decade.

Early in 1940 it was decided to fly home the four H.P.42Es 'Hannibal', 'Horsa', 'Hadrian' and 'Helena'. 'Hannibal', in India at the time, left Delhi on 1 March 1940 with four crew and four passengers en route for Cairo and after take-off from Jask passed an E.T.A. to Sharjah but was never seen again, despite a massive air and sea search in the Gulf of Oman. The others were reunited with their brethren at Whitchurch but 'Hanno' and 'Heracles' became partially airborne at the end of their picketing ropes during a gale at Whitchurch on 19 March 1940 and were blown together and wrecked, leaving only three H.P.42s to be impressed.

Thus 'Horsa', 'Hadrian' and 'Helena' were posted to the strength of No. 271 Squadron, Doncaster as AS981 to AS983 and delivered in civil markings on 30 May, 4 June and 8 June 1940 respectively but these ungainly old aircraft were scarcely suited to military service in the field and in less than three months engine failures resulted in 'Hadrian' making a forced landing at Acklington while flying from Doncaster to Turnhouse on 12 July; irreparable damage to 'Helena' while rounding out to touch down at Donibristle on 1 August; and the destruction by fire of 'Horsa' following a forced landing near Whitehaven, Cumberland on 7 August while transporting ammunition from Ringway to Stornoway.

'Helena's' removable equipment was collected by 'Hadrian' on 9 September and in the summer of 1941 the airframe was dismantled by the Royal Navy who mounted the metal-clad passenger cabin on a wooden trestle and used it as a Squadron office.

'Hadrian', last survivor, broke from its pickets in a gale at Doncaster on 6 December 1940 and was blown down an embankment on to the railway and overturned. During attempts to clear the line it was eventually carried away altogether and disintegrated in an adjoining field.

SPECIFICATION

Manufacturers: Handley Page Ltd., Cricklewood, London, N.W.2, and Radlett Aerodrome, Herts.

Power Plants: (H.P.42W) Four 555 h.p. Bristol Jupiter XFBM.
(H.P.42E) Four 490 h.p. Bristol Jupiter XIF.

Dimensions: Span, 130 ft. 0 in. Length, 89 ft. 9 in. Height, 27 ft. 0 in. Wing area, 2,989 sq. ft.

Weights: All-up weight (H.P.42W), 29,500 lb. (H.P.42E), 28,000 lb.

Performance: (H.P.42W) Maximum speed, 127 m.p.h. Cruising speed, 100 m.p.h. Initial climb, 670 ft./min.
(H.P.42E) Maximum speed, 120 m.p.h. Cruising speed, 100 m.p.h. Initial climb, 790 ft./min.

Production: Eight aircraft only: (c/n 42/1 to 42/8) G-AAGX; G-AAUC to 'UE; G-AAXC to 'XF.

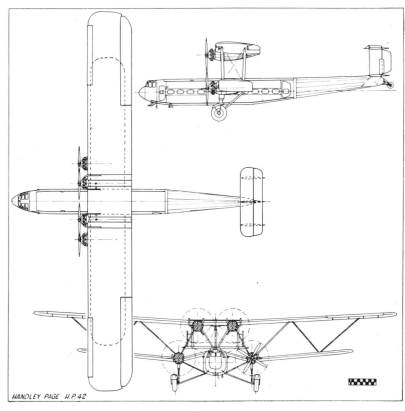

HANDLEY PAGE H.P.42

G-AIWK, second Halifax C. Mk.8 to bear the name 'Port of Sydney'.
(*E. J. Riding*)

Handley Page Halifax and Halton

The all-metal Halifax bomber of the 1939–45 war first became a civilian aircraft in February 1946 with the arrival at Radlett of NR169, an H.P.61 Halifax 3 which Handley Page Ltd. converted into a 15 passenger aircraft to the order of A.T.A. Flight Captain G. N. Wikner, of pre-war Wicko fame. Named 'Waltzing Matilda' and with civil markings G-AGXA emblazoned in white on night camouflage, the Halifax left Hurn on 26 May en route to Australia. Piloted by the owner and carrying two crew and 13 other Australian repatriates, the aircraft touched down at Mascot, Sydney, on 20 June in a flying time of 71 hours. After exhibition in aid of R.A.F. charities it was disposed of to Air Carriers Pty., but made only one commercial flight, to Singapore with a load of dogs in June 1947. Afterwards it limped back to Sydney with an unserviceable port outer engine, suffered dismemberment by local vandals and never flew again.

As soon as the new H.P.70 Halifax C. Mk. 8 transports erected at Radlett in 1945, came up for disposal, Dr. Graham Humby acquired six and founded London Aero and Motor Services Ltd. They were ferried from High Ercoll to Elstree and converted for freighting duties, for which their large panniers made them eminently suitable and in its blue colour scheme with white markings, the first civil Halifax 8, G-AHZJ, formerly PP247, became the first British civil aeroplane to land at Barcelona after the war. One aircraft, G-AHZM, fully civilianised, suffered undercarriage collapse when taxying out for its first civil test flight on 16 September 1946, and was cannibalised to become a welcome source of spares, but the other five did a brisk trade with fruit from Italy and the South of France. Positioning flights were made to London/Heathrow for each trip, but to eliminate dead flying the firm moved to Stansted on 14 December 1946. Ten more Halifax 8s, G-AIWI–'WR and 'WT, were then acquired, 'WO and 'WP being cannibalised during the conversion of the others, which, with the originals, were named after their ports of call. By July 1947 the fleet was importing 500 tons of fruit a month and the expansion of business into full-scale tramping was also attempted with the departure of G-AIWT 'Port of Sydney', Capt. Thiele in command, from Stansted on 23 April 1947. He flew the Halifax to New Zealand via Iceland and the U.S.A., the long haul of 2,500 miles from San Francisco to

Honolulu being completed in $11\frac{1}{2}$ hours. Several charters were secured between New Zealand and Australia and the aircraft returned to Stansted on 5 June carrying 7 tons of dripping. As a result, L.A.M.S. (Australia) Ltd. was formed and flights were made between Sydney and the Philippines with turkeys, as well as to the United Kingdom. L.A.M.S. (Africa) Ltd. began operations with G-AIWR 'Port of Durban', re-registered at the Cape as ZS-BUL for the pilgrim traffic between Istanbul, Nairobi and Jeddah, where on 25 November 1947, its undercarriage was damaged on arrival. The Halifax then flew south to Port Sudan, where it was written off in a crash landing. In spite of this very considerable activity, the company wound up in 1948 and G-AIWK, named 'Port of Sydney' in place of 'WT, finding itself marooned at Mascot, was picketed alongside 'Waltzing Matilda' until it suffered a similar fate.

In 1946–48 a demand also developed for the rapid transport of ship's crews and spares, the delivery of machinery to the Overseas Food Corporation in East Africa and for the carriage of pilgrims in the Near East. Civil Halifaxes played a prominent part in these charters, notably the fleet of the Lancashire Aircraft Corporation based at Squires Gate and of smaller concerns, such as Skyflight, Alpha Airways, Payloads, Bond Air Services, British American Air Services, Chartair, Air Freight, World Air Freight, Eagle Aviation, Westminster Airways and Petair. A shortage of spares was overcome when 33 H.P.61 Halifax B. Mk. 6s were allotted civil markings for ferrying to Bovingdon and Stansted where they were broken up by the Lancashire Aircraft Corporation and London Aero and Motor Services Ltd. This fate also overtook G-ALOM, ferried from Hawarden to Southend by Aviation Traders Ltd.

Stansted, Bovingdon, Thame, Southend and Blackbushe became the principal Halifax bases in the south and in 1947 G-AGPC, 'TK, G-AHKK, 'VT, 'WL, G-AJBK and 'XD were ferried through Gatwick to the French operator Aero Cargo. Payloads Ltd. sold G-AJNV, G-AKBP and 'CT to Air Globe, Geneva, but they were never used commercially and were sold eventually to the Egyptian Air Force.

Three other Halifax C. Mk. 8s, G-AJNU, 'NX and 'NY, were converted for Pakistan Airways at Thame in 1948 and flown to Karachi as AP-ACH, 'BZ and 'CG but AP-ABZ, commanded by Capt. Pearson and carrying 27 drums of cable, ran out of fuel en route and was forced down and wrecked on the inhospitable coast near Basra on 10 May 1948. Three days later, F-BCJX, the former

G. N. Wikner's Halifax 3 'Waltzing Matilda' being readied for the Australia flight, May 1946. (*Aeroplane*)

'Falkirk', first of the Halton conversions for B.O.A.C. (*B.O.A.C.*)

G-AGTK, inward from Lyons, blocked the Hemel Hempstead road after over-shooting at Bovingdon. These were but two of the 14 major accidents to converted Halifaxes, the destruction of G-AIZO of Bond Air Services Ltd. at Berkhampsted on 23 May 1948, caused by the cargo of apricots shifting in the air, was believed to be the first such case on record. G-AJPJ of British American Air Services Ltd. met a different fate when an unauthorised pilot flew it away from White Waltham on 20 July 1948, to an undisclosed destination, although unconfirmed reports suggested that it eventually limped into Lydda on two engines and crash landed, thus just failing to become an Israeli bomber.

The Halifax was also used for airline duties at a time when British Overseas Airways Corporation was faced with fleet shortages caused by the non-delivery of the Avro Tudors. Twelve Halifax C. Mk. 8s were reworked at Belfast by Short and Harland Ltd. into transports for 10 passengers, with 8,000 lb. of baggage, freight and mail in the pannier. A large entrance door was fitted in the starboard side of the rear fuselage and square windows provided in the cabin. While retaining the designation H.P.70, a new type name Halton 1 was allotted, the prototype G-AHDU 'Falkirk' being christened by Lady Winster at Radlet on 18 July 1946. The sole Halton 2, G-AGZP, was originally a V.I.P. Halifax operated on behalf of the Maharajah Gaekwar of Baroda by British American Air Services Ltd., which, after transporting the owner from India in April 1946, was converted to special standards at Radlett. Following a period in South Africa as ZS-BTA with Alpha Airways, it finished its career in the service of Lancashire Aircraft Corporation.

The 12 B.O.A.C. aircraft flew for a year or so on the desert routes from London to Accra until replaced by Canadair C-4s. All 12 then lined up at London Airport until G-AHDR 'Foreland' was sold to the Louis Breguet concern in France and the rest left for Southend on delivery to Aviation Traders Ltd. to join the firm's 22 H.P.71 Halifax A. Mk. 9 paratroop transports granted civil status for ferrying from Hawarden prior to servicing for the Egyptian Air Force. An embargo on arms to Egypt early in 1950 resulted in only half a dozen, G-ALOP, 'OR and 'VJ–'VM leaving for Cairo, the last mentioned being the former RT938, 6,176th and last Halifax built. In Egypt it carried the serial 1161 in Arabic, the others becoming 1155, 1157, 1159, 1160 and 1162 respectively.

243

In 1948, when the initial post war boom in air freighting collapsed, the future of the civil Halifaxes was again in jeopardy until they were pressed into used on the Berlin airlift, together with the Haltons and G-ALON and 'OS, the only two Halifax 9s converted for civil use. During the period from 24 June 1948, to the last Halifax flight on 15 August 1949, they operated a continuous round-the-clock service into Gatow from their bases at Schleswigland and Wunsdorf. The fleet consisted of 41 Halifaxes operated by the Lancashire Aircraft Corporation (13), Bond Air Services Ltd. (12), Westminster Airways Ltd. (4), Eagle Aviation Ltd. (4), British American Air Services Ltd. (3), World Air Freight Ltd. (3) and Skyflight Ltd. (2). The phenomenal total of 4,653 freight sorties was flown with an additional 3,509 by Westminster Airways, the Lancashire Aircraft Corporation and British American Air Services, whose Halifaxes were converted for the bulk carriage of diesel fuel. Loads averaged $6\frac{1}{2}$ tons, and operations were carried out under extreme difficulties for with few spares available, even minor accidents often resulted in aircraft being scrapped. Thus nine Halifaxes were lost during the operation, many on the ground at Schleswigland and Tegel, and one, World Air Freight's G-AKGZ, at Gatow on 8 October 1948.

G-ALOS, formerly RT937, was one of two Halifax A.Mk.9 aircraft fully civilianised by Aviation Traders Ltd. It flew 161 sorties for Bond Air Services Ltd. on the Berlin airlift. (*A. J. Jackson*)

The end of the Berlin airlift marked the end of the Halifax as a civil aeroplane. The majority returned to Squires Gate, Woolsington, Southend and Bovingdon, where they were reduced to produce, melted down on site and taken away as ingots. A few survived for a while, including G-AITC, one of two originally civilianised for the College of Aeronautics, which crash landed at Brindisi on 20 January 1950 while in service with World Air Freight Ltd. and carrying a cargo of cloth from Milan to Teheran. Later in the year, one of the surviving Lancashire Halifaxes G-AKEC 'Air Voyager' was sportingly entered for the *Daily Express* Air Race and on 20 September Capt. A. N. Marshall flew it low round the South Coast from Hurn to Herne Bay to come 24th at an average speed of 267 m.p.h., surely the Halifax's only race!

Halifax C.Mk.8 AP-ACG, formerly G-AJNY, taxying out at Stansted on 8 May 1948 at the beginning of its delivery flight to Pakistan Airways. (*A. J. Jackson*)

Halifax C.Mk.8 F-BCJS, originally intended as G-AGPC, at Gatwick in October 1947 awaiting delivery to Aero Cargo, Lyons. (*E. J. Riding*)

Halifax A.Mk.9 G-ALVK at Southend on 17 February 1950 with Arabic serial 1160 in readiness for delivery to the Egyptian Air Force. (*A. J. Jackson*)

SPECIFICATION

Manufacturers: Handley Page Ltd., Cricklewood, London, N.W.2 and Radlett Aerodrome, Herts.

Power Plants: (Halifax 3 and 9) Four 1,615 h.p. Bristol Hercules 16.
(Halifax 6 and 8) Four 1,675 h.p. Bristol Hercules 100.
(Halton 1 and 2) Four 1,675 h.p. Bristol Hercules 100.

	Halifax 3	Halifax 6	Halifax 8	Halifax 9
Span	103 ft. 8 in.	103 ft. 8 in.	103 ft. 8 in.	103 ft. 8 in.
Length	70 ft. 1 in.	73 ft. 7 in.	73 ft. 7 in.	73 ft. 7 in.
Height	21 ft. 7 in.	21 ft. 7 in.	22 ft. 8 in.	21 ft. 7 in.
Wing area	1,275 sq. ft.	1,275 sq. ft.	1,275 sq. ft.	1,275 sq. ft.
Tare weight	—	38,900 lb.	37,750 lb.	37,830 lb.
All-up weight	65,000 lb.	65,000 lb.	68,000 lb.	65,000 lb.
Maximum speed	—	320 m.p.h.	320 m.p.h.	270 m.p.h.
Cruising speed	—	195 m.p.h.	260 m.p.h.	—
Initial climb	—	950 ft./min.	740 ft./min.	700 ft./min.
Ceiling	—	24,000 ft.	21,000 ft.	21,000 ft.
Range	—	2,350 miles	2,530 miles	2,050 miles

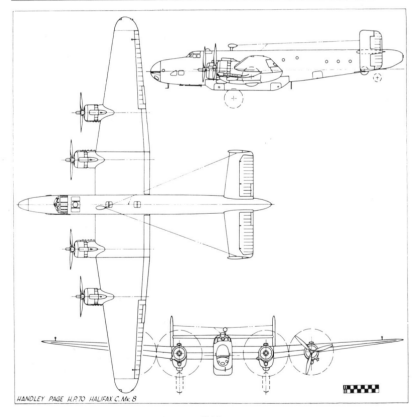

HANDLEY PAGE H.P.70 HALIFAX C.Mk.8

The Handley Page H.P.81 Hermes 4 'Hero' (*B.O.A.C.*)

Handley Page Hermes

The H.P.68 Hermes 1 four engined transport was designed during the 1939–45 war for use on future peacetime air routes. A specification issued in 1944 disclosed that seven crew and either 34 first class or 50 tourist class passengers would be accommodated in a pressurised fuselage, making the Hermes the first British pressurised passenger aircraft. The prototype, G-AGSS, of all metal construction powered by four Bristol Hercules engines, was built at Cricklewood during 1944–45, and in common with all Handley Page aircraft since the H.P.42, its component parts were taken by road to Radlett Aerodrome for final erection. On Sunday 3 December 1945, the aircraft took off on its first flight piloted by Flt. Lt. J. R. Talbot, the firm's chief test pilot, but proved unmanageable, probably because of elevator overbalance, stalled and dived upside down into the ground at Kendall's Hall, three miles south of the aerodrome and was destroyed by fire with the loss of the pilot and flight observer E. A. Wright.

In spite of this set-back, work proceeded on a military counterpart, the Hastings, the first of which flew successfully during the year. A second civil prototype, the H.P.74 Hermes 2 G-AGUB, was then constructed and made a successful maiden flight in the hands of the company's chief test pilot Sqn. Ldr. H. G. Hazelden at Radlett on 2 September 1947, in time to participate in the S.B.A.C. Show held there a week later. It was a stretched version of the H.P.68 with a 13 ft. extension to the front fuselage and seating 50 passengers in pressurised comfort. Built primarily for development flying, 'UB had a long and useful life which paved the way for the tricycle undercarriage version, the H.P.81 Hermes 4, 25 of which had been ordered by the Ministry of Supply on behalf of B.O.A.C. in April 1947. Construction of the first, G-AKFP, went ahead rapidly, Sqn. Ldr. Hazelden making the first test flight at Radlett on 5 September 1948. Such was his confidence in the new machine that before landing he flew past at an Elstree air display, and once more a new Hermes was able to put in the qualifying hours before the S.B.A.C. Show. It was publicised as a medium/long range type for 63 passengers and seven crew, the total payload being 7 tons and the ultimate range 3,500 miles. Its Hercules 763 power plants drove four bladed de Havilland fully feathering, reversible pitch airscrews and were installed in quick-access cowlings, notable for their clean aerodynamic form and beauty of line. Two such power units were installed in the outer nacelles of the Hermes 2 prototype, delivered by air to the B.O.A.C. Development Flight at Hurn on 9 May 1949 for a 250 hour programme of test flying under simulated airline conditions. Its work done, the Hermes 2 returned to Radlett, where it languished until fitted with modified windows, a solar compass and camera in 1953 for geophysical research by the Ministry of Supply as VX234. In 1958 it was delivered to the Royal Radar Establishment, Defford (later transferred to Pershore) and when retired in 1969 was the last operational Hermes.

The Ministry of Supply also ordered two H.P.82 Hermes 5 development aircraft G-ALEU and 'EV, the first of which made its initial flight on 23 August 1949. Both Hermes 5s, exhibited at the 1949, 1950 and '51 S.B.A.C. Shows, were powered by Bristol Theseus turbines and in their day were the world's largest propeller turbine aircraft. The engines, lighter than the Hercules, were installed farther forward, with the bifurcated jet orifices on each side of the nacelles and passing under the wing. Both were subjected to intensive research flying, during which 'EU, flown by a Handley Page pilot, W. Burton, ended its career in a wheels-up landing short of the Chilbolton runway on 10 April 1951 due to engine trouble. The second Mk. 5 'EV, fully furnished to airline standards, was flown the 215 miles from London Airport to Orly by D. Bloomfield on 5 June 1951, in the remarkable time of 43 minutes at an average speed of 300 m.p.h. After demonstration to the French authorities it returned to end its career unspectacularly under the breaker's hammer at Farnborough in 1953.

The B.O.A.C. Hermes 4s were delivered in rapid succession throughout 1950, an achievement made possible by B.O.A.C.'s acceptance of a slight weight penalty resulting partly from the use of Hastings jigs and partly from the tricycle undercarriage. The main oleo attachments for this were moved from the front to the rear spar, which for speed of production was strengthened by modification rather than by redesign. B.O.A.C. accepted the first aircraft on 22 February 1950, the fleet being based initally at Hurn for crew training. After route proving trials in June, the Hermes fleet took over the West Africa route to Tripoli, Kano, Lagos and Accra, the inaugural service being flown by G-ALDJ on 6 August. A new London–Entebbe–Nairobi service began on 24 September, replacing the pre-

The Handley Page H.P.68 Hermes 1 at Radlett in December 1945.

248

G-ALEU, first prototype Handley Page H.P.82 Hermes 5, at Farnborough, September 1949. (*Topical Press*)

vious Southampton–Lake Naivasha route operated by Short Solents and on 7 November the Hermes took over their Johannesburg schedules, becoming the first British aircraft of post-war construction to enter B.O.A.C. service. In regular airline use they carried five crew and 40 passengers and perpetuated and extended the famous range of mythological names once carried by their illustrious forebears the H.P.42s. Their career was short, and on being replaced by Canadair C-4s in 1952, G-ALDJ was fatigue checked at 3,500 hours flying time. This resulted in a programme of main spar modification, after which they were cocooned at London Airport although one did not return to suffer this humiliation. G-ALDN 'Horus', victim of a navigational error on the night of 25–26 May 1952, forced landed 11 hours out from Tripoli and lies under the Sahara sand in French West Africa. Several were unexpectedly recommissioned, however, when the Comets were grounded, and equipped with 56 seats, the Hermes 4s began weekly tourist services between London, Nairobi and Dar es Salaam on 18 July 1954, the last service being flown early in December.

The second phase in the career of the Hermes 4 began in 1952, when four were sold to Airwork Ltd. for trooping to Kenya and the Egyptian Canal Zone. The Hercules 763 engine, running on special 115 octane fuel, depended on pre-arranged supplies not always available in the remote areas served by charter operations. It was therefore necessary to modify the engines to burn standard 100 octane fuel, with a change in Hercules nomenclature to 773 and in aircraft designation to Hermes 4A. The first so modified, G-ALDB, went to Entebbe for tropical trials piloted by Sqn. Ldr. Hazelden and the Airwork chief test pilot, Capt. C. D. Stenner.

G-ALDB and 'DF were lost in accidents during July and August of 1952, so that when the trooping system was extended, two additional Hermes 4s were acquired by Airwork Ltd. for this purpose, the fleet then comprising G-AKFP, G-ALDA, 'DC and 'DG, all fitted with 68 strengthened, rearward facing seats. To conform to international agreement, the Airwork Hermes adopted R.A.F. colours and military serials for these flights as did G-ALDI, 'DJ, 'DK, 'DP, 'DU and 'DX operated by Britavia Ltd. out of Blackbushe. The last two of these were short leased to Kuwait Airways Ltd. in 1956 and all but one of the remainder were sold to Skyways Ltd., Bovingdon (later Stansted) on trooping and scheduled services to

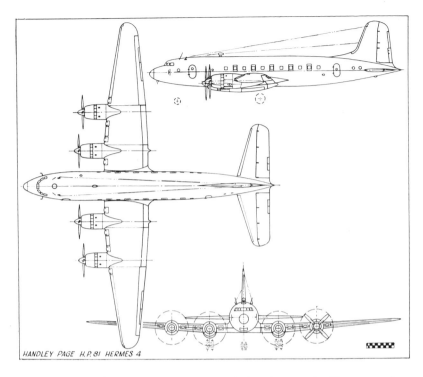

HANDLEY PAGE H.P. 81 HERMES 4

the Near and Middle East. Several were lost during these semi-military operations including Skyways' G-ALDW blown up by a saboteur's bomb on the ground at Nicosia, Cyprus, on 4 March 1956. The Skyways fleet provided the only Hermes aircraft to adopt foreign marks viz. G-ALDT and 'DY leased to Middle East Airlines as OD-ACB and 'CC for the 1956 pilgrim traffic; and G-ALDE and 'DL transferred to Bahamas Airways Ltd. as 78 seaters at the end of 1959 for the Nassau–Miami route. Registered VP-BBO and 'BP respectively, they were joined by VP-BBQ (G-ALDT) in 1960.

In 1957 fuel supplies were such that reversion to Hermes 4 standard took place on nearly all aircraft but during the following year the Hermes began to be withdrawn from service although on 2 June 1959 Skyways' G-ALDO opened a new London–Tunis service and the Britavia/Silver City Airways 'Silver Arrow' route between Manston and Le Touquet was inaugurated by G-ALDP 'City of Truro' on 15 June. Silver City also operated G-ALDG, 'DI, 'DM (on lease from Air Safaris Ltd.) and 'DU. The type was also used later by two new inclusive tour firms, Falcon Airways Ltd. which operated G-ALDA, 'DC and 'DG until the end of 1960 (losing 'DC at Southend on 9 October in the first accident in the United Kingdom officially attributed to aquaplaning), and Air Safaris Ltd. which acquired G-ALDM, 'DA from Falcon Airways, and the three Bahamas Airways machines in time for the 1961 season.

During 1961 and '62 nearly all the remaining Hermes were scrapped, mainly at Hurn and Stansted, and the final Hermes operation began when Air Links Ltd. bought three of the Air Safari aircraft and ferried them to Southend where

G-ALDL and 'DT were cannibalised to service G-ALDA which entered service at Gatwick in 82 seat configuration in December 1962. After two years service it completed the last revenue earning Hermes flight when it landed at Gatwick on 13 December 1964, and nine days later flew to Southend where it was scrapped during the following year. The last Hermes 'in service' was G-ALDG, the fuselage of which became a familiar sight close to the London–Brighton road at Gatwick where it was used for training British United Airways cabin staff.

SPECIFICATION

Manufacturers: Handley Page Ltd., Cricklewood, London, N.W.2 and Radlett Aerodrome, Herts.

Power Plants: (Hermes 1)   Four 1,650 h.p. Bristol Hercules 101.
(Hermes 2)   Four 1,675 h.p. Bristol Hercules 121.
(Hermes 4)   Four 2,100 h.p. Bristol Hercules 763.
(Hermes 4A) Four 2,125 h.p. Bristol Hercules 773.
(Hermes 5)   Four 2,490 h.p. Bristol Theseus 502.

	Hermes 1	Hermes 2	Hermes 4	Hermes 5
Span	113 ft. 0 in.	113 ft. 0 in.	113 ft. 0 in.	113 ft. 0 in.
Length	81 ft. 6 in.	96 ft. 10 in.	96 ft. 10 in.	96 ft. 10 in.
Height	21 ft. 0 in.	22 ft. 6 in.	29 ft. 11 in.	29 ft. 11 in.
Wing area	1,408 sq. ft.	1,408 sq. ft.	1,408 sq. ft.	1,408 sq. ft.
Tare weight	37,642 lb.	41,689 lb.	55,350 lb.	50,900 lb.
All-up weight	70,000 lb.	80,000 lb.	86,000 lb.	85,000 lb.
Maximum speed	340 m.p.h.	337 m.p.h.	350 m.p.h.	351 m.p.h.
Cruising speed	210 m.p.h.	289 m.p.h.	276 m.p.h.	343 m.p.h.
Initial climb	1,010 ft./min.	750 ft./min.	1,030 ft./min.	2,010 ft./min.
Ceiling	—	23,600 ft.	24,500 ft.	28,600 ft.
Range	2,000 miles	2,000 miles	2,000 miles	2,500 miles

Production:
One H.P.68 Hermes 1; one H.P.74 Hermes 2; twenty-five H.P.81 Hermes 4; two H.P.82 Hermes 5 built at Radlett.

The last production Hermes 4, G-ALDY, at Blackbushe in July 1956 ready for delivery to Middle East Airlines as OD-ACC.

'Millersdale', a Marathon 1A in airline service with Derby Aviation Ltd., Burnaston from 1955 to 1960.

Handley Page (Reading) H.P.R.1 Marathon

The Marathon originated in 1944 when Fred and George Miles and J. H. Lowden of Miles Aircraft Ltd. produced an imaginative design conforming to the Brabazon 5a and 18/44 specifications, three prototypes of which were ordered. Piloted by the Miles chief test pilot K. H. F. Waller, the M.60 Marathon, first Miles aeroplane to have four engines, all metal construction and a retractable nose wheel undercarriage, made an uneventful maiden flight under B conditions as U-10 on 19 May 1946, only 14 months after construction began. It was a high-wing, cantilever monoplane with a capacious monocoque fuselage capable of seating two crew and 20 passengers, the fuselage being set low to the ground for ease of entry. The design incorporated Miles pneumatically operated retractable, auxiliary, high-lift flaps and on the power of four supercharged Gipsy Queen 71 engines was the only aircraft of its class that could maintain its climb even if two engines failed. Boscombe Down trials were interrupted to permit exhibition at the Radlett S.B.A.C. Show in September, and fully furnished as G-AGPD, the Marathon was again exhibited in 1947.

During 1946 it became evident that tooling could be planned only for a minimum of 100 Marathons, but total orders amounted to only 25 for the Ministry of Supply and a further 25 for British European Airways which were to be Mamba powered and designated Miles M.69 Marathon 2. The second Marathon, G-AILH, first flown on 27 February 1947, had two fins and rudders instead of the standard three, and was unfurnished for the purpose of testing the thermal de-icing and cabin heating provided by the Daniel petrol-burning heater, the air intake for which protruded from the top of the rear fuselage. Only the two prototypes had been built before financial difficulties overtook Miles Aircraft Ltd. and work on the Marathon practically ceased. A second blow fell in May 1948, when G-AGPD was totally destroyed in a crash soon after take off from Boscombe Down, with the loss of test pilot Brian Bastable and his flight test observer.

Negotiations to save the aircraft finally resulted in Handley Page Ltd. taking over Marathon production at Woodley, and for this purpose the name of the firm's historic subsidiary, Handley Page Transport Ltd., was changed to Handley Page (Reading) Ltd. on 5 July 1948. The Marathon design was then broken down into seven major assemblies and production began at once. Forty aircraft were built during the next three years with the amended designation Handley Page (Reading) H.P.R.1 Marathon 1, and the Mamba powered Marathon 2 G-AHXU was completed. This had been designed to Specification 15/46 and a full-scale mock-up of the curiously shaped nacelle was test flown on the starboard outer wing of the prototype Miles Aerovan G-AGOZ during 1947. G-AHXU became the third British-built propeller turbine transport to fly when it took off with Handley Page test pilot Hugh Kendall at the controls on 23 July 1949. After exhibition at Farnborough in 1949 and 1950, 'XU was flown by the same pilot into seventh place in the *Daily Express* race from Hurn to Herne Bay on 16 September 1950 at 280·5 m.p.h. It was then transferred to the Ministry of Supply as VX231 and fitted with D.H. reversible pitch airscrews, the first fitted to turbine engines. It was flown for the first time with these airscrews at Hatfield on 23 July 1951 and demonstrated backward taxying at the 1951 Farnborough S.B.A.C. Show.

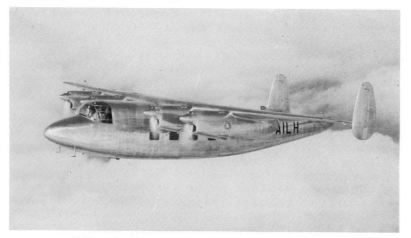

The second prototype Marathon in its original form without the central fin.

The first production Marathon 1, G-ALUB, left Woodley on 14 January 1950, also piloted by Hugh Kendall, accompanied by A. F. 'Bush' Bandidt, on a 40,000 miles sales tour to New Zealand. Demonstrations were staged en route and in Australia and New Guinea, the aircraft returning to Woodley in the following May. A year later it was delivered at Northolt for B.E.A. acceptance tests, but as had already been foreseen, neither the Marathon 1 nor 2 would be a really suitable Rapide replacement on Scottish services. Thus only seven names were allotted in the proposed Clansman Class, the order was reduced to seven Marathon 1s and some 20 undelivered machines were lined up at Woodley and Blackbushe that summer, many of which were later flown to Stansted for storage. G-ALUB reappeared at London Airport in September 1951 in full B.E.A. livery with the

The Mamba powered Marathon 2. (*Aeroplane*)

name 'Rob Roy', but in February 1952 the Corporation finally abandoned the Marathon and the Ministry of Supply diverted 30 aircraft for modification to Marathon T.Mk.11 advanced navigation trainers for the R.A.F. serialled XA249 to XA278. These were preceded by G-AILH, now fitted with the third fin, which was converted as the prototype T.Mk.11, VX229, during 1952. In October 1957 it was sold to Dan-Air Services Ltd. and moved to Lasham by road but was not restored to the civil register.

The 12th production Marathon, G-AMEO, was loaned to West African Airways Corporation in March 1951 as VR-NAI for evaluation over the Nigeria–Gold Coast–Sierra Leone–Gambia network. As a result six Marathons, G-AMGW, 'GX, 'HR, 'HS, 'HV and 'HW were delivered to the Corporation for regular airline service at the end of 1952 as VR-NAN, 'AO, 'AR, 'AS, 'AT and 'AU respectively, and fitted with Gipsy Queen 70-4s which changed the designation to Marathon 1A. Within two years they were replaced by Herons and all six returned for storage at Cranfield or Lasham to await sale, G-AMHW going to Jordan in September 1954 as VK-501, a VIP transport for King Hussein, later to be destroyed in a take-off accident. The remaining five and the evaluation aircraft G-AMEO were disposed of in the following year and in July 1955 'EO went to Düsseldorf as D-CFSA for radio calibration duties with the West German Civil Aviation Board. G-AMHS and 'HV were delivered to the R.A.E., Farnborough in March 1955 as XJ830 and XJ831 and were converted for special duties as Marathon 1Cs. G-AMGX was fitted out as a juke box showroom by the Balfour Marine Engineering Co. Ltd. at Southend and tried unsuccessfully to reach the U.S.A. by the northern route in August 1955. The remaining pair, G-AMGW and 'HR, were acquired by Derby Aviation Ltd. in October that year and flew on scheduled services between Burnaston, the Channel Islands, Isle of Man and Renfrew until retired in 1960.

The long distance tour of 1950 resulted, two years later, in the sale of the last three production Mk.1A aircraft, G-AMIA, 'IB and 'IC, to Union of Burma Airways in Rangoon. Registered XY-ACX, 'CY and 'CZ, they had increased tankage giving a range of 1,400 miles and although 'CX crashed and burned landing at Myaungmya on 4 August 1953, the others flew for several years on services to Akyab, Calcutta, Singapore and Bangkok. An order for two placed by Far East Airlines, Japan, in 1954 was met by releasing the last two earmarked for T.Mk.11 conversion, G-AMHY and 'HZ, which then went east to become JA-6009 and JA-6010. They were taken over by All Nippon Airways in 1957 and in 1968 JA-6009 was to be seen atop a building at Nagoya Airport. JA-6010 was at that time parked at Tama-Tec near Tokyo.

The Marathon's R.A.F. career was short and it enjoyed only limited service with No. 2 A.N.S., Thorney Island. XA271/G-AMGT crashed at Calne, Wilts. on 30 September 1954 and others were struck off charge following minor accidents, the survivors being sold at Hullavington in October 1958, the majority to scrap dealers but a few found airline customers. G-AMET was purchased by Derby Aviation Ltd. as spares for G-AMEW which they had acquired in August 1957 and converted to Marathon 1A; and East Anglian Flying Services Ltd. bought G-AMEU and 'EV purely for their engines. G-ALVY, G-AMER, 'GR and 'HT were repurchased by F. G. Miles Ltd. and flown to Shoreham for refurbishing but the first three were dismantled in February 1962 and G-AMHT, which made a number of test flights in the same month, soon followed them to the scrap yard. In September 1958 the Air Navigation and Trading Co. Ltd. collected the two R.A.E. machines and moved them first to Lasham and then to Hurn for overhaul where G-AMHS was eventually broken up but G-AMHV was delivered to Squires Gate on 21 June 1960 and in the following March flew to Wymes-wold where it was repainted for a Canadian customer as CF-NUH but never delivered.

The Mamba Marathon, re-engined with Alvis Leonides Major two-row radials and first flown with them at Woodley on 15 March 1955, was not only a test bed but was fitted with nacelles designed for the projected H.P.R.3 Herald. In this form, redesignated H.P.R.5, it was based at Baginton with Alvis Motors Ltd. until it was moved to Bitteswell in 1958 for the installation of the new Armstrong Siddeley P.181 engines and broken up there in October 1959.

Marathon 1C XJ831 (G-AMHV) which, with XJ830 (G-AMHS), was used for communications flights between Farnborough and R.A.E. Bedford 1955–1958.
(*F. G. Swanborough*)

SPECIFICATION

Manufacturers: Handley Page (Reading) Ltd., Woodley Aerodrome, Reading, Berks.
Power Plants: (Miles M.60) Four 330 h.p. de Havilland Gipsy Queen 71.
  (Miles M.69) Two 1,010 e.h.p. Armstrong Siddeley Mamba 502.
  (Marathon 1) Four 340 h.p. de Havilland Gipsy Queen 70-3.
  (Marathon 1A) Four 340 h.p. de Havilland Gipsy Queen 70-4.
  (H.P.R.5) Two 870 h.p. Alvis Leonides Major 701/1.
Dimensions: Span, 65 ft. 0 in. Length, 52 ft. 1½ in. Height, 14 ft. 1 in. Wing area,
  498 sq. ft.

	M.60	M.69	Marathon 1
Tare weight	11,200 lb.	10,850 lb.	11,688 lb.
All-up weight	16,240 lb.	18,000 lb.	18,250 lb.
Maximum speed	230 m.p.h.	290 m.p.h.	232·5 m.p.h.
Cruising speed	210 m.p.h.	260 m.p.h.	201 m.p.h.
Initial climb	682 ft./min.	2,100 ft./min.	595 ft./min.
Ceiling	22,000 ft.	35,000 ft.	18,000 ft.
Range	960 miles	900 miles	935 miles

Production:

Three prototype aircraft by Miles Aircraft Ltd. and forty production machines by Handley Page (Reading) Ltd.

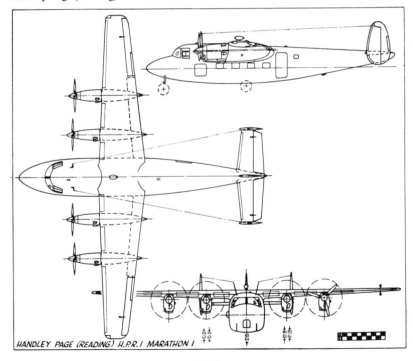

HANDLEY PAGE (READING) H.P.R.1 MARATHON 1

The second prototype Dart Herald after conversion to Series 200, flying in Maritime Central Airways colours as G-ARTC, August 1961.

Handley Page H.P.R.7 Dart Herald

During the early 1950s the Handley Page (Reading) Ltd. designer E. W. Gray and his team began drawings for a short haul airliner which, when revealed in 1953, bore a marked resemblance to an enlarged Marathon with cantilever high-wing, three fins and rudders, and a pressurised semi-monocoque fuselage seating up to 44 passengers. Four Alvis Leonides Major radial piston engines were selected to power the aircraft since intensive market research indicated that potential customers in Australasia, Asia and South America still regarded the propeller turbine as unproven and possibly difficult to maintain in the field. By the end of 1954 the design was finalised as an essentially similar aircraft with large single fin and rudder and designated H.P.R.3 Herald. Two prototypes were laid down and flight testing began in the following year with two Leonides Majors mounted in Herald nacelles fitted to VX231, the sole Marathon 2. The prototype Herald, G-AODE, first flew at Radlett on 25 August 1955 in the colours of Queensland Airlines and appeared at the S.B.A.C. Show, Farnborough, in the following month, the second prototype, G-AODF, making its first flight on 3 August 1956 in time for that year's S.B.A.C. Show.

A production batch of 25 aircraft was laid down under the designation H.P.R.4 but none were completed as such due to a decision taken in May 1957 to change the power plants to two Rolls-Royce Dart propeller turbines. This decision stemmed both from the success of the Vickers Viscount, which had proved the simplicity, reliability and economy of the Dart and from strong competition by the Dart powered Fokker Friendship which was otherwise similar to the Herald.

The prototype Herald was withdrawn from flight testing in June 1957 for conversion and two 2,105 e.h.p. Dart 527 engines were installed in new nacelles about 30 in. further outboard than the inner Leonides but the undercarriage position was retained, giving an asymmetric shape which necessitated a short inverted slot at the tailplane leading edge root to smooth out airflow over the elevator. The fuselage was also lengthened by 20 in. and a large dorsal fillet was

The second prototype H.P.R.3 Herald, G-AODF, with Leonides Major radials, flying to the Farnborough S.B.A.C. Show, September 1957. (*Flight*)

fitted forward of the fin. Now redesignated H.P.R.7 Dart Herald, G-AODE was again flown from Woodley on 11 March 1958 and obtained a preliminary C. of A. on 22 April but on 30 August, while en route to the Farnborough S.B.A.C. Show piloted by chief test pilot Sqn. Ldr. H. G. Hazleden, it suffered an engine failure followed by fire and was destroyed despite a masterly forced landing at Milford near Godalming, Surrey. Dart conversion of G-AODF was completed in time for a first flight on 17 December 1958 and in the following April it commenced the first of three extensive demonstration tours, visiting the Indian sub-continent and returning to England via Iran, Turkey, Greece and Crete. In June it left for South America fitted with long range fuel tanks for the $8\frac{1}{2}$ hour Atlantic crossing from Dakar to Recife and returned in time to participate in the 1959 S.B.A.C. Show. The third tour, to Australasia and the Far East, was timed to include a visit to the official opening of the new airport at Wellington, New Zealand on 24 October.

To assist Handley Page Ltd. to establish a production line in competition with the Friendship, the Ministry of Aviation announced an order for three Dart Heralds on 11 June 1959, registered G-APWB, 'WC and 'WD, to be known as Series 101 for use by B.E.A. on the Scottish 'highlands and islands' services, and G-AODF was accordingly painted in B.E.A. livery. The first production aircraft and company demonstrator, G-APWA, flew on 30 October 1959, also in B.E.A. colours, and left England on 16 March 1960 at the start of a further South American sales tour. Its arrival at Recife coincided with calls for help from flood victims at Fortaleza, and 5,500 lb. of clothing and medical supplies were flown immediately to the stricken area. During this tour G-APWA repeatedly demonstrated its ability to climb, fully laden, straight out from Rio de Janeiro over the top of the 1,430 ft. Sugarloaf Mountain situated only $2\frac{1}{4}$ miles from the end of the runway—a feat accomplished only once before.

In September 1960 Jersey Airlines Ltd. ordered six Dart Heralds, G-APWE to 'WJ with a 42 inch extension to the front fuselage and capable of seating 56 passengers in high density configuration. The second prototype, G-AODF, was converted to this standard, designated Series 200, and resumed flight trials on 8 April 1961 but in the following August it was fitted with a nose radome, re-registered G-ARTC and painted in the livery of Maritime Central Airways, a Canadian operator which had ordered two Dart Heralds. It then took part in that year's S.B.A.C. Show. The demonstrator G-APWA and B.E.A.'s first Series 101, G-APWB, were leased to Jersey Airlines during the summer of 1961 and the first production Series 201, G-APWE, was delivered to them on 4 January 1962, one day before the delivery of G-APWC, first received by B.E.A. The B.E.A. aircraft in fact were the only Series 100 machines to be built and during 1962 G-APWA and 'WC were fitted with pylon-mounted wing tanks for use by H.R.H. Prince Phillip, Duke of Edinburgh, on his 19,000 mile South American tour during which he personally flew G-APWA for 99 hours.

Maritime Central's two Dart Herald Series 202s were delivered to a subsidiary, Nordair Ltd., as CF-NAC and 'AF in February and March 1962 and two more, CF-MCK and 'CM, were ordered but cancelled when the company was taken over in May 1963 by Eastern Provincial Airways Ltd. This operator already had Series 206s CF-EPI and 'PC, and had recently lost CF-NAF with all hands soon after take-off from Halifax, Nova Scotia on 17 March following an explosive decompression resulting from corrosion of the lower fuselage skinning caused by an accumulation of 'bilge fluid'. CF-MCK was then allocated to Cruz Airways as the first of two Series 211s but although it was fully painted as PI-C910, the airline went into liquidation before delivery. The aircraft was therefore registered G-ASKK and leased to Sadia SA Transportes Aereos as PP-ASU for nine months during 1964 alongside the demonstrator G-APWA which was re-registered PP-ASV. CF-MCM became HB-AAG 'Herald of Bern', first of four eventually operated by Globe Air A.G., and was delivered to Basle on 4 May 1963 for inclusive tour and charter work. Small orders and repeat orders kept a slow trickle of Dart Heralds coming off the production line, first at Cricklewood and, from mid-1966, at Radlett and a number flew initially in British marks. British United Airways Ltd. took delivery of Series 204 G-ASBP at Southend on 9 October 1962 and furnished it for executive use.

Aerolinee Itavia purchased four Series 203s, I-TIVA, 'VE, 'VI, and 'VU; Arkia-Israel Inland Airlines acquired five Series 209s, 4X-AHQ to 'HT and the last Dart

Dart Herald Ser.213 D-BEBE 'Herald of Bavaria' landing at Heathrow 1965. It became British Island Airways' G-AYMG in 1971. (*Brian M. Service*)

Herald built, 4X-AHN; Bavaria Flug bought two Series 213s, D-BEBE 'Herald of Bavaria' and D-BIBI 'Herald of Munich'; and British Midland Airways Ltd. ordered two although only G-ASKK was delivered in February 1965 at the end of its lease to SADIA. This company eventually purchased six Series 214s PP-SDG to 'DJ, 'DL and 'DN; Air Manila acquired the Series 215 PI-C866; and Globe Air added HB-AAH 'Herald of Zürich', HB-AAK 'Herald of Basel' and HB-AAL 'Herald of Geneva'. In addition a number of machines went out on short lease

Airline liveries—Itavia's second Dart Herald Ser.203 I-TIVE; British United Airways' Ser.201 G-APWG (*Aviation Photo News*); SADIA's Ser.214 PP-SDJ

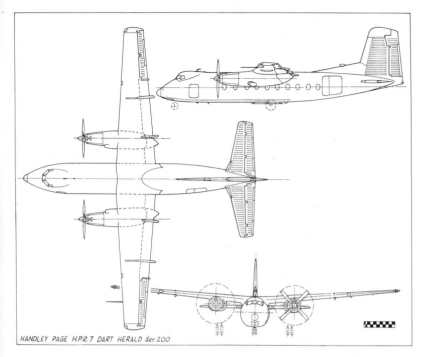

HANDLEY PAGE H.P.R.7 DART HERALD Ser. 200

including Globe Air's HB-AAK prior to delivery to Alia-Royal Jordanian Airlines as G-ASPJ; and Bavaria Flug's D-BIBI to Itavia as G-AVPN. B.U.A.'s Series 204, G-ASBP, was leased to Air Manila as PI-C867 for two months during 1966 and then sold outright.

Military customers comprised the Royal Jordanian Air Force (later the Royal Arab Air Force) which received Series 207s serialled 109 and 110 in 1963. They were transferred to Alia-Royal Jordanian Airlines in December that year as JY-ACR and 'CQ respectively and although the latter crashed near Damascus during the night of 10 April 1965, the former returned to Handley Page Ltd. as G-ATHE for brief service with British Midland Airways Ltd. before sale to Bavaria Flug as D-BOBO 'Herald of the Alps'. In March 1963 the Royal Malaysian Air Force ordered four Series 401s, a version of the Series 200 with strengthened floor, underwing lugs for external stores and a special door able to be opened in flight for making air drops. Serialled FM1020 to FM1023, they were delivered between November 1963 and February 1964 and were followed by four more, the first of which, FM1024, was demonstrated at the 1964 S.B.A.C. Show.

In 1966 the three B.E.A. Series 101s, G-APWB, 'WC and 'WD were sold to Autair International Airways Ltd., Luton and used on scheduled services to the North and Scotland until late in 1969, eventually being sold to Lineas Aereas la Urraca, Colombia as HK-718, HK-715 and HK-721 respectively. Jersey Airlines Ltd. (later renamed British United C.I. Airways Ltd., British United Island Airways Ltd. and finally, in 1970, British Island Airways Ltd.) was operating five of its original Series 201s in 1971 on scheduled services to London, the Channel

261

Islands, Isle of Man, Eastleigh, Exeter, Dublin, Belfast, Squires Gate, Abbotsinch, Turnhouse, Paris, Hanover and Düsseldorf. The sixth aircraft, G-APWI, was sold to Far East Air Transport as B-2009 at the end of 1968 but crashed at Cheluchien, Taiwan on 24 February 1969 and was replaced by G-ATHE re-registered as B-2011 to join B-2001 (the former G-ATHB) acquired in February 1966.

British Island Airways Ltd. also operated G-AVEZ, the former Globe Air HB-AAH, purchased in December 1966 and leased to SADIA early in 1968 as PP-ASW to replace PP-SDJ which had been lost in a crash at Curitiba on 3 November 1967. After Globe Air's financial collapse in 1968 its remaining Dart Heralds HB-AAK and HB-AAL were acquired by the Perpignan-based Europe Aero Service, first as F-OCLY and 'LZ and later as F-BLOY and F-BOIZ.

SPECIFICATION

Manufacturers: Handley Page Ltd., Cricklewood, London, N.W.2 and Radlett Aerodrome, Herts.

Power Plants: (Herald) Four 870 h.p. Alvis Leonides Major 701/1.

(Dart Herald) Two 1,910 s.h.p. Rolls-Royce Dart R.Da.7/2 Mk.527.

	H.P.R.3 Herald	Dart Herald 100	Dart Herald 200
Span	94 ft. 9 in.	94 ft. 9 in.	94 ft. 9 in.
Length	70 ft. 3 in.	71 ft. 11 in.	75 ft. 5 in.
Height	22 ft. 4 in.	24 ft. 0 in.	24 ft. 0 in.
Wing area	886 sq. ft.	886 sq. ft.	886 sq. ft.
Tare weight	25,240 lb.	24,200 lb.	24,960 lb.
All-up weight	37,500 lb.	39,000 lb.	43,000 lb.
Cruising speed	224 m.p.h.	275 m.p.h.	270 m.p.h.
Maximum range	1,640 miles	1,730 miles	1,635 miles

Production: (a) Prototypes

Two conversions of Handley Page (Reading) Ltd. H.P.R.3 Heralds: (c/n 147) G-AODE; (148) G-AODF flown as G-ARTC

(b) Production

Fifty aircraft for British and overseas operators: (c/n 149) Ser.100 G-APWA; (150–152) Ser.101 G-APWB to 'WD; (153–158) Ser.201 G-APWE to 'WJ; (159) Ser.202 CF-NAC; (160) 202 CF-NAF; (161) 211 G-ASKK; (162) 202 CF-MCM/210 HB-AAG, later G-ATHB; (163) 204 G-ASBP; (164) 203 G-ASBG; (165) 207 Jordan Air Force 109/JY-ACR, later G-ATHE; (166) 206 CF-EPI; (167) 206 CF-EPC/VP-BCG; (168) 203 I-TIVE; (169) 210 HB-AAH, later G-AVEZ; (170) 207 Jordan Air Force 110/JY-ACQ; (171) 401 R.M.A.F. FM1020; (172) 401 FM1021; (173) 210 G-ASPJ; (174) 209 G-8-2/4X-AHS; (175) 401 FM1022; (176) 213 D-BIBI, later G-AVPN; (177) 214 G-ATIG; (178) 401 FM1023; (179) 213 D-BEBE, later G-AYMG; (180–182) 401 FM1024 to FM1026; (183) 209 G-8-1/4X-AHR; (184) 203 I-TIVU; (185) 214 G-8-3/G-ASVO; (186) 214 PP-SDH; (187) 401 FM1027; (188) 210 HB-AAL; (189) 209 G-ATDS; (190) 214 PP-SDJ; (191) 214 PP-SDL; (192) 215 PI-C866; (193) Series 200 structural test airframe; (194) 214 PP-SDN; (195) 209 4X-AHQ; (196) 203 I-TIVI; (197) 209 4X-AHN

The first prototype Jetstream, G-ATXH, on test in 1968. (*Aviation Photo News*)

Handley Page H.P.137 Jetstream

By the mid 1960s it was apparent to Handley Page Ltd. that its long association with military aircraft was ending and, with Dart Herald sales also tapering off, a new commercial project was required to carry the company through the next decade. Attention was directed towards the small feeder liner market and detail design work began late in 1965 on the Jetstream, announced publicly on 19 January 1966.

It was revealed as a sleek monoplane with semi-monocoque pressurised fuselage seating up to 18 passengers with genuine 'walk-around' capability, powered by two 840 e.h.p. Turboméca Astazou propeller turbines. Aimed principally at world third level and executive markets, maximum all-up weight was set at 12,500 lb. for F.A.A. certification and later in the year C.S.E. International Ltd. was appointed distributor for Europe, Africa and the Middle East with options on 100 aircraft, and the International Jetstream Corporation was formed, with 65 options, to handle sales in North America.

As a result of forecasts of a potential market for 1,000 Jetstreams, Handley Page Ltd. commenced large scale production, built a new assembly hangar at Radlett and sub-contracted a number of major components including the complete mainplane to Scottish Aviation Ltd., Prestwick and the tail unit to Northwest Industries Ltd., Edmonton, Alberta.

Four prototypes, G-ATXH to 'XK, and a static test airframe were laid down initially and chief test pilot J. W. Allam made the first 100 minute test flight in G-ATXH with the lower powered 690 e.h.p. Astazou 12s at Radlett on 18 August 1967. The first flight with the specified Astazou AZ 14-C01s was made on 29 November and the next Jetstream to fly was G-ATXJ on 28 December. Both aircraft were then evaluated at the Turboméca airfield at Pau, south west France in order to take advantage of its factory facilities and the superior winter weather. The third aircraft, G-ATXI, flown on 8 March 1968, was followed a month later by G-ATXK, the International Jetstream Corporation demonstrator which remained permanently in the U.S.A. and later flew in the livery of Cal-State Air Lines, Long Beach, California.

In December 1967 Handley Page also negotiated a contract to supply the United States Air Force with 11 Jetstream 3M utility transports powered by 904 e.h.p. Garrett AiResearch TPE-331-3W-301A propeller turbines. Featuring a large forward hinging cargo door, strengthened floor and accommodation for 12 passengers (or 6 stretcher cases) at the increased all-up weight of 14,500 lb., this version received the U.S.A.F. designation C-10A, the allocated serials being 68-10378 to 68-10388. The Jetstream 3M was the first transport aircraft ever ordered by the U.S.A.F. outside North America and a fuselage mock-up in its livery appeared at the September 1968 Farnborough S.B.A.C. Show.

The prototype, G-AWBR, first flew on 21 November 1968 and G-ATXI was later re-engined and first flew with the Garrett TPE-331s on 7 May 1969 prior to static display at the Paris Air Show. Both aircraft were then used for airframe and engine certification and this programme had actually been completed and the production C-10As were well advanced when, in October 1969, the order was cancelled. G-ATXI and G-AWBR were then broken up and during 1970 their cockpit sections went to the Stansted Fire School, the production airframes ending up in a scrap yard at Cove, Hants.

The second production Jetstream, which flew on 2 January 1969 under Class B marking G-8-4, was delivered to C.S.E. International Ltd. at Kidlington the following day to become their demonstrator G-AXEK. During the Paris Air Show in June 1969 it flew a daily Kidlington—Le Bourget service piloted by Hugh Field and immediately afterwards was evaluated by Dan-Air Services Ltd. on its Bristol—Cardiff—Liverpool—Newcastle route but in mid-June C.S.E. International Ltd. announced the termination of its distributorship and G-AXEK returned to Handley Page Ltd.

The next aircraft, G-AXEL, was subjected to prolonged fitting out at Kidlington and delivered to the British Steel Corporation on 28 September but on the following day crash landed at Courtyard Farm, Norfolk. A later aircraft, G-8-12, delivered to Kidlington as a replacement, was never finished. G-AXEM

Jetstream 1 N1035S of Cal-State Air Lines at Long Beach in 1969. Formerly G-AWVK, it returned to England via Prestwick on 20 December 1970. (*Aviation Photo News*)

The Jetstream 3M prototype, G-AWBR, showing the changed nacelle shape and totally enclosed undercarriage of the Garrett powered version.

was delivered to Bavaria Flug, Munich as D-INAH on 3 October but crashed on approach to Samaden, St. Moritz, Switzerland on 6 March 1970 at the end of a charter flight from Munich.

High structural weight made it impossible to achieve performance targets but G-ATXI completed $51\frac{1}{2}$ hours of intensive route proving which led to British and United States certification in March 1969 by which time the first and third production aircraft, G-AWSE and G-AWVI, were already in the United States for delivery to Sun Airlines of St. Louis, Missouri. Transatlantic deliveries in British ferry markings then increased rapidly, six going to Cal-State Air Lines as N1035S to N1040S, including the two originally ordered by Sun Airlines, while others such as the Hoover Corporation's N5V, National Steel's N340 and Standard Oil's N815M, were sold for executive purposes. The International Jetstream Corporation used G-AWYP, appropriately re-registered N137HP, as a new demonstrator, while G-AXHB, which went to Northwest Industries Ltd., the Canadian distributors, as CF-QJB, was painted in the livery of Airspur Ltd. which had ordered 20 Jetstreams.

By the summer of 1969, however, Handley Page Ltd. was already in financial difficulties due to excessive Jetstream development costs combined with disappointing sales in Britain and Europe which, in turn, led to a loss of confidence in the United States. It also became clear that the original performance targets could be met only by fitting more powerful 1,073 e.h.p. Astazou AZ 16-C engines but there was no finance available for such a conversion and on 8 August the company went into liquidation. The Receiver created a trading company styled Handley Page Aircraft Ltd. to continue Jetstream production, and in the following October the American-owned K. R. Cravens Corporation financed development of the Astazou AZ 16-C powered Jetstream 2.

Prototype G-ATXH was fitted with these engines and allocated to Rolls-Royce Ltd., Filton for engine trials and a production Jetstream 1, G-AXFV, was similarly fitted for performance testing. This programme too was nearly complete when, on 27 February 1970, Handley Page Aircraft Ltd. also went into liquidation, leaving G-ATXH engaged in tropical trials at Fort Lamy, Chad and

The Jetstream 2 development aircraft G-AXFV showing the ventral fin fitted to all production aircraft.

demonstrator G-AXEK stranded at Brisbane during an Australian sales tour. On 2 March the Radlett works closed down and most of its semi-complete aircraft were scrapped.

Later in the year Terravia Trading Services Ltd., which had been responsible for Jetstream transatlantic delivery flights, announced that it had acquired all production rights, a number of complete aircraft, and sufficient spares to ensure continued product support. After discussions with the International Jetstream Corporation, Jetstream 1 N666WB was shown at the N.B.A.A. Convention at Denver, Colorado in September 1970 and Terravia, later restyled Jetstream Aircraft Ltd., delivered G-AXUI and 'UM to the Cranfield Institute of Technology to be equipped as flying classrooms; and G-AXUN, 'UO and 'XS to Sywell for furnishing and sale. N1035S, which returned to Blackbushe from the U.S.A. in Cal-State livery on 20 December 1970 to act as demonstrator, won the 135 mile *Daily Express* Air Race from Sywell to Biggin Hill on 12 June 1971 piloted by the company's managing director, Capt. W. J. Bright and the first sale was completed at Leavesden, the new Jetstream base, on 26 January 1972 when G-AXUO was handed over to the Metz-based French operator Air Wasteels.

Handling trials towards Jetstream 2 certification were completed with the development aircraft G-AXFV, which competed in the London–Victoria B.C. transatlantic air race in July 1971 piloted by Capt. Bright; it was flown to Dubai on the Persian Gulf by chief test pilot J. W. Allam in the following September for tropical trials; and then evaluated at Boscombe Down as a possible R.A.F. Varsity replacement.

Future plans were to market the Jetstream in two versions to be known as Series 200 and Series 300 operating at all-up weights of 12,500 lb. and 14,000 lb. respectively and built on a new production line set up at Prestwick by Scottish Aviation (Jetstream) Ltd. who acquired the production rights when they received an order for 25 aircraft for the R.A.F. in February 1972.

SPECIFICATION

Manufacturers: Handley Page Ltd., Radlett Aerodrome, Herts.; Scottish Aviation (Jetstream) Ltd., Prestwick Aerodrome, Ayrshire.

Power Plants: (Jetstream 1)   Two 840 e.h.p. Turboméca Astazou AZ 14-C01.
(Jetstream 200) Two 996 e.h.p. Turboméca Astazou AZ 16-C.
(Jetstream 3M) Two 904 e.h.p. Garrett TPE 331-3W-301A.

Dimensions: Span, 52 ft. 0 in. Length, 47 ft. $1\frac{1}{2}$ in. Height, 17 ft. $5\frac{1}{2}$ in. Wing area, 270 sq. ft.

	Jetstream 1	Jetstream 200	Jetstream 3M
Tare weight	8,450 lb.	8,850 lb.	—
All-up weight	12,500 lb.	12,500 lb.	14,500 lb.
Cruising speed	250 m.p.h.	285 m.p.h.	—
Ceiling	30,000 ft.	—	27,000 ft.
Maximum range	1,900 miles	2,480 miles	1,455 miles*

* Ten passengers in executive layout.

Production: (a) Handley Page H.P.137 Jetstream 1

Forty-five British registered aircraft and the following flown only in Class B markings:
(c/n 222) G-8-9; (234) G-8-12; (243) G-8-13

(b) Handley Page H.P.137 Jetstream 3M

One aerodynamic prototype (c/n 258) G-AWBR and eleven unfinished C-10A aircraft laid down for the U.S.A.F.: (c/n 219) 68-10378; (226) 68-10379; (228) 68-10380; (232) 68-10381; (236) 68-10382; (239) 68-10383; (242) 68-10384; (244) 68-10385; (247) 68-10386; (250) 68-10387; (260) 68-10388

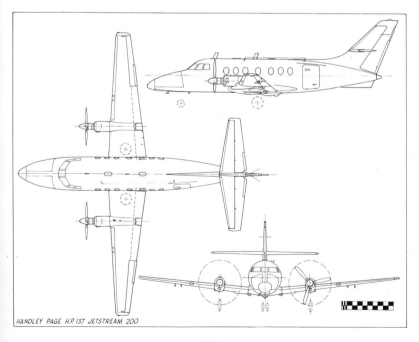

HANDLEY PAGE H.P. 137 JETSTREAM 200

The sole remaining Tomtit in 1948 with standard uncowled engine and Spitfire windscreen. (*Hawker Aircraft Ltd.*)

Hawker Tomtit

In the late 1920s the Air Ministry forsook wooden construction and issued a specification for an all-metal Mongoose powered trainer. Hawker's interpretation of this specification was the Tomtit, a fabric covered, two seat biplane with Handley Page automatic slots, Frise ailerons on the lower wing only and cockpits behind the centre section for ease of parachute escape. It was fully aerobatic and a delight to fly. Thirty-six were built between 1929 and 1931, mostly for the R.A.F. but four went to the R.N.Z.A.F. and five were registered by the makers as civil aeroplanes. The first two, fitted with Mongoose IIIA radials, were G-AALL and G-ABAX, flown in the 1930 King's Cup Race by Sqn. Ldr. D. S. Don and the Hon. F. E. Guest respectively, the latter coming 12th, to record the first of many Tomtit racing failures. A third machine G-AASI appeared in September 1930 fitted experimentally with a Cirrus Hermes I in-line engine and despite its low power put up good aerobatic performances at Brooklands, piloted by P. E. G. Sayer and others.

The original pair were sold to the Hon. F. E. Guest, after which 'LL was fitted with a Mongoose IIIC, standard engine of the R.A.F. machines. After coming 8th piloted by Flg. Off. E. C. T. Edwards in the *Morning Post* Race at Heston on 21 May 1932, it competed for the King's Cup against G-AASI. The latter now boasted a Mongoose IIIC in place of the Hermes, but the pilots, F. E. Guest and H. Wilcox, were unlucky and retired. Last of the civil Tomtits, G-ABII and 'OD, almost certainly the last two built, were registered in 1931. In May 1933 'SI, 'AX and 'OD were sold to Wolseley Motors Ltd. and went to Castle Bromwich as engine test beds, and for that year's King's Cup Race, 'SI and 'AX fitted with geared Wolseley A.R.9 Mk. Ia radials and 'OD with a direct drive A.R.9 Mk. IIa, were flown by Brookland's strongest team, P. W. S. Bulman, P. E. G. Sayer and

G. E. Lowdell. Although they averaged 137 m.p.h., the handicapper was not to be beaten, and they faired no better in the following year. In the Hanworth–Isle of Man Race on 30 May 1936, however, Charles Hughesdon came 2nd in G-AASI at 107 m.p.h.

Various trial engine installations were made at Castle Bromwich in ensuing years, including that of a Wolseley Aries in 1935. In 1938 'OD, with a Wolseley Aquarius, became personal mount of Hawker test pilot W. Humble, its A.R.9 powered stable mates spending the last year of peace with the Tollerton Aero

Messrs. Bulman, Sayer and Lowdell flying the Wolseley engined Tomtits prior to the 1933 King's Cup Race. Note the ungeared engine of G-ABOD. (*Flight Photo 7566*)

Tomtit G-AASI in 1930 with Cirrus Hermes engine.

Club. The Tomtit G-ABII served inconspicuously as the maker's communications aircraft for 12 years, going camouflaged to Gloster Aircraft Ltd. for the same purpose in 1943. It reappeared at Fairoaks after the war but it was damaged beyond repair at Cowes in 1948.

A second chapter in the history of the type opened in 1935, when the R.A.F. disposed of its obsolete Tomtits by public tender. Nine were civilianised by L. J.

Tomtit G-ABOD with the experimental Wolseley Aquarius engine.

Anderson, Hanworth; C. B. Field, Kingswood Knoll; the Leicestershire Aero Club, Braunstone and Southern Aircraft (Gatwick) Ltd. First to appear, G-AEES, performed aerobatics and pleasure flying with Campbell Black's British Empire Air Displays in 1936–37, eventually going to private ownership at Marylands. G-AEXC saw a year's service at Broxbourne with the Herts and Essex Aero Club; and a fleet of four, G-AFIB, 'KB, 'TA and 'VV, operated at the Leicester Club. H. D. Rankin flew his private G-AFFL from Southend, where it was wantonly smashed up at the outbreak of war. C. Plumridge's G-AEVO, on the other hand, survived at Redhill until 1947, when it was burned in an adjacent field.

Six Hawker Tomtits were unique in wartime because G-ABII, G-AFIB, 'KB, 'TA, 'VV and G-AGEF all flew continuously on communications duties as camouflaged civil aeroplanes and somehow resisted impressment. G-AFIB and its successors, 'TA and G-AGEF, were mainly used as personal mounts of Alex Henshaw, test pilot of Spitfires built by the Castle Bromwich Aeroplane Factory.

Following the post-war loss of G-ABII, the only surviving Tomtit was G-AFTA, fitted with a Spitfire windscreen and a streamlined headrest, legacy of its wartime Henshaw ownership. After spending 1948 at Chalgrove with R. C. S. Allen, 'TA became the property of Hawker's chief test pilot Neville Duke, thereby becoming well known for its air racing and aerobatic prowess until Hawker Aircraft Ltd. purchased it in July 1950 and maintained it in immaculate condition as a flying museum piece. Based at Dunsfold, it appeared annually at any air display where biplane nostalgia was appreciated until it was eventually handed over to the Shuttleworth Trust, Old Warden but returned temporarily to Dunsfold in 1967 to be repainted in its original R.A.F. colours as K 1786.

SPECIFICATION

Manufacturers: H. G. Hawker Engineering Co. Ltd., Canbury Park Road, Kingston-on-Thames and Brooklands Aerodrome, Byfleet, Surrey.

Power Plants: One 155 h.p. Armstrong Siddeley Mongoose IIIA.
One 150 h.p. Armstrong Siddeley Mongoose IIIC.
One 105 h.p. A.D.C. Cirrus Hermes I.
One 185 h.p. Wolseley A.R.9 Mk. Ia or IIa.
One 170 h.p. Wolseley Aquarius.
One 225 h.p. Wolseley Aries.

Dimensions: Span, 28 ft. 6 in. Length, 23 ft. 8 in. Height, 8 ft. 8 in. Wing area, 238 sq. ft.

*Weights: Tare weight, 1,100 lb. All-up weight, 2,100 lb.

*Performance: Maximum speed, 124 m.p.h. Cruise, 105 m.p.h. Initial climb, 1,000 ft./min. Ceiling, 19,500 ft. Range, 350 miles.

* With Mongoose IIIC engine.

Production:

One prototype: J9772 built 1927–28. Five British civil aircraft: G-AALL, G-AASI, G-ABAX, G-ABII, G-ABOD built 1929–31.

First production batch of ten for the R.A.F.: J9773–J9782 built 1929. Second batch of six: K1448–K1453 built 1929–30. Third batch of eight: K1779–K1786 built 1930.

Two for the R.C.A.F.: serials 139 and 140 built 1930. Four for the R.N.Z.A.F.: serials 50–53 built 1930–31.

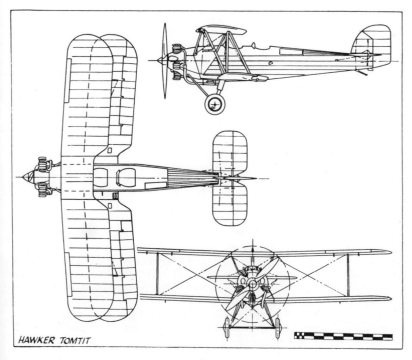

HAWKER TOMTIT

271

AP-ATK, first Trident 1E for Pakistan International Airlines, first flown in November 1965 as G-ATNA, on a pre-delivery flight near Hatfield in March 1966.

Hawker Siddeley H.S.121 Trident

In 1957 the de Havilland Aircraft Co. Ltd. commenced design studies to meet a B.E.A. requirement for a 600 m.p.h. jetliner capable of flying 1,000 mile stage lengths. These were eventually finalised as the D.H.121 low-wing cantilever monoplane seating up to 111 passengers and powered by three 12,000 lb. s.t. Rolls-Royce RB.141 Medway turbojet rear-mounted engines, two in side-pods and the third in the extreme rear of the fuselage below a high-set tailplane. Then, in 1958, B.E.A. asked for a smaller aircraft which necessitated a major re-design from which the aircraft emerged in scaled-down form around three 10,100 lb. s.t. Rolls-Royce RB.163 Spey turbofan engines and seating up to 101 passengers. Among its unconventional features were the all-flying tailplane, sideways retracting nose leg offset 24 inches to port and a Bristol Siddeley Artouste auxiliary power unit permanently fitted under the floor of the rear cabin.

Construction of 24 aircraft, G-ARPA to 'PP, 'PR to 'PU and 'PW to 'PZ, began at Hatfield in July 1959 but when de Havillands became part of the Hawker Siddeley Group in 1960 the prototype became the H.S.121 Trident and first flew at Hatfield on 9 January 1962 piloted by John Cunningham and Peter Buggé. G-ARPB and 'PC, first flown on 20 May and 25 August 1962 respectively, were followed by G-ARPD on 17 January 1963, all four being used for the intensive certification programme which culminated in a full C. of A. issued on 18 February 1964. The first revenue earning flight followed on 11 March and full scheduled services on 1 April.

Only 23 aircraft were actually delivered because G-ARPY crashed at Felthorpe, Norfolk during its maiden flight on 3 June 1966 as the result of a deep stall with the loss of test pilots Peter Barlow and the redoubtable George Errington and two other crew. The fleet thereafter gave uneventful service until 3 July 1968 when the rear fuselage was sliced from G-ARPI, and G-ARPT totally destroyed, by the crashing Airspeed Ambassador G-AMAD as they stood parked at Heathrow. G-ARPI was repaired on site and flew again on 10 February 1969.

Being tailored to B.E.A. requirements the Trident had little outside appeal. Accordingly a number of variants were evolved, the first being the Trident 1C with increased tankage in the centre section and all B.E.A. aircraft of the original

Airline liveries: YI-AEB, Iraqi Airways' second Trident 1E; 5B-DAB, second Trident 1E for Cyprus Airways; G-AVYD, second Trident 1E-140 operated by Northeast Airlines Ltd. (*Aviation Photo News*); G-AVYE, the second Channel Airways Trident 1E-140. (*John Goring*)

The third Trident 3B flying in B.E.A.'s revised livery at the Farnborough S.B.A.C. Show, September 1970. (*Richard Riding*)

order were, in fact, fitted with 9,850 lb. s.t. Spey Mk. 505/5F engines as Trident 1Cs carrying 109 passengers at the increased all-up weight of 117,300 lb.

In August 1962 the 115 passenger Trident 1E was announced with Spey Mk. 511/5 engines, increased span, tankage and all-up weight, and also the Trident 1F with a 110 inch fuselage extension and seats for 125 passengers. The Artouste auxiliary power unit was moved to the base of the fin and full span leading edge slats, first flown on Trident 1C G-ARPD as part of the 1E development programme, replaced the drooped leading edge of the earlier mark.

Kuwait Airways ordered three Trident 1Es, 9K-ACF to 'CH, the first of which flew on 2 November 1964 as G-ASWU before delivery from Hatfield via Heathrow as 9K-ACF on 18 March 1966. The second aircraft, flown initially as G-ASWV, was written off in a non-fatal undershoot at Kuwait Airport on 30 June 1966, a month after delivery. Iraqi Airways, which purchased Trident 1Es YI-AEA to 'EC, was the first operator actually to take delivery, YI-AEA being handed over on 1 October 1965. Pakistan International Airlines followed suit with an order for four, AP-ATK to 'TM and AP-AUG, the first of which was test flown as G-ATNA and left Hatfield on delivery on 1 March 1966. AP-AUG was repainted briefly in Pakistan Air Force colours before delivery in P.I.A. livery in February 1967. Three years later three of the Pakistani Tridents were sold to the People's Republic of China and the first, AP-AUG, left Karachi for Pekin on 29 June 1970.

Five more Trident 1Es, G-AVYA to 'YE, were also laid down and the first rolled out in Kuwait Airways livery in January 1966 but they remained unsold until October 1967 when Channel Airways Ltd. signed a contract for all five. Operating at an all-up weight of 135,580 lb. and fitted with 139 passenger seats, this version was redesignated Trident 1E-140. Only two, G-AVYB and 'YE, were delivered to Channel Airways Ltd. at Stansted May–June 1968, 'YC and 'YD being delivered to B.K.S. Air Transport Ltd. (restyled Northeast Airlines in 1970) for scheduled London–Newcastle and other services. The fifth aircraft, which never carried British markings, was completed as a Trident 1E and delivered to Air Ceylon as 4R-ACN on 16 July 1969.

In December 1971–January 1972 the two Channel Trident 1E-140s were delivered to B.E.A. at Heathrow to be prepared for service with Northeast and the two surviving Kuwait 1Es, 9K-ACF and 'CH, also arrived for overhaul and delivery to Cyprus Airways.

Discussions with B.E.A. concerning a Trident 1F order, begun during 1962, resulted in the improved Trident 2E of 1964. The fuselage remained unchanged but wing span was again increased and, with extra fuel in the fin and more powerful Spey Mk. 512/5W engines, the long London–Beirut stage could at last be flown nonstop. B.E.A. ordered 15 Trident 2Es, G-AVFA to 'FO, on 26 August 1965 equipped to carry 97 tourist class passengers. The first aircraft flew on 27 July 1967, scheduled services began on 18 April 1968 and deliveries were completed in 1969. Two Trident 1Es were also supplied to Cyprus Airways Ltd. as 5B-DAA and 'AB and the first, flown on 28 August 1969, was delivered on 18 September. During 1971–72 twelve Trident 2Es were ordered by the Republic of China which were test flown as G-AZFT to 'FY and G-BABP to 'BV.

The Trident was built from the outset for automatic landing in bad weather and Trident 1C G-ARPB, retained by Hawker Siddeley for 'Autoflare' and 'Autoland' development, made its first fully automatic landing at Bedford on 5 March 1964 flown by test pilot J. Phillips who, with John Cunningham, was at the controls when 'PB made the first fully automatic landing by a civil aircraft in fog when it landed at Heathrow in nil visibility on 4 November 1966. The world's first automatic touchdown on a commercial service was made by Trident 1C G-ARPR when it arrived at Heathrow from Paris on 10 June 1965.

Following further discussions with B.E.A. in May 1966, Hawker Siddeley proposed a high capacity variant, the Trident 3, for medium range inter-city routes which, later in the year, became the Trident 3B with a small booster engine for take-off from difficult airfields. This was basically a Trident 2E with a 16 ft. 5 in. fuselage extension and accommodating up to 179 tourist class passengers.

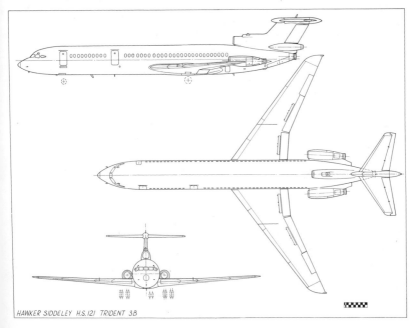

HAWKER SIDDELEY H.S.121 TRIDENT 3B

Wing span remained unchanged but wing area and span of t' flaps were bot' increased and a 5,250 lb. s.t. Rolls-Royce RB.162-86 turbojet eng was installed at the base of the fin to provide extra take-off thrust, allowing either a 1,800 ft. reduction in take-off run or 14,500 lb. greater payload. A Garrett AiResearch GTCP 85C auxiliary power unit was also mounted inside the fin and all-up weight rose to 150,000 lb. B.E.A. ordered 26 Trident 3Bs, G-AWYZ and 'ZA to 'ZZ although for operational convenience G-AWZY was re-registered G-AYVF before delivery. G-AWYZ made its first flight on 11 December 1969 without the RB.162 engine installed and deliveries commenced in the following year.

SPECIFICATION

Manufacturers: Hawker Siddeley Aviation Ltd., Hatfield Aerodrome, Herts.

Power Plants: (Trident 1C) Three 9,850 lb. s.t. Rolls-Royce Spey 505/5F.

(Trident 1E) Three 11,400 lb. s.t. Rolls-Royce Spey 511/5.

(Trident 2E) Three 11,930 lb. s.t. Rolls-Royce Spey 512/5W.

(Trident 3B) Three 11,930 lb. s.t. Rolls-Royce Spey 512/5W and one 5,250 lb. s.t. Rolls-Royce RB.162.

Dimensions, Weights and Performance:

	Trident 1C	Trident 1E	Trident 2E	Trident 3B
Span	89 ft. 10 in.	95 ft. 0 in.	98 ft. 0 in.	98 ft. 0 in.
Length	114 ft. 9 in.	114 ft. 9 in.	114 ft. 9 in.	131 ft. 2 in.
Height	27 ft. 0 in.	27 ft. 0 in.	27 ft. 0 in.	28 ft. 3 in.
Wing area	1,358 sq. ft.	1,446 sq. ft.	1,456 sq. ft.	1,493 sq. ft.
Tare weight	68,071 lb.	69,700 lb.	73,800 lb.	81,250 lb.
All-up weight	117,300 lb.	130,000 lb.*	142,500 lb.	150,000 lb.
Maximum cruise	610 m.p.h.	590 m.p.h.	590 m.p.h.	550 m.p.h.
Economical cruise	579 m.p.h.	580 m.p.h.	580 m.p.h.	540 m.p.h.
Maximum range	1,300 miles	2,700 miles	2,700 miles	2,235 miles

* Trident 1E-140, 135,580 lb.

Production: (a) Trident 1C and 1E

Twenty-four Trident 1Cs for British European Airways commencing (c/n 2101) G-ARPA; and the following Trident 1Es for Kuwait, Iraq, Ceylon and Cyprus: (c/n 2114) 9K-ACF/G-ASWU; (2118) 9K-ACG/G-ASWV; (2125) YI-AEA; (2127) YI-AEB; (2129) YI-AEC; (2130) AP-ATK/G-ATNA; (2131) AP-ATL; (2132) AP-ATM; (2133) AP-AUG; (2134) 9K-ACH, later G-AZND; (2135) 4R-ACN/ G-AYVA; (2154) 5B-DAA; (2155) 5B-DAB

(b) Trident 1E-140

Four aircraft only: (c/n 2136–2139) G-AVYB to G-AVYE

(c) Trident 2E

Fifteen aircraft for B.E.A. commencing (c/n 2140) G-AVFA; twelve for China (2157) G-AZFT to (2162) G-AZFY and (2163) G-BABP to (2168) G-BABV

(d) Trident 3B

Twenty-six aircraft for B.E.A. commencing (c/n 2301) G-AWYZ

Hawker Siddeley H.S.125 Series 1B HB-VAU, originally built for Transair A.G., Geneva, was delivered Luton–Dakar for Nigeria Airways as 5N-AER in December 1966 but later went to the U.S.A. as N2246.

Hawker Siddeley H.S.125

In March 1961 a team led by de Havilland designer J. Goodwin began work on the two crew/6–8 passenger D.H.125 'mini jetliner' known for a short time as the Jet Dragon and powered by two 3,000 lb. static thrust Bristol Siddeley Viper 20 turbojets mounted externally in the rear. An initial batch of 30 aircraft was laid down in the Chester factory but the two prototypes, slightly shorter in span and length, were constructed in the experimental shop at Hatfield.

The first, G-ARYA, rolled out only 15 months later in July 1962, made a maiden flight of 56 minutes on 13 August piloted by C. A. Capper and the second, G-ARYB, followed on 12 December. Both aircraft then embarked on an intensive proving and certification programme in which they were joined later by the first production D.H.125, G-ARYC, delivered to Bristol Siddeley Engines Ltd. at Filton on 24 July for flight trials of the Viper 520 engine destined for subsequent aircraft. G-ASEC, the fourth D.H.125, flown on 30 April 1963, operated a simulated airline schedule between Gatwick and Le Bourget during the Paris Air Show in the following June.

The next two aircraft, first for customer operation, were G-ASNU flown on 26 February 1964 and delivered to Fried. Krupp GmbH, Essen as D-COMA on 10 October; and HB-VAG, to the Swiss charter organisation Chartag AG at Zürich on 10 September.

Only nine production aircraft, designated Series 1, were completed before cabin windows were reduced from six to five and Viper 521 and 522 engines substituted to permit an increase in all-up weight to 21,000 lb. Like most later variants this model was marketed as the Series 1A for operation under American F.A.A. certification, and as the Series 1B for sale elsewhere.

The company was determined to follow up the success its Dove had had on the American continent and three distributors were appointed to cover the area, followed by a North American tour by the 8th aircraft, G-ASSI, in the autumn of 1964 and the issue of a Series 1A demonstrator to each. The 13th D.H.125, G-ASSJ, delivered to Atlantic Aviation Sales Corporation of Wilmington,

H.S.125 Series 2 Dominie T.Mk.1 XS730 'H' of No.1 Air Navigation School, Stradishall 1966. (*Aviation Photo News*)

Delaware via Prestwick on 11 September 1964 (and later registered N125J) was followed on 23 September by G-ASSK which became N125G with AiResearch Aircraft Sales Corporation of Los Angeles, and by G-ASSL which left Prestwick on 16 December for Timmins Aviation Ltd. of Montreal where it was registered CF-RWA.

By this time de Havillands had become part of the newly created Hawker Siddeley Group but in North America the de Havilland reputation was such that the aircraft continued to be marketed as the D.H.125 instead of H.S.125. Large numbers of this and later variants were sold, transatlantic deliveries being made under British registration in primer finish for final furnishing and painting to customer requirements by the distributors.

A smaller number of H.S.125 Series 1s and 1Bs were sold elsewhere, principally in Britain and Europe, and also as V.I.P. transports with foreign air forces. British operators included C. A. Parsons Ltd. of Newcastle with G-ASSI; Shell Aviation Ltd. with G-ATPD and 'PE at Heathrow; the Board of Trade Civil Aviation Flying Unit with G-ATPC at Stansted; and Gregory Air Taxis Ltd. with the former Krupps aircraft restored as G-ASNU and based at Luton. The last made the headlines when it was hijacked over the Mediterranean on 30 June 1967 while carrying the former Congolese prime minister Moise Tsombe. It was flown to Algeria and impounded for 42 weeks before it was released and flown back to Gatwick on 18 April 1968.

In 1963 the R.A.F. ordered twenty H.S.125s, designated Series 2 but similar to the Series 1B while retaining the Viper 520 engines of the Series 1. Known as the H.S. Dominie T.Mk.1 in Service use, the first, XS709, flew on 30 December 1964 and the majority served as navigation trainers initially with No. 1 Air Navigation School at Stradishall but XS710 was delivered to the A. & A.E.E., Boscombe Down and XS732–XS736 went initially to the College of Air Warfare, Manby. In March 1971 an additional order was placed for four aircraft for operation as V.I.P. transports by No.32 Squadron, Northolt.

VH-ECE and 'CF, Series 3 crew trainers with cockpit layouts similar to the Boeing 707, were specially built for QANTAS in 1965 and by July 1966 production reached one per week and 100 aircraft had been completed. Series 3A and 3B models with improved air conditioning, auxiliary power units and Viper 522 engines were then introduced, British operators including the Beecham Group Ltd. whose G-AVGW, lost in a crew training accident at Luton on 23 December 1967, was replaced by G-AVVB; the British Aircraft Corporation which based G-AVPE and 'RF at Filton; and the Rank Organisation and Rio Tinto Zinc Corporation which operated G-ATZN and G-AWMS respectively from Heathrow.

G-AVAI, 'DX, 'OI and 'XL all became demonstrators in turn and various improvements followed which permitted an increase in maximum take-off weight which was used to provide additional fuel capacity in a large tank faired into the underside of the fuselage. This, in turn, necessitated the addition of a ventral fin, first tested on the company-owned Series 1B G-ATWH and on the prototype G-ARYA, all H.S.125s being built to this standard from mid-1967 as Series 3A-RA and 3B-RA. In September 1968 the Series 400A and 400B were announced with luxury seating for 7 passengers, integral airstair door, flight deck improvements and increase in all-up weight to 23,300 lb. G-AWXN and G-AXYJ served as demonstrators and other British registered aircraft included the Green Shield Stamp Company's G-AWXO; G-AXDM of Birmingham Sound Reproducers Ltd.; G-AYEP of the British Steel Corporation; and G-AYFM of the Ford Motor Co. Ltd., Stansted.

During 1969 negotiations took place with the American Beechcraft Corporation for the joint design, construction and marketing of a family of business jet aircraft and as a first step H.S.125 marketing in North America was transferred to Beechcraft with an associated change in designation to B.H.125 signifying the creation of the Beechcraft Hawker Aircraft Corporation. Appropriately G-AXYE was re-registered N41BH in the U.S.A. and many subsequent exports initially carried marks in this sequence. By February 1972 production of all variants exceeded 270 aircraft, the majority for export.

A larger, faster version of the B.H.125, designated Series 600, with higher powered Viper 600 turbojets, was soon announced and a partial conversion of the fourth D.H.125 G-ASEC was made to speed the certification process. The prototype, Series 600B G-AYBH, which first flew at Chester on 21 January 1971, was followed by the first production example G-AZHS.

H.S.125 Series 1B demonstrator G-ATWH modified to Series 1B-R as aerodynamic prototype of the Series 3A-RA and 3B-RA with integral air stairs, long range tank under fuselage and ventral fin. (*Richard Riding*)

The first and second prototypes, G-ARYA and 'YB, were sent by road to Hawker Siddeley apprentice training schools at Chester and Hatfield respectively as instructional airframes in the summer of 1968 so that in 1971, when in use for Viper 600 engine trials, the first production aircraft, G-ARYC, was the oldest flying H.S.125.

The H.S.125 Series 400 carried up to 10 passengers, one example, Series 400B D-CBVW being delivered to the German Volkswagenwerke A.G. in August 1970. (*Aviation Photo News*)

SPECIFICATION

Manufacturers: de Havilland Aircraft Co. Ltd., Hatfield Aerodrome, Herts. and Hawarden Aerodrome, Chester (style changed to Hawker Siddeley Aviation Ltd. in 1964).

Power Plants:

(Prototypes)	Two 3,000 lb. s.t. Bristol Siddeley Viper 20.
(Series 1)	Two 3,000 lb. s.t. Bristol Siddeley Viper 520.
(Series 1A/1B)	Two 3,100 lb. s.t. Bristol Siddeley Viper 521/522.
(Series 3, 3A/3B, 3A-RA/3B-RA)	Two 3,360 lb. s.t. Bristol Siddeley Viper 522.
(Series 400A/B)	Two 3,600 lb. s.t. Bristol Siddeley Viper 522.
(Series 600A/B)	Two 3,750 lb. s.t. Bristol Siddeley Viper 601-22.

	Series 1	Series 1B	Series 3B-RA	Series 400B
Span	47 ft. 0 in.	47 ft. 0 in.	47 ft. 0 in.	47 ft. 0 in.
Length	47 ft. 5 in.	47 ft. 5 in.	47 ft. 5 in.	47 ft. 5 in.
Height	16 ft. 6 in.	16 ft. 6 in.	16 ft. 6 in.	16 ft. 6 in.
Wing area	353 sq. ft.	353 sq. ft.	353 sq. ft.	353 sq. ft.
Tare weight	9,768 lb.	10,300 lb.	11,500 lb.	11,275 lb.
All-up weight	20,000 lb.	21,200 lb.	23,100 lb.	23,300 lb.
Max. cruise	485 m.p.h.	472 m.p.h.	500 m.p.h.	510 m.p.h.
Econ. cruise	420 m.p.h.	420 m.p.h.	440 m.p.h.	450 m.p.h.
Maximum range	2,000 miles	1,930 miles	2,050 miles	1,940 miles

Prototype dimensions: Span, 44 ft. 0 in. Length, 43 ft. 6 in.
Height, 14 ft. 0 in. Wing area, 342 sq. ft.

Production: (a) H.S.125 Series 1

Two prototypes, six other British registered aircraft and (c/n 25006) HB-VAG for Chartag

(b) H.S.125 Series 1A

Sixty-two built, 34 with Viper 521, 28 with Viper 522, mainly British registered but the following were exported in foreign marks: (c/n 25015) VH-CAO; (25018) CF-DOM; (25025) D-COME/HB-VAR/F-BOHU; (25027) CF-SEN; (25028) Ghana G-511; (25034) CF-HLL; (25036) CF-PQG; (25039) CF-SIM/N413G; (25042) CF-ANL; (25053) CF-IPJ; (25058) D-COMI/N9308Y/N215G/N632PB/N470R; (25080) VQ-ZIL/3D-AAB; (25086) CF-DSC

(c) H.S.125 Series 1B

Thirteen built, three with Viper 521, ten with Viper 522 including six British registered and the following for export: (c/n 25063) HB-VAN; (25067) 9J-RAN; (25068) XB-BEA/XA-BEM; (25090) HB-VAT, later G-AWYE; (25099) HB-VAU/5N-AER; (25105) D-CKOW/D-CKCF, later G-AYRY; (25106) HZ-BIZ, later G-AWUF

(d) H.S.125 Series 2 Dominie T.Mk.1

Twenty aircraft for the R.A.F.: (c/n 25011) XS709; (25012) XS710; (25024) XS711; (25040) XS712; (25041) XS713; (25044) XS726; (25045) XS727; (25048–25050) XS728–XS730; (25054) XS714; (25055) XS731; (25056) XS732; (25059) XS733; (25061) XS734; (25071) XS735; (25072) XS736; (25076) XS737; (25077) XS738; (25081) XS739

(e) H.S.125 Series 3

Two special aircraft for QANTAS only: (c/n 25062) VH-ECE; (25069) VH-ECF

(f) H.S.125 Series 3A

Fifteen aircraft exported with British registrations

(g) H.S.125 Series 3B

Twelve British registered aircraft and the following for export in foreign marks: (c/n 25117) 5N-AET; (25132) OY-DKP; (25135) HB-VAY, later G-AXPS; (25147) PK-PJR; (25154) EP-AHK; (25157) D-CAMB

(h) H.S.125 Series 3A-RA

Nineteen aircraft exported with British registrations

The first production H.S.125 Series 600B, G-AZHS, showing the larger cabin with six-a-side windows.

281

(i) H.S.125 Series 3B-RA

Five British registered aircraft and the following for export: (c/n 25162) Brazilian Air Force VC93-2120; (25164) EC93-2125; (25165) VC93-2121; (25166) VC93-2122; (25167) VC93-2123; (25168) VC93-2124; (25171) HB-VBT, later G-AXPU

(j) H.S.125 Series 400A

A large number of aircraft for export, mainly with British registrations but the following flew out in foreign marks: (c/n 25192/NA724) CF-SDH; (25193/NA725) CF-CFL, crashed in Labrador 11.11.69 and replaced by G-AXTT q.v.; (25221/NA746) N42BH/CG-BNK; (25228/NA751) N47BH/N640M; (25229/NA752) N48BH/ N9148D; (25230/NA753) N49BH/N400BH; (25232/NA754) CF-TEC; (25233/ NA755) N50BH/N701Z; (25234/NA756) N51BH; (25236/NA757) N52BH/N125BH; (25237/NA758) N53BH/N6709; (25239/NA759) G-5-19/N54BH/N6702; (25241/ NA760) N55BH/N731X; (25244/NA761) N56BH; (25245/NA762) N57BH; (25251/NA763) N58BH; (25253/NA764) N59BH; (25255/NA765) N62BH; (25258/NA766) N63BH; (25261/NA767) N64BH; (25263/NA768) N65BH

Note: Export c/n NA769 to NA780 were registered N66BH to N77BH inclusive. Hawker
  Siddeley c/n for these and previous Series 400A aircraft are unconfirmed.

(k) H.S.125 Series 400B

A large number of British registered aircraft and the following for export in foreign marks: (c/n 25197) PP-EEM; (25209) Malaysian Air Force FM1201; (25215) HB-VBZ; (25231) D-CBVW; (25235) HB-VCE, later G-AYNR; (25242) VH-TOM; (25248) D-CFCF; (25252) G-5-17; (25257) G-5-19

(l) B.H.125 Series 600A

Production commenced 1972 with (c/n 6001) G-AZUF

(m) H.S.125 Series 600B

Two British registered aircraft by July 1972: (c/n 25256) G-AYBH; (25268) G-AZHS

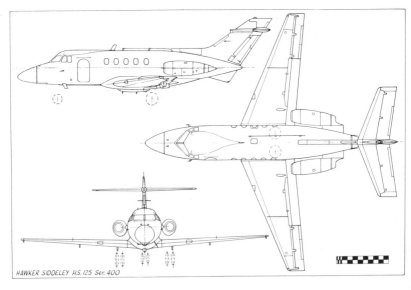

HAWKER SIDDELEY H.S.125 Ser. 400

The prototype Armstrong Whitworth A.W.650 Argosy Series 100, G-AOZZ, on an early test flight in 1959

Hawker Siddeley H.S.650 Argosy

In 1955 Sir W. G. Armstrong Whitworth Aircraft Ltd. prepared design studies for a general purpose transport with two 3,000 h.p. propeller turbine engines and conventional fuselage to which designations A.W.65 and A.W.66 were allotted in its civil and military forms. These studies eventually crystallised as the four engined A.W.650 medium range, twin boom freighter with podded fuselage which Hawker Siddeley developed as the private venture H.S.650 Argosy.

Operators showed interest and an initial batch was laid down comprising ten aeroplanes and two structural test airframes. The first machine, G-AOZZ, was first flown for 62 minutes at Bitteswell by chief test pilot Eric Franklin on 8 January 1959, only 23 months after the issue of the first drawings. Six Argosies were flown in the first ten months, a rapid production rate achieved by using a mainplane based on that of the Avro Shackleton 3 constructed at Manchester by A. V. Roe and Co. Ltd. under type number Avro 733; a Gloster-built tail unit; and Vickers Viscount-type nacelles to house the four Rolls-Royce Dart 526 turbine engines.

The crew occupied a raised flight deck above the pressurised freight pod of 3,680 cu. ft. capacity, sufficient to accommodate six 80 in. pallets loaded through nose and tail doors by means of the Gloster-designed Rolamat cargo handling system.

The first four Argosies were all used to speed the certification programme. The second, G-APRL, left Elmdon on 31 August 1959 for tropical trials at Khartoum and Nairobi; the third, G-APRM, was used for detail performance measurements; and the fourth, 'RN, for a European sales tour following its appearance at the September 1959 Farnborough S.B.A.C. Show in company with the fifth, G-APVH.

Riddle Airlines Inc. of Miami, U.S.A. placed an order for four Argosies and the demonstrator G-APRN, which first flew in their colours for publicity purposes, gave a convincing demonstration of its ability to handle awkward loads by flying 8 tons of electronic equipment from Heathrow to Benbecula. Commanded by test pilot Eric Franklin and equipped for mixed traffic with 24 seats and a 10,000 lb. specimen load, the same Argosy began a 300 hr. route proving programme in May 1960 to simulated airline schedules between Elmdon and the European capitals. The aircraft made a sales tour to Athens, Beirut and Malta between 14 and 17 June and on 17 July it left for a ten day tour of India carrying components for the first Indian-built H.S.748s.

After considerable modification the second Argosy, G-APRL, flew again at Bitteswell on 28 July 1960 as the aerodynamic prototype of the H.S.660 military transport. The nose door was sealed to take a radome; 'clam shell' doors with integral loading ramp for large vehicles or air-dropping supplies were fitted in the rear; and two exit doors were cut in the starboard side for use when carrying paratroops.

The Riddle order was increased to seven Series 101 aircraft commencing N6501R when a MATS contract was awarded on 17 June 1960 for a Logair outsize cargo freight operation. This called for five Argosies to ply daily over three routes originating and terminating at Tinker A.F.B., Oklahoma, carrying spares and materials to 27 U.S.A.F. bases; and two held permanently available for U.S. Government emergency use.

The second Argosy, G-APRL, flying in July 1960 as aerodynamic prototype of the military A.W.660 (later H.S.660) version with rear 'clam shell' doors.

Commencing with N6501R on 12 December 1960, the Riddle Argosies were delivered via Prestwick and the North Atlantic and the first Logair flight was made on 15 January 1961, departing in the early hours of the morning as Flight 80 on a 3,444 mile circuit embracing 16 States and reaching Wright-Patterson Field in the north and Kelly Field in the south. Flight 81 also left each morning on a 4,837 mile schedule via 11 States to Grand Forks Base in the north and McChord in the north west while Flight 82 was an evening departure to the north east through 16 States as far afield as Loring A.F.B.

A purely commercial freight service was also inaugurated between Miami and San Juan on February 21 but when the contract ended in June 1962 Riddle traded all seven Argosies back to the manufacturers who sold five to Capitol Airlines of Berry Field, Nashville, Tennessee, for a similar MATS contract, and the remaining two were leased to Zantop Air Transport of Detroit, Michigan. These were

G-APRL flying over Coventry in Riddle colours as N6507R before delivery in August 1961.

N6501R and N6505R (re-registered respectively as N601Z and N600Z) operated on domestic cargo services and a daily 3,421 mile military supply route emanating from Wright-Patterson A.F.B. with ten traffic stops at stage lengths varying from 156 to 801 miles. Later a third Capitol Argosy, the former G-APRL/N6507R, was transferred to Zantop as N602Z but on 14 October 1965, N601Z forced landed on a highway south of Piqua, Ohio, and was wrecked.

When British European Airways signed a contract on 27 April 1961 for the purchase of G-AOZZ, G-APRM and 'RN, all ten Argosies of the initial batch had been sold, the works at this time being fully engaged with the completion of fifty-six H.S.660 Argosy C.Mk.1 transports for the R.A.F., the first of which, XN814, had flown at Bitteswell on 6 March 1961. The first B.E.A. Argosy freight service was flown on 14 November 1961 and all three aircraft, known as Series 102, were in service by January 1962 and by the following April replaced all Dakota and York aircraft on scheduled freight services between London, Manchester, Copenhagen and Milan. A night freight service between London, Düsseldorf and Frankfurt was opened on 2 January 1962 under contract to Deutsche Lufthansa and in 1963 B.E.A. operated twice weekly to Guernsey where (to quote the *BEA Magazine*) the Argosy '. . . caught all eyes when she waddled on to the apron and opened up like an Easter egg to discharge her goodies. . . .'

On 9 March 1964 the first of a batch of ten Series 200 Argosies, G-ASKZ, made its first flight at Bitteswell piloted by Eric Franklin. The new version had an enlarged freight hold with wider front and rear doors enabling six standard MATS-type 108 in. cargo pallets to be transferred from intercontinental jet aircraft to the Argosy for European distribution. Powered by four 2,100 e.h.p. Rolls-Royce Dart 532/1s, maximum range was increased to 1,160 miles with a 20,000 lb. payload by abandoning the Shackleton-type wing and fitting a main-plane with a redesigned fail-safe box spar giving a 400 lb. saving in structural weight. Within a month of the first flight of G-ASKZ, the manufacturers agreed to repurchase B.E.A.'s Argosy Series 102s in part exchange for five newer models, G-ASXL to 'XP, to be known as Series 222. The last was delivered at Heathrow

Zantop Argosy Series 101, N601Z, formerly Riddle's N6501R, flying near Detroit in 1963.

The prototype Argosy G-AOZZ at Bitteswell in December 1968 before delivery to Universal Airlines as N896U.

The former Universal Airlines N893U in service with Sagittair Ltd. as G-AZHN in 1972.
(*P. J. Bish*)

286

on 16 June 1965 but 'XL was lost when it struck high ground during an approach to Milan in bad weather on 4 July and was replaced by the final Argosy, G-ATTC, c/n 6805, delivered on 21 November 1966. When G-ASXP was burned out in a crew training accident at Stansted a fortnight later no replacement was considered.

In 1966 Capitol's four remaining Argosy Series 101s were also transferred to Zantop, which, in the same year, changed its name to Universal Airlines and in 1968 acquired the former B.E.A. aircraft G-AOZZ and G-APRN. The entire fleet of eight was then re-registered with 'U' suffixes as N890U to N897U. G-APRM, delivered to Filton in April 1969 for airlifting Concorde engines to and from Toulouse, became the last U.K.-based Argosy, the unsold G-ASKZ and incomplete airframe c/n 6806 having been reduced to spares in September 1967.

In 1970 export aircraft began to trickle back, commencing with N867U leased to Nittler Air Transport, Luxembourg until restored to Sagittair Ltd., Heathrow as G-APRN in May 1971. N893U, which followed in August, was airtested at Castle Donington for Sagittair Ltd. on 26 October as G-AZHN, and N892U arrived on 6 January 1972 for restoration as G-APWW. The former B.E.A. G-ASXM was ferried back to Dublin from Canada on 3 November 1971 as EI-AVJ 'The Consortium' for Aer Turas International.

G-ASXO, fourth Argosy Series 222, was delivered to B.E.A. on 28 April 1965 and sold to Midwest Airlines Ltd., Winnipeg exactly five years later.

SPECIFICATION

Manufacturers: Sir W. G. Armstrong Whitworth Aircraft Ltd., Baginton Aerodrome, Coventry and Bitteswell Aerodrome, Warwicks. (re-styled the Avro Whitworth Division of Hawker Siddeley Aviation Ltd. w.e.f. 8 July 1963).

Power plants: (Ser.100) Four 2,100 e.h.p. Rolls-Royce Dart 526.
(C.Mk.1) Four 2,680 e.h.p. Rolls-Royce Dart 101.
(Ser.200) Four 2,100 e.h.p. Rolls-Royce Dart 532/1.

	Series 100	C.Mk.1	Series 200
Span	115 ft. 0 in.	115 ft. 0 in.	115 ft. 0 in.
Length	86 ft. 9 in.	89 ft. 0 in.	86 ft. 9 in.
Height	27 ft 0 in.	27 ft. 0 in.	29 ft. 3 in.
Wing area	1,458 sq. ft.	1,458 sq. ft.	1,458 sq. ft.
Operating wt. empty	48,000 lb.	57,400 lb.	48,830 lb.
Max.loaded weight	88,000 lb.	97,000 lb.	93,000 lb.
Optimum cruise	276 m.p.h.	269 m.p.h.	285 m.p.h.
Initial climb	900 ft./min.	1,000 ft./min.	900 ft./min.
Range (max. fuel)	1,610 miles	3,250 miles	1,850 miles

Production: (a) Argosy Series 101 and 102

Ten aircraft only: (c/n 6651) G-AOZZ; (6652) G-APRL; (6653) G-APRM; (6654) G-APRN; (6655) G-APVH; (6656) G-APWW; (6657) G-1-4/Riddle N6505R/Zantop N600Z/N893U; (6658) G-1-5/N6506R; (6659) G-1-6/N6501R/N601Z; (6660) G-1-7/N6502R/N895U

(b) Argosy C.Mk.1

Fifty-six aircraft for the R.A.F.: (c/n 6743–6798) XN814–XN821; XN847–XN858; XP408–XP413; XP437–XP450; XR105–XR109; XR133–XR143

(c) Argosy Series 222

Eight aircraft only: (c/n 6799) G-ASKZ; (6800) G-ASXL; (6801) G-ASXM; (6802) G-ASXN; (6803) G-ASXO; (6804) G-ASXP; (6805) G-ATTC; (6806) incomplete airframe.

Note: The 9th and 10th aircraft (c/n 6807–6808) existed only as components.

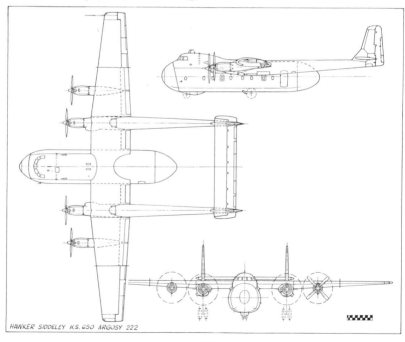

HAWKER SIDDELEY H.S. 650 ARGOSY 222

APPENDIX A

Other British-built Civil Aircraft

This section of the book describes civil aircraft of British design which existed only in prototype form or in small numbers and includes designs intended for amateur construction which, although of foreign origin, have been built in Britain from British materials to British standards of airworthiness.

Whenever possible, registration details are included in the text but when this is prevented through lack of space, they are listed in Appendix E. Omission of the date of issue of C. of A. indicates that none was issued. Dates are given in the British way, viz. day, month, year.

Abbreviations are confined to:

C.C.A	Controller of Civil Aviation
d.b.r	Damaged beyond economical repair
f/f	First flown
F/G	Flying Group
P.F.A.	Popular Flying Association
R.A.E.	Royal Aircraft Establishment
w.f.u	Withdrawn from use

(*Aeroplane*)

Chrislea L.C.1 Airguard

Side-by-side cabin two seater powered by one 62 h.p. Walter Mikron 2, designed for Civil Air Guard training by R. C. Christophorides and B. V. Leak and built by the Chrislea Aircraft Co. Ltd. at Heston 1938. One aircraft only: G-AFIN, c/n L.C.1, owned by J. W. Haggas, Throssington, Leics. from 1940 but later stored near Salisbury, Wilts. Collected by the Northern Aircraft Preservation Society 2.70, reassembled at Irlam, Lancs. 1972 with new fuselage constructed at R.A.F. Finningley. Span, 35 ft. 9 in. Length, 21 ft. 5 in. Tare wt., 812 lb. A.U.W., 1,300 lb. Max. speed, 118 m.p.h. Cruise, 104 m.p.h.

(*E. J. Riding*)

Cierva W.11 Air Horse

Experimental 24 seat or freight helicopter, with three rotors driven via a gearbox by one 1,620 h.p. Rolls-Royce Merlin 24, built at Eastleigh by the Cierva Autogiro Co. Ltd. 1948. Two aircraft only: G-ALCV, c/n W.11/1, static exhibit at 1948 S.B.A.C. Show, first flown by H. A. Marsh as VZ724 at Eastleigh 7.12.48 at an A.U.W. of 14,000 lb., the greatest lift by helicopter at that time. Crashed at Eastleigh due to fatigue failure of the rotor hub, H. A. Marsh and crew killed 13.6.50; G-ALCW, c/n W.11/2, flown as WA555 before storage at M.o.S. Sub-Depot at Byley, Cheshire. Rotor diameter 47 ft. 0 in. Length, 88 ft. 7 in. Tare wt., 12,140 lb. A.U.W., 17,500 lb. Cruise, 116 m.p.h.

(*A. J. Jackson*)

Cierva W.14 Skeeter 1

Two seat experimental helicopter powered by one 110 h.p. Jameson FF-1, built at Eastleigh 1948. One aircraft only: G-AJCJ, c/n W.14/1, static exhibit at 1948 S.B.A.C. Show, first flown by H. A. Marsh at Eastleigh 10.48. Used for test and exhibition flying, broken up at Eastleigh 11.52. Rotor diameter, 29 ft. 0 in. Length, 35 ft. 7 in. Tare wt., 810 lb. A.U.W., 1,210 lb. Cruise, 75 m.p.h.

Cierva W.14 Skeeter 2

Two seat experimental all-metal helicopter powered by one 145 h.p. de Havilland
Gipsy Major 10, built at Eastleigh 1949. One aircraft only: G-ALUF, static
exhibit at 1949 S.B.A.C. Show, first flown by H. A. Marsh at Eastleigh 15.10.49.
Broken up by vibration due to ground resonance, Eastleigh 26.6.50. Rotor dia-
meter, 32 ft. 0 in. Length, 38 ft. 4½ in. Tare wt., 1,200 lb. A.U.W., 1,800 lb.
Cruise, 77 m.p.h.

(Air Portraits)

Cierva CR. LTH-1 Grasshopper 3

Four seat helicopter powered by two 135 h.p. Rolls-Royce Continental O-300 flat
four engines driving two co-axial, contra-rotating, two bladed rotors and built at
Redhill by Cierva Rotorcraft Ltd. in conjunction with Servo-Tec Ltd. Three
prototypes initially: G-AWRP, c/n GB-1, began tests 1969, P. to F. 13.5.71;
G-AXFM, c/n GB-2, first flown 8.69, P. to F. 12.2.70; G-AZAU, c/n
GB-3, registered 6.71. Rotor diameter, 32 ft. 0 in. Length, 34 ft. 5 in. Tare wt.,
1,650 lb. A.U.W., 3,050 lb. Cruise, 116 m.p.h. Range, 250 miles

(*E. J. Riding*)

C.L.W. Curlew

Two seat all-metal trainer powered by one 90 h.p. Pobjoy Niagara III and built by Messrs. S. W. Cole, A. Levell and F. S. Welman at Bexleyheath, Kent 1936, embodying the C.L.W. lightweight cantilever wing. One aircraft only: G-ADYU, c/n C.L.W.1, first flight by A. N. Kingwill at Gravesend 9.36, C. of A. issued 19.11.36. Sold to Essex Aero Ltd., Gravesend, 9.9.36, stored during the war, scrapped at Gravesend 1948. Span, 26 ft. 6 in. Length, 21 ft. 6 in. Tare wt., 970 lb. A.U.W., 1,500 lb. Max. speed, 127 m.p.h.

(*Flight Photo 7790*)

Clarke Cheetah Biplane

Single seat convertible monoplane/biplane using the lower wings of Halton Mayfly G-EBOO and some D.H.53 components, powered by one 35 h.p. Blackburne Thrush, designed and built 1929 by Flg. Off. J. Clarke, R.A.F. One aircraft only: G-AAJK, c/n C.C.1, C. of A. 17.9.29. Following the death of its designer in a Siskin crash at Brough 11.10.29, it was acquired by Lord Malcolm Douglas Hamilton and flown at the Suffolk Aero Club's meeting in June 1930. Span, 29 ft. 0 in.

Clarke Cheetah Monoplane

The original Clarke Cheetah acquired in September 1930 by A. C. Thomas and three other airmen of No. 600 (City of London) Squadron, Hendon and converted to monoplane. Flown at Hendon and Tangmere until disposed of to F. G. Miles at Shoreham in 1935. Sold to R. A. Hopkinson at Hanworth (later Abingdon) 5.36. Scrapped in 1937. Span, 29 ft. 0 in. Tare wt., 450 lb. A.U.W., 678 lb.

Clutton Fred

Wood and fabric monoplane designed and built by E. C. Clutton and E. W. Sherry 1957–63 and designated FRED (Flying Runabout Experimental Design). One aircraft only: G-ASZY, c/n EC/ES.1A, first flown at Meir, Stoke-on-Trent, 3.11.63 as Fred Mk. 1 with 27 h.p. Triumph 5T motor cycle engine. Flown 1965 with 37 h.p. Scott Squirrel; taxying trials 1966 as Fred Mk. 2 with 37 h.p. Lawrance L-5 radial; flown 1968 with 66 h.p. converted Volkswagen (illustrated). Span, 22 ft. 6 in. Length, 17 ft. 0 in. Tare wt., 533 lb. A.U.W., 773 lb. Cruise, 63 m.p.h.

(*Aeroplane*)

Comper Mouse

Three seater with retractable undercarriage, powered by one 130 h.p. de Havilland Gipsy Major, built at Heston 1933. One aircraft only: G-ACIX, c/n M.33/1, C. of A. issued 22.5.34. Flown in the 1934 King's Cup Race by E. H. Newman at an average speed of 132·75 m.p.h. Span, 37 ft. 6 in. Length, 25 ft. 1 in. Tare wt., 1,300 lb. A.U.W., 2,215 lb. Cruise, 130 m.p.h.

(*Aeroplane*)

Comper Streak

Single seat sporting monoplane with retractable undercarriage, powered by one 146 h.p. de Havilland Gipsy Major high compression engine. One aircraft only: G-ACNC, c/n S.T.33/1, first flown by Comper at Heston 12.4.34, C. of A. issued 18.5.34. Built for the Coupe Deutsch Race in which it was flown by Comper at Etampes 27.5.34 but withdrew with undercarriage trouble. Forced down at Wittering in 1934 King's Cup Race after averaging 175·5 m.p.h. Flown in 1935 King's Cup Race by Philip de Walden Avery at 173·5 m.p.h. Scrapped at Heston 1937. Span, 23 ft. 6 in. Length, 18 ft. 0 in. Tare wt., 880 lb. A.U.W., 1,500 lb.

Comper Kite

Two seat tourer version of the Comper Streak, powered by one 90 h.p. Pobjoy Niagara, built by the Comper Aircraft Co. Ltd. at Heston 1934. One aircraft only: G-ACME, c/n K.34/42, C. of A. issued 10.7.34. Flown in the 1934 King's Cup Race by Flt. Lt. E. A. Healey at an average speed of 143·5 m.p.h. Scrapped at Heston 1935. Span, 23 ft. 6 in. Length, 19 ft. 3 in. Tare wt., 750 lb. A.U.W., 1,350 lb. Max. speed, 155 m.p.h. Cruise, 140 m.p.h.

Cranwell C.L.A.2

Side-by-side two seat ultra light designed by Flt. Lt. N. Comper and built by the Cranwell Light Aeroplane Club for the 1924 Air Ministry trials at Lympne. One aircraft only: G-EBKC, powered by one 32 h.p. Bristol Cherub, first flown by Comper at Cranwell 14.9.24. Completed 17 hours 53 minutes flying at Lympne, covering 762·5 miles to win the £300 Reliability Prize. Later crashed while under evaluation at Martlesham. Span, 29 ft. 8 in. Length, 23 ft. 3 in. Tare wt., 540 lb. A.U.W., 897 lb.

Cranwell C.L.A.3

Single seat ultra light powered by one 32 h.p. Bristol Cherub built at Cranwell 1925. One aircraft only: G-EBMC, won the International Speed Race at its first public appearance at Lympne 1.8.25, making fastest time of 86·92 m.p.h. Fitted with 36 h.p. Cherub III and metal airscrew for 1926 King's Cup Race but Comper was forced down. It was scrapped in 1929. Span, 21 ft. 0 in. Length, 18 ft. $6\frac{1}{2}$ in. Tare wt., 325 lb. A.U.W., 530 lb. Max. speed, 100 m.p.h.

Cranwell C.L.A.4A

Two seat inverted sesquiplane built at Cranwell for the 1926 Lympne Trials. Two aircraft only: G-EBPB, C. of A. issued 12.4.27, flown by Comper in the trials but eliminated with damaged undercarriage, flown in Bournemouth Races 1927, Blackpool Races 1928 and Orly Meeting 1928. Sold to J. T. H. Baldwin, Catterick 5.30, scrapped at Heston 1933; G-EBPC intended as C.L.A. 4 with Pobjoy P, but in its absence was fitted with 36 h.p. Cherub III and crashed 4.3.27. Span, 27 ft. 4 in. Length, 22 ft. $3\frac{1}{2}$ in. Tare wt., 480 lb. A.U.W., 874 lb.

(E. J. Riding)

Cunliffe-Owen Concordia

Medium range 10 seat transport powered by two 550 h.p. Alvis Leonides L.E.
4M, designed by W. Garrow-Fisher and built by Cunliffe-Owen Aircraft Ltd. at
Eastleigh 1947. Two aircraft only: prototype Y-0222, c/n 1, first flown at
Eastleigh by A. Corbin 19.5.47; G-AKBE, c/n 2, shown at 1947 Radlett S.B.A.C.
Show, C. of A. issued 15.10.47. Made extensive European sales tour. Work
suspended 18.11.47 on production batch of six, including G-AKBF/VT-CQT, c/n
3, for Nawab of Bhopal and two for B.E.A. as sufficient market did not exist.
Span, 56 ft. 7 in. Length, 44 ft. 10 in. Tare wt., 4,450 lb. A.U.W., 12,500 lb. Max.
speed, 216 m.p.h. Cruise, 160 m.p.h.

(A. R. Weyl)

Dart Flittermouse

Single seat ultra light powered by one 25 h.p. Scott Squirrel, designed by A. R.
Weyl and built by Dart Aircraft Ltd. at Dunstable 1936 to the order of Dr. H. N.
Bradbrooke. One aircraft only: G-AELZ, c/n H.N.B.1, A. to F. 28.8.36, flown at
Witney until sold to A. Carpenter, Whitley, 5.38. Rear skid then removed,
undercarriage moved back and castoring nose wheel fitted. Few straight hops
only. Sold to G. A. Chamberlain 1950, scrapped at Blackbushe 1951. Span,
40 ft. 6 in. Length, 22 ft. 6 in. A.U.W., 640 lb. Max. speed, 64 m.p.h.

(*A. R. Weyl*)

Dart Pup

Single seat, ultra light pusher with one 27 h.p. Ava 4a-00 flat four, designed by A. R. Weyl and built by Zander and Weyl Ltd at Dunstable 1936 as the Dunstable Dart. Renamed Pup when the company reformed as Dart Aircraft Ltd. One aircraft only: G-AELR, c/n Dart Mk. II, first flown 7.36, A. to F. 8.8.36, modified 1937 with horn balanced rudder, taller undercarriage and 36 h.p. Bristol Cherub III. Sold to A. E. Green, Tachbrook 9.37, crashed on take-off 8.38. Span, 29 ft. 7½ in. Length, 19 ft. 8½ in. Tare wt., 485 lb. A.U.W., 705 lb. Cruise, 62 m.p.h.

(*Aeroplane*)

Dart Kitten

Single seat ultra light with 27 h.p. Ava 4a-00 flat four, designed by A. R. Weyl and constructed by Dart Aircraft Ltd., Dunstable. Prototype Mk. I, G-AERP, built 1936 followed by one Mk. II, G-AEXT, with 36 h.p. Aeronca-J.A.P. J-99, revised decking and simplified undercarriage in 1937 and one Mk. III, G-AMJP, with wheel brakes in 1951. A fourth, VH-WGL, home built at Port Moresby, New Guinea, was registered 9.11.60 to A. P. Baglee. Span, 31 ft. 9 in. Length, 21 ft. 4 in. Tare wt., 440 lb. A.U.W., 682 lb. Cruise, 65 m.p.h. (Mks. II/III) Tare wt., 582 lb. A.U.W., 835 lb. Cruise, 83 m.p.h. Range, 340 miles

De Bolotoff SDEB 14

Two seat general utility biplane powered by one 200 h.p. Curtiss 8 cylinder water-cooled geared engine. Designed by Prince Serge de Bolotoff and built by the de Bolotoff Aeroplane Works at Sevenoaks, Kent, 1919. One aircraft only, G-EAKC, c/n 14, registered to de Bolotoff and Company 14.8.19. Span, 'about 36 ft.'

De Bruyne Snark

Experimental four seat, low-wing monoplane powered by one 130 h.p. de Havilland Gipsy Major, designed by Dr. N. A. de Bruyne and built by Aero Research Ltd., Hinxton Road, Duxford, Cambs., formed by the designer to investigate low weight, bakelite-bonded plywood, stressed skin, wing and fuselage structures. One research aircraft only: G-ADDL, c/n D.B.2, first flown at Cambridge by Dr. de Bruyne 16.12.34, C. of A. issued 25.4.35. Transferred to the R.A.E., Farnborough 5.36 as L6103 for research into the aerodynamic behaviour of thick wing monoplanes. Span, 42 ft. 6 in. Length, 24 ft. 7 in. Tare wt., 1,200 lb. A.U.W., 2,200 lb. Max. speed, 123 m.p.h. Cruise, 110 m.p.h. Range, 450 miles

De Bruyne-Maas Ladybird

Shoulder wing single seater with monocoque wooden fuselage, powered by one 25 h.p. Scott Squirrel. Designed by Dr. N. A. de Bruyne, construction begun by Aero Research Ltd. at Duxford in 1936 was completed by J. N. Maas in 1937. One aircraft only: G-AFEG, c/n D.B.3/M.1, flown at Cambridge by R. G. Doig. Fitted with 36 h.p. Bristol Cherub (illustrated) in 1938. Still stored in a barn near Peterborough in 1960. Span, 32 ft. 0 in. Length, 20 ft. 0 in. Tare wt., 420 lb. A.U.W., 800 lb. Max. speed, 95 m.p.h. Cruise, 75 m.p.h.

Deekay Knight

Side-by-side two seater powered by one 90 h.p. Blackburn Cirrus Minor, designed by S. C. Hart-Still and built and flown by the Deekay Aircraft Corporation Ltd. at Broxbourne, 1937. One aircraft only: G-AFBA, c/n 237/1, scrapped during war. Span, 31 ft. 6 in. Length, 22 ft. 10 in. Tare wt., 850 lb. A.U.W., 1,450 lb. Max. speed, 125 m.p.h. Cruise, 105 m.p.h.

De Havilland D.H.29

Ten passenger monoplane powered by one 450 h.p. Napier Lion, built at Stag Lane 1921. One civil aircraft only, ordered by the Air Ministry as the second prototype Doncaster J6850 but became G-EAYO, c/n 8, on completion. Registered to the de Havilland Aircraft Co. Ltd. 28.9.21, to Martlesham trials 9.11.22, not used commercially, registration lapsed. Span, 54 ft. 0 in. Length, 43 ft. 0 in. Tare wt., 4,370 lb. A.U.W., 7,500 lb. Max. speed, 116 m.p.h. Cruise, 100 m.p.h.

De Havilland D.H.37

Three seater powered by one 270 h.p. Rolls-Royce Falcon III. Two aircraft only: G-EBDO 'Sylvia', c/n 43, built for A. S. Butler and first flown 6.22, C. of A. 11.7.23, owner came 5th in 1922 King's Cup Race and made two trips to Prague in 1924. First flown 5.27 as D.H.37A 'Lois' with 300 h.p. A.D.C. Nimbus, second in Hamble races 15.5.27, crashed during Bournemouth races 4.6.27, pilot H. Hemming. G-AUAA, c/n 105, C. of A. 15.5.24, C.C.A., Australia, to Guinea Gold Co. Ltd., Lae 1927, crashed at Crowdy Head, N.S.W. 25.3.32. Span, 37 ft. 0 in. Length, 28 ft. 9 in. Tare wt., 2,507 lb. A.U.W., 3,550 lb. Max. speed, 133 m.p.h.

(*Aviation Photo News*)

De Havilland D.H.51

Three seat tourer powered by one 120 h.p. Airdisco. Three aircraft only: G-EBIM first flown with 90 h.p. R.A.F. 1A; G-EBIQ; and G-EBIR 'Miss Kenya', taken to Nairobi 1.26, became VP-KAA in 1929, flown back for the Shuttleworth Trust, Old Warden 7.65 in an R.A.F. Beverley. G-EBIM was fitted with single bay wings as D.H.51A and flown by C. D. Barnard in the 1925 King's Cup Race; to Australia 4.27 as G-AUIM; converted to D.H.51B floatplane in 1929. Span, 37 ft. 0 in. (D.H. 51A) 32 ft. 0 in. Length, 26 ft. 6 in. Tare wt., 1,342 lb. (D.H. 51A) 1,437 lb. A.U.W., 2,240 lb. Cruise, 90 m.p.h.

(*Flight Photo*)

De Havilland D.H.54 Highclere

Transport for two crew and 12 passengers powered by one 650 h.p. Rolls-Royce Condor IIIA, equipped with jettisonable undercarriage to facilitate ditching and also camber changing flaps. One aircraft only: G-EBKI, c/n 151, registered to the Air Council 17.11.24, first flown by H. S. Broad 18.6.25, shown at Hendon R.A.F. Display 25–26.6.25, used by R.A.E., Farnborough, from 7.3.26, C. of A. 23.4.26. Loaned to Imperial Airways Ltd. for evaluation 7.11.26, destroyed at Croydon when hangar collapsed in heavy snow 1.2.27. Span, 68 ft. 0 in. Length, 51 ft. 0 in. Tare wt., 6,768 lb. A.U.W., 11,250 lb. Max. speed, 110 m.p.h.

302

(*Topical Press*)

De Havilland D.H.71 Tiger Moth

Single seat research and racing monoplane built at Stag Lane 1927. Two aircraft only: G-EBQU, c/n 323, 130 h.p. Gipsy Experimental, C. of A. issued 29.7.27, world's closed circuit class record 24.8.27 at 186·4 m.p.h., world's altitude record 19,191 ft. 29.8.27, pilot H. S. Broad, sold in Australia 1930 as VH-UNH, crashed at Mascot 17.9.30; G-EBRV, c/n 324, 85 h.p. A.D.C. Cirrus II, C. of A. issued 28.7.27, flown in 1927 King's Cup Race by H. S. Broad, preserved by makers until destroyed by enemy bombing, Hatfield 1940. Span, 22 ft. 6 in. Length, 18 ft. 7 in. Tare wt., 618 lb. A.U.W., 905 lb. Max. speed, 197 m.p.h.

(*Tony Leigh*)

Druine D.31 Turbulent

Single seat ultra light designed in France by Roger Druine for amateur construction using converted 30 h.p. (1,200 c.c.) Volkswagen or similar engines. G-APCM constructed at Belfast by Rev. P. J. O'Kelly and first flown at Ards 22.12.58 was first of 25 British registered home-builts which included G-APWP built at St. Albans 1961 by C. F. Rogers, powered by a 40 h.p. Pollman Hepu KFM. 40/350 and later fitted with cantilever spring steel undercarriage, spats and canopy. Two originated abroad: G-ASTA built in France 1959 as F-PJGH and G-ATHP begun at Calcutta 1961 as VT-XAG. See also Rollason Turbulent. Span, 21 ft. 5 in. Length, 17 ft. $4\frac{1}{2}$ in. Tare wt., 349 lb. A.U.W., 620 lb. Max. speed, 93 m.p.h. Cruise, 82 m.p.h.

(*Chris Morris*)

Druine D.53 Turbi

Open cockpit two seater designed by Roger Druine for amateur construction. Two British-built aircraft only: G-AOTK with 62 h.p. Walter Mikron 2 engine constructed at Hatfield 1957–58 by D.H. Technical School students and first flown by W. P. I. Fillingham 9.5.58; and G-APBO, also fitted with a Mikron 2 engine, built by P. F. A. Group No. 39 at Rutherglen, Glasgow 1959–60 and first flown from the Group's private airstrip at Strathaven 22.7.60. Span, 28 ft. 6 in. Length, 20 ft. 4 in. Tare wt., 684 lb. A.U.W., 1,100 lb. Max. speed, 99 m.p.h. Cruise, 82 m.p.h.

(*Tony Leigh*)

Druine D.54 Turbi

Open cockpit two seater similar to D.53 Turbi but powered by one 65 h.p. Coventry Victor Flying Neptune engine. One aircraft only: G-APFA built by Britten-Norman Ltd. at Bembridge, Isle of Wight 1956–57 and first flown there 13.5.57. Rebuilt at Elstree by Ulair Ltd. 1958 with 65 h.p. Continental engine and glazed cockpit canopy. Flown by the Wolverhampton Ultra Light Flying Group at Halfpenny Green from 1962. Data similar to D.53 Turbi

(*Flight Photo 8621*)

Dudley Watt D.W.2

Two seater with exceptional slow flying qualities designed for Dudley N. Watt by K. N. Pearson and built at Brooklands 1929–30. One aircraft only: G-AAWK, c/n 1, powered by one 90 h.p. A.D.C. Cirrus III, public debut at Brooklands 17.5.30 piloted by Dudley Watt. Sold to F. C. H. Allen, Selsey, 19.2.34, dismantled by Brian Field at Kingswood Knoll, Surrey, 12.34. Span, 39 ft. 8 in. Length, 25 ft. 10 in. Tare wt., 1,050 lb. A.U.W., 1,500 lb. Max. speed, 90 m.p.h. Cruise, 75 m.p.h.

(*P. R. March*)

E.A.A. Sport Biplane

Single seat, fabric covered sporting biplane with welded steel tube fuselage and wooden wings designed for home construction using plans issued by the Experimental Aircraft Association of Hales Corner, Wisconsin, U.S.A. Three British registered examples only: G-ATEP (PFA.1301), 75 h.p. Continental C-75-12F, built in Guernsey by E. L. Martin, first flown 3.4.67, P. to F. 11.4.67; G-AVZW (PFA.1314), under construction 1971 by R. G. Maidment, Billingshurst, Kent; G-AYFY (PFA.1319), 65 h.p. Lycoming, H. Kuchling, Rhoose, first shown at Sywell 11–12.7.70. Span, 20 ft. 0 in. Length, 17 ft. 0 in. A.U.W., 1,150 lb. Max. speed, 105 m.p.h. Cruise, 90 m.p.h.

(*P. J. Bish*)

Edwards Gyrocopter

Single seat gyrocopter similar to the American-designed Adams-Wilson XH-1 Hobbycopter, built by N. A. F. Edwards at Gillingham, Kent 1961–62. One aircraft only: G-ASDF, c/n NAFE.1 (650 cc. Triumph motor cycle engine), registered 10.62, believed damaged in trials, dismantled and sold 9.63. Under reconstruction (illustrated) by B. L. King at Coulsdon, Surrey in 1972. Two Hobbycopters built by P. Zabell at Canewdon, Essex and D. Purser at Birmingham were unregistered. Rotor diameter, 21 ft. 6 in. Length, 14 ft. 0 in. A.U.W., 555 lb. Cruise, 45 m.p.h. Range, 55 miles

English Electric Wren

Single seat ultra light powered by one 398 c.c. A.B.C., designed by W. O. Manning and built by the English Electric Co. Ltd. at Lytham St. Annes. Three aircraft only, Air Ministry J6973 built 1921 and two for the 1923 Lympne Trials: (c/n 4) flown by Sqn. Ldr. M. E. A. Wright as No. 3, registered 9.4.26 as G-EBNV by Alan Smith at Sherburn-in-Elmet, stored at Bradford 1929 (later by R. H. Grant, Dumfries), used as spares by E.E.C. for rebuilding Wren No. 4 (c/n 3, Lympne pilot Flt. Lt. W. Longton), flown again at Warton 1.57 by P. Hillwood and at later displays. Preserved by the Shuttleworth Trust. Span, 37 ft. 0 in. Length, 24 ft. 3 in. Tare wt., 232 lb. A.U.W., 420 lb. Max. speed, 50 m.p.h.

(*D. A. Conway*)

Evans VP-1 Volksplane

All-wood, strut braced, single seater designed for amateur construction by W. S. Evans of La Jolla, California. Powered by one 1,300 cc. Volkswagen, equipped with all-moving tail surfaces and removable mainplane panels for ease of road transport. At least 16 under construction in Britain by 1972, but only three registered (with dates): G-AYUJ (PFA.1538), 17.3.71, R. F. Selby, Ashford, Kent; G-AYXW (PFA.1544), 30.4.71, J. S. Penny, Netherthorpe and first flown 20.6.72; G-BAAD (PFA.1540), Super VP-1, 27.7.72, R. W. Husband, Netherthorpe. Span, 24 ft. 0 in. Length, 18 ft. 0 in. Tare wt., 440 lb. A.U.W., 750 lb. Max. speed, 120 m.p.h.

Fairey Gyrodyne

Four seat helicopter powered by one 505 h.p. Alvis Leonides LE.22.HM, built at Hayes, Mx. 1947. Two prototype aircraft only: G-AIKF, c/n F.B.1, exhibited Radlett S.B.A.C. Show 9.47, first flown at Heston by B. H. Arkell 7.12.47, broke International helicopter 3 Km closed circuit record at 124·3 m.p.h., White Waltham 28.6.48, crashed at Ufton near Reading 17.4.49, chief test pilot F. H. Dixon killed; G-AJJP, c/n F.B.2, exhibited at Farnborough S.B.A.C. Show 9.48, converted to Jet Gyrodyne XD759 in 1954. Rotor diameter, 52 ft. 0 in. Tare wt., 3,270 lb. A.U.W., 4,500 lb. Max. speed, 124 m.p.h. Cruise, 100 m.p.h.

(*Fairey Aviation Co. Ltd.*)

Fairey Primer

Trainer developed from the Tipsy M, built at Hamble 1948. Two prototype aircraft only: G-ALBL, c/n F.8455, one 145 h.p. de Havilland Gipsy Major 10, C. of A. issued 22.10.48, test flown as G-6-4, later flown without rear decking, dismantled 1949; G-ALEW, c/n F.8456, one 155 h.p. Blackburn Cirrus Major 3, evaluated against the Chipmunk at Boscombe Down 11.48 as G-6-5, dismantled 1951. Span, 32 ft. 10 in. Length, 27 ft. 6 in. Tare wt., 1,572 lb. A.U.W., 1,960 lb. Max speed (Cirrus Major 3), 141 m.p.h. Cruise, 125 m.p.h.

(*Richard Riding*)

Fairtravel Linnet

French-designed Piel CP-301 Emeraude low-wing, side-by-side two seater, modified to meet British airworthiness requirements, fitted with one 90 h.p. Continental C-90-14F and built initially at White Waltham as the Garland-Bianchi Linnet 1958. Prototype, G-APNS, was first flown by Sqn. Ldr. Neville Duke at Fairoaks 1.9.58 and one other, G-APRH, was flown in 1962. Three more, G-ASFW, 'MT and 'ZR were completed with 100 h.p. Rolls-Royce Continental O-200-A engines as Fairtravel Linnets by Fairtravel Ltd. 1963–65, the last two (with one-piece sliding canopies) at Blackbushe. Span, 26 ft. 4 in. Length, 20 ft. 9 in. Tare wt., 810 lb. A.U.W., 1,400 lb. Cruise, 104 m.p.h. Range, 415 miles

Falconar F-9

Up-dated version of the Jodel D.9 Bébé single seater built from drawings issued by Falconar Aircraft of Edmonton, Alberta, Canada, the basic differences being less dihedral, wide track spring steel undercarriage and redesigned cockpit. One British-built aircraft only: G-AYEG, c/n PFA.1321, built at Gerrards Cross, Bucks. 1964–71 by G. R. Gladstone and powered by one 1,500 c.c. Volkswagen. First flown at Denham, A. to F. issued 9.2.71. Span, 22 ft. 11 in. Length, 17 ft. 10$\frac{1}{2}$ in. Tare wt., 480 lb. A.U.W., 705 lb. Cruise, 92 m.p.h. Range, 300 miles

Firth Helicopter

Two seat twin rotor helicopter powered by two 145 h.p. de Havilland Gipsy Major 10 engines, designed by Messrs. Heenan, Winn and Steele to American Landgraf principles and built at Thame by Firth Helicopters Ltd. 1954, using the magnesium alloy monocoque fuselage of the second prototype Planet Satellite. One aircraft only, G-ALXP, c/n FH-01/4, construction not completed, airframe presented to the museum of the College of Aeronautics, Cranfield, in 1955. Cruise, 125 m.p.h. Range, 250 miles

Gadfly H.D.W.1

Two seat cabin autogyro of metal clad, welded steel tube construction with tricycle undercarriage, two bladed rotor and engine-driven spin-up gear. It was powered by one 165 h.p. Rolls-Royce Continental IO-346-A driving a pusher airscrew between twin booms which carried the tail unit. One prototype only: G-AVKE, c/n H.D.W.1, designed by E. Smith and completed at Andover 1967 by the Gadfly Aircraft Co. Ltd. Tested at Thruxton; loaned to Southend Historic Aircraft Museum 1.73. Rotor diameter, 37 ft. 0 in. Length, 22 ft. 0 in. A.U.W., 1,600 lb. Estimated cruise, 110 m.p.h. Minimum flying speed, 25 m.p.h. Range, 460 miles

General Aircraft Monospar ST-18 Croydon

Transport for 10 passengers, powered by two 450 h.p. Pratt & Whitney Wasp Junior SB-9, built at Hanworth 1935. One aircraft only, G-AECB, c/n 501, first flown as T-22, C. of A. issued 16.6.36. Sold to Maj. C. R. Anson 2.7.36, left Croydon for Australia 30.7.36 piloted by H. Wood. Abandoned on return journey on Seringapatam Reef, 175 miles off N.W. coast of Australia 7.10.36. Failed to make landfall across Timor Sea due to compass error. Span, 59 ft. 6 in. Length, 43 ft. 3 in. Tare wt., 7,974 lb., A.U.W., 11,500 lb. Max. speed, 203 m.p.h. Cruise, 190 m.p.h.

General Aircraft G.A.L.45 Owlet

All-metal, two seat trainer with tricycle undercarriage developed from the G.A.L.42 Cygnet. One aircraft only: G-AGBK, c/n 134, powered by one 150 h.p. Blackburn Cirrus Major 1, built Hanworth 1940, first flown 5.9.40, C. of A. 10.1.41. Impressed 1.5.41 as DP240 for training with No. 51 O.T.U., Cranfield. To No. 605 Sqn., Ford (Douglas Bostons) 3.7.42, crashed near Arundel, Sussex 30.8.42. Span, 32 ft. 5 in. Length, 24 ft. 7 in. Tare wt., 1,563 lb. A.U.W., 2,300 lb. Max. speed, 125 m.p.h. Cruise, 110 m.p.h.

Gloster Mars I Bamel

Single seat racer, 450 h.p. Napier Lion II, developed from the Nieuport Nighthawk by H. P. Folland, built by the Gloucestershire Aircraft Co. Ltd. One aircraft only: G-EAXZ, f/f at Hucclecote by J. H. James 20.6.21, won the Aerial Derby 17.7.21 at 163·3 m.p.h. Wing area reduced for Coupe Deutsch Race at Etampes 1.10.21, retired with slack wing fabric. Set up British speed record of 196·4 m.p.h. at Martlesham 19.12.21. Fastest time in Aerial Derby 7.8.22 at 177·8 m.p.h. S.E.5-type tail fitted for 1922 Coupe Deutsch. Span, 22 ft. 0 in. Length, 23 ft. 0 in. Tare wt., 1,890 lb. A.U.W., 2,500 lb. Max. speed, 202 m.p.h.

(*Gloster Aircraft Co. Ltd.*)

Gloster Gannet

Single seat ultra light with folding wings built for the 1923 Daily Mail Light Aeroplane Competitions at Lympne. One aircraft only: G-EBHU, c/n 1, first flown 23.11.23, powered by one 750 c.c. Carden two stroke. Retired with engine trouble. Re-engined 1924 with 698 c.c. Blackburne Tomtit. Kept airworthy until exhibited at the Olympia Aero Show, London 7.29. With Tomtit engine: Span, 18 ft. 0 in. Length, 16 ft. 6 in. Tare wt., 330 lb. A.U.W., 460 lb. Cruise, 64 m.p.h. Range, 140 miles

(*Leonard Bridgman*)

Gloster I

Bamel modified in 1923 with strutted centre section, internal tanks and updated wing section. Won the Aerial Derby at Croydon 6.8.23 at 192·4 m.p.h. piloted by Larry Carter. To Martlesham 12.33 as J7234; converted to training seaplane for 1925 and 1927 Schneider Trophy contests; wing radiator trials 1926; still at Felixstowe 4.30. Span, 20 ft. 0 in. Length, 23 ft. 0 in. Tare wt., 1,970 lb. (seaplane) 2,440 lb. A.U.W., 2,650 lb. (seaplane 3,120 lb). Max. speed, 220 m.p.h.

(*Gloster Aircraft Co. Ltd.*)

Gloster II

Racing seaplane developed from the Bamel, built at Sunningend, Cheltenham, to Air Ministry order and powered by one 585 h.p. Napier Lion. One civil aircraft only, G-EBJZ, c/n Gloster II, racing number 1. Registered for participation in the 1924 Schneider Trophy Race in the U.S.A. By road to Felixstowe 12.9.24. Flight trials by Hubert Broad, undercarriage collapsed after landing 19.9.24, aircraft sank and was written off. 1924 contest postponed till 1925. Span, 29 ft. 0 in.

(*via H. G. Martin*)

Gloster III

Successor to Gloster II, fitted with twin floats and powered by one special 680 h.p. Napier Lion VII, built at Sunningend for the Schneider Trophy Race at Baltimore, U.S.A. 26.10.25. Two Air Ministry aircraft N194 and N195 only, the former registered G-EBLJ 3.6.25, C. of A. issued 4.10.25, as principal contender, racing number 5. Piloted by Hubert Broad, gained second place at 199·169 m.p.h. Reverted to R.A.F. use and converted to Gloster IIIA trainer for 1927 contest. Span, 20 ft. 0 in. Length, 26 ft. 10 in. Tare wt., 2,028 lb. A.U.W., 2,687 lb. Max. speed, 225 m.p.h.

(*Flight Photo 7817*)

Gloster A.S.31 Survey

Developed from the D.H.67 design, the A.S.31 was the first Gloster twin engined aircraft. Carrying two pilots and camera operator it was used by the Aircraft Operating Co. Ltd. for the survey of Northern Rhodesia. One civil aircraft only, G-AADO, no c/n, powered by two 525 h.p. Bristol Jupiter XI, first flown 6.29, C. of A. 30.1.30. Left Heston 20.3.30 and delivered by air to Cape Town by A. S. and Mrs. Butler. Sold to S.A.A.F. 3.33, serial '250', broken up at Waterkloof 12.42. Span, 61 ft. 6 in. Length, 48 ft. 6 in. Tare wt., 5,615 lb. A.U.W., 8,570 lb. Max. speed, 131 m.p.h. Cruise, 110 m.p.h. Range, 495 miles

(*Glos-Air Ltd.*)

Glos-Airtourer

All-metal, aerobatic two seater designed by H. Millicer and built by Victa Aircraft, Bankstown, Sydney, 1962–66 as the Airtourer 100 with 100 h.p. Rolls-Royce O-200-A or 115 h.p. Lycoming O-235-Cl. Twelve erected by Glos-Air Ltd. at Staverton 1965–66. From 1967 built by Aero Engine Services Ltd. (AESL), Hamilton, N.Z. Assembled in U.K. as the Glos-Airtourer 115 (or T2); with 130 h.p. Rolls-Royce O-300-A as the T3; with 150 h.p. Lycoming O-320-E2A as the Airtourer 150 (or T4); with c.s. airscrew and revised cockpit as T6 or T6/24 Super 150. Data for T6: Span, 26 ft. 0 in. Length, 22 ft. 0 in. Tare wt., 1,190 lb. A.U.W., 1,900 lb. Cruise, 138 m.p.h. Range, 530 miles

Gnosspelius Gull

Single seat ultra light with wooden monocoque fuselage, powered by one 698 c.c. Blackburne Tomtit with twin chain driven pusher airscrews, designed by Major O. T. Gnosspelius for the 1923 Lympne Trials and built at Rochester by Short Bros. Ltd. Two aircraft only: G-EBGN, c/n 1, rudder projecting above fin, first flown by J. Lankester Parker 26.5.23; c/n 2, unregistered, equal fin and rudder, flown at Lympne as No. 19, crashed at Cramlington, S. A. Packman killed 18.6.26. Span, 36 ft. 4 in. Length, 19 ft. 6 in. Tare wt., 360 lb. A.U.W., 570 lb. Max. speed, 70 m.p.h. Cruise, 45 m.p.h.

Gordon Dove

Single seat ultra light powered by one 750 c.c. Douglas Sprite, designed by S. C. Buszard and built at Maylands Aerodrome, Romford, by Premier Aircraft Constructions Ltd., 1937. Three aircraft only: G-AETU, c/n S.C.B. III, first flown 3.3.37, A. to F. issued 4.3.37, Romford Flying Club, burned in hangar fire Maylands 6.2.40; G-AEZA, c/n S.B.IV, A. to F. issued 1.7.37, Earl of Cardigan, Marlborough, scrapped 5.39; G-AEZB, c/n 3, A. to F. issued 24.8.37, J. K. Flower, damaged beyond repair at Tilbury, Essex 9.9.37, G-AFAC–'AG not built. Span, 27 ft. 3 in. Length, 18 ft. 3 in. Tare wt., 382 lb. A.U.W., 600 lb. Max. speed, 95 m.p.h. Cruise, 81 m.p.h.

(*Air Portraits*)

Gowland GWG.2 Jenny Wren

Single seat cabin monoplane designed and built at Brookmans Park, Herts. by G. W. Gowland and erected at Panshanger in September 1966. It used modified Luton Minor wings once fitted to G-AGEP, had a child's jump seat in the rear, and was powered by one 55 h.p. Lycoming O-145-A2, closely cowled and fitted with exhaust augmenter tubes. One aircraft only: G-ASRF, c/n GWG.2/PFA.1300, A. to F. 12.10.66. Span, 27 ft. 4 in. Length, 21 ft. 6 in. A.U.W., 900 lb. Cruise, 70 m.p.h.

Grahame-White G.W.E.6 Bantam

Single seat sporting biplane powered by one 80 h.p. Le Rhône rotary, designed by M. Boudot and built by The Grahame-White Aviation Co. Ltd. at Hendon 1919. Two British registered aircraft only: K-150/G-EAFK, c/n G.W.E.6; K-153/G-EAFL, c/n G.W.E.6A; both raced in 1919 Aerial Derby and at Hendon where K-150 crashed into a hangar 6.7.19. G-EAFL stored until reconditioned by Gnat Aero Co. at Shoreham 1926. A third, unregistered, Bantam flown by A. V. Everitt at agricultural shows in South Africa 1920. Span, 20 ft. 0 in. Length, 16 ft. 6 in. Tare wt., 640 lb. A.U.W., 995 lb. Max. speed, 100 m.p.h.

(Royal Aeronautical Society)

Grahame-White G.W.E.7

Luxury transport with folding wings designed by M. Boudot to seat four passengers in the cabin in the nose and the pilot in a glazed compartment between the centre section struts. One aircraft only, G-EALR, c/n G.W.E.7, powered by two 320 h.p. Rolls-Royce Eagle V, built at Hendon by The Grahame-White Aviation Co. Ltd. 8.19, damaged beyond repair in forced landing at Hendon (illustrated) in 1919, burned 1920. Span, 60 ft. 0 in. Length, 39 ft. 0 in. Tare wt., 5,785 lb. A.U.W., 7,947 lb. Max. speed, 116 m.p.h. Cruise, 104 m.p.h.

(D. Napier and Son Ltd.)

Grahame-White G.W.E.9 Ganymede

The twin fuselage three engined G.W.E.4 Ganymede bomber of 1918, converted for civil use by The Grahame-White Aviation Co. Ltd., at Hendon 1919. One aircraft only, G-EAMW, c/n G.W.E.9, powered by two 450 h.p. Napier Lion, formerly C3481, registered to the manufacturers 12.9.19, burned 9.20. Two pilots in an open cockpit sat ahead of about 12 passengers in a glazed central nacelle. Span, 89 ft. 3 in. Length, 49 ft. 9 in.

Granger Archaeopteryx

Single seater with pterodactyl wing but retaining normal rudder. Designed with the assistance of C. H. Latimer-Needham and built at Attenborough, Notts, 1926–30 by R. F. T. and R. J. T. Granger. One aircraft only: G-ABXL, c/n 3A, powered by one 32 h.p. Bristol Cherub I, first flown at Hucknall 10.30, flown without markings until registered 3.6.32. Regularly flown at Tollerton, longest flight was to R.A.F. Flying Club Display, Hatfield 15.6.35. Overhauled by the Shuttleworth Trust at Old Warden and flown again by Sqn. Ldr. J. Lewis 6.71. Span, 27 ft. 6 in. Length, 15 ft. 0 in. Max. speed, 95 m.p.h. Cruise, 75 m.p.h.

(*Airmaster Helicopters Ltd.*)

H2-B1 Helicopter

Light utility helicopter designed in co-operation with the builders of the U.S.-built Helicom and powered by one 100 h.p. Rolls-Royce Continental O-200. One aircraft only: G-AYNS, c/n 1, registered 21.12.70, built at Camberley, Surrey by Airmaster Helicopters Ltd. and first flown at Redhill 12.9.72 as prototype of the H2-B2 production model. Rotor diameter, 23 ft. 0 in. Length, 19 ft. 6 in. Tare wt., 780 lb. A.U.W., 1,200 lb. Cruise, 100 m.p.h.

Hafner A.R.III Mk. 2 Gyroplane

Single seat, experimental, vertical lift autogyro with variable incidence rotor blades, designed by Raoul Hafner and built by the A.R.III Construction Co. in the Martin-Baker Aircraft Company's factory, Denham, 1936. One aircraft only G-ADMV, c/n A.R.III (A.R. signifying 'Auto Rotation'), one 90 h.p. Pobjoy Niagara, registered to T. V. Welsh, Heston 26.7.35. First flown 6.2.37 and later tested at Farnborough by A. E. Clouston. Leased to R.A.E. for research, scrapped during war. Rotor diameter, 32 ft. 10 in. Length, 17 ft. 10 in. Tare wt., 640 lb. A.U.W., 900 lb. Max. speed, 120 m.p.h. Cruise, 110 m.p.h.

Halton H.A.C.I Mayfly

Two seater powered by one 32 h.p. Bristol Cherub III, designed by C. H. Latimer-Needham and built by the Halton Aero Club 1926–27. One aircraft only, G-EBOO, c/n 1, first flown by Flt. Lt. C. F. Le Poer Trench 31.1.27. Converted to single seater, C. of A. issued 13.5.27, won the President's, Selfridge and Leeming Cups, £150 in prize money and competed in the King's Cup Race. Completed 2,700 miles in 40 flying hours as a biplane. Span, 28 ft. 6 in. Length, 22 ft. 0 in. Tare wt., 480 lb. A.U.W., 920 lb. Max. speed, 83·5 m.p.h. Cruise, 75 m.p.h.

(*Flight Photo*)

Halton H.A.C.II Minus

The Mayfly single seater converted to parasol monoplane. Second in the Blackpool Open Handicap Race 7.7.28 at 87·75 m.p.h., won the Wakefield Trophy, Hamble, piloted by Flt. Lt. C. F. Le Poer Trench. Flown by same pilot in 1928 King's Cup Race, retired at Leeds with broken magneto drive. Entered by C. H. Latimer-Needham and flown by Flt. Lt. G. R. Ashton in 1929 King's Cup Race, retired at Newcastle. Dismantled at Halton 1930. Tare wt., 450 lb. A.U.W., 720 lb. Max. speed, 95 m.p.h. Cruise, 85 m.p.h.

(*Flight Photo 4112*)

Handley Page H.P.32 Hamlet (Lucifer)

Transport for six passengers, powered by three 120 h.p. Bristol Lucifer IV three-cylinder radials, fitted with full span slots and slotted flaps, built to Air Ministry order at Cricklewood 1926. One aircraft only, G-EBNS, c/n 1, first flown 19.10.26 by A. S. Wilcockson; flown to Croydon 21.10.26 for inspection by Dominion Premiers; last flight with Lucifers 25.10.26. Span, 52 ft. 0 in. Length, 34 ft. 10 in. Tare wt., 3,105 lb. A.U.W., 5,000 lb. Max. speed, 118 m.p.h. Cruise, 100 m.p.h.

(Flight Photo 4560)

Handley Page H.P.32 Hamlet (Lynx)

G-EBNS with smaller fin and larger rudder, re-engined with two 220 h.p. Armstrong Siddeley Lynx radials due to excessive vibration of the Lucifer installation. First flown 19.5.27 by T. H. England. Flown at Hendon R.A.F. Display 2.7.27. Further re-engined 3.28 with three 150 h.p. Armstrong Siddeley Mongoose radials with which it was airborne once only—during delivery to the R.A.E., Farnborough 25.9.28. Scrapped 1929. A.U.W. (Lynx), 5,000 lb. Max. speed (Lynx), 114 m.p.h.

Handley Page H.P.39 Gugnunc

Two seat biplane fitted with Handley Page full span slots and flaps, powered by one 155 h.p. Armstrong Siddeley Mongoose II, built at Cricklewood 1929 for the Guggenheim air safety competition in the U.S.A. One aircraft only, G-AACN, no c/n, runner up in competition; flown in 1930 Hendon R.A.F. Display by Flg. Off. H. H. Leech, transferred to the R.A.E. 12.30 as K1908, stored by the Science Museum at Hayes, Middlesex, 1972. Span, 40 ft. 0 in. Length, 26 ft. 9 in. Tare wt., 1,362 lb. A.U.W., 2,150 lb. Max. speed, 112·5 m.p.h. Min. speed, 33·5 m.p.h.

321

Hants. and Sussex Herald

Single seat ultra light with tricycle undercarriage, powered by one 40 h.p. Aeronca-J.A.P. J-99, built at Portsmouth 1949 by Hants. and Sussex Aviation Ltd. One aircraft only, G-ALYA, c/n HS/AC/001, few ground hops only at Portsmouth 1953, dismantled 1954. Span, 29 ft. 0 in. Length, 21 ft. 6 in. Tare wt., 580 lb. A.U.W., 800 lb. Max. speed, 92 m.p.h. Cruise, 82 m.p.h.

(Hawker Aircraft Ltd.)

Hawker Cygnet

Two seater designed by W. G. Carter and S. Camm for the 1924 Lympne Trials. Two aircraft only: G-EBJH, c/n 1, 30 h.p. A.B.C. Scorpion, flown as No. 15 by F. P. Raynham, to R.A.E. Aero Club 1.26, fitted with 32 h.p. Bristol Cherub III, C. of A. 21.8.26, second in 1926 Trials piloted by J. S. Chick, crashed at Lympne 8.27 on take-off for Bucharest piloted by R. L. Ragg; G-EBMB, c/n 2, 1,100 cc. Anzani, flown in 1924 Trials as No. 14 by W. H. Longton, C. of A. 28.8.26 with Cherub III, won 1926 Trials piloted by P. W. S. Bulman, stored Brooklands 1927, airworthy at Langley 1949, to R.A.F. Museum, Hendon 1972. Span, 28 ft. 0 in. Length, 20 ft. 3 in. Tare wt., 370 lb. A.U.W., 780 lb. Max. speed, 65 m.p.h.

Military Types Used For Civil Purposes

Aircraft listed in this section were either demilitarised in small numbers for normal commercial or private usage or were military aircraft flown with civil markings for demonstration, test or overseas delivery. As it constitutes a breach of international law to fly an aircraft over foreign soil in military marks without permission, British military aircraft often receive temporary civil status when being delivered by air.

The introductory notes to Appendix A apply equally to this section. British military types civilianised overseas are outside the scope of this book.

(*Flight Photo 483*)

De Havilland D.H.10

Two seat bomber powered by two 400 h.p. Liberty XII, built by the Aircraft Manufacturing Co. Ltd. at Hendon 1918, converted for Aircraft Transport and Travel Ltd. for the carriage of airmail 1919. One civil aircraft (without type name) only: G-EAJO, formerly E5488, C. of A. issued 18.8.19, flown to the First Air Traffic Exhibition at Amsterdam and on regular flights between Hendon and Renfrew with mails by Capt. G. Gathergood during the railway strike 10.19, crashed 4.20. Span, 65 ft. 6 in. Length, 39 ft. $7\frac{1}{2}$ in. Tare wt., 5,488 lb. A.U.W., 8,500 lb. Max. speed, 131 m.p.h.

De Havilland D.H.14A

Unfinished D.H.14 day bomber, J1940, completed by the Aircraft Manufacturing Co. Ltd. at Hendon 1919 as a long range two seater with 450 h.p. Napier Lion. One civil aircraft only: G-EAPY, c/n E.46, left Hendon 4.2.20 fitted with four wheel undercarriage and piloted by F. S. Cotton and W. A. Townsend on attempted Cape flight. Crashed near Messina, Italy. Shipped home, repaired, damaged in forced landing at Hertford during Aerial Derby 24.7.20, written off 2.2.21. Span, 50 ft. 5 in. Length, 37 ft. 7 in. Tare wt., 4,006 lb. Max. speed, 117 m.p.h.

(de Havilland Aircraft Co. Ltd.)

De Havilland D.H.65 Hound

Two seat general purpose biplane, one 550 h.p. Napier Lion XI, built at Stag Lane 1926. Two aircraft only, G-EBNJ and 'NK (c/n 250–251), registered 15.1.26 to de Havillands and A. S. Butler respectively. G-EBNJ first flown 17.11.26; converted 1927 to D.H.65A with modified nose and rudder; to the R.A.F. 1.28 as J9127; World's record 26.4.28 carrying 1,000 kg. load over 100 km. at 160·861 m.p.h., pilot H. S. Broad. G-EBNK not completed. (Data for D.H.65A) Span, 45 ft. 0 in. Length, 31 ft. 0 in. Tare wt., 2,981 lb. A.U.W., 4,934 lb. Max. speed, 153 m.p.h. Initial climb, 1,490 ft./min.

(*P. T. Capon*)

De Havilland D.H.115 Vampire T.Mk. 55

Side-by-side two seater powered by one 3,350 lb. s.t. de Havilland Goblin 35, designed in 1950, in production 1951–58. Three British civil aircraft only, registered to the manufacturers for overseas delivery: G-ANVF, c/n 15485, flown 9.54, sold to the Finnish Air Force 4.55 with serial VT-1; G-AOXH, c/n 15798, shipped to Buenos Aires 11.56, demonstration tour of S. America by George Errington, to the Chilean Air Force 16.4.57; G-APFV, c/n 15802, flown 9.57, sold to the Lebanese Air Force with serial L-160, shown at Farnborough 9.57. Span, 38 ft. 0 in. Length, 34 ft. 6 in. Tare wt., 7,380 lb. A.U.W., 11,150 lb. Max. speed, 538 m.p.h.

(*Air Portraits*)

English Electric Canberra

The Canberra B.Mk.2 was an all-metal, three seat unarmed bomber powered by two 6,500 lb. s.t. Rolls-Royce Avon 101 turbojets which entered R.A.F. service in 1951. Three British civil registered examples only: the E.E.C. trials aircraft WD937 (c/n 71018), registered 5.10.66 for undisclosed experimental work as G-ATZW; and the first two of a batch of two-crew, 7,500 lb. s.t. Avon 109 powered, Canberra B.Mk.6 aircraft reworked as B.Mk.62s for the Argentine Air Force and registered G-AYHO and 'HP for the Farnborough S.B.A.C. Show 9.70. Data for B.Mk.6: Span, 63 ft. $11\frac{1}{2}$ in. Length, 65 ft. 6 in. Tare wt., 21,679 lb. A.U.W., 55,000 lb. Max. speed, 518 m.p.h. Max. range, 3,790 miles

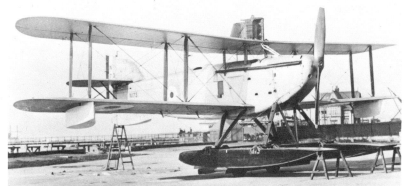

(*Imperial War Muesum MH.2945*)

Fairey Fremantle

Four seat, long range seaplane powered by one 650 h.p. Rolls-Royce Condor III, designed 1922 for projected round-the-world flight piloted by R. H. McIntosh but construction not completed until 1925. One aircraft only, G-EBLZ, c/n F.420, registered to the Air Council but flown in Service markings as N173. Handed over to the R.A.E. for radio navigation development 1926. Span, 68 ft. 6 in. A.U.W., 12,550 lb. Max. speed, 100 m.p.h. Cruise, 80 m.p.h. Range, 1,100 miles

(*Aeroplane*)

Fairey Fox I

Two seat day bomber powered by one 450 h.p. Curtiss D-12 (Fairey Felix), built at Hayes, Middlesex, for No. 12 Sqn. R.A.F. in 1926, put up for civilian disposal 1932. Three civil aircraft only, detailed in Appendix E: G-ACAS of Luxury Air Tours Ltd., flown by Flt. Lt. J. B. Pugh with C. W. A. Scott's Circus 1933; G-ACXO and 'XX flown in MacRobertson Race to Australia October 1934, former by R. J. P. Parer and G. E. Hemsworth, latter by J. K. C. Baines and H. D. Gilman. Span, 37 ft. 8½ in. Length, 31 ft. 2 in. Tare wt., 2,600 lb. A.U.W., 4,300 lb. Max. speed, 156·5 m.p.h.

(*Fairey Aviation Co. Ltd.*)

Fairey Fox II

All-metal development of Fox I powered by one 480 h.p. Rolls-Royce Kestrel IIB. Built Hayes, Middlesex, 1929. One civil aircraft only: G-ABFG, c/n F.1138, formerly the prototype J9834, C. of A. issued 6.10.30. Demonstrated to Belgian Air Force at Evere, Brussels, by C. S. Staniland 1930, converted to demonstration two seat fighter 1931, withdrawn from use 11.32. Span, 38 ft. 0 in. Length, 24 ft. 6 in. Max. speed, 190 m.p.h.

(*Fairey Aviation Co. Ltd.*)

Fairey Fox III

Three seat variant of Fox III day bomber, powered by one 525 h.p. Rolls-Royce Kestrel IIMS, built Hayes, Middlesex, 1932. One aircraft only: G-ABYY, c/n F.1842, C. of A. issued 23.6.33. Exhibited at Hendon S.B.A.C. Show 26.6.33, later shipped to Shanghai for demonstration to Chinese military authorities. Span, 38 ft. 0 in. Length, 29 ft. 8 in. A.U.W., 5,000 lb. Max. speed, 185 m.p.h.

(*Aeroplane*)

Fairey Firefly IIM

Prototype single seat interceptor fighter powered by one 480 h.p. Rolls-Royce Kestrel IIS, built Hayes, Middlesex 1929. One civil aircraft only: G-ABCN, c/n F.1130, first flown at Northolt 5.2.29, registered 9.7.30, C. of A. issued 10.7.30. Flown at Hendon R.A.F. Display 28.6.30 and employed as demonstrator at home and on the continent until the end of 1932. Span, 32 ft. 0 in. Length, 24 ft. 6 in. A.U.W., 3,404 lb. Max. speed, 212 m.p.h.

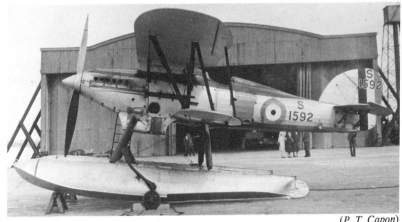

(*P. T. Capon*)

Fairey Firefly III

Ship-borne version of Firefly II with increased span, powered by one 480 h.p. Rolls-Royce Kestrel IIS, built Hayes, Middlesex, 1931. One aircraft only: S1592, c/n F.1137, first flown 17.5.29, allotted civil markings G-ABFH during manufacture, used as floatplane trainer for 1931 Schneider Trophy team. Fitted with land undercarriage and demonstrated by C. S. Staniland at major air displays 1932. Span, 33 ft. 6 in. Length, 25 ft. 6 in. A.U.W., 3,500 lb. Max. speed, 214 m.p.h.

(*Fairey Aviation Co. Ltd.*)

Fairey Fox III Trainer

Two seat trainer variant of Fox III with full dual control, powered by one 340 h.p. Armstrong Siddeley Serval, built Hayes, Middlesex, 1933. One British civil aircraft only: G-ACKH, c/n F.1925, later allotted Avions Fairey c/n A.F.3032, C. of A. issued 22.12.33, sold to the Belgian Air Force 3.34. Span, 38 ft. 0 in. Length, 31 ft. 4 in. A.U.W., 4,296 lb. Max. speed, 138 m.p.h.

(*Fairey Aviation Co. Ltd.*)

Fairey Fantôme

Single seat fighter powered by one 925 h.p. Hispano-Suiza 12 Ycrs, built at Hayes, Middlesex 1935 for the Belgian Government's International Fighter Competition. One civil aircraft only: G-ADIF, c/n F.6, first flown under B conditions 6.35 as F-6. Demonstrated at Hendon S.B.A.C. Show 1.7.35 by C. S. Staniland. Crashed at Evere, Brussels, 17.7.35 during the Competition and test pilot S. H. G. Trower killed. Span, 34 ft. 6 in. Length, 27 ft. 6 in. A.U.W., 4,120 lb. Max. speed, 270 m.p.h.

Fairey Swordfish

(A. J. Jackson)

Three seat torpedo-bomber in production 1935–45. One British civil aircraft only: G-AJVH, formerly LS326, powered by one 750 h.p. Bristol Pegasus 30, built at Brough 1943 by Blackburn Aircraft Ltd. Flown postwar in Service marks for communications and demonstration, exhibited at Fifty Years of Flying Exhibition, Hendon, 7.51, civilianised at Hamble 10.55 as flying museum piece for preservation by the Fairey Aviation Co. Ltd. Reverted to military marks 6.59, airworthy as LS326 at the Fleet Air Arm Museum, Yeovilton in 1972 and flown annually at displays. Span, 45 ft. 6 in. Length, 35 ft. 8 in. Tare wt., 4,700 lb. A.U.W., 7,510 lb. Max. speed, 138 m.p.h. Cruise, 104–129 m.p.h. at 5,000 ft.

Fairey Fulmar 2

(Charles E. Brown)

Two seat naval fighter built by the Fairey Aviation Co. Ltd. at Heaton Chapel, Stockport. One civil aircraft only: G-AIBE, c/n F.3707, formerly the prototype N1854, first flown at Ringway 4.1.40. Civilianised at Ringway 1946 as communications aircraft powered by one 1,300 h.p. Rolls-Royce Merlin 30F, C. of A. issued 26.2.47. Preserved by makers as a flying museum piece (in naval markings as N1854 after 6.59). Donated to the Royal Navy. Hangared at Lossiemouth in 1971. Span, 46 ft. 4½ in. Length, 40 ft. 3 in. A.U.W., 9,672 lb. Max. speed, 280 m.p.h.

330

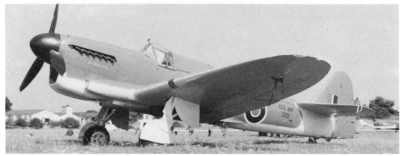

Fairey Firefly F.Mk.1

Two seat carrier-borne fighter powered by one 1,730 h.p. Rolls-Royce Griffon
IIB, in production at Hayes and Hanworth, Middlesex, from 1942. One British
civil aircraft only: Royal Navy Z2033, c/n F.5607, sold to Svensk Flygtjänst 3.49
for target towing as SE-BRD. Presented by owners to Skyfame Museum and
allotted markings G-ASTL for ferrying from Gothenburg to Staverton 5.5.64,
piloted by Tage Paller. Permanently exhibited in naval markings as Z2033
'Sir Richard Fairey' (illustrated). Span, 44 ft. 6 in. Length, 37 ft. 7½ in. Tare wt.,
9,750 lb. A.U.W., 14,020 lb. Max. speed, 316 m.p.h. Max. range, 1,300 miles

Fairey Firefly Trainer Mk.1

Two seat naval trainer powered by one 1,815 h.p. Rolls-Royce Griffon XII,
developed from Firefly 1 two seat fighter. One British civil aircraft only:
G-AHYA, formerly MB750, first flown at Heston 7.46 as F-1, demonstrated at Les
Mureaux, France, and Valkenburg, Netherlands, 11.46–2.47. Then reverted to the
Admiralty as MB750, coming 3rd in Lympne High Speed Handicap 31.8.47
piloted by Grp. Capt. R. G. Slade at 290·21 m.p.h. Span, 44 ft. 6 in. Length,
37 ft. 7¼ in. Tare wt., 9,906 lb. A.U.W., 12,300 lb. Max. speed, 305 m.p.h.

Fairey Gannet T.Mk.5

Trainer version of the Gannet A.S.4 naval strike aircraft powered by one 3,035 e.h.p. Armstrong Siddeley Double Mamba 10. Prototype, WN365, c/n F.9137, (illustrated), f/f at Northolt 16.8.54 as the first T.Mk.2, was later brought up to T.Mk.5 standard and flown to White Waltham 3.3.60 as G-APYO. Temporarily Indonesian Navy 'AS-14' for Indonesian pilot training programme, C. of A. 12.10.60, stored 10.61. Reworked 1966 for the Royal Navy as XT752. Span, 54 ft. 4 in. Length, 43 ft. 0 in. Tare wt., 14,000 lb. A.U.W., 21,000 lb. Max. speed, 299 m.p.h. Range, 660 miles

Fairey Ultra Light Helicopter

A.O.P. two seater powered by one 252 lb. s.t. Blackburn Turboméca Palouste 505 supplying compressed air to pressure jet rotor tip burners, built at Hayes, Mx. 1955–58. Three prototypes only: G-AOUK, c/n F.9426, first flown at White Waltham 8.55, fitted with triple tail 1957, withdrawn from use 1958; G-AOUJ, c/n F.9424, modified version built 1956, shown with 'UK at the S.B.A.C. Shows 9.56 and 9.57, C. of A. issued 30.9.58; G-APJJ, c/n F.9428, shown at the S.B.A.C. Show 9.58, C. of A. issued 2.10.58, evaluated by the Royal Navy with 'UJ 1958. Preserved at Cranfield and Stockport respectively in 1972. Rotor diameter, 28 ft. $3\frac{1}{2}$ in. Length, 14 ft. 8 in. A.U.W., 1,650 lb. Cruise, 80 m.p.h.

(Aeroplane)

Fane F 1/40

Two seat Air Observation Post with fully flapped and slotted wing, developed by Capt. Gerard Fane from the Comper Scamp design, powered by one 80 h.p. Continental A-80 driving a pusher airscrew. Built at Norbury by the Fane Aircraft Co. Ltd. 1941. One aircraft only, c/n F.1, on charge at Heston D.G.R.D. 21–26.3.41 as T1788, registered G-AGDJ 11.9.41, A. to F. issued 17.9.41, scrapped during the 1939–45 war. Span, 37 ft. 0 in. Length, 23 ft. 5 in. A.U.W., 1,500 lb.

F.E.2B

Two seat fighter powered by one 160 h.p. Beardmore, designed by the Royal Aircraft Factory, Farnborough, 1915 and widely sub-contracted. One British civil aircraft only, G-EAHC, formerly D3832, built by Richard Garrett and Sons at Leiston, Suffolk. Registered 14.7.19 to J. Carter Smith, C. of A. issued 8.8.19, sold to the Bournemouth Aviation Co. Ltd. 31.3.20 for instruction and joyriding. Crashed prior to 10.1.23. Span, 47 ft. 9 in. Length, 32 ft. 3 in. Tare wt., 2,061 lb. A.U.W., 3,037 lb. Max. speed, 91·5 m.p.h.

Felixstowe F.3

Patrol boat designed by John Porte, powered by two 345 h.p. Rolls-Royce Eagle VIII. Two British civil aircraft only: G-EAQT, c/n S.607, ex N4019, built by Short Bros. Ltd. at Rochester 1918, remodelled with cabin for L. Horden 3.20, shipped to Botany Bay, not erected; G-EBDQ, ex N4177, built by the Phoenix Dynamo Co. Ltd., Bradford, 1918, registered to the Aircraft Disposal Co. Ltd. 26.7.22 for the final, Atlantic, section of Major W. T. Blake's abortive world flight, registration cancelled 11.22. Span, 102 ft. 0 in. Length, 49 ft. 2 in. Tare wt., 7,958 lb. A.U.W., 12,235 lb. Max. speed, 91 m.p.h.

General Aircraft G.A.L.47

Two seat, twin boom Air Observation Post powered by one 90 h.p. Blackburn Cirrus Minor driving a pusher airscrew, built at Hanworth 1940. One aircraft only: G-AGBL, c/n 135, first flown as T-47 and later as T-0224, civil registration not used. Destroyed 2.4.42. Span, 37 ft. 10 in. Length, 25 ft. 9 in. A.U.W., 1,615 lb. Cruise, 75 m.p.h.

Gloster Mars III Sparrowhawk II

Two seat trainer powered by one 230 h.p. Bentley B.R.2 rotary, designed by H. P. Folland and built by the Gloucestershire Aircraft Co. Ltd. at Sunningend 1921. One British aircraft only: G-EAYN, c/n Mars III, fitted with S.E.5 tail unit in 1922, C. of A. 24.7.22, flown in Aerial Derby round London 7.8.22 by L. R. Tait-Cox who averaged 103·2 m.p.h. before retiring at the end of the first lap. Converted to Grouse I in 1923. Span, 27 ft. 0 in. Length, 19 ft. 8 in. Tare wt., 1,675 lb. A.U.W., 2,010 lb. Max. speed, 127 m.p.h. Range, 300 miles.

(*Gloster Aircraft Co. Ltd.*)

Gloster Grouse I

Sparrowhawk demonstrator rebuilt 1923 with square-cut vertical tail surfaces and single bay sesquiplane wings incorporating the Gloster H.L.B. high and medium lift feature. One aircraft only: G-EAYN, c/n 1, shown at the Gothenburg International Aeronautical Exhibition 8.23, converted to Grouse II in 1924. Span, 27 ft. 0 in. Length, 19 ft. 0 in. Tare wt., 1,357 lb. A.U.W., 2,120 lb. Max. speed, 128 m.p.h. Endurance, $3\frac{3}{4}$ hr.

(*Gloster Aircraft Co. Ltd.*)

Gloster Grouse II

Grouse I prototype re-engined 1924 with 180 h.p. Armstrong Siddeley Lynx II radial as ab initio trainer. One British civil demonstrator only: G-EAYN, c/n 2, C. of A. 21.4.25, later fitted with oleo undercarriage, sold abroad 9.12.25. Span, 27 ft. 10 in. Length, 20 ft. 4 in. Tare wt., 1,365 lb. A.U.W., 2,120 lb. Max. speed, 120 m.p.h. Endurance, $3\frac{3}{4}$ hr.

(*Flight Photo*)

Gloster Grebe I

Single seat fighter designed by H. P. Folland and built for the R.A.F. by the Gloucestershire Aircraft Co. Ltd. at Sunningend. One civil aircraft only: G-EBHA, no c/n, demonstrator powered by one 385 h.p. Armstrong Siddeley Jaguar IIIA, first flown 6.7.23, C. of A. issued 11.7.23. Scratch machine in 1923 King's Cup Race, piloted by L. L. Carter, retired at Manchester. Span, 29 ft. 4 in. Length, 20 ft. 3 in. Tare wt., 1,720 lb. A.U.W., 2,570 lb. Max. speed, 152 m.p.h. Endurance, $2\frac{3}{4}$ hr.

Gloster Grebe

G-EBHA rebuilt 1926 with one 425 h.p. Bristol Jupiter IV and Gamecock-type undercarriage, tail unit and top ailerons, C. of A. renewed 30.3.27. Used to flight test and demonstrate Gloster-Hele-Shaw-Beacham experimental v.p. airscrew. Withdrawn from use at C. of A. expiry 29.7.29. Scrapped in 1930. Dimensions as Grebe I, Tare wt., 1,695 lb. A.U.W., 2,538 lb. Max. speed, 152 m.p.h.

Gloster Gamecock (Special)

Standard aircraft J8047 rebuilt by Glosters with lengthened fuselage, modified fin and rudder, narrow chord ailerons and wide track undercarriage, delivered to the R.A.E. 28.11.28. Temporarily fitted with one 530 h.p. Bristol Jupiter VII and Hele-Shaw variable pitch airscrew 1929–30, disposed of to scrap dealer at Hornchurch 10.4.34, sold to J. W. Tomkins 5.34 and rebuilt for private use with one 490 h.p. Jupiter VIIFP as G-ADIN at Apethorpe, Northants, C. of A. issued 24.9.35. Flown at Apethorpe and Sywell, withdrawn from use 1936.

Gloster Gamecock I

Single seat fighter of wood and fabric construction, developed from the Grebe and powered by one 460 h.p. Bristol Jupiter VI radial. Eighty-two built at Hucclecote for the R.A.F. and two for civil purposes. The first, G-EBNT, c/n 95/12877, was a standard aeroplane with Jupiter VI, registered to the Gloucestershire Aircraft Co. Ltd. 17.3.26 as a demonstrator, C. of A. issued 26.3.26, withdrawn from use in 3.27, registration cancelled 4.27.

The second civil Gamecock, G-EBOE, c/n not recorded, was a special aircraft registered 20.5.26 for the experimental private venture installation of the 495 h.p. Bristol Orion exhaust-turbo-supercharged version of the Jupiter which was not completed as the result of unsuccessful bench tests. R.A.F. serial J9248 was allotted in 1927 for projected Service flight trials of the Orion engine. Registration cancelled 3.28.

Span, 29 ft. $7\frac{1}{2}$ in. Length, 19 ft. $10\frac{1}{2}$ in. Tare wt., 1,052 lb. A.U.W. (Jupiter), 2,750 lb. (Orion), 2,823 lb. Max. speed, 150 m.p.h.

(*Gloster Aircraft Co. Ltd.*)

Gloster Gladiator

Single seat fighter, one 840 h.p. Bristol Mercury VIIIA, 527 built at Hucclecote 1937–40. One civil aircraft only: G-AMRK, mainly ex R.A.F. L8032, made airworthy by V. H. Bellamy at Eastleigh 1952. To Gloster Aircraft Ltd. 1956 and to Shuttleworth Trust 7.11.60 with incorrect serial K8032. Span, 32 ft. 3 in. Length, 27 ft. 5 in. Tare wt., 3,745 lb. A.U.W., 5,420 lb. Max. speed, 250 m.p.h. Cruise, 212 m.p.h.

(*Sport and General*)

Gloster Meteor 4

Single seat fighter powered by two 3,500 lb. s.t. Rolls-Royce Derwent 5, in large-scale production at Hucclecote from 1946. One British civil aircraft only: G-AIDC, demonstrator built 1946, finished in carmine and cream, C. of A. issued 14.4.47, left same day on Continental tour piloted by Sqn. Ldr. D. V. Cotes-Preedy. Established Brussels–Copenhagen record 22.4.47 at 630 m.p.h. Seriously damaged by a Belgian pilot at Melsbroek 5.47. Major components salvaged and returned to manufacturers. Span, 37 ft. 2 in. Length, 41 ft. 0 in. Tare wt., 11,217 lb. A.U.W., 14,545 lb. Max. speed, 580 m.p.h.

Gloster Meteor T.Mk.7

Two seat trainer powered by two 3,500 lb. s.t. Rolls-Royce Derwent 5, built in quantity at Hucclecote. One British civil aircraft only: G-AKPK, prototype, c/n G.5/201, constructed from wings, rear fuselage and tail unit of Meteor 4 G-AIDC, first flown 19.3.48, C. of A. issued 12.4.48, sales tour of Turkey 5.48, flew Lord Mayor's letter from Biggin Hill to Orly 30.9.48 in 27·5 minutes. Sold to Royal Netherlands Air Force 11.48 as I-1. Span, 37 ft. 2 in. Length, 43 ft. 6 in. Tare wt., 10,645 lb. A.U.W., 14,230 lb. Max. speed, 590 m.p.h.

Gloster Meteor P.V.7–8

Two seat demonstration and photographic aircraft powered by two 3,600 lb. s.t. Rolls-Royce Derwent 8. One aircraft only: G-ANSO, c/n G.5/1525, constructed 1954 by fitting a Mk. 7 two seat cockpit to the demilitarised P.V. ground attack prototype G-7-1. First flown 9.8.51, C. of A. 9.7.54, exhibited at the Farnborough S.B.A.C. Show 9.54 in larkspur blue and ivory finish as Hawker Siddeley Group camera ship. To Svensk Flygtjänst, Bromma, 8.59 as SE-DCC for target towing with WF833/SE-CAS and WH128/SE-CAT. Span, 42 ft. 0 in. A.U.W., 18,500 lb.

(*Gloster Aircraft Co. Ltd.*)

Gloster Meteor Mk.8

Single seat, private venture attack fighter powered by two 3,600 lb. s.t. Rolls-Royce Derwent 8, modified from a production Meteor F. Mk. 8 to carry RATOG, external rockets, ventral cannon and tip tanks. Rectilineal vertical tail surfaces without underkeel. One aircraft only: G-AMCJ, c/n G.5/1210, first flown 4.9.50, exhibited at the Farnborough S.B.A.C. Show 9.50, to the Danish Air Force 2.51 as '490'. Span, 37 ft. 2 in. Length, 44 ft. 7 in. Tare wt., 10,684 lb. A.U.W., 15,700 lb. Max. speed, 598 m.p.h.

(*Rolls-Royce Ltd.*)

Gloster Meteor N.F. Mk.14

Two seat night fighter with clear-view canopy, powered by two 3,600 lb. s.t. Rolls-Royce Derwent 8 or 9 turbojet engines. One hundred built for the R.A.F. by Armstrong Whitworth Aircraft Ltd. at Baginton 1953–55, two received civil registrations G-ARCX and G-ASLW for development work by Ferranti Ltd. and Rolls-Royce Ltd., and a third became G-AXNE for a ferry flight to Africa in 1969. See individual histories. Span, 43 ft. 0 in. Length, 51 ft. 4 in. Tare wt., 12,620 lb. A.U.W. (civil), 18,700 lb. Max. speed, 578 m.p.h. Range, 795 miles

Gosport Flying-boat

Felixstowe F.5 four seater powered by two 345 h.p. Rolls-Royce Eagle VIII. One civil aircraft only: G-EAIK, c/n G6/100, an R.A.F. aircraft, N4634, built at Northam 1919 by the Gosport Aviation Co. Ltd., C. of A. issued 7.8.19, registered to the makers as a 'Gosport Flying Boat'. Flown to Amsterdam 8.8.19 by Lt. Col. R. Hope-Vere for exhibition at the First Air Traffic Exhibition and demonstration flights from the River Ij. Returned to Felixstowe 28.8.19, withdrawn from use at C. of A. expiry. Span, 102 ft. 0 in. Length, 49 ft. 2 in. Tare wt., 7,958 lb. A.U.W., 12,235 lb. Max. speed, 93 m.p.h.

Handley Page H.P.33 Clive I

Transport for 16 passengers powered by two 550 h.p. Bristol Jupiter IX, built at Cricklewood 1927. One civil aircraft only: c/n H.P.33, first flown 2.28 as the wooden prototype J9126. Registered to the Air Council 13.8.32 as G-ABYX, C. of A. issued 9.9.32. Sold to Sir Alan Cobham 4.33 and named 'Youth of Australia' for joyriding and flight refuelling experiments. Renamed 'Astra', scrapped 1935 after carrying 120,000 passengers. Registration G-ABIP reserved by the Air Council 2.2.31, but not used, for the metal prototype H.P.35 Clive II, J9949, c/n H.P.35/1. Span, 75 ft. 0 in. Length, 59 ft. 2 in. A.U.W., 14,500 lb. Max. speed, 111 m.p.h.

(*Flight Photo 7060*)

Handley Page H.P.34 Hare

Two seat day bomber of metal construction, designed by G. R. Volkert, powered by one 485 h.p. Bristol Jupiter VIII, built at Cricklewood 1928. One aircraft only: J8622, first flown 24.2.28, struck off R.A.F. charge 1932, sold to J. N. Addinsell and registered G-ACEL for proposed long distance flight. Flown to Hanworth 3.33, where it was redoped in a civil colour scheme of blue and silver but was not flown again. Progressively broken up by vandals until the remains were scrapped in 1937. Span, 50 ft. 0 in. Length, 32 ft. 2 in. Tare wt., 3,050 lb. A.U.W., 5,720 lb. Max. speed, 145 m.p.h. Range, 1,000 miles

(*J. McNulty*)

Handley Page H.P.54 Harrow II

Short range tanker, powered by two 925 h.p. Bristol Pegasus XX. Three R.A.F. aircraft built at Cricklewood 1936–37, loaned to Sir Alan Cobham for refuelling experiments 1939: G-AFRG, prototype Mk.I K6933, C. of A. issued 4.4.39; G-AFRH, K7029, C. of A. issued 4.4.39; G-AFRL, K7027, C. of A. issued 20.7.39. The first two arrived by sea in Montreal 30.4.39 to refuel the transatlantic Empire Boats off Newfoundland. Impressed by the R.C.A.F. at Rockliffe, Ottawa, where 'RG became '794' and 'RH was cannibalised. G-AFRL refuelled the Empire Boats over Foynes and was destroyed by enemy action at Ford, Sussex, 6.40. Span, 88 ft. 5 in. Length, 82 ft. 2 in. Tare wt., 13,600 lb. A.U.W., 25,240 lb. Max. speed, 200 m.p.h. Cruise, 163 m.p.h.

(*via R. P. Howard*)

Hanriot HD-1

Single seat fighter powered by one 110 h.p. Le Rhône, in production by Hanriot et Cie. at Billancourt, France 1916–18. One British aircraft only: Belgian Air Force N75 (later H-1), civil 1934 as OO-APJ, ferried Brussels–Old Warden 5.38 by R. O. Shuttleworth. Shown at R.Ae.S. Garden Party, Heathrow 8.5.38 as G-AFDX, lost a wheel on take-off from Brooklands 17.6.39 and turned over landing at Old Warden. Wings destroyed in air raid on Brooklands 1940, fuselage stored at Old Warden until sold to M. K. Hand, San Francisco 1963. Flown again 1968 at Sonoma Valley, California. Span, 28 ft. $6\frac{1}{2}$ in. Length, 19 ft. $1\frac{7}{8}$ in. Tare wt., 904 lb. A.U.W., 1,521 lb. Max. speed, 100 m.p.h.

(*Flight Photo 3106*)

Hawker Hedgehog

Three seat fleet reconnaissance biplane to Specification 37/22, powered by one 400 h.p. Bristol Jupiter IV, built at Kingston-on-Thames and first flown by F. P. Raynham about 3.24. One prototype only, registered to H. G. Hawker Engineering Co. Ltd. 16.7.24 as G-EBJN for ferrying to Martlesham but civil marks not used. Taken on Air Ministry charge 9.24 as N187 with modified undercarriage (illustrated). Span, 40 ft. $0\frac{1}{2}$ in. Length, 30 ft. $8\frac{3}{4}$ in. Tare wt., 2,995 lb. A.U.W., 4,791 lb. Max. speed, 120 m.p.h. Cruise, 89 m.p.h. Endurance, $2\frac{1}{2}$ hr.

(*Flight Photo*)

Hawker Woodcock Mk.II

Single seat fighter of wooden construction powered by one 420 h.p. Bristol Jupiter IV, designed by W. G. Carter, built at Kingston-on-Thames, Surrey, 1925–27 by the H. G. Hawker Engineering Co. Ltd. The fourth production R.A.F. aircraft, J7515, prepared for Scandinavian Tour as G-EBMA. Entered by T. O. M. Sopwith and flown in the King's Cup Race 3.7.25 by Flt. Lt. P. W. S. Bulman, crash landed in fog at Luton. Span, 32 ft. 6 in. Length, 23 ft. 3 in. Tare wt., 2,075 lb. A.U.W., 3,040 lb. Max. speed, 138 m.p.h. Cruise, 103 m.p.h. Endurance, $2\frac{3}{4}$ hr.

(*Flight Photo 5262*)

Hawker Hawfinch

Single seat fighter to Specification F.9/26, designed by W. G. Carter, powered by one 450 h.p. Bristol Jupiter VIIF, built at Kingston-on-Thames and first flown at Brooklands 3.27. Prototype only, J8776, registered to Hawkers 27.7.29 as G-AAKH for flights with experimental aerofoil sections at Brooklands and Farnborough. Scrapped 1931. Span, 33 ft. 6 in. Length, 24 ft. 4 in. Max. speed, 171 m.p.h.

(Hawker Aircraft Ltd.)

Hawker Heron

Single seat fighter powered by one 455 h.p. Bristol Jupiter VI, designed by W. G. Carter and built at Kingston-on-Thames. The first Hawker metal aircraft. Prototype only, J6989, c/n 1B, first flown by P. W. S. Bulman at Brooklands 1925. To Martlesham 1926, civilianised as G-EBYC, C. of A. 21.5.28 for King's Cup Race 20.7.28. Collided with car at Hendon before the start. In store at Minster Lovell in 1966. Span, 35 ft. 0 in. Length, 23 ft. 2 in. A.U.W., 2,780 lb. Max. speed, 164 m.p.h.

(Hawker Aircraft Ltd.)

Hawker Hart II (Kestrel)

Two seat day bomber designed by Sydney Camm, in production from 1931. One civil demonstrator: G-ABMR, c/n H.H.1, C. of A. 1.8.31, initially with one 525 h.p. Rolls-Royce Kestrel IB. Fitted 1938 with 525 h.p. Kestrel IIS and Osprey rudder (illustrated) for icing experiments. Fitted 1949 with 560 h.p. Kestrel IIIS and redoped blue and gold. Averaged 170 m.p.h. in 1952 King's Cup Race piloted by G. F. Bullen. Repainted 1959 as J9933, based at Dunsfold 1971 in No. 57 Sqn. colours as J9941. Span, 37 ft. 3 in. Length, 29 ft. 4 in. Tare wt., 2,530 lb. A.U.W., 4,635 lb. Max. speed, 184 m.p.h. Cruise, 140 m.p.h.

Hawker Hart (Jupiter)

Hart bomber initially fitted with 480 h.p. Bristol Jupiter VIII, built at Kingston 1931. One British civil aircraft only: G-ABTN, c/n H.H.3, re-engined with 595 h.p. Jupiter XFAM, first flown thus 1.3.32, C. of A. 25.6.32; re-engined with 570 h.p. Bristol Pegasus IM.2, first flown 24.11.32. Flown from Heston to the Paris Aero Show 27.11.32 by P. E. G. Sayer, lost at sea off Ostend on the return journey, 30.11.32, pilot rescued. Span, 37 ft. 3 in. Length (Jupiter VIII) 36 ft. 10 in. (Jupiter XFAM) 35 ft. 10 in. (Pegasus) 35 ft. $9\frac{1}{2}$ in. Tare wt., 2,937 lb. A.U.W. (Jupiter VIII) 4,500 lb. (Pegasus) 4,852 lb. Max. speed (Jupiter VIII) 161 m.p.h. (Pegasus) 177 m.p.h.

Hawker Osprey

Deck landing, fighter-reconnaissance version of the Hart. One British civil aircraft only: G-AEBD, c/n S.O.1 (i.e. Spanish Osprey 1), powered by one 600 h.p. Rolls-Royce Kestrel V, for demonstration tour of Spain 1935. Specially fitted and first flown 24.2.36 with 595 h.p. Hispano-Suiza 12 Xbrs engine for Spanish Government, delivered 6.36 as EA-KAJ. Used in the Civil War. Span, 37 ft. 0 in. Length, 29 ft. 4 in. A.U.W., 4,750 lb. Max. speed, 164 m.p.h.

Hawker Fury I

Developed, private venture version of the Fury single seat fighter powered initially by one 525 h.p. Rolls-Royce Kestrel IIS. One aircraft only: G-ABSE, c/n H.F.4, first flown at Brooklands by P. E. G. Sayer 13.4.32, C. of A. 10.5.32, used as test vehicle during development work on Hawkers' F.7/30 design. Loaned to Air Service Training Ltd., Hamble for aerobatic training in 1936. Scrapped 1938. Span, 30 ft. 0 in. Length, 26 ft. $8\frac{1}{2}$ in. Tare wt., 2,623 lb. A.U.W., 3,367 lb. Max. speed, 207 m.p.h.

Hawker Hurricane Mk.I

Single seat fighter of fabric covered, metal construction with retractable undercarriage, designed by Sydney Camm, in production by Hawker Aircraft Ltd. from 1938. One civil aircraft only: G-AFKX, c/n W/O 5436, formerly L1606 of No. 56 Sqn. powered by one 1,030 h.p. Rolls-Royce Merlin III, first civil flight at Brooklands 24.1.39, C. of A. 25.5.39, first flown with metal wings and experimental 1,210 h.p. Merlin RM4S 9.6.40. Flown at Langley 3.5.41 with 1,585 h.p. Merlin 45; last recorded flight 4.5.41. Span, 40 ft. 0 in. Length, 31 ft. 5 in. Tare wt., 4,670 lb. A.U.W., 6,600 lb. Max. speed, 316 m.p.h.

(*Hawker Aircraft Ltd.*)

Hawker Hurricane Mk.IIC

Four cannon version powered by one 1,280 h.p. Rolls-Royce Merlin 20, in production from 1940. The 12,780th and final Hurricane, PZ865 'Last of the Many', first flown by P. W. S. Bulman at Langley 8.44, stripped of armament as flying museum piece. First appearance in blue and gold at R.Ae.S. Garden Party, White Waltham, 14.5.50, C. of A. 23.5.50. Second in King's Cup Race 17.6.50 at 283 m.p.h. piloted by Grp. Capt. P. Townsend. Fitted Merlin 502 and camouflaged as PZ865 in 1963. Flew in film 'Battle of Britain' 1968, based at Coltishall 1972. Span, 40 ft. 0 in. Length, 32 ft. 0 in. Tare wt., 5,800 lb. A.U.W., 7,600 lb. Max. speed, 340 m.p.h.

(*Richard Riding*)

Hawker Hurricane Mk.XII

Version with 4 cannon and 8 Browning guns built for the R.C.A.F. by Canadain Car and Foundry Co. Ltd., Montreal from 1941. One British civil example only: G-AWLW, c/n 42012, formerly R.C.A.F. 5588, refurbished at Carman, Manitoba, by R. E. Diemert with 1,635 h.p. Rolls-Royce Merlin 25, flown 1966 as CF-SMI. Airfreighted to U.K. 1967 for film 'Battle of Britain'. Registered 10.7.68 to N. A. W. Samuelson, Elstree, C. of A. 6.5.69, to W. J. D. Roberts, Shoreham 7.70. Span, 40 ft. 0 in. Length, 31 ft. 5 in. Tare wt., 5,590 lb. A.U.W., 8,600 lb. Max. speed, 335 m.p.h. Range, 700 miles

Hawker Fury F.Mk.1

Single seat fighter powered by one 2,500 h.p. Bristol Centaurus 18. First prototype, first flown at Brooklands 1.9.44 as NX798, allotted civil marks G-AKRY 1948 for overseas delivery, C. of A. 13.4.48, crashed in Egypt 1949. Third prototype, LA610, first flown at Brooklands 27.11.44 with one Rolls-Royce Griffon 81 engine, converted in 1946 to take one 2,700 h.p. Napier Sabre 7 with leading edge radiators. Civil marks G-AKRZ reserved by Hawker Aircraft Ltd. 29.1.48, scrapped 1949. Span, 38 ft. $4\frac{3}{4}$ in. Length, 34 ft. 8 in. Tare wt., 9,240 lb. A.U.W., 12,500 lb. Max. speed, 460 m.p.h.

(*J. M. G. Gradidge*)

Hawker Hunter T.Mk.66A

All metal, two seat fighter trainer powered by one 10,050 lb. s.t. Rolls-Royce Avon 207C turbojet. One civil aircraft only: G-APUX, c/n H.IF.19, erected at Dunsfold 7.59 using the nose section of Indian Hunter 66 BS369 and fuselage of Belgian Hunter 6-IF.19. Fitted with braking nose wheel, C. of A. 4.9.59, demonstrated at the S.B.A.C. Show 9.59 by chief test pilot A. W. Bedford. Loaned to Iraqi Air Force 5.63 as '567'; to Lebanon 1964; returned to Dunsfold 18.12.65, became G-9-232; to Chile 8.67 as J718. Span, 33 ft. 8 in. Length, 48 ft. $10\frac{1}{2}$ in. A.U.W., 17,420 lb. Max. speed, 700 m.p.h.

(*Hawker Siddeley Aviation Ltd.*)

Hawker Siddeley Harrier GR.Mk.1

Single seat vertical take-off reconnaissance fighter, one 19,000 lb. s.t. Bristol Siddeley Pegasus 101 turbofan, built at Kingston-on-Thames for the R.A.F. and U.S. Marines from 1967. One R.A.F. aircraft, XV742, given temporary civil markings G-VSTO for demonstrations at Lugano, Grenchen and Zürich, Switzerland by test pilot John Farley 11–13.6.71. Reverted to R.A.F. marks 8.71. Span, 25 ft. 3 in. Length, 45 ft. 8 in. Basic operational weight, 12,200 lb. A.U.W. above 25,000 lb. Max. cruise, above 737 m.p.h.

(*Hawker Siddeley Aviation Ltd.*)

Hawker Siddeley Harrier T.Mk.52

Export version of the Harrier T.Mk.2 trainer, similar to the Harrier GR.Mk.1 but with two crew in tandem in a lengthened nose, extended tail cone and increased fin area. One civil demonstrator, initially with one 20,000 lb. s.t. Pegasus 102 and other equipment loaned by the aircraft industry: G-VTOL, c/n B3/41H/735795, registered 27.7.70 to Hawker Siddeley Aviation Ltd., first flown 15.9.71, C. of A. 31.9.71, damaged landing at Dunsfold 6.10.71, rebuilt with 21,500 lb. s.t. Pegasus 103. Flew again 8.6.72; to Indian Navy and Kuwait A/F trials 7.72. Span, 25 ft. 3 in. Length, 55 ft. 10 in. A.U.W., 26,500 lb.

Foreign and Commonwealth Types

This section of the book describes all aircraft of foreign or Commonwealth design and construction flown in British civil markings since the inception of the registration system in 1919 and should be read in conjunction with Appendix E.

The introductory notes to Appendix A apply equally to this section.

(Imperial War Museum CH.14931)

Consolidated Model 28 Catalina

Commercial version of the U.S. Navy PBY all-metal patrol boat, two 1,200 h.p. P. & W. Twin Wasp R-1830-S1C3-G, first produced by the Consolidated Aircraft Corp. at San Diego, California in 1937. Seven British registered examples listed in Appendix E were mainly Lend-Lease R.A.F. machines with a range of 4,650 miles at 130 m.p.h. used on B.O.A.C. Poole–Lagos and QANTAS Ceylon–Perth nonstop services 1940–45. A Mk.3 amphibian, G-APZA, was registered in 1960. Span, 104 ft. 0 in. Length, 65 ft. 1¾ in. Tare wt., 14,240 lb. A.U.W., 35,100 lb. Max. speed, 160 m.p.h.

(Air Ministry)

Consolidated Model 32 Liberator

Bomber with four 1,200 h.p. P. & W. Twin Wasp R-1830-S3C4-G demilitarised as the LB-30A Liberator I, LB-30 Liberator II (long nose) or Liberator III (S4C4-G engines), initially for the R.A.F./B.O.A.C. Transatlantic Ferry Service and the U.K.–Egypt link 1941. Twenty-six allotted civil marks for long distance communications 1941–46 comprised 17 for B.O.A.C., 4 for the QANTAS Ceylon–Perth route and 5 for Scottish Aviation Ltd. One Liberator VII instructional airframe, G-AKAG, at Cranfield from 1947. Span, 110 ft. 0 in. Length, 63 ft. 9 in. A.U.W., 53,600 lb. Cruise, 228 m.p.h. (LB-30) Length, 66 ft. 4 in. A.U.W., 60,000 lb. Range, 2,850 miles

(P. R. Keating)

Convair 240-5

Medium range 40 seat transport powered by two 1,900 h.p. Pratt & Whitney Double Wasp R-2800-CA18, built by Consolidated Vultee Aircraft Corporation at San Diego, California, U.S.A. One British aircraft only: G-AOFC, c/n 64, built 1948, originally Trans-Australia Airlines VH-TAQ 'John Forrest'. Delivered to Kuwait Government as N9853F by U.S. crew 10.56, overhauled by Swissair at Zurich, C. of A. 22.5.57, sold to the Jap-Arabian Oil Co. 7.58 as JA-5048. Span, 91 ft. 9 in. Length, 74 ft. 8 in. Tare wt., 27,600 lb. A.U.W., 41,790 lb. Max. speed, 347 m.p.h. Cruise, 272 m.p.h.

(*D. Napier and Son Ltd.*)

Convair 340-D2

Larger version with an eleventh window, to seat 44 first class or 52 tourist passengers. One British aircraft only: G-ANVP, c/n 153, built San Diego 1954 as N8458H, delivered by air to D. Napier and Son Ltd. at Luton 12.54. Fitted with Napier Eland 503 propeller turbine engines in place of the Pratt & Whitney R-2800-CB16 radials, thus flown 6.55, C. of A. 21.10.57 under the designation Napier Eland Convair Series 2. Left Prestwick 15.11.57 for Santa Monica for C.A.A. airworthiness trials as N340E. Span, 105 ft. 4 in. Length, 79 ft. 2 in. Tare wt., 29,500 lb. A.U.W., 53,200 lb. Cruise, 310 m.p.h.

(*A. J. Jackson*)

Curtiss T-32 Condor

Fifteen seat biplane with retractable undercarriage, powered by two 700 h.p. Wright Cyclones, built by the Curtiss Wright Corporation at St. Louis, Missouri, U.S.A. Four British aircraft only: G-AEWD, 'WE, 'WF and 'ZE, delivered new to Eastern Air Transport 1933, sold to International Air Freight Ltd., Croydon, 1937 and converted into freighters. Stored at Croydon 9.38 when the firm closed down, bought by the Air Ministry 10.38, allotted R.A.F. serials as flying class-rooms but never used. See Appendix E. Span, 82 ft. 0 in. Length, 49 ft. 1 in. Tare wt., 11,235 lb. A.U.W., 16,800 lb. Max. speed, 170 m.p.h. Cruise, 150 m.p.h.

(*Aeroplane*)

Curtiss Wright CW-20

Thirty-six seat transport powered by two 1,700 h.p. Wright Double Row Cyclone 586-C14-BA2, built at St. Louis 1939, and at that time the world's largest twin engined aircraft. First flown at St. Louis 26.3.40 as NX19436 and transferred to the U.S.A.A.F. as the C-55-CS, serial 41-21041. One aircraft only: c/n 101, sold to B.O.A.C. as G-AGDI, 'St. Louis' and converted to 24 seater with long range tanks, C. of A. 22.11.41. Ferried to Prestwick by A. C. P. Johnstone 12.11.41 in 9 hours 40 minutes. Used on long haul routes and the Gibraltar–Malta run 1942, scrapped at Filton 10.43. Span, 108 ft. 0 in. Length, 75 ft. 0 in. Tare wt., 29,500 lb. A.U.W., 45,000 lb. Max. speed, 243 m.p.h. Cruise, 195 m.p.h.

(*J. M. G. Gradidge*)

Curtiss C-46A

Commercial adaptation of war surplus Commando transport built in quantity for U.S.A.A.F. 1942–45, powered by two 2,000 h.p. P. & W. R-2800-51 Double Wasps. One British aircraft only: G-ATXV, c/n 430, ex 43-47360 and PP-ITH, operated in Brazil by SADIA S.A. Transportes Aereos as PP-SLK, registered to Handley Page Ltd. 26.7.66 and flown to Fort Lauderdale, Florida as part exchange for a Dart Herald. Unused British marks cancelled 9.68. Span, 108 ft. 1 in. Length, 76 ft. 4 in. Tare wt., 29,483 lb. A.U.W., 45,000 lb. Max. speed, 241 m.p.h. Cruise, 227 m.p.h.

Darmstadt D 22

Two seat sporting biplane with cantilever mainplanes built by the Academic Flying Group of the Darmstadt Technical High School, Germany in 1931. Two aircraft only, the first of which was built with 120 h.p. de Havilland Gipsy III engine for the Brooklands-trained Indian long distance pilot Man Mohan Singh, for whom registration G-ABPX was reserved 25.9.31. The second aircraft, D-2222, later D-EQIN, 150 h.p. Argus As 8R, crashed in 1935. Span, 24 ft. 3½ in. Length, 21 ft. 10½ in. Tare wt., 816 lb. A.U.W., 1,477 lb. Cruise, 130 m.p.h. Range, 500 miles

De Havilland D.H.A.3 Drover 2

Transport for 8 passengers resembling the D.H. Dove but with fixed undercarriage and three 145 h.p. D.H. Gipsy Major 10 Mk. 2. Twenty aircraft built by de Havilland Aircraft Pty. Ltd. at Sydney 1948–53 of which three, VH-EBQ (illustrated), VH-BMU and VH-EAS were registered in Britain 1949–59 as G-ALLK, G-APPP and G-APXX respectively but only the last actually arrived and this is permanently exhibited at the Southend Historic Aircraft Museum. Span, 57 ft. 0 in. Length, 37 ft. 0 in. Tare wt., 4,100 lb. A.U.W., 6,500 lb. Cruise, 140 m.p.h. Range, 500 miles

356

(*de Havilland Aircraft Co. Ltd.*)

De Havilland D.H.C.2 Beaver 1

Utility transport for pilot and six passengers powered by one 450 h.p. Pratt & Whitney Wasp Junior, 1,632 built at Toronto from 1947. Five British civil aircraft: G-ALOW and G-AMVU for demonstration by de Havillands, Hatfield 1949–56; G-ARTR used for oil drilling support in Libya by B. L. R. Pocock 1961–64; G-ASTK by Martin Cowley Ltd. during the rebuilding of the Damascus–Medina railway 1964–66; and G-AZLU for crop spraying by A. D. S. (Aerial) Ltd. 1972. Span, 48 ft. 0 in. Length, 30 ft. 3 in. Tare wt., 2,810 lb. A.U.W., 4,820 lb. Max. speed, 179 m.p.h. Cruise, 137 m.p.h.

(*de Havilland Aircraft Co. Ltd.*)

De Havilland D.H.C.2 Beaver 2

Utility transport for pilot and six passengers powered by one 550 h.p. Alvis Leonides 502/4 and fitted with revised vertical tail surfaces and mainplanes of increased span. One aircraft only: G-ANAR, c/n 80, formerly CF-GQE, C. of A. 15.9.53, first demonstrated at S.B.A.C. Show 1953, temporarily to R.A.F. 9.54 as XH463. Army trials 1958 as XN142, operated by Alvis Ltd.; returned to Canada 8.71 as CF-CNR. Span 48 ft. 8 in. Length, 31 ft. 9 in. Tare wt., 3,255 lb. A.U.W., 5,100 lb. Max. speed, 196 m.p.h. Cruise, 156 m.p.h.

(*de Havilland Aircraft Co. Ltd.*)

De Havilland D.H.C.3 Otter

Utility transport for two crew and 14 passengers powered by one 600 h.p. Pratt & Whitney Wasp, produced at Toronto by de Havilland Aircraft of Canada Ltd. Two British civil aircraft only, both for D.H. demonstration and communication: G-ANCM, c/n 17, delivered at Hatfield 9.9.53, C. of A. 13.2.56, R-1340-S1H1-G engine, sold to Indian Air Force 3.57; G-AOYX, c/n 204, C. of A. 9.5.57, R-1340-S3H1-G-AN2 engine, sold in Portugal 7.61. Span, 58 ft. 0 in. Length, 42 ft. 0 in. Tare wt., 4,165 lb. A.U.W., 7,600 lb. Max. speed, 163 m.p.h. Cruise, 151 m.p.h.

Dornier Do J Wal

Four seat flying boat powered by two 360 h.p. Rolls-Royce Eagle IX, built by S.A.I. di Construzioni Mecchaniche at Marina di Pisa, Genoa, 1925 for the Amundsen–Ellsworth polar expedition. Reached latitude 87 degrees 44 minutes North, (farthest North by air), 21.5.25, bearing Norwegian markings N-25. To F. T. Courtney 3.27 as G-EBQO, c/n 37, re-engined at Genoa with two 450 h.p. Napier Lions for Atlantic flight, C. of A. 13.7.27. Left Calshot 2.9.27, forced landed off Corunna, Spain 3.9.27, returned to Calshot 31.10.27, left for Friedrichshafen 13.11.27. To Germany 10.28 as D-1422 'Amundsen Wal'. Span, 74 ft. 9 in. Length, 59 ft. 9 in. A.U.W., 9,021 lb. Max. speed, 117 m.p.h.

Dornier Do 28

All-metal cantilever monoplane with STOL performance, accommodating six passengers and two crew, built by Dornier-Werke GmbH at Munich, Germany, from 1960. Two British civil aircraft only: G-ASUR, c/n 3051, Do 28A-1 (two 250 h.p. Lycoming O-540-A1D), C. of A. 1.9.64, Sheffair Ltd., Tollerton in 1972; G-ATAL, c/n 3067, Do 28B-1 (two 290 h.p. Lycoming IO-540-A1A5), delivered at Ringway 7.8.65, C. of A. 17.9.65, Richard Hayes Investments Ltd., Cardiff 10.71. Span, 45 ft. 3½ in. Length, 29 ft. 6 in. Tare wt., 3,810 lb. A.U.W., 6,000 lb. Max. speed, 188 m.p.h. Cruise, 174 m.p.h.

Douglas DC-1

Transport for two crew and 10 passengers, powered by two 875 h.p. Wright Cyclone R-1820-F.25, built by Douglas Aircraft Co. Inc. at Santa Monica, California 1933. One aircraft only: X223Y, c/n 1137, first flown 1.7.33. Saw service with T.W.A. and Howard Hughes in America until sold to Lord Forbes 5.38 as G-AFIF, C. of A. 29.7.38, based at Croydon. Sold in France 9.38, thence to Lineas Aereas Postales Espanolas as EC-AGJ, to Iberia 1940 as EC-AAE 'Negron', crashed at Malaga, Spain 12.40. Span, 85 ft. 0 in. Length, 61 ft. 6 in. A.U.W., 17,500 lb. Cruise, 190 m.p.h.

(*Peter Barrington*)

Douglas DC-2

Transport for 14 passengers and 2 crew, built by Douglas at Santa Monica. G-ADHO, licence-built Airspeed A.S.23 version contemplated 1935, was not built. Two British civil aircraft only, constructed 1935: SP-ASL, c/n 1378, two 775 h.p. Bristol Pegasus VI, purchased from Polskie Linie Lotnicze by Imperial Airways Ltd. as G-AGAD at Bucharest 11.39, was interned by the Rumanian Govt.; PH-ALE 'Edelvalk', c/n 1584, C. of A. 15.4.36, two 710 h.p. Wright Cyclone GR-1820-F52s, K.L.M. refugee based at Whitchurch, Bristol 1939–45 as G-AGBH, returned to Dutch Govt. 2.46 as NL203, later K.L.M. PH-TBB, rest. 7.46 to Southampton Air Services Ltd., crashed in Malta 3.10.46. Span, 85 ft. 0 in. Length, 62 ft. 0 in. Tare wt., 12,010 lb. A.U.W., 18,200 lb. Cruise, 191 m.p.h. Range, 1,060 miles

Douglas DC-3

All-metal transport for 21 passengers and two crew developed from the DC-2, powered by two 900 h.p. Wright Cyclone GR-1820-G102A radials and built in quantity by Douglas Aircraft Co., Inc. at Santa Monica, California from 1935. Ten British registered examples only: five K.L.M. DC-3s which escaped to England to join the B.O.A.C. fleet in 1940; G-AGEN flown in India in 1942; G-AICV (Skyways Ltd. 1946); G-AJDC and 'DG (Starways Ltd. 1950–53); and G-ATXS, ex SADIA, delivered to Handley Page Ltd. at Fort Lauderdale, Florida 1966. Span, 95 ft. 0 in. Length, 64 ft. 6 in. Tare wt., 18,289 lb. A.U.W., 24,000 lb. Cruise, 185 m.p.h.

Douglas Dakota 3 and 4

Military transport version of the DC-3 with strengthened floor, freight door and two 1,200 h.p. Pratt & Whitney Twin Wasp R-1830-92 radials (Dakota 3) or 1,200 h.p. supercharged R-1830-90Cs and air filters on top of the nacelles (Dakota 4). Over 10,000 built during 1939–45 war, including large numbers for the R.A.F., some diverted to B.O.A.C. After the war, stocks of surplus Dakotas were sufficient to supply world short haul needs for a generation. Data for Dakota 3: Span, 95 ft. 0 in. Length, 64 ft. 6 in. Tare wt., 16,600 lb. A.U.W., 28,200 lb. Cruise, 185 m.p.h. Range, 1,500 miles

Douglas Dart Dakota

Three experimental aircraft only: KJ829, c/n 14168, delivered to Rolls-Royce Ltd., Hucknall 1.6.49 and used for Rolls-Royce Dart propeller-turbine development for 13 years, eventually as G-37-2 and temporarily G-AOXI for tropical trials at Dakar with one Dart 510 and one 526, C. of A. 14.11.56; G-ALXN and G-AMDB, c/ns 14661 and 14987, fitted with 1,547 e.h.p. Dart 505s by Field Aircraft Services Ltd., Tollerton for B.E.A. familiarisation in readiness for the Viscounts, Cs. of A. 8.6.51 and 15.8.51 and used on freight runs for 18 months commencing Northolt–Hanover 15.8.51 with G-ALXN. Dimensions as Dakota 3/4, A.U.W., 28,000 lb. Cruise, 207 m.p.h.

Douglas DC-4/C-54 Skymaster

Designed in 1941 as a four engined development of the DC-3, the DC-4 was mass produced during the 1939–45 war with four 1,540 h.p. Pratt & Whitney Twin Wasp R-2000-3 radials as the C-54 Skymaster (C-54A, cargo doors and Twin Wasp R-2000-7; C-54B, extra fuel; C-54D and E, Twin Wasp R-2000-11; C-54G, Twin Wasp R-2000-9). Postwar DC-4s and war surplus C-54s used by world airlines in large numbers as 36–81 seaters from 1946, 31 under British registry. Span, 117 ft. 6 in. Length, 93 ft. 11 in. Tare wt., 40,806 lb. A.U.W., 73,800 lb. Cruise, 246 m.p.h. Range, 1,680 miles

Douglas DC-6A and DC-6B

The DC-6 was a stretched and pressurised version of the DC-4 with four 2,100 h.p. Pratt & Whitney R-2800-CA15 radials in production from 1945. Further stretching with fore and aft freight doors and 2,500 h.p. R-2800-CB17 engines produced the DC-6A freighter and the 60-170 passenger DC-6B airliner; 175 DC-6, 77 DC-6A and 286 DC-6B aircraft built by Douglas at Santa Monica, California 1951–58. Two new and 13 secondhand aircraft registered in Britain. Span, 117 ft. 6 in. Length, 105 ft. 7 in. Tare wt., 54,148 lb. A.U.W., 106,000 lb. Cruise, 307 m.p.h. Range, 3,860 miles

(*Richard Riding*)

Douglas DC-7C

Ultimate development of the DC-4 with four 3,400 h.p. Wright R-3350-18EA1 turbo compound radials, increased span, a further fuselage stretch, taller fin, increased tankage and nonstop transatlantic capability with 99 passengers. Total production 121 aircraft including over 40 DC-7CF freighters. Ten new DC-7Cs delivered to B.O.A.C. 1956–57; ten secondhand, mainly from SABENA and Pan American, used by Caledonian and Trans Meridian from 1961. Span, 127 ft. 6 in. Length, 112 ft. 3 in. Tare wt., 72,763 lb. A.U.W., 140,000 lb. Cruise, 338 m.p.h. Range, 4,635 miles

Enstrom F-28

Three seat helicopter powered by one 205 h.p. Lycoming HIO-360-C1A built from 1966 by the R. J. Enstrom Corporation, Menominee, Michigan, U.S.A. Two British aircraft by 8.72: G-AVUK, c/n 12, N4460, airfreighted to Heathrow 22.9.67, C. of A. 6.10.67, imported by Twyford Moors (Helicopters) Ltd., Eastleigh with the intention of manufacturing the type as the Twyford-Enstrom F-28A Solent. To Spooner Aviation Ltd., Fairoaks 3.72. G-BAAU, c/n 92, imported 8.72 for John E. Clark & Co. (Bournemouth) Ltd. Rotor diameter, 32 ft. 0 in. Length, 29 ft. 0 in. Tare wt., 1,430 lb. A.U.W., 1,950 lb. Max. speed, 100 m.p.h. Cruise, 95 m.p.h.

Ercoupe 415

Two seater with linked rudder and aileron controls built by Engineering and Research Corp., Riversdale, U.S.A. from 1937. One Model 415-C, 75 h.p. Continental C-75-12F; two 415-CD, 90 h.p. C-90-14F; and two 415-D, 85 h.p. C-85-12F, imported 1947–70. Fifteen conventionally controlled Forney F-1As, 90 h.p. C-90-12F, built by Fornaire Aircraft Inc., Fort Collins, Colorado, imported 1955–60 were followed 1966–67 by three improved Alon A-2 Aircoupes (see Vol. 1), 90 h.p. C-90-16F, built by Alon Inc., McPherson, Texas. Span, 30 ft. 0 in. Length, 20 ft. 2 in. Tare wt., 750–800 lb. A.U.W., 1,260–1,450 lb. Cruise, 110 m.p.h. Range, 500 miles

Fairchild 24C8-C and 24C8-E

Fabric covered three seater, with welded steel tube fuselage, wooden wing and 145 h.p. Warner Super Scarab radial, in production by the Fairchild Aircraft Corp. at Hagerstown, Maryland, U.S.A. from 1935. Two British registered examples only: G-AECO (24C8-C), c/n 2718, C. of A. 14.4.36, imported for W. L. S. MacLeod, High Post; impressed 12.40 as BK869, later 3129M. G-AFKW (24C8-E), c/n 2817, imported by A. S. Van Goës, Hatfield as VH-AAW in 1938, C. of A. 17.3.39, impressed 12.40 as BK868. Span, 36 ft. 4 in. Length, 23 ft. 9 in. Tare wt., 1,390 lb. A.U.W., 2,400 lb. Cruise, 120 m.p.h. Range, 525 miles

(*W. K. Kilsby*)

Fairchild 24C8-F

Improved version of the Fairchild 24C8-C and E with 150 h.p. Ranger 6-390-D3 inverted in-line engine, introduced in 1936. Two British registered examples only: G-AEOU, c/n 3126, C. of A. 9.11.36, imported for Lord Willoughby de Broke and based at Kineton, Warwicks. private airstrip, impressed 10.40 as BS817, later 2759M. G-AFFK, c/n 3120, C. of A. 10.6.38, imported for J. H. Thompson, Heston, impressed 7.41 as EF523. Span, 36 ft. 4 in. Length, 24 ft. 10 in. Tare wt., 1,577 lb. A.U.W., 2,400 lb. Cruise, 113 m.p.h. Range, 500 miles

Fairchild 24W-41A Argus 2

The 24W-41A was a four seat version of the Fairchild 24C8-C and E with 165 h.p. Warner Super Scarab radial built in quantity for U.S.A.A.F. communications during the 1939–45 war and supplied to the R.A.F. under Lend-Lease as the Argus 2. Fifty-four war surplus aircraft flown postwar as British registered civil aeroplanes, see Appendix E. Span, 36 ft. 4 in. Length, 23 ft. 9 in. Tare wt., 1,482 lb. A.U.W., 2,562 lb. Cruise, 112 m.p.h. Range, 720 miles

Fairchild 24R Argus 3

Four seater similar to the Argus 2 but powered by one 175 h.p. Ranger 6-440-C2 inverted in-line engine. Entire output of 306 aircraft supplied to the R.A.F. in the Near East, South Africa and Pacific area under Lend-Lease but the engine did not qualify for validation of American C. of A. so that G-AJDD and G-AMBA converted by Gulf Aviation Ltd. at Bahrein and G-AKPX by R. L. Whyham at Squires Gate could not be certificated. Span, 36 ft. 4 in. Length, 25 ft. 10 in. A.U.W., 2,562 lb. Cruise, 117 m.p.h. Range, 640 miles

(*John Goring*)

Fairchild-Hiller FH.1100

Four/five seat utility helicopter powered by one 317 s.h.p. Allison 250-C18 turbine engine, built by the Fairchild Aircraft Corporation at Germantown, Maryland, U.S.A. from 1966. Three British aircraft by 7.72: G-AVTG (c/n 10), formerly N517FH, C. of A. 21.11.67, crashed at Paris Air Show, Le Bourget 5.6.69; G-AYTE (45), EI-ART, C. of A. 25.3.71; G-AZYT (79), 5N-AGX, registered 12.7.72; both used by Twyford Moors (Helicopters) Ltd., Southampton Heliport. Rotor diameter, 35 ft. 5 in. Length, 29 ft. 10 in. Tare wt., 1,396 lb. A.U.W., 2,750 lb. Max. speed, 127 m.p.h. Cruise, 120 m.p.h.

Fiat G.212

Twenty-six seat transport powered by three 1,215 h.p. Pratt & Whitney Twin Wasp R-1830-92, built by Aeronautica D'Italia S.A. (Fiat) at Turin 1948. One British aircraft only: G-ANOE, c/n 10, formerly F-BCUX, originally I-ENEA, C. of A. 31.5.54, owner H. E. Shaikh Du-ag Salman al-Sabah, operating Arabian Desert Airlines. Dismantled at Kuwait after C. of A. expiry 12.1.56. Span, 96 ft. 4 in. Length, 75 ft. 7 in. Tare wt., 24,640 lb. A.U.W., 39,600 lb. Max. speed, 236 m.p.h. Cruise, 199 m.p.h.

Fleet F.7C-2

Two seater powered by one 135 h.p. Armstrong Siddeley Genet Major, built 1937 by Fleet Aircraft Ltd. at Fort Erie, Ontario, Canada. One British civil aircraft only: G-AEJY, c/n 69, imported by Amalgamated Aircraft Builders Ltd., first flown at Gatwick 14.7.38, C. of A. 26.7.38. Sold to A. G. A. Fisher, Croydon; to Aero Industries Ltd., Heston 1939; C. R. Dunn, Langley 1943; C. W. Blankley 1946. Damaged landing at Kidlington 14.4.46, stored until transferred to Ringway 5.58, scrapped at Altrincham 7.59. Span, 28 ft. 0 in. Length, 21 ft. 8 in. Tare wt., 1,100 lb. A.U.W., 1,750 lb. Max. speed, 113 m.p.h. Cruise, 98 m.p.h.

(*via Bruce Robertson*)

Focke-Wulf Fw 200B Condor

Transport for 26 passengers powered by four 880 h.p. B.M.W. Hornet 132-G/1, built at Bremen, Germany 1938. One British civil aircraft only: G-AGAY, c/n 2894, formerly Danish Air Lines OY-DAM 'Dania', Danish C. of A. 21.7.38. Seized at Shoreham 5.40, flown to Whitchurch with a prize crew, allotted B.O.A.C. name 'Wolf', impressed by the R.A.F. 1.41 as DX177, damaged beyond repair at White Waltham 12.7.41. Span, 108 ft. 0 in. Length, 78 ft. 0 in. Tare wt., 24,860 lb. A.U.W., 32,600 lb. Max. speed, 267 m.p.h. Cruise, 258 m.p.h.

(*P. R. Duffy*)

Fokker Dr. I Triplane

Single seat fighter of wood and fabric construction, with one 110 h.p. Oberursel rotary engine, built by Fokker Flugzeug-Werke A.G., Schwerin and used by the Germans on the Western Front from August 1917. Two replica aircraft constructed by John Bitz GmbH at Munich for Twentieth Century-Fox Productions Ltd. and airfreighted to Shannon for the film 'Blue Max', shot at Baldonnel/Casement in 1965: G-ATIY, c/n 001, A. to F. 23.9.65; G-ATJM, c/n 002, A. to F. 23.9.65; both to Shillelagh Productions Inc. 6.67 as EI-APW and EI-APY respectively. Span, 23 ft. 7 in. Length, 19 ft. 0 in. A.U.W., 1,540 lb. Max. speed, 121 m.p.h.

(*Air Portraits*)

Fokker E.III

Single seat fighter of wood and fabric construction, with one 130 h.p. Oberursal rotary engine, built by Fokker Flugzeug-Werke A.G., Schwerin and used by the Germans on the Western Front in 1915. One replica aircraft G-AVJO, c/n PPS/FOK/1, powered by one 75 h.p. Continental A-75, built at White Waltham by D. E. Bianchi and first flown by Miss Joan Hughes 4.65. Registered 12.4.67 to Personal Plane Services Ltd., A. to F. 19.7.69, based at Booker. Span, 37 ft. 9 in. Length, 24 ft. 0 in. A.U.W., 910 lb. Max. speed, 95 m.p.h.

(*via Hans Kofoed*)

Fokker F.III

Transport monoplane with fabric covered, welded steel tube fuselage and wooden cantilever wing, seating five cabin passengers with the pilot in an open cockpit on the starboard side of the single 240 h.p. Siddeley Puma engine. Built by Deutscher Aero Lloyd A.G. at Staaken, Germany from 1923. Two British registered examples only, delivered to Det Danske Luftfartselskab, Kastrup in 1925 and acquired by British Air Lines Ltd., Croydon as G-AALC and G-AARG respectively in 1929. Joint log book preserved by Shuttleworth. Span, 52 ft. 6 in. Length, 33 ft. 10 in. Tare wt., 2,645 lb. A.U.W., 4,187 lb. Cruise, 84 m.p.h.

Fokker F.VIIA

Eight passenger/two crew development of the Fokker F.III powered by one 450 h.p. Gnome-Rhône Jupiter 9AB radial and built by Fokker at Amsterdam from 1925. Five British registered, ex K.L.M., aircraft only: G-EBPL used by the Rt. Hon. F. E. Guest in 1926; G-EBTQ 'St. Raphael' lost on a transatlantic flight 31.8.27; and G-EBTS 'Princess Xenia' used on the McIntosh/Fitzmaurice transatlantic attempt 16.9.27 and the McIntosh/Hinkler India flight 1927 (renamed 'The Spider' with 500 h.p. Jupiter XI for the C. D. Barnard/Duchess of Bedford India and Cape flights 1929–30); G-AEHE and 'HF for the League of Nations 1936. Span, 63 ft. $3\frac{3}{4}$ in. Length, 47 ft. $10\frac{1}{4}$ in. Tare wt., 4,299 lb. A.U.W., 7,936 lb. Cruise, 93 m.p.h. Range, 560 miles

Fokker F.VIIA/3m

Three engined version of the Fokker F.VIIA powered by three 215 h.p. Armstrong Siddeley Lynx IVC, in production from 1925. Three British registered aircraft built to special order for the personal use of wealthy owners: G-EBPV for the Rt. Hon. F. E. Guest 12.26; G-EBYI, registered 5.28 to D. H. Drew, personal pilot to Albert Lowenstein, Belgian financier; G-EBZJ for Maj. A. P. Holt 7.28. See Appendix E. Span, 63 ft. $3\frac{3}{4}$ in. Length, 47 ft. $10\frac{1}{4}$ in. Tare wt., 4,730 lb. A.U.W., 7,920 lb. Cruise, 106 m.p.h.

Fokker F.VIIB/3m

A more powerful version of the F.VIIA/3m with increased span and improved performance to carry two crew and 8 passengers. Two British registered aircraft only, both fitted with 330 h.p. Wright Whirlwind J-6-9 radials: G-AADZ, c/n 5105, PH-AGP, 8.2.29, Van Lear Black 'Maryland Free State', London–Tokio flight 9.2.30–7.4.30, sold abroad 12.30, to Ala Littoria 8.35 as I-UEBI; G-AATG, c/n 5026, PH-AGW, 10.2.30, W.Z. Ltd., Dübendorf, Switzerland 'Extra Dry', sold abroad 6.35. Span, 71 ft. $2\frac{1}{4}$ in. Length, 47 ft. $6\frac{3}{4}$ in. Tare wt., 6,724 lb. A.U.W., 11,464 lb. Range, 520 miles

Fokker F.VIII

A larger, twin engined transport carrying two crew and 15 passengers, in production from 1928. Two British registered aircraft only, both fitted with 500 h.p. Pratt & Whitney Wasp T1D1 radials, bought from K.L.M. by British Airways Ltd., Gatwick in 1937 for its cross-Channel services: G-AEPT, c/n 5043, PH-AEF, 13.1.37, w.f.u. 5.38; G-AEPU, c/n 5046, PH-AEI, 21.5.37, to Sweden 4.39 as SE-AHA. Span, 73 ft. 5 in. Length, 54 ft. 10 in. Tare wt., 7,400 lb. A.U.W., 12,800 lb. Cruise, 96 m.p.h.

Fokker Universal

A small strut braced monoplane for six passengers and two crew built initially in Holland as the F.XI. One British registered aircraft only: G-EBUT, c/n 422, 300 h.p. Wright Whirlwind J-5, American version without type number built by Atlantic Aircraft Corp., Teterboro, New Jersey for Mrs. Maia Carberry, Nairobi, Kenya, as NC3199 'Miss Africa'. Flown to Croydon by Sir Piers Mostyn 5.28, flown back to Kenya by John Carberry 12.28, temporarily VP-KAB, returned to Croydon 3.29 for Air Taxis Ltd. as G-EBUT, Surrey Flying Services Ltd., Croydon 8.32, to Australia 12.35 as VH-UTO. Span, 47 ft. 9 in. Length, 33 ft. 0 in. Tare wt., 2,100 lb. A.U.W., 4,189 lb. Cruise, 98 m.p.h. Range, 600 miles

(*A. J. Jackson*)

Fokker F.XII

Successor to the F.VIIB/3m to carry 16 passengers and two crew, in production for K.L.M. from 1931 and powered by three 420 h.p. Pratt & Whitney Wasp C radials. Six K.L.M. aircraft sold to Crilly Airways Ltd. as G-ADZH to 'ZK, G-AEOS and 'OT, the last two with 500 h.p. Wasp T1D1 engines. Used between Heston, Croydon, Gatwick and the Continent during 1936. See Appendix E. Span, 88 ft. 6 in. Length, 60 ft. 8 in. Tare wt., 11,790 lb. A.U.W., 19,836 lb. Cruise, 109 m.p.h. Range, 700 miles

Fokker F.XXII

Transport monoplane with fabric covered, circular section, fuselage seating 22 passengers (as indicated by the designation) and powered by four 525 h.p. Pratt & Whitney Wasp T1D1 radials. Two of the four built at Amsterdam in 1936 were sold in Britain 'in 1939: G-AFXR, K.L.M. PH-AJR 'Roerdomp', to British American Air Services Ltd., Heston and G-AFZP, K.L.M. PH-AJP 'Papegaai' to Scottish Aviation Ltd., Prestwick as a navigation trainer. G-AFZP fitted with 600 h.p. Wasp R-1340-S3H1 for Scottish Airlines 1946. Span, 99 ft. 0 in. Length, 68 ft. 10 in. Tare wt., 17,475 lb. A.U.W., 28,600 lb. Cruise, 162 m.p.h. Range, 980 miles

Fokker F.XXXVI

Transport monoplane for 4 crew and 32 passengers from which the smaller F.XXII was derived. One aircraft only: PH-AJA, c/n 5348, K.L.M. 'Arend', built at Amsterdam 1934 and powered by four 750 h.p. Wright Cyclone SGR-1820-F2 radials. Sold to Scottish Aviation Ltd. 1939 as G-AFZR, C. of A. 29.8.39, as a navigators' flying classroom for No.12 E.F.T.S./No.1 A.O.N.S., Prestwick. Burned out in take-off accident at Prestwick 21.5.40. Span, 108 ft. 2 in. Length, 78 ft. 8 in. Tare wt., 22,700 lb. A.U.W., 36,366 lb. Cruise, 165 m.p.h. Range, 160 miles

Fokker F.27 Friendship

All metal transport for two crew and up to 48 passengers, in production at Amsterdam from 1956. Three British registered aircraft initially, powered by two 2,230 e.h.p. Rolls-Royce Dart 532-7 propeller turbines: G-AVDN, Ser.200, c/n 10316, PH-FKL, C. of A. 6.1.67; and mixed traffic Ser.400s G-AWFU, c/n 10325, PH-FKV, PH-SAR, C. of A. 3.4.68 and G-AZFD, c/n 10323, PH-FKT, HB-AAW, all used by Gulf Aviation Ltd. on local services out of Bahrein. Span, 95 ft. $1\frac{3}{4}$ in. Length, 77 ft. 1 in. Tare wt., 23,197 lb. A.U.W., 43,500 lb. Cruise, 295 m.p.h. Max. range, 1,286 miles

(Flight Photo 9509)

Ford 4AT-E

All metal transport accommodating two crew and 11 passengers, in production at Dearborn, Michigan, U.S.A., by the Stout Metal Airplane division of the Ford Motor Co. from 1926 and powered by three 300 h.p. Wright Whirlwind J-6-9 radials. Two British registered examples only: Ford's demonstrator NC9678 registered to their English agent H. S. Cooper 10.30 as G-ABEF; and NC8406 which had been with the Spanish Ford agents CLASSA as EC-KKA 1930–31, imported for H. S. Cooper 10.32 as G-ACAK. See Appendix E. Span, 74 ft. 0 in. Length, 49 ft. 10 in. Tare wt., 6,500 lb. A.U.W., 10,130 lb. Cruise, 107 m.p.h. Range, 570 miles

(*Flight Photo 10875*)

Ford 5AT-C and 5AT-D

Larger version of the all metal 4AT-E accommodating 14 passengers and powered by three 420 h.p. Pratt & Whitney Wasp radials. The 5AT-D had increased cabin headroom, square door and 450 h.p. Wasp C radials. Two Ford 5AT-Cs, G-ABFF (later re-registered with Henry Ford's initials as G-ABHF) and G-ABHO, imported by H. S. Cooper and the Earl of Lovelace respectively in 1930; and one Ford 5AT-D, G-ACAE, purchased by Hon. A. E. Guinness 1933. See Appendix E. Span, 77 ft. 10 in. Length, 50 ft. 3 in. Tare wt., 7,600 lb. A.U.W., 13,500 lb. Cruise, 115 m.p.h. Range, 560 miles

(*Flight Photo F68 16/6*)

Fournier RF-3, RF-4 and SF-531 Milan

The RF-3 wood and fabric, single seat, powered sailplane with 39 h.p. Rectimo 4AR-1200 engine and retractable wheel, was designed by René Fournier and built at Gap, France by Alpavia from 1963. The improved RF-4D, built in numbers from 1967 by Sportavia-Pützer GmbH at Dahlemer-Binz, Germany was followed by the long-span SF-531 Milan with 1:29 glide angle. Two RF-3s, a number of RF-4Ds and one SF-531 (G-AYRL, c/n 6606, C. of A. 5.11.71) imported by Sportair Aviation Ltd. and Aspenair Ltd., Biggin Hill. RF-4D: Span, 37 ft. 0 in. Length, 19 ft. 0 in. Tare wt., 595 lb. A.U.W., 860 lb. Cruise, 112 m.p.h.

(*Sportair Aviation Ltd.*)

Fournier RF-5

Two seat, dual control, trainer version of the RF-4D powered by one 68 h.p. Umbach SL 1700E engine, in production by Sportavia-Pützer at Dahlemer-Binz from 1969. Eight aircraft imported initially by Sportair Aviation Ltd. for the Sportair Flying Club at Biggin Hill and for private owners, are listed in Appendix E. Span, 45 ft. 0 in. Length, 25 ft. 10 in. Tare wt., 925 lb. A.U.W., 1,430 lb. Cruise, 115 m.p.h. Range, 435 miles

(*D. A. Conway*)

Fuji FA-200-180

All-metal four seater of stressed skin construction, powered by one 180 h.p. Lycoming IO-360-B1B, in production from 1968 by Fuji Jukogyo Kabushiki Kaisha (Fuji Heavy Industries, successors to the Nakajima Aircraft Co.) at their Utsunomiya City factory, Japan. The first British-owned example, G-AZTJ, c/n 166, (illustrated), registered 28.4.72 to Air Associates Ltd., Fairoaks, was delivered 8.72. Span, 30 ft. 9 in. Length, 26 ft. 2 in. Tare wt., 1,433 lb. A.U.W., 2,535 lb. Max. speed, 145 m.p.h. Cruise, 123 m.p.h. Range, 800 miles

Gardan GY-20 Minicab

Two seater (90 h.p. Continental C-90) designed in France by M. Yves Gardan, first flown 1949 and built by Constructions Aéronautiques du Béarn but after its closure, exclusive rights were acquired by A. W. J. G. Ord-Hume who anglicised the drawings and improved the design for amateur constructors. Six registered initially: G-ATPV known as the Barritault JB.01; G-AVRW, G-AWEP and G-AZJE amateur-built; G-AWUB and 'WM (60 h.p. Continental A-65) built at Béarn, the last a differently equipped GY-201. Span, 25 ft. 0 in. Length, 17 ft. 0 in. Tare wt., 600 lb. A.U.W., 1,232 lb. Cruise, 112 m.p.h. Range, 460 miles

Gardan GY-80 Horizon

M. Gardan's four seat, all-metal Horizon, first flown in 1960, featured an all-moving tailplane and retractable undercarriage, the latter linked electrically to four Fowler flaps. Built in numbers by Sud-Aviation at Toulouse from 1962. Eleven British registered aircraft in 1972 comprised one Horizon 150, G-ATXF; six Horizon 160s G-ASJY, 'ZS, G-ATDG, 'DH, 'GY and 'JT; and four Horizon 180s G-AVMA, 'RS, G-AWAC and G-AYOL. See Appendix E. Span, 31 ft. 10 in. Length, 21 ft. $9\frac{1}{2}$ in. (Horizon 180) Tare wt., 1,360 lb. A.U.W., 2,535 lb. Max. cruise, 150 m.p.h. Range, 770 miles

(*John Goring*)

Globe GC-1B Swift

Two seater built at Dallas, Texas, U.S.A., by the Texas Engineering and Manufacturing Co. Inc. Four British aircraft only: G-AHUU, c/n 1003, 125 h.p. Continental C-125-1, imported by Helliwells Ltd., Walsall, C. of A. 26.2.47, to Norway 5.54 as LN-BDE; G-AHWG, c/n 1, to have been Helliwells-built, not proceeded with; G-AHWH, c/n 1243, 125 h.p. Continental C-125-2, C. of A. 19.3.47, w.f.u. at Wombleton 6.61; G-ARNN, c/n 1272, formerly N3279K, ZS-BMX, VP-RDA and VP-YMJ, C. of A. 23.8.62, Nottingham F/G, Tollerton. Span, 29 ft. 4 in. Length, 20 ft. 10¾ in. Tare wt., 1,139 lb. A.U.W., 1,710 lb. Cruise, 140 m.p.h.

(*R. W. Brown*)

Grumman G.21A Goose

All-metal amphibian for two crew and six passengers, powered by two 450 h.p. Pratt & Whitney Wasp Junior R-985-SB2, in production 1937 by the Grumman Aircraft Engineering Corp. at Bethpage, Long Island, N.Y., U.S.A. Two British civil aircraft only: G-AFCH, c/n 1009, registered to Lord Beaverbrook 26.10.37, sold in the Dutch East Indies 7.38; G-AFKJ, c/n 1049, C. of A. 4.1.39, same owner, impressed 2.41 as HK822, sank off Benghazi, Libya 9.12.42. Span, 49 ft. 0 in. Length, 38 ft. 4 in. Tare wt., 5,425 lb. A.U.W., 8,500 lb. Max. speed, 205 m.p.h. Cruise, 191 m.p.h.

(*Aviation Photo News*)

Grumman G.21A Super Goose

Modernised version of the Goose with retractable wing tip floats and two 450 h.p. Pratt & Whitney Wasp Junior R-985-AN6 radials, operating at an increased all-up weight. One British registered aircraft only: G-ASXG, c/n 1083, formerly R.C.A.F. 926, CF-BZY, N36992 and N3692, C. of A. 16.10.64, based at Hawarden by The Grosvenor Estates for executive flights between London, the Continent and Scottish and Irish lakes. Converted to G.21C Turbo Goose in 1968. A.U.W., 9,200 lb. Cruise, 150 m.p.h.

(*Aviation Photo News*)

Grumman G.21C Turbo Goose

The Grosvenor Estates' Super Goose G-ASXG re-engined to McKinnon specification by Marshalls of Cambridge (Engineering) Ltd. with two 550 e.h.p. Pratt & Whitney PT-6A-20 propeller turbine units, 1 ft. 3 in. further inboard than the original Wasps, and driving Hartzell three-bladed feathering and reversible airscrews. C. of A. re-issued 19.7.68. Cocooned at Leavesden 1972. A.U.W., 9,200 lb. Cruise, 207 m.p.h. Endurance, $5\frac{1}{2}$ hr.

Grumman G.73 Mallard

Commercial amphibian for 10 passengers and two crew, powered by two 600 h.p. Pratt & Whitney Wasp R-1340-S3H1, built by the Grumman Aircraft Engineering Corp'n. at Bethpage, Long Island, New York, U.S.A. 1949. Two British aircraft only: G-ALLJ, c/n J-41, C. of A. 6.4.49, Shell Refining & Marketing Co. Ltd., to N.V. Bataafsche Petroleum Maatschappij 5.49 as PK-AKE, burned out at Djakarta 27.1.51: G-ASCS, c/n J-55, formerly N2985, CF-HAV and CF-PQE, C. of A. 19.8.62, to Canada 4.69 as CF-YQC. Span, 66 ft. 8 in. Length, 48 ft. 4 in. Tare wt., 9,350 lb. A.U.W., 12,750 lb. Cruise, 180 m.p.h.

(*Aviation Photo News*)

Grumman G.159 Gulfstream I

Executive transport for two crew and 14 passengers powered by two 2,190 e.s.h.p. Rolls-Royce Dart 529-8E propeller turbine engines in production at Bethpage, N.Y. from 1965. Two British registered aircraft only: G-ASXT, c/n 135, N755G, C. of A. 20.10.64, Shell Aircraft Ltd., Heathrow, to Ford Motor Co. Ltd., Stansted 7.67; G-AWYF, c/n 48, formerly N748G, VR-BBY and N302K, C. of A. 26.4.69, Ford Motor Co. Ltd., Stansted. Span, 78 ft. 4 in. Length, 64 ft. 0 in. Tare wt., 20,993 lb. A.U.W., 36,000 lb. Economical cruise, 288 m.p.h. Max. range, 2,540 miles

(*Aviation Photo News*)

Grumman G.1159 Gulfstream II

Swept wing version of the Gulfstream I for up to 30 passengers, powered by two aft-mounted 11,400 lb. s.t. Rolls-Royce Spey 511-8 turbofans, in production at Bethpage from 1967. One British registered aircraft only: G-AYMI, c/n 91, N17586, C. of A. 16.8.70, delivered to R.T.Z. Services Ltd., Heathrow 2.71. Span, 68 ft. 10 in. Length, 79 ft. 11 in. Tare wt., 38,000 lb. A.U.W., 60,000 lb. Max. cruise, 565 m.p.h. Max. range, 3,460 miles

(*A. J. Jackson*)

Grumman G.164 Ag-Cat

Single seat agricultural biplane powered by one 450 h.p. P. & W. Wasp Junior R-985-AN3, built by Schweizer Aircraft, Elmira, U.S.A. from 1957. Three British aircraft only: G-ATVY, c/n 287, N725Y and 6Y-JDP, C. of A. 6.7.66 and G-ATVZ, c/n 288, N726Y and 6Y-JDR, C. of A. 29.6.66, both to Agrarflug, Worms, Germany 11.68 as D-FADA and D-FACU; G-AYTM (G.164A), c/n 797, N6555, C. of A. 27.4.71, Aerocare Agricultural Services Ltd., Breighton, Yorks. Span, 35 ft. 8 in. Length, 24 ft. 4 in. Tare wt., 2,300 lb. A.U.W., 4,375 lb. Max. speed, 110 m.p.h. Spraying speed, 75–90 m.p.h.

APPENDIX D

This section of the book gives details of British civil aircraft for which illustrations have not been found despite many years of intensive search. It also describes those which were not completed and therefore not photographed and also those under construction at the time of going to press.

The introductory notes to Appendix A apply equally to this section.

Coates Swalesong SA.2 and SA.3

Open cockpit, side-by-side low wing two seater of wooden construction designed by J. R. Coates, builder of Luton Minor G-AMAW (Swalesong SA.1) in 1950. One SA.2 only: G-AYDV, c/n PFA.1353, powered by one 90 h.p. Continental G.P.U. converted to C-90 standard, nearing completion at Hitchin, Herts. in 1972. One SA.3, G-BAAH, c/n PFA.1590, registered 31.7.72, simplified version for amateur construction. Span, 26 ft. 5 in. Length, 19 ft. 0 in. Tare wt., 640 lb. A.U.W., 1,150 lb. Max. cruise, 110 m.p.h. Max. range, 450 miles

Comper C.97 Trimster

Reservation dated 7.12.31 for Comper monoplane of undisclosed specification. One aircraft only: G-ABSG, c/n 3097, construction abandoned.

C.W. Swan

Six—eight seat low wing passenger monoplane of sleek appearance with twin fins and rudders built in mock-up form by Messrs. C. R. Chronander and J. I. Waddington (designers of the C.W. Cygnet G-AEMA*) at their Slough, Middlesex, works in 1937. Two versions envisaged were one with underslung 200 h.p. de Havilland Gipsy Six Series I or II engines, and the other with 450 h.p. Pratt & Whitney Wasp Junior (or Wright Whirlwind) radials. The aircraft was not built and registration G-AERO reserved in January 1937 was eventually allotted to an Auster J-1 Autocrat (see Vol. 1) in 1946. Span, 46 ft. 0 in. Length, 36 ft. 0 in. Tare wt. (Gipsy Six Series II), 3,660 lb. A.U.W., 6,000 lb. Cruise, 175 m.p.h. Range, 700 miles

de Havilland D.H.23

Four seat biplane flying boat powered by one 450 h.p. Napier Lion mounted under the top centre section and driving a tractor airscrew. Reservation dated 9.3.20 for one aircraft only: G-EARN, c/n E.58, construction abandoned.

de Havilland D.H.92 Dolphin

Modernised Rapide with D.H.86A nose accommodating two pilots side-by-side, increased span, retractable undercarriage and two 204 h.p. Gipsy Six Series II engines driving constant speed airscrews. One aircraft only, c/n 6400, flown at Hatfield in the summer of 1936 but was too heavy structurally and no others were built. Registration G-AEMX allotted to the de Havilland Aircraft Co. Ltd. 27.8.36 was not painted on the aircraft which was scrapped 10.36 and unique as the only D.H. type to have flown without being photographed. Span, 53 ft. 7 in. Wing area, 393 sq. ft. A.U.W., 6,600 lb. Max. speed, 161 m.p.h.

* See General Aircraft Cygnet

Falconar F-11-3

The two seat Jodel D.11 up-dated for home construction by Falconar Aircraft of Edmonton, Alberta, Canada. Two British examples under construction in 1972: G-AWHY, c/n PFA.1322, one 90 h.p. Continental C-90-12F, registered 17.4.68 to W. M. Greenwood, Henley-in-Arden, Warwicks; G-AXDY, c/n PFA.906, registered 21.4.69 to G. K. Ellis, Saxmundham, Suffolk. Span, 27 ft. 6 in. Length, 22 ft. 0 in. Tare wt., 870 lb. A.U.W., 1,350 lb. Cruise, 100 m.p.h. Range, 450 miles

Farman S-11 Shorthorn

Two seat pusher biplane powered by one 80 h.p. Renault, designed 1914 by Henri and Maurice Farman. One British civil aircraft only: G-EAAZ, formerly R.A.F. trainer B4674, built at Hendon by the Aircraft Manufacturing Co. Ltd. in August 1917. Registered 3.5.19 to Maj. H. S. Shield who made the delivery flight from Old Sarum to Squires Gate in the same month. Span, 53 ft. 0 in. Length, 30 ft. 8 in. Tare wt., 1,441 lb. A.U.W., 2,046 lb. Max. speed, 66 m.p.h.

Fenton Cheel

Two seat light aircraft designed and built 1930–31 by J. B. Fenton at Beggar's Roost, Stanmore, Middlesex. One aircraft only: G-ABHZ, c/n F.Mk.1, registered 5.1.31, construction abandoned, registration cancelled 15.8.45

Fokker D.VII

Single seat fighter powered by one water-cooled 160 h.p. Mercedes, or similar engine, built for the German Air Force by Fokker Flugzeug-Werke, Schwerin and sub-contractors 1918. One British civil aircraft only: G-EANH, registered 18.9.19 to J. Forgan Potts, registration cancelled 9.20. Span, 29 ft. $3\frac{1}{2}$ in. Length, 23 ft. 0 in. Tare wt., 1,540 lb. A.U.W., 1,936 lb. Max. speed, 120 m.p.h.

Grahame-White G.W.15

Two seat box kite pusher trainer, normally powered by one 80 h.p. Gnome or 80 h.p. Le Rhône rotary, built by The Grahame-White Aviation Co. Ltd. at Hendon 1916–17. Three civil aircraft only: K-111 to K-113, later G-EABB, 'BC and 'BD, c/n 401–403, registered 6.5.19 to the manufacturers for use by the Grahame-White Flying School, Hendon where one, believed to be K-113, was flying in September 1919 with racing number 24. Dimensions, weights and performance are not recorded.

Griffiths G.H.4 Gyroplane

Single seat gyroplane, c/n G.1, registered 20.7.65 as G-ATGZ to Mr. G. Griffiths who was building it at Normanton, Derby from a kit marketed by Enugh of Kansas, U.S.A.

Gunton Special

Single seat ultra light monoplane powered by one 40 h.p. A.B.C. Scorpion, designed and built by T. F. W. Gunton at Spalding, Lincs. 1939. One aircraft only: G-AFRW, c/n T.F.W.G.1, registered 21.3.39, construction not completed. Sold to R. G. Bracewell at Gorleston, Norfolk 5.45 and converted into the Pivot single seat parasol monoplane G-AGOO, construction of which was also not completed. Scrapped 12.46

Register of British Civil Aircraft

Temporary civil registrations beginning at K-100 and reaching K-175, used for approximately one month from 30 April 1919, were supplanted by a lettered sequence commencing G-EAAA but by international agreement in 1928 a new system began at G-AAAA after G-EBZZ had been reached. The letter Q was discontinued in 1927, the last aircraft to carry it being the Fokker F.VIIA G-EBTQ described in this volume.

Class B registrations before 1947 comprised a manufacturer's identifying letter and an aircraft number, e.g. D.H.88 Comet E-1 where E indicated the de Havilland Aircraft Co. Ltd. and 1 the particular aircraft. This system was replaced by one comprising the national G, manufacturers' numbers and aircraft identity digits, e.g. Dart Herald G-8-3 where 8 indicated Handley Page Ltd. and 3 the individual aircraft.

This appendix is the second instalment of more than 16,500 individual aircraft registrations issued in Great Britain since 1919. They are grouped alphabetically by types and variants, following precisely the same order as that in which they are described in the chapters and appendixes.

As in Volume 1, details for each aircraft are given in the following order: constructor's number in parentheses; variant number (where necessary); previous identities; date of issue of Certificate of Airworthiness or Authorisation to Fly; representative ownership changes; fate or disposal. If no C. of A. was issued or the date of issue of an export C. of A. was not available for publication, the date of registration is substituted.

Where first flight dates are included, or where certification came late in the life of an aircraft, this is made clear. Airworthy aircraft and those on overhaul in August 1972 have no disposal details.

Space considerations compel a condensed form for all foreign types as well as for British machines built in very large numbers and if, in these cases, the last recorded fact is the date of issue of C. of A., the aircraft was still active in August 1972.

Abbreviations are limited to those included in the introductory notes to Appendix A, those common to aviation parlance, and the following:

A/F	Air Force	d/d	delivered
A/S	Air Services Ltd.	F/C	Flying Club
A/T	Air Transport Ltd.	F/S	Flying Services Ltd.
A/W	Airways Ltd.	ntu	registration not taken up
canc.	registration cancelled	rest.	registration restored
d.b.f.	destroyed by fire	t/a	trading as

Chrislea CH.3 Ace and Super Ace

G-AHLG (100), 7.1.48, Chrislea Aircraft Ltd., Heston; scrapped at Exeter 4.52

G-AKFD (101), 7.5.48, Chrislea Aircraft Ltd.; crated for Australia 3.49 as VH-BRP, burned out in a ship's fire as deck cargo at Port Said, Egypt 1949

G-AKUV (104), 30.6.48, Chrislea Aircraft Ltd.; Mrs. R. Morrow-Tait, 'Thursday's Child' 1948; J. Chapman, Cambridge 6.51; d.b.r. at Thruxton 23.6.53

G-AKUW (105), 12.8.48, Chrislea Aircraft Ltd.; F. G. Fox, Fairoaks/Redhill 11.50; J. M. Lovett and S. W. Ward, Panshanger 5.69; E. M. Woodhams, Baginton 2.72

G-AKUX (106), 6.9.48, Sqn. Ldr. J. L. Patient (Arab Airways), Amman; Enterprise Aviation Services Ltd., Beirut, Lebanon 1949; scrapped at Beirut 4.66

G-AKUY (107), 6.9.48, Chrislea Aircraft Ltd., Exeter; to the Argentine 9.48 as LV-XAX, re-registered LV-RXV on arrival; w.f.u. 10.58

G-AKUZ (108), 6.9.48, Chrislea Aircraft Ltd., Exeter; to the Argentine 9.48 as LV-XAY, re-registered LV-RXW on arrival; w.f.u. Ascuncion 9.61

G-AKVA (109), 18.11.48, Suffolk Trust Ltd., Fairoaks; Autowork (Winchester) Ltd., Eastleigh 2.50; W. A. Eley, Denham 5.51; to the Gold Coast 9.54 as VP-AAE, subsequently registered in Ghana as 9G-ABJ; to South Africa as ZS-DPR

G-AKVB (110), 4.1.49, Chrislea Aircraft Ltd.; J. Chapman, Cambridge 6.53; E. F. Thurston, Stapleford 5.55; crashed at Rettenden, Essex 22.5.55

G-AKVC (111), 19.5.49, Chrislea Aircraft Ltd.; to A. Grut, Malaya 4.49 as VR-RBI; scrapped at Kallang 4.55

G-AKVD (112), 19.5.49, Chrislea Aircraft Ltd.; P. F. de Mulder, Brough 4.52; to Honda Motors, Yokohama 2.53 as JA-3062; crashed at Fujisawa 31.8.58

G-AKVE (113), 22.5.50, Chrislea Aircraft Ltd.; to Brazil 5.50 as PT-AJG, owned by A. X. da S. J. Machado 6.59

G-AKVF (114), 25.8.50, Chrislea Aircraft Ltd.; to Pakistan via Croydon 27.8.50 as AP-ADT; rest. 11.59 to J. H. Southern, Barton; D. L. Rugg-Easey, Wolverhampton 12.61; D. F. Redman, Wolverhampton 6.67; J. N. Scott, Hurn 1.71; J. Stanbridge, Biggin Hill 5.72

G-AKVG (115), 9.5.50, Chrislea Aircraft Ltd.; to Switzerland 12.50 as HB-EAA

G-AKVH to G-AKVL (116–120), construction completed by 4.49 but never flown

G-AKVM (121) and G-AKVN (122), partially completed, construction abandoned

The original Ace in revised form with twin fins and rudders. (*Aeroplane*)

Chrislea CH.4 Skyjeep

G-AKVO (123) and G-AKVP (124), partially completed, construction abandoned

G-AKVR (125), Chrislea Aircraft Ltd.; to Australia 9.51 as VH-BRP; fitted with 200 h.p. D.H. Gipsy Six engine in 1957 as VH-RCD

G-AKVS (126), 14.6.50, Chrislea Aircraft Ltd.; to French Indochina 10.52 as F-OAMP

G-AKVT (127), Chrislea Aircraft Ltd., Exeter; to Uruguay 1.51 as CX-AMR

Cierva Autogiros (*experimental machines*)

G-EBQG (Pl/5281), C.11, Parnall-built, registered to the Cierva Autogiro Co. Ltd. 4.2.27; never flown; to instructional airframe at Hamble 1931

G-EBTW (5114), C.6D, registered to the Cierva Autogiro Co. Ltd., Hamble 9.9.27; converted to Cierva C.8R; scrapped in 1929

G-EBTX (5113), C.8V, registered to the Cierva Autogiro Co. Ltd., Hamble 9.9.27; converted from Avro 552A G-EAPR and converted to Avro 552A G-ABGO in 1930

G-EBYY (nil), C.8L Mk.II, 14.7.28, Air Commodore J. G. Weir; flown Croydon–Paris 18.9.28; preserved in British marks in the Musée de l'Air, Paris

G-AABP (nil), C.17 Mk.I, registered to the Cierva Autogiro Co. Ltd. 14.9.28; first flown 23.10.28, dismantled in 1931

G-AAGJ (5129), C.17 Mk.II, registered to the Cierva Autogiro Co. Ltd., Hamble 19.4.29, Avro Alpha engine; to instructional airframe at Hamble 1931; converted to Avro Avian II G-ADEO in 1935

G-AAGK (5130), C.19 Mk.I, 2.8.29, Cierva Autogiro Co. Ltd.; sold abroad 1.30

G-AAGL (5131), C.19 Mk.I, 30.8.29, Cierva Autogiro Co. Ltd., Hamble; crashed at Haldon Aerodrome, Teignmouth 21.9.29

G-AAHM (5132), C.19 Mk.I, 22.3.32, Cierva Autogiro Co. Ltd., Hamble; converted to C.19 Mk.IV; crashed at White City Stadium, London 29.9.32

G-AAIH (18), C.18, built in France by Weymann-Lepère, registered to the Cierva Autogiro Co. Ltd. 5.6.29; believed taken to the U.S.A. by Loel Guinness

G-ABLM (710), C.24, 23.4.32, built by de Havillands at Stag Lane; Cierva Autogiro Co. Ltd.; stored by the Science Museum at Hayes, Middlesex in 1972

G-ABTO (G.31/1), C.25, built by Comper at Hooton; dismantled at Heston 12.33

Cierva C.19 Mk.II

G-AAKY (5133), registered to the Cierva Autogiro Co. Ltd. 9.8.29; sold in the U.S.A. 12.29 to H. Pitcairn, believed as NC311V

G-AAKZ (5134), 26.9.29, Cierva Autogiro Co. Ltd.; written off in accident at Sherburn-in-Elmet, Yorks. 31.5.31; H. M. Scolefield injured

G-AALA (5135), 24.12.29, Cierva Autogiro Co. Ltd.; converted to Cierva C.19 Mk.III; crashed 5.32

G-AAUA (5136), C.19 Mk.IIA (rotor head modifications and long range tanks), 1.8.30, Cierva Autogiro Co. Ltd.; sold abroad, believed in Spain, 3.31

Cierva C.19 Mk.III

G-AAYN (5137), registered to the Cierva Autogiro Co. Ltd. 9.5.30; sold abroad 10.30; believed damaged beyond repair in Argentina 6.3.33

G-AAYO (5138), 10.9.30, Cierva Autogiro Co. Ltd.; on R.A.F. charge 6.11.30 as K1696, struck off charge 21.2.31

Photographs showing the precise configuration of the first two C.19 Mk.I aircraft are rare. The second, with uncowled 80 h.p. Genet radial, is seen after its accident at Haldon on 21 September 1929. (*W. K. Kilsby*)

G-AAYP (5139), 10.9.30, Cierva Autogiro Co. Ltd.; modified to Cierva C.19 Mk.IV; scrapped in 1932

G-ABCK (5140), 14.10.30, Cierva Autogiro Co. Ltd.; to New Zealand 12.30 as ZK-ACL; crashed at Oamaru 5.31; wreck shipped back to the U.K.

G-ABCL (5141), 20.10.30, Cierva Autogiro Co. Ltd.; crashed 29.11.30 after striking tree during take-off from Hounslow Heath, pilot A. H. Rawson

G-ABCM (5142), 13.12.30, Cierva Autogiro Co. Ltd.; delivered Hamble–Farnborough 5.1.31; on R.A.F. charge 16.1.31 as K1948; struck off charge 14.3.34

Cierva C.19 Mk.IV

G-ABFZ (5143), 24.3.31, J. N. Young; National Aviation Day Displays Ltd. 1.34; Capt. H. R. S. Howe, Ford 12.35; scrapped in 1937

G-ABGA (5145), 26.3.31, Cierva Autogiro Co. Ltd.; withdrawn from use 12.31

G-ABGB (5144), 2.4.31, Cierva Autogiro Co. Ltd.; National Aviation Day Displays Ltd. 4.32; to S. Africa 12.32; crashed in display at Cape Town 17.2.33

G-ABUC (5148), 24.5.32, J. A. McMullen, Hanworth; Nat. Aviation Day Displays Ltd. 3.33; F. G. Lundon, Shoreham 8.36; to Singapore F/C 11.36 as VR-SAR

G-ABUD (5149), 26.5.32, Cierva Autogiro Co. Ltd., used by the Autogiro Flying School at Hanworth; crashed 3.33

G-ABUE (5150), 26.5.32, Cierva Autogiro Co. Ltd.; sold abroad, believed in Germany 5.32

G-ABUF (5151), 25.6.32, Cierva Autogiro Co. Ltd., used by the Autogiro Flying School at Hanworth; scrapped 5.35

G-ABUG (5152), 16.6.32, J. A. McAlpine, Yeadon; to Sweden 12.35 as SE-ADU

G-ABUH (5153), 12.7.32, Kent Flying Club, Bekesbourne; to Australia 12.34 as VH-USO; Australian marks cancelled 12.35

G-ABXD (5154), 6.8.32, Cierva Autogiro Co. Ltd.; sold abroad, believed Japan, 8.32

G-ABXE (5155), 6.8.32, Cierva Autogiro Co. Ltd.; sold abroad, believed Japan, 8.32

G-ABXF (5156), 25.8.32, Cierva Autogiro Co. Ltd.; to Japan 8.32 as J-BAYA

G-ABXG (5157), 15.9.32, Cierva Autogiro Co. Ltd., Hanworth; J. A. McMullen and
J. C. Campion, Hanworth 4.35; crashed at Hanworth 25.4.37

G-ABXH (5158), 4.10.32, Cierva Autogiro Co. Ltd.; left Heston on delivery to Spain
7.12.32 as EC-W13; later EC-ATT, 30-62, EC-CAB and EC-AIM

G-ABXI (5159), 4.10.32, Cierva Autogiro Co. Ltd.; left Heston on delivery to the
Spanish Air Force 7.12.32 as 49-1

Cierva Autogiros (*direct control experimental*)

G-ABXP (nil), C.19 Mk.V, registered to the Cierva Autogiro Co. Ltd. 13.6.32; flown at
Hanworth; scrapped in 1935

G-ACFI (1), C.30, built by N.F.S. Ltd., Hanworth; registered to the Cierva Autogiro
Co. Ltd. 21.3.33; first flown 4.33; scrapped in 1938

G-ACKA (A.H.1), C.30P Mk.II, built by Airwork Ltd., Heston; registered to the Cierva
Autogiro Co. Ltd. 1.9.33; scrapped in 1938

G-ACYI (WA.2351F), CL.20, built by Westland Aircraft Ltd., Yeovil; registered to the
Cierva Autogiro Co. Ltd. 24.9.34; scrapped in 1938

G-AFDP (1001), C.40, erected by the British Aircraft Mfg. Co. Ltd., Hanworth; registered to Cierva Autogiro Co. Ltd. 18.12.37; lost in France 6.40

G-AFDR (1002), C.40, details the same as for G-AFDP; impressed into the R.A.F. 6.40,
possibly as T1419

Cierva C.30P (*Avro-built*)

G-ACIM (658), 21.12.33, Cierva Autogiro Co. Ltd., Hanworth; sold abroad 3.34

G-ACIN (659), 2.1.34, Cierva Autogiro Co. Ltd., Hanworth; scrapped in 1938

G-ACIO (660), 2.1.34, Cierva Autogiro Co. Ltd., Hanworth; scrapped in 1937

Cierva C.30A (*Avro-built*)

G-ACUI (705), 27.7.34, Hon. A. E. Guinness; M. of Dufferin, Heston 9.35; Autogiro
F/C 2.39; impressed 9.42 as HM581; restored 11.6.46 as G-AHTZ q.v.

G-ACUT (725), 18.9.34, Airwork Ltd., Heston; C. W. A. Scott's Flying Display 3.36;
Malcolm & Farquharson Ltd., Heston 3.37; registration cancelled 12.37

G-ACUU (726), 14.9.34, Air Service Training Ltd., Hamble; impressed 9.42 as HM580;
restored 3.12.46 to Ciervas; G. S. Baker, Elmdon 'Billy Boy' 4.50; withdrawn
from use at Elmdon 4.60; loaned to Skyfame Museum, Staverton

G-ACVC (706), 28.7.34, Cierva Autogiro Co. Ltd., Hanworth; sold abroad 8.34

G-ACVX (707), 2.10.34, Hon. Mrs. Victor Bruce; Redhill Flying Club 9.36; to N. V.
Autogiro Import 10.37 as PH-ASA; d.b.r. at Oostwold 25.5.38

G-ACWF (708), 31.7.34, Cierva Autogiro Co. Ltd., Hanworth; impressed 6.41 as
DR624; restored 8.5.46 as G-AHMI q.v.

G-ACWG (709), 11.9.34, Cierva Autogiro Co. Ltd.; to France 9.34 as F-AOHY

G-ACWH (710), 26.9.34, Cierva Autogiro Co. Ltd., Hanworth; impressed 6.41 as
DR623; restored 26.4.46 as G-AHLE q.v.

G-ACWI (711), 23.8.34, Cierva Autogiro Co. Ltd.; to France 9.34 as F-AOIO

G-ACWJ (712), 5.9.34, Cierva Autogiro Co. Ltd.; to N.V. Autogiro Import 1.35 as
PH-HHH 'Donna Dulcinea'; impressed 6.40 as AP508 after storage at Hanworth from 1938; lost at sea off Seaton, Devon 16.4.41

G-ACWK (713), 3.11.34, Cierva Autogiro Co. Ltd.; to Focke-Wulf 11.34 as D-EKOM

G-ACWL (714), 16.11.34, Cierva Autogiro Co. Ltd.; to Focke-Wulf 11.34 as D-EKOP

G-ACWM (715), 18.4.35, A. Batchelor, Ramsgate; Thanet Aero Club, Ramsgate 1.39;
impressed 6.40 as AP506; rest. 5.46 to H. R. Philp; to Staverton 1965

H. A. Marsh demonstrating G-ACWF with 'jump start' modifications at Hounslow Heath, Middlesex on 23 July 1936. (*Aeroplane*)

G-ACWN (716), 12.11.34, Austin Dobson; damaged in forced landing at owner's property, Haslemere 18.5.35; sold abroad 2.37

G-ACWO (717), 21.12.34, Cierva Autogiro Co. Ltd.; Autogiro Flying Club, Hanworth 3.39; impressed 12.39 as V1187; to Belgium as spares 1949

G-ACWP (728), 16.11.34, E. J. Jobling Purser, Hanworth; J. S. Meikle, Macmerry 10.38; Autogiro F/C, Hanworth 3.39; impressed 6.40 as AP507; sold to the Science Museum 5.45; permanently exhibited at South Kensington, London

G-ACWR (731), 1.8.34, J. G. Weir, Dalrymple, Ayrshire; Autogiro F/C 3.39; impressed 12.39 as V1186; fell in sea off Worthing 24.10.43 and scrapped

G-ACWS (732), 23.8.34, J. H. Moller, Teviothead Lodge, Hawick; Hon. J. D. Kemp, Barton 9.38; Autogiro Flying Club 6.39; impressed 6.40 as AP509; restored 6.46 to Cierva Autogiro Co. Ltd. as G-AHUC q.v.

G-ACWT (733), 5.7.35, Cierva Autogiro Co. Ltd.; to France 12.34 as F-AOLK

G-ACWU (736), 10.1.35, Cierva Autogiro Co. Ltd.; d/d to Alpar 19.1.35 as HB-MAB

G-ACWZ (752), 31.12.34, Cierva Autogiro Co. Ltd.; Redhill Flying Club 2.35; withdrawn from use at Redhill 3.38

G-ACXA (753), 8.5.35, Cierva Autogiro Co. Ltd.; to Italy 8.35 as I-CIER; to Italian Air Force as MM30030; preserved in Milan Museum as I-CIER

G-ACXB (754), registered to Cierva Autogiro Co. Ltd. 4.4.35, no other information

G-ACXC (755), as G-ACXB above

G-ACXG (743), 19.9.34, A. A. Noer & Co. Ltd.; Cierva Autogiro Co. Ltd. 8.36; to N.V. Autogiro Import 6.37 as PH-ARA; written off at Waalhaven 6.6.37

G-ACXP (772), 28.9.34, Bristol & Wessex Aeroplane Club, Whitchurch; to Australia 12.34 as VH-USQ; withdrawn from use 7.40

G-ACXR (760), 15.12.34, L. E. Venn, Hanworth; withdrawn from use 5.38

G-ACXV (744), 3.1.35, A. V. Roe and Co. Ltd., Woodford; sold abroad 12.35

G-ACXW (737), 6.10.34, Light Planes (Lancs.) Ltd., Barton; impressed 1.41 as BV999; rest. 4.46 to Fairey Aviation Co. Ltd., White Waltham; w.f.u. after C. of A. expiry 10.7.47; presented to Twickenham A.T.C. Squadron

G-ACYC (776), 21.9.34, Henlys Ltd., Heston; to France 9.35 as F-AOHZ
G-ACYE (775), 21.11.34, The Earl of Essex, Manorbier; A. Q. Cooper, Hanworth 5.35; impressed 6.40 as AP510; rest. to Mrs. Maxwell-Channell 12.46; withdrawn from use at Eastleigh 7.47; reduced to spares 12.51
G-ACYH (777), 24.1.35, Henlys Ltd., Heston; National Aviation Day Displays Ltd. 5.35; H. R. Starkey-Howe, Hanworth 4.39; impressed 6.41 as DR622; restored 4.46 to J. Gillam as G-AHRP q.v.
G-ACYP (745), 30.11.34, Cierva Autogiro Co. Ltd.; to the Polish Ministry of Communications, Warsaw 10.34 as SP-ANN
G-ACZV (791), 17.1.35, A. A. Nathan, Hanworth; sold abroad 4.37
G-ADBJ (798), 21.6.35, A. Q. Cooper, Hanworth; registration cancelled 1.4.40
G-ADCK (780), registered to the Cierva Autogiro Co. Ltd. 5.2.35; to Australia 7.35 as VH-UUQ; Australian marks cancelled 7.36
G-ADKY (749), 11.7.35, Cierva Autogiro Co. Ltd.; sold abroad 8.35

Cierva C.30A G-AIOC at White Waltham in 1947. Originally K4239, it later passed into possession of the Shuttleworth Trust, Old Warden. (*A. J. Jackson*)

Cierva C.30A (*postwar conversions*)
G-AHLE (710), G-ACWH, DR623, 22.6.46, Cierva Autogiro Co. Ltd., Eastleigh; withdrawn from use at Eastleigh 6.47; scrapped by A.T.C., Shoreham 2.52
G-AHMI (708), G-ACWF, DR624, 11.7.46, Fairey Aviation Co. Ltd., White Waltham; dismantled 7.47 and handed over to the Shuttleworth Trust, Old Warden
G-AHMJ K4234, 11.7.46, Fairey Aviation Co. Ltd., White Waltham; dismantled 7.47 and given to Hayes & Harlington Sea Cadets; to Shuttleworth Trust
G-AHRP (771), G-ACYH, DR622, registered to J. Gillam 28.5.46; Cierva Autogiro Co. Ltd. 3.47; C. of A. 25.7.47; w.f.u. at White Waltham 7.48
G-AHTZ (705), G-ACUI, HM581, 12.2.47, Essex Aero Ltd., Gravesend; Rota Towels Ltd., Elmdon 'Billy Boy' 7.49; crashed and burned at Elmdon 4.3.58
G-AHUC (732), G-ACWS, AP509, 11.7.46, Cierva Autogiro Co. Ltd., Eastleigh; to A.B. Helikopterflyg, Bromma 7.46 as SE-AZA; w.f.u. in 1958
G-AHXI (R3/CA/41), K4233, 28.4.48, Southern Aircraft (Gatwick) Ltd.; to Belgium 7.48 as OO-ADK
G-AIOC K4239, 25.4.47, B. H. Arkell, White Waltham; G. S. Baker, Ludlow 6.49; damaged beyond repair at Rearsby 10.7.49; to Shuttleworth Trust

Civilian C.A.C. I Coupé

G-AAIL   (1), 5.6.30, Civilian Aircraft Co. Ltd.; T. E. Richardson, Hedon 10.32; to J. Gilmore, Baldonnel 8.33 as EI-AAV; Irish reg'n. cancelled 1.49

G-ABFI   (0.2.1), 9.6.31, Civilian Aircraft Co. Ltd., Hedon; to Stadtverkeer Eindhoven 4.33 as PH-BBC; damaged beyond repair at Mijdrecht 30.12.33

G-ABFJ   (0.2.2), 14.4.31, Civilian Aircraft Co. Ltd., Hedon; Flt. Lt. V. S. Bowling 6.31; not flown after forced landing at Sandbach 8.7.31

G-ABNT   (0.2.3), 10.9.31, Civilian Aircraft Co. Ltd., Hedon; S. B. Cliff, Woodley 2.33; G. O. Rees, Cardiff 10.33; in store at Carmarthen in 1972

G-ABPW   (0.2.5), 27.8.32, Civilian Aircraft Co. Ltd., Hedon; to Germany 10.32 as D-EPAN; withdrawn from use circa 1940

Comper C.L.A.7 Swift

G-AARX   (C.L.A.7/1), 16.4.30, prototype with Scorpion engine, Comper Aircraft Ltd., Hooton; scrapped 12.31

G-AAZA   (S.30/2), registration not used; sold to Aerofotos, Buenos Aires 1931 as R222 (Andes flight); later to Ing. K. A. de Atencio as LV-FBA

G-AAZB   (S.30/3), registered 4.6.30 to Brian Lewis & C. D. Barnard Ltd., Heston; sold to G. N. Stringer, Ratcliffe; scrapped 2.31

G-AAZC   (S.30/4), 23.10.30, W. Taylor; F. R. Walker, Hooton 11.31; L. H. Riddell, Doncaster 4.33; Airwork Ltd., Heston 5.38; w.f.u. 4.43

G-AAZD   (S.30/5), 23.2.31, A. H. Youngman, Heston; M. J. Parish, Donibristle 1.33; to Egypt 11.33 as SU-AAJ; rest. 8.8.35 to F. B. Chapman, Gosport; M. N. Mavrogordato, Witney 7.38; crashed at Witney 31.7.38

G-AAZF   (S.30/7), 28.6.30, Gerard Fane, Brooklands; scrapped in Coley and Atkinson's yard at Hounslow, Middlesex in 1937

G-ABJR   (S.31/1), 23.6.31, H. C. Mayers, Hooton; Air Taxis Ltd., Stag Lane 1.33; C. R. Shillingford 10.33; crashed at Brooklands 28.1.34

G-ABMY   (S.31/2), 4.8.31, P. E. L. Gethin; to Tanganyika 6.32 as VR-TAF

G-ABNH   (S.31/4), 19.8.31, Lt. C. Byas R.N.; to South Africa 12.31 as ZS-AEU

G-ABPE   (S.31/3), 4.9.31, C. Clarkson, Heston; Dr. E. Robertson, Kuala Lumpur 'Vital Spark' 2.35; D. F. W. Atcherley, Andover 3.36; E. A. Boulter, Sywell 11.43; A. B. Golay, Heston 5.44; crashed at St. Albans 26.4.47

G-ABPR   (S.31/5), 17.9.31, Brian Lewis, Heston; F. R. Walker, Hooton 7.33; H. G. Everett, Leamington 5.36; J. Hassall, Coleshill, Birmingham 1942; destroyed in hangar fire at Broxbourne 30.6.47

G-ABPY   (S.31/6), 10.11.31, National Aviation Day Ltd.; H. S. Griffiths, Walsall 11.36; L. Lipton, Gravesend 8.37; to Australia 12.38 as VH-UZB

G-ABRE   (S.31/8), 27.10.31, Comper Aircraft Co. Ltd., Hooton; Victor Smith 12.32; sold in South Africa pre-1939; registration cancelled 15.8.45

G-ABTC   (S.32/1), I. C. Maxwell, Hooton; C. E. Gardner, Warlingham 3.36; D. L. Dodwell, Hinckley 10.38; J. F. Reed, Cricklade 1944–45; J. A. Kent, Lasham 1951; J. P. Forsyth, Sywell 6.61; J. D. Menzies, Blackbushe 9.65

G-ABUA   (S.32/2), 23.3.32, Miss Fidelia Crossley, Heston; A. H. Cook, Lympne 4.33; delivered in Java 28.11.34 as PK-SAQ

G-ABUS   (S.32/4), 18.3.32, Shell Mex & B.P. Ltd., Hanworth; R. Frogley, Broxbourne 1.35; A. G. Poole, Broxbourne 3.36; L. C. G. M. Le Champion, Sywell 12.36; A. L. Cole, Shoreham 7.48; A. J. Linnell, Sywell 5.58; J. Edwards, Baginton 1.64; J. Anning, Yeadon 1.66; K. Sedgwick, Halfpenny Green 6.70

G-ABUU (S.32/5), 13.4.32, M. A. Lacayo, Barton; E. C. T. Edwards 4.33; Miss C. R. Leathart, Cramlington 5.34; No. 131 A.T.C. Sqn., Newcastle 1942; D. Heaton, Speeton 1951; I. Imrie, Turnhouse 3.57; I. Tretheway, Fairoaks 8.60; A. W. Offen, Fairoaks 2.62; N. D. Norman, Bembridge 4.62; J. Pothecary, Christchurch 8.62, later Slinfold strip, Sussex

G-ABWE (S.32/7), 9.5.32, R. O. Shuttleworth, Old Warden; S. T. Lowe, Abridge 9.35; C. H. Tutt, Gravesend 6.38; sold abroad 2.40

G-ABZZ (S.32/8), 24.8.32, S. P. Symington, Desford; to Jugoslavia 8.36 as YU-PDS; destroyed by enemy action 4.41

G-ACAG (S.32/10), 16.11.32, Comper Aircraft Co. Ltd., Hooton; to Australia 12.34 as VH-UVC; flying at Moorabin in 1967

G-ACDS (S.33/2), 5.4.33, M. A. Lacayo, Hooton; delivered to Evreux, France 28.2.33; crashed 1.34; rebuilt as F-AOTP in 1936

G-ACDT (S.33/3), 16.2.33, A. Harrison, Heston; d/d to G. Aversing, Algeria via Lympne 20.2.33; destroyed in German air attack on Paris 6.40

G-ACFD (S.33/5), CH-353 ntu, 3.4.33, I. C. Maxwell, Heston; sold to G. Reginensi, Buc 9.34 as F-ANIY

G-ACGL (S.33/6), 23.6.33, A. Henshaw, Sywell; Airwork Ltd., Heston 8.35; D. L. Lloyd, Sywell 12.35; P. G. Leeson, Braunstone 3.39; scrapped 1942

G-ACML (S.33/10), 28.12.33, R. P. Pope, Hamble; P. de Walden Avery, Heston 11.34; to M. Rouvroy, Deurne 4.35 as OO-OML; crashed at Keerbergen 5.6.35

G-ACTF (S.32/9), VT-ADO 'Scarlet Angel', 27.8.32, G. B. S. Errington, Heston; R. E. Clear, Christchurch 1951; J. C. Quinney, Baginton 7.55; Proctor Flying Group, Baginton 12.60; E. M. Woodhams, Baginton 11.67

Comper C.L.A.7 Gipsy Swift

G-ABWH (GS.32/2), 28.6.32, British Air Navigation Co. Ltd., Heston; to U.S.A. 12.33 as NC27K; rest. 7.35 to W. L. Hope; to Australia 7.39 as VH-ACG

G-ABWW (GS.32/1), 28.6.32, Flt. Lt. E. H. Fielden, Hendon; R. O. Shuttleworth, Old Warden 8.35; T. Richardson, Eastleigh 7.36; S. T. Lowe, Gravesend 12.37; H. O. Winters, Gravesend 9.38; to Tonbridge, Kent A.T.C. Squadron 1943

G-ACBY (GS.32/3), 19.1.33, R. O. Shuttleworth, Old Warden; crashed at Moulton, Northants. during the King's Cup Race 8.7.33, pilot F. R. Walker

Consolidated Model 28 Catalina (*B.O.A.C./Qantas aircraft*)

G-AGBJ (3), Model 28, NC777 'Guba', 13.12.40, to Ministry of Aircraft Production 1.44 as SM706 sunk off Pwllheli 1944; G-AGDA, Catalina 1, AH563, 24.6.41, crashed and burned in Poole Harbour, Dorset 23.3.43; G-AGFL (122), PBY-5B, FP221, 31.10.42, Qantas No.1 'Vega Star', scuttled off Fremantle W.A. 28.11.45; G-AGFM (145), PBY-5B, FP244, 31.10.42, Qantas No.2 'Altair Star', scuttled off Fremantle, W.A. 28.11.45; G-AGID (182), PB2B-1, U.S. Navy 08215, JX575, 21.7.43, Qantas No.3 'Rigel Star', scuttled off Fremantle, W.A. 28.11.45; G-AGIE, PB2B-1, U.S. Navy 08217, JX577, Qantas No.4 'Antares Star', scuttled off Fremantle, W.A. 28.11.45; G-AGKS, PBY-5B, JX287, 2.5.44, Qantas No.5 'Spica Star', scuttled off Sydney, N.S.W. 3.46

Consolidated PBY-5A Catalina 3 (*amphibian*)

G-APZA (1619), N94574, delivered Rotterdam–Southend 17.2.60 for T. D. Keegan and partners, did not fly again, scrapped at Southend 11.60

Unlike the wartime civil Catalina flying-boats, G-APZA (seen here at Southend in 1960), was an amphibian with tricycle undercarriage. (*W. L. Lewis*)

Consolidated Model 32-2 Liberator I (LB-30A) (*B.O.A.C. aircraft*)

G-AGCD (2), AM259, 15.5.41, returned to the R.A.F. 7.44; G-AGDR (9), AM918, 5.1.42, shot down in error off the Eddystone Light 15.2.42; G-AGDS (6), AM263, registered 1.42, to the R.A.F. 6.42 as AM263, rest. 4.43, returned to the R.A.F. 8.44 as AM263; G-AGHG (5), AM262, 10.6.43, markings not used, operated as AM262, returned to the R.A.F. 9.44; G-AHYB (11), AM920, 30.9.46, to France 4.51 as F-BEFR, to Emperor Bao Dai of Vietnam 5.52 as F-VNNP, to ACANA, Rabat 6.55 as F-OASS

Consolidated Model 32-3 Liberator II (LB-30) (*B.O.A.C. aircraft*)

G-AGEL (10), AL512, 16.8.42, markings not used, operated as AL512, crashed at Gander, Newfoundland 27.12.43; G-AGEM (26), AL528, 7.8.42, markings not used, operated as AL528, crashed landing at Charlottetown, P.E.I. 21.2.46; G-AGJP (12), AL514, 13.11.43, to Ste Alpes Maritimes 4.51 as F-BEFX; G-AGKT (117), AL619, 21.5.44, operated by Qantas, to spares at Mascot, Sydney 12.47; G-AGKU (45), AL547, 24.7.44, operated by Qantas, to spares at Mascot, Sydney 12.47; G-AGTI (39), AL541, 28.11.45, to Qantas Empire Airways Ltd. 6.47 as VH-EAI, dismantled at Mascot 8.50; G-AGTJ (22), AL524, 7.3.46, to Qantas Empire Airways Ltd. 4.47 as VH-EAJ, dismantled at Mascot 11.50; G-AHYC (5), AL507, 2.10.46, d.b.r. landing at Prestwick 13.11.48; G-AHYD (20), AL522, 26.9.46, to France 4.51 as F-BFGJ; G-AHYE (27), AL529, 27.9.46, dismantled at Prestwick 12.48; G-AHYF (90), AL592, 28.9.46, to France 4.51 as F-BEFY; G-AHYG (101), AL603, 30.9.46, to France 4.51 as F-BFGK; G-AHYJ (125), registered 29.8.46, to spares 2.47

Consolidated Model 32-3 Liberator II (LB-30) (*Scottish Aviation Ltd.*)

G-AGZH (69), AL571, 2.3.46, scrapped at Prestwick 4.50; G-AGZI (55), AL557, 21.9.46, to Hellenic Airlines, Athens 2.48 as SX-DAA 'Maid of Athens'; G-AHZP (14), AL516, 12.8.46, crashed at Speke 13.10.48; G-AHZR (50), AL552, 3.12.46, to Hellenic Airlines 11.49 as SX-DAB

Consolidated Model 32-4 Liberator III (*B.O.A.C. or *Scottish Aviation Ltd.*)

G-AGFN, FL909, 11.11.42, returned to the R.A.F. 1.45; G-AGFO, FL915, 28.7.43, to the R.A.F. 3.45; G-AGFP, FL917, 16.1.44, to the R.A.F. 1.45; G-AGFR, FL918, 12.5.43, to the R.A.F. 1.45; G-AGFS, FL920, 15.4.43, to the R.A.F. 1.45; *G-AHDY, 41-1087, 27.5.46, dismantled at Prestwick 10.50

Consolidated C-87 Liberator VII

G-AKAG, EW611, 44-39219, registered 25.6.47 to the College of Aeronautics for ferrying to Cranfield as instructional airframe, scrapped by International Alloys Ltd., Aylesbury in 1959

Currie Wot

G-AFCG (C.P.A.1/1), A. to F. 22.11.37, Cinque Ports Aviation Ltd., Lympne; destroyed in German air raid on Lympne 5.40

G-AFDS (C.P.A.1/2), A. to F. 21.3.38, Cinque Ports Flying Club Ltd., Lympne; destroyed in German air raid on Lympne 5.40

G-APNT (H.A.C.3), A. to F. 22.10.58, V. H. Bellamy, Eastleigh; H. J. Penrose, Yeovil 'Airy Mouse' 3.59; W. M. Hodgkins, Yeovilton 5.64; L. W. Richardson, Usworth 12.65

G-APWT (H.A.C.4), A. to F. 28.10.59, V. H. Bellamy, Eastleigh; M.P.M. Flying Group, Elstree 1.62

G-ARZW (1), A. to F. 2.5.63, Dr. J. H. B. Urmston, King's Somborne; N. H. Jones (The Tiger Club), Fairoaks 3.70

G-ASBA (A.E.1), A. to F. 5.8.66, A. Etheridge, Clothall Common, Baldock; R. J. Miller, Panshanger 8.66; A. J. Howlett, Swanton Morley 2.69

G-AVEY (PFA.3006), Super Wot with Pobjoy engine registered 31.1.67 to K. Sedgwick, Wolverhampton; A. Eastelow, Halfpenny Green 8.70; A. to F. 16.4.71

G-AXOL (PFA.3012), registered 26.9.69, built at Morested Farm near Winchester by E. F. Tomlinson and B. Dyke, f/f at Compton Abbas 3.72, C. of A. 23.3.72

G-AYMP (PFA.3014), Wot Special, Mikron III, 13.6.72, E. H. Gould, Henstridge 'Que Mas'

G-AYNA (PFA.3016), registered 25.11.70 to R. W. Hart; under construction at Three Bridges, Sussex in 1972 with 65 h.p. Continental A-65

Currie Wot G-APWT on the Hamble River with float undercarriage in November 1959.
(*J. O. Isaacs*)

Currie Wot (*Slingsby Type 56 S.E.5A scale replica*)

G-AVOT to G-AVOY (c/n 1590–1595), registered 8.6.67 to Slingsby Sailplanes Ltd., Kirkbymoorside; ferried to Ireland 6.67 and delivered to Shillelagh Productions Inc.; re-registered EI-ARH to EI-ARM respectively but for film purposes carried bogus R.F.C. serials A5435, A4850, A7001, A5202, A6262 and A5435, the duplicated serial being changed later to A1313. EI-ARH and EI-ARM sold in the U.S.A. 1971

Curtiss T-32 Condor

G-AEWD (29), delivered to Eastern Air Transport 12.6.33 as NC12367; to U.K. 1937; C. of A. 20.5.37, International Air Freight Ltd., Croydon; to Air Ministry 10.39, allotted serial P5723; by road to No.30 M.U., Sealand 26.10.39 and scrapped

G-AEWE (30), d/d to E.A.T. 24.6.33 as NC12368; British C. of A. 13.5.37, International Air Freight Ltd., Croydon; allotted P5725; scrapped as above

G-AEWF (36), d/d to E.A.T. 16.8.33 as NC12375; British C. of A. 13.5.37, International Air Freight Ltd., Croydon; allotted P5726; scrapped as above

G-AEZE (28), d/d to E.A.T. 3.6.33 as NC12366; British C. of A. 12.8.37, International Air Freight Ltd., Croydon; allotted P5724; scrapped as above

Dart Kitten

G-AERP (121), Mk.I, A. to F. 31.12.36, first flown 15.1.37, E. C. Peacock, Tollerton 9.37; stored at Rearsby 1939–45; re-engined with Aeronca-J.A.P. J-99; W. S. Ogilvie, Broxbourne 4.49; crashed at Broxbourne 23.11.52

G-AEXT (123), Mk.II, A. to F. 30.4.37, W. B. Shaw, Ipswich; F. Dawson Paul, Gatwick 4.38; W. G. Harrison, Booker 8.50; loaned to Southend Flying School 1951; R. M. Long, Navestock 8.61; crashed at Willingale 29.11.64

G-AMJP (131), Mk.III, C. of A. 15.1.52, Dart Aircraft Ltd., Denham 1.53, leased to Thruxton Flying Group 1958; Grimsby Flying Club 4.59; G. Bramhill, Skegness 7.63; crashed at Hillington, King's Lynn 5.6.66

de Havilland D.H.4

G-EAEW (G7/67), K-141, registered to Aircraft Transport & Travel Ltd., Hendon 16.6.19 as D.H.4R racing aircraft with Napier Lion; scrapped in 1920

G-EAEX (G7/63), K-142, registered to Aircraft Transport & Travel Ltd., Hendon 16.6.19 for racing purposes; scrapped in 1920

G-EAMU H5939, 16.10.19, Instone Air Line Ltd. 'City of Cardiff'; converted to cabin type D.H.4A in 1920 q.v.

G-EANK F2670, 4.10.19, Aircraft Transport & Travel Ltd.; sold abroad 4.20

G-EANL F2671, 25.9.19, Aircraft Transport & Travel Ltd.; sold abroad 4.20

Note: For civil registrations used for ferrying 19 D.H.4s to the Belgian Air Force in 1921 see page 44.

de Havilland D.H.4A

G-EAHF F2699, 12.8.19, Aircraft Transport & Travel Ltd., Hendon; crashed at Caterham, Surrey 11.12.19

G-EAHG F2694, 12.8.19, Aircraft Transport & Travel Ltd., Hendon; crashed in the English Channel in poor weather conditions 10.19

G-EAJC   F2702, 19.8.19, Aircraft Transport & Travel Ltd., Hendon; withdrawn from use 8.20

G-EAJD   F2704, 25.8.19, Aircraft Transport & Travel Ltd., Hendon; withdrawn from use 8.20

G-EAMU   H5939, 19.2.20, Instone Air Line Ltd. 'City of York'; Imperial Airways Ltd., Croydon 6.24; withdrawn from use

G-EAVL   H5905, 11.11.20, Handley Page Ltd., Cricklewood; crashed 4.21

G-EAWH   F5764, 18.4.21, Handley Page Ltd., Cricklewood; withdrawn in 1922

de Havilland D.H.6 (*R.A.F. 1A engine unless otherwise stated*)

G-EAAB   K-100, 23.7.19, Aircraft Transport & Travel Ltd., Hendon; Marconi's Wireless Telegraph Co. Ltd., Croydon 3.20; crashed at Croydon 11.21

G-EAFT   B2943, 24.9.19, Bournemouth Aviation Co. Ltd.; withdrawn from use 9.20

G-EAFY   C7390, registered 3.7.19 to C. V. Maddocks t/a Kingsford Smith-Maddocks Aeros Ltd.; marks not used; sold to the Nelson Aviation Co. as G-EAJM

G-EAFZ   C7320, registered 3.7.19 to C. V. Maddocks t/a Kingsford Smith-Maddocks Aeros Ltd.; marks not used; sold to the Nelson Aviation Co. as spares

G-EAGE   C5224, 9.9.19, Grahame-White Aviation Co. Ltd., Hendon; C. B. Wilson, Manchester 7.22; withdrawn from use 9.24

G-EAGF   C5220, Curtiss OX-5 engine, 22.8.19, Grahame-White Aviation Co. Ltd., Hendon; C. of A. expired 21.8.21; to Hon. Elsie Mackay 9.21 without C. of A.

G-EAGG   C2101, registered 4.7.19 to the Aircraft Manufacturing Co. Ltd., Hendon; aircraft sold and registration not used

G-EAHD   B2934, 2.8.19, Golden Eagle Aviation Co. Ltd., Squires Gate; withdrawn from use 2.20

G-EAHE   B2917, 2.8.19, Golden Eagle Aviation Co. Ltd., Squires Gate; withdrawn from use 2.20

G-EAHH   F3435, 13.8.19, Warwick Aviation Co. Ltd.; withdrawn from use 8.20

G-EAHI   C6889, Curtiss OX-5 engine, 7.8.19, Warwick Aviation Co. Ltd.; Manchester Aviation Co. Ltd., Alexandra Park 10.20; withdrawn from use 7.22

G-EAHJ   C9432, reservation for H. V. David, Aberystwyth; reg'n. cancelled 7.19

G-EAJM   C7390, G-EAFY, 7.8.19, Nelson Aviation Co. Ltd.; withdrawn from use 8.20

G-EAKU   R.A.F. serial not given, C. of A. 18.9.19, Kingsbury Aviation Co. Ltd.; Astra Engineering Works Ltd. 5.20; withdrawn from use 9.20

G-EALS   C7620, registered 29.8.19 to the Cambridge School of Flying Ltd., Hardwicke; registration lapsed

G-EALT   B3094, 29.12.19, Cambridge School of Flying Ltd., Hardwicke; withdrawn from use 12.20

G-EAMK   C9448, 19.9.19, F. H. Solomon; shipped to South Africa for use by Cape Coast Resorts Aviation Ltd.; crashed 1921

G-EAML   C9449, 19.9.19, details are the same as for G-EAMK above

G-EAMS   B2689, registered 11.9.19 to J. H. T. Carr; conversion abandoned

G-EAMT   A9613, details as for G-EAMS above

G-EANJ   B2861, Curtiss OX-5 engine, 19.1.20, J. T. Rogers; J. F. Stallard trading as Stallard Airways, Herne Bay 7.20; withdrawn from use 4.22

G-EANU   C5230, Curtiss OX-5 engine, 17.12.19, Leatherhead Motor Co., Croydon; J. V. Yates, Croydon 5.22; de Havilland Aircraft Co. Ltd., Stag Lane 1.23; withdrawn from use 5.24

G-EAOT   C7434, 31.10.19, A. B. Ford; to Transalpina, Lausanne 2.21 as CH-45

G-EAQC, the Martin Aviation Company's joyriding D.H.6, on the beach at Cleethorpes in 1920.

G-EAPG   C7430, 13.4.20, Golden Eagle Aviation Co. Ltd., Squires Gate; registration cancelled 11.20

G-EAPH   C7739, registered 8.11.19 to the Golden Eagle Aviation Co. Ltd., Squires Gate; civil conversion abandoned; cancelled 2.20

G-EAPW   C6503, registered 2.12.19 to Dr. E. D. Whitehead Reid, Bekesbourne; not certificated; registration lapsed

G-EAQB   C7815, 6.7.20, By Air Ltd., Baginton; withdrawn from use after death of owner in crash of Armstrong Whitworth F.K.8 G-EALW

G-EAQC   C7436, 29.3.20, By Air Ltd., Baginton; B. Martin, Nottingham 6.20; written off 11.21

G-EAQQ   C2136, 9.9.22, E. Milton; P. A. A. Boss trading as The Airadvert Co., Hendon 4.24; registration cancelled 10.24

G-EAQY   B2885, 29.5.23, H. B. Elwell, Lytham St. Annes; withdrawn from use 5.24

G-EARA   C5527, 8.4.20, International Aviation Co. Ltd., Hooton; crashed 5.20

G-EARB   C5533, 9.4.20, International Aviation Co. Ltd., Hooton; w.f.u. 3.21

G-EARC   C5547, 1.6.20, International Aviation Co. Ltd., Hooton; Giro Aviation Co. Ltd., Hesketh Park, Southport 5.20; withdrawn from use 8.24

G-EARD   C7768, 8.4.20, International Aviation Co. Ltd., Hooton; crashed 8.20

G-EARJ   B3061, Renault engine, 27.4.20, Golden Eagle Aviation Co. Ltd., Squires Gate; Giro Aviation Co. Ltd., Southport 7.21; withdrawn from use 7.23

G-EARK   B3065, Renault engine, 27.4.20, Golden Eagle Aviation Co. Ltd., Squires Gate; Giro Aviation Co. Ltd., Southport 3.21; withdrawn from use 5.22

G-EARL   B3003, Renault engine, 27.4.20, Golden Eagle Aviation Co. Ltd., Squires Gate; H. B. Elwell, Lytham St. Annes 12.20; withdrawn from use 4.21

G-EARM   B3068, Renault engine, 12.4.20, Golden Eagle Aviation Co. Ltd., Squires Gate; Giro Aviation Co. Ltd., Southport 3.21; withdrawn from use 4.23

G-EARR   B3067, 1.6.20, A. Patchett, Lincoln; Capt. J. S. Hyde 11.20; C. Hudson, Retford 5.21; used by The Midland Aviation Service Ltd.; fitted with 80 h.p. Renault 1922 and stored; C. Matthews, Wickham Bishops, Essex 1927; lapsed

G-EATI   (G5/100), 10.6.20, C. B. Wilson, Manchester; withdrawn from use 7.22

G-EAUS   C7763, Renault engine, 9.7.21, Blackpool Flying Services; withdrawn from use 7.23; sold to the Manchester Aviation Co. as spares

G-EAUT   C9436, 20.5.21, Blackpool Flying Services; withdrawn from use 5.22

G-EAVG R.A.F. serial not given, registered 16.8.20 to the Giro Aviation Co. Ltd., Southport; forced landed on the Ribble mud flats and set on fire to attract rescuers from the shore; registration cancelled 3.21

G-EAVR C7797, 15.1.21, Humphrey's Film Productions Ltd.; H. B. Elwell, Aintree 4.25; withdrawn from use 4.26

G-EAWD (c/n given as 649), 21.6.22, de Havilland Aircraft Co. Ltd., Stag Lane; used by G. de Havilland; later to D.H. School of Flying; crashed at Stanford Rivers, Essex 27.8.23

G-EAWT F3437, Renault engine, 23.5.21, Brompton Motor Co. Ltd.; Martin Aviation Co. Ltd., Isle of Wight 8.22; withdrawn from use 8.24

G-EAWU F3439, 23.5.21, Renault engine, Brompton Motor Co. Ltd.; Martin Aviation Co. Ltd., Isle of Wight; crashed 31.3.22

G-EAWV F3440, Renault engine, 23.5.21, Brompton Motor Co. Ltd.; Martin Aviation Co. Ltd., Isle of Wight 6.24; registration lapsed

G-EBEB Built from spares, 17.4.24, Giro Aviation Co. Ltd., Southport 'Maysbus'; withdrawn from use 9.30; stored at Hesketh Park; burned circa 1940

G-EBPN C7823, 7.7.27, F. J. V. Holmes, Witney; British Flying & Motor Services Ltd., Maylands, Romford 4.28; withdrawn from use and scrapped 7.28

G-EBVS F3443, 27.4.28, F. J. V. Holmes, Witney; British Flying & Motor Services Ltd., Maylands, Romford; withdrawn from use and scrapped 4.29

G-EBWG C7291, 9.3.28, R. J. Bunning, Pontypool; Giro Aviation Co. Ltd., Southport 'Silver Wings' 5.29; withdrawn from use 4.31; burned circa 1940

G-AARN B2868, registered 24.9.29 to V. N. Dickinson, St. Albans; scrapped 1933

de Havilland D.H.9

G-EAAA C6054, registered 30.4.19 to Aircraft Transport & Travel Ltd., Hendon; crashed on Portsdown Hill, north of Portsmouth, Hants. 1.5.19

G-EAAD H9273, registered 30.4.19 to Aircraft Transport & Travel Ltd., Hendon; sold abroad 9.19

G-EALJ D2884, registered 26.8.19 to Aircraft Transport & Travel Ltd., Hendon; conversion for civil use abandoned; registration cancelled 10.20

G-EAMX D5622, registered 15.9.19 to Aircraft Transport & Travel Ltd., Hendon; sold abroad 4.20

G-EAOP H5579, registered 20.10.19 to Aircraft Transport & Travel Ltd., Hendon; written off 9.20

G-EAQM F1278, 2.1.20, R. J. P. Parer; left Hounslow 8.1.20, flown to Australia by Parer and J. C. McIntosh; preserved at the Australian War Memorial 1972

G-EAVM H9243, 15.9.20, Handley Page Ltd.; delivered to Det Danske Luftfartselskab, Copenhagen 18.9.20; re-registered T-DOKL; reduced to spares 1927

Temporary British civil registrations issued to military D.H.9s for ferry flights to the Belgian Air Force December 1921 to May 1922:

H5619/G-EAYW; H5629/G-EAZA; H5705/G-EAZB; H5607/G-EAZC; H5856/ G-EAZD; H5757/G-EAZE; H5666/G-EAZJ; H5865/G-EAZM; H5707/G-EAZN; H5845/G-EAZO; H5868/G-EAZP; H5706/G-EAZY; H5668/G-EAZZ; H5783/ G-EBAA; H5851/G-EBAB; H5621/G-EBAD; H5736/G-EBAE; H5712/G-EBAI; H5716/G-EBAO; H5741/G-EBAP; H5753/G-EBAQ; H5747/G-EBAR; H5662/ G-EBAS; H5735/G-EBBA; H5709/G-EBBB; H5711/G-EBBJ; H5719/G-EBBK; H5836/G-EBCH; H5742/G-EBCI; H5820/G-EBCJ

The penultimate civil D.H.9, G-AACR, operating as a flight refuelling tanker in 1932. (*Flight Photo 12258*)

G-EAYY   H5833, registered 31.10.21 to the Aircraft Disposal Co. Ltd., Croydon; delivered to Alfred Comte in Switzerland 12.21 as CH-82

G-EAYZ   H5848, registered 31.10.21 to the Aircraft Disposal Co. Ltd., Croydon; delivered to Alfred Comte in Switzerland 12.21 as CH-83

G-EAZH   H5839, registered 14.11.21 to the Aircraft Disposal Co. Ltd., Croydon; delivered to Ad Astra Aero A.G., Zürich via Paris 7.2.22; became CH-81

G-EAZI   H5860, registered 14.11.21 to the Aircraft Disposal Co. Ltd., Croydon; delivered to Ad Astra Aero A.G., Zürich via Paris 7.2.22; became CH-84

G-EBDE   H5652, registered 19.5.22 to Maj. W. T. Blake for world flight; abandoned after accident near Istres, France 28.5.22; flight continued in G-EBDL

G-EBDF   H5738, registered 23.5.22 to Maj. W. T. Blake for Canadian section of the flight but not used; C. of A. issued to the Aircraft Disposal Co. Ltd. 4.7.23; leased to the D.H. Aeroplane Hire Service Ltd. Sold in Canada to the Laurentide Air Service as G-CAEU and modified to D.H.9C

G-EBDL   H5678, registered 17.6.22 to Maj. W. T. Blake; replaced G-EBDE in France; repainted as G-EBDE and flown to Calcutta; presented to Univ. of Benares

Replacement aircraft ferried to various destinations 1922–27:
H5775/G-EBEF; D1347/G-EBEG; D5777/G-EBEH; F1286/G-EBEI; F1216/G-EBEJ

G-EBEN   H5688, registered 24.8.22 to the Aircraft Disposal Co. Ltd.; to the British & Egyptian Tea Co. Ltd.; C. of A. 3.1.24; sold abroad 11.24

G-EBEP   D5799, 26.9.22, Surrey Flying Services Ltd., Croydon; crashed at West Hill, Sanderstead, Surrey 17.11.29

G-EBEZ   (66), registered 12.2.22 to the de Havilland Aircraft Co. Ltd.; fitted with Napier Lion and named 'Eileen' for 1923 King's Cup; converted to D.H.9J

G-EBFQ   (76), 15.5.23, de Havilland Aircraft Co. Ltd., Stag Lane (Reserve School dual trainer); converted to D.H.9J in 1926

G-EBGQ   H5632, 7.7.23, William Beardmore and Co. Ltd., Renfrew (Reserve School dual trainer); crashed 30.10.24

G-EBHP   H9203, 19.9.23, William Beardmore and Co. Ltd., Renfrew (Reserve School dual trainer); withdrawn from use 1.26

G-EBHV   H5844, 12.11.23, Sir W. G. Armstrong Whitworth Aircraft Ltd., Whitley (Reserve School dual trainer); converted to D.H.9J in 1926

G-EBJR	H9289, 1.8.24, float seaplane; overhauled by de Havillands and allotted c/n 158; to the British & Egyptian Tea Co. Ltd. 11.24; sold abroad 11.24
G-EBJW	H9333, 30.8.24, Messrs. Greig and Higgs t/a Northern Air Lines, Manchester; Air Taxis Ltd., Stag Lane 6.27; withdrawn from use 7.28
G-EBJX	H9147, 17.9.24, Messrs. Greig and Higgs t/a Northern Air Lines, Manchester; G. B. H. Mundy 6.26; Air Taxis Ltd. 3.27; crashed 1.29
G-EBKO	H9319, 17.4.25, Aircraft Disposal Co. Ltd., Croydon; Aircraft Operating Co. Ltd., Hinaidi, Iraq; withdrawn from use 2.29; scrapped in 1930
G-EBKV	H9337, 17.4.25, Aircraft Disposal Co. Ltd.; sold abroad 7.26
G-EBLH	(181), 27.6.25, de Havilland Aircraft Co. Ltd., Stag Lane (Reserve School dual trainer); converted to D.H.9J in 1926
G-EBPE	(284), 21.12.26, Aircraft Operating Co. Ltd., Northern Rhodesia; converted to float seaplane on Zambesi River; withdrawn from use 12.27
G-EBPF	(285), 21.12.26, Aircraft Operating Co. Ltd., Northern Rhodesia; converted to float seaplane on Zambesi River; withdrawn from use 12.27
G-EBQD	H9205, 21.4.27, A.D.C. Aircraft Ltd.; Aircraft Operating Co. Ltd., Bulawayo, Southern Rhodesia; withdrawn from use 5.29; scrapped in 1930
G-EBTR	H9369, 11.1.28, A.D.C. Aircraft Ltd., Croydon (Nimbus engine demonstrator); sold abroad 9.30
G-EBXR	H9276, 13.8.28, A.D.C. Aircraft Ltd., Croydon; to Australia 1928 as G-AUJA; crashed at Salamaua, New Guinea 2.11.29
G-AACP	H9248, 28.2.29, A.D.C. Aircraft Ltd.; Surrey Flying Services Ltd., Croydon 2.32; Sir Alan Cobham, Ford, 2.33; C. B. Field, Kingswood Knoll 5.35; Aerial Sites Ltd., Hanworth 6.36; dismantled at Hanworth 1938
G-AACR	H9324, 22.6.32, A.D.C. Aircraft Ltd., Croydon; Sir Alan Cobham, Ford 6.32 and used for flight refuelling experiments; cancelled 9.33
G-AACS	H9327, registered 7.11.28 to A.D.C. Aircraft Ltd., Croydon; civil conversion abandoned
G-AADU	R.A.F. serial not given; C. of A. 13.7.29, Surrey Flying Services Ltd., Croydon; C. E. B. Winch, Halton 7.33; scrapped during 1939–45 war

de Havilland D.H.9A

G-EAHT	(GR/1), K-172, D.H.9R racing conversion with Lion engine, registered to Aircraft Transport & Travel Ltd., Hendon 23.7.19; scrapped 1922
G-EAOF	E750, 31.10.19, The British Government (operated by Aircraft Transport & Travel Ltd., on Hawkinge–Cologne air mail service); returned to the R.A.F. 6.20 as E750
G-EAOG	E752, 31.10.19, details as above; returned to the R.A.F. 6.20 as E752
G-EAOH	E753, 10.11.19, details as above; returned to the R.A.F. 4.20 as E753
G-EAOI	E754, 31.10.19, details as above; returned to the R.A.F. 6.20 as E754
G-EAOJ	E756, 5.11.19, details as above; returned to the R.A.F. 6.20 as E756
G-EAOK	E757, 7.11.19, details as above; returned to the R.A.F. 6.20 as E757
G-EAXC	E8791, registered 1.6.21 to the Aircraft Disposal Co. Ltd.; written off 13.11.22
G-EBAC	E8788, registered 5.12.21 to the Aircraft Disposal Co. Ltd.; ferried Croydon–Le Bourget by F. J. Ortweiler 29.12.21; sold abroad 12.1.22
G-EBAN	F2867, registered 21.12.21 to the Aircraft Disposal Co. Ltd.; ferried Croydon–Brussels by E. D. C. Herne 28.1.22; thence to Spanish A/F 3.22
G-EBCG	F2868, 11.7.23, Aircraft Disposal Co. Ltd. 'Bellini'; withdrawn from use in 1924; Rolls-Royce Eagle VIII engine; registration cancelled 1.27

G-EBGX F2872, registered 16.6.23 to the Aircraft Disposal Co. Ltd., named 'Aurora' with Napier Lion engine for the 1923 King's Cup Race; lapsed

G-EBLC E8781, 30.12.25, Aircraft Disposal Co. Ltd., Croydon; Liberty engine; withdrawn from use at Croydon 8.29

de Havilland's veteran D.H.9 G-EAAC as a two seat dual trainer in 1925. Originally a D.H.9B, it was later converted to D.H.9J with a total civil life of 14 years from 1919 to 1933.

de Havilland D.H.9B

G-EAAC H9277, K-109, 7.5.19, Aircraft Transport & Travel Ltd., Hendon; de Havilland Aircraft Co. Ltd., 'Antiopa' 3.21; converted to D.H.9J

G-EAGX H9255, 7.8.19, Aircraft Transport & Travel Ltd., Hendon 'Ancuba'; crashed 8.20

G-EAGY H9258, 12.8.19, Aircraft Transport & Travel Ltd., Hendon; sold abroad 1.21

G-EAOZ (P.32E), H5889, 17.11.19, Aircraft Transport & Travel Ltd., Hendon and Croydon; to K.L.M., Amsterdam 7.21 as H-NABF; written off 2.26

G-EAPL (P.33E), H5890, 28.11.19, Aircraft Transport & Travel Ltd., Croydon; to K.L.M., Amsterdam 7.21 as H-NABE; written off 5.22

G-EAPO (P.34E), 6.12.19, Aircraft Transport & Travel Ltd., Croydon; written off 9.20

G-EAPU (P.35E), 29.12.19, Aircraft Transport & Travel Ltd., Croydon; written off 11.20

G-EAQA (P.36E), 12.1.20, Aircraft Transport & Travel Ltd., Croydon; crashed 1.21

G-EAQL (P.38E), 24.1.20, Aircraft Transport & Travel Ltd., Croydon; sold abroad 7.21

G-EAQN (P.37E), 28.1.20, Aircraft Transport & Travel Ltd., Croydon; crashed at Le Bourget 9.11.20

G-EAQP (P.39E), 9.2.20, Aircraft Transport & Travel Ltd., Croydon; sold to F. S. Cotton and operated in Newfoundland in A.T. & T. markings 1922

G-EATA H9271, 14.5.20, Handley Page Ltd., Cricklewood; sold abroad 4.21

G-EAUC H9282, 6.7.20, Handley Page Ltd., Cricklewood; withdrawn from use 7.21, scrapped in 1922

G-EAUH   H9196, 24.7.20, Handley Page Ltd., Cricklewood; to K.L.M., Amsterdam 7.21 as H-NABP; written off in accident at Waalhaven 2.9.21

G-EAUI   H9197, 13.7.20, Handley Page Ltd., Cricklewood; Surrey Flying Services Ltd., Croydon 3.23; sold abroad 6.23, believed in Spain

G-EAUN   H9128, 18.8.20, Handley Page Ltd., Cricklewood; Surrey Flying Services Ltd., Croydon 3.23; to Cia Española del Trafico Aereo 6.23 as M-AGAG

G-EAUO   H9187, 20.8.20, Handley Page Ltd., Cricklewood; to K.L.M., Amsterdam 7.21 as H-NABO; written off in accident at Schiphol 17.11.22

G-EAUP   H9176, 8.9.20, Handley Page Ltd., Cricklewood; withdrawn from use 9.21

G-EAUQ   H9125, 31.7.20, Handley Page Ltd., Cricklewood; withdrawn from use 3.21

G-EAVK   (P.60E), 20.9.20, Aircraft Transport & Travel Ltd., Hendon; sold abroad 3.22

de Havilland D.H.9C

G-EAXG   (16), D516, 5.9.21, de Havilland Aircraft Co. Ltd., Stag Lane; to K.L.M., Amsterdam 6.22; believed used as spares

G-EAYT   (14), 13.1.22, de Havilland Aircraft Co. Ltd., Stag Lane 'Atlanta'; landed in the sea off Venice Lido in fog 2.10.22

G-EAYU   (15), 10.1.22, de Havilland Aircraft Co. Ltd., Stag Lane; sold to the Hedjaz Government 11.24

G-EBAW   (25), 10.3.22, de Havilland Aircraft Co. Ltd., Stag Lane; crashed 10.9.23

G-EBAX   (26), 6.3.22, de Havilland Aircraft Co. Ltd., Stag Lane; written off 23.4.24

G-EBCZ   (38), 29.5.22, de Havilland Aircraft Co. Ltd., Stag Lane; crashed 7.11.23

G-EBDD   (39), 16.6.22, de Havilland Aircraft Co. Ltd., Stag Lane; written off 6.11.25

G-EBDG   H4890*, 27.7.23, Manchester Aviation Co. Ltd., Alexandra Park; Northern Aviation Co. Ltd., Alexandra Park 3.24; Wm. Beardmore & Co. Ltd., Renfrew 7.24; Northern Air Lines Ltd., Alexandra Park 2.30; scrapped 1930

G-EBGT   (82), 2.7.23, de Havilland Aircraft Co. Ltd., Stag Lane 'Nulli Secundus'; converted to D.H.9J in 1926

G-EBGU   (83), 19.9.23, de Havilland Aircraft Co. Ltd., Stag Lane; sold abroad 9.24

G-EBIG   H5886, 25.10.23, Wm. Beardmore & Co. Ltd., Renfrew; Northern Air Lines (Manchester) Ltd., Wythenshaw; dismantled 12.31

G-EBUM   H9370, O-BATA, 22.12.27, J. S. Newall & N. Vintcent; U.K.–India flight machine; re-registered in India 1.29 as VT-AAK

G-EBUN   F1223, O-BELG, 22.12.27, J. S. Newall & N. Vintcent; U.K.–India flight machine; re-registered in India 1.29 as VT-AAL

* As documented

de Havilland D.H.9J

G-EAAC   H9277, formerly D.H.9B K-109, weighed for C. of A. renewal as D.H.9J 2.7.26, de Havilland Aircraft Co. Ltd., Stag Lane; scrapped in 1933

G-EBEZ   (66), 17.2.26, formerly D.H.9 trainer q.v.; fitted with Lion engine in 1923; de Havilland Aircraft Co. Ltd., Stag Lane; scrapped in 1933

G-EBFQ   (76), 11.12.26, formerly D.H.9 trainer certificated in 1923; de Havilland Aircraft Co. Ltd., Stag Lane; withdrawn from use 7.32

G-EBGT   (82), 19.8.26, formerly D.H.9C certificated in 1923; de Havilland Aircraft Co. Ltd., Stag Lane; d.b.r. in accident at Hatfield 16.10.32

G-EBHV   H5844, 29.9.27, formerly D.H.9 trainer certificated in 1924; Sir W. G. Armstrong Whitworth Aircraft Ltd., Whitley; withdrawn from use 9.28

The SNETA conversion O-BATA after modernisation at Stag Lane in 1927 as G-EBUM
for the Vintcent–Newall India Flight. (*D. C. Fuller*)

G-EBLH (181), 25.8.26, formerly D.H.9 trainer certificated in 1925; de Havilland
Aircraft Co. Ltd., Stag Lane; crashed at White Waltham 12.5.27

G-EBOQ (282), 17.8.26, Sir W. G. Armstrong Whitworth Aircraft Ltd., Whitley;
crashed near Coventry 9.7.29

G-EBOR (283), 15.9.26, Sir W. G. Armstrong Whitworth Aircraft Ltd., Whitley; withdrawn from use 1.29

G-EBTN (326), 14.9.27, de Havilland Aircraft Co. Ltd., Stag Lane; withdrawn from use
4.33

G-AARR (397), 4.10.29, Sir W. G. Armstrong Whitworth Aircraft Ltd., Whitley; Air
Service Training Ltd., Hamble 5.31; scrapped in 1936

G-AARS (398), 17.10.29, Sir W. G. Armstrong Whitworth Aircraft Ltd.; Serval test
bed; Air Service Training Ltd., Hamble 5.31; pilot fell out and parachuted
safely, aircraft crashed in a field near Hamble 9.9.34

G-AART (399), 5.11.29, Sir W. G. Armstrong Whitworth Aircraft Ltd., Whitley; Air
Service Training Ltd., Hamble 5.31; scrapped in 1936

G-AASC (704), 20.12.29, de Havilland Aircraft Co. Ltd., Stag Lane; scrapped in 1931

G-ABPG (1990), 14.10.31, built by D. H. Technical School; operated by the D.H.
Reserve School, Hatfield; scrapped in 1933

de Havilland D.H.16

G-EACT (D.H.16 No. 1), K-130, 25.5.19, Aircraft Transport & Travel Ltd., Hendon;
crashed 3.20

G-EALM (4), 9.9.19, Aircraft Transport & Travel Ltd., Croydon; de Havilland Aircraft
Co. Ltd., Stag Lane 8.22; crashed at Stanmore 10.1.23

G-EALU (P.1), 22.9.19, Aircraft Transport & Travel Ltd., Croydon 'Arras'; to the de
Havilland Aircraft Co. Ltd. 8.22 as spares

G-EAPM (P.2), 28.11.19, Aircraft Transport & Travel Ltd., Croydon 'Agincourt'; taken
over by the de Havilland Aircraft Co. Ltd. 11.22; w.f.u. 11.23

G-EAPT (P.3), 8.12.19, Aircraft Transport & Travel Ltd., Croydon; de Havilland
Aircraft Co. Ltd., Stag Lane 7.22; dismantled 6.7.23

403

G-EAQG (P.4), 24.1.20, Aircraft Transport & Travel Ltd.; to the River Plate Aviation Co. Ltd., Buenos Aires 4.20; later re-registered as R-137

G-EAQS (P.5E), 29.3.20, Aircraft Transport & Travel Ltd., Croydon; stored at Croydon 12.20, scrapped in 1922

G-EARU (P.59), 21.5.20, Aircraft Transport & Travel Ltd., Croydon; stored at Croydon 12.20, scrapped in 1922

G-EASW (P.6), 30.6.20, Aircraft Transport & Travel Ltd., Croydon; stored at Croydon 12.20, scrapped in 1922

de Havilland D.H.18

G-EARI (1), D.H.18, delivered to Aircraft Transport & Travel Ltd., Croydon 5.3.20; C. of A. 22.7.20; crashed at Wallington, Surrey 16.8.20

G-EARO (2), D.H.18A, delivered to Aircraft Transport & Travel Ltd., Croydon 21.5.20, C. of A. 15.9.20; Air Council 3.21; loaned to Instone Air Line Ltd. as 'City of Cardiff'; to R.A.E., Farnborough 4.24; last flew 10.11.27

G-EAUF (3), D.H.18A, delivered to Aircraft Transport & Travel Ltd., Croydon 31.7.20; C. of A. 11.8.20; Air Council 3.21; loaned to Instone Air Line Ltd., Croydon as 'City of Paris'; crashed 13.5.21

G-EAWO (4), D.H.18A, delivered to Aircraft Transport & Travel Ltd., Croydon 21.5.21; Daimler Hire Ltd. 4.22; destroyed in air collision with Farman Goliath F-GEAD over Grandvilliers, Northern France 7.4.22

G-EAWW (5), D.H.18B, Air Council (ordered 7.21 as J6899); C. of A. 17.12.21; loaned to Instone Air Line Ltd. as 'City of Brussels'; ditched off Felixstowe in Air Ministry flotation test 2.5.24

G-EAWX (6), D.H.18B, Air Council (ordered 7.21 as J6900); C. of A. 23.1.22; loaned to Instone Air Line Ltd.; Handley Page Ltd. 3.22; w.f.u. 11.23

de Havilland D.H.34

G-EBBQ (27), 6.5.22, Daimler Hire Ltd., Croydon; crashed 8.23

G-EBBR (28), 6.5.22, Instone Air Line Ltd., Croydon 'City of Glasgow'; Imperial Airways Ltd. 4.24; burned out in take-off crash at Ostend 27.5.24

G-EBBS (29), 6.5.22, Daimler Hire Ltd., Croydon; crashed near Ivinghoe Beacon, Bucks. 14.9.23

G-EBBT (30), 28.4.22, Instone Air Line Ltd., Croydon 'City of New York'; Imperial Airways Ltd. 4.24; converted to D.H.34B in 1925; dismantled 3.26

G-EBBU (31), 6.5.22, Daimler Hire Ltd., Croydon; crashed at Berck, Northern France 3.11.22

G-EBBV (32), 19.7.22, Instone Air Line Ltd., Croydon 'City of Washington'; Imperial Airways Ltd. 4.24; withdrawn from use and dismantled 3.26

G-EBBW (34), 25.8.22, Instone Air Line Ltd., Croydon 'City of Chicago'; Imperial Airways Ltd. 4.24; withdrawn from use and dismantled 3.26

G-EBBX (35), 19.9.22, Daimler Hire Ltd., Croydon; converted to D.H.34B by 2.24; Imperial Airways Ltd. 4.24; crashed at Purley, Surrey 24.12.24

G-EBBY (36), 25.9.22, Daimler Hire Ltd., Croydon; Imperial Airways Ltd. 4.24; converted to D.H.34B in 1925; withdrawn from use and dismantled 3.26

G-EBCX (40), 30.12.22, Daimler Hire Ltd., Croydon; Imperial Airways Ltd. 4.24; withdrawn from use and dismantled at Croydon 12.24

G-EBCY (41), registered 28.4.22 to the de Havilland Aircraft Co. Ltd., Stag Lane; it is believed that this aircraft was not completed

The fourth production D.H.34 at Croydon in April 1924 bearing both Imperial Airways and Instone Air Line titling.

de Havilland D.H.50* and D.H.50A

G-EBFN* (73), 2.8.23, de Havilland Aircraft Co. Ltd., Stag Lane 'Galatea'; to West Australian Airways Ltd., Perth, W.A. 2.26 as G-AUEY; w.f.u. 4.35

G-EBFO* (74), 12.11.23, de Havilland Aircraft Co. Ltd., Stag Lane; converted to D.H.50J, C. of A. as such 14.11.25; to West Australian Airways Ltd. 1.29 as VH-UMC, reconverted to D.H.50; w.f.u. 9.34

G-EBFP* (75), 12.11.23, de Havilland Aircraft Co. Ltd., Stag Lane; Imperial Airways Ltd., Croydon 11.24; Iraq Petroleum Transport Co. Ltd., Haifa 10.32; Imperial Airways Ltd., Croydon 5.33; scrapped later in 1933

G-EBIW (116), 28.5.24, de Havilland Aircraft Co. Ltd.; to QANTAS 5.24 as G-AUER 'Hermes', later 'Victory'; to Rockhampton Aerial Services Ltd. 4.34; ditched at Caloundra, north of Bribie Island, Queensland 8.12.35

G-EBKJ (132), 1.12.24, de Havilland Aircraft Co. Ltd., Stag Lane; to the Czech Government 1.25 as L-BAHG, later OK-AHG

G-EBKZ (133), 11.6.25, Imperial Airways Ltd., Croydon; stalled on take-off from Roborough, Plymouth 23.10.28; aircraft written off

G-EBOP (281), 21.12.26, North Sea Aerial & General Transport Co. Ltd., Khartoum 'Pelican'; crashed at Kisumu, Kenya 17.10.27

G-EBQI (136), 5.5.27, Air Taxis Ltd., Stag Lane; Sir P. Richardson, Brooklands 3.29; Northern Air Lines Ltd., Barton 6.30; Brooklands S. of F. Ltd. 11.30; scrapped at Brooklands 4.33

de Havilland D.H.51

G-EBIM (100), first flown 7.24 with R.A.F.1A; fitted with Airdisco, C. of A. 22.10.24; first flown 8.11.24 as D.H.51A, C. of A. 1.5.25; G. E. F. Boyes 5.26; to Golden Aviation Co., Mascot 4.27 as G-AUIM; to A. S. Elkin 1929; converted to D.H.51B seaplane; capsized in Sydney Harbour 3.1.31

G-EBIQ (101), first flown 27.3.25, C. of A. 29.6.25, Air Commodore J. G. Weir, Renfrew; Taxiplanes Ltd., Weston-super-Mare 8.28; L. G. Anderson, Hanworth 6.31; scrapped at Hanworth in 1933

G-EBIR (102), 12.9.25, de Havilland Aircraft Co. Ltd.; to J. E. Carberry, Nairobi 1.26, became G-KAA 9.28 and VP-KAA 1.29; airfreighted to Hatfield 7.65 and handed over to the Shuttleworth Trust; restored to flying condition at Hawarden 1972

de Havilland D.H.53 Humming Bird

G-EBHX (98), de Havilland Aircraft Co. Ltd., Stag Lane; f/f 9.23; F. J. V. Holmes, Witney 2.26; E. W. Kennett, Walmer 1935; C. of A. 28.10.37; f/f at Hatfield 4.8.60 after rebuild by D.H. Tech. School for the Shuttleworth Trust

G-EBHZ (99), A. S. Butler, Stag Lane; Flg. Off. G. E. F. Boyes (Seven Aero Club), Eastchurch 7.25; registration lapsed after last appearance at Lympne 9.26

G-EBQP (114), J7326, 13.5.27, R.A.E. Aero Club, Farnborough; Flg. Off. A. F. Scroggs, Henlow 1.28; destroyed in crash at Hamble 21.7.34

G-EBRA (109), J7270, registered to R. P. Cooper, Boxmore 26.4.27; to de Havillands 9.28; sold abroad 1.30, believed as spares

G-EBRJ (108), J7269, 28.11.27, Tellus Super Vacuum Cleaner Co. Ltd., Brooklands; withdrawn from use 11.28; scrapped at Woodley in 1930

G-EBRK (112), J7273, 4.6.29, R. W. H. Knight, Duxford; crashed 3.32

G-EBRW (107), J7268, 25.6.27, Flt. Lt. D. V. Carnegie; F. Gough 10.27; R.A.E. Aero Club, Farnborough 2.29; R. L. Burnett, Broxbourne 8.33; w.f.u. 6.34

G-EBTT (111), J7272, registered 5.9.27 to W. B. Ellis, Cramlington, Newcastle; conversion abandoned; registration cancelled 7.28. See G-ABPS below

G-EBXM (113), J7325, 26.5.28, K. V. Wright, Farnborough; A. V. C. Douglas, Bekesbourne, Canterbury 1.29; withdrawn from use at Brooklands 8.31

G-EBXN (110), J7271, 25.5.28, R.A.E. Aero Club, Farnborough; T. S. Fisher, Stag Lane 11.32; J. Gillett, Squires Gate 7.35; E. D. Ward, Hooton 8.38; stored at Hooton Park Racecourse until destroyed in grandstand fire 8.7.40

G-ABPS Registration reserved 8.9.31 for unspecified D.H.53 for J. K. Lawrence, Cramlington; believed for the unconverted J7272/G-EBTT; not taken up

de Havilland D.H.60 Moth (Cirrus I)

G-EBKT (168), 25.6.25, crashed at Stanmore, Mx. 21.8.27; G-EBKU (169), 23.6.25, crashed at Calcutta 22.7.27; G-EBLI (183), 13.8.25, crashed at Stanmore, Mx. 9.10.27; G-EBLR (184), 13.8.25, crashed at Hale, Cheshire 12.6.27; G-EBLS (185), 13.8.25, written off 2.28; G-EBLT (186), 13.8.25, w.f.u. 11.36; G-EBLU (187), 13.8.25, crashed at Stag Lane 8.1.26; G-EBLV (188), 13.8.25, airworthy at Hatfield in 1972; G-EBLW (189), 9.9.25, crashed 11.29; G-EBLX (190), 13.9.25, crashed at Blyth, Northumberland 20.5.31; G-EBLY (191), 28.9.25, crashed at Cramlington 24.2.27; G-EBME (193), 20.12.25, to Australia 9.27 as G-AUME; G-EBMF (194), 31.10.25, w.f.u. 3.35, scrapped at Gatwick 1948; G-EBMO (197), 8.7.26, sold in India 6.27; G-EBMP (198), 21.1.26, to Sweden 11.29 as SE-ACD; G-EBMQ (201), 4.2.26, w.f.u. 8.34; G-EBMU (234), 27.2.26, to Canada 4.29 as CF-AEN; G-EBMV (235), 9.4.26, crashed 8.29

G-EBNM (249), 29.4.26, to Denmark 1.28 as T-DMOL, later OY-DOF; G-EBNN (260), 16.6.26, crashed at Lympne 27.3.29; G-EBNO (261), 8.7.26, to Sweden 7.28 as S-AABS; G-EBNP (280), 1.5.26, one-off variant known as D.H.60X (actually the prototype Cirrus II Moth), crashed at Stag Lane 22.11.26; G-EBNX (262), 19.6.26, to U.S.A. 9.27 as C1686; G-EBNY (263), 5.7.26, crashed 11.29; G-EBOH (269), 23.7.26, d.b.r. at Ewshot, Surrey 15.5.30; G-EBOI (270), 23.7.26, impressed 5.40 as 2061M; G-EBOS (268), crashed at Mill Hill 20.10.28; G-EBOT (272), 7.8.26, crashed at Nazeing, Essex 13.12.31; G-EBOU (271), Genet engine, 8.9.26, to Germany 6.29 as D-1651; G-EBVD (247), J8031, 4.6.28, w.f.u. 7.39, scrapped at Coulsdon, Surrey 1949

de Havilland D.H.60 Moth (Cirrus II)

G-EBPG (359), 2.4.27, registration cancelled 1.28; G-EBPM (353), 27.1.27, crashed near Lympne 27.2.30; G-EBPP (355), registered to de Havillands 1.12.26, to Australia

1927 as G-AUPP; G-EBPQ (357), 6.4.27, crashed at Newhaven 20.6.32; G-EBPR (358), 20.5.27, crashed at Halton 22.10.30; G-EBPS (360), 20.8.27, crashed at Duxford 20.1.29; G-EBPT (361), 3.2.27, crashed 10.30; G-EBPU (373), 19.2.27, crashed 1930; G-EBQE (370), 31.3.27, sold abroad 7.31; G-EBQJ (371), 21.5.27, crashed at Aurangabad, India 4.8.27; G-EBQV (375), 13.4.27, w.f.u. 4.36; G-EBQW (378), 22.4.27, w.f.u. 12.30; G-EBQX (385), 25.5.27, w.f.u. 10.37, scrapped at Beddington, Surrey 6.51; G-EBQY (376), 13.5.27, w.f.u. 1.29; G-EBQZ (386), 1.6.27, w.f.u. 7.35; G-EBRU (387), 9.6.27, wrecked at Rakos, Budapest 6.8.27; G-EBRX (388), 11.6.27, to Holland 6.33 as PH-KLG; G-EBRY (389), 19.8.27, impressed 6.40 as AW147; G-EBVN, reservation for Genet Moth not taken up; G-EDCA (379) J8818, Genet engine, 13.12.27, returned to the R.A.F. 2.28 as J8818; G-AADB (372), U.S.N. 7564, 2.5.27, crashed near Eastleigh 29.6.37

Twenty production Cirrus II Moths lined up at Stag Lane Aerodrome, Edgware in May 1927. (*Aerofilms*)

de Havilland D.H.60X Moth

G-EBQH (276), 14.4.27, w.f.u. 9.37; G-EBRH (404), seaplane, 21.7.27, crashed at Kastrup 4.9.27; G-EBRI (405), 1.7.27, impressed 12.39 as X5128; G-EBRT (410), 5.7.27, crashed at Ashingdon, Essex 20.6.36; G-EBRZ (413), 18.7.27, crashed near Sherburn-in-Elmet 23.9.27; G-EBSA (414), 29.6.27, crashed 10.30; G-EBSF (415), 22.7.27, crashed at Tabora, Tanganyika 8.4.28; G-EBSI (416), 22.7.27, to Denmark 10.27 as T-DALF, later OY-DEF; G-EBSK (417), 28.7.27, crashed near Hucknall 22.8.28; G-EBSN (418), 26.7.27, crashed at Filton 6.5.28; G-EBSO (419), 26.8.27, crashed at Brooklands 28.5.32; G-EBSP (420), 6.8.27, w.f.u. 12.33; G-EBSQ (421), 8.8.27, crashed at Nairobi 12.3.28; G-EBSR (422), 8.8.27, sold abroad 2.29; G-EBSS (423), 20.8.27, crashed near Lympne 13.10.28; G-EBST (427), 8.9.27, impressed 7.40 as AX793; G-EBSU (428), 23.8.27, to Norway as N-38, crashed at Calais during delivery flight 19.3.29

G-EBTD (430), 1.9.27, impressed 6.40 as AW153; G-EBTG (469), 18.11.27, struck furniture van landing at Maylands 24.8.38; G-EBTH (429), 8.9.27, burned at Sheldon, Birmingham 1951; G-EBTI (431), 26.8.27, sold in Johore 9.34; G-EBTJ (432), 13.9.27, to South Africa 2.28 as G-UAAD; G-EBTV (436), 19.10.27, crashed in the sea off Skegness 23.4.33; G-EBTZ (437), 22.9.27, impressed 6.40 as AW146; G-EBUA (438), 19.9.27, to Denmark 10.27 as T-DALP, to Sweden 1.28 as S-AABR; G-EBUF (441), 6.10.27, to France 6.33 as F-ANHN; G-EBUJ (450), seaplane, 13.1.28, registered in Singapore 9.34; G-EBUK (451), seaplane, 16.1.28, registered in Singapore 9.34; G-EBUL (443), 10.10.27, w.f.u. at Nairobi 6.31; G-EBUO (452), 10.11.27, to Southern Rhodesia 11.30 as VP-YAB; G-EBUR (446), 19.10.27, crashed at Detling 20.7.30; G-EBUS (444), 19.10.27, stored at Southsea 6.40, cancelled 11.45; G-EBUU (471), 31.10.27, crashed at Renfrew 1.5.28; G-EBUV (474), seaplane, 21.12.27, written off 2.29; G-EBUW (475),

D.H.60X Moth seaplane G-EBUJ of the Royal Singapore Flying Club with locally installed Hermes I engine.

2.12.27, crashed at Odsey, Cambs. 18.5.29; G-EBUX (476), 18.11.27, crashed at Brooklands 23.3.31; G-EBUZ (478), 10.12.27, to India 1933 as VT-AEE

G-EBVC (483), 13.1.28, crashed 11.30; G-EBVJ (501), 13.12.27, to Southern Rhodesia 12.30 as VP-YAE; G-EBVK (467), 16.12.27, d.b.r. at Broxbourne 6.7.37; G-EBVT (537), 7.2.28, crashed at Lumloch Colliery, Glasgow 10.2.29; G-EBVX (538), 27.2.28, crashed at Sollum, Egypt 17.5.28; G-EBWA (539), 15.6.28, crashed near Buxton, Derbyshire 10.34; G-EBWC (553), 27.3.28, re-registered G EBZN but written off in collision with hangar at Lympne 17.7.28 before it could be repainted; G-EBWD (552), 25.5.28, preserved 1972 in airworthy condition with Hermes I engine by the Shuttleworth Trust, Old Warden; G-EBWI (557), 2.3.28, w.f.u. 5.36; G-EBWL (556), 21.3.28, cancelled 12.31; G-EBWS (558), 13.3.28, exhibited in Barcelona 6.28, believed sold in Spain 1.29; G-EBWT (590), 5.5.28, crashed at Nazeing, Essex 24.3.34; G-EBWX (583), 28.4.28, w.f.u. 4.31; G-EBWY (584), 5.4.28, w.f.u. 10.32; G-EBWZ (509), 15.3.28, crashed at Addlestone, Surrey 18.1.30

G-EBXB (592), 2.4.28, to the Argentine 4.28; G-EBXF (609), 23.5.28, sold abroad 5.35; G-EBXG (615), 18.4.28, crashed at Chilwell, Notts. 3.11.34; G-EBXP (626), 12.5.28, to Canada 7.28 as G-CAXP, to U.S.A. 1931 as NC9305; G-EBXS (593), 17.5.28, crashed at South Mitford, Yorks. 28.4.36; G-EBXT (548), 30.4.28, impressed 6.40 as AW157; G-EBXU (627), seaplane, 14.6.28, w.f.u. 12.31; G-EBXW (594), 14.6.28, to Portugal 7.28 as C-PAAB; G-EBYD (672), 4.7.28, crashed near Stag Lane 3.8.28; G-EBYG (337), 5.7.28, cancelled 3.33; G-EBYH (338), 3.7.28, crashed at Theydon Bois, Essex 25.1.37; G-EBYJ (647), 11.6.28, crashed near Lyons, France 25.9.29; G-EBYV (648), seaplane later landplane, 2.7.28, to Ireland 6.31 as EI-AAG, rest. 9.32 as D.H.60G, crashed at Medomsley, Durham 30.6.36

G-EBZC (678), 4.7.28, impressed 6.40 as AW158; G-EBZE (643), 7.7.28, w.f.u. 4.33; G-EBZF (644), 27.7.28, to Spain 1.29 as M-CAAK; G-EBZG (676), 16.7.28, w.f.u. at Abu Sueir, Egypt 2.37; G-EBZH (679), 24.7.28, to Germany 7.32 as D-2298; G-EBZI (650), 20.7.28, w.f.u. 4.38; G-EBZL (682), 2.8.28, impressed 6.40 as AW159; G-EBZN, marks not taken up, see G-EBWC; G-EBZO (683), 28.7.28, crashed 1.8.29; G-EBZP

(681), 28.7.28, w.f.u. 11.36; G-EBZS (684), 28.7.28, crashed near Radlett 18.7.29; G-EBZT (685), 1.8.28, to Denmark 5.31 as OY-DUD; G-EBZU (686), 28.7.28, crashed at Irlam, Lancs. 9.10.32; G-EBZW (687), 28.7.28, crashed at Mousehold 19.5.32; G-EBZX (649), 26.7.28, to Poland 8.28 as SP-ALH; G-EBZZ (691), 9.8.28, crashed at Stansted Abbots, Essex 23.6.34; G-EDCA(2) (529), 23.2.28, to the R.A.F. 12.29

G-AAAC (694), 16.8.28, impressed 1.41 as DG587; G-AAAD (695), 17.8.28, w.f.u. 2.34; G-AAAG (697), 22.8.28, crashed in sea off Spithead 7.11.34; G-AABA (700), 8.9.28, crashed in North Sea 9.3.29: G-AABH (699), 17.9.28, impressed 1.40 as V4738; G-AABL (702), 19.9.28, crashed at Kingsbury, Mx. 15.10.30; G-AADJ (920), seaplane, 31.1.29, re-registered in Singapore 9.34; G-AADK (921), seaplane, 31.1.29, re-registered in Singapore 9.34; G-AAKJ (1162), 19.8.29, crashed at Southall, Mx. 18.10.35; G-AAMM (1228), 29.3.30, crashed at Woodley 4.7.32; G-AAMN (1229), 29.3.30, w.f.u. 12.33; G-AAMO (1281), 25.7.30, crashed at Port Meadow, Oxford 4.9.32; G-AAMP (1279), 17.7.30, last flight 2.6.39, scrapped near Brough 1950; G-AAMR (1280), 18.7.30, burned out at Maylands 6.2.40; G-AAMS (1285), 31.7.30, impressed 2.40 as X5018; G-AAMT (1809), 21.10.30, crashed at Cotgrove, Tollerton 9.11.30; G-AAMU (1826), 8.1.31, scrapped at Hanworth 11.46; G-AAMV (1828), 8.1.31, impressed 9.40 as BK844; G-AAMW (1831), 9.2.31, w.f.u. 2.40

G-AAPA (1164), 17.8.29, crashed at Hedon, Hull 17.7.35; G-AAPB (1165), 17.8.29, crashed near Sheffield 28.3.30; G-AAPC (1166), 22.8.29, crashed at Yeadon 22.3.36; G-AAPD (1167), 22.8.29, w.f.u. 12.32; G-AAPE (1168), 22.8.29, w.f.u. 12.30; G-AAPF (1169), 22.8.29, w.f.u. 12.33; G-AAPG (1170), 29.8.29, impressed 6.40 as AV996; G-AAPH (1171), 29.8.29, impressed 11.39 as X5020; G-AAPI (1172), 29.8.29, w.f.u. 12.30; G-AAPJ (1173), 29.8.29, crashed at Chilworth, Oxon 16.8.36; G-AAPL (1198), 28.9.29, crashed at Waltham, Grimsby 18.5.32; G-AAPM (1199), 1.10.29, w.f.u. 12.33; G-AAPN (1200), 4.10.29, crashed at Hampton, Mx. 6.5.30; G-AAPO (1201), 4.10.29, crashed at Hanworth 20.2.32; G-AAPV (1215), 3.11.29, crashed at Truro 21.4.35; G-AAPW (1216), 9.11.29, impressed 2.40 as W7945; G-AARM (477), C-PAAA, 28.12.27, reg'd. 26.9.29 to G. L. P. Henderson, Brooklands, crashed in Port Meadow, Oxford 4.11.29; G-AAYS (1232), 22.5.30, crashed in Southampton Water 4.12.32

G-ABAO (1247), 6.6.30, impressed 8.40 as BD163; G-ABBD (1266), 24.6.30, impressed 2.40 as W9367

de Havilland D.H.60X Moth (*Gipsy conversions*)

G-EBWV (566), registered 28.3.28 to de Havilland Aircraft Co. Ltd.; left St. John's, Newfoundland on Atlantic flight 17.10.28; lost at sea 18.10.28

G-ABUB (363), G-AUFT/VH-UFT, Mollison record Australia–U.K. flight 7.31; C. of A. 27.4.32, Sir Alan Cobham; F. C. J. Butler 12.33; R. J. B. Seaman, Roborough 5.36; Norfolk & Norwich Aero Club 11.38; impressed 11.39 as X5029

G-ACMB (526), J9119, 21.4.34, Hon. Mrs. Victor Bruce, Croydon; Surrey Flying Services Ltd., Croydon 6.36; impressed 4.40 as X9302

G-ACXF (425), G-AUGX/VH-UGX, Australia–U.K. flight 1934; C. of A. 9.8.34, D. L. Rawnsley; I. Scott, Dyce 7.38; R. J. Bunning, Pershore 2.30; w.f.u. 9.42

G-ADIL (522), J9115, 21.12.35, Surrey Flying Services Ltd., Croydon; Horton Kirby Flying Club, Dartford, Kent 8.39; impressed 11.39 as X5050

de Havilland D.H.60G Gipsy Moth

G-EBYK (825), 18.7.28, crashed at Arborfield, Berks. 18.7.31; G-EBYS (829), 8.9.28, S. S. Halse, left Stag Lane for South Africa 9.9.28; G-EBYZ (801), 18.7.28, crashed near

Cambridge 20.9.32; G-EBZR (844), 14.9.28, to S. Rhodesia 6.33 as VP-YAM; G-EBZY (806), 15.10.28, to Fiji 9.29 as ZK-ABV

G-AAAA (805), 12.9.28, impressed 11.39 as X5038; G-AAAE (826), 17.9.28, w.f.u. 12.31; G-AAAH (804), 11.12.28, permanent exhibit at Science Museum, London; G-AAAI (817), 27.9.28, sold abroad 8.33; G-AAAJ (803), 2.10.28, sold abroad 8.29; G-AAAK (807), 5.2.29, sold abroad 1.30; G-AAAL (809), 21.9.28, w.f.u. 2.40; G-AAAM (814), 15.10.28, to U.S.A. 10.28 believed as NC9704; G-AAAO (808), 10.10.28, impressed 11.39 as X5019; G-AAAS (810), 15.10.28, sold abroad 2.37; G-AAAV (815), 10.10.28, impressed 8.40 as BK826; G-AABI (845), 21.3.29, impressed 2.41 as DG658; G-AABJ (827), 12.10.28, impressed 11.39 as X5034; G-AABK (811), 5.10.28, converted to Gipsy III, impressed 11.39 as X5031; G-AABM (816), 2.1.29, to Shanghai 12.28; G-AABN (802), 8.4.29, crashed at Stanmore, Mx. 3.6.31; G-AABO (865), 27.9.28, w.f.u.

B. de Skorsewski (*left*), de Havilland agent in Poland, with Gipsy Moth G-AACM at Krakow early in 1929 at the end of a delivery tour from Stag Lane via Tunis, Sicily and Vienna.

1936; G-AACK (831), 26.10.28, to Spain 12.28 as EC-DAA; G-AACL (887), 17.4.29, lost in English Channel 1.3.31; G-AACM (991), 20.11.28, temporarily SP-ACT in 1929, crashed near Maidstone 3.5.33; G-AACO (874), 20.11.28, w.f.u. 12.34; G-AACY (841), 28.11.28, impressed 5.40 as AV991; G-AACZ (1021), 18.12.28, w.f.u. 6.42

G-AADA (1019), 21.12.28, w.f.u. 12.36; G-AADC (917), 22.12.28, w.f.u. 2.30; G-AADD (1017), 21.12.28, to Canada 7.30 as CF-ANY; G-AADH (889), 19.1.29, impressed 11.39 as X5028; G-AADI (970), 4.2.29, crashed 6.35; G-AADP (1022), 22.1.29, crashed at Abridge Aerodrome, Essex 8.9.34; G-AADS (1028), 5.2.29, sold abroad 4.29; G-AADV (998), amphibian, 5.2.29, ditched off Folkestone 24.12.29; G-AADW (988), 28.1.29, cancelled 12.46; G-AADX (1002), 27.2.29, crashed at Dagenham, Essex 2.2.31; G-AAEA (1030), 28.2.29, to Ireland 5.33 as EI-AAR; G-AAEB (1003), 15.2.29, sold abroad 10.32; G-AAEE (981), 20.1.29, to Sheffield A.T.C. 1.41; G-AAEF (1059), 12.2.29, sold abroad 2.37; G-AAEG (1027), 13.2.29, to Germany 4.29 as D-1599; G-AAEH (1083), 8.2.29, impressed 11.39 as X5025; G-AAEI (993), 25.2.29, crashed near Stag Lane 1.11.30; G-AAEL (994), 21.3.29, crashed at Doncaster 1.8.32; G-AAEN (990), 16.3.29, w.f.u. 1930; G-AAEO (1079), 26.3.29, to India 7.36 as VT-AJP; G-AAEP (1096), 15.4.29, to Brazil 2.30 as P-BABM; G-AAER (1097), 27.3.29, sold abroad 4.29; G-AAET (1080), 31.5.29, impressed 6.40 as AW126; G-AAEU (916), 21.3.29, crashed at Adisham, Kent 2.9.34; G-AAEW (1043), 28.3.29, impressed 5.40, crashed near Netheravon 11.41; G-AAEX (997), 15.4.29, impressed 11.39 as X5021

G-AAFC (1037), 17.4.29, to France 3.31 as F-ALHI; G-AAFI (1095), 15.5.29, impressed 1.41 as DG579; G-AAFK (1040), 30.4.29, to India 2.33 as VT-AEZ; G-AAFL (1005), 8.5.29, ditched off Bournemouth 4.31; G-AAFM (1006), 4.5.29, cancelled 6.42; G-AAFO (989), 19.4.29, impressed 11.39 as X5053; G-AAFS (1012), 15.5.29, impressed 2.41, DG589 ntu; G-AAFY (999), 26.4.29, to South Africa 10.37 as ZS-AKV; G-AAGA (1058), 7.5.29, impressed 9.40 as BK834; G-AAGD (1008), 3.5.29, sold abroad 5.29; G-AAGI (1010), 26.4.29, sold in India 11.32; G-AAGM (1009), 27.4.29, to Switzerland 12.31 as HB-OLA, rest. 10.38, cancelled 6.41; G-AAGS (1042), 30.4.29, crashed at Barmouth 30.8.33; G-AAGT (1052), 23.5.29, w.f.u. 4.37; G-AAGZ (1007), 10.5.29, to South Africa 9.30 as ZS-ABW; G-AAHF (1051), 25.5.29, crashed at Croydon 29.6.30; G-AAHG (1085), 22.5.29, impressed 1.41 as DG580/2547M; G-AAHI (1082), 28.5.29, cancelled 1.47; G-AAHO (1056), 25.5.29, to India 1.35 as VT-AGZ; G-AAHP (1067), 28.6.29, crashed 6.36; G-AAHR (1068), 28.6.29, crashed 5.35; G-AAHS (1011), 31.7.29, sold abroad 2.29; G-AAHT (1089), 28.5.29, to India 12.29 as VT-ABN; G-AAHU (1099), 28.5.29, impressed 8.40 as BK827; G-AAHX (1062), 30.5.29, crashed near Dungeness 18.6.29; G-AAIA (1090), 30.5.29, impressed 11.39 as X5037; G-AAIB (1110), 6.6.29, crashed at Renfrew 15.5.30; G-AAIC (1100), 4.6.29, to Holland 5.34 as PH-AJM; G-AAIE (1094), 4.6.29, impressed 6.40 as AW160; G-AAIM (1153), 27.6.29, cancelled 12.46; G-AAIU (1055), 10.7.29, w.f.u. 2.39; G-AAIV (1104), 21.6.29, impressed 6.40 as AW127; G-AAIW (1081), 20.6.29, impressed 12.39 as X5030

G-AAJA (1106), 20.6.29, crashed at Gosport 2.5.36; G-AAJG (1130), 25.6.29, w.f.u. 12.37; G-AAJJ (1105), 25.6.29, temporarily EI-ABA in 1934, impressed 8.40 as BD164; G-AAJL (1054), 28.6.29, impressed 2.41 as DG657; G-AAJM (1091), 1.7.29, to India 6.34 as VT-AFH; G-AAJN (1049), 4.7.29, crashed near Brooklands 3.10.36; G-AAJO (1101), 5.6.29, sold abroad 3.35; G-AAJP (1123), 4.7.29, impressed 2.40 as W7947; G-AAJR (1050), 4.7.29, lost in Bristol Channel 20.9.31; G-AAJS (1139), 18.7.29, impressed 1.40 as X5055; G-AAJT (1084), 4.7.29, to U.S.A. 1.30; G-AAJU (1103), 11.7.29, destroyed in air collision with Gipsy Moth G-AAKL over Stag Lane 29.7.29; G-AAJV (1108), 12.7.29, to Kenya 7.31 as VP-KAL; G-AAJW (1135), 12.7.29, impressed 11.39 as X5040; G-AAJZ (1134), 19.7.29, impressed 1.41 as DG586

G-AAKC (1149), 1.8.29, to South Africa 3.37 as ZS-AKJ; G-AAKD (1150), 30.7.29, sold abroad 8.34; G-AAKE (1151), 1.8.29, w.f.u. at Barton-in-the-Clay, Beds. 7.39; G-AAKF (1127), 25.7.29, to New Zealand 11.29 as ZK-ABM; G-AAKG (1126), 27.7.29, sold abroad 12.34; G-AAKI (1152), 1.8.29, impressed 7.40 as AX789; G-AAKK (1093), 23.7.29, re-registered in New Zealand 1930 as ZK-AKK 'Elijah' on floats; G-AAKL (1129), destroyed over Stag Lane in air collision with Gipsy Moth G-AAJU 29.7.29 before registration and certification details were complete; G-AAKM (1142), 2.8.29, to Ireland 11.34 as EI-ABB, rest. 7.37, to India 4.41 as VT-APU; G-AAKN (1146), 29.7.29, crashed in Langstone Harbour, Portsmouth 15.10.36; G-AAKO (1045), 26.7.29, impressed 11.39 as X5035; G-AAKU (1092), 31.7.29, impressed 11.39 as X5047; G-AAKX (1154), 10.8.29, lost in Thames Estuary 1.6.33

G-AALD (1137), 21.8.29, to Kenya 1.30 as VP-KAG; G-AALE (1140), 22.8.29, sold abroad 7.35, rest., cancelled 12.46; G-AALJ (1087), 5.9.29, destroyed 7.34; G-AALK (1174), 10.9.29, w.f.u. 4.37; G-AALM (1160), 20.1.30, crashed near Poix, France 21.4.30; G-AALN (1047), 31.8.29, impressed 11.39 as X5041; G-AALR (1159), 4.9.29, to Brazil 12.31 as PP-TAD; G-AALT (1184), 23.9.29, w.f.u. 12.38; G-AALU (1178), 17.9.29, crashed 9.32; G-AALV (1179), 13.9.29, impressed 11.39 as X5032; G-AALW (1180), 12.9.29, impressed 11.39 as X5027; G-AALY (1175), to France 11.29 as F-AJKM; G-AALZ (1177), 12.9.29, crashed 12.31; G-AARA (1186), 21.9.29, impressed 11.39 as X5046; G-AARC (1187), 5.10.29, impressed 1.41 as DG584; G-AARE (1176),

411

17.5.30, crashed on Cross Fell, Penrith 21.4.36; G-AARW (1209), 30.10.29, sold abroad 9.30; G-AASB (1053), 20.11.29, to Sweden 12.36 as SE-AFP; G-AASG (1203), 16.11.29, destroyed 3.39; G-AASN (839), ex Sarawak Govt., 26.10.28, registered 14.11.29 to Kuala Lumpur F/C, sold abroad 9.34; G-AASY (1048), 21.12.29, to Ireland 2.35 as EI-ABE, rest. 12.37, impressed 6.40 as AW128; G-AAUR (1245), 16.6.30, rebuilt 2.33 as G-ACCY; G-AAVC (1238), amphibian, 7.5.30, crashed 12.30; G-AAVY (1230), 9.4.30, impressed 11.39 as X5023

G-AAWL (1231), 15.4.30, to Portugal 12.30 as CS-AAG; G-AAWN (1234), 6.5.30, to New Zealand 2.33 as ZK-ACY; G-AAWO (1235), 3.5.30, still flying in 1972; G-AAWP (1236), 13.6.30, sold in Egypt 6.32; G-AAWR (1237), 17.5.30, impressed 8.40 as BD166; G-AAWS (1239), 3.5.30, w.f.u. 12.36; G-AAWX (1241), 3.5.30, crashed at Charing, Kent 3.5.33; G-AAXA (1246), 20.6.30, re-registered 1.32 as G-AAZE; G-AAYJ (1248), 29.5.30, crashed 40 miles S.W. of Nairobi 16.1.33; G-AAYL (1252), 6.6.30, impressed 9.40 as BK835; G-AAYT (1233), 30.5.30, impressed 3.41 as DR606; G-AAYY (1251), 26.6.30, to Ceylon 12.36 as VP-CAC; G-AAZE (1246), ex G-AAXA, impressed 9.40 as BK843; G-AAZG (1253), 16.6.30, to Spain 6.30 as MW-133; G-AAZL (1254), 13.6.30, to Jugoslavia via Lympne 29.8.30 as UN-PAH; G-AAZR (1275), 7.7.30, w.f.u. 12.37, components at Clifton, York. until 6.51; G-AAZZ (1255), 17.6.30, to South Africa 5.32 as ZS-ADA

G-ABAD (1256), 30.5.30, to Egypt 6.32 as SU-ABD; G-ABAE (1257), 30.5.30, impressed 6.40 as AW129; G-ABAF (1258), 26.6.30, w.f.u. 11.35; G-ABAG (1259), 1.7.30, crashed at Perth 27.2.55; G-ABAH (1260), 16.7.30, to Jugoslavia 1.32 as UN-PAV; G-ABAK (1265), 11.7.30, crashed at Hyde, near Manchester 13.5.31; G-ABAL (1264), 6.6.30, impressed 11.39 as X5118; G-ABAM (1263), 19.6.30, crashed 3.40; G-ABBA (1261), 27.6.30, impressed 6.40 as AW130; G-ABBG (1262), 20.6.30, to Ireland 4.31 as EI-AAF; G-ABBI (1267), 15.7.30, sold in Jugoslavia 4.31; G-ABBJ (1268), 9.4.31, impressed 4.40 as X9303; G-ABBK (1270), 10.7.30, impressed 2.41 as DG659; G-ABBM (1271), 5.7.30, sold abroad 1.34; G-ABBO (1272), 23.7.30, sold abroad 10.33; G-ABBP (1273), 23.7.30, to Belgium 7.30 as OO-AAA, later to France as F-AMZM; G-ABBV (1276), 26.7.30, to Ireland 9.31 as EI-AAK, rest. 6.36, crashed 8.39; G-ABBW (1277), 11.7.30, ditched off Shoreham 27.6.39; G-ABBX (1278), 19.7.30, impressed 6.40 as AW131; G-ABCG (1288), 22.7.30, sold abroad 3.39; G-ABCS (1282), 24.7.30, impressed 11.39 as X5039; G-ABCT (1286), 31.7.30, impressed 11.39 as X5048

Gipsy Moth G-AAYY at Stanley Park Aerodrome, Blackpool in November 1935 while it was in use by United Airways Ltd. for club flying. (*E. J. Riding*)

J. R. Micklethwaite taking off in the smart Gipsy Moth G-ABHM which he based at Yeadon 1932–1939. (*Aeroplane*)

G-ABDA (1284), 24.7.30, impressed 1.41 as DG583; G-ABDE (1827), 6.1.31, to India 2.33 as VT-ADX; G-ABDK (1804), 18.12.30, impressed 2.40 as X5033; G-ABDR (1287), 1.8.30, crashed at Erdington, Birmingham 12.7.31; G-ABDU (1290), 19.8.30, impressed 11.39 as X5024; G-ABDV (1291), 18.9.30, w.f.u. 12.34; G-ABDX (1294), 22.8.30, to Switzerland 11.34 as HB-UAS; G-ABEB (1298), 6.9.30, sold abroad 12.30; G-ABEK (1289), 27.9.30, written off 6.40; G-ABEN (1812), 25.9.30, to Australia 3.31 as VH-UPV; G-ABEO (1813), 27.9.30, impressed 8.40 as BK828; G-ABEP (1292), 4.9.30, ditched in the English Channel 7.3.33; G-ABER (1296), 5.9.30, impressed 2.40 as W7946; G-ABES (1299), 6.9.30, impressed 7.40 as AX792

G-ABFD (1800), 13.9.30, impressed 9.40 as BK845; G-ABFT (1817), 4.11.30, impressed 9.40 as BK836; G-ABFW (1820), 6.11.30, crashed at Sabzawar, Persia 2.5.31; G-ABGC (1802), 20.11.30, sold abroad 12.30; G-ABGL (1808), 27.1.31, to Ireland 1.32 as EI-AAH; G-ABGM (1811), impressed 12.39 as X5112; G-ABGN (1814), 12.1.31, w.f.u. 6.33; G-ABGP (1816), 17.12.30, sold abroad 3.32; G-ABGU (1819), 4.12.30, sold in Malaya 12.31; G-ABGV (1822), 4.12.30, sold in Malaya 12.31; G-ABGY (1807), 18.12.30, to Kenya 6.32 as VP-KAQ; G-ABHM (1830), 28.5.31, impressed 9.40 as BK841; G-ABHS (1824), 6.1.31, to Poland 9.33 as SP-ALK; G-ABIO (1846), 9.4.31, to Sweden 4.35 as SE-ABG; G-ABJC (1825), 4.3.31, to India 2.34 as VT-AEO; G-ABJE (1841), 9.3.31, to France 9.31 as F-ALQA; G-ABJH (1838), 14.4.31, impressed 12.39 as X5111; G-ABJI (1839), 24.3.31, impressed 11.39 as X5036; G-ABJJ (1840), 28.3.31, impressed 9.40 as BK842, rest. 1.46, to Canada 1962 as CF-AAA*; G-ABJL (1837), 17.3.31, crashed 11.34; G-ABJN (1851), impressed 6.40 as AW119; G-ABJT (1244), 10.3.30, impressed 6.40 as AW132; G-ABJZ (1842), 27.3.31, crashed 7.39

G-ABLH (1848), 24.4.31, crashed 3.40; G-ABLN (1850), 4.4.31, written off 6.40; G-ABLT (1852), 18.6.31, impressed 12.39 as X5113; G-ABLZ (1853), 14.5.31, impressed 8.40 as BD162; G-ABMA (1854), 22.5.31, to Mozambique 10.37 as CR-AAI; G-ABND (1845), 15.6.31, to Egypt 5.33 as SU-ABF; G-ABOA (1859), 31.7.31, sold abroad 4.37; G-ABOE (1856), 17.8.31, impressed 11.39 as X5017; G-ABOG (1857), 17.7.31, impressed 6.40 as AW149; G-ABON (1865), 10.8.31, to South Africa 5.33 as ZS-ADY; G-ABOU (1862), 8.8.31, impressed 1.40 as W6415; G-ABOV (1868), written off 2.42;

* Registration first allotted to D.H.60M, c/n 1302, in 1929

413

G-ABOW (1860), 12.8.31, to Ireland 8.31 as EI-AAI; G-ABOY (1863), 7.8.31, impressed 11.39 as X5022; G-ABOZ (1866), 12.8.31, to Ireland 8.31 as EI-AAJ

G-ABPC (1867), 15.8.31, impressed 4.40 as AX784; G-ABPD (1869), 21.8.31, impressed 6.40 as AW133; G-ABPK (1871), 4.9.31, crashed at Exeter 14.11.37; G-ABPP (1879), 13.10.31, to Belgium 10.31 as OO-AMO; G-ABPT (1874), 11.9.31, to India 7.33 as VT-AEH; G-ABRD (1877), 8.10.31, impressed 6.40 as AW134; G-ABRO (1870), 29.10.31, impressed 12.39 as X5129; G-ABRT (1884), 29.10.31, to India 10.31 as VT-ACO; G-ABSD (1883), 26.11.31, crashed at Bungendore, N.S.W., Australia 14.10.32; G-ABSH (1885), 14.11.31, crashed 2.1.39; G-ABTP (1891), 12.2.32, impressed 2.41 as DG660; G-ABTS (1900), 21.3.32, impressed 6.40 as AW135; G-ABTW (1893), 9.2.32, to Poland 2.33 as SP-AHD

G-ABVA (1894), 15.3.32, to France 3.32 as F-ALVV; G-ABWL (1896), 10.5.32, registration cancelled 2.43; G-ABWM (1898), 20.5.32, to South Africa 11.37 as ZS-AMX; G-ABWN (1897), 20.5.32, to Holland 6.33 as PH-AJF, rest. 5.36, cancelled 3.40; G-ABWY (1899), 27.5.32, cancelled 11.40; G-ABXB (1902), 14.6.32, impressed 8.40 as BK848; G-ABXC (1903), 6.6.32, to France 6.32 as F-AMAR; G-ABXR (1905), 5.7.32, impressed 6.40 as AW111; G-ABXT (1901), 19.7.32, sold abroad 12.32; G-ABXZ (1904), 1.7.32, impressed 11.39 as X5052; G-ABYA (1906), 12.7.32, crashed near Biggin Hill 21.5.72; G-ABYI (1907), 14.7.32, to India 11.34 as VT-AFK; G-ABZE (1908), 9.9.32, impressed 1.41 as DG585

G-ACAM (1915), 25.1.33, to India 6.34 as VT-AFJ; G-ACBU (1849), ZS-ADB, 9.7.31, reg'd. to G. A. Williams 26.1.33, to Ireland 1.34 as EI-AAW; G-ACCY (1245), ex G-AAUR, 16.6.30, crashed at Redhill 20.6.38; G-ACJG (1921), 4.8.33, impressed 6.40 as AW136; G-AEDZ (1031), D-1644/D-EONA, 22.5.29, crashed 26.2.37; G-AFDZ (1924), 16.8.38, impressed 1.40 as X5056; G-AFKA (1000), EI-AAC, 16.4.29, reg'd. to Redhill F/C 27.9.38, impressed 1.41 as DG582; G-AFKY (1887), OO-AMR, 17.12.31, reg'd. to Southern Motors and Aircraft Ltd., Hamsey Green 24.10.38, impressed 11.39 as X5042; G-AFLV (1847), OO-ARG, 9.6.31, reg'd. to Eastbourne F/C 29.10.38, impressed 6.40 as AW145; G-AFPY (RC/SA/1), reconstructed by Southern Aircraft (Gatwick) Ltd., 10.3.39, impressed 11.39 as X5059; G-AFTG (1927), HB-OFI, 19.11.38, impressed 11.39 as X5054; G-ATBL (1917), CH-353/HB-OBA, 13.3.33, reg'd. to E. Eves, Baginton 2.65, to Mrs. M. S. and C. C. Lovell, Worthy Down 3.70, C. of A. 25.9.71, A. Haig-Thomas, Horsey Island, Essex 5.72

de Havilland D.H.60GIII Moth

G-ABUI   (5000), 13.5.32, J. M. B. Benson, Stag Lane; Eastern Counties Aero Club, Ipswich 12.35; Ipswich Aero Club, 5.36; crashed and burned at Nacton, Suffolk 11.6.37

G-ABVW   (5003), 28.6.32, Amy Mollison 'Jason 4'; L. Lipton, Hatfield 5.33; to N.V. Nederlandsch Instituut voor Zweefvliegen 8.37 as PH-ART

G-ABWT   (5004), 24.6.32, H. W. Sear; re-registered in Kenya 6.32 as VP-KAR

G-ABXX   (5005), 14.7.32, H. Vaughan, Brooklands; w.f.u. 1.37

G-ABYV   (5007), 12.8.32, Hon. Brian Lewis, Heston; to Austria 6.35 as OE-DAC

G-ABYZ   (5008), 31.8.32, H. A. C. Gregory; damaged at Spezia, Italy 20.12.32; sold abroad 8.37

G-ABZB   (5011), 16.9.32, K. A. Whittome, Whitchurch; to Sweden 4.39 as SE-AIA

G-ABZK   (5012), 7.10.32, Marquis of Douglas and Clydesdale, Renfrew; M. R. Cooke, Heston 11.34; Midland Aero Club, Castle Bromwich 4.38; scrapped 11.45

G-ABZS   (5014), 14.10.32, Scottish F/C, Renfrew; impressed 8.40 as BD177

G-ABZT   (5015), 21.10.32, Scottish F/C, crashed on Isle of Islay 24.5.36

A. J. Linnell's D.H.60GIII Moth at Hanworth in 1936. This had previously spent some time in Kenya as VP-KAU. (*A. J. Jackson*)

G-ABZU (5016), 28.10.32, Scottish F/C, Renfrew; impressed 8.40 as BD178
G-ABZV (5017), 28.10.32, Scottish F/C, Renfrew; impressed 8.40 as BD179
G-ACBX (5020), 28.1.33, W. L. Everard, Ratcliffe; Leicestershire Aero Club 5.36; Hull Aero Club 10.38; London Transport Flying Club, Broxbourne 8.39; impressed 12.39 as X5132
G-ACCW (5022), 10.2.33, Hon. R. Westenra, Haldon; Blackpool & Fylde A/C, Stanley Park 9.36; R. Ridley & H. V. Armstrong, Hooton 6.39; impressed as X5114
G-ACDV (5023), 7.3.33, T. G. Bishop, Renfrew; Scottish Flying Club, Renfrew 1.34; impressed 8.40 as BD174
G-ACGD (5025), 27.4.33, A. Fraser, Renfrew; Midland & Scottish Air Ferries Ltd. 7.34; Edinburgh F/C, Macmerry 5.35; crashed on Broad Law 25.7.36
G-ACGX (5029), 30.5.33, D. H. Whitbread, Heston; Hillmans Airways Ltd., Stapleford 12.34; Cinema Press Ltd., Croydon 6.36; London Transport Flying Club, Broxbourne 2.39; impressed 12.39 as X5131
G-ACGZ (5030), 2.6.33, Lt. Col. W. Duncan, Heston; to India 10.34 as VT-AFW
G-ACHH (5026), 30.5.33, H. E. Evans, Heston; Cinque Ports Flying Club Ltd., Lympne 9.35; sold abroad 2.38
G-ACIA (5033), 21.7.33, T. G. Bishop, Renfrew; sold abroad 7.36
G-ACIB (5034), 1.8.33, Scottish F/C, Renfrew; impressed 8.40 as BD175
G-ACII (5036), 28.7.33, H. E. Evans, Heston; sold abroad 3.34
G-ACIK (5037), 4.8.33, Vickers (Aviation) Ltd., Brooklands; sold in South Africa 3.40
G-ACJB (5035), 11.8.33, J. M. Barbour, Newtownards; Miss E. Barbour 1.36; Scottish Flying Club, Renfrew 9.37; impressed 8.40 as BD176
G-ACKF (5042), 27.10.33, R. Meeuwenvord; sold abroad 10.33
G-ACKV (5024), 14.3.33 (for Flt. Lt. H. von Schinkel as SE-ADO ntu); Hon. J. D. Kemp, Barton; sold abroad 9.36
G-ACMF (5047), 8.12.33, London Aeroplane Club, Hatfield; sold abroad 9.37
G-ACMY (5055), 9.2.34, Sir Malcolm Campbell; to Italy 1.35 as I-RAFF
G-ADAT (5019), VP-KAU, 21.2.33, Henlys Ltd., Heston; H. G. Linnell, Sywell 8.35; A. J. Linnell 2.36; London Transport F/C 12.38; impressed 1942 as X5124
G-AFWX (5032), EI-AAU, 5.7.33, Southern Aircraft Ltd., Gatwick; scrapped at Gatwick in 1945; registration cancelled 12.46

de Havilland D.H.60GIII Moth Major

G-ACNL (5061), 9.3.34, Hon. Brian Lewis, Heston; Rollason Aircraft Services Ltd., Croydon 7.35; sold abroad 8.37

G-ACNM (5062), 17.3.34, Sqn. Ldr. R. F. Leslie; Hon. D. Fortescue, Heston 4.35; to Southern Rhodesia 7.37 as VP-YBP

G-ACNP (5057), 21.2.34, Peter de Havilland, Hatfield; to Jugoslavia 3.34 as YU-PCH

G-ACNR (5067), 5.4.34, E. Hicks; Midland Aero Club 2.35; sold abroad 5.40

G-ACNS (5068), 10.4.34, Hon. Brian Lewis, Heston; Air Hire Ltd., Heston 4.35; British Airways Ltd., Stanley Park 12.35; sold in South Africa 3.40

G-ACOF (5058), 23.2.34, A. Schmidt; sold abroad 5.34

G-ACOG (5070), 9.4.34, Midland Aero Club, Castle Bromwich; sold abroad 9.40

G-ACOH (5071), 14.4.34, Midland Aero Club; destroyed in air collision with Hawker Hart over Castle Bromwich Aerodrome 9.12.34

G-ACOI (5072), 14.4.34, Midland Aero Club, Castle Bromwich; sold abroad 9.40

G-ACPH (5073), 24.4.34, T. A. K. Aga, Hatfield; Sir Geo. Lewis, Heston 12.35; Cinema Press Ltd., Croydon 11.36; to the Penang F/C 9.37 as VR-SAZ

G-ACPI (5077), 19.5.34, Household Brigade Flying Club, Heston; Airwork Ltd., Heston 3.37; A. M. Lee, Firbeck 12.37; sold abroad 5.40

G-ACPT (5080), 1.6.34, Bristol and Wessex Aero Club, Whitchurch; O. R. Guard, Portsmouth 6.37; Portsmouth Aero Club 3.39; impressed 6.40 as AW161

G-ACRI (5079), 30.5.34, Scottish Motor Traction Co. Ltd., Renfrew; Edinburgh Flying Club, Macmerry; impressed 8.40 as BK833

G-ACRR (5082), 15.6.34, G.L.A. France; Hon. Brian Lewis, Heston 1.36; M. G. Christie, Hanworth 7.36; impressed 2.40 as W7949

G-ACSA (5087), 9.7.34, R. K. C. Marwood; sold abroad 11.34

G-ACST (5088), 13.8.34, T. C. Place; Tollerton Aero Club 5.35; to the Penang Flying Club 11.37 as VR-SBA

G-ACTW (5091), 27.7.34, Hon. Brian Lewis, Heston; Midland Aero Club, Castle Bromwich 9.34; to India 2.37 as VT-AIO

G-ACUC (5084), 13.6.34, Miss Freda Thompson, Hatfield; Australia flight machine; to Australia 4.35 as VH-UUC; registration cancelled 10.47

G-ACUR (5097), 6.9.34, Duchess of Bedford, Woburn; lost in the North Sea off Great Yarmouth 23.3.37

G-ACXK (5095), 20.8.34, Lady Joan Hoare, Bucharest; reg'n. cancelled 11.45

G-ACYD (5100), 28.9.34, Luis Fontes, Woodley; to Kenya 3.38 as VP-KCP

G-ACZX (5113), 30.11.34, Nottingham Airport Ltd., Tollerton; Tollerton Aero Club Ltd. 2.36; crashed at Mansfield, Notts. 21.8.37

G-ADAN (5122), 20.2.35, London Transport Flying Club, Broxbourne; impressed 4.40 as W7976

G-ADFK (5143), 11.5.35, Portsmouth Aero Club; impressed 6.40 as AW162

G-ADFL (5144), 15.5.35, Portsmouth Aero Club; to Austria 12.35 as OE-TAT

G-ADFM (5145), 22.5.35, Portsmouth Aero Club; to Austria 12.35 as OE-TET

G-ADHE (5147), 12.6.35, H. E. Evans, Heston; Miss N. Garsed, Stanley Park 6.38; W. Westoby, Squires Gate 6.48; S. Wood, Squires Gate 1.49; N. D. Norman, Staverton 4.51; P. E. Hindmarsh, White Waltham 12.52; H. J. Warwick, Denham 9.55; V. B. Nightscale 12.57; crashed at Rickmansworth 22.3.58

G-ADIO (2263), built by D.H. Tech. School, 12.6.35, de Havilland Aircraft Co. Ltd.; to the Austrian Aero Club 7.35 as OE-DIO. The last ex-works Moth.

The single-seat, long range D.H.60M Moth G-ABHY in which C. W. A. Scott lowered the England–Australia record to 9 days 4 hours 11 minutes, 1–10 April 1931. (*Flight Photo 9822*)

de Havilland D.H.60M Moth

G-AAAR (339), 29.10.28, to Canada 11.28 as G-CAVX; G-AACD (340), 31.10.28; G-AACU (342), 10.4.29, impressed 6.40 as AV995; G-AAFB (1336), 23.3.29, to Germany 3.29 as D-1600; G-AAFF (1338), 26.4.29, to Jugoslavia 4.29 as YU-PDH; G-AAGE (1332), 30.5.29, sold abroad 7.34; G-AAHB (1352), 18.5.29, crashed at Hambrook, Bristol 23.9.29; G-AAHY (1362), 10.6.29, to Switzerland 7.37 as HB-AFI; G-AAIF (1363), 10.6.29, sold abroad 1.32; G-AAJX* (1374), 17.7.29, w.f.u. 12.31; G-AAKB (1365), 2.8.29, to France 1.30 as F-AJOA; G-AAKP* (1394), 3.8.29, impressed 6.40 as AW148; G-AAKR* (1395), 3.8.29, crashed at New Inn Green, Kent 17.9.31; G-AAKS* (1396), 3.8.29, crashed at Hessenthal am Main, Germany 24.3.30; G-AAKV (1369), 8.8.29, to India 1.34 as VT-AEX; G-AAKW (1380), 10.8.29, to Germany 3.35 as D-EKIV, rest. 2.36, sold abroad 4.37

G-AALF (1402), 29.8.29, w.f.u. in Sweden circa 1935; G-AALG (1411), 5.9.29, sold abroad 12.33, rest. 1.35, impressed 1.40 as X5104; G-AALS (1409), 12.9.29, sold abroad 10.34; G-AALX (1410), 27.9.29, w.f.u. 9.37; G-AARB (1412), 23.9.29, sold abroad 7.33, rest. 11.33, burned in hangar fire at Maylands 6.2.40; G-AARD (1414), 27.9.29, sold abroad 1.36; G-AARH (1417), 27.9.29, impressed 6.40 as AV997; G-AARI (1413), 25.9.29, sold abroad 1.33; G-AARL (1416), 27.9.29, sold abroad 9.31; G-AARU (1424), 17.10.29, impressed 11.39 as X5119; G-AASA (1438), 9.11.29, to New Zealand as ZK-ACK; G-AASD (1440), 9.11.29, to Iraq 3.32 as YI-ASD; G-AASF (1439), 23.11.29, sold in India 12.31; G-AASL (1430), 6.6.30, impressed 12.39 as X5127; G-AASM (1433), 16.11.29, crashed at Cheam, Surrey 22.4.34; G-AASR (1441), 2.12.29, impressed 6.40 as AW110; G-AASZ (1434), 18.12.29, impressed 11.39 as X5043

G-AATA (1460), 13.1.30, to Egypt 9.32 as SU-AAF; G-AATB (1467), 15.1.30, to India 8.31 as VT-ABY; G-AAUH (1462), 15.2.30, burned in hangar fire, Gravesend 3.8.37; G-AAUI (1495), 26.3.30, registration cancelled circa 1933; G-AAUS (1477), 11.3.30, to Australia 5.33 as VH-UQT; G-AAVE (1493), 10.4.30, registration cancelled 8.40; G-AAVR (1482), 29.3.30, destroyed in air collision with Hawker Hart K5800 over Horley, Surrey 8.5.39; G-AAVU (1485), 9.4.30, crashed at Hendon 8.11.31; G-AAVV

* Delivered initially to National Flying Services with Cirrus III engines

(1486), 5.4.30, impressed 1.41 as DG581; G-AAVZ (1480), 11.4.30, to Holland 8.37 as PH-ARS; G-AAWU (1474), 29.4.30, to India 1.34 as VT-AEW; G-AAWV (1476), 17.4.30, crashed at Tomas, Burma 3.7.30; G-AAXG (1542), 26.6.30, to France 1.31 as F-AJZB, rest. 2.33, to France 1.34 as F-AJZB, rest. 8.34, to New Zealand 12.35 as ZK-AEJ; G-AAYF (1535), 15.5.30, registration cancelled 12.32; G-AAYG (1546), 20.6.30, impressed 12.39 as X5126; G-AAZJ (1538), 24.5.30, sold abroad 12.33

G-ABAI (1472), 27.5.30, impressed 2.40 as W7948; G-ABAN (1549), 12.9.30, to New Zealand 9.30 as ZK-ACC; G-ABAS (1539), 6.6.30, crashed near Redhill 20.3.35; G-ABAT (1540), 13.6.30, impressed 1.41 as DG588; G-ABBL (1547), 11.7.30, to India 4.31 as VT-ACU; G-ABCH (1553), 10.7.30, to Holland 6.33 as PH-AJE; G-ABCW (1552), 16.7.30, to India 4.33 as VT-AEC; G-ABCZ (1555), 31.7.30, to Kenya 10.31 as VP-KAO, later to Tanganyika as VR-TAH; G-ABDB (1557), 22.8.30, to Norway 8.35 as LN-BAU; G-ABDT (1543), 4.7.30, sold abroad 3.32; G-ABHN (1680), 6.1.31, impressed 12.39 as X5130; G-ABHY (1685), 9.3.31, to Australia 12.31 as VH-UQH; G-ABID (1514), K1202, 25.3.31, to India 3.35 as VT-AGJ, rest. 8.35 as G-ADLJ q.v.; G-ABMX (1698), 25.4.31, w.f.u. at Amman, Jordan 6.39; G-ABMZ (1420), VT-ABM, 11.10.29, registration cancelled 8.40

G-ABNA (1711), 17.6.31, to India 12.31 as VT-ACW; G-ABNE (1384), J9922, 22.7.31, to Germany 10.31 as D-2296, rest. 12.35, sold abroad 1.36; G-ABNR (1706), 26.6.31, impressed 2.40 as X9296; G-ABPA (1712), 24.9.31, to India 12.31 as VT-ACU; G-ABPJ (1556), EI-AAE, 28.10.30, impressed 11.39 as X5026; G-ABRF (1794), 29.10.31, crashed 9.37; G-ABSF (1337), ex U.S. Embassy, 29.4.29, to Denmark 2.33 as OY-DAG; G-ABTF (1798), 1.3.32, impressed 8.40 as BK829; G-ABXM (3028), 6.6.32, to Jugoslavia 7.32 as UN-SAI, later YU-SAI

G-ACOA (1566), VH-UQA, 11.4.34, crashed at Hanworth 20.8.36; G-ADEZ (1669), VP-KAI, 12.12.30, impressed 7.40 as AX794; G-ADLJ (1514), K1202, G-ABID, 10.8.35, registration cancelled 8.45; G-ADLK (1661), K1828, 31.8.35, to India 7.37 as VT-AJO; G-AFKM (1509), K1227, 25.1.39, sold abroad 8.40; G-AFMY (1657), K1907, 18.1.39, impressed 11.39 as X5051; G-AFWJ (1600), K1860, 31.7.39, impressed 2.40 as W9368; G-AFZB (1595), K1845, nil C. of A., impressed 4.40 as X9438

de Havilland D.H.60T Moth Trainer

G-ABKM (1700), 15.5.31, de Havilland Aircraft Co. Ltd., Stag Lane; to the Swedish Air Force 6.31 as Fv.5103

G-ABKN (1701), 16.5.31, de Havilland Aircraft Co. Ltd., Stag Lane; to the Swedish Air Force 6.31 as Fv.5104, civil 3.48 as SE-AZW, crashed 6.12.50

G-ABKO (1702), 16.5.31, de Havilland Aircraft Co. Ltd., Stag Lane; to the Swedish Air Force 6.31 as Fv.5105

G-ABKP (1703), 16.5.31, de Havilland Aircraft Co. Ltd., Stag Lane; to the Swedish Air Force 6.31 as Fv.5106

G-ABKR (1704), 16.5.31, de Havilland Aircraft Co. Ltd., Stag Lane; to the Swedish Air Force 6.31 as Fv.5107

G-ABKS (1705), 16.5.31, de Havilland Aircraft Co. Ltd., Stag Lane; second prototype E-4, sold abroad 12.31

G-ABKU (1672), 13.5.31, de Havilland Aircraft Co. Ltd., Stag Lane; first prototype E-3, sold abroad 12.31

de Havilland D.H.61 Giant Moth

G-EBTL (325), 14.1.28, de Havilland Aircraft Co. Ltd., Stag Lane 'Canberra'; to MacRobertson Miller Aviation Co. Ltd. 2.28 as G-AUTL 'Old Gold'

G-AAAN (331), 8.10.28, Associated Newspapers Ltd. 'Geraldine'; National Flying
Services Ltd., Hedon 'Leone' 2.30; to New Guinea 1.32 as VH-UQJ
G-AAEV (335), 15.5.29, Alan Cobham Aviation Co. Ltd. 'Youth of Britain'; Imperial
Airways Ltd. 1.30; crashed at Broken Hill, Northern Rhodesia 19.1.30

D.H.66 Hercules G-EBMX at Swartkop as South African Air Force '262' in 1935 after
reconversion to open cockpits. (S.A.A.F.)

de Havilland D.H.66 Hercules
G-EBMW (236), 18.12.26, Imperial Airways Ltd. 'City of Cairo'; crashed near Koepang,
Timor 19.4.31
G-EBMX (237), 23.12.26, Imperial Airways Ltd. 'City of Delhi'; to the South African
Air Force 11.34 as '262'; scrapped at Broken Hill 11.39
G-EBMY (238), 17.12.26, Imperial Airways Ltd. 'City of Baghdad'; withdrawn from use
and dismantled at Kisumu, Kenya in 1933
G-EBMZ (239), 21.2.27, Imperial Airways Ltd. 'City of Jerusalem'; destroyed by fire
after stalling on night approach to Jask, Persia 6.9.29
G-EBNA (240), 7.3.27, Imperial Airways Ltd. 'City of Teheran'; damaged beyond repair
in forced landing at Gaza, 14.2.30
G-AAJH (393), 26.10.29, Imperial Airways Ltd. 'City of Basra'; to the South African
Air Force 4.34 as '260'; written off 4.43
G-AARY (703), 25.1.30, Imperial Airways Ltd. 'City of Karachi'; withdrawn from use
12.35
G-ABCP (347), G-AUJR, 30.4.29, to Imperial Airways Ltd. 7.30 as 'City of Jodhpur';
crashed near Salisbury, Southern Rhodesia 23.11.35
G-ABMT (346), G-AUJQ, 30.4.29, to Imperial Airways Ltd. 6.31 as 'City of Cape
Town'; Sir Alan Cobham, Germiston 10.32; Imperial Airways Ltd. 3.33; to
the South African Air Force 7.34 as '261'; written off 4.43

de Havilland D.H.75 Hawk Moth
G-EBVV (327), D.H.75, de Havilland Aircraft Co. Ltd., Stag Lane; first flown 7.12.28,
no C. of A. issued, scrapped in 1930
G-AAFW (343), D.H.75A, 7.11.29, de Havilland Aircraft Co. Ltd.; to Canadian
Controller of Civil Aviation 7.30 as CF-CCA; to R.C.A.F. 1931 as G-CYVD

G-AAFX (348), D.H.75A, 22.2.30, de Havilland Aircraft Co. Ltd.; to Australia 12.30 as
VH-UNW; withdrawn from use at Alice Springs in 1951

G-AAUZ (705), D.H.75A, 26.6.30, de Havilland Aircraft Co. Ltd.; Air Taxis Ltd., Stag
Lane 6.32; sold abroad 12.38

de Havilland D.H.80

G-AAHZ (396), E-1, registered to the de Havilland Aircraft Co. Ltd., Stag Lane 30.5.29;
first flown 9.9.29; converted to engine test bed in 1930–31

Maurice Jackaman's 1930 model Puss Moth G-AAYE, showing the original small rudder
and wire wheels. (*Aeroplane*)

de Havilland D.H.80A Puss Moth

G-AAFA (2038), 27.6.30, to Sweden 10.36 as SE-AFH; G-AARF (2059), 20.8.30, to
Kenya 10.31 as VP-KAT, later VP-KBO and SU-ACN, rest. 2.41, impressed 2.41 as
HK866; G-AATC (2001), 22.5.30, to Australia 12.30 as VH-UON, later ZK-ADU;
G-AAVA (2002), 2.7.30, to Holland 6.38 as PH-ATI; G-AAVB (2003), 28.8.30, to Egypt
5.31 as SU-ABB, rest. 7.33, impressed 5.41 as DR755; G-AAXI (2024), reg'd. to C. S.
Wynne-Eaton 26.5.30, crashed at Lester Field, Newfoundland 6.7.30; G-AAXJ (2006),
22.5.30, to Ceylon 7.31 as VT-ACZ; G-AAXL (2010), 16.6.30, d.b.f. on sandbank 5 miles
off Hunstanton 26.5.32; G-AAXM (2011), 13.6.30, to Belgium 3.33 as OO-ANH;
G-AAXN (2012), 14.6.30, in the sea, Goodwin Sands 22.6.30; G-AAXO (2041), 26.6.30,
impressed 4.40 as X9404; G-AAXR (2007), 11.9.30, impressed 2.41 as DG661;
G-AAXS (2009), 17.7.30, sold abroad 7.35; G-AAXT (2013), 27.6.30, to France 1.37 as
F-APZX; G-AAXU (2014), 20.6.30, to Egypt 3.32 as SU-ABE; G-AAXV (2026), 5.7.30,
to South Africa 3.37 as ZS-AIB; G-AAXW (2027), 27.6.30, crashed 4.37; G-AAXX
(2028), 15.7.30, reg'n. cancelled 12.34; G-AAXY (2029), 25.7.30, impressed 2.41 as
DJ711; G-AAXZ (2030), 27.6.30, reg'n. cancelled 5.37

G-AAYA (2031), 12.7.30, destroyed by enemy action 3.43; G-AAYB (2033), 17.7.30,
crashed at St. Moritz, Switzerland 31.1.33; G-AAYC (2035), 28.6.30, reg'n. cancelled
12.46; G-AAYD (2036), 19.7.30, crashed on Edgworth Moor, Bolton 15.11.35; G-AAYE
(2037), 25.7.30, sold abroad 11.32; G-AAYK (2034), 11.7.30, d.b.r. landing at Heston
1.4.32; G-AAZM (2042), 7.7.30, sold abroad 7.33; G-AAZN (2043), 6.9.30, crashed at
Leek, Staffs. 23.11.34; G-AAZO (2045), 23.7.30, impressed 7.40 as AX870; G-AAZP
(2047), 24.6.30, to Egypt 6.32 as SU-AAC, rest. 12.36, impressed 9.41 as HL537, rest.
11.46, airworthy in 1972; G-AAZS (2061), 25.8.30, to Kenya 8.30 as VP-KAH, rest.

10.31, as G-ABNV; G-AAZT (2063), 9.7.30, impressed 3.40 as 2063M; G-AAZU (2076), 7.10.30, sold abroad 2.33; G-AAZV (2077), 16.9.30, impressed 4.40 as X9402; G-AAZW (2090), 28.8.30, impressed 5.41 as ES916; G-AAZX (2101), 1.11.30, impressed 4.40 as X9401; G-AAZY (2025), 3.7.30, crashed 12.30

G-ABBH (2005), 12.6.30, crashed at Verneuil sur Avre, France 14.6.31; G-ABBS (2020), 28.7.30, sold abroad 12.34; G-ABCR (2083), 9.9.30, impressed 11.40 as DD820; G-ABCX (2040), 18.8.30, sold abroad 4.38; G-ABDF (2057), 18.9.30, stored during 1939–45 war, rest. at Sealand 10.48, crashed near Dunmow, Essex 29.5.55; G-ABDG (2070), 5.9.30, sold abroad 12.34, rest. 9.35, impressed 7.40 as AX869; G-ABDH (2081), 6.9.30, crashed at Kettlebury Hill, Churt 27.7.32; G-ABDI (2091), 14.8.30, reg'n. cancelled 5.38; G-ABDJ (2065), 29.10.30, to South Africa 12.30 as ZS-ACF; G-ABDL (2106), 21.10.30, sold abroad 9.33, rest. 11.33, impressed 8.40 as BD181; G-ABDM (2105), 8.10.30, impressed 7.41 as ES953; G-ABDW (2051), 11.9.30, to Australia 12.33 as VH-UQB

G-ABEC (2055), 13.9.30, to France 3.34 as F-ANEC; G-ABEH (2072), 18.9.30, sold abroad 2.33, rest. 3.34, impressed 8.41 as HH981, rest. at Eastleigh 11.46, d.b.r. landing at Thruxton 15.8.48; G-ABEI (2073), 17.10.30, impressed 9.40 as BK846; G-ABEJ (2074), 3.10.30, to India 12.30 as VT-ACJ; G-ABEL (2075), 13.10.30, to Belgium 2.35 as OO-AEL; G-ABEM (2109), 13.11.30, to Holland 5.38 as PH-ATL; G-ABFU (2123), 10.1.31, reg'n. cancelled 12.32; G-ABFV (2122), 18.12.30, impressed 1.40, no serial; G-ABFY (2115), 24.11.30, sold abroad 11.32

G-ABGD (2104), 8.11.30, sold abroad 12.33; G-ABGR (2116), 1.1.31, sold abroad 11.32; G-ABGS (2117), 15.1.31, impressed 7.40 as AX872; G-ABGT (2120), 24.12.30, reg'n. cancelled 12.46; G-ABGX (2121), 19.1.31, sold abroad 12.34; G-ABGZ (2071), 28.9.30, to Jugoslavia 9.30 as UN-PAI, later YU-PAI; G-ABHB (2113), 4.12.30, impressed 4.40 as X9405; G-ABHC (2125), 16.1.31, to New Zealand 12.32 as ZK-AEV; G-ABIA (2127), 16.1.31, impressed 5.41 as ES917; G-ABIH (2140), 23.2.31, to U.S.A. 11.31 as NC770N; G-ABIJ (2141), 17.4.31, to India 4.35 as VT-AGM; G-ABIN (2135), 14.3.31, impressed 1.41 as DJ712; G-ABIT (2137), 12.3.31, to Belgium 9.35 as OO-EIT; G-ABIU (2139), 27.3.31, to South Africa 12.31 as ZS-ADO, rest. 12.38, impressed 5.41 as DR608; G-ABIY (2134), 28.2.31, crashed 4.35; G-ABIZ (2136), 27.2.31, impressed 1.40 as W9369

G-ABJB (2147), 28.3.31, to Czechoslovakia 4.32 as OK-OFK; G-ABJD (2144), 27.3.31, to France 10.36 as F-APFZ; G-ABJO (2145), 31.3.31, crashed 12.35; G-ABJU (2156), 30.4.31, impressed 5.41 as ES918; G-ABJV (2154), 9.5.31, sold abroad 11.35; G-ABJY (2155), 24.4.31, reg'n. cancelled 12.37; G-ABKD (2143), 30.3.31, impressed 4.40 as X9403; G-ABKG (2157), 22.5.31, impressed 1.40 as W6416; G-ABKZ (2132), 3.2.31, impressed 5.41 as DR607, rest. 2.46, scrapped at Southend 5.49; G-ABLB (2149), 11.4.31, impressed 4.40 as X9400; G-ABLC (2150), 16.4.31, sold abroad 2.38; G-ABLD (2158), 27.6.31, to Holland 6.35 as PH-ATB; G-ABLG (2159), 12.5.31, impressed 2.41 as DG662; G-ABLO (2167), 22.5.31, to France 11.33 as F-AMUY; G-ABLP (2162), 16.5.31, impressed 12.40 as EM995; G-ABLR (2163), 16.5.31, impressed 10.40 as BK871; G-ABLS (2164), 28.5.31, stored at Dyce 1939–1968, airworthy in 1972; G-ABLX (2173), 10.6.31, impressed 5.41 as EM996; G-ABLY (2189), 21.7.31, impressed 5.41 as ES919

G-ABMC (2160), 11.5.31, impressed 3.41 as DP849; G-ABMD (2168), 12.5.31, destroyed by fire at Hooton 11.7.40; G-ABMG (2172), 6.6.31, to France 7.34 as F-ANEZ; G-ABMH (2174), 25.6.31, to France 5.34 as F-ANBR; G-ABMN (2176), 20.6.31, to India 6.32 as VT-ADN; G-ABMP (2185), 23.6.31, impressed 3.41 as DP850; G-ABMS (2166), 22.5.31, impressed 3.41 as DP854; G-ABNC (2170), 12.6.31, sold abroad 12.33, rest. 2.34, to France 3.38 as F-AQOR; G-ABNF (2188), 4.9.31, ntu, to U.S. Air Attaché, rest. 8.35 as G-ADOC; G-ABNN (2190), 17.7.31, sold abroad 5.35; G-ABNO (2161), 7.6.31, crashed near Denbigh 6.9.33; G-ABNS (2178), 2.7.31, reg'n. cancelled 11.45; G-ABNV (2061), G-AAZS, VP-KAH, 25.8.30, sold abroad 12.35, rest. 6.37, to Italy 7.38 as I-BIGA; G-ABNZ (2200), 20.8.31, to Ireland 10.37 as EI-ABM, rest. 11.38, impressed 1.40 as 2065M

G-ABOC (2201), 24.7.31, to Kenya 5.38 as VP-KCN; G-ABOF (2191), 17.7.31, impressed 10.40, no serial; G-ABPB (2196), 20.8.31, impressed 1.40 as 2064M; G-ABPF (2207), 31.8.31, sold abroad 10.31, rest. 12.33, sold abroad 10.34; G-ABRR (2209), 15.9.31, impressed 3.40 as X9378; G-ABSA (2203), 19.11.31, crashed 10.32; G-ABSB (2213), 24.11.31, reg'n. cancelled during 1939–45 war; G-ABSO (2217), 30.12.31, impressed 4.40 as X9439; G-ABTD (2216), 7.1.32, impressed 2.41 as HK861; G-ABTV (2218), 9.2.32, impressed 3.31 as DP846; G-ABUJ (2219), 21.3.32, ditched off Seaview, I.O.W. 15.7.33; G-ABUX (2220), 15.2.32, impressed 12.40 as DD821; G-ABVT (2223), 18.4.32, to Spain 3.34 as EC-AAV; G-ABVX (2228), 22.4.32, impressed 11.39 as X5044

G-ABWA (2229), 21.4.32, reg'n. cancelled 12.37; G-ABWG (2232), 9.5.32, impressed 1.40 as 2069M; G-ABWZ (2236), 13.6.32, reg'n. cancelled 11.40; G-ABXJ (2238), 21.6.32, sold in Ceylon 7.33; G-ABXY (2241), 4.8.32, 'The Hearts Content', crashed near Genholac, Cevennes, France 29.3.34; G-ABYP (2233), 10.8.32, impressed 10.40 as BK870, rest. 7.46, crashed at Eaton Bray, Beds. 31.8.47; G-ABYU (2234), 23.9.32, to France 6.37 as F-AQCE; G-ABYW (2240), 2.9.32, sold abroad 2.37; G-ACAB (2247), 8.11.32, burned out at Hooton 8.7.40; G-ACBL (2246), 8.12.32, to Spain 1.33 as EC-VAA; G-ACDU (2142), UN-SAA, 17.3.31, crashed 7.38; G-ACFE (2259), 10.5.33, to France 5.34 as F-AMYR; G-ACIV (2131), ZS-ACH, 30.1.31, impressed 7.41 as ES954; G-ACSB (2053), VH-UPJ, 26.8.30, to Holland 3.35 as PH-AMN; G-ACTV (2080), VT-ACA, 3.9.30, impressed 7.40 as AX868; G-ACYT (2231), E-8, 23.11.34, impressed 5.41 as ES920

G-ADLP (2111), VT-ACI, 28.11.30, crashed at Dane Hill, Sussex 5.9.36; G-ADOC (2188), G-ABNF, U.S. Air Attaché, 4.9.31, reg'n. cancelled 5.41; G-AEEB (2089), VH-UQO, destroyed during 1939–45 war; G-AEIV (2067), VH-UQK, 30.6.36, impressed 3.41 as DP853; G-AEOA (2184), UN-PAX, 9.7.31, impressed 5.41 as ES921, rest. 2.46; G-AFDH (2054), ZK-ABR, 18.9.30, reg'n. cancelled 12.46; G-AFKV (2118), VP-KAK, 9.2.31, to Sweden 12.38 as SE-AHO; G-AHLO (2187), U.S.N. 8877, HM534, 27.7.46, to Canada 10.69 as CF-PEI

Jim Mollison's immortal Puss Moth 'The Hearts Content' showing the extra windows and the tiny entrance door in the rear of the cabin. (*Flight Photo 12144*)

The Tiger Club's Puss Moth G-AHLO (enlarged rudder) flying near Redhill in 1969.
(*John Goring*)

de Havilland D.H.60T Tiger Moth

G-ABNG (1725), 1.10.31 ⎫
G-ABNI (1726), 29.8.31 ⎪
G-ABNJ (1727), 26.8.31 ⎪ registered to the de Havilland Aircraft Co. Ltd.,
G-ABNK (1728), 1.10.31 ⎬ all delivered to the Swedish Air Force 1931
G-ABNL (1729), 1.10.31 ⎪
G-ABNM (1730), 1.10.31 ⎪
G-ABNY (1724), 28.9.31 ⎭
G-ABPH (1732), 8.9.31, de Havilland Aircraft Co. Ltd., sold to the Portuguese
Government 12.31

de Havilland D.H.82 Tiger Moth

G-ABRC (1733), 18.3.32, impressed 10.40 as BB723; G-ABSK (1796), 29.12.31, sold
in Portugal 12.32; G-ABSW (3102), 12.2.32, to India 9.40; G-ABSX (3103), 24.2.32, to
India 9.40; G-ABSY (3104), 26.2.32, to India 9.40; G-ABSZ (3105), 26.2.32, to India
9.40; G-ABTA (3106), 1.3.32, to India 9.40; G-ABTB (3101), 21.3.32, to Holland 12.33
as PH-AJO, rest. 4.35, impressed 8.40 as BD153; G-ABUL (3107), 9.3.32, impressed
9.40 as BB792; G-ABYJ (3137), 22.7.32, crashed at Winkfield 13.7.36

G-ACBA (3152), 6.2.33, landed on Hawker Hart K4372 at Filton 3.5.39; G-ACBB
(3153), 6.2.33, destroyed in air collision with G-ACBE over Yate 25.6.34; G-ACBC
(3154), 9.2.33, crashed at Shipperdine 11.3.40; G-ACBD (3155), 13.2.33, to India 9.40;
G-ACBE (3156), 16.2.33, see G-ACBB above; G-ACBF (3157), 17.2.33, to India 9.40;
G-ACBG (3158), 18.2.33, spun in at Filton Junction 20.5.39; G-ACBN (3148), 16.11.32,
sold in Spain 12.32

de Havilland D.H.82A Tiger Moth

G-ACDA (3175), 10.3.33, impressed 10.40 as BB724; G-ACDB (3176), 13.3.33,
impressed 10.40 as BB725; G-ACDC (3177), 10.3.33, impressed 10.40 as BB726, rest.
12.53; G-ACDE (3178), 13.3.33, impressed 10.40 as BB727; G-ACDF (3179), 15.3.33,
impressed 10.40 as BB741; G-ACDG (3180), 17.3.33, impressed 10.40 as BB728, rest.
6.44, to Holland 3.47 as PH-UAY; G-ACDH (3181), 20.3.33, crashed 7.38; G-ACDI

(3182), 24.3.33, impressed 10.40 as BB742, rest. 4.48, crashed at Christchurch 10.7.54; G-ACDJ (3183), 29.3.33, impressed 10.40 as BB729, rest. 12.53; G-ACDK (3184), 29.3.33, impressed 10.40 as BB730; G-ACDY (3189), 6.4.33, crashed in River Don, Aberdeen 26.8.33

G-ACEH (3185), 14.3.33, sold in Poland 2.34; G-ACEZ (3186), 7.4.33, impressed 9.40 as BB790, rest. 3.55, crashed near Andover 23.8.61; G-ACFA (3187), 4.4.33, to India 1.35 as VT-AGD; G-ACGE (3188), 27.4.33, to Holland 6.33 as PH-AJD, rest. 3.36, sold abroad 1.38; G-ACJA (3191), 15.8.33, sold abroad 10.34; G-ACPS (1993), 19.4.34, to France 6.37 as F-AQDP; G-ACSK (3223), 11.5.34, sold abroad 12.39; G-ACVK (3224), 16.8.34, to India 9.40; G-ACVL (3225), 16.8.34, to India 9.40 as VT-AOG; G-ACWB (3226), 14.8.34, to R.N.Z.A.F. 12.39 as NZ737; G-ACYN (3314), 24.10.34, sold in Palestine 10.34; G-ACZY (3315), 21.2.35, to India 9.40; G-ACZZ (3316), 21.2.35, crashed 12.36

G-ADCG (3318), 29.4.35, impressed 10.40 as BB731; G-ADCH (3319), 2.5.35, impressed 10.40 as BB732; G-ADGF (3345), 15.7.35, impressed 9.40 as BB704; G-ADGG (3346), 11.7.35, impressed 9.40 as BB695; G-ADGH (3347), 11.7.35, impressed 9.40 as BB696; G-ADGO (2262), 20.2.35, crashed 3.40; G-ADGS (3337), 28.6.35, impressed 9.40 as BB705; G-ADGT (3338), 28.6.35, impressed 9.40 as BB697, rest. 4.57, reduced to spares at Ludham 5.67; G-ADGU (3339), 28.6.35, impressed 9.40 as BB693; G-ADGV (3340), 29.6.35, impressed 9.40 as BB694; G-ADGW (3341), 6.7.35, impressed 9.40 as BB706; G-ADGX (3342), 13.7.35, impressed 9.40 as BB698, rest. 9.51, crashed at Thruxton 11.7.53; G-ADGY (3343), 9.7.35, impressed 9.40 as BB699; G-ADGZ (3344), 16.7.35, impressed 9.40 as BB700

G-ADHA (3348), 23.7.35, to Canada 7.35 as CF-AVG; G-ADHN (3474), 4.3.36, impressed 10.40 as BB811; G-ADHR (3371), 4.9.35, impressed 10.40 as BB743; G-ADHS (3372), 3.9.35, impressed 10.40 as BB744; G-ADHT (3373), 3.9.35, impressed 10.40 as BB733; G-ADHU (3374), 5.9.35, impressed 10.40 as BB734; G-ADHV (3375), 7.9.35, impressed 10.40 as BB735, rest. 9.53 as G-ANBV q.v.; G-ADHW (3376), 10.9.35, crashed 1.38; G-ADHX (3377), 12.9.35, crashed at Sywell 27.8.40 prior to impressment as BB793; G-ADHY (3366), 30.8.35, impressed 10.40 as BB745; G-ADHZ (3367), 23.8.35, impressed 10.40 as BB746

G-ADIA (3368), 24.8.35, impressed 10.40 as BB747, rest. 5.46; G-ADIB (3369), 26.8.35, impressed 10.40 as BB748, rest. 1.54, to France 5.54 as F-BGZU; G-ADIC

G-ADJJ at Tollerton in 1966, thirty-one years old and newly restored to near-mint condition. (*A. J. Jackson*)

424

(3370), 28.8.35, spun in at White Waltham 23.2.40; G-ADIH (3349), 23.7.35, impressed 9.40 as BB789, rest. 11.46, crashed in Broadstairs 20.11.52; G-ADII (3350), 23.7.35, impressed 9.40 as BB701; G-ADIJ (3351), 23.7.35, impressed 9.40 as BB788, rest. 3.47, to New Zealand 12.52 as ZK-BBS; G-ADIW (3352), 29.7.35, to India 9.40; G-ADIX (3353), 29.7.35, to India 9.40; G-ADIY (3354), 29.7.35, to India 9.40; G-ADIZ (3355), 30.7.35, to India 9.40

G-ADJA (3356), 30.7.35, to India 9.40; G-ADJB (3378), 18.11.35, crashed 12.36; G-ADJC (3379), 18.11.35, impressed 10.40 as BB815; G-ADJD (3380), 18.11.35, impressed 10.40 as BB816; G-ADJE (3381), 19.11.35, impressed 11.39 as W5015; G-ADJF (3382), 19.11.35, impressed 9.40 as BB791; G-ADJG (3383), 20.11.35, impressed 10.40 as BB817, rest. 9.46 as G-AIHO q.v.; G-ADJH (3384), 19.11.35, impressed 11.39 as X5045; G-ADJI (3385), 20.11.35, impressed 10.40 as BB818, rest. 12.53, to France 6.55 as F-BHII; G-ADJJ (3386), 19.11.35, impressed 10.40 as BB819, rest. 12.53; G-ADKG (3361), 22.8.35, impressed 10.40 as BB749; G-ADLU (3357), 31.7.35, to R.N.Z.A.F. 12.39 as NZ735; G-ADLV (3364), 12.8.35, impressed 10.40 as BB750, rest. 5.56 as G-AORA q.v.; G-ADLW (3365), 13.8.35, impressed 10.40 as BB751; G-ADLX (3360), 12.8.35, crashed at White Waltham 1.7.39; G-ADLZ (3362), 16.8.35, impressed 10.40 as BB752

G-ADMA (3363), 17.8.35, impressed 10.40 as BB753, to Rollason, Croydon 10.54, to Australia 12.56 as VH-PCG; G-ADNP (3411), 28.11.35, to India 9.40; G-ADNR (3412), 27.11.35, to India 9.40; G-ADNS (3413), 27.11.35, crashed at Yatesbury 23.8.40; G-ADNT (3414), 28.11.35, crashed 10.38; G-ADNU (3415), 29.11.35, to India 9.40; G-ADNV (3416), 29.11.35, impressed 8.40 as BD155; G-ADNW (3417), 29.11.35, reg'n. cancelled 3.41; G-ADNX (3418), 29.11.35, to India 9.40; G-ADNY (3419), 27.11.35, to India 9.40; G-ADNZ (3420), 1.1.36, to India 9.40

G-ADOA (3421), 3.1.36, crashed near Marlborough 26.9.39; G-ADOB (3422), 7.1.36, to India 9.40; G-ADOF (3399), 18.12.35, impressed 9.40 as BB672; G-ADOG (3400), 11.1.36, impressed 9.40 as BB673; G-ADOH (3401), 11.1.36, impressed 9.40 as BB674; G-ADOI (3402), 11.1.36, impressed 9.40 as BB675, to D. H. Witney 11.46, to Ethiopia 1947; G-ADOJ (3403), 11.1.36, impressed 9.40 as BB676; G-ADOK (3404), 11.1.36, impressed 9.40 as BB677, rest. 1.48, to Holland 7.51 as PH-UEX; G-ADOL (3405), 11.1.36, impressed 9.40 as BB678; G-ADOM (3406), 13.1.36, impressed 9.40 as BB679, rest. 3.52 to G-AMRC q.v.; G-ADON (3407), 11.1.36, impressed 9.40 as BB680; G-ADOO (3408), 13.1.36, impressed 9.40 as BB681; G-ADOP (3409), 13.1.36, impressed 9.40 as BB682; G-ADOR (3410), 13.1.36, impressed 9.40 as BB683, misapplied as BB687, rest. 5.47, to Pakistan 11.48; G-ADOW (3387), 18.11.35, impressed 1.41 as BB856; G-ADOX (3388), 18.11.35, impressed 1.41 as BB857; G-ADOY (3389), 18.11.35, impressed 1.41 as BB858; G-ADOZ (3390), 18.11.35, impressed 1.41 as BB859

G-ADPA (3391), 18.11.35, impressed 1.41 as BB851; G-ADPB (3392), 18.11.35, d.b.r. landing at Stoughton, Leics. 27.5.40; G-ADPC (3393), 18.11.35, impressed 1.41 as BB852; G-ADPD (3394), 19.11.35, crashed at Desford 5.3.36; G-ADPE (3395), 19.11.35, d.b.r. in forced landing at Kirkbymoorside 10.5.40; G-ADPF (3396), 20.11.35, impressed 1.41 as BB853; G-ADPG (3397), 19.11.35, crashed at Desford 27.2.40 prior to impressment as BB854; G-ADPH (3398), 19.11.35, impressed 1.41 as BB855; G-ADSH (3424), 25.11.35, impressed 10.40 as BB754; G-ADSI (3423), 4.10.35, crashed 1.7.38; G-ADUC (3425), 23.11.35, impressed 10.40 as BB812; G-ADUK (3426), 26.10.35, to R.N.Z.A.F. 12.39 as NZ732; G-ADVN (3427), 6.1.36, impressed 9.40 as BB684; G-ADVO (3428), 7.1.36, crashed at Perth 8.2.36; G-ADVP (3429), 8.1.36, impressed 9.40 as BB685

G-ADVX (3441), 8.1.36, impressed 10.40 as BB799; G-ADVY (3442), 8.1.36, impressed 10.40 as BB795; G-ADVZ (3443), 8.1.36, impressed 10.40 as BB796, rest. 5.54, to Norway 9.54 as LN-BDL; G-ADWA (3444), 8.1.36, impressed 10.40 as BB797; G-ADWB (3445), 18.1.36, impressed 10.40 as BB798; G-ADWC (3446), 13.1.36, impressed 10.40 as BB794; G-ADWD (3447), 15.1.36, crashed 1.40; G-ADWE (3448), 20.1.36, impressed 10.40 as BB800; G-ADWF (3449), 20.1.36, impressed 10.40 as BB801; G-ADWG (3492), 7.4.36, to India 1.40 as VT-AMA; G-ADWJ (3450), 21.1.36, impressed 10.40 as BB803; G-ADWK (3451), 16.1.36, impressed 10.40 as BB802; G-ADWL (3452), 23.1.36, impressed 10.40 as BB804, rest. 6.51, to Germany 4.57 as D-ECUT; G-ADWM (3453), 24.1.36, impressed 10.40 as BB805; G-ADWN (3454), 25.1.36, impressed 10.40 as BB808; G-ADWO (3455), 24.1.36, impressed 10.40 as BB807, rest. 3.51 using major components of BB860/G-ADXT, d.b.r. at Christchurch 31.7.58; G-ADWP (3456), 27.1.36, impressed 10.40 as BB806, used in S. Rhodesia, sold locally 7.52 as VP-YJM

G-ADXB (3430), 28.11.35, impressed 10.40 as BB736; G-ADXC (3431), 30.11.35, crashed at Parndon, Essex 16.11.36; G-ADXD (3432), 30.11.35, impressed 10.40 as BB737; G-ADXE (3433), 6.12.35, impressed 10.40 as BB755; G-ADXI (3434), 23.12.35, impressed 10.40 as BB756; G-ADXJ (3435), 14.12.35, impressed 10.40 as BB738; G-ADXK (3457), 31.1.36, impressed 9.40 as BB686; G-ADXN (3458), 6.2.36, impressed 9.40 as BB687, permanently mispainted as BB683; G-ADXO (3459), 13.2.36, impressed 9.40 as BB688; G-ADXP (3460), 4.2.36, impressed 9.40 as BB689; G-ADXR (3461), 6.12.35, impressed 9.40 as BB690; G-ADXT (3436), 5.12.35, impressed 1.41 as BB860; G-ADXU (3437), 5.12.35, impressed 1.41 as BB861; G-ADXV (3438), 7.12.35, impressed 1.41 as BB862; G-ADXW (3439), 18.12.35, crashed 12.37; G-ADXX (3440), 16.12.35, impressed 1.41 as BB863; G-ADXZ (3475), 3.3.36, crashed 25.6.38; G-ADYA (3476), 13.2.36, impressed 10.40 as BB810; G-ADYB (3477), 22.2.36, impressed 10.40 as BB809

G-AEBY (3485), 15.2.36, impressed 9.40 as BB702; G-AEBZ (3486), 18.2.36, impressed 9.40 as BB703; G-AECG (3488), 20.3.36, crashed 12.37; G-AECH (3489), 20.3.36, impressed 1.41 as BB864; G-AECI (3490), 23.3.36, impressed 1.41 as BB865; G-AECJ (3491), 24.3.36, impressed 1.41 as BB866; G-AEEA (3495), 7.4.36, impressed 9.40 as BB691; G-AEID (3498), 1.7.36, crashed landing at Desford 27.9.40; G-AELA (3509), 13.8.36, crashed near Woolsington 6.3.37; G-AELB (3510), 1.8.36, impressed 7.40 as AX781; G-AELC (3511), 8.8.36, impressed 7.40 as AX782; G-AELD (3512), 19.8.36, crashed near Prestatyn 11.4.37; G-AELP (3513), 26.8.36, impressed 10.40 as BB757

G-AEMF (3514), 19.9.36, impressed 10.40 as BB758; G-AEMU (3516), 18.9.36, reg'n. cancelled 8.40; G-AENK (3517), 9.10.36, d.b.r. at Filton 1.6.40; G-AEOE (3521), 7.12.36, sold abroad 6.40; G-AERM (3280), K4284, 18.12.36, returned to the R.A.F. 10.37 as K4284; G-AERW (3543), 1.3.37, reg'n. cancelled 12.37; G-AESA (3544), 1.3.37, impressed 8.40 as BD161; G-AESC (3545), 11.3.37, crashed 9.37; G-AESD (3552), 4.3.37, impressed 8.40 as BD156; G-AESM (3582), 15.4.37, crashed at Yatesbury 30.5.40; G-AESN (3586), 19.4.37, to India 9.40; G-AESO (3587), 16.4.37, crashed near Avebury, Wilts. 30.3.40; G-AETO (3561), 22.4.37, to Australia 3.40 as VH-ACP; G-AETP (3574), 15.4.37, civil during 1939–45 war, to Holland 3.46 as PH-UCA; G-AEUV (3599), 2.7.37, impressed 9.40 as BB692; G-AEVB (2264), 8.4.37, impressed 10.40 as BB739; G-AEWG (3589), 24.4.37, impressed 1.40 as X5105; G-AEXG (3584), 5.5.37, impressed 7.40 as AX786; G-AEZC (3624), 13.10.37, impressed 8.40 as BD152

G-AFAI (3602), 29.7.37, to Turkey 9.37 as TC-KUR; G-AFAR (3627), 20.10.37, impressed 1.41 as BB867; G-AFAS (3628), 24.11.37, impressed 1.41 as BB868;

426

The Midland Aero Club's G-AFNR, impressed in 1940 as W7952 and seen here at Wolverhampton in July 1950, was restored briefly as G-ANBU in 1953. (*W. K. Kilsby*)

G-AFCA (3637), 20.11.37, impressed 8.40 as BD154; G-AFDC (3594), 15.6.37, to South Africa 12.37 as ZS-ANR; G-AFDD (3595), 15.6.37, to South Africa 12.37 as ZS-ANS; G-AFEJ (3664), 18.2.38, to India 3.40 as VT-AMC; G-AFFA (3706), 12.10.38, impressed 10.40 as BB813; G-AFFO (3674), 19.3.38, to South Africa 5.38 as ZS-AIY; G-AFGJ (3679), 14.4.38, impressed 7.40 as AX791 mispainted as AX787; G-AFGT (3681), 2.5.38, impressed 1.40 as W7955, rest. 9.50, to Thai Navy 1.51; G-AFGW (3684), 25.5.38, sold abroad 2.40; G-AFGY (3699), 13.7.38, impressed 10.40 as BB740; G-AFGZ (3700), 13.7.38, impressed 10.40 as BB759, rest. 1.51 as G-AMHI q.v.; G-AFHI (3682), 20.5.38, impressed 8.40 as BD151; G-AFHT (3695), 18.6.38, impressed 7.40 as BD142, rest. 3.42 as G-AMRD q.v.

G-AFJF (3722), 30.9.38, to R.N.Z.A.F. 12.39 as NZ734; G-AFJG (3724), 28.9.38, impressed 7.40 as AX787 mispainted as AX791, rest. 8.51 as G-AMLB q.v.; G-AFJH (3725), 8.10.38, impressed 7.40 as AX788; G-AFJI (3747), 18.10.38, to R.N.Z.A.F. 12.39 as NZ733; G-AFJK (3748), 20.10.38, impressed 10.40 as BB760, rest. 8.52, d.b.r. landing Squires Gate 16.4.54; G-AFJL (3749), 26.10.38, to R.N.Z.A.F. 12.39 as NZ730; G-AFJM (3766), 19.11.38, impressed 8.40 as BD170; G-AFJN (3767), 19.11.38, impressed 8.40 as BD171; G-AFLX (3790), 26.10.38, to India 9.40 as VT-AOD; G-AFMC (3793), 6.12.38, impressed 7.40 as AX783; G-AFMD (3794), 6.12.38, impressed 7.40 as AX785; G-AFNL (82185), 27.6.39, to R.N.Z.A.F. 12.39 as NZ736; G-AFNM (82186), 29.6.39, sold abroad 2.40; G-AFNP (3881), 2.2.39, to India 5.40 as VT-AMH; G-AFNR (3882), 2.2.39, impressed 1.40 as W7952, rest. 9.53 as G-ANBU q.v.; G-AFNS (3883), 3.2.39, sold abroad 6.40; G-AFNT (3884), 3.2.39, sold abroad 6.40; G-AFNU (3885), 3.2.39, sold abroad 5.40; G-AFNV (3886), 3.2.39, to South Africa 5.40 as ZS-ATP, re-reg'd. ZS-ATN (2)

G-AFSG (82097), 19.5.39, impressed 1.40 as W7954; G-AFSH (82139), 8.6.39, impressed 1.40 as X5106, rest. 1.52, to New Zealand 3.52 as ZK-BAT; G-AFSI (82142), 9.6.39, impressed 1.40 as X5107; G-AFSJ (82182), 23.6.39, impressed 1.40 as X5108, rest. 3.51, crashed at Padgate 26.6.55; G-AFSK (82140), 8.6.39, crashed at Wooperton, Northumberland 27.6.39; G-AFSL (82141), 8.6.39, impressed 1.40 as W7950; G-AFSM (82183), 29.6.39, impressed 1.40 as X5109, rest. 2.48, to Pakistan A.F. 11.48, civil 11.56 as AP-AHU; G-AFSN (82184), 28.6.39, impressed 1.40 as X5110; G-AFSP (82584), 9.6.39, impressed 1.40 as W7951; G-AFSR (82585), 22.6.39, impressed 1.40 as W7953; G-AFSS (82586), 21.6.39, impressed 3.40 as X9318; G-AFST (82587), 5.7.39, impressed 1.40 as W7956; G-AFSU (82588), 5.7.39, impressed 1.40 as W7970, rest. 9.53 as G-ANCZ q.v.; G-AFSX (82004), 20.4.39, impressed 7.40 as AX856

G-AFTI (82233), 21.8.39, sold abroad 5.40; G-AFTJ (82575), 4.5.39, sold abroad 1.40; G-AFWC (82589), 14.7.39, impressed 1.40 as W6417; G-AFWD (82590), 14.7.39, impressed 1.40 as W6418; G-AFWE (82591), 21.7.39, impressed 1.40 as W6419, rest. 3.56 as G-AOHC q.v.; G-AFWF (82592), 21.7.39, impressed 1.40 as W6420, rest. 6.52 as G-AMTL q.v.; G-AFWI (82187), 24.7.39, impressed 10.40 as BB814, rest. 8.72; G-AFXZ (82234), 22.8.39, sold abroad 5.40; G-AFYA (82235), 22.8.39, sold abroad 6.40; G-AFYB (82593), 23.8.39, sold abroad 5.40; G-AFYC (82594), 22.8.39, sold abroad 5.40; G-AFZC (82293), 24.10.39, to Australia 2.40 as VH-ACT; G-AFZD (82595), 23.8.39, sold abroad 6.40; G-AFZF (3524), OE-DIK, 29.8.39, impressed 11.39 as W5014, rest. 7.55, to Germany 8.55 as D-EDER

G-AGAP (3688), F-AQOX, 13.6.38, to Australia 3.40 as VH-ADK; G-AGRA, NL690, 13.9.45, to Ireland 1.54 as EI-AGG; G-AGRB, NL905, 25.8.45, to Belgium 4.53 as OO-EVN; G-AGYU (85265), DE208, 6.4.46; G-AGYV (82029), N6751, 29.1.46, to Belgium 7.46 as OO-TWD; G-AGYW (3857), N6544, 22.3.46, to Pakistan 2.49 as AP-AEP; G-AGZY (82287), N9176, 6.6.46, to India 2.49 as VY-DBC

G-AHDD (86051), EM849, 2.3.46, crashed at Calais 6.8.55; G-AHDE (86113), EM919, 12.3.46, to Morocco 4.50 as F-OAGR; G-AHDF, EM981, 9.4.46, to Hong Kong 3.49 as VR-HEM; G-AHDG (85213), DE143, 1.5.46, sold in France 4.50; G-AHIZ, PG624, 1.5.46; G-AHKZ (83636), T7170, 27.10.47, d.b.r. at Baginton 26.7.50 in ground collision with Avian G-ACKE

G-AHLA (84103), T7726, 29.8.46, to Portugal 9.53 as CS-AAB; G-AHLB (82691), R4750, 16.7.46, to New Zealand 11.54 as ZK-BJN; G-AHLC (83822), T5892, 6.7.46, crashed at Fairoaks 22.8.48; G-AHLD (85111), T6864, 6.7.46, to New Zealand 7.50 as ZK-AUY; G-AHLP (83041), R5179, 6.6.46, crashed at Fairoaks 2.9.47; G-AHLR (83885), T7461, 28.6.46, to New Zealand 6.50 as ZK-AUU; G-AHLS (3799), N6462, 8.5.46, burned in hangar fire at Broxbourne 23.6.47; G-AHLT (82247), N9128, 14.5.47; G-AHME (84163), T7790, 5.7.46, withdrawn from use at Apethorpe 9.56; G-AHMF (83904), T7475, 13.7.46, burned in hangar fire at Broxbourne 23.6.47; G-AHMK (82077), N6807, to Holland 8.46 as PH-UAX; G-AHML (84316), T7963, 16.1.47, crashed at Sywell 13.6.48; G-AHMM, EM870, 9.8.46, crashed near Newport Pagnell 10.7.54; G-AHMN (82223), N6985, 19.8.46

W. A. Rollason Ltd.'s G-AFZF at Croydon in October 1955 after restoration ex W5014 and awaiting delivery to Germany as D-EDER.

G-AHNC (85881), DF132, 3.1.47, withdrawn from use 2.66; G-AHND (85142), T6913, 20.3.47, crashed near Biggin Hill 8.4.66; G-AHNX (83622), T7163, 21.6.46, crashed at Luton 30.5.48; G-AHNY (82172), N6928, 20.6.46, to spares at Lympne 9.48; G-AHPZ (83794), T7280, 4.11.46, to Ireland 1.52 as EI-AFJ; G-AHRC (83589), T6064, 28.3.47, ditched in Irish Sea 23.8.71; G-AHRL (84736), T6362, to New Zealand 1.52 as ZK-AZH; G-AHRM (3861), N6548, 14.8.46, d.b.r. landing at Fairoaks 18.8.58; G-AHRN (82553), T5841, 14.8.46, crashed near Newbury, Berks. 24.5.52; G-AHRR (85753), DE855, 7.10.47, to New Zealand 5.52 as ZK-BBH; G-AHRS (85035), T6748, 4.10.46, d.b.r. at Broxbourne 27.2.47; G-AHRT (84957), T6643, 14.1.47, to Kuala Lumpur 6.49 as VR-RBJ; G-AHRU (84258), T7883, 30.8.46, to India 2.49 as VT-DBZ; G-AHRV (82104), N6849, 1.11.46, to Denmark 9.68 as OY-DNR; G-AHRW (85189), T6980, 24.7.46, to Holland 12.50 as PH-NEB; G-AHRX (83669), T7359, 4.10.46, crashed at Kidlington 23.7.53

G-AHUB (86232), NL763, 9.7.46, to New Zealand 3.54 as ZK-BFM; G-AHUE (84240), T7868, 26.7.46, destroyed in air collision with glider at Meir 5.4.70; G-AHUO (83688), T7218, 7.9.48, crashed at Eastleigh 15.7.53; G-AHUP (84211), T7846, to Holland 12.46 as PH-UAU; G-AHUR (83856), T7452, to Holland 12.46 as PH-UAT; G-AHUS (85006), T6706, to Holland 12.46 as PH-UCC; G-AHUT (85506), DE526, 26.7.46, crashed near Woking 9.1.55, rebuilt for Germany 5.62 as D-EDIS; G-AHUV (3894), N6593, 18.10.46

G-AHVU (84728), T6313, 27.8.46, w.f.u. 6.61; G-AHVV (86123), EM929, 23.7.46, crashed at Lympne 12.12.71; G-AHVW (84626), T6178, 25.4.47, to New Zealand as spares 11.51; G-AHVX (86127), EM944, 17.7.46, to Indo-China 2.54 as F-OAPE; G-AHVY (83315), T5617, 12.8.46, crashed at Christchurch 12.10.58; G-AHVZ, NM113, 24.7.46, crashed at Hamble 26.11.47; G-AHWA (85711), DE813, 24.7.46, d.b.r. at Dusseldorf 7.8.53; G-AHWB (85710), DE812, 24.7.46, crashed near Winchester 24.4.55; G-AHWC (83880), T7456, 17.7.46, crashed at Old Warden 29.6.58; G-AHWE, NL995, 24.9.46, destroyed in ground collision with Auster J-1 G-AJIP at Exeter 24.7.55

G-AHXB (84114), T5978, 20.1.47, to New Zealand 2.54 as ZK-BFL; G-AHXC (85032), T6745, 19.9.46, crashed at Hatfield Park, Herts. 28.6.52; G-AHXD (85856), DE996, 29.11.46, crashed at St. Mellons, Mon. 24.7.49; G-AHXN (82339), N9244, 28.3.47, crashed at Caxton, Cambs. 22.4.62; G-AHXO, EM966, 31.7.46, crashed near Pulborough 16.1.47; G-AHYP (84487), T8195, 6.5.47, to France 8.50 as F-BDJM; G-AHYR (83639), T7173, to Holland 10.46 as PH-UCD; G-AHYS (82022), N6744, to Holland 10.46 as PH-UAV; G-AHYT (82076), N6806, 5.9.46, sold abroad 10.46; G-AHYU (83887), T5897, 5.9.46, to S. Rhodesian A/F 10.46 as SR-D1; G-AHYV (83398), T5683, 17.7.46, to India 2.49 as VT-DBF; G-AHZH (85903), DF154, 20.9.46, crashed at Portsmouth 24.3.57

G-AIAK (85130), T6901, to Holland 12.46 as PH-UAW; G-AIAL (83642), T7176, to Switzerland 9.46 as HB-UBE; G-AIAM (84259), T7884, to Holland 1.47 as PH-UCB; G-AIBN (84320), T7967, 3.10.46, to Ireland 11.65 as EI-AOP; G-AIDA (83311), T7030, 20.10.46, to Holland 8.52 as PH-UFF; G-AIDB (85839), DE979, 31.10.46, to Germany 11.57 as D-ECOF; G-AIDD (83224), T5491, 13.3.47, w.f.u. at Roborough 11.57; G-AIDP, NL697, burned in hangar fire at Broxbourne 23.6.47 before conversion; G-AIDR (83323), T5625, 14.11.47, to New Zealand 1.54 as ZK-BEF; G-AIDS (84546), T6055, 11.11.46, w.f.u. 8.62; G-AIDT (84717), T6302, 22.1.47, to Germany 10.57 as D-EJOM; G-AIDU (84485), T8193, burned in hangar fire at Broxbourne 23.6.47 before conversion; G-AIDV (83489), T5832, 5.12.46, given to Enfield A.T.C. 4.54; G-AIEL (3957), N6653, 2.8.47, crashed at Sherburn-in-Elmet 15.9.51

The Hampshire Aero Club's Tiger Moth G-AISR flying over Netley in 1947. (*E. J. Riding*)

G-AIHO (3383), G-ADJG, BB817, 26.6.47, crashed at Baginton 6.9.53; G-AIHP (84880), T6551, 30.4.47, sold in Pakistan 11.48; G-AIHR (84129), T7747, to S. Rhodesian A/F 10.46 as SR-D4; G-AIHS (84681), T6255, to S. Rhodesian A/F 10.46 as SR-D3; G-AIHT (85237), DE167, to India 2.49 as VT-DBE; G-AIIV (86211), NL730, 21.1.47, to Nigeria 8.49 as VR-NAE; G-AIIZ (84959), T6645, 7.2.47; G-AIJA (85520), DE553, 30.11.46, crashed at Sandown 22.8.57; G-AIJB (84734), T6319, to Holland 11.46 as PH-UDB; G-AIJC (3279), N5461, to Holland 11.46 as PH-UDA; G-AILR (83634), T7168, 13.12.46, burned in hangar fire at Broxbourne 23.6.47; G-AILS (84958), T6644, burned in hangar fire at Broxbourne 23.6.47 before conversion complete; G-AILT (85857), DE997, burned in hangar fire at Broxbourne 23.6.47 before certification

G-AINU (82330), N9213, 2.11.46, crashed at Boughton, Kent 23.5.48; G-AINV (82107), N6852, 3.9.47, to Pakistan 2.49 as AP-ACJ; G-AINW (83011), R5129, 28.1.47, to India 2.49 as VT-DBI; G-AINX (85764), DE879, not converted, to spares at Tollerton 1949; G-AINY (83812), T7416, 28.12.46, to New Zealand 2.52 as ZK-AYC; G-AIRI (3761), N5488, 3.7.51, stored at Sherburn-in-Elmet in 1970; G-AIRJ (84326), T7973, 30.4.47, w.f.u. at White Waltham 8.52; G-AIRK (82336), N9241, 15.4.48; G-AIRR (84086), T7692, 3.12.46, crashed at Newtownards 3.4.60; G-AISR (84559), T6068, 29.4.47, to Italy 2.65 as I-GIVI; G-AISY (82018), N6740, 9.1.47, to India 7.48 as VT-CZV; G-AISZ (83661), T7294, 2.5.47, to Ceylon 5.48 as VP-CBB

G-AITA (85859), DE999, 2.12.47, crashed at Ayot, Herts. 26.6.48; G-AITD (85617), DE676, 12.8.47, crashed near Yeadon 7.7.59; G-AITE (85202), DE132, 13.7.49, crashed at Speeton, Yorks. 15.8.52; G-AITH (85525), DE558, 19.6.47, crushed in hangar collapse at Taif, Saudi Arabia 2.4.49; G-AITI (84000), T7603, 2.7.47, sold in Saudi Arabia 10.50; G-AIVU (85244), DE174, 20.8.47, crashed at Woolsington 19.6.49; G-AIVV (85103), T6856, 4.6.47, damaged in forced landing near Grange-over-Sands 9.49; G-AIVW (83135), T5370, 11.12.46, first flown as seaplane 20.7.63; G-AIVZ (82291), N9180, 14.12.46, to New Zealand 3.53 as ZK-BCN; G-AIXD (82224), N6986, 27.10.47; G-AIXF (84956), T6642, 7.1.48, sold abroad 11.48; G-AIXG (85430), DE422, 10.6.47, crashed at Cranfield 3.11.51; G-AIXH (85652), DE722, 4.3.47, to Hong Kong 3.49 as VR-HEL; G-AIXI (83129), T5364, 10.6.47, scrapped after heavy landing at Cranfield 21.10.51; G-AIXJ (85434), DE426, 10.6.47, d.b.r. near Woburn, Beds. 14.5.50; G-AIXK, EM924, 7.1.48, sold abroad 11.48; G-AIXL (82999), R5117, 28.2.47, d.b.r. at

Portsmouth 21.6.55; G-AIZF (83412), T5697, 6.6.47, crashed at Gayton, Northants. 21.2.64

G-AJDU (82045), N6781, 7.1.48, to Pakistan 11.48 as AP-ALJ; G-AJHI, NL897, 7.5.47, d.b.r. in forced landing at Haddington, East Lothian 26.4.51; G-AJHN (85664), DE734, 22.5.47, burned out at Elstree 15.9.47; G-AJHR (85349), DE315, 7.6.47, to New Zealand 7.50; G-AJHS (82121), N6866, 12.5.47, stored at Farnborough in 1970; G-AJHT (83740), T7399, 23.3.49, to New Zealand 12.53 as ZK-BEE; G-AJHU (83900), T7471, 9.9.47; G-AJKD (233 Australian-built), A17-232, VH-AUU, 1.8.47, d.b.r. landing at Sutton Park, Birmingham 17.5.48; G-AJOA (83167), T5424, 14.5.47; G-AJTW (82203), N6965, 19.6.47, d.b.r. in forced landing at Little Warley, Essex 8.4.55; G-AJVE (85814), DE943, 25.4.49, crashed at Turnhouse 24.1.60; G-AJVF (83911), T5901, 3.4.48, sold abroad 11.51; G-AJVS (84257), T7882, registered 3.6.47, to Holland 7.47 as PH-UDC; G-AJXJ (DHP.26), to Holland 7.47 as PH-UDE; G-AJXM (3711), N5448, to Thai Navy 1.51 as No.4; G-AJXN (3915), N6614, to Thai Navy 2.51; G-AJXP (3938), N6634, to Thai Navy 2.51; G-AJXR (82457), N9387, to Thai Navy 2.51; G-AJXT (82816), R4899, to Thai Navy 2.51; G-AJYJ (84621), T6173, not converted, to spares at Croydon 12.50

G-AKCG (124 Australian-built), A17-127, VH-AVD, 15.8.47, sold in Saudi Arabia 10.50; G-AKCH (83043), R5181, VH-BDJ, 16.1.48, crashed near Stirling 29.8.57; G-AKCI (229 Australian-built), A17-228, VH-BDK, 30.8.48, dismantled at Perth 2.56; G-AKCL (85928), DF192, 28.1.49, to India 2.49 as VT-DCA; G-AKCM (83303), T5610, 19.2.48, sold abroad 10.50; G-AKEE (83645), T7179, to Ceylon 9.47 as VP-CAW, later CY-AAB; G-AKGF (85916), DF180, 23.3.48, crashed at Thruxton 28.7.62; G-AKGG (3959), N6655, 14.9.48, to Thai Navy 12.50 as No.1; G-AKGT (83095), R5236, 13.10.47, to India 2.49 as VT-DBB; G-AKGU (83588), T5852, 20.10.47, to India 1.49 as VT-DBK; G-AKIG (85888), DF139, 26.4.48, w.f.u. at Blackbushe 2.53; G-AKIY (82799), R4882, VH-AQZ, to Pakistan 5.49 as AP-ACK

G-AKMX (83474), T7089, reduced to spares at Broxbourne 4.49; G-AKTE (3848), N6535, 5.4.49, to Belgium 5.50 as OO-RMU; G-AKVY (85789), DE904, 26.6.48, to India 1.49 as VT-DBJ; G-AKWX (3739), N5471, 7.10.48, to Belgium 10.48 as OO-TMB; G-AKWY (83138), T5371, 17.8.48, crashed at Bembridge 30.5.50; G-AKWZ,

The Tiger Club's Sea Tiger G-AIVW moored on the River Deben during a refuelling stop at Waldringfield, Suffolk on 6 November 1971. (*A. J. Jackson*)

431

NL782, 13.10.48, scrapped at Barton 9.49; G-AKXA (85141), T6912, 11.8.48, crashed at Barton 8.10.49; G-AKXB (85754), DE856, 7.10.48, to Belgium 10.48 as OO-TMA; G-AKXC (82040), N6776, 27.7.48, to New Zealand 10.52 as ZK-BCE; G-AKXD (84136), T7749, 6.7.48, d.b.r. in forced landing in Lincolnshire 10.2.60; G-AKXE (82065), N6795, 12.7.51, to New Zealand 10.51 as ZK-BAI; G-AKXF (84742), T6368, to Belgium 3.50 as OO-AJM; G-AKXG (84572), T6105, 8.6.49, to Australia 10.57 as VH-KYA; G-AKXH (84568), T6101, 9.8.50, to New Zealand 9.50 as ZK-AVB; G-AKXO (83548), T7121, 16.7.49, crashed at Shoreham 13.3.64; G-AKXS (83512), T7105, 1.6.48; G-AKXU, NL776, to spares at Hamble 1948; G-AKXV (85648), DE718, to spares at Hamble 1948; G-AKXW (83820), T7441, scrapped unconverted at Barton 12.52

G-AKYL (225 Australian-built), A17-224, VH-BKV, to New Zealand 12.50 as ZK-AXT; G-AKYM (137 Australian-built), A17-140, VH-AUE, to New Zealand 12.50 as ZK-AXU; G-AKYN (85072), T6803, to spares at Croydon in 1949; G-AKYO (83899), T7470, 22.5.56, to Germany 6.56 as D-EMUT; G-AKYP (84068), T7679, 26.7.51, to Portuguese East Africa 8.51 as CR-LCN; G-AKYR (83022), R5140, 12.7.48, crashed near Stapleford 4.6.58; G-AKZK (83815), T7436, 26.8.48, to French Equatorial Africa 9.55 as F-OATP; G-AKZL (85750), DE852, 30.7.48, to Madagascar 10.55 as F-OASJ; G-AKZM (85909), DF173, 30.7.48, to New Zealand 10.53 as ZK-BES; G-AKZZ (84105), T7728, 4.4.51, in the sea off Bournemouth 6.6.53

G-ALAA, NL825, 17.4.51, sold abroad 7.51; G-ALAD (84711), T6296, 24.7.51, to New Zealand 2.52 as ZK-BAW; G-ALBD (84130), T7748, 23.12.48; G-ALFG (83038), R5176, 1.3.50, to Sweden 12.60 as SE-COT; G-ALGD (3819), N6482, 14.4.49, sold in France 9.49; G-ALGF (83127), T5362, burned out in crash landing at Twinholme, Kirkcudbrightshire 11.12.49; G-ALGX (83147), T5380, 22.4.49, crashed at Grennforth, Germany 2.3.54; G-ALIU (84623), T6175, 14.8.51, to Holland 10.51 as PH-UEY; G-ALIV (84673), T6247, to spares at Wolverhampton, reg'n. cancelled 4.53; G-ALIX (84576), T6109, 8.7.49, to Holland 4.56 as PH-NGO; G-ALIY (3951), N6647, 8.2.51, to French Equatorial Africa 8.51 as F-OAJS; G-ALIZ (82439), N9369, 19.8.49, to Ireland 9.49 as EI-AFI; G-ALJL (84726), T6311, 29.9.49, scrapped at Hamble 1.51; G-ALMV (3256), K4260, 6.11.52, to New Zealand 11.52 as ZK-BCD

G-ALNA (85061), T6774, 25.5.49; G-ALND (82308), N9191, 5.9.49; G-ALOX (82704), R4763, 23.12.49, d.b.r. at Wimbledon Common 31.7.54; G-ALRI (83350), T5672, 28.12.51, to New Zealand 2.52 as ZK-BAB; G-ALSE (85812), DE941, to Holland 5.49 as PH-UDX; G-ALSF (83157), T5414, to Holland 5.49 as PH-UDY; G-ALSG (83607), T7148, to Holland 5.49 as PH-UDZ; G-ALSH (85786), DE901, 22.7.49, crashed at Thruxton 6.8.60; G-ALTW (84177), T7799, 20.10.49; G-ALUC (83094), R5219, 29.7.49, d.b.r. landing at Baginton 4.2.61; G-ALVP (82711), R4770, 3.3.50, w.f.u. at Shoreham 2.61; G-ALWS (82413), N9326, not converted, to spares at Hamble 2.51; G-ALWT (85106), T6859, 12.4.50, to New Zealand 1.53 as ZK-BCF; G-ALWU (83717), T7227, 25.5.50, to Australia 11.55 as VH-BTC; G-ALWV (85973), EM742, not converted, to spares at Hamble 2.51; G-ALWW, NL932, 31.3.50; G-ALWZ (82245), N9126, 6.4.50, to New Zealand 6.50 as ZK-AUV; G-ALZA (83589), T5853, to New Zealand 9.53 as ZK-BAH; G-ALZI (84013), T7611, to New Zealand 11.51 as ZK-AZO

G-AMAJ (83256), T5537, 22.2.52, to New Zealand 9.53 as ZK-BAM; G-AMAR (82119), N6864, 31.8.50, to Switzerland 9.53 as HB-UBF; G-AMBB (85070), T6801, not converted, reg'n. cancelled in 1952; G-AMBD (8286 sic), 10.10.50, crashed at Le Touquet 24.6.55; G-AMBI, NL994, 1.8.50, d.b.r. in forced landing at Stourpaine, Dorset 14.2.61; G-AMBJ (84960), T6646, 16.6.50, to Pakistan 8.50 as AP-AEB; G-AMBK, NM115, 16.6.50, w.f.u. at Whitchurch, Bristol 10.54; G-AMBR (85447), DE451, to Ceylon 5.51 as VP-CBG, later CY-AAH; G-AMCK (84641), T6193, to Switzerland 5.51 as HB-UAC;

432

G-AMCL (84884), T6555, 10.8.50, to New Zealand 9.51 as ZK-AVC; G-AMCM (85295), DE249, 26.1.51, crashed at Somerton, Hants. 25.9.55; G-AMCN (84236), T7864, 13.3.52, crashed at Gosport 29.7.54

G-AMDF (83838), T7327, to Thai Navy 1.51 as No. 3; G-AMDI (85216), DE146, to Thai Navy 1.51 as No.2; G-AMDK (82207), N6969, to Thai Navy 10.50 as No.7; G-AMDL (82727), R4783, to Thai Navy 10.50; G-AMDM (82939), R5038, to Thai Navy 11.50; G-AMDP (3980), N6707, to New Zealand 1.51 as ZK-AXZ; G-AMDR (3708), N5445, to French Equatorial Africa 2.50 as F-OAIQ; G-AMDT (84564), T6097, 16.11.50, to Thai Navy 12.50 as No.8; G-AMDU (82057), N6787, Thai Navy 12.50; G-AMDV (83578), T7127, to Thai Navy 11.50 as No.13; G-AMDW (83479), T7094, to Thai Navy 12.50; G-AMDX (84173), T6025, to Thai Navy 11.50 as No.11; G-AMDY (85883), DF134, to Thai Navy 12.50

The Auckland Aero Club's ZK-BBB, originally G-ADOM operated by Airwork Ltd., Perth and impressed in 1940 as BB679, was restored briefly in 1952 as G-AMRC.
(*K. Meehan*)

G-AMEA (85315), DE269, to Denmark 2.51 as OY-ACD; G-AMEB (85667), DE737, to Thai Navy 2.51 as No.14; G-AMEC (86052), EM850, 18.6.51, to New Zealand 10.51 as ZK-BAJ; G-AMEE (82722), R4778, to Thai Navy 2.51; G-AMEF (85149), T6920, to Thai Navy 2.51; G-AMEG (84187), T7809, to Thai Navy 1.51; G-AMEH (83613), T7154, to Thai Navy 2.51; G-AMES (83424), T5703, 9.3.60, to the U.S.A. 4.66 as N5300; G-AMEX (83346), T5639, to New Zealand 5.51 as ZK-AYA; G-AMEY (85545), DE578, 17.11.50, crashed at Little Snoring 16.5.68, rebuilt as Rumpler C IV replica at Kirkbymoorside 1969; G-AMEZ (85828), DE957, 15.5.53, crashed at Verden-Scharnhorst, Germany 16.8.64; G-AMFA (83296), T5603, to Thai Navy 1.51; G-AMFB (84212), T6033, to Thai Navy 1.51; G-AMFC (3822), N6485, to Thai Navy 2.51; G-AMFD (85440), DE432, to Thai Navy 11.50; G-AMFE (83475), T7090, to Thai Navy 11.50; G-AMFF (82883), R4973, to Thai Navy 11.50; G-AMFG (84630), T6182, to Thai Navy 11.50; G-AMFH, NL824, to Thai Navy 11.50; G-AMFI (82377), N9276, to Thai Navy 11.50; G-AMFN (83454), T5819, 2.8.51, to New Zealand 8.54 as ZK-BJQ; G-AMFW (83557), T5845, 17.5.51, to New Zealand 9.51 as ZK-AZY; G-AMFX, NL827, to Belgium 1.51 as OO-AAS; G-AMFY (3986), N6713, to Thai Navy 1.51; G-AMFZ (84680), T6254, to Thai Navy 1.51

G-AMGA (82157), N6913, to Thai Navy 2.51; G-AMGB (82794), R4877, to Thai Navy 1.51; G-AMGC (83677), T7191, 15.10.53, d.b.r. near Hawarden 10.11.63; G-AMGZ, NM157, to New Zealand 5.51 as ZK-AYD; G-AMHA (85304), DE258, sold abroad 6.51; G-AMHF (83026), R5144, 22.3.51, crashed at Bovington, Dorset 26.10.63; G-AMHG, NM128, 22.3.51, w.f.u. at Portsmouth 7.54; G-AMHH (84275), T6045, to Thai Navy 2.51; G-AMHI (3700), G-AFGZ, BB759, 7.8.51, crashed at Petersfield 25.7.58; G-AMHL (84006), T7609, application for C. of A. cancelled 3.51; G-AMHN (3757), N5484, to French Equatorial Africa 5.51 as F-OAJQ; G-AMHO (84607), T6159, 19.6.51, to New Zealand 9.51 as ZK-AYI; G-AMHP (85326), DE280, 17.4.51, crashed at Thruxton 23.4.57; G-AMIE (84647), T6199, 22.9.51, d.b.r. in forced landing at Finedon, Northants. 30.9.51; G-AMIF (3841), N6528, 30.5.51, to French Equatorial Africa 8.51 as F-OAJR; G-AMIG (82405), N9318, to New Zealand 10.51 as ZK-AYM

The following Tiger Moths were registered to Short Bros. and Harland Ltd. in 1951 but were all dismantled at Portsmouth before civil conversion and their registrations cancelled 23.5.53: G-AMIJ (84702), T6287; G-AMIK (84709), T6294; G-AMIL (84930), T6616; G-AMIM (84953), T6639; G-AMIN (84986), T6686; G-AMIO (84135), T5984; G-AMIP (84053), T5963; G-AMIR (83591), T5855; G-AMIS (83347), T5669; G-AMIT (83257), T5538; G-AMIW (3996), N6723; G-AMIY (85128), T6899; G-AMIZ (85143), T6914; G-AMJA (85169), T6960; G-AMJB (85177), T6968; G-AMJC (84610), T6162

G-AMIU (83228), T5495, 23.8.51; G-AMIV (83111), R5246, 3.9.51, w.f.u. at Boxted 11.65; G-AMIX (85208), DE138, 9.3.54, to New Zealand 3.54 as ZK-BFA; G-AMJD (83728), T7238, 7.11.52, to Belgium 10.52 as OO-SOI; G-AMJF (84712), T6297, 3.7.51, d.b.r. landing at Dunstable 5.8.62; G-AMJG (84674), T6248, 4.6.51, to New Zealand 10.51 as ZK-AYS; G-AMJL (82070), N6800, 3.8.51, crashed near Woolsington 30.4.52; G-AMJN (85212), DE142, 23.5.52, to Germany 12.55 as D-EJIF; G-AMJO (84192), T6029, not converted, registration cancelled 1953; G-AMJR (85167), T6958, 18.9.51, to Finland 10.51 as OH-ELA; G-AMJS (84570), T6103, 28.9.51, to New Zealand 1.51 as ZK-AXW

G-AMKH (3554), L6921, 11.9.51, w.f.u. at Fairoaks 10.54; G-AMKI (84643), T6195, 15.8.51, to Ireland 3.52 as EI-AGC; G-AMKJ (85892), DF143, 28.11.51, to Finland 3.52 as OH-ELB; G-AMKN (84903), T6564, to New Zealand 12.51 as ZK-BAA; G-AMKO (84772), T6398, to New Zealand 8.51 as ZK-BBD; G-AMKP (84031), T5956, sold abroad 7.51; G-AMKR (84194), T6031, sold abroad 7.51; G-AMKV (84551), T6060, not converted, reg'n. cancelled in 1953; G-AMLA (83076), R5214, 2.10.51, to New Zealand 10.51 as ZK-BAP; G-AMLB (3724), G-AFJG, AX787, mispainted as AX791, not reconverted, scrapped at Wolverhampton 1953; G-AMLD (84723), T6308, 27.11.51, to New Zealand 9.51 as ZK-AZG; G-AMLE (84910), T6570, 23.1.52, to New Zealand 1.51 as ZK-AXX; G-AMLF, PG675, 21.5.52, sold in U.S.A. 7.71; G-AMLG (85686), DE772, 28.9.51, to New Zealand 9.51 as ZK-AZV; G-AMLH (85534), DE567, 29.1.52, crashed at Woolsington 14 11.53; G-AMLV (83754), T7244, not converted, scrapped at Gatwick 3.55

G-AMMF (85225), DE155, 3.3.52, to New Zealand 9.51 as ZK-AZW; G-AMMG (82793), R4876, 27.11.51, to New Zealand 11.51 as ZK-BAL; G-AMMH (83644), T7178, 7.1.52, to New Zealand 1.52 as ZK-BAK; G-AMMK (82524), N9497, 19.10.51, to New Zealand 10.51 as ZK-AYY; G-AMML (84134), T5893, 17.10.51, to New Zealand 10.51 as ZK-AYX; G-AMMN (83707), T7386, 9.10.52, to New Zealand 11.52 as ZK-BCB; G-AMMO (85151), T6942, 12.2.52, to New Zealand 12.52 as ZK-BAX; G-AMMP (85184), T6975, 24.6.52, to New Zealand 11.52 as ZK-BCA;

G-AMMT (84153), T6020, 5.12.51, to New Zealand 12.51 as ZK-AZP; G-AMMV (3985), N6712, 29.11.51, to New Zealand 12.51 as ZK-AZQ; G-AMMW (82215), N6977, 14.2.52, to New Zealand 3.52 as ZK-BBL; G-AMMX (83478), T7093, 19.3.52, to New Zealand 4.52 as ZK-BAN

G-AMND (85383), DE361, to New Zealand 1.52 as ZK-BAV; G-AMNE (84526), T8253, 30.5.52, to New Zealand 6.52 as ZK-BBK; G-AMNF (84648), T6200, 21.2.52, to New Zealand 3.52 as ZK-BAD; G-AMNG (84649), T6201, 23.1.52, to New Zealand 3.52 as ZK-BAC; G-AMNH, NM131, to New Zealand 4.52 as ZK-BAO; G-AMNN, NM137, 16.5.52, crashed at Redhill 27.5.64; G-AMNO (3709), N5446, 18.1.52, crashed at Turnhouse 24.3.57; G-AMNP (84775), T6401, to Malaya 4.52 as VR-RBY; G-AMOU (84695), T6269, 3.4.52, to Malaya 4.52 as VR-RBZ

G-AMPD (85874), DF125, 3.3.52, to New Zealand 4.52 as ZK-BAS; G-AMPM (86128), EM945, 21.3.52, to New Zealand 4.52 as ZK-BBF; G-AMPN (85829), DE969, 14.3.52, to New Zealand 4.52 as ZK-BBG; G-AMRC (3406), G-ADOM, BB679, 16.4.52, to New Zealand 5.52 as ZK-BBB; G-AMRD (3695), G-AFHT, BD142, 9.4.52, to New Zealand 5.52 as ZK-BBC; G-AMRH, NL979, to Belgium 5.52; G-AMRM (83209), T7016, to New Zealand 6.52 as ZK-BBI; G-AMSC (84676), T6250, 29.5.52, to Madagascar 5.52 as F-OAMB; G-AMSD (84738), T6364, 28.5.52, to Madagascar 5.52 as F-OAMC; G-AMSE (85005), T6705, 10.7.52, to Holland 8.52 as PH-UFG; G-AMSY (82205), N6967, 6.6.52, d.b.r. landing at Southend 6.11.55

G-AMTF (84207), T7842, 3.10.52, to New Zealand 10.52 as ZK-AVE; G-AMTG (3787), N6457, 5.9.52, to New Zealand 10.52 as ZK-BBW; G-AMTH (85325), DE279, 13.1.53, to New Zealand 1.53 as ZK-AVZ; G-AMTK (3982), N6709, 3.12.52, w.f.u. at Speke 5.66; G-AMTL (82592), G-AFWF, W6420, 23.7.52, to Belgium 1.53 as OO-SOF; G-AMTO (84655), T6229, 26.8.52, stored at Rush Green 1970; G-AMTP (84857), T6534, 29.8.52, to Belgium 10.52 as OO-ETP; G-AMTT (83420), T5699, 5.2.53, to New Zealand 3.53 as ZK-BCO; G-AMTU (82698), R4757, 21.8.53, to New Zealand 9.53 as ZK-BEJ; G-AMTV (3858), N6545, 26.9.52, to Belgium 10.52 as OO-SOE; G-AMTW (84730), T6315, 2.10.52, to Belgium 11.52 as OO-SOH; G-AMTX (83850), T7446, not converted as Tiger Moth, rebuilt 1958 as Thruxton Jackaroo G-APJV; G-AMTY (84256), T7781, reg'n. not used, converted in 1954 as G-ANNP; G-AMUA (84675), T6249, 9.9.52, to New Zealand 10.52 as ZK-BBQ; G-AMUB (3975), N6671, partially converted at Barton 1954, derelict at Squires Gate 1956; G-AMUO (84631), T6183, 10.10.52, to Holland 10.52 as PH-UFH; G-AMUY (85291), DE245, 7.11.52, to Belgium 11.52 as OO-SOD

G-AMVE (84581), T6114, 4.12.52, to New Zealand 1.53 as ZK-BCG; G-AMVF (84660), T6234, 17.4.57, to Australia 8.60 as VH-SCI; G-AMVG (84663), T6237, 24.7.53, to New Zealand 10.53 as ZK-BEY; G-AMVH (84671), T6245, 12.10.53, to New Zealand 11.53 as ZK-BEN; G-AMVI (85010), T6710, 12.10.53, to New Zealand 11.53 as ZK-BEP; G-AMVJ (83413), 4.6.53, to French Equatorial Africa 7.53 as F-OANB; G-AMVO (85547), DE580, 4.12.52, to New Zealand 1.53 as ZK-BCH; G-AMVS (82784), R4852, 22.12.52, to Belgium 1.53 as OO-SOJ; G-AMVX (82060), N6790, 7.5.53, scrapped 8.61

G-ANAY (83890), T5900, 27.8.53, burned out at Fairoaks 8.10.53; G-ANBT (83626), T7167, 19.10.53, to New Zealand 11.53 as ZK-BEC; G-ANBU (3882), G-AFNR, W7952, to Belgium 1.54 as OO-BYL; G-ANBV (3375), G-ADHV, BB735, 8.11.57, temporarily D-EHYB 2.58, derelict at Las Palmas 3.67; G-ANBW (83564), T5807, 5.2.54, to New Zealand 3.54 as ZK-BFF; G-ANBX (85644), DE714, 19.10.53, to New Zealand 11.53 as ZK-BEB; G-ANBY (86042), EM840, not converted, derelict at Hesketh Park, Southport 5.58; G-ANBZ (85621), DE680, 28.4.54, to the Saar 1.55 as SL-AAF;

G-ANCK (82301), N9184, to New Zealand 3.54 as ZK-BFC; G-ANCL (84596), T6126, 26.11.53, to New Zealand 12.53 as ZK-BFZ; G-ANCN (85521), DE744, sold in France 4.55; G-ANCP, NM155, 6.8.54, to New Zealand 9.54 as ZK-BJK; G-ANCR (86157), EM964, 19.3.54, to New Zealand 4.54 as ZK-BFW; G-ANCS (82824), R4907, 7.10.53, dismantled at Little Snoring 6.58; G-ANCT (85467), DE471, not converted, scrapped at Christchurch 1956; G-ANCU (84692), T6266, not converted, scrapped at Christchurch 1956; G-ANCV (85009), T6709, 31.8.55, crashed at South Fambridge, Essex 15.3.63; G-ANCW (84349), T7996, not converted, scrapped at Christchurch 1956; G-ANCX (83719), T7229, 6.10.53; G-ANCY (85234), DE164, 2.12.53, to Belgium 3.55 as OO-DLA; G-ANCZ (82588), G-AFSU, W7970, 24.2.54, crashed at Panshanger 16.1.59

G-ANDA (83768), T7269, 2.11.53, crashed near Fairoaks 21.3.67; G-ANDB (83343), T7035, 29.1.54, to New Zealand 2.54 as ZK-BFH; G-ANDC (82814), R4897, to Luxembourg 12.53 as LX-JON; G-ANDD (85668), DE738, 6.6.55, to No.2 R.C.A.F. G/C in France 8.56; G-ANDE (85957), EM726, 2.11.53; G-ANDF (85530), DE563, 9.5.54, crashed at Onslow, Surrey 5.7.55; G-ANDG (82472), N9402, 1.1.54, destroyed in take-off collision with Turbulent G-APBZ at Fairoaks 6.9.59; G-ANDH (3579), L6944, 27.11.53, crashed in Germany in 1954; G-ANDI (3946), N6642, 14.3.58, to the U.S.A. 12.70 as N40DH; G-ANDJ (82437), N9367, 30.3.54, d.b.r. in forced landing at Theale, Berks. 5.5.56; G-ANDK (83554), T5842, not converted, scrapped at White Waltham 3.56; G-ANDL (85339), DE305, 5.2.57, crashed near White Waltham 10.1.58; G-ANDM (82335), N9240, 4.3.54, to Ireland 11.56 as EI-AGP, rest. 8.65, to Ireland 4.66 as EI-AGP; G-ANDN (85882), DF133, 11.12.53, to Sweden 12.60 as SE-COY; G-ANDO (84841), T6500, 22.1.54, to Germany 3.55 as D-EBIC; G-ANDP (82868), R4960, 6.1.54, to Germany 2.55 as D-EBEC, rest. 12.63; G-ANDR (82089), N6840, 27.11.53, to Germany 3.55 as D-EGOH; G-ANDS, NL915, 19.10.53, to New Zealand 11.53 as ZK-BEA; G-ANDT, NL996, 14.10.53, to New Zealand 11.53 as ZK-BDZ; G-ANDV (83771), T7272, 26.2.54, d.b.r. on take-off from Wisley 5.6.66; G-ANDW (84739), T6365, not converted, reg'n. cancelled 10.54; G-ANDZ (85689), DE775, not converted, scrapped at Rochester in 1955

Note: Previous identities and constructor's numbers for G-ANDI and G-ANDM are as documented but they were, in fact, reversed during civil conversion.

G-ANEA (85611), DE670, 3.2.60, crashed near New Romney, Kent 24.6.60; G-ANEB (82326), N9209, 15.4.54, to Sweden 4.57 as SE-CGB; G-ANEC (86102), EM908, 29.4.57, crashed at Letterkenny, Donegal 21.6.60; G-ANED (82913), R5018, not converted, dismantled at Perth in 1956; G-ANEE (83161), 29.12.53, to Ireland 10.64 as EI-ANN; G-ANEF (83226), T5493, 17.5.60; G-ANEH (82067), N6797, 14.7.54, w.f.u. at Blackbushe 7.64; G-ANEI (82960), R5065, 28.1.55, sold in the U.S.A. 10.64; G-ANEJ (85597), DE638, 7.11.53, d.b.r. landing at Owstwick, Yorks. 15.5.65; G-ANEK (82303), N9186, 7.11.53, crashed at Frankfurt, Germany 10.3.54; G-ANEL (82333), N9238, 7.11.53; G-ANEM (82943), R5042, 14.11.53, to Ireland 3.54 as EI-AGN; G-ANEN (85418), DE410, to Belgium 10.53 as OO-ACG; G-ANEO (85549), DE582, to Ireland 1.54 as EI-AGL, rest. 6.58, crashed at Keston, Kent 16.4.61; G-ANER (82041), N6777, 26.2.54, crashed at Staverton 16.6.60; G-ANES (82911), R5016, 27.10.53, w.f.u. at Ipswich 10.54; G-ANEV (83813), T7417, 2.4.54, crashed at Pengam Moors, Cardiff 22.7.58; G-ANEW, NM138, 19.12.53, w.f.u. at Thruxton in 1962; G-ANEX (84541), T6050, 12.5.54, in the sea off Margate 3.9.54; G-ANEY (85964), EM733, 11.12.53, w.f.u. 12.59; G-ANEZ (84218), T7849, 30.12.53

P. W. Kennedy's EI-AGP flying at Weston, Leixlip in 1967 after its second spell in England as G-ANDM. (*G. Flood*)

G-ANFA (83825), T7297, 26.2.54, to New Zealand 4.54 as ZK-BGJ; G-ANFB (82032), N6754, 28.10.53, to New Zealand 2.54 as ZK-BFG; G-ANFC (85385), DE363, 14.5.54; G-ANFI (85577), DE623, 19.11.53; G-ANFJ (82822), R4905, 1.12.53, crashed at Walsgrave, Coventry 6.4.57; G-ANFK (84231), T7862, 6.11.53, crashed in 1957; G-ANFL (84617), T6169, 25.7.58, w.f.u. at Boxted 5.64; G-ANFM (83604), T5888, 25.4.58; G-ANFN (83375), T5678, 24.2.58, crashed at South Petherton, Somerset 17.6.60; G-ANFO, NL914, 25.10.57, crashed at Little Snoring 17.3.62; G-ANFP (82530), N9503, 16.1.59, to spares at Rush Green 6.63; G-ANFR (85299), DE253, 30.12.53, to Switzerland 5.54 as HB-UBF; G-ANFS (83569), T5812, 4.12.53, crashed near Port Talbot 22.12.53; G-ANFT (84206), T7841, 27.11.53, crashed in the Blue Nile, Sudan 6.11.60; G-ANFV (85904), DF155, 31.12.53; G-ANFW (3737), N5469, 29.5.54; G-ANFX (85238), DE168, 12.2.54, to the Cameroons 2.54 as F-OAPF; G-ANFY, NL906, 8.12.53, converted to Thruxton Jackaroo; G-ANFZ (82013), N6735, 2.5.55, to Belgium 4.56 as OO-ZAC

G-ANGD (83683), T7213, 12.3.54, to Germany 4.57 as D-EKAL; G-ANGJ (84771), T6397, 24.12.53, to New Zealand 1.54 as ZK-BEW; G-ANGT (83830), T7302, 24.12.53, to New Zealand 1.54 as ZK-BEX; G-ANGY (85314), DE268, not converted, reg'n. cancelled 7.56; G-ANGZ (85949), DF213, to France 8.55 as F-BHIX; G-ANHG (3763), N5490, to France 8.55 as F-BHIN; G-ANHH (3865), N6552, to France 6.54 as F-BHAN; G-ANHI (83002), R5120, 9.4.57, crashed at Lutterworth, Leics. 2.10.65; G-ANHJ (84230), T7861, to France 8.55 as F-BHIT; G-ANHK (82442), N9372, to France 8.55 as F-BHIM, rest. 10.69, C. of A. 4.3.70; G-ANIV (86109), EM915, 29.6.54, to New Zealand 7.54 as ZK-BGW; G-ANIW (85450), DE454, 29.6.54, to New Zealand 7.54 as ZK-BGV; G-ANIX (84764), T6390, 24.11.54, to Germany 11.55 as D-ELOM; G-ANIY (84137), T7750, 24.3.54, crashed at Doncaster 27.6.61; G-ANIZ (83896), T7467, 8.9.54, w.f.u. at Wyberton 11.62, to U.S.A. 12.67

G-ANJA (82459), N9389, 17.9.55; G-ANJD (84652), T6226, 2.10.54, crashed near Irmington, Devon 30.9.67; G-ANJE (82014), N6736, 1.8.58, crashed at Plymouth 27.2.60; G-ANJF (85802), DE931, 19.5.54, to Germany 1.56 as D-EMAX; G-ANJG (83875), T7349, to France 6.54 as F-BGZT; G-ANJH (85887), DF138, to France 5.54 as F-BGZX; G-ANJI (85099), T6830, to France 8.55 as F-BHIQ; G-ANJJ (84766), T6392,

Tiger Moth G-ANKW at Croydon in June 1954 while being prepared for delivery to France as F-BHAQ. (*A. J. Jackson*)

to France 8.55 as F-BHIC; G-ANJK (84557), T6066, 5.9.57; G-ANJL (84920), T6581, to France 6.54 as F-BHAM; G-ANJM (84078), T7684, to France 5.54 as F-BGZR; G-ANJN, NM133, to France 8.55 as F-BHIY; G-ANJO, NM203, to France 8.55 as F-BHIZ; G-ANJP (85783), DE898, to France 10.55 as F-BHIV; G-ANJW (85233), DE163, to France 6.54 as F-BGZS; G-ANJX (85585), DE631, not converted, destroyed by gale at Croydon 16.1.54; G-ANJY (86098), EM904, to France 6.54 as F-BHAO; G-ANJZ, NL693, to France 8.55 as F-BHIF

G-ANKA (3742), N5474, 8.2.60, to Italy 2.60 as I-LUNI; G-ANKB (82155), N6911, 30.1.58, shipped to Canada 3.72; G-ANKC (82163), N6919, to France 8.55 as F-BHIJ; G-ANKD (82289), N9178, to France 8.55 as F-BHIK; G-ANKE (84627), T6179, to France 8.55 as F-BHIP; G-ANKF (83803), T7289, to France 8.55 as F-BHIE; G-ANKG (86164), EM971, 12.3.54, crashed at Ipswich 11.9.58; G-ANKH (82323), N9206, 3.5.57, to Holland 9.57 as PH-NIG; G-ANKJ, NL929, 4.9.59, to Sweden 11.62 as SE-COO; G-ANKK (83590), T5854, 27.1.56; G-ANKL (85470), DE474, not converted, reg'n. cancelled 7.56; G-ANKM (3989), N6716, to France 6.54 as F-BGZV; G-ANKN (82700), R4759, 6.1.56, to Canada 8.57 as CF-JJI; G-ANKO (82995), R5113, to France 5.54 as F-BGZP; G-ANKP (83006), R5124, to France 8.55 as F-BHIB; G-ANKR (82114), N6859, not converted, reg'n. cancelled 9.56; G-ANKS (84659), T6233, to France 8.55 as F-BHIH; G-ANKT (85087), T6818, 1.6.56, w.f.u. 10.70; G-ANKU (85866), DF117, 27.3.54, crashed at Kilpadder, Co. Wicklow 10.8.65; G-ANKV (84166), T7793, not converted, reg'n. cancelled 9.56; G-ANKW (86101), EM907, to France 6.54 as F-BHAQ; G-ANKX (82438), N9368, to France 6.54 as F-BGZQ; G-ANKY (84110), T7733, 28.2.57, to Sweden 8.57 as SE-CGE; G-ANKZ (3803), N6466, to France 8.55 as F-BHIO

G-ANLA (83000), R5118, to France 8.55 as F-BHIG; G-ANLB (83857), T7453, 15.2.57, d.b.r. at Southam, Warwicks. 17.3.62; G-ANLC (85154), T6945, converted to Rumpler C V replica at Croydon in 1961; G-ANLD (85990), EM773, not converted, registration cancelled 7.56; G-ANLE, NM142, 19.7.56, w.f.u. 3.64; G-ANLG, NL777, 6.4.54, crashed at Luton 11.5.58; G-ANLH, PG637, 24.12.54, to Belgium 3.55 as OO-EVO; G-ANLP (85872), DF123, 2.8.55, crashed at Brookbridge, Worcs. 23.8.58; G-ANLR (82111), N6856, 22.9.58, crashed at Syderstone, Norfolk 23.4.66; G-ANLS

(85862), DF113, 30.9.57, to spares at Croydon 1970; G-ANLX (84165), T7792, 5.3.54, crashed at Luton 31.12.55

G-ANME (82866), R4958, 30.4.54, w.f.u. at Wolverhampton 5.62; G-ANMK (82440), N9370, 29.1.54, to Australia 11.55 as VH-BQM; G-ANML (84553), T6062, to France 8.55 as F-BHIR; G-ANMM (83552), T5840, to France 6.54 as F-BGZZ; G-ANMN (83299), T5606, to France 8.55 as F-BHIS; G-ANMO (3255), K4259, to France 8.55 as F-BHIU, rest. 6.70, crashed at Weston-super-Mare 30.7.72; G-ANMP (86126), EM943, 25.7.57, crashed in Langstone Harbour, Portsmouth 29.7.57; G-ANMR (84817), T6463, to France 5.54 as F-BGZN; G-ANMS (84876), T6547, not converted, to Australia 5.57 as VH-SCD; G-ANMT (85058), T6771, to France 5.54 as F-BGZO; G-ANMU (85132), T6903, 2.8.57, to Germany 8.57 as D-ECOR; G-ANMV (83745), T7404, to France 6.54 as F-BHAZ, rest. 12.67, C. of A. 2.4.69, destroyed in landing collision with Cessna F.150H G-AVTO at Swanton Morley 14.11.71; G-ANMW (82173), N6929, to France 6.54 as F-BHAX; G-ANMX (82433), N9346, to France 8.55 as F-BHIL; G-ANMY (85466), DE470, 8.8.57, to Belgium 8.57 as OO-SOC; G-ANMZ (85588), DE634, 2.9.60

G-ANNA (83598), T5882, 13.8.54, to Morocco 8.54 as F-OASE; G-ANNB (84233), T6037, 13.6.57, to Germany 8.57 as D-EGYN; G-ANNC (84569), T6102, 17.3.58, to Belgium 4.58 as OO-SOM; G-ANND (83689), T7219, to Sweden 10.62 as SE-CPW; G-ANNE (83814), T7814, 31.5.57, to Belgium 6.57 as OO-CCI; G-ANNF (83028), R5146, converted to Rumpler C V replica at Croydon in 1961; G-ANNG (85504), DE524, 16.10.57, w.f.u. 10.70; G-ANNH (83102), R5243, to Germany 10.57 as D-ECOB; G-ANNI (85162), T6953, 29.1.58, crashed at Yelden, Beds. 18.4.63; G-ANNJ (83764), T7265, to France 6.54 as F-BHAR; G-ANNK (83804), T7290, 3.7.57, to France 8.57 as F-BFDO, rest. 4.70, crashed near Banbury 13.2.72; G-ANNL (83826), T7299, 25.6.56, to Switzerland 1.57; G-ANNM (85148), T6919, to France 5.54 as F-BHAP; G-ANNN (84073), T5968, not converted, derelict at Southend in 1970; G-ANNP (84256), T7881, G-AMTY, 29.3.54, crashed at Munich 12.8.55; G-ANNR, NM182, 19.2.54, to New Zealand 2.54 as ZK-BFI; G-ANNS (85712), DE814, 19.2.54, to New Zealand 2.54 as ZK-BFJ; G-ANNU (86166), EM973, 9.3.54, to New Zealand 3.54 as ZK-BFB

G-ANOD (84588), T6121, 14.4.54, w.f.u. at Kidlington 2.60; G-ANOF, NL780, 30.6.55, crashed at Boxted 23.6.59; G-ANOG (83327), T7021, not converted, derelict at Panshanger in 1958; G-ANOH (86040), EM838, 23.7.56, to Denmark 6.69; G-ANOI (82864), R4956, not converted, believed scrapped at Panshanger 1954; G-ANOJ (86031), EM814, 5.12.55, to French Somaliland 12.55 as F-OAVT; G-ANOM (82086), N6837, 11.5.54, d.b.r. in taxying accident at Fairoaks 17.12.61; G-ANON (84270), T7909, 28.7.54; G-ANOO (85409), DE401, 14.5.54; G-ANOP (85446), DE450, 25.3.55, to Australia 4.55 as VH-BFW; G-ANOR (85635), DE694, 27.9.55, stored at Rochester 1972; G-ANOS (85461), DE465, 18.4.55, w.f.u. at Roborough 2.70, rest. 6.72; G-ANOT (84242), T7870, 13.5.54, to New Zealand 5.54 as ZK-BGD; G-ANOU (82862), 13.5.54, to New Zealand 5.54 as ZK-BFS; G-ANOX (84155), T6022, 25.3.54, to Spain 1.56 as EC-AMF; G-ANOY (84069), T7680, to France 6.54 as F-BHAS; G-ANOZ (3983), N6710, 27.8.54, crashed at Yeovil 17.8.56

G-ANPB (82485), N9431, 28.6.54, crashed near Fairoaks 24.7.57; G-ANPC (82858), R4950, 15.4.54, crashed near Loch Leven 2.1.67; G-ANPD, NM174, to France 6.54 as F-BHAU; G-ANPE (83738), T7397, to France 5.54 as F-BHAT, rest. 9.70; G-ANPF (82378), N9277, to France 7.55 as F-BHID; G-ANPI (85219), DE149, 16.3.56, crashed at Mursley, Bucks. 12.4.57; G-ANPJ (82503), N9449, not converted, see G-ANUL; G-ANPK (3571), L6936, 4.6.58, stored at Netheravon in 1970; G-ANPL (85624), DE683, 12.5.55, w.f.u. 4.64; G-ANPM (82322), N9205, 7.5.54, to Germany 10.56 as D-EGUR;

439

G-ANPN (82391), N9310, 17.5.54, to Germany 6.56 as D-ECUP; G-ANPO (85309), DE263, stored at Croydon as spares 1958; G-ANPS (83168), T5425, to France 6.54 as F-BHAY; G-ANPT (82536), N9509, to France 5.54 as F-BHAV; G-ANPU (86165), EM972, 20.2.56, crashed at Stapleford 31.3.56; G-ANPW (85557), DE603, to Australia as spares 12.55; G-ANPX (85378), DE356, not converted, to spares at Croydon 7.56; G-ANPY (85358), DE336, not converted, to spares at Croydon 1956; G-ANPZ (83145), T5378, 14.6.54, to New Zealand 6.54 as ZK-BFX

G-ANRA (83096), R5237, 19.5.54, to Sweden 4.57 as SE-CGC; G-ANRB (85487), DE507, 15.6.54, to New Zealand 6.54 as ZK-BFY; G-ANRD (3860), N6547, 6.12.54, crashed at Coolham, Sussex 20.4.58; G-ANRE (82106), N6851, 8.7.54, crashed in the S. Cameroons 12.9.57; G-ANRF (83748), T5850, 2.6.55; G-ANRH (86032), EM816, 8.9.55, crashed in the South Cameroons 29.11.57; G-ANRI (83036), R5174, 31.10.55, to Germany 10.55 as D-EGAL; G-ANRJ (85400), DE378, not converted, believed reduced to spares at Portsmouth in 1954; G-ANRK (85215), DE145, 29.6.56, to Germany 8.57 as D-ENOX; G-ANRL (84536), T8263, 8.9.55, w.f.u. 8.60; G-ANRM (85861), DF112, 15.12.54, w.f.u. 10.65; G-ANRN (83133), T5368, 23.5.56; G-ANRO (84281), T7917, 6.3.58, w.f.u. at Foulsham 9.61; G-ANRU (82036), N6772, 6.8.54, crashed near Morbihan, France 17.5.58; G-ANRV (82381), N9300, 11.6.54, scrapped 9.57; G-ANRW (86029), EM812, not converted, to Stapleford 1961 as spares; G-ANRX (3863), N6550, 5.11.55, w.f.u. at Boxted 6.61; G-ANRY (85240), DE170, 25.6.54, crashed at Croydon 3.1.57; G-ANRZ (83097), R5238, 6.7.54, to Belgium 7.54 as OO-SOG

The special, bespatted Tiger Moth coupé G-ANSA at White Waltham in 1955.

G-ANSA (82194), N6944, 13.5.55, crashed in River Mersey off Speke 30.3.58; G-ANSB (85328), DE282, 9.9.54, to Norway 9.54 as LN-BDN; G-ANSC (85294), DE248, 9.9.54, to Norway 9.54 as LN-BDM; G-ANSD (82229), N9116, not converted, reg'n. cancelled 10.56; G-ANSE (85738), DE840, 25.6.54, to Norway 6.54 as LN-BDO; G-ANSG (85569), DE615, 14.8.54, crashed at Caen, France 15.6.57; G-ANSH, NL873, 14.1.55, to Sweden 8.59 as SE-CHH; G-ANSI (86120), EM926, 12.11.54, to New Zealand 11.56 as ZK-BQF; G-ANSJ (85071), T6802, 14.12.54, to New Zealand 10.55 as ZK-BLV; G-ANSK (83740), T7399, 9.12.54, to New Zealand 10.55 as ZK-BKF; G-ANSL (84120), T7738, 4.11.54, to New Zealand 10.55 as ZK-BLQ; G-ANSM (82909), R5014, 20.3.55, to Torbay Aircraft Museum 1971; G-ANSN (85781), DE896, 21.3.56, crashed at Glan-y-Mor, North Wales 23.9.56; G-ANSP (85762), DE877, 24.12.54, to South Africa 2.70 as ZS-JVZ; G-ANSR (83861), T7335, 13.8.54, crashed in Studland Bay, Dorset 4.3.61; G-ANST (85826), DE955, 30.7.54, to New Zealand 8.54 as ZK-BGX; G-ANSU (85768), DE883, 30.7.54, to New Zealand 8.54 as ZK-BGY; G-ANSX (83610), to Holland 8.58 as PH-NIS

G-ANTA, NM146, 31.8.54, to French West Africa 9.54 as F-OASD; G-ANTE (84901), T6562, 24.11.55; G-ANTL (82844), R4974, 4.7.55, to Germany 8.56 as D-EHAG; G-ANTM (83329), T7023, 27.8.54, to Germany 4.56; G-ANTN (85878), DF129, 30.3.55, to New Zealand 5.55 as ZK-BLJ; G-ANTR (85676), DE746, 29.11.55, to Germany 11.56 as D-ECEB; G-ANTS (3845), N6532, not converted, reg'n. cancelled 11.54; G-ANTT (82462), N9392, 2.9.55, destroyed 5.56; G-ANTU (82489), N9435, 25.7.55, to Germany 1.60 as D-ENYG; G-ANTV (84589), T6122, 23.9.55, to Germany 11.55 as D-EKUR; G-ANTW (83580), T7129, 2.3.56, to Germany 4.56 as D-EGIT; G-ANUD (83435), T5714, 5.4.55, crashed at Fairoaks 29.7.60; G-ANUE (83757), T7247, 22.10.54, crashed near Stapleford 7.1.62; G-ANUF (84156), T7783, 29.10.54, w.f.u. at Roborough 8.55; G-ANUG (84523), T8250, 29.10.54, crashed near High Wycombe 17.9.55; G-ANUH (85410), DE402, 17.1.55, crashed at Kings Norton, Birmingham 16.6.59; G-ANUI (85532), DE565, 20.4.55, to Australia 4.55 as VH-BQN; G-ANUJ (85942), DF206, 24.11.55, crashed at Aslacton, Norfolk 18.11.61; G-ANUL (82503), N9449, 11.4.56, to Australia 1.57 as VH-RSF

G-ANVE (83223), T5490, 14.2.55, to Germany 3.56 as D-EBUN; G-ANVI (82028), N6750, 24.5.55, to Austria 7.55 as OE-AAF; G-ANVV (83098), R5239, to Belgium 1.55 as OO-ACI; G-ANXS (85623), DE682, 24.3.55, to Australia 4.55 as VH-BEY; G-ANXT (83110), R5251, 28.2.55, to Australia 3.55 as VH-BIC; G-ANXU (84646), T6198, 1.3.55, to Australia 3.55 as VH-BEW; G-ANYN (85083), T6814, 18.3.55, crashed at Le Touquet 30.7.60; G-ANYX (3888), N6587, 5.8.55, crashed at Thruxton 24.11.57; G-ANZR (82997), R5115, 9.9.55, to Germany 5.56 as D-EGER; G-ANZS (85082), T6813, 10.1.56, to Australia 11.59 as VH-DCH; G-ANZT (84176), T7798, 16.1.56, converted to Thruxton Jackaroo in 1957; G-ANZU (3583), L6938, 22.9.55, d.b.r. 5.70; G-ANZY (85242), DE172, 4.8.55, sold in Nigeria 8.57; G-ANZZ (85834), DE974, 9.2.56

G-AOAA (85908), DF159, 1.12.55; G-AOAB, NL911, 27.10.55, to Sweden 4.57 as SE-CGD; G-AOAC (82216), N6978, 21.7.55; G-AOAD (82533), N9506, 5.10.55, w.f.u. 6.60; G-AOAE (82015), N6737, 4.2.58, crashed at Tadcaster, Yorks. 21.1.59; G-AOAF (82812), R4895, 19.4.55, to New Zealand 5.55 as ZK-BLK; G-AOAH (85980), EM749, 14.11.55, to Australia 11.55 as VH-BTD; G-AOBH (84350), T7997, 2.6.55, w.f.u. at Cranwell 5.63; G-AOBJ (85830), DE970, 12.8.55, to Germany 8.55 as D-EBIG; G-AOBK (82152), N6908, 3.6.55, to Germany 9.55 as D-EKYN; G-AOBO (3810), N6473, 8.7.55; G-AOBP (82795), R4878, 2.6.55, to Germany 7.55 as D-EDIR; G-AOBR (85133), T6904, 23.5.55, to Germany 7.55 as D-EDAR; G-AOBS (84768), T6394, 9.3.56, to Holland 3.56 as PH-UFN; G-AOBT, PG701, 20.2.56, to Holland 2.56 as PH-UFO; G-AOBX (83653), T7187, 20.9.57, d.b.r. at Rochester 16.7.67; G-AOCG (83369), T7039, 1.7.55, to Australia 7.55 as VH-KYC; G-AOCS, NM156, TJ-AAG, registered 1956, believed abandoned at Amman, Jordan; G-AOCV (3974), N6670, 6.10.56; G-AOCW (83172), T5429, 30.8.56, to Germany 10.56 as D-ECEF; G-AOCX (84661), T6235, 20.8.56, to Sweden 8.57 as SE-CGI

G-AODR, NL799, 18.5.56, d.b.r. at Nympsfield 18.9.61; G-AODS (82942), R5041, 25.5.56, crashed at Sherburn 5.7.70; G-AODT (83109), R5250, 29.12.55; G-AODU (85835), DE975, 10.12.55, crashed 17.4.68, parts used in Slingsby Type 58 Rumpler C IV replica in 1969; G-AODW, NM185, 30.8.55, to Germany 3.56 as D-EMOR; G-AODX (83437), T5716, 20.8.56; G-AOEA (85436), DE428, 17.11.55, to Germany as D-EFYN but crashed at Ostend 6.12.55 during delivery; G-AOEB (83524), T5838, 28.9.55, to New

Zealand 11.55 as ZK-BNF; G-AOEC (82078), N6808, 28.9.55, to New Zealand 11.55 as ZK-BNG; G-AOED (83091), R5216, 25.5.56, to Germany 6.56 as D-EKIF; G-AOEE (84186), T7808, 2.3.56, to Germany 4.56 as D-EKUL; G-AOEF (85138), T6909, 9.1.56, to Germany 1.56 as D-EMUS; G-AOEG (83547), T7120, 19.6.59; G-AOEI (82196), N6946, 16.7.58; G-AOEL (82537), N9510, 28.10.55; G-AOEM (84554), T6063, 25.11.55, sold in Germany 12.55; G-AOES (84547), T6056, 7.9.56; G-AOET (85650), DE720, 1.2.61, crashed at Hardwick, Norfolk 23.7.65; G-AOEU, NL704, 17.4.56, to Germany 4.56 as D-EFYN (reallotted); G-AOEV (82765), R4833, to Germany 11.55 as D-EKUN; G-AOEW, NM211, 8.12.55, to Germany 11.55 as D-EDOR; G-AOEX, NM175, converted as Thruxton Jackaroo in 1957; G-AOEY (85899), DF150, converted as Thruxton Jackaroo in 1957; G-AOFB (83170), T5427, 6728M, 27.12.56, to French Equatorial Africa 12.56; G-AOFD (85930), DF194, 19.4.61, crashed at Tewin, Herts. 16.9.62; G-AOFG (84529), T8256, 17.11.56, to Australia 12.56 as VH-AWI; G-AOFH, 7043M, 12.10.56, crashed at Wolverhampton 20.10.57; G-AOFO (82120), N6865, 14.6.56, crashed at Tollerton 29.9.62; G-AOFP (84185), T7807, 28.5.56, to Germany 10.57 as D-EMEC; G-AOFR, NL913, 28.2.58, to Sweden 12.60 as SE-COX; G-AOGB (83140), T5373, 9.12.55, crashed at Uffington, Berks. 19.4.62; G-AOGI (85922), DF186, 29.12.55, to Belgium 12.55 as OO-SOA; G-AOGJ (83283), T7025, 16.1.56, to Belgium 1.56 as OO-SOB; G-AOGP (85586), DE632, to Malaya 5.56 as VR-RBQ; G-AOGR (84566), T6099, 20.7.56, to the Royal Navy 10.56 as XL714; G-AOGS (3815), N6478, 24.5.56, sold in Germany 2.71 as N82TM; G-AOGT (83594), T5878, 28.3.56, to Spain 5.56, scrapped at Madrid in British markings 1960; G-AOGY (82918), R5023, 11.4.56, to Australia 1.57 as VH-RSE

XL714, formerly G-AOGR, was one of four machines ferried to Gosport in temporary civil markings for overhaul by the Royal Navy in 1956.

G-AOHC (82591), G-AFWE, W6419, 13.4.56, crashed at Holywell, Flintshire 26.5.56; G-AOHY (3850), N6537, 22.3.56, used as spares 8.60; G-AOIK (85403), DE395, 3.9.56, to the Royal Navy 10.56 as XL715; G-AOIL (83673), T7363, 5.10.56, to the Royal Navy 10.56 as XL716; G-AOIM (83287), T7019, 7.12.56; G-AOIN (3964), N6660, 16.3.56, crashed at Wattisham 4.9.65; G-AOIO (82151), N6907, converted as Thruxton Jackaroo in 1958; G-AOIP (82706), R4765, 8.3.56, crashed near Fakenham 31.5.60; G-AOIR (82882), R4972, converted as Thruxton Jackaroo in 1958; G-AOIS (83034), R5172, 7.3.56; G-AOIT (83190), T5465, converted as Thruxton Jackaroo in

1958; G-AOIU (84615), T6167, 27.2.56, to Germany as spares 11.57; G-AOIV (85146), T6917, converted as Thruxton Jackaroo in 1958; G-AOIW (85147), T6918, converted as Thruxton Jackaroo in 1959; G-AOIX (83472), T7087, converted as Thruxton Jackaroo in 1958; G-AOJJ (85877), DF128, 4.5.56, crashed at Thruxton 9.11.63; G-AOJK (82813), R4896, 31.12.56, crashed near Shaftesbury 27.10.62; G-AOJX (3272), K4276, 29.5.56, to Belgium 6.56 as OO-EVS

G-AORA (3364), G-ADLV, BB750, 6.6.56, to Sweden 7.63 as SE-CWG; G-AORX (83866), T7340, 2.8.56, to Switzerland 8.56 as HB-UBB; G-AORY (85508), DE528, 12.10.56, to Sweden 5.57 as SE-CGA; G-AORZ (84122), T7740, 14.7.56, to New Caledonia 8.56 as F-OAZV; G-AOSD (83483), T5826, 3.8.56, crashed at Syerston 30.3.58; G-AOSM (84906), T6567, 27.7.56, crashed at Fishtoft, near Boston, Lincs. 30.1.60; G-AOUI (85374), DE352, 18.9.56, to Italy 2.65 as I-CEDI; G-AOUR, NL898, 14.3.57, crashed at Newtownards 6.6.65; G-AOUW (82356), N9255, 9.11.56, to France 1.57 as F-BDVJ; G-AOUX (3956), N6652, 2.11.56, to Switzerland 11.56 as HB-UBC; G-AOUY (3796), N6459, 10.1.57, crashed at Nelson, Glam. 24.5.62; G-AOUZ (85348), DE314, 22.3.57, to Ireland 5.57 as EI-AJP

G-AOXF (85454), DE458, 27.12.56, to French Morocco 1.57 as F-OBAK; G-AOXG (83805), T7291, 1.11.56, to the Royal Navy 5.57 as XL717; G-AOXJ (84542), T6051, 18.1.57, crashed at Bawdsey, Suffolk 22.4.60; G-AOXN (85958), EM727, 14.6.57, w.f.u. at Burnaston 6.59; G-AOXS (85425), DE417, 1.3.57, crashed near Reigate Heath 28.2.60; G-AOXX (84797), T6443, 11.4.58, scrapped at Rochester 7.60; G-AOXY (84762), T6388, 21.2.58, crashed at Cheltenham 6.7.59; G-AOYU (82270), N9151, 25.9.58; G-AOZB (3917), N6616, 13.5.57; G-AOZC (84635), T6187, 18.4.57, to Holland 9.57 as PH-EAA; G-AOZH, NM129, 4.7.57

G-APAI (85838), DE978, converted as Thruxton Jackaroo 1958; G-APAJ (83314), T5616, converted as Thruxton Jackaroo 1958; G-APAK (84286), T7922, used as spares at Thruxton 1962; G-APAL (82102), N6847, converted as Thruxton Jackaroo 1959; G-APAM (3874), N6580, converted as Thruxton Jackaroo 1959; G-APAO (82845), R4922, converted as Thruxton Jackaroo 1959; G-APAP (83018), R5136, converted as Thruxton Jackaroo 1959; G-APAW (85263), DE206, 30.9.57, crashed at Redhill 20.12.59; G-APAX (3813), N6476, 17.6.57, to Switzerland 8.57 as HB-UBF; G-APAY (85200), T6991, 20.5.57, to Italy 8.60 as I-SUDD; G-APBI (86097), EM903, 1.11.57; G-APBY (82166), N6922, 24.7.57, to Belgium 7.57 as OO-SOK; G-APCC, PG640, 3.7.57, stored at Compton Abbas 1970; G-APCU (82535), N9508, 6.6.58; G-APDZ (83699), T7369, 24.4.58, crashed at Little Snoring 12.5.60

G-APFS (3741), N5473, 5.3.58, crashed near Wickham Market, Suffolk 4.7.63; G-APFT (83584), T7145, 22.11.57, to Holland 11.57 as PH-NIK; G-APFU (86081), EM879, 10.4.58, crashed at Denham 26.12.68; G-APFX (82353), N9252, 19.12.57, crashed in Langstone Harbour, Portsmouth 29.4.58; G-APGL, NM140, not converted, stored at Kirkham, Lancs. 1.58; G-APHZ (82168), N6924, converted as Thruxton Jackaroo 1958; G-APIG (84882), T6553, 30.1.58; G-APIH (82981), R5086, 2.1.58, to Germany 4.58 as D-EMEX; G-APIO (84005), T7608, not converted, scrapped at Fairoaks 1959; G-APIP (83555), T5843, 31.7.58, crashed at Hayes Common, Kent 28.7.63

G-APJK, NL760, 25.6.58, to Italy 3.59 as I-RIBI; G-APJL (85642), DE712, 21.10.58, to the U.S.A. 7.69 as N126B; G-APJO, NM126, 28.3.58, crashed at Ross-on-Wye 5.8.58; G-APJP (82869), R4961, G-AOCV ntu, 15.3.58, w.f.u. at Christchurch 6.62, to spares at Boxted; G-APJR (83712), T7391, 18.12.57, crashed at Princethorpe, Warks. 28.5.61; G-APJV (83850), N7446, G-AMTX ntu, converted as Thruxton Jackaroo 1958; G-APKE, NL989, 22.5.58, crashed at Rearsby 22.8.64; G-APLB (86099), EM905, 1.5.58,

G-APJL in R.A.F. training yellow with Tiger Club rudder badge at Boulder, Colorado as N126B in June 1970 after an immaculate rebuild by Rollasons at Croydon. (*H. B. Adams*)

in the sea off Bembridge 8.5.58; G-APLC (3277), K4281, 1.5.58, crashed near Sherborne, Dorset 15.7.60; G-APLI (85593), DE639, 21.4.60, to Sweden 6.60 as SE-COG; G-APLR (84682), T6256, 30.7.58, to Italy 8.58 as I-JENA; G-APLU (85094), T6825, 2.7.58, to French Somaliland 8.58 as F-OBKK; G-APLV, PG653, 16.4.59, to Italy 4.59 as I-RIBU; G-APMM (85427), DE419, 1.1.62, damaged on take-off at Boscombe Down 11.6.63; G-APMX (85645), DE715, 18.7.58

G-APOC (85496), DE516, 7.11.58, to Italy 11.58 as I-PUMA; G-APOG (82499), N9445, 27.2.59, to Switzerland 2.59 as HB-UBH; G-APOU (85867), DF118, 22.5.59, to Sweden 5.59 as SE-CHG; G-APOV (83012), R5130, converted as Rollason Jackaroo 1960; G-APPB (82062), N6792, 17.12.58, crashed at St Lawrence Bay, Essex 21.2.64; G-APPN (83839), T7328, 3.9.59, crashed at Mendlesham, Suffolk 14.7.64; G-APPT (84567), T6100, to Belgium 11.58 as OO-SOW; G-APRA (85347), DE313, 27.4.59, crashed near Moynalty, Co. Meath 23.3.63; G-APRB (3971), N6667, intended as Thruxton Jackaroo, conversion abandoned 1962; G-APRC (84489), T8197, intended as Thruxton Jackaroo, conversion abandoned 1962; G-APRG (82332), N9215, 24.2.59, to Finland 9.60 as OH-ELC; G-APRX (85302), DE256, 13.4.59, crashed at Compton Abbas 6.10.68; G-APRY (85482), DE486, 22.5.59, to Italy 5.59 as I-BANG; G-APSS (84653), T6227, 20.4.59, w.f.u. 6.66; G-APSU (3879), N6585, intended as Thruxton Jackaroo, conversion abandoned 1962; G-APSV (85590), DE636, intended as Thruxton Jackaroo, conversion abandoned 1962; G-APTI (82783), R4851, 16.5.60, crashed at Vinon, France 17.8.63; G-APTV (83790), T7276, 12.6.59, to Italy 7.59 as I-MOMI

G-APVP (85758), DE873, 3.9.59, crashed at Ellingham, Norfolk 21.7.68, rest. 5.72; G-APVT (3250), K4254, 25.9.59, crashed at Swanton Morley 21.5.67, rest. 5.72; G-ARAZ (82867), R4959, 6.4.60; G-AREH (85278), DE241, 22.12.60, stored at Usworth in 1966; G-ARMS (85698), DE784, 12.5.61, crashed at George, South Africa 27.5.61; G-ARTL (83795), T7281, AP-AEV, 25.5.63; G-ASES, NM145, not converted, stored at Croydon in 1972; G-ASET, NL775, 9.2.72, shipped to Canada 3.72; G-ASKP (3889), N6588, 26.6.64; G-ASPV (84167), T7794, not converted, registration cancelled 3.69; G-ASPZ (83666), T7356, D-EDUM, 29.10.64, w.f.u. at Geilenkirchen, Germany 9.69; G-ASSC (82720), R4776, 5.6.64, sold in the U.S.A. 9.71; G-ASXB (3852), N6539, 7152M, 21.4.66; G-ATWI (83741), T7400, F-BGZY, not imported; G-AVPJ, NL879, 1.8.67, d.b.r. 6.70

G-AXAN (85951), EM720, F-BDMM, 15.4.69; G-AXBW (83595), T5879, 6854M, 2.7.71; G-AXBZ, PG643, F-BGDF, 5.8.71; G-AXTY (85970), EM739, F-BDMP, 16.2.71; G-AXWM, NM193, F-BGCK, to the U.S.A. 12.70 as N5984; G-AXXE, PG626, F-BGDD, 6.5.70; G-AXXV (85852), DE992, F-BGJI, 2.7.70; G-AYDI (85910), DF174, F-BDOE, 21.9.70; G-AYHU, NL875, F-BGEU, to the U.S.A. 11.70 as N5050C; G-AYIT, NL896, F-BGEZ, 8.3.71; G-AYJV, NM136, F-BDOC, 16.7.71; G-AYKC (85729), DE831, F-BGEO, 27.10.70; G-AYUX, PG651, F-BDOQ, awaiting conversion in 1972; G-AYVH, PG735, F-BGEG, to Germany 5.71 as N45TM; G-AYVY, PG617, F-BGCZ, awaiting conversion in 1972; G-AZDY, PG650, F-BGDJ, awaiting conversion in 1972; G-AZGZ, NM181, F-BGCF, awaiting conversion in 1972; G-AZZZ, NL864, F-BGJE, registered 27.7.72; G-BABA, PG687, F-BGDT, registered 11.8.72

de Havilland D.H.83 Fox Moth

G-ABUO   (4000), 20.5.32, de Havilland Aircraft Co. Ltd., Stag Lane; first flown 29.1.32; to Canadian Airways Ltd. 1.33 as CF-API; scrapped in 1950

G-ABUP   (4001), 17.6.32, Aviation Tours Ltd., crashed in 1934

G-ABUT   (4002), 28.6.32, W. L. Hope; Surrey Flying Services Ltd., Croydon 9.32; impressed 4.40 as X9304; scrapped 11.41

G-ABVI   (4004), 17.6.32, Hillman's Airways Ltd., Maylands; Essex Aero Ltd., Maylands 7.36; burned out in hangar fire due to enemy bombing 6.2.40

G-ABVJ   (4006), 24.6.32, Hillman's Airways Ltd., Maylands; Eastern Air Transport Ltd., Skegness 4.33; Midland Airways Ltd., Sywell 9.35; d.b.f. 1937

G-ABVK   (4005), 23.6.32, Hillman's Airways Ltd., Maylands; British Airways Ltd., Stapleford 1.36; L. Lipton, Stapleford 4.36; Pines Airways Ltd., Porthcawl, 2.39; impressed 12.39 as X2867; scrapped 8.41

G-ABWB   (4007), 5.7.32, de Havilland Aircraft Co. Ltd.; Blackburn Aircraft Ltd., Grimsby 1.37; G. H. Jackson, Eastleigh 3.38; to India 12.38 as VT-AKV

G-ABWD   (4009), 27.7.32, de Havilland Aircraft Co. Ltd., Stag Lane; sold in Switzerland to Marcel Genens 7.32 as CH-344

G-ABWF   (4008), 8.7.32, Scottish Motor Traction Co. Ltd., Renfrew; crashed at Haslingden, near Bury, Lancs. during forced landing 31.1.33

G-ABXS   (4015), 7.9.32, H. G. Travers, Stag Lane; P. A. Wills, Stag Lane 1.33; to Australia 8.35 as VH-UVL; R.A.A.F. impressment 10.42 as A41-2

G-ABYO   (4012), 16.8.32, de Havilland Aircraft Co. Ltd., Stag Lane; Norman Edgar, Whitchurch, Bristol 1.33; crashed at Caerwent, Mon. 16.6.34

G-ABYR   (4017), 22.11.32, de Havilland Aircraft Co. Ltd., Stag Lane; to de Havilland Aircraft Pty. Ltd., Sydney 11.32 as VH-UQR; destroyed by Japanese 1942

G-ABZA   (4014), 30.8.32, T. G. Mapplebeck, Belgrade; re-registered in Jugoslavia 9.32 as UN-SAK, later YU-SAK

G-ABZD   (4026), 27.10.32, de Havilland Aircraft Co. Ltd., Stag Lane; sold in the United States 12.32 as NC12739, later N12739

G-ABZM   (4018), 23.9.32, de Havilland Aircraft Co. Ltd.; left Heston for Oslo 23.1.33, pilot W. Omsted; wing washed up on Norwegian coast 2.2.33

G-ABZN   (4022), 1.11.32, Airwork Ltd., Heston; to Misr Airwork Ltd., Cairo 3.33 as SU-ABA; rest. to Airwork Ltd. 7.35; to Sweden 9.36 as SE-AFL

G-ACAJ   (4033), registered 19.11.32 to Flt. Lt. E. H. Fielden, Hendon; registration cancelled 6.12.32 in favour of double letter sequence G-ACDD q.v.

G-ACBO   (4036), 17.1.33, Mrs. E. J. Richardson, Stag Lane; sold in Kenya 5.35 as VP-KBH; to Southern Rhodesia 2.37 as VP-YBM

The Royal Fox Moth G-ACDD with coupé top and spats, flying near Stag Lane in 1933.
(*Flight*)

G-ACBZ (4040), 2.2.33, Midland & Scottish Air Ferries Ltd., Renfrew; to Australia 12.36 as VH-UZD; crashed at Tapini, New Guinea 3.10.49

G-ACCA (4041), 2.2.33, Hon. Brian Lewis, Heston; Portsmouth, Southsea & I.O.W. Aviation Ltd., Portsmouth 9.33; to Australia 6.35 as VH-UTY

G-ACCB (4042), 10.2.33, Midland & Scottish Air Ferries Ltd., Renfrew; Giro Aviation Ltd., Southport 1.36; ditched at Southport 25.9.56

G-ACCF (4046), 23.2.33, C. W. A. Scott; Provincial Airways Ltd., Croydon 11.33; British A/T Ltd., Redhill 5.36; impressed 8.41, no serial

G-ACCS (4044), 8.2.33, Mount Everest Flight Expedition, Heston; to Australia 8.36 as VH-UUS; R.A.A.F. impressment 7.43 as A41-3

G-ACCT (4047), 7.3.33, Midland & Scottish Air Ferries Ltd., Renfrew; West of Scotland Air Services Ltd., Renfrew 8.35; to Australia 11.37 as VH-ABU

G-ACCU (4048), 3.3.33, Midland & Scottish Air Ferries Ltd., Renfrew; to Australia 12.36 as VH-UZC; R.A.A.F. impressment 7.43 as A41-4

G-ACDD (4033), G-ACAJ, 17.12.32, Flt. Lt. E. H. Fielden, Hendon on behalf of H.R.H. Prince of Wales; sold in Belgium 7.35 as OO-ENC; to New Zealand 1.36 as ZK-AEK; to Fiji as VQ-FAT; w.f.u. at Nausori 1960

G-ACDZ (4054), 28.3.33, Scottish Motor Traction Co. Ltd., Renfrew; West of Scotland Air Services Ltd., Renfrew 11.34; Border Flying Club Ltd., Carlisle 5.38; impressed 12.39 as X2865; scrapped 8.41

G-ACEA (4055), 30.3.33, Scottish Motor Traction Co. Ltd., Renfrew; Sussex Aero Club, Wilmington 6.36; Sandown & Shanklin F/S, Lea 7.36; Isle of Wight Flying Club 7.39; impressed 6.40 as AW124; scrapped 4.44

G-ACEB (4058), 13.4.33, Scottish Motor Traction Co. Ltd., Renfrew; Southend Flying Services Ltd. 6.34; to Australia 7.35 as VH-USJ

G-ACEC (4059), 13.4.33, Scottish Motor Traction Co. Ltd., Renfrew; West of Scotland Air Services Ltd., Renfrew 4.35; to Australia 4.37 as VH-AAX

G-ACED (4064), 6.5.33, Scottish Motor Traction Co. Ltd., Renfrew; Northern & Scottish Airways Ltd., Renfrew 7.35; to Australia 3.37 as VH-UZL

G-ACEE (4065), 6.5.33, Scottish Motor Traction Co. Ltd., Renfrew; crashed while joyriding at Riverside Park, Dundee, Angus 31.7.34

G-ACEI (4068), 27.5.33, Scottish Motor Traction Co. Ltd., Renfrew; crashed at Alva, Clackmannanshire 1.7.33 and burned out

G-ACEJ   (4069), 30.5.33, Scottish Motor Traction Co. Ltd., Renfrew; Giro Aviation Co. Ltd., Southport 7.36; N. H. Jones (The Tiger Club), Redhill 6.66

G-ACEX   (4056), 7.4.33, National Aviation Day Ltd., Ford; Provincial Airways Ltd., Croydon 5.34; Pines Airways Ltd., Porthcawl 4.36; impressed 12.39 as X2866; overturned and beyond repair landing at Wroughton 6.4.41

G-ACEY   (4057), 7.4.33, National Aviation Day Ltd., Ford; Provincial Airways Ltd., 5.34; Crilly A/W Ltd., Braunstone 4.35; burned out, Hooton 8.7.40

G-ACFC   (4053), 24.3.33, Blackpool & West Coast A/S Ltd.; Olley Air Service Ltd., Croydon 1.36; Gt. Western & Southern Air Lines Ltd., Shoreham 9.38; impressed 5.40 as AX859; later to instructional airframe as 2583M

G-ACFF   (4060), 22.4.33, Blackpool & West Coast A/S Ltd.; Gt. Western & Southern Air Lines Ltd., Shoreham 7.39; impressed 4.40 as X9305, later 2613M

G-ACGB   (4062), 29.4.33, H. W. Noble, Heston; to India 3.35 as VT-AGI

G-ACGN   (4063), 18.5.33, Gravesend Aviation Ltd., Gravesend; L. J. Rimmer, Hooton 8.35; to Australia 11.35 as VH-UDD; destroyed by Japanese 1942

G-ACGW   (4067), 27.5.33, C. Lloyd; crashed and burned out in Jersey 1.10.33

G-ACID   (4039), D-3408, 17.2.33, L. Ingram, Heston; to Australia 1.35 as VH-UTF

G-ACIG   (4072), 12.7.33, Portsmouth, Southsea & I.O.W. Aviation Ltd.; impressed 3.40 as X9299; instructional airframe with A.T.C. at Hampstead to 1946

G-ACIY   (4077), 17.8.33, Brooklands Aviation Ltd.; H. Deterding, Sywell 8.34; impressed 6.41 as DZ213 for Royal Navy, Lee-on-Solent

G-ACKZ   (4083), 7.11.33, P. L. Palmer; to India 1.38 as VT-AJW

G-ACRK   (4090), E-10, 11.7.34, interchangeable float u/c for John Grierson's U.K.–Canada flight; to Australia 5.35 as VH-UBB; destroyed by Japanese 1942

G-ACRU   (4089), 11.7.34, British Graham Land Expedition; to Australia 4.38 as VH-AAZ

G-ACSW   (4091), 14.6.34, H. F. Broadbent; to India 1.35 as VT-AFT

G-ADNF   (4024), SU-ABG, 3.11.32, C. T. Berry, Hunstanton; to Australia 10.38 as VH-ABQ; destroyed by Japanese 1942

G-AEPB   (134, origin not known), registered 5.11.36 to Essex Aero Club, Stapleford; not certificated; registration cancelled 'sold abroad' 11.38

G-AFKI   (4003), EI-AAP, 15.7.32, H. G. Aitcheson, Croydon, later Shoreham; impressed 8.41, no serial, no record of service

G-AOJH   (FM.42), AP-ABO, 26.3.59, H. Paterson, Barton; J. S. Lewery, Squires Gate 6.63

de Havilland D.H.84 Dragon 1

G-ACAN   (6000), E-9, 16.12.32, Hillman's Airways Ltd. 'Maylands'; Aberdeen Airways Ltd., Dyce 'The Starling' 9.34; crashed near Dunbeath 21.5.41

G-ACAO   (6001), 3.2.33, Hillman's Airways Ltd. 'Goodmayes'; Lady Apsley, Whitchurch 10.35; Western Airways Ltd. 7.38; impressed 4.40 as X9398

G-ACAP   (6002), 9.2.33, Hillman's Airways Ltd., Maylands; Commercial Air Hire Ltd., Croydon 2.36; fatal night crash at Lyndhurst, Hants. 26.3.36

G-ACBW   (6009), 13.4.33, Hillman's Airways Ltd., Maylands; Provincial Airways Ltd., Croydon 7.34 'Neptune'; Air Dispatch Ltd., Cardiff 11.39, impressed 10.40 as BS816 for No.6 A.A.C.U., Ringway; scrapped 10.41

G-ACCE   (6010), 21.4.33, Hon. Brian Lewis, Heston; leased to Highland Airways Ltd., Inverness; crashed on take-off from Kirkwall 29.8.34

G-ACCR (6011), 3.4.33, W. A. Rollason, Croydon; Barnstaple & N. Devon A/S 10.33; Commercial Air Hire Ltd. 12.34, in Channel off French coast 22.1.36

G-ACCV (6014), 2.6.33, Mrs. J. A. Mollison, Stag Lane 'Seafarer'; crashed at Bridgeport, Conn., U.S.A. 23.7.33 at end of transatlantic flight

G-ACCZ (6015), 11.5.33, Midland & Scottish Air Ferries Ltd., Renfrew; Crilly Airways Ltd., Leicester 5.35; Air Dispatch Ltd., Cardiff 6.40; impressed 7.40 as AW154; scrapped at West Hartlepool Tech. College 12.42

G-ACDL (6016), 12.5.33, Midland & Scottish Air Ferries Ltd.; Provincial A/W Ltd., Croydon 9.34; Luxury Air Tours Ltd. 6.36; sold abroad 8.36

G-ACDM (6017), 18.5.33, Scottish Motor Traction Co. Ltd., Renfrew; to South Africa 11.33 as ZS-AEI; S.A.A.F. impressment 1940 as '1570'

G-ACDN (6018), 29.5.33, Scottish Motor Traction Co. Ltd.; Crilly A/W Ltd. 5.35; Commercial Air Hire Ltd., Croydon 5.37; impressed 7.40 as AW170

G-ACEK (6019), 11.5.33, W. L. Everard, Ratcliffe 'Leic. Vixen II'; Olley A/S Ltd., Croydon 6.36; Commercial Air Hire Ltd. 8.39; impressed 7.40 as AX867

G-ACET (6021), 3.6.33, Scottish Motor Traction Co. Ltd.; Highland Airways Ltd., Inverness 5.35; Air Dispatch Ltd., Cardiff 2.40; impressed 7.40 as AW171

G-ACEU (6022), 10.5.33, Hillman's Airways Ltd. 'Brentwood'; Airwork Ltd., Heston 1.36; sold abroad 3.37

G-ACEV (6023), 12.6.33, Hillman's Airways Ltd. 'Ilford'; Airwork Ltd., Heston 1.36; sold abroad 8.36

G-ACFG (6027), 28.6.33, de Havilland Aircraft Co. Ltd.; Northern & Scottish Airways Ltd., Renfrew 12.34; sold abroad 2.37

G-ACGG (6025), 6.6.33, Flt. Lt. E. H. Fielden, Hendon (Royal Flight); R. O. Shuttleworth, Old Warden 2.35; L. H. Stace, Heston 4.36; to Australia 12.37 as VH-AAC; R.A.A.F. impressment 4.41 as A34-10

G-ACGK (6033), 30.6.33, E. C. Gordon England, Hanworth; Highland Airways Ltd., Inverness 7.34; ditched off Inverness 8.1.35

G-ACGU (6034), 28.6.33, Blackpool and West Coast Air Services Ltd., Squires Gate; burned out in take-off crash at Heston 16.7.35

G-ACHV (6035), 4.7.33, Anglo Persian Oil Co. Ltd., Abadan; Railway Air Services Ltd. 8.35; Air Taxis Ltd., Croydon 12.38; impressed 3.40 as X9379

G-ACHX (6036), 11.7.33, Wrightson & Pearce Ltd., Heston; Wrightways Ltd., Croydon 11.35; crashed at Purley, Surrey 25.4.38

G-ACIE (6032), 27.6.33, V. A. Schmidt; to Bata 12.34 as OK-ATO; rest. 5.38 to Airwork Ltd., Shoreham; to Misr Airwork, Cairo 3.39 as SU-ABZ

G-ACIT (6039), 29.7.33, Highland Airways Ltd. 'Aberdeen'; Scottish Airways Ltd., 'Orcadian' 6.38; Assoc. Airways Joint Committee 6.40; B.E.A., Inverness 2.47; Air Navigation & Trading Co. Ltd., Squires Gate 1.52; Beagle Aircraft Ltd., Rearsby 3.62; Southend Historic Aircraft Museum 6.71

G-ACIU (6041), 5.8.33, Viscount Furness; Maddox Airways Ltd., Brooklands 4.35; Surrey Flying Services Ltd., Croydon 7.35; impressed 4.40 as X9395

G-ACIW (6038), 29.7.33, W. N. McEwen; to France 7.34 as F-ANGE

G-ACJH (6040), 23.8.33, S. T. Weedon; to France 11.33 as F-AMTM

G-ACJM (6049), 6.9.33, Mrs. J. A. Mollison 'Seafarer II'; J. R. Ayling 'Trail of the Caribou' 5.34; damaged beyond repair landing at Hamble 12.8.34

G-ACJS (6042), 4.8.33, Midland & Scottish Air Ferries Ltd., Renfrew; Northern and Scottish Airways Ltd., Renfrew 1.35; registration cancelled 11.36

G-ACJT (6043), 26.8.33, Western Airways Ltd., Whitchurch; Sir Derwent Hall Caine 9.33; Western Airways Ltd. 5.35; crashed at Weston-s-Mare 20.12.39

G-ACKB   (6055), 6.11.33, Iraq Petroleum Transport Co. Ltd.; Commercial Air Hire Ltd., Croydon 9.36; impressed 7.40 as AX863; scrapped 2.41

G-ACKC   (6056), 9.11.33, Iraq Petroleum Transport Co. Ltd.; Commercial Air Hire Ltd., Croydon 4.36; sold abroad 8.36

G-ACKD   (6052), 15.9.33, Hon. Brian Lewis, Heston; Provincial Airways Ltd., Croydon 7.34; League of Nations Union, Croydon 12.35; sold abroad 12.35

G-ACLE   (6044), YI-AAC, 5.9.33, Airwork Ltd.; Crilly Airways Ltd. 9.35; North Eastern Airways Ltd. 2.37; Allied Airways Ltd., Dyce 12.37; Western Airways Ltd., Whitchurch 9.39; impressed 4.40 as X9397

G-ACLP   (6057), 6.11.33, G. Descampes; re-registered in France 11.33 as F-AMTR

G-ACMC   (6053), 24.11.33, Jersey Airways Ltd. 'St. Brelade's Bay'; Airwork Ltd., Heston 1.36; to Australia 8.36 as VH-UXK; crashed at Mundoo, Q. 29.8.38

G-ACMJ   (6058), 7.12.33, Jersey Airways Ltd. 'St. Aubin's Bay'; Airwork Ltd., Heston 1.36; Western Airways Ltd. 7.36; impressed 4.40 as X9396

G-AEKZ   (6028), SU-ABH, 14.6.33, Airwork Ltd., Heston; L. H. Stace, Heston 8.36; Air Dispatch Ltd., Cardiff 4.39; impressed 6.40 as AW163

G-AJKF   (Australian 2081), A34-92, registered 28.3.47 to Butlins Ltd.; not imported; registered in Australia 4.48 as VH-BDS

de Havilland D.H.84 Dragon 2

G-ACKU   (6066), 24.11.33, W. L. Everard, Ratcliffe; Wrightways Ltd., Croydon 2.34; Commercial Air Hire Ltd., Croydon 2.39; impressed 7.40 as AW172

G-ACMO   (6062), 31.1.34, Jersey Airways Ltd. 'St. Ouen's Bay'; Northern and Scottish Airways Ltd., Renfrew 7.35; to Australia 3.38 as VH-ABK

G-ACMP   (6063), 20.2.34, Jersey Airways Ltd. 'St. Clement's Bay'; crashed on mudflats near Splott, Cardiff 23.7.35 while in service with Western Airways Ltd.

G-AEMI, one of the last British-built Dragons, photographed from the control tower at Croydon by the author on 10 October 1936.

G-ACNA (6067), 28.2.34, Olley Air Service Ltd., Croydon; sold abroad 8.36

G-ACNG (6069), 23.3.34, Jersey Airways Ltd. 'Portelet Bay'; Spartan Airlines Ltd., Cowes 6.35; British Airways Ltd., Abridge 3.36; Northern & Scottish Airways Ltd. 1.37; Scottish Airways Ltd. 6.38; crashed at Kirkwall 19.4.40

G-ACNH (6070), 26.3.34, Jersey Airways Ltd. 'Bouley Bay'; Northern & Scottish Airways Ltd., Renfrew 7.35; registration cancelled 1.37

G-ACNI (6071), 28.3.34, Jersey Airways Ltd. 'Bonne Nuit Bay'; British Airways Ltd., Eastleigh 2.36; Airwork Ltd., Heston 12.36; sold abroad 3.37

G-ACNJ (6072), 28.3.34, Jersey Airways Ltd. 'Rozel Bay'; Allied Airways (Gandar Dower) Ltd., Dyce; dismantled for spares at Dyce 1946

G-ACOR (6073), 19.5.34, G. Mackinnon, Hatfield 'Fiona'; British Continental A/W Ltd., Croydon 10.35; British Airways Ltd., Gatwick 3.37; Northern and Scottish Airways Ltd., Renfrew 3.37; to Australia 2.38 as VH-AEA

G-ACPX (6075), 26.4.34, Railway Air Services Ltd.; Brian Allen Aviation Ltd., Croydon 7.35; Western Airways Ltd. 7.38; impressed 4.40 as X9399

G-ACPY (6076), 10.5.34, Olley Air Service Ltd., Croydon; Blackpool & West Coast Air Services Ltd., Squires Gate 2.35; to Aer Lingus 5.36 as EI-ABI; rest. 3.38 to Olley; shot down by German fighter off Scilly Is. 3.6.41

G-ACRF (6077), 18.5.34, Portsmouth, Southsea & Isle of Wight Aviation Ltd.; to Australia 2.36 as VH-UXG; crashed at Archerfield 19.4.54

G-ACRH (6078), 21.6.34, Aberdeen Airways Ltd., Dyce 'Aberdonian'; burned out after take-off crash at Dyce 13.7.34

G-ACRO (6079), 4.5.34, de Havilland Aircraft Co. Ltd.; to Kenya 10.34 as VP-KBG

G-ACVD (6084), 24.7.34, Railway Air Services Ltd., Eastleigh; re-registered 9.37 as VH-UZX; crashed at Beddington, Surrey 26.2.38

G-ACXI (6087), 18.8.34, Railway Air Services Ltd.; sold abroad 12.35

G-ADCP (6092), 30.3.35, Blackpool & West Coast Air Services Ltd., Squires Gate; Isle of Man Air Services Ltd. 10.37: impressed 4.40 as X9440

G-ADCR (6094), 6.4.35, Blackpool & West Coast Air Services Ltd., Squires Gate; crashed 25.6.38

G-ADCT (6095), 28.5.35, Highland Airways Ltd. 'Orcadian'; Scottish Airways Ltd., Inverness 6.38; crashed at Longman Aerodrome, Inverness 14.2.40

G-ADDI (6096), 18.5.35, Railway Air Services Ltd. 'City of Cardiff'; Great Western & Southern Air Lines Ltd., Lands End 1.39; Vickers-Armstrongs Ltd. 7.43; B.E.A., Inverness 2.47; Air Navigation & Trading Co. Ltd., Squires Gate 2.51; Aero Enterprises (J.H.S.) Ltd., Charing 4.63; to the U.S.A. 2.71 as N34DH

G-ADDJ (6097), 25.5.35, Railway Air Services Ltd., 'City of Plymouth'; to Australia 3.37 as VH-UZZ; R.A.A.F. impressment 1.40 as A34-3

G-ADED (6098), 27.5.35, Railway Air Services Ltd.; crashed on take-off from Ronaldsway, Isle of Man 1.7.35

G-ADEE (6099), 13.6.35, Railway Air Services Ltd.; crashed 1,550 ft. up on slopes of Fairsnape Fell, 19 miles E.N.E. of Blackpool 26.10.35

G-ADFI (6100), 4.9.35, Aberdeen Airways Ltd. 'The Silver Ghost'; burned out in crash at Thurso, Caithness 3.7.37

G-ADOS (6103), E-4, 3.9.35, Smith's Aircraft Instruments Ltd., Hatfield; impressed 6.42 as HM569; crashed when landing at Squires Gate 24.6.42

G-AECZ (6105), 18.4.36, Air Cruises Ltd., Hatfield; Ramsgate Airport Ltd., 11.37; Southern Airways Ltd., Ramsgate 3.39; impressed 5.40 as AV982; rest. 6.46 to Air Taxis Ltd., Croydon; to Ireland 3.50 as EI-AFK

G-AEFX (6106), 5.5.36, W. S. Shackleton Ltd., Hanworth; to Australia 5.36 as VH-UVN; crashed at Broome, Western Australia 7.1.42

G-AEIS   (6107), 13.6.36, de Havilland Aircraft Co. Ltd.; sold abroad 12.36

G-AEIT   (6108), 9.6.36, de Havilland Aircraft Co. Ltd.; sold abroad 12.36

G-AEIU (6109), 18.6.36, de Havilland Aircraft Co. Ltd.; sold abroad 12.36

G-AEMI (6110), 5.9.36, Union Founders Trust Ltd.; Commercial Air Hire Ltd., Croydon 9.36; impressed 7.40 as AW173; crashed in Warwickshire 14.12.40

G-AEMJ (6111), 13.4.37, Union Founders Trust Ltd.; sold to the Portuguese Air Force immediately after certification

G-AEMK (6112), 3.9.36, Union Founders Trust Ltd.; Commercial Air Hire Ltd., Croydon 9.36; to Australia 6.38 as VH-AAO; to the R.A.A.F. as A34-5

Registrations of the first four Leopard Moths (Gordon Selfridge's G-ACGS, Butler's 'HB, Hall Caine's, HC and de Havilland's 'HD) all included their owners' initials or variations thereof. (*Hunting Aerosurveys Ltd.*)

de Havilland D.H.85 Leopard Moth

G-ACGS (7002), 27.7.33, Gordon Selfridge Jnr., Heston; to Holland 6.36 as PH-ALM; restored 3.39 to C. Randrup, Heston; impressed 4.40 as AX858

G-ACHB (7001), 30.6.33, A. S. Butler, Hatfield; Flt. Lt. R. L. Wilkinson, Upavon 7.38; R. E. Velten, Brooklands 3.39; impressed 7.40 as BD144

G-ACHC (7003), 30.6.33, Sir Derwent Hall Caine; A. B. Crankshaw, Braunstone 3.38; Newcastle Aero Club 2.39; impressed 8.40 as BD167

G-ACHD (7000), E-1, 29.6.33, de Havilland Aircraft Co. Ltd.; registration cancelled at census 1.12.46

G-ACKJ   (7006), 6.12.33, Peter de Havilland; to France 12.33 as F-AMXQ (re-allocation of French registration first carried by c/n 7043)

G-ACKK (7008), 1.12.33, Sir Pyers Mostyn, Nairobi; to South Africa 7.37 as ZS-ALL; to Southern Rhodesia 10.39 as VP-YCB

G-ACKL (7009), 4.1.34, Hon. Brian Lewis, Heston; Scottish Flying Club, Renfrew 10.35; impressed 8.40 as BD169; crashed at Halfpenny Green 17.8.41

G-ACKM (7026), 2.2.34, W. L. Everard, Ratcliffe; Household Brigade Flying Club, Heston 12.36; impressed 6.40 as AW169; scrapped at Witney 9.10.42

G-ACKN (7013), 20.12.33, Hon. Brian Lewis, Heston; F. Wallis, Eastleigh 5.36; impressed 5.40 as AV975; crashed at Blackdown, Hants. 5.2.42

451

G-ACKO (7014), 16.12.33, W. H. Whitbread, Heston; to Belgium 4.38 as OO-GEJ

G-ACKP (7200), 19.3.34, Capt. G. de Havilland, Hatfield; impressed 10.40 as BK867; damaged beyond repair landing at Aston Down 10.5.41

G-ACKR (7023), 16.1.34, J. R. Bryans, Heston; L. H. Stace, Heston 9.35; Air Commerce Ltd., Heston 3.40; impressed 3.40 as X9294

G-ACKS (7033), 7.3.34, British Air Transport Ltd., Croydon; Yorkshire Airways Ltd., Yeadon 4.36; Yorkshire Aeroplane Club, Yeadon 12.37; impressed 6.40 as AW120; crashed on take-off from Netheravon 13.8.42

G-ACKY (7016), 22.12.33, Miss Delphine Reynolds, Hanworth; G. M. Tonge, Croydon 7.35; to Australia 12.37 as VH-ADV, later VH-RSL and VH-BAH

G-ACLK (7027), 31.1.34, T. L. E. B. Guinness, Heston; J. G. Crammond, Redhill 11.36; A. J. Mulder, Redhill 3.38; impressed 12.39 as W9370

G-ACLL (7028), 5.2.34, F. H. Matusch, Heston; impressed 7.40 as AW165; rest. 8.46 to W. A. Rollason Ltd., Croydon; Morton Air Services Ltd., Croydon 11.46; C. P. Godsal, Croydon 12.49; Derby Aviation Ltd., Burnaston 9.59; British Midland Airways Ltd. 12.64; J. V. Skirrow, Wymeswold 7.71

G-ACLM (7032), 3.3.34, Hon. Brian Lewis, Heston; Olley A/S, Croydon 3.36; Birkett A/S, Heston 10.38; impressed 3.40 as X9380, scrapped 8.44

G-ACLN (7044), 7.4.34, Hon. Mrs. E. Montague, Heston; sold abroad 12.37

G-ACLO (7048), 10.4.34, A. Henshaw, Skegness; W. Humble, Doncaster 9.37; sold abroad 3.38

G-ACLW (7046), 10.4.34, Sir Phillip Sassoon, Lympne; London Air Park Flying Club 10.37; W. Silcock, Old Warden 6.39; impressed 6.40 as AX862

G-ACLX (7036), 15.3.34, Bernard Rubin, Lympne; crashed 9.34

G-ACLY (7012), 14.12.33, Shell Mex & B.P. Ltd., Heston; Rollason Aircraft Serv. Ltd., Croydon 1.36; Southend F/S Ltd. 8.37; impressed 7.40 as AW166

G-ACLZ (7040), 23.3.34, W. G. Robson, Heston; York County Aviation Club, Sherburn 7.36; Airwork Ltd., Heston 3.37; impressed 6.40 as AW121

G-ACMA (7042), 29.3.34, National Benzole Ltd., Heston; impressed 8.40 as BD148; rest. 3.46 to de Havillands; J. P. Filhol Ltd., Baginton 3.61

G-ACMN (7050), 24.4.34, Norman Holden, Selsey; Personal Airways Ltd., Croydon 4.36; impressed 3.40 as X9381; rest. 6.46 to de Havillands, Christchurch; Alvis Ltd., Baginton 6.57; J. J. Parkes, Baginton 8.67

G-ACMS (7024), 17.1.34, Lt. Col. Sir F. Humphreys; to India 4.35 as VT-AGN

G-ACMV (7025), 22.1.34, F. E. Clifford; crashed 12.35

G-ACNN (7011), 7.12.33, Nigel Norman, Heston; impressed 5.40 as AX861

G-ACOO (7054), 7.5.34, F. J. A. Cameron, Hamble; Mrs. Beryl Urquhart, Croydon 3.38; impressed 8.40 as BD172; d.b.r. landing at St. Eval 7.4.41

G-ACOS (7038), 9.3.34, H. S. Broad, Hatfield; to Belgium 3.34 as OO-CAA

G-ACOT (7057), 28.5.34, S. Wales and Monmouthshire Airways Ltd.; T. F. Neale, Hatfield 2.34; to South Africa 3.35 as ZS-AFN; crashed 7.4.35

G-ACPF (7049), 27.4.34, Wrightson & Pearce Ltd., Heston; Air Hire Ltd., Heston 3.35; J. J. Hofer, Heston 8.38; impressed 6.40 as AW123

G-ACPG (7051), 25.4.34, W. E. Davies, Lympne; Cinque Ports Flying Club, Lympne 3.38; impressed 5.40 as AV988; d.b.r. landing Weston Zoyland 10.6.41

G-ACPK (7056), 28.5.34, E. Hicks, Heston; Marquess of Douglas and Clydesdale, Renfrew 4.35; Olley Air Service Ltd., Croydon 10.36; impressed 3.40 as X9382; damaged beyond repair landing at Lichfield 31.8.41

G-ACRC (7058), 4.6.34, N. Rankin; Merseyside Aero & Sports Ltd. (Liverpool Aero Club), Speke 2.36; impressed 6.40 as AW168; crashed 1.10.41

G-ACRJ (7052), 8.5.34, R. E. Gardner, Hamsey Green; R. E. Tonge, Heston 8.37; de
        Havillands, Karachi 5.38; re-registered in India 6.38 as VT-AKH
G-ACRV (7060), 13.6.34, F. C. Clifford, Heston; Marshall's Flying School Ltd.,
        Cambridge 7.38; impressed 5.40 as AV986; crashed Rushup Edge 30.8.41
G-ACRW (7061), 22.6.34, D. H. Rhodes Moorhouse, Heston; J. Cunliffe Lister, Heston
        10.35; N. R. Harben, Derby 10.38; impressed 7.40 as AX873; rest. 3.47 to
        F. T. Bingham, Eastleigh; to Norway 5.52 as LN-TVT
G-ACSE (7062), 9.7.34, to Austrian Aero Club as A-145, later OE-ABC; later to
        Germany as D-EABC; returned to Britain 8.39 as G-AFZG q.v.
G-ACSF (7065), 7.7.34, Dunlop Rubber Co. Ltd.; Leicestershire Aero Club,
        Braunstone 2.38; impressed 7.40 as BD147; scrapped 5.42
G-ACSG (7066), 12.7.34, Wrightson Air Hire Ltd., Heston*; J. W. Adamson,
        Sunderland 9.35; to India 5.36 as VT-AHO
G-ACSH (7067), 13.7.34, K. C. Gandar Dower; R. J. B. Seaman, Heston 7.35; L. H.
        Stace, Heston 1.36; Birkett A/S Ltd. 6.37; impressed 3.40 as X9384
G-ACSI (7068), 20.7.34, Lt. Col. A. H. Gault; to India 6.37 as VT-AJC
G-ACSJ (7070), 27.7.34, E. L. Maddox, Brooklands; L. J. Marr, Stanley Park,
        Blackpool 2.35; Yorkshire A/C, Yeadon 6.38; impressed 6.40 as AW117
G-ACSU (7071), 3.8.34, G. L. Prendergast; Marquess of Kildare, Lympne 12.35;
        Brooklands Aviation Ltd. 6.36; impressed 5.40 as AV984
G-ACTG (7073), 3.8.34, Morris Motors Ltd., Witney; impressed 5.40 as BD140
G-ACTH (7074), 23.8.34, Mrs. Edith Riley, Tripoli; re-registered locally 3.36 as
        I-ACIH
G-ACTJ (7075), 23.8.34, J. A. Henderson; Brooklands Av. Ltd. 1.35; Silentbloc Ltd.,
        Croydon 4.36; T. W. Shipside, Tollerton 2.38; impressed 7.40 as BD146; rest.
        4.46 to Graviner Mfg. Co. Ltd., Langley; A. R. Frogley, Broxbourne 5.48; to
        Switzerland 5.50 as HB-UAB
G-ACTL (7076), 24.8.34, A. R. Coleman, Mousehold; R. Ince, Heston 6.38; P. J.
        Urlwin Smith, Heston 8.38; impressed 6.40 as AW125; scrapped 12.40
G-ACUJ (7079), 7.8.34, Brooklands Av. Ltd.; Epidaurus Trust Ltd., Brooklands 2.35;
        to Switzerland 12.37 as HB-ABA
G-ACUK (7080), 15.9.34, R. F. Fox-Carlyon; British American Air Services Ltd.,
        Heston 4.35; L. H. G. Ltd., Heston 2.37; impressed 4.40 as X9295
G-ACUO (7081), 24.9.34, J. M. Barbour, Heston; A. S. Butler, Hatfield 11.37;
        impressed 7.40 as AX865; beyond repair landing at Hooton 6.6.44
G-ACUS (7082), 15.10.34, Ariane Dufaux, direct to Switzerland as HB-OXA
G-ACVS (7064), 6.7.34, Alexander Tucker; to Poland 10.34 as SP-BSZ
G-ACXH (7077), 31.8.34, Graham Mackinnon, Hatfield; J. R. Bryans, Croydon 7.35;
        Edinburgh Flying Club, Macmerry 8.37; D. Fairweather and Hon. Mrs. M.
        Fairweather, Renfrew 12.38; impressed 8.40 as BD173; later 2993M
G-ADAA (7087), 2.1.35, C. Macdonald, Hatfield; to India 4.39 as VT-AKX
G-ADAP (7090), 8.4.35, A. Ellison, Castle Bromwich; to Kenya 10.35 as VP-KBU; rest.
        to Wing Cdr. F. O. Soden, Finningley 11.36; impressed 5.40 as AV989
G-ADAR (7091), 6.2.35, Birkett Air Services Ltd., Heston; burned out 10.7.35
G-ADBH (7030), F-AMXR, 21.2.34, Lady Loch, Hatfield; Birkett Air Services Ltd.,
        Heston 4.36; W. Andrews, Heston 1.39; impressed 5.40 as AV983
G-ADCO (7093), 27.2.35, Airwork Ltd., Heston; Birkett Air Service Ltd., Heston 2.36;
        impressed 3.40 as X9383; crashed near York 11.8.41

* Total wreck in fatal crash at Heston 17.3.35 but rebuilt.

Constructed at White Waltham in 1963 using parts of G-ACGS, Leopard Moth G-APKH
flies past at the Hatfield Open Day, July 1969. (*Aviation Photo News*)

G-ADFG (7100), 18.5.35, G. L. Harrison, Hatfield; to France 7.38 as F-AREP

G-ADFJ (7103), 18.6.35, Hon. Brian Lewis, Heston; sold to André Bailly, Paris 6.35 as F-AOHS

G-ADHB (7104), 2.7.35, Brooklands Air Taxis Ltd.; J. A. Henderson, Heston 6.36; A. F. Wigram, Brooklands 3.37; impressed 12.39 as W9371

G-ADHD (7106), not certificated, reservation only; not taken up

G-ADUL (7072), D-EGYV, 26.7.34, Airwork Ltd., Heston; Miss Betty Malcolm, Brooklands 11.35; fatal take-off crash at Alicante, Spain 23.1.36

G-ADWY (7117), 14.12.35, J. B. Wild, Croydon; Air Taxis Ltd., Croydon 6.38; impressed 3.40 as X9385; to instructional airframe 5.42 as 2991M

G-AEFR (7125), 23.4.36, H. R. A. Kidston, Brooklands; impressed 5.40 as AV985

G-AENB (7128), 5.9.36, T. H. A. Tucker, Brooklands; to Jugoslavia 9.36 as YU-PEA

G-AEZI (7113), VP-KBV, I-NENO, 21.10.35, Yorkshire Aeroplane Club, Yeadon; impressed 6.40 as AW122; to instructional airframe 3.42 as 2992M

G-AFDV (7120), VH-AHB, 7.2.36, S. Harris, Redhill; Yorkshire Aeroplane Club, Yeadon 8.39; impressed 1.40 as W5783; burned out at Ringway 19.4.41

G-AFZG (7062), G-ACSE ntu, A-145, OE-ABC, D-EABC, 9.7.34, Airwork Ltd., Heston; impressed 7.40 as AW156; believed destroyed in flying accident 31.1.42

G-AIYS (7089), SU-ABM, YI-ABI, 4.3.47, Birkett Air Service Ltd., Croydon; H. F. Buckmaster, White Waltham 6.49; T. P. Norman, White Waltham 8.52; Surrey Flying Club, Croydon 6.56; Chrisair Ltd., Panshanger 3.61; J. H. Stevens, Charing 12.62; stored at Blackbushe in 1972

G-APKH (PPS 85/1/7131), first flown 8.8.63, C. of A. 31.10.63, P. Franklin, White Waltham

G-ATFU (7007), CH-366, HB-OTA, 22.11.65, W. F. Harries, Biggin Hill; J. K. Pickett, Rhoose 4.67; Allcycles (Finance) Ltd., Rhoose 7.69; J. W. Benson, Bicester 2.71

de Havilland D.H.86 (*single pilot type*)

G-ACPL (2300), 30.1.34, Railway Air Services Ltd., Croydon; rebuilt for 2 crew as Imperial Airways 'Delphinus'; impressed at Cairo 12.41 as HK844

G-ACVY (2302), 15.8.34, Railway Air Services Ltd., Croydon 'Mercury'; in regular airline service for 14 years; scrapped at Langley in 1948

G-ACVZ (2303), 7.12.34, Railway Air Services Ltd., Croydon 'Jupiter'; crashed at Elsdorf, near Cologne, Germany on the night of 15–16.3.37

de Havilland D.H.86 (*two crew type*)

G-ACWC (2304), 5.3.35, Imperial Airways Ltd., Croydon 'Delia'; crashed at Minaa, Nigeria 17.6.41

G-ACWD (2305), 28.2.35, Imperial Airways Ltd., Croydon 'Dorado'; impressed at Cairo 11.41 as HK829; beyond repair landing at Noffution North 17.3.43

G-ACWE (2306), 14.2.35, Imperial Airways Ltd., Croydon; transferred to QANTAS as VH-UUA 'Adelaide'; to Tata Airlines Ltd. 1940 as VT-AKM, later HX789

G-ACYF (2313), 6.2.35, Jersey Airways Ltd. 'Giffard Bay'; to Wearnes Air Services Ltd. 6.38 as VR-SBD; later to Australia as VH-ADN and A31-2

G-ACYG (2314), 8.3.35, Jersey Airways Ltd. 'Grouville Bay'; impressed for the Royal Navy 7.40 as AX840; scrapped at Donibristle in 1945

G-ACZN (2316), 22.3.35, Jersey Airways Ltd. 'St. Catherine's Bay'; crashed at Jersey Airport 4.11.38

G-ACZO (2318), 9.4.35, Jersey Airways Ltd. 'Ouaine Bay'; impressed for the Royal Navy 7.40 as AX841; destroyed in air raid, Lee-on-Solent 16.7.40

G-ACZP (2321), 11.5.35, Jersey Airways Ltd. 'Belcroute Bay'; impressed 7.40 as AX843; rest. 8.40 to Railway Air Services Ltd.; Skytravel Ltd. 1948; Lancashire Aircraft Corporation 1950; Silver City Airways Ltd. 1957; V. H. Bellamy, Eastleigh 1958; beyond repair at Barajas, Madrid 21.9.58

G-ACZR (2322), 29.5.35, Jersey Airways Ltd. 'La Saline Bay'; impressed for the Royal Navy 7.40 as AX844; spun in at Donibristle 31.3.43

G-ADCM (2317), 30.3.35, Imperial Airways Ltd., Croydon 'Draco'; crashed at Zwettl, Austria 22.10.35

G-ADCN (2319), 15.4.35, Imperial Airways Ltd., Croydon 'Daedalus'; destroyed by fire at Bangkok 3.12.38

G-ADEA (2323), 5.6.35, Hillmans Airways Ltd.; to British Airways Ltd. 1936; to Wearnes Air Services Ltd. 6.38 as VR-SBC; to Australia as VH-UZX

Jersey Airways' two crew type D.H.86 G-ACYF at Jersey in June 1938 ready for delivery to Wearnes Air Service as VR-SBD 'Governor Murchison'.

G-ADEB (2324), 20.6.35, Hillmans Airways Ltd.; to British Airways Ltd. 1936; crashed near Altenkirchen, Germany 12.8.36

G-ADEC (2325), 1.7.35, Hillmans Airways Ltd.; to British Airways Ltd. 1936; to P.L.U.N.A., Uruguay 9.38 as CX-AAH

G-ADMY (2327), 10.8.35, Wrightways Ltd., Croydon; British Continental Airways Ltd., Croydon 'St. George' 2.37; British American Air Services Ltd., Croydon 7.38; impressed for the Royal Navy 11.40 as X9442

de Havilland D.H.86A (*converted to D.H.86B in 1937*)

G-ADFF (2328), 13.1.36, Imperial Airways Ltd., Croydon 'Dione'; impressed 8.41 for the Lydda Communications Flight as AX760; d.b.r. 26.11.41

G-ADUE (2333), 20.1.36, Imperial Airways Ltd., Croydon 'Dardanus'; impressed in Egypt 9.41 as AX762 but mispainted as AX672; d.b.r. at Siwa 23.6.42

G-ADUF (2334), 24.1.36, Imperial Airways Ltd., 'Dido'; impressed 11.41 as HK828 but delivered instead to Misrair as SU-ACR 'Beirut'; rest. 5.48 to Field Aircraft Services Ltd.; Gulf Aviation Ltd. 10.51; w.f.u. 5.52

G-ADUG (2335), 7.2.36, Imperial Airways Ltd., Croydon 'Danae'; impressed at Cairo 11.41 as HK831 but believed cannibalised

G-ADUH (2336), 7.3.36, Imperial Airways Ltd., Croydon 'Dryad'; to Aer Lingus 10.38 as EI-ABT 'Sasana'; rest. 11.46 to Steiner's Air Services Ltd., Speke; Gulf Aviation Ltd. 5.51; written off after ground collision with Auster J-1 G-AIBO at Bahrein about 6.51

G-ADUI (2337), 18.2.36, Imperial Airways Ltd., Croydon 'Denebola'; impressed in Egypt 11.41 as HK830; damaged at Bilbeis 11.3.42

G-ADVJ (2338), 8.4.36, Blackpool and West Coast Air Services Ltd. 'Ronaldsway'; to Aer Lingus 9.36 as EI-ABK 'Eire'; rest. 10.46 to Bond Air Services Ltd., Gatwick; Gulf Aviation Ltd. 7.51; derelict at Bahrein 8.52

G-ADVK (2339), 21.4.36, Blackpool and West Coast Air Services Ltd.; abandoned at Jersey Airport while on C. of A. overhaul 6.40

G-ADYC (2340), 14.5.36, British Airways Ltd., Gatwick; to the R.A.F. as a flying classroom for wireless telegraphy 11.37 as L8037

G-ADYD (2341), 19.5.36, British Airways Ltd., Gatwick; to the R.A.F. as a flying classroom for navigation training 11.37 as L8040

G-ADYE (2346), 28.7.36, British Airways Ltd., Gatwick; to P.L.U.N.A. 11.37 as CX-ABG

G-ADYF (2347), 2.9.36, British Airways Ltd., Gatwick; crashed on night take-off at Gatwick 15.9.36

G-ADYG (2343), 30.6.36, British Airways Ltd., Gatwick; to No.24 Squadron, R.A.F., Hendon 6.38 as N6246

G-ADYH (2344), 21.7.36, British Airways Ltd., Gatwick; Railway Air Services Ltd. 8.40; Skytravel Ltd., Speke 10.46; to Australia 10.48; w.f.u. Bandoeng

G-ADYI (2345), 26.8.36, British Airways Ltd., Gatwick; Wrightways Ltd., Croydon 3.40; impressed 7.40 as AX795 initially for No.24 Squadron, R.A.F.

G-ADYJ (2348), 19.5.36, British Airways Ltd., Gatwick; to No.24 Squadron 10.37 as L7596; crashed at Ulverston, Lancs. 29.7.39

G-AEAP (2349), 17.3.36, Imperial Airways Ltd., Croydon 'Demeter'; impressed in Egypt 10.41 as HK843; burned out at Pachino, Sicily 23.7.43

G-AEFH (2350), 10.8.36, Railway Air Services Ltd., Croydon 'Neptune'; lost during the evacuation from France 6.40

G-AEJM (2351), 24.9.36, Wrightways Ltd., Croydon; impressed 4.40 as X9441 for No.24 Squadron and named 'The Cathedral'; burned out at Hendon 17.2.43

de Havilland D.H.86B
G-AENR (2352), 8.2.37, Blackpool and West Coast Air Services Ltd.; Guernsey Airways Ltd., Jersey 11.39; impressed for the Royal Navy 7.40 as AX842; rest. 8.40; to Railway Air Services Ltd.; scrapped at Langley 11.48
G-AETM (2353), 29.6.37, Allied Airways Ltd., Woolsington 'Silver Star'; Western Airways Ltd. 4.39; to Finland 12.39 as OH-SLA, later OH-IPA; to the Finnish Air Force; destroyed in ground collision at Malmö
G-AEWR (2354), 29.6.37, Railway Air Services Ltd., Croydon 'Venus'; lost during the evacuation from France 6.40
G-AFAJ (2355), 18.8.37, de Havilland Aircraft Co. Ltd.; to Hürkus Airlines, Turkey as TC-ERK; still flying in 1963
G-AFAK (2356), 8.9.37, de Havilland Aircraft Co. Ltd.; to Hürkus Airlines, Turkey 9.37 as TC-FER
G-AFAL (2357), 30.9.37, de Havilland Aircraft Co. Ltd.; to Hürkus Airlines, Turkey 9.37 as TC-GEN
G-AFAM (2358), 29.10.37, de Havilland Aircraft Co. Ltd.; to Turkey 12.37 as TC-HEP
G-AJNB (2342), D.H.86A SU-ABV, 1.1.37, Peacock Air Charter, Alexandria 'Paul'; derelict at Wadi Halfa in 1949

Imperial Airways Ltd.'s D.H.86B G-AEAP 'Demeter' in service with No.1 Air Ambulance Unit, R.A.A.F. as HK843 in the Western Desert 1943. (*via J. Hopton*)

de Havilland D.H.87 Hornet Moth
G-ACTA (1997), E-6, 6.7.34, scrapped at Hatfield 2.46; G-ADIR (8000), E-1, 1.6.35, impressed 2.40 as W9387; G-ADIS (8001), 25.6.35, impressed 2.40 as W9391; G-ADJU (8002), 4.9.35, to Hong Kong 10.37 as VR-HCX; G-ADJV (8003), 25.9.35, impressed 7.40 as AX857 rest. 4.46, crashed at Fairoaks 13.10.51; G-ADJW (8004), 24.9.35, to France 4.36 as F-AOVY; G-ADJX (8005), 27.9.35, impressed 5.40 as X9443; G-ADJY (8006), 25.9.35, crashed 4.37; G-ADJZ (8008), 27.9.35, impressed 5.40 as X9444; G-ADKA (8007), 19.10.35, impressed 1.40 as W5746; G-ADKB (8012), 7.10.35, impressed 1.40 as W6421; G-ADKC (8064), 31.3.36, impressed 5.40 as X9445, rest. 5.46; G-ADKD (8016), 22.10.35, impressed 2.40 as X9321, rest. 7.46, w.f.u. at Croft 10.47; G-ADKE (8018), 29.10.35, impressed 10.39 as W5830; G-ADKF (8019), 4.11.35, to Australia 6.37 as VH-AAV

G-ADKH (8068), 22.2.36, impressed 1.40 as W5747; G-ADKI (8029), 1.11.35, impressed 7.40 as AV951; G-ADKJ (8032), 25.11.35, impressed 1.40 as W5748; G-ADKK (8033), 22.11.35, impressed 1.40 as W5749, rest. 6.46; G-ADKL (8035), 17.12.35, impressed 1.40 as W5750, rest. 5.46, to France 4.47 as F-BCJO, rest. 7.59, crashed on take-off at Roborough 9.7.66; G-ADKM (8037), 29.11.35, impressed 1.40 as W5751, rest. 5.46; G-ADKN (8073), 25.2.36, impressed 1.40 as W6422; G-ADKO (8042), 24.3.36, crashed 3.38; G-ADKP (8081), 29.4.36, impressed 2.40 as X9322; G-ADKR (8045), 20.12.35, impressed 1.40 as W5752; G-ADKS (8046), 19.4.36, impressed 3.40 as X9458; G-ADKT (8014), 11.10.35, to Australia 12.37 as VH-ABO; G-ADKU (8051), 27.3.36, impressed 2.40 as W9386; G-ADKV (8054), 13.3.36, impressed 3.40 as W9372; G-ADKW (8074), 9.4.36, impressed 1.40 as W5754, rest. 5.46, w.f.u. at Panshanger 7.48

G-ADLY (8020), 4.11.35, impressed 2.40 as W9388, rest. 5.46; G-ADMJ (8066), 14.3.36, impressed 2.40 as W9389, rest. 4.46, to Australia 9.51 as VH-AMJ; G-ADMK (8067), reservation only, aircraft certificated as G-AEIY q.v.; G-ADML (8069), 22.2.36, impressed 2.40 as X9323; G-ADMM (8072), 4.3.36, impressed 1.40 as W5755; G-ADMN (8076), 27.3.36, impressed 1.40 as W5770; G-ADMO (8086), 26.5.36, impressed 4.40 as AV969, rest. 7.46 as OY-DTI, rest. 11.47 as G-ADMO, sold abroad 9.49 believed as CR-LCE; G-ADMP (8082), 26.3.36, impressed 9.40 as BK837; G-ADMR (8087), 26.5.36, impressed 4.40 as X9310; G-ADMS (8044), 12.2.36, impressed 1.40 as W5771; G-ADMT (8093), 10.6.36; G-ADNB (8080), 22.4.36, impressed 1.40 as W5772, rest. 6.46, to U.S.A. 3.72 as N36DH; G-ADNC (8084), 14.5.36, impressed 1.40 as W5773; G-ADND (8097), 8.8.36, impressed 2.40 as W9385, rest. 6.46; G-ADNE (8089), 16.4.36, impressed 2.40 as X9325, rest. 7.46

G-ADOT (8027), 1.11.35, impressed 2.40 as X9326, rest. 5.46, w.f.u. at Stapleford 10.59; G-ADSJ (8096), 20.5.36, registration not used, sold direct to New Zealand as ZK-ACP; G-ADSK (8091), 9.4.36, impressed 7.40 as AV952, rest. 5.46, to Pakistan 8.50 as AP-AES, to Germany 1956 as D-EJOM, rest. 8.58; G-ADSL (8098), 7.8.36, registration not used, direct to South Africa as ZS-AII, later S.A.A.F. 1572 and VP-YIH; G-ADUR (8085), 25.3.36; G-AEET (8092), 28.4.36, impressed 3.40 as X9319, rest. 3.42, to Canada 6.69 as CF-EEJ; G-AEIY (8067), G-ADMK ntu, 23.5.36, impressed 6.40 as AW114; G-AEKP (8101), 3.7.36, impressed 4.40 as AV972; G-AEKS (8100), 20.7.36, impressed 1.40 as W5753; G-AEKY (8102), 18.7.36, impressed 3.40 as W9383, rest. 7.46, w.f.u. at Croydon 8.53; G-AELO (8105), 26.8.36; G-AEMG (8071), 22.8.36, to India 3.38 as VT-AKA; G-AEPV (8106), 1.2.37, impressed 1.40 as W5774; G-AESE (8108), 8.1.37, impressed 1.40 as W5775, rest. 5.46 by Short Bros. and Harland Ltd. with their c/n SH.44C; G-AETC (8109), 8.2.37, impressed 1.40 as W5776; G-AEVU (8112), 20.3.37, to India 7.38 as VT-AKE; G-AEWM (8114), 1.5.37, to South Africa 7.38 as ZS-AOS; G-AEWY (8116), 5.5.37, impressed 1.40 as W5777, rest. 4.46, crashed at Barton 18.4.64; G-AEXM (8122), 21.5.37, to Uruguay 10.37 as CX-ABD; G-AEZG (8131), 2.7.37, impressed 8.40 as BK830, rest. 5.46; G-AEZH (8132), 13.7.37, impressed 3.40 as W9381; G-AEZT (8133), 8.5.37, impressed 1.40 as W5778; G-AEZY (8138), 22.7.37, impressed 3.40 as W9384

G-AFAT (8137), 12.8.37, crashed at Lympne 7.7.39; G-AFBG (8140), 7.10.37, registration not used, direct to France as F-AQEB; G-AFBH (8141), 13.10.37, impressed 2.40 as X9324; G-AFDF (8145), 7.4.38, impressed 3.40 as W9382; G-AFDG (8146), 11.5.38, impressed 3.40 as W9390; G-AFDT (8150), 18.5.38, impressed 1.40 as W5779, rest. 5.46, crashed at Dinas Powis, Penarth 20.12.51; G-AFDU (8160), 23.7.38, impressed 1.40 as W9379; G-AFDW (8154), 23.7.38, impressed 3.40 as W9380; G-AFDY (8149), 11.5.38, impressed 1.40 as W5780; G-AFEC (8157), 15.7.38, impressed 4.40 as X9446;

G-AFED (8162), 15.10.38, to S.A.A.F. 1939 as '2037', later ZS-BKD; G-AFEE (8155), 20.6.38, impressed 1.40 as W5781; G-AFEF (8156), 29.6.38, impressed 3.40 as X9447; G-AFHE (8158), 20.7.38, to South Africa 2.40 as ZS-CAA; G-AFHX (8022), OE-DKS, 29.10.35, to France 6.38 as F-ARAX; G-AFMP (8120), EI-ABO, 21.4.37, impressed 1.40 as W5782; G-AFRE (8107), EI-ABL, 30.1.37, impressed 1.40 as W5784, rest. 5.46, to the Gold Coast 3.52 as VP-AAC

G-AHBL (8126), CF-BFJ, P6785, 18.2.48; G-AHBM (8135), CF-BFN, P6786, 4.11.52; G-AMZO (8040) VR-RAI, SE-ALD, 30.11.35

Note: Previous identities and c/ns of G-AHBL and 'BM given above are as documented. In actual fact they were reversed.

The original D.H.88 Comet in Portuguese markings as CS-AAJ 'Salazar'.
(*Flight Photo 14573*)

de Havilland D.H.88 Comet

G-ACSP   (1994), E-1, 9.10.34, J. A. Mollison 'Black Magic'; to the Portuguese Government 3.35 as CS-AAJ 'Salazar'; still extant in 1937

G-ACSR   (1995), 12.10.34, Bernard Rubin; named 'Reine Astrid' 12.34; to the French Government 4.35 as F-ANPY

G-ACSS   (1996), 12.10.34, A. O. Edwards 'Grosvenor House'; to the R.A.F. 6.35 as K5084; damaged landing at Martlesham 2.9.36; rest. 6.37 to F. E. Tasker, Gravesend as 'The Orphan', later 'The Burberry'; stored at Gravesend 1937–1950 and at Leavesden 1951–65; to Old Warden 30.10.65

G-ADEF   (2261), 6.8.35, C. A. Nicholson, Hatfield 'Boomerang'; crashed in the Sudan 22.9.35, south of Atbara, after the crew parachuted

de Havilland D.H.89 Dragon Rapide

G-ACPM   (6251), 5.7.34, Hillman's Airways Ltd., Maylands; hit sea in bad visibility four miles off Folkestone and disintegrated 2.10.34

G-ACPN   (6252), 2.8.34, Hillman's Airways Ltd., Maylands (later Abridge); British Airways Ltd., Heston 4.36; sold abroad 9.36

G-ACPO   (6253), 4.9.34, Hillman's Airways Ltd., Maylands (later Abridge); British Airways Ltd., Speke 3.36; to Australia 5.36 as VH-UBN

G-ACPP   (6254), 12.3.35, Railway Air Services 'City of Bristol'; Great Western and Southern Air Lines Ltd., Shoreham 3.39; B.E.A., Northolt 7.47; Yellow Air Taxis Ltd., Elmdon 6.48; to Canada 6.61 as CF-PTK

Railway Air Services' first Rapide, G-ACPP 'City of Bristol', ready to leave Whitchurch in 1935. (*W. K. Kilsby*)

G-ACPR (6255), 18.3.35, Railway Air Services 'City of Birmingham'; Great Western and Southern Air Lines Ltd. 2.39; d.b.r. at Burford 19.2.40

G-ACTT (6257), 20.10.34, Anglo American Oil Co. Ltd.; Flt. Lt. E. H. Fielden, Hendon (King's Flight) 2.35; Olley Air Service Ltd., Croydon 3.36; impressed 3.40 as X8509; damaged beyond repair in accident 14.7.41

G-ACTU (6258), 24.8.34, C. R. Anson, Heston; Western Airways Ltd., Weston-super-Mare 11.38; impressed 6.40 as AW115; crashed at Cardiff 15.2.41

G-ACYM (6269), 6.3.35, Olley Air Service Ltd., Croydon; Great Western and Southern Air Lines Ltd. 4.39; impressed 3.40 as X9320

G-ACYR (6261), 2.2.35, Olley Air Service Ltd., Croydon; Miles Aircraft Ltd., Woodley 7.46; Reid & Sigrist Ltd., Desford 8.46; withdrawn from use 4.53

G-ACZE (6264), 15.12.34, Anglo Persian Oil Co. Ltd., Abadan; Airwork Ltd., Heston 4.39; impressed 7.40 as Z7266; rest. 7.42 to Allied Airways (Gandar Dower) Ltd., Dyce; crashed at Grimsetter, Orkney 27.12.45

G-ACZF (6268), 11.2.35, Anglo Persian Oil Co. Ltd., Abadan; Airwork Ltd., 4.39; Allied Airways (Gandar Dower) Ltd., Dyce 6.39; scrapped 8.48

G-ACZU (6274), 25.3.35, Viscount Furness, Melton Mowbray; Cinema Press Ltd., Croydon 1.37; sold abroad 7.37

G-ADAE (6272), 17.4.35, Northern & Scottish Airways Ltd., Renfrew; British Airways Ltd., Eastleigh 3.36; to Denmark 5.38 as OY-DIN; rest. 6.46 to Southampton Air Services Ltd.; Air Charter Experts Ltd., Ronaldsway 5.47; scrapped 8.48

G-ADAG (6266), 6.2.35, Hillman's Airways Ltd., Abridge; British Airways Ltd., Eastleigh 1.36; Northern & Scottish Airways Ltd., Renfrew 8.36; Airwork Ltd., Shoreham 9.37; impressed 7.40 as Z7264; withdrawn from use 8.43

G-ADAH (6278), 19.2.35, Hillman's Airways Ltd., Abridge; British Airways Ltd., Abridge 2.36; Northern & Scottish Airways Ltd., Renfrew 8.36; Airwork Ltd., Shoreham 8.37; Allied Airways (Gandar Dower) Ltd., Dyce 'Pioneer' 10.38; reduced to spares at Booker 1969; some components to Old Warden 1970

G-ADAI (6287), 14.5.35, Hillman's Airways Ltd., Abridge; British Continental Airways Ltd., Croydon 5.35; British Airways Ltd., Gatwick 2.37; Airwork Ltd., Shoreham 8.37; impressed 7.40 as X7262

460

G-ADAJ (6276), 5.6.35, Hillman's Airways Ltd., Abridge; British Airways Ltd., Abridge 1.36; Highland Airways Ltd., Inverness 9.36; Scottish Airways Ltd., Renfrew 6.38; B.E.A., Renfrew 2.47; to France 11.47 as F-BEDY

G-ADAK (6281), 14.5.35, British Continental Airways Ltd., Croydon; C. H. Stave, Croydon 9.36; Air Dispatch Ltd., Cardiff 6.40; impressed 7.40 as AW155

G-ADAL (6263), 2.3.35, Hillman's Airways Ltd., Abridge; British Airways Ltd., Heston 3.36; Wrightways Ltd., Croydon 6.36; impressed 4.40 as X9448

G-ADAO (6275), 5.4.35, Ethyl Export Corporation, Heston; sold abroad 9.36

G-ADBU (6280), 29.4.35, United Airways Ltd., Heston; British Airways Ltd., Stanley Park 1.36; Northern & Scottish Airways Ltd., Renfrew 8.36; damaged beyond repair 11.36

G-ADBV (6286), 6.6.35, Jersey Airways Ltd. 'St. Ouens Bay II'; J. Dade, Croydon 5.37; Western Airways Ltd. 11.38; impressed 3.40 as X8511

G-ADBW (6288), 27.6.35, Jersey Airways Ltd.; Isle of Man Air Services Ltd., 10.37; Airwork Ltd., Heston 4.39; impressed 7.40 as Z7265

G-ADBX (6289), 4.7.35, United Airways Ltd., Heston; British Airways Ltd., Heston 1.36; crashed into hangar landing at Ronaldsway 16.5.36

G-ADCL (6277), 4.5.35, Anglo American Oil Co. Ltd., Heston; Airwork Ltd., Heston 12.35; sold in Spain 8.36

G-ADDD (6283), 8.6.35, Flt. Lt. E. H. Fielden, Hendon (King's Flight); Western Airways Ltd., Weston-super-Mare 11.38; impressed 6.40 as AW116

G-ADDE (6282), 31.5.35, Aberdeen Airways Ltd., Dyce; North Eastern Airways Ltd., Croydon 11.37; impressed 3.40 as X9386; sold to E. L. Gandar Dower 3.47

G-ADDF (6284), 8.8.35, Aberdeen Airways Ltd., Dyce; Hillman's Airways Ltd., Abridge 9.35; British Airways Ltd., Heston 1.36; Northern & Scottish Airways Ltd., Renfrew 8.36; Airwork Ltd. 8.37; sold abroad 9.37

G-ADFX (6290), 22.7.35, British American Air Services Ltd., Heston; L.H.G. Ltd., Heston 2.37; impressed 4.40 as X9457; d.b.r. at Sywell 17.5.43

G-ADFY (6291), 26.7.35, W. H. Rhodes Moorhouse, Heston; C. E. Gardner, Hamsey Green; sold abroad 8.36

G-ADIM (6293), 31.7.35, British Continental Airways Ltd., Croydon; British Airways Ltd., Gatwick 2.37; Airwork Ltd., Shoreham 8.37; impressed 7.40 as Z7263; crashed and burned at Doncaster 11.4.42

G-ADNG (6297), 5.10.35, Iraq Petroleum Transport Co. Ltd., Haifa; crashed 8.36

G-ADNH (6300), 11.10.35, Iraq Petroleum Transport Co. Ltd., Haifa; Hon. Mrs. Victor Bruce, Cardiff 11.39; impressed 1.40 as W6423

G-ADNI (6301), 17.10.35, Iraq Petroleum Transport Co. Ltd., Haifa; Anglo European Airways Ltd., Croydon 11.39; impressed 4.40 as W9365

G-ADUM (6315), 30.4.36, de Havilland Aircraft Co. Ltd., Hatfield; to Devlet Hava Yollari (Turkish State Air Line) 5.36 as TC-ARI

G-ADUN (6316), 30.4.36, de Havilland Aircraft Co. Ltd., Hatfield; to Devlet Hava Yollari (Turkish State Air Line) 5.36 as TC-BAY

G-ADUO (6317), 30.4.36, de Havilland Aircraft Co. Ltd., Hatfield; to Devlet Hava Yollari (Turkish State Air Line) 5.36 as TC-CAN

G-ADUP (6319), registration not taken up; re-registered VH-UVT and delivered to Adelaide Airways Ltd., South Australia with C. of A. 11.2.36

G-ADWZ (6309), 9.11.35, de Havilland Aircraft Co. Ltd.; Personal Airways Ltd., Croydon 3.36; North Eastern Airways Ltd., Croydon 11.38; impressed 4.40 as X9449; crashed at Llanrhaiadr-ym-Mochnant, N. Wales 2.8.40

G-ADYK (6310), 10.12.35, de Havilland Aircraft Co. Ltd.; sold abroad 2.36

G-ADYL (6311), 10.12.35, de Havilland Aircraft Co. Ltd.; sold abroad 2.36; returned to Croydon 1955 as 4X-AEI; rest. 8.55 to Aeroservices Ltd., Croydon; F. G. Fox, Fairoaks 3.56; withdrawn from use at Fairoaks 12.58

G-ADYM (6312), 10.12.35, de Havilland Aircraft Co. Ltd.; sold abroad 2.36

G-AEAJ (6320), 14.3.36, Railway Air Services 'Star of Lancashire'; Isle of Man Air Services Ltd., Derbyhaven 10.37; impressed 1.40 as W6425

G-AEAK (6324), 4.4.36, Railway Air Services 'Star of Mona'; Isle of Man Air Services Ltd., Derbyhaven 10.37; crashed at Speke 5.39

G-AEAL (6325), 25.4.36, Railway Air Services 'Star of Yorkshire'; Isle of Man Air Services Ltd. 10.37; Hunting Aerosurveys Ltd., Luton 3.46; Wolverhampton Aviation Ltd. 4.53; to the Ivory Coast 4.56 as F-OAUE

G-AEAM (6326), 5.5.36, Railway Air Services 'Star of Ulster'; Isle of Man Air Services Ltd. 10.37; impressed 1.40 as W6424; abandoned at Amiens 5.40

G-AEBW (6327), 13.5.36, Railway Air Services 'Star of Renfrew'; Isle of Man Air Services Ltd. 10.37; abandoned at Bordeaux 18.6.40

G-AEBX (6328), 20.5.36, Railway Air Services 'Star of Scotia'; crashed 3.7.38

G-AEGS (6335), 7.8.36, Iraq Petroleum Transport Co. Ltd., Haifa; crashed 30.12.36

G-AEKF (6332), 15.6.36, T. G. Mapplebeck, Belgrade; sold in Jugoslavia 6.36 as YU-SAS

G-AEMH (6336), 5.9.36, Personal Airways Ltd., Croydon; North Eastern Airways Ltd., Croydon 11.38; impressed 3.40 as X9387; rest. 3.47 to Air Charters Ltd., Ronaldsway; G. Clifton, Horsey Toll 2.49; East Anglian Flying Services Ltd., Southend 6.52; dismantled at Ipswich 1961 and stored

G-AEML (6337), 26.9.36, Wrightways Ltd., Croydon; impressed 4.40 as X9450; rest. 3.46 to Armstrong Whitworth Aircraft Ltd., Baginton; Neil Tool Co. Ltd., Panshanger 9.62; Liverpool Aero Engineering Co. Ltd., Speke 2.68; J. P. Filhol Ltd., Baginton 12.69

G-AEMM (6339), 10.10.36, Anglo Iranian Oil Co. Ltd., Abadan; taken over by the R.A.F. in the Near East during 1939–1945 war; reg'n. cancelled 3.46

G-AENN (6340), 25.11.36, Olley Air Service Ltd., Croydon; C. W. Wood, Dar-es-Salaam 11.36; Olley Air Service Ltd. 12.37; impressed 1.40 as W6455

G-AENO (6341), 10.11.36, Blackpool and West Coast Air Services Ltd., Squires Gate; to Aer Lingus 2.38 as EI-ABP; to Australia 6.40 as VH-ADE, later A33-7

G-AFEP in camouflage at Croydon in 1946 after nearly seven years with Air Commerce Ltd. on wartime internal services. (*E. J. Riding*)

de Havilland D.H.89A Dragon Rapide

G-AEOV   (6342), 3.3.37, de Havilland Aircraft Co. Ltd., Hatfield; Mrs. H. Wood, Croydon 2.38; W. D. Gairdner, Renfrew 8.39; impressed 1.40 as W6456

G-AEPE   (6344), 24.2.37, Personal Airways Ltd., Croydon; Olley Air Service Ltd., Croydon 7.37; impressed for No.24 Squadron 7.40 as BD143

G-AEPF   (6353), 17.4.37, Air Commerce Ltd., Heston; abandoned in France 18.6.40

G-AEPW   (6350), 15.3.37, Olley Air Service Ltd., Croydon; impressed 3.40 as X8510

G-AERE   (6355), 26.5.37, L.H.G. Ltd., Heston; Mrs. L. H. Falk, Heston 6.38; crashed at Forest-in-Teesdale, Co. Durham 20.6.39

G-AERN   (6345), 24.3.37, Blackpool and West Coast Air Services Ltd., Squires Gate; Olley Air Service Ltd., Derbyhaven I.O.M. 10.39; B.E.A., Northolt 2.47; Gibraltar Airways Ltd. 10.47; to Spain 1.54 as EC-AKO

G-AERZ   (6356), 7.5.37, Air Commerce Ltd., Heston; crashed at Craigavad, Co. Down while on service with Railway Air Services Ltd. 1.4.46

G-AESR   (6363), 25.6.37, Iraq Petroleum Transport Co. Ltd., Haifa; Airwork Ltd., Perth 5.48; Air Kruise (Kent) Ltd., Lympne 3.53; w.f.u. in Libya 11.56

G-AEWL   (6367), 18.6.37, Highland Airways Ltd., Inverness; British Airways Ltd., Inverness 11.37; Scottish Airways Ltd., Renfrew 11.39; B.E.A., Northolt 2.47; M. G. Fletcher, Croydon 9.48; Air Kruise (Kent) Ltd., Lympne 4.50; to the Ivory Coast 1.56 as F-OATT

G-AEXO   (6368), 19.7.37, North Eastern Airways Ltd., Doncaster; impressed 3.40 as X8507 for use by No.24 Sqn., Hendon; struck off charge 6.41

G-AEXP   (6369), 19.7.37, North Eastern Airways Ltd., Doncaster; impressed 3.40 as X8505; damaged by enemy action at St. Omer, France 21.5.40

G-AFAH   (6377), 27.8.37, Personal Airways Ltd., Croydon; Capt. G. S. Whitelaw, Barton 6.38; impressed 3.30 as X8508; burned at Merville, France 21.5.40

G-AFAO   (6372), 4.8.37, de Havilland Aircraft Co. Ltd.; to Turkey 9.37 as TC-DAG

G-AFEN   (6399), 25.4.38, Sir Wm. Firth, Heston; to Palestine 12.38 as VQ-PAC; rest. 12.40 to Sec. of State for Air, Heliopolis; impressed 2.42 as HK864; rest. 4.47 to W. A. Rollason Ltd., Croydon; to Argentina 12.48

G-AFEO   (6405), 9.5.38, North Eastern Airways Ltd., Croydon; impressed 3.40 as X8506 for No.24 Sqn., Hendon; abandoned in France 5.40

G-AFEP   (6406), 13.5.38, North Eastern Airways Ltd., Croydon; impressed 3.40 as X9388; rest. 11.40 to Air Commerce Ltd., Speke; Olley Air Service Ltd., Croydon 12.46; F. A. White and H. C. D. Haytor, Croydon 9.47; to Mrs. E. M. Noon, Nairobi 6.48 as VP-KFV; d.b.f. at Masindi 29.11.49

G-AFEY   (6402), 11.4.38, Scottish Airways Ltd., Renfrew; crashed at Kirkwall, Orkney 18.3.40

G-AFEZ   (6408), 21.6.38, Wrightways Ltd., Croydon; impressed 4.40 as X9451; rest. 9.40 to Isle of Man Air Services Ltd., Speke; B.E.A., Northolt 'Lord Shaftesbury' 2.47; to Laos Air Service 11.56 as F-LAAL

G-AFFB   (6409), 27.5.38, Iraq Petroleum Transport Co. Ltd., Haifa; Air Transport Charter (C.I.) Ltd., Jersey 7.47; Island Air Services Ltd., Heathrow 4.54; Trans European Airways Ltd., Baginton 7.59; w.f.u. Baginton 2.62

G-AFFC   (6410), 2.6.38, Iraq Petroleum Transport Co. Ltd., Haifa; impressed in the Near East 2.42 as HK862; to Iraq and Persia Communication Flt.

G-AFFF   (6386), 16.3.38, de Havilland Aircraft Co. Ltd.; Railway Air Services Ltd., Renfrew 7.38, named 'Juno' in 1945; crashed at Milngavie 27.9.46

463

G-AFHY   (6417), 1.9.38, Anglo Iranian Oil Co. Ltd., Abadan; Aircraft & Engineering Services Ltd., Croydon 10.46; Air Charter Ltd., Haddenham 3.47; sold in Belgium 6.50

G-AFHZ   (6418), 15.9.38, Anglo Iranian Oil Co. Ltd., Abadan; W. A. Rollason Ltd., Croydon 6.47; to the Uganda Co. 9.47 as VP-UAX; later VP-KFH

G-AFIA   (6419), 22.9.38, Anglo Iranian Oil Co. Ltd., Abadan; destroyed by fire at Abadan 20.8.42

G-AFLY   (6426), 30.11.38, Airwork Ltd., Perth; impressed 7.40 as Z7253

G-AFLZ   (6429), 14.12.38, Airwork Ltd., Perth; impressed 7.40 as Z7254; rest. 5.46 to Field Consolidated Aircraft Services Ltd., Hanworth as G-AHPX; to The Aircraft Operating Co. of Africa Pty. Ltd. 8.46 as ZS-AYF

G-AFMA   (6430), 3.1.39, Airwork Ltd., Perth; impressed 7.40 as Z7255; rest. 6.47 to Ciros Aviation Ltd.; Wm. Dempster Ltd., Heathrow 1.49; to Portugal 4.50 as CS-AEB; re-registered in Angola as CR-LCO

G-AFME   (6431), 13.1.39, Airwork Ltd., Perth; impressed 7.40 as Z7257

G-AFMF   (6432), 20.1.39, Airwork Ltd., Perth; impressed 7.40 as Z7256; rest. 1.46 to N. R. Harben, Burnaston; D. L. Steiner, Speke 1.47; British Cellulose Co. Ltd., Ringway 3.48; J. W. Adamson t/a Oldstead Aircraft, Yeadon 4.50; crashed at Hexham, Northumberland 19.2.54

G-AFMG   (6433), 1.2.39, Airwork Ltd., Perth; impressed 7.40 as Z7259; rest. 12.46 to Portsmouth Aviation Ltd.; to Weston Air Services 5.48 as EI-AEA

G-AFMH   (6434), 6.2.39, Airwork Ltd., Perth; impressed 7.40 as Z7258 'Women of the Empire' for ambulance duties at Abbotsinch; struck off charge 7.45

G-AFMI   (6435), 20.2.39, Airwork Ltd., Perth; impressed 7.40 as Z7260

G-AFMJ   (6436), 27.2.39, Airwork Ltd., Perth; impressed 7.40 as Z7261 as 'Women of Britain' for ambulance duties at Wick; rest. 12.47 to Air Enterprises Ltd., Gatwick, named 'Shanklin Flyer'; Airwork Ltd. 4.53; to Aero-Carga, Paraguay 9.56 as ZP-TDH

G-AFNC   (6442), 21.6.39, Aircraft Operating Co. Ltd., Hatfield; impressed 10.39 as V4724; rest. 6.46 to Field Consolidated Aircraft Ltd., Hanworth; to the Belgian Congo 8.46 as OO-CCD; Belgian registration cancelled 7.47

The Air Jordan Rapide JY-ABP, formerly TJ-ABP and originally Channel Islands Airways' G-AGSK, in use by the Dead Sea (1,292 ft. below sea level) in 1956. (*P. R. Keating*)

G-AFND (6443), 29.6.39, Aircraft Operating Co. Ltd., Hatfield; impressed 10.39 as
V4725; rest. 12.47 to W. A. Rollason Ltd., Croydon; to Arab Airways
Association Ltd., Amman 7.48 as TJ-AAP
G-AFOI (6450), 28.8.39, Scottish Airways Ltd., Renfrew; B.E.A., Northolt 2.47;
Gibraltar Airways Ltd. 1.49; Airmotive (Liverpool) Ltd. 1.50; Handley Page
Ltd., Radlett 6.52; scrapped at Tollerton 9.57
G-AFRK (6441), 8.5.39, Isle of Man Air Services Ltd., Derbyhaven; Scottish Airways
Ltd., Renfrew 8.39; B.E.A., Northolt 'Rudyard Kipling' 2.47; Airviews Ltd.,
Barton 6.56; reduced to spares at Christchurch 3.59
G-AFSO (6445), 22.5.39, Western Airways Ltd., Weston-super-Mare; impressed 1.40
as W6457; destroyed by enemy action, Aneuil, France 31.5.40
G-AGDM (6584), 8.11.41, Allied Airways (Gandar Dower) Ltd., Dyce 'Eldorado';
B.E.A., Northolt 11.47; Sivewright Airways Ltd., Barton 6.49; Airviews Ltd.,
Barton 9.51; modified to Mk.4; to French Guiana 3.57 as F-OAXK
G-AGDP (6403), F-AQOH, 5.5.38, Iraq Petroleum Transport Co. Ltd., Haifa; Modern
Transport Ltd., Wolverhampton 4.49; Don Everall (Aviation) Ltd., Elmdon
1.52; w.f.u. 7.58; burned at Wolverhampton 8.69

de Havilland D.H.89B Dominie (*conversions to civil D.H.89A*)
  G-AGDG (6547), X7387, 21.10.41, to French Indo China 11.47 as F-OADX;
G-AGDH (6548), X7388, 10.10.41, d.b.r. by gale, Stornoway 25.11.41; G-AGED
(6621), X7504, 25.4.42, crashed at Renfrew 2.2.43; G-AGEE (6622), X7505, to Iceland
7.53 as TF-KAA; G-AGFU (6463), R5926, 4.8.43, derelict at Brussels 1952; G-AGHI
(6455), P9588, 18.3.44, w.f.u. at Croydon 9.50; G-AGIC (6522), X7349, 20.8.43, to
French Indo China 11.47 as F-OADZ; G-AGIF (6509), X7336, 20.7.43, to spares at
Newtownards 10.50; G-AGJF (6499), X7326, 29.10.43, crashed at Barra, Hebrides
6.8.47; G-AGJG (6517), X7344, 15.2.44; G-AGLE (6784), NR685, 12.2.45, w.f.u.
at Croydon 12.51; G-AGLN (6795), NR696, 1.12.44, crashed at Abadan, Persia
15.12.46; G-AGLO reservation not taken up; G-AGLP (6780), NR681, 2.2.45, w.f.u.
at Croydon 9.50; G-AGLR (6781), NR682, 13.1.45, crashed at Berkswell, Warwicks
7.10.56
  G-AGNH (6803), NR715, 16.5.45, to Kenya 8.46 as VP-KCT, rest. 8.49, to Aden 2.57
as VR-AAP; G-AGOJ (6850), NR774, 27.9.45, d.b.r. at Lympne 1.5.61; G-AGOP
(6873), NR797, 3.8.45, crashed in Syria 25.6.48; G-AGOR (6877), NR801, 3.8.45, to
Kenya 9.53 as VP-KLB; G-AGOT (6876), NR800, 21.7.45, to Kenya 8.46 as VP-KCX;
G-AGOU (6875), NR799, 21.7.45, to Kenya 8.46 as VP-KCW; G-AGOV (6874),
NR798, 29.8.45, to Kenya 8.46 as VP-KCY; G-AGOW (6849), NR773, 6.7.45, to Kenya
8.46 as VP-KCV, rest. 11.56, w.f.u. at Croydon 12.57; G-AGOX (6848), NR772, 6.7.45,
to Kenya 8.46 as VP-KCU; G-AGPH (6889), NR813, 30.6.45, d.b.r. at Barra, Hebrides
6.12.51; G-AGPI (6885), NR809, 30.6.45, crashed at Cowes 16.6.49; G-AGSH (6884),
NR808, 25.8.45, to Ireland 4.57 as EI-AJO, rest. 7.57; G-AGSI (6886), NR810, 15.8.45,
to Australia 10.54 as VH-BFS; G-AGSJ (6888), NR812, 15.8.45, to Denmark 12.49 as
OY-ACZ; G-AGSK (6887), NR811, 27.8.45, to Jordan 10.53 as TJ-ABP
  G-AGTM (6746), NF875, 6.12.45, to the Lebanon 4.53 as OD-ABP, rest. 3.64;
G-AGTN (6749), NF878, sold in the U.S.A. 6.52; G-AGUF (6855), NR779, 29.10.45,
crashed at Ramsgate 29.6.57; G-AGUG (6859), NR783, 8.11.45, to Pakistan 6.53 as
AP-AGL, rest. 9.56, to Dakar 1.63 as F-OCAG; G-AGUP (6911), NR847, 20.12.45, to
the Ivory Coast 4.58 as F-OBGY; G-AGUR (6910), NR846, 20.12.45, crashed at Frankfurt 2.8.54; G-AGUU (6908), NR844, 10.1.46, to Borneo 9.52 as VR-OAA; G-AGUV
(6912), NR848, 9.1.46, burned out near Bahrein 26.4.54; G-AGWC (6916), NR852,

21.1.46, to Pakistan 8.52 as AP-ADM; G-AGWP (6918), RL936, 18.1.46, to the Congo 9.60; G-AGWR (6917), NR853, 25.1.46, to Denmark 5.54 as OY-DYA; G-AGZJ (6936), RL954, 1.4.46, w.f.u. at Cardiff 1.52; G-AGZK (6937), RL955, 21.3.46, w.f.u. at Beirut 12.51; G-AGZO (6913), NR849, 11.2.46, to France 6.52 as F-BGZJ; G-AGZU (6773), NR674, 12.2.46, to South Africa 7.55 as ZS-DLS

G-AHAG (6926), RL944, 18.2.46, airworthy in 1972; G-AHEA (6946), RL964, 12.4.46, to France 1.55 as F-BHCF; G-AHEB (6945), RL963, 17.4.46, to Ireland 8.47 as EI-ADP, rest. 4.55, to France 4.57 as F-BHVQ; G-AHED (6944), RL962, 25.4.46, w.f.u. at Leavesden 3.69, to R.A.F. Museum, Hendon; G-AHFJ (6545), X7385, 28.5.46, to Kenya 6.48 as VP-KFW; G-AHGC (6583), X7442, 25.6.46, w.f.u. 7.68; G-AHGD (6862), NR786, 17.5.46; G-AHGF (6903), NR839, 19.11.45, to New Zealand 7.54 as ZK-BFK; G-AHGG (6902), NR838, 26.11.45, to Liberia 4.52 as EL-AAA; G-AHGH (6934), RL952, 6.3.46, to Sweden 6.53 as SE-BXZ; G-AHGI (6935), RL953, 18.3.46, to French Indo China 11.52 as F-OANF; G-AHIA (6948), RL966, 8.4.46, d.b.r. at Maritse, Rhodes 5.3.51

G-AHJA (6486), R9558, 8.5.47, w.f.u. 4.70; G-AHJS (6967), TX309, 18.7.46, w.f.u. at Blackbushe 5.66; G-AHKA (6839), NR751, 20.5.46, to French Guiana 2.54 as F-OAQL; G-AHKB (6596), X7454, to France 10.61 as F-BEKB; G-AHKR (6824), NR736, 9.7.46, crashed in the Isle of Man 15.4.47; G-AHKS (6812), NR724, 26.8.46, to Borneo 6.55 as VR-OAC; G-AHKT (6811), NR723, 22.6.46, to French Guiana 2.58 as F-OAUG; G-AHKU (6810), NR722, 14.6.46, w.f.u. 5.72; G-AHKV (6792), NR693, 25.7.46, w.f.u. at Elmdon 9.69; G-AHLF (6494), X7321, 20.6.46, scrapped and burned at Portsmouth 12.62; G-AHLL (6576), X7416, 28.6.46, to spares 2.60; G-AHLM (6708), HG723, 13.7.46, crashed at St. Mary's, Scilly Is. 20.7.63; G-AHLN (6754), NF883, 6.10.46, to France 4.53 as F-BGOQ; G-AHLU (6633), X7516, 30.7.46, to Australia 11.49 as VH-AHI

G-AHPT (6478), R9550, 6.10.46, crashed near Leverstock, Herts. 7.7.59; G-AHPU (6963), TX305, 29.6.46, to Sierra Leone 4.58 as VR-LAD; G-AHPV (6759), NF888, registered 22.5.46, to South Africa 8.46 as ZS-AYG; G-AHPW (6678), HG693, registered 22.5.46, to South Africa 10.46 as ZS-BCO; G-AHPX (6429), G-AFLZ, Z7254, registered 22.5.46, to South Africa 8.46 as ZS-AYF; G-AHPY (6561), X7401, registered 22.5.46, to South Africa 10.46 as ZS-BCP; G-AHRH (6823), NR735, 18.10.46, to Algeria 2.60 as F-OBOH; G-AHTR (6964), TX306, 4.7.46, burned out at Abadan, Persia 7.50; G-AHTS (6962), TX304, 22.6.46, crashed 29.4.47; G-AHTT (6966), TX308, 18.7.46, to Persia 11.51 as EP-AAX; G-AHTY (6608), X7491, 1.8.46, to France 9.52 as F-BGIS; G-AHWF (6965), TX307, 4.7.46, to Persia 11.51 as EP-AAW; G-AHXV (6747), NF876, 16.8.46, d.b.r. at Ronaldsway 15.1.49; G-AHXW (6782), NR683, 16.8.46, to the U.S.A. 2.71 as N683DH; G-AHXX (6800), NR701, 9.8.46, to Borneo 9.52 as VR-OAB; G-AHXY (6808), NR720, 13.9.46, crashed at Renfrew 27.12.48; G-AHXZ (6825), NR737, 5.9.46, burned out at Renfrew 28.8.51

G-AIBB (6813), NR725, 6.5.48, to Dakar 8.61 as F-OBVJ; G-AIDL (6968), TX310, 5.9.46; G-AIHN (6498), X7325, 25.10.46, to South Africa 10.54 as ZS-DJT; G-AIIJ (6675), HG690, 29.5.47, crashed in the Isle of Man 10.6.48; G-AIUJ (6724), NF853, registered 8.11.46, to India 5.47 as VT-CHZ; G-AIUK (6640), X7523, 26.9.47, to Kenya 2.55 as VP-KND; G-AIUL (6837), NR749, 8.5.47, w.f.u. 10.70; G-AIUM (6519), X7346, 19.2.47, to Sweden 7.50 as SE-BTA; G-AIUN (6602), X7485, 7.8.47, registration cancelled 5.50; G-AIUO (6467), R5930, 20.6.47, to Sweden 8.51 as SE-BTT; G-AIWG (6497), X7324, 6.1.47, to Australia 2.50 as VH-AIK; G-AIWY (6775), NR676, 26.11.46, to Denmark 1.47 as OY-AHO; G-AIWZ (6867), NR791, 13.1.47, crashed at Brough 30.7.49; G-AIYE (6815), NR727, 23.12.46, to Algeria 3.57 as F-OAYS; G-AIYP

G-AKIF 'The Rothman Skydriver', one of a fleet of Rapides sponsored by this tobacco firm for dropping parachutists. (*Chris Morris*)

(6456), P9589, 17.1.47, forced landed and burned out near Pwllheli 5.7.53; G-AIYR (6676), HG691, 26.2.48, airworthy in 1972; G-AIYY (6854), NR778, 23.1.47, w.f.u. at Rochester 4.64; G-AIZI (6861), NR785, 25.3.47, crashed at Wallington, Surrey 14.9.52

G-AJBJ (6765), NF894, 26.3.47, dismantled at Squires Gate 9.61; G-AJCL (6722), NF851, 29.5.49, dismantled at Fairoaks 6.71; G-AJDN (6860), NR784, 30.4.47, to Algeria 8.58 as F-OBIV; G-AJFJ (6587), X7445, 27.6.47, dismantled at Croydon 6.51; G-AJFK (6552), X7392, 29.4.47, to Pakistan 3.52 as AP-AFN; G-AJFL (6631), X7514, registered 29.1.47, to Uganda 3.47 as VP-UAW; G-AJFM (6496), X7323, registered 29.1.47, to Kenya 4.47 as VP-KEE; G-AJFN (6520), X7347, to Belgium 4.47 as OO-CDE, rest. 7.47, C. of A. 23.7.47, burned out at Kosti, Sudan 4.12.47; G-AJFO (6726), NF855, to Belgium 4.47 as OO-CDF, rest. 7.47, C. of A. 23.7.47, burned out at Kosti, Sudan 4.12.47; G-AJGS (W.1001), 12.3.48, sold in the U.S.A. 8.70; G-AJGV (6589), X7447, 30.4.47, sold in Paraguay 6.55; G-AJGZ (6883), NR807, 13.5.47, burned out at Agha Jari, Persia 16.7.49; G-AJHO (6835), NR747, 27.6.47, airworthy in 1972; G-AJHP (6770), NR671, 16.5.47, to Algeria 7.60 as F-OBOI

G-AJKE (6555), X7395, 28.8.47, to France 5.52 as F-BEFU; G-AJKH (6763), NF892, 8.1.48, seized in Persia 10.51 as EP-AAV; G-AJKI (6768), NR792, 31.10.47, seized in Persia 10.51 as EP-AAY; G-AJKW (6539), X7379, 30.7.48, d.b.r. at Halfpenny Green 7.5.67; G-AJKX (6457), R5921, 18.7.47, to Pakistan 5.53 as AP-AGI, crated back to Croydon 7.56, scrapped at Biggin Hill 1962; G-AJKY (6553), X7393, 17.2.48, to French Indo China 6.54 as F-OAQZ; G-AJMY (6511), X7338, 17.2.48, to Portuguese Guinea 10.52 as CR-GAK; G-AJNA (6516), X7343, 23.7.47, to France 12.47 as F-BEDI; G-AJSJ (6826), NR738, 25.7.47, crashed in Tunisia 18.9.47; G-AJSK (6500), X7327, 27.4.48, to Kenya 5.54 as VP-KMD; G-AJSL (6801), NR713, 26.10.49, scrapped 1.71; G-AJTU (6558), X7398, 7.10.47, to Kenya 12.48 as VP-KGS; G-AJVA (6600), X7483, 1.3.48, w.f.u. at Tripoli, Lebanon 10.52; G-AJVB (6753), NF882, 10.5.48, to Jordan 10.52 as JY-AAZ; G-AJXB (6530), X7370, 15.12.48, to Sweden 8.56 as SE-BCU

G-AKBW (6585), X7443, registered 18.7.47, not converted, scrapped 5.48; G-AKDW (6897), NR833, YI-ABD, 23.10.45, to France 7.58 as F-BCDB; G-AKDX (6898), NR834, YI-ABE, 24.10.45, to Kenya 2.51 as VP-KIO; G-AKED (6487), R9559,

Rapide G-ALWJ converted to Mk.4 with Gipsy Queen IIs and constant speed airscrews with large spinners as VP-KLL for Noon and Pearce Air Charters Ltd., Nairobi in 1953.
(*Flight*)

20.1.48, to French Morocco 1.56 as F-DABY; G-AKEU (6672), HG673, 3.6.48, sold in the Lebanon 8.51; G-AKFO (6460), R5924, registered 3.9.47, not converted; G-AKGV (6796), NR697, 17.10.47, to France 8.50 as F-BFPU; G-AKGY (6723), NF852, 20.5.48, to France 9.57 as F-BFEH; G-AKIF (6838), NR750, 22.12.47, to Norway 8.71 as LN-BEZ; G-AKJS (W.1002), E-0228, 2.12.47, to France as spares 8.65; G-AKJY (6447), R2486, 13.5.48, to Algeria 5.54 as F-OAPT; G-AKJZ (6880), NR804, 3.6.49, w.f.u. at Biggin Hill 7.59

G-AKLA (6764), NF893, 18.1.50, d.b.r. near Jodhpur, India 15.6.54; G-AKMD (6802), NR714, 10.9.48, to Senegal 1.52 as F-OAKD; G-AKME (6767), NF896, 7.5.48, burned out at Lympne 30.6.50; G-AKMF (6617), X7500, 11.5.48, cancelled by M.C.A. 12.48; G-AKMG (6635), X7518, 13.5.48, to France 3.52 as F-BGPI; G-AKMH (6704), HG719, 16.6.48, sold in the Congo 10.64; G-AKND (6515), X7342, 1.4.48, to Kenya 8.48 as VP-KGE; G-AKNE (6519), X7449, 30.5.49, to Madagascar 9.57 as F-OBDV; G-AKNF (6518), X7345, 2.5.49, to Persia 8.55 as EP-ADP; G-AKNN (6598), X7456, 22.4.48; G-AKNV (6458), R5922, 24.3.48, to Ireland 12.53 as EI-AGK, rest. 6.55, to Belgium 12.56 as OO-AFG; G-AKNW (6469), R5932, 7.4.48, to the Lebanon 6.50 as OD-ABH; G-AKNX (6629), X7512, 13.2.48, to Gabon 9.55 as F-OATD; G-AKNY (6470), R5933, 25.3.48, to Dakar 10.60 as F-OBRX; G-AKNZ (6550), X7390, 9.3.48, to the Argentine 12.48

G-AKOA (6618), X7501, 18.3.48, to Persia 8.55 as EP-ADO; G-AKOB (6492), R9564, 19.3.48, to Kenya 12.55 as VP-KNS; G-AKOC (6814), NR726, 20.7.48, sold in Australia 8.49; G-AKOD (6566), X7406, 30.9.48, to French Indo China 6.54 as F-OAQY; G-AKOE (6601), X7484, 26.5.48, w.f.u. 7.65; G-AKOF (6538), X7378, 18.6.48, crashed in the River Mersey 11.11.48; G-AKOG (6878), NR802, 12.7.48, to Northern Rhodesia 10.51 as VP-RCH; G-AKOH (6582), X7441, 21.5.48, sold in France 6.53; G-AKOI (6546), X7386, 7.5.48, destroyed 9.48; G-AKOJ (6580), X7439, 20.4.48, to Jordan 5.48 as TJ-AAJ; G-AKOK (6474), R9546, 2.6.48, to France 3.52 as F-BGPK; G-AKOM (6758), NF887, 12.7.50, to Belgium 2.52 as OO-DCB; G-AKON (6620), X7503, 29.1.48, to Kenya 7.48 as VP-KFX; G-AKOO (6468), R5931, 2.12.48, sold in Chile 4.52; G-AKOP (6636), X7519, 14.1.48, cancelled by M.C.A. 5.48;

G-AKOR (6577), X7417, 1.3.48, to Fiji 12.52 as VQ-FAN; G-AKOV (6612), X7495, 18.9.48, to Kenya 2.55 as VP-KNC; G-AKOY (6504), X7331, 21.5.48, to Pakistan 6.53 as AP-AGM

G-AKPA (6709), HG724, 25.6.48, to Ireland 6.62 as EI-AML; G-AKRE (6606), X7489, 16.2.48, to French Indo China 1.49 as F-OABH; G-AKRN (6513), X7340, 24.3.48, w.f.u. at Ipswich 6.60; G-AKRO (6480), R9552, 11.5.48, to Algeria 2.54 as F-OAOY; G-AKRP (6940), RL958, 14.2.48, to Dakar 10.58 as F-DAFS; G-AKRR (6950), RL968, 25.2.48, to the Sudan 8.52 as SN-ABB, rest. 12.52, to Ethiopa 8.53 as ET-P-16; G-AKRS (6952), RL981, 9.4.48; G-AKSB (6951), RL980, 14.2.48, to the Gold Coast 2.50 as VP-AAA; G-AKSC (6779), NR680, 16.3.48, to New Caledonia 9.55 as F-OATC; G-AKSD (6949), RL967, 26.11.48, to Dakar 9.61 as F-OBVI; G-AKSE (6870), NR794, 10.3.48, to Ireland 5.59 as EI-AKH, rest. 10.59, to France 4.63 as F-BLHE; G-AKSF (6491), R9562, 23.6.48, burned out at Prestwick 23.7.49; G-AKSG (6931), RL949, 25.8.49, to France 7.56 as F-BHAF; G-AKSH (6471), R5934, 14.5.48, to Fiji 1.52 as VQ-FAM; G-AKSL (6865), NR789, 28.5.48, to France 5.52 as F-BGPL; G-AKTD (6791), NR692, 14.4.48, to France 5.51 as F-BFVM; G-AKTX (6639), X7522, 8.4.48, cancelled by M.C.A. 5.50; G-AKTY (6563), X7403, 5.5.48, to France 5.51 as F-BFVR; G-AKTZ (6482), R9554, 5.5.48, d.b.r. near Benghazi 27.5.57

G-AKUB (6488), R9560, 2.4.48, to Persia 8.55 as EP-ADN; G-AKUC (6565), X7405, 14.5.48, to Persia 8.55 as EP-ADM; G-AKUS (6805), NR717, 19.8.48, cancelled by M.C.A. 5.50; G-AKVU (6476), R9548, 25.3.49, to France 3.52 as F-BGPM; G-AKYW (6581), X7440, 2.11.48, sold in the Argentine 11.48; G-AKYX (6864), NR788, 29.7.48, to the Argentine 11.48 as LV-AEN; G-AKYY (6822), NR734, 2.11.48, sold in the Argentine 11.48; G-AKYZ (6789), NR690, 6.9.48, to the Argentine 9.48 as LV-AEO; G-AKZA (6892), NR828, 2.7.48, to South Africa 10.48 as ZS-BZC; G-AKZB (6790), NR691, 13.7.48, crashed at Lands End 12.12.61; G-AKZH (6529), X7369, 10.8.48, to Portuguese West Africa 5.52 as CR-GAJ; G-AKZI (6536), X7376, 29.7.48, cancelled by M.C.A. 5.50; G-AKZJ (6549), X7389, 29.6.48, cancelled by M.C.A. 6.50; G-AKZO (6575), X7415, 24.7.48, to France 8.60 as F-BHFM; G-AKZP (6882), NR806, 2.6.49, to France 8.65 as spares; G-AKZT (6894), NR830, LR-AAE, 1.10.45, to Ceylon 4.52 as CY-AAK; G-AKZV (6843), NR755, LR-AAD, 16.10.45, sold in South America 12.48; G-AKZW (6896), NR832, LR-AAF, 8.10.45, to Portuguese West Africa 5.52 as CR-GAI

G-ALAS (6484), R9556, registered 1.6.48, re-registered same day as G-ALEJ q.v.; G-ALAT (6851), NR775, 31.7.48, to France 1.55 as F-BHCE; G-ALAU (6609), X7492, 21.9.48, sold abroad 10.48; G-ALAX (6930), RL948, 4.9.48, scrapped at Luton 3.67; G-ALAY (6942), RL960, 29.7.48, sold in South America 12.48; G-ALAZ (6932), RL950, registered 17.7.48, to Belgian Congo 7.48 as OO-CFI; G-ALBA (6821), NR733, 24.7.48, w.f.u. at Baginton 9.61; G-ALBB (6829), NR741, 10.9.48, crashed at Heathrow 1.8.52; G-ALBC (6572), X7412, 2.7.48, crashed at Edale, Derbyshire 30.12.63; G-ALBH (6607), X7490, 9.8.49, sold in the Congo 9.60; G-ALBI (6525), X7352, 17.7.49, to Luxembourg as LX-LAD, rest. 7.51, to Dakar 8.60 as F-OBRV; G-ALEJ (6484), R9556, G-ALAS, 1.4.49, crashed near Eccleshall, Staffs. 14.9.56; G-ALET (6832), NR744, 21.11.49, to French Indo China 9.51 as F-OALD; G-ALGB (6706), HG721, 5.11.49, to France 10.54 as F-BHCD; G-ALGC (6906), NR842, YI-ABF, 17.12.45, in storage 1972; G-ALGE (6907), NR843, YI-ABG, 17.12.45, to Ireland 10.62 as EI-AMN; G-ALGI (6909), NR845, YI-ABH, 20.12.45, to Gabon 9.53 as F-OAND; G-ALGM (6559), X7399, registered 17.2.49, to France 7.52 as F-BGOL; G-ALGN (6943), RL961, 11.10.51, to Madagascar 1.52 as F-OAKE; G-ALGO (6830), NR742, 2.12.49, crashed at Abadan, Persia 10.7.51

G-ALNS (6778), NR679, 16.9.49, sold in the Congo 1.65; G-ALNT (6713), HG728, 8.7.49, to Australia 2.52 as VH-CFA; G-ALOV (6638), X7521, 30.5.49, to Gabon 3.54 as F-OAPS; G-ALPK (6757), NF886, 17.8.49, to spares at Netheravon 4.66; G-ALRW (6941), RL959, 29.7.49, to France 10.53 as F-BGXT; G-ALVU (6526), X7353, not converted, burned at Squires Gate 1962; G-ALWI (6703), HG718, 28.3.50, to France 3.52 as F-BGPJ; G-ALWJ (6777), NR678, 21.4.50, to Kenya 11.53 as VP-KLL; G-ALWK (6856), NR780, 12.4.50, to Algeria 4.57 as F-OBAL; G-ALWL (6778), NR679, 25.1.51, to France 3.52 as F-BGPH; G-ALWM (6755), NF884, registered 26.1.50, to France 6.50 as F-OAGP; G-ALWN (6729), NF858, 24.7.50, to France 3.52 as F-BGPG; G-ALWO (6840), NR752, 10.5.50, to Southern Rhodesia 6.51 as VP-YHE; G-ALWP (6707), HG722, 26.7.50, to Fiji 6.51 as VQ-FAL; G-ALWY (6741), NF870, 24.3.50, d.b.r. Isle of Islay 19.4.52

G-ALXA (6727), NF856, 8.6.50, burned out at Hanoi 4.6.52; G-ALXI (6690), HG705, 25.5.50, to Austria 11.55 as OE-FAA; G-ALXJ (6863), NR787, 6.4.50, crashed in sea off Laxey Head, I.O.M. 10.7.51; G-ALXS (6715), HG730, registered 24.1.50, to Jordan 5.50 as TJ-AAU; G-ALXT (6736), NF865, 2.5.50, to Ceylon 6.51 as CY-AAI; G-ALXU (6797), NR698, registered 24.1.50, to Jordan 5.50 as TJ-AAV; G-ALZF (6541), X7381, 5.7.50, to France 9.52 as F-BGON; G-ALZH (6448), R2487, 24.5.50, to Madagascar 4.52 as F-OAKF; G-ALZJ (6573), X7413, 21.4.50, to Tunisia 11.56 as F-OAME

G-AMAI (6879), NR803, 7.7.50, to Spain 8.52 as EC-AGP; G-AMAM (6571), X7411, 29.3.51, w.f.u. at Wymeswold 11.60; G-AMCT (6714), HG729, 9.10.50, to France 8.56 as F-BHTH; G-AMDG (6818), NR730, 26.2.51, to French Indo China 5.51 as F-OAIR; G-AMJK (given as 83908), VT-ARV, 24.9.51, to French Guiana 10.61 as F-OBVL

G-ANAH (6786) NR687, 3.3.54, to Uruguay 9.54 as CX-API; G-ANET (6700), HG715, 18.11.53, to Aden 6.55 as VR-AAL; G-ANEU (6836), NR748, 27.11.53; to Gabon 9.54 as F-OAQU; G-ANJR (6816), NR728, 15.4.54, to Madagascar 7.54 as F-OAKX; G-ANZP (6682), HG697, 9.9.55, w.f.u. at Speke 7.62

G-AOAO (6844), NR756, 7.1.56, to France 1.56 as F-BHGR; G-AOZG (6603), X7486, 18.10.57, to Sierra Leone 1.58 as VR-LAC; G-APBJ (6872), NR796, Dutch V-2, PH-VNB, to Tunisia unconverted 9.57 as F-OBGE; G-APBM (6748), NF877, Dutch V-1, PH-VNA, 3.9.57, to Dakar 8.60 as F-OBRU; G-APBN (6787), NR688, Belgian D-5, OO-ARI, to Algeria unconverted 4.58 as F-OBIA; G-APJW (6578), X7437, 20.5.58, to France 8.62 as F-BHOB; G-APKA (6827), NR739, 6.5.58, to Sierra Leone 7.58 as VR-LAE; G-APSD (6556), X7396, 19.7.60, scrapped at Shoreham 7.64; G-ASFC (6679), HG694, 5.7.63, w.f.u. 8.65; G-ASIA (6718), NF847, not converted, dismantled at Abingdon 1963; G-ASKI (6858), NR782, converted 1965, to Italy 3.65 as I-BOBJ; G-ASKO (6735), NF864, 13.3.64, to French Guiana 3.66 as F-OCHF; G-ASRJ (6959), TX301, TJ-AAD, 26.5.64, w.f.u. 3.70; G-ASRM (6961), TX303, TJ-AAE, to the Congo 8.64 in British markings

de Havilland D.H.90 Dragonfly

G-ADNA (7500), E-2, 17.1.36, de Havilland Aircraft Co. Ltd.; A. Batchelor, Ramsgate 1.38; Southern A/W Ltd., Heston 4.39; impressed 4.40 as X9452

G-ADXM (7509), 20.6.36, Sir W. L. Everard, Ratcliffe 'Leicestershire Vixen II'; impressed 2.40 as X9327; struck off charge 22.7.44

G-AEBU (7501), 15.2.36, de Havilland Aircraft Co. Ltd., Hatfield; to France 5.38 as F-AQEU

G-AECW (7504), 28.7.36, London Aeroplane Club, Hatfield; de Havilland Aircraft Co.
Ltd., Hatfield 3.38; company wartime communications; scrapped 11.45

G-AECX (7505), 20.5.36, A. H. Youngman, Heston; to India 3.38 as VT-AKC; rest.
8.39 to International Air Freight Ltd., Croydon; Hon. Mrs. Victor Bruce,
Cardiff 12.39; impressed 6.40 as AX855; struck off charge 22.2.42

G-AEDG (7516), 28.7.36, J. V. Fairbairn, Heston 'Spirit of Flanders'; re-registered in
Australia 10.37 as VH-ADG; withdrawn from use 1.48

G-AEDH (7510), 2.7.36, S. Harris, Redhill; Plymouth Airport Ltd. 9.37; Western
Airways Ltd.,.Weston-super-Mare 2.39; impressed 5.40 as AV987

G-AEDI (7511), 13.10.36, British Continental Airways Ltd., Croydon; sold in
Singapore 10.36 as VR-SAX

G-AEDJ (7515), 3.7.36, Loel Guinness, Heston; A. J. Jameson, Heston 11.37; Hon.
Mrs. Victor Bruce, Cardiff 6.40; impressed 6.40 as AV992

After three years in France as F-AOYK, Dragonfly c/n 7521 was briefly G-AFVJ
from June 1939 until impressed for Army Co-operation duties in March 1940.
(*E. J. Riding*)

G-AEDK (7517), 5.9.36, C. J. Donada, Heston; Mutual Finance Ltd., Croydon 11.39;
Anglo European Airways Ltd., Cardiff 6.40; impressed 6.40 as AW164

G-AEDT (7508), 22.6.36, Sir P. Sassoon, Lympne; to Australia 7.38 as VH-AAD; rest.
12.63 to Lord Trefgarne, Shoreham; to the U.S.A. 8.64 as N2034

G-AEDU (7509), registration not used; aircraft completed and flown as G-ADXM

G-AEDV (7524), 8.10.36, Hon. C. F. Winn, Croydon; Birkett Air Services Ltd., Heston
12.39; impressed 3.40 as X9389; crashed at Chedzoy, Som. 3.9.41

G-AEDW (7503), 9.5.36, H. B. Legge & Sons Ltd., Warlingham; to Rhodesia and
Nyasaland Airways Ltd., Salisbury 2.38 as VP-YBR; crashed at Kasama 1939

G-AEEK (7518), 11.9.36, Sir William Firth, Heston; crashed at Beeding, Sussex just
north of Shoreham Aerodrome, owner and pilot uninjured, 17.8.37

G-AEFN (7507), 6.6.36, W. G. Robson, Heston; Air Commerce Ltd., Heston 5.39;
impressed 3.40 as X9390; crashed at Cosford 10.9.41

G-AEHC (7514), 14.7.36, Lord Beaverbrook, Croydon; London Express Newspapers
Ltd., Croydon 1.37; crashed at Newton Stewart, Wigtownshire 2.2.37

G-AESW (7544), 4.3.37, W. A. Rollason, Croydon; Air Taxis Ltd., Croydon 12.39; impressed 5.40 as AV976; reduced to spares'at Ringway 11.40

G-AEWZ (7555), 9.7.37, Air Service Training Ltd., Hamble; impressed 1.41 as DJ716; rest. 5.46 to Short Bros. Ltd., Rochester; F. T. Bingham, Eastleigh 12.48; V. H. Bellamy, Eastleigh 6.49; Silver City Airways Ltd., Blackbushe 7.50; V. H. Bellamy, Eastleigh 7.60; d.b.r. at Elmdon 3.3.61

G-AEXI (7554), 27.5.37, Lt. Col. E. T. Peel, Heston; to Kenya 11.38 as VP-KCS

G-AEXN (7559), 16.6.37, de Havilland Aircraft Co. Ltd.; E. D. Spratt, Hatfield 7.37; Hon. Max Aitken, Hendon 3.38; Mutual Finance Ltd., Croydon 1.39; crashed at Hampden, in the Chilterns near High Wycombe 21.7.39

G-AFAN (7556), 5.8.37, de Havilland Aircraft Co. Ltd., Hatfield; to Devlet Hava Yollari (Turkish State Air Line) 9.37 as TC-IDE

G-AFRF (7519), F-AOZC, 27.8.36, Mutual Finance Ltd., Croydon; Anglo European Airways Ltd., Cardiff 5.40; impressed 6.40 as AV993

G-AFRI (7536), F-APAX, 7.12.36, Hon. Mrs. Victor Bruce, Croydon; Anglo European Airways Ltd., Cardiff 5.40; impressed 6.40 as AV994

G-AFTF (7533), VH-UXA, 21.10.36, E. E. Noddings, Croydon; impressed 8.40 as BD149; struck off charge 21.5.42

G-AFVJ (7521), F-AOYK, 14.9.36, Airwork Ltd., Heston (leased to Allflight Ltd.); impressed 3.40 as X9337; d.b.r. taking off from Old Sarum 24.6.41

G-AIYJ (7553), SU-ABW, 22.7.37, C. G. M. Alington, Elmdon; w.f.u. at Gatwick 3.49

G-ANYK (7529), F-APDE, EC-BAA, EC-AAQ, OO-PET, F-OAMS, first flown 27.3.59 after rebuild at Eastleigh, C. of A. 27.5.59, O. Hill, Eastleigh; J. Jarvis and B. Winslett, Portsmouth 12.59; Metropolitan Air Movements Ltd., Gatwick 1.61; crashed on landing at La Baule, France 22.6.61

de Havilland D.H.91 Albatross (*mail carrier*)

G-AEVV (6800), E-2, K8618 ntu, 29.9.38, Sec. of State for Air; to Imperial Airways Ltd. 8.39 as 'Faraday'; to B.O.A.C. 1940; impressed for No.271 Sqn. 9.40 as AX903; swung into Fairey Battle L5547 landing Reykjavik 11.8.41

G-AEVW (6801), E-5, K8619 ntu, 3.7.40, Sec. of State for Air; to B.O.A.C. as 'Franklin'; impressed for No.271 Sqn. 9.40 as AX904; beyond repair when undercarriage collapsed during landing run at Reykjavik 7.4.42

de Havilland D.H.91 Albatross (*passenger carriers*)

G-AFDI (6802), 17.10.38, Imperial Airways Ltd., Croydon 'Frobisher'; destroyed on the ground during German air raid on Whitchurch, Bristol 20.12.40

G-AFDJ (6803), 1.11.38, Imperial Airways Ltd., Croydon 'Falcon'; scrapped 9.43

G-AFDK (6804), 6.1.39, Imperial Airways Ltd., Croydon 'Fortuna'; crash landed near Shannon Airport, Ireland 6.7.43

G-AFDL (6805), 4.4.39, Imperial Airways Ltd., Croydon 'Fingal'; crash landed near Pucklechurch, Gloucestershire 6.10.40

G-AFDM (6806), 16.6.39, Imperial Airways Ltd., Croydon 'Fiona'; scrapped 9.43

de Havilland D.H.94 Moth Minor (*open cockpit models*)

G-AFMZ (94029), 27.7.39, Kent Flying Club, Bekesbourne; impressed 6.40 as AW151; written off after undercarriage collapsed at Wymeswold 13.9.42

G-AFNA (94058), de Havilland Aircraft Co. Ltd., Hatfield; application for C. of A. cancelled; aircraft sold in South Africa

G-AFNB (94066), de Havilland Aircraft Co. Ltd., Hatfield; application for C. of A. cancelled; aircraft sold in South Africa

G-AFNE (94019), 8.7.39, Marquess of Londonderry, Ards; sold abroad 2.40

G-AFNF (94010), 30.6.39, Newcastle-on-Tyne Aero Club, Woolsington; Hartlepools and Tees-side Flying Club, West Hartlepool 2.40; impressed 9.40 as BK838; rest. 3.46 to W. A. Rollason Ltd., Croydon; to France 10.51 as F-BFYR; fitted with sliding canopy 1.59 and re-registered F-PFYR

G-AFNG (94014), 4.7.39, Cambridge Aero Club; impressed 6.40 as AW112; rest. 5.46 to D. G. S. Cotter, White Waltham; converted to coupé at Panshanger in 1954; A. J. Baggarley, Shoreham 2.69; A. Haig-Thomas, Horsey Is. 5.72

G-AFNH (94023), 15.7.39, Newcastle-on-Tyne Aero Club, Woolsington; Hartlepools and Tees-side Flying Club, West Hartlepool 2.40; impressed 9.40 as BK839; rest. 2.46 to Newman Aircraft Ltd., Panshanger; G. S. Meek, Perth 8.48; crashed in the Isle of Skye 15.4.49

G-AFNI (94035), 27.7.39, Newcastle-on-Tyne Aero Club, Woolsington; impressed 1.40 as W7972; rest. 3.46 to G. A. R. Malcolm, White Waltham; converted to cabin model at Panshanger 1954; reduced to spares in 1967

G-AFNJ (94038), 28.7.39, Cambridge Aero Club; impressed 6.40 as AW113; rest. 6.46 to the R.A.F. Flying Club, Panshanger; to France 5.54 as F-BAOG

G-AFNK (94048), 24.8.39, Hull Aero Club, Hedon; impressed 9.40 as BK847

G-AFNN (94067), de Havilland Aircraft Co. Ltd., Hatfield; application for C. of A. cancelled; shipped to Australia; became VH-ACR, later A21-42

The London Aeroplane Club's second Moth Minor G-AFON after restoration in New Zealand 1947 as ZK-AKM. (*K. Meehan*)

G-AFNO (94103), registration not taken up; aircraft completed as E-14/G-AGAO

G-AFNX (94072), de Havilland Aircraft Co. Ltd., Hatfield; application for C. of A. cancelled; shipped to Australia; became VH-ACQ; w.f.u. 5.47

G-AFNZ (94050), 24.8.39, Hon. Lady Mary Bailey D.B.E.: reg'n. cancelled 10.39

G-AFOA (94074), de Havilland Aircraft Co. Ltd., Hatfield; application for C. of A. cancelled; shipped to Australia for the R.A.A.F.

G-AFOB (94018), 7.7.39, Norfolk & Norwich Aero Club; impressed 11.39 as X5117; rest. 11.46 to W. R. Scott, White Waltham; G. S. Meek, Perth 2.52; J. H. Stevens, Charing, Kent 3.59; being restored at Woodley in 1972

G-AFOC (94042), 29.7.39, Norfolk & Norwich Aero Club; impressed 11.39 as X5115

The author photographing the Hornet Moth camera ship from the West London Aero Club's Moth Minor G-AFPT over White Waltham in July 1946. (*E. J. Riding*)

G-AFOD   (94022), 11.7.39, Airwork Flying Club, Heston; impressed 12.39 as X5120; rest. 2.46 to Sqn. Ldr. W. C. Potter, Heston; E. I. H. Ward, Shoreham 9.46; reduced to spares at Eastleigh 11.49

G-AFOE   (94024), 14.7.39, Airwork Flying Club, Heston; impressed 12.39 as X5121

G-AFOF   (94056), 28.8.39, Airwork Flying Club, Heston; reg'n. cancelled 10.39

G-AFOG   (94063), de Havilland Aircraft Co. Ltd., Hatfield; application for C. of A. cancelled; shipped to Australia for the R.A.A.F.

G-AFOM   (94008), 12.7.39, London Aeroplane Club, Panshanger; to Australia 3.40 as VH-AED; withdrawn from use 8.54

G-AFON   (94012), 12.7.39, London Aeroplane Club, Panshanger; to New Zealand 2.40 as ZK-AHK; impressed 10.42 as NZ597; rest. 2.47 as ZK-AKM

G-AFOO   (94033), 20.7.39, London Aeroplane Club, Panshanger; to Australia 2.40 as VH-AEE; later VH-CBE; wrecked at Traverston, Qld. 11.6.49

G-AFOP   (94041), 28.8.39, London Aeroplane Club, Panshanger; Leicestershire Aero Club 8.39; to N.V. National Luchtvaartschool 3.40 as PH-AZG

G-AFOS   (94070), de Havilland Aircraft Co. Ltd.; application for C. of A. cancelled; shipped to Australia for the R.A.A.F.

G-AFOT   (94021), 7.7.39, Bristol & Wessex Aeroplane Club, Whitchurch; impressed 5.40 as AV977; struck off charge 6.44

G-AFOU   (94039), 29.7.39, Bristol & Wessex Aeroplane Club, Whitchurch; impressed 2.40 as X9298; struck off charge 12.44

G-AFOV   (94053), 26.8.39, Bristol & Wessex Aeroplane Club, Whitchurch; to Australia 7.39 as VH-ADJ; withdrawn from use 12.50

G-AFOW   (94047), 18.8.39, Yorkshire Aviation Services Country Club Ltd., York; to Australia 10.39 as VH-ACS; withdrawn from use 10.48

G-AFOX   (94027), 17.7.39, Redhill Flying Club, Redhill; impressed 1.40 as W7973; struck off charge 6.43

G-AFOY   (94043), 15.8.39, Redhill Flying Club, Redhill; impressed 1.40 as W7974; struck off charge 7.44

G-AFOZ   (94055), 26.8.39, Redhill Flying Club; impressed 1.40 as W7975; rest. 4.46 to R.A.F. Flying Club, Panshanger; C. P. Burrell, Compton Abbas 3.70; W. J. D. Roberts, Shoreham 3.72

G-AFPA   (94065), de Havilland Aircraft Co. Ltd., Hatfield; application for C. of A. cancelled; shipped to Australia for the R.A.A.F.

G-AFPB   (94015), 7.7.39, British Aviation Insurance Group Ltd., Brooklands; impressed 1.40 as W7971; to instructional airframe 1941 as 2609M

G-AFPC   (94007), 23.6.39, R.A.F. Flying Club, Hatfield; impressed 12.39 as W6458; struck off charge 12.43

G-AFPD   (94034), 20.7.39, R.A.F. Flying Club, Hatfield; impressed 12.39 as W6459; rest. 2.46 to J. V. Campbell; to Ireland 6.59 as EI-AKU

G-AFPE   (94104), registration not taken up; aircraft completed as G-AFYT

G-AFPG   (94009), Light Planes (Lancs.) Ltd., Barton; impressed 8.40 as BD182; to No. 1220 A.T.C. Sqn., March, Cambs. 7.41 as 2630M

G-AFPH   (94016), 1.7.39, Light Planes (Lancs.) Ltd., Barton; impressed 1.40 as X5133; rest. 4.47 to Warden Aviation & Engineering Ltd.; F. P. Heath, Fairoaks 9.50; re-registered to him in Singapore 11.51 as VR-SDI

G-AFPI   (94057), 28.8.39, Norfolk & Norwich Aero Club; impressed 11.39 as X5116; struck off charge 10.43

G-AFPJ   (94030), 19.7.39, W. S. Shackleton Ltd.; Lt. R. Kent, Almaza, Cairo 6.39; registration cancelled 4.42; believed to U.S.A.A.F. as 42-94128

G-AFPK   (94013), 3.7.39, North Eastern Airways Ltd., Doncaster; Doncaster Aero Club 7.39; impressed 7.40 as AX790; to No. 650 A.T.C. Sqn., Uppingham

G-AFPM   (94032), 28.7.39, Hartlepools & Tees-side Flying Club, West Hartlepool; impressed 9.40 as BK840; rest. 2.46 to J. M. Rollo, Perth; G. Whyte, Perth 11.48; crashed at Kirby Overblow, near Harrogate 12.5.51

G-AFPN   (94044), 1.7.39, L. A. K. Halcombe, Firbeck; impressed 2.40 as X9297; rest. 2.46 to J.N. & R.H.B. Enterprises Ltd., Croft; D. R. Robertson, Ipswich 10.51; K. C. Moore, Sleap 8.70

G-AFPO   (94052), 21.8.39, A. R. Senior, Firbeck; impressed 10.42 as HM544; rest. 1.46 to J. V. Rushton, Wolverhampton; A. Carnegie, Panshanger 9.46 as 'Bugs I'; M. W. Woodard, Shoreham 11.47; crashed at Prautoy, Fr. 30.1.48

G-AFPR   (94031), 14.7.39, Herts. & Essex Aero Club, Broxbourne; impressed 12.39 as X5122; rest. 10.46 to West London Aero Club, White Waltham; Miss J. L. Bird 9.49; G. C. S. Whyham 2.55; dismantled at Squires Gate in 1956

G-AFPS   (94059), 29.8.39, Grimsby Aviation Ltd., Waltham; impressed 12.39 as W6460; d.b.r. in forced landing at Wootton Bassett, Wilts. 16.2.45

G-AFPT   (94026), 15.7.39, Edinburgh Flying Club, Macmerry; impressed 8.40 as BK831; rest. 3.46 by West London Aero Club, White Waltham; crashed at White Waltham 17.9.47

G-AFPU   (94045), 16.8.39, Edinburgh Flying Club, Macmerry; impressed 8.40 as BK832; stored at Woolsington 1944; to Croft 1946; not restored to reg.

G-AFPW   (94064), de Havilland Aircraft Co. Ltd., Hatfield; application for C. of A. cancelled; shipped to Australia for the R.A.A.F.

G-AFRD   (94001), 15.5.39, de Havilland Aircraft Co. Ltd.; to Australia 3.40 as VH-AAQ; to New Zealand as ZK-AHI; impressed as NZ596; later ZK-ALN

G-AFRJ   (94068), C. H. and Mrs. Willis, Gravesend; application for C. of A. cancelled; shipped to Australia for the R.A.A.F.

G-AFSE   (94089), registration not taken up; shipped to Australia for R.A.A.F.

G-AFSF   (94100), registration not taken up; shipped to Australia for R.A.A.F.

G-AFTH   (94040), 29.8.39, de Havilland Aircraft Co. Ltd., Hatfield; impressed 10.42 as HM585; d.b.r. in precautionary landing in Cornwall 31.10.43

G-AFUU   (94084), registration not taken up; shipped to Australia for R.A.A.F. with G-AFUV (94095); G-AFYP (94082); G-AFYR (94083); G-AFYS (94086); G-AFYT (94104); G-AFZM (94105); G-AFZN (94106)

G-AGAO   (94103), G-AFNO ntu, E-14, 16.2.40, de Havilland Aircraft Co. Ltd.; to the Maharajah of Jaipur 5.40 as VT-AMG; still flying in 1947

de Havilland D.H.94 Moth Minor (*cabin model*)

G-AFNY (9401), 22.6.39, Capt. the Hon. L. J. O. Lambart, D.S.O., R.N., Ret'd., Lee-on-Solent; believed destroyed there by German bombing raid 7.40

G-AFOJ (9407), 21.7.39, de Havilland Aircraft Co. Ltd., Hatfield but flown as E-0236, restyled E-1 in 1946; London Aeroplane Club, Panshanger 6.49; R. V. Fox, Jenkins Farm, Navestock 6.62; R. M. Long, Jenkins Farm 7.66

G-AFOR (9404), 25.8.39, Women's Legion Air Wing; to Australia 8.39 as VH-AGL

G-AFPL (9408). 28.2.40, de Havilland Aircraft Co. Ltd., Hatfield; impressed 2.42 as HM584; crashed into the sea off Saunton, Devon 28.10.43

G-AFRR (9403), 30.6.39, R. A. Walley; impressed 8.42 as HM579; rest. 3.46 to A. R. Ward, Hungerford; to New Zealand 3.54 as ZK-BFP

G-AFRY (9402), 1.7.39, de Havilland Aircraft Co. Ltd., Hatfield; impressed 12.39 as X5123; rest. 3.46 to W. A. Rollason Ltd., Croydon; converted to open cockpits; R. A. Gunton, Tollerton 5.47; Morgan Aviation Ltd., Cowes 2.48; G. S. Meek, Perth 9.49 withdrawn from use at Perth 7.56

G-AFSD (9400), E-6, 15.5.39, de Havilland Aircraft Co. Ltd., Hatfield; to India 5.40 as VT-AMF; to Ceylon 1.41 as VP-CAG; impressed 7.42 as NP490; rest. 10.42 to Campling Bros., Nairobi as VP-KDB; crashed at Rumuruti 15.10.50

G-AGAM (9405), E-7, 16.2.40, de Havilland Aircraft Co. Ltd., Hatfield; to India 5.40 as VT-AMD; impressed 1941 as HX796; crashed at Calcutta 2.43

G-AGAN (9406), 16.2.40, de Havilland Aircraft Co. Ltd., Hatfield; to India 5.40 as VT-AME; impressed 1941 as HX797; struck off charge 4.44

Maintenance in progress on British Air Transport's Flamingo G-AFYH at Redhill in 1949. (*E. J. Riding*)

de Havilland D.H.95 Flamingo

G-AFUE (95001), 30.6.39, de Havilland Aircraft Co. Ltd., Hatfield; to No.24 Sqn., 10.39; repainted 11.39 as T5357; lost in flying accident 4.10.40

G-AFUF (95002), E-1, 12.1.40, Guernsey Airways Ltd.; delivered direct to No.24 Sqn., Hendon; impressed 3.40 as X9317; scrapped at Hendon 10.42

G-AFYE (95007), 10.9.40, B.O.A.C. 'King Arthur'; delivered via St. Eval to Cairo 8.42; dived vertically into the ground from 800 ft., Asmara, Eritrea 15.2.43

G-AFYF (95009), 13.9.40, B.O.A.C. 'King Alfred'; delivered via St. Eval to Cairo 8.40; shipped back to Britain 1945; scrapped at Redhill 1950

G-AFYG (95010), 19.10.40, B.O.A.C. 'King Harold'; delivered via St. Eval to Cairo 8.40; damaged beyond repair on take-off, Addis Ababa 18.11.42

G-AFYH (95011), f/f 29.11.40; to No.782 Sqn., Donibristle 30.11.40 as BT312 'Merlin VI' (later 'Merlin 27'); rest. 10.46 to Southern Aircraft (Gatwick) Ltd.; C. of A. 7.6.47; British Air Transport Ltd., Redhill 6.47; scrapped 5.54

G-AFYI (95012), 14.12.40, B.O.A.C. 'King Henry'; delivered via St. Eval to Cairo 12.40; wrecked in landing accident at Adana, Turkey 13.9.42

G-AFYJ (95013), 14.1.41, B.O.A.C. 'King Richard'; delivered via St. Eval to Cairo 1.41; shipped back to Britain 1945; scrapped at Redhill 1950

G-AFYK (95014), E-17, 18.3.41, B.O.A.C. 'King James'; delivered via St. Eval to Cairo 3.41; shipped back to Britain 1945; scrapped at Redhill 1950

G-AFYL (95015), 15.4.41, B.O.A.C. 'King Charles'; delivered via St. Eval to Cairo 1.42; shipped back to Britain 1945; scrapped at Redhill 1950

G-AFYZ Registration not taken up. Believed reserved originally for Jersey Airways Ltd.

G-AFZA Registration not taken up. Believed reserved originally for Jersey Airways Ltd.

G-AGAZ (95005), E-16, 17.7.40, de Havilland Aircraft Co. Ltd., Hatfield; delivered to No.24 Sqn., Hendon 8.6.40; impressed immediately as AE444 'Lady of Ayr'; last flight 18.7.44; struck off charge 11.44

G-AGBY (95020), BK822, 19.9.41, B.O.A.C. 'King William'; delivered via St. Eval to Cairo 9.41; shipped back to Britain 1945, stored at Witney as spares

G-AGCC (95008), R2766, 28.6.40, Wing. Cdr. E. H. Fielden, Benson (King's Flight); to No.24 Sqn., Hendon 2.41 as R2766; named 'Lady of Glamis' 1942; to de Havillands 11.44; to Donibristle 10.3.45 as spares for BT312

de Havilland D.H.98 Mosquito

G-AGFV Mk.4, DZ411, 30.1.43, B.O.A.C., Leuchars; returned to the R.A.F. 1.45

G-AGGC Mk.6, HJ680, 1.5.43, B.O.A.C., Leuchars; returned to the R.A.F. 1.46

G-AGGD Mk.6, HJ681, 7.5.43, B.O.A.C., Leuchars; undershot and crashed when making emergency landing at Sarenas, Sweden 3.1.44

G-AGGE Mk.6, HJ718, 7.5.43, B.O.A.C., Leuchars; returned to the R.A.F. 6.45

G-AGGF Mk.6, HJ720, 15.5.43, B.O.A.C., Leuchars; burned out in crash at Invermairk, Glen Esk when approaching to land at Leuchars 17.8.43

G-AGGG Mk.6, HJ721, 22.5.43, B.O.A.C., Leuchars; crashed near Leuchars when returning from Stockholm 25.10.43

G-AGGH Mk.6, HJ723, 15.5.43, B.O.A.C., Leuchars; returned to the R.A.F. 6.45; to instructional airframe 12.45 as 5755M; scrapped 2.46

G-AGKO Mk.6, HJ667, 10.6.44, B.O.A.C., Leuchars; returned to the R.A.F. 6.45

G-AGKP Mk.6, LR296, 27.5.44, B.O.A.C., Leuchars; crashed in the North Sea 5 miles off the Scottish coast inbound from Stockholm 19.8.44

G-AGKR Mk.6, HJ792, 21.5.44, B.O.A.C., Leuchars; posted missing between Gothenburg and Leuchars 29.8.44

G-AIRT Mk.16, NS812, registered 23.10.46 to V.I.P. Association Ltd., Cambridge; H. L. White 5.48; flown to Nice en route to Israel 5.7.48

G-AIRU Mk.16, NS811, registered 23.10.46 to V.I.P. Association Ltd., Cambridge; H. L. White 5.48; flown to Nice en route Israel 16.7.48

G-AJZE Mk.34, RG231, 1.3.48, Ministry of Supply, Cranfield (on loan to B.E.A. Gust Research Unit); returned to the R.A.F. at Waterbeach 8.49

G-AJZF Mk.34, RG238, 9.6.48, Ministry of Supply, Cranfield (on loan to B.E.A. Gust Research Unit); returned to the R.A.F. at Waterbeach 8.49

A Flight Refuelling Ltd. Mosquito Mk.19 at Tarrant Rushton in 1950.

G-ALFL Mk.36, RL150, 30.11.48, Ministry of Supply; prepared for C. of A. at Hatfield; returned to the R.A.F. 11.49; scrapped 1950

G-ALGU Mk.19, TA299, 7.10.49, Flight Refuelling Ltd., Tarrant Rushton; withdrawn from use at Tarrant Rushton 4.53

G-ALGV Mk.19, TA343, registered 16.2.49 to Flight Refuelling Ltd., Tarrant Rushton and there reduced to spares to service G-ALGU

G-AOCI Mk.16, NS639, registered 5.56 to R. A. Short, Thruxton; not civilianised; became derelict at Thruxton and was burned there 10.60

G-AOCJ Mk.16, NS742, registered 5.56 to R. A. Short, Thruxton; to Hurn for overhaul 8.56; to the Israeli Air Force 1957 as 4X-FDG-91

G-AOCK Mk.16, NS753, registered 5.56 to R. A. Short, Thruxton; not civilianised; became derelict at Thruxton and was burned there 10.60

G-AOCL Mk.16, RG173, registered 5.56 to R. A. Short, Thruxton; not civilianised; became derelict at Thruxton and was burned there 10.60

G-AOCM Mk.16, RG174, registered 5.56 to R. A. Short, Thruxton; to Hurn for overhaul 8.56; to the Israeli Air Force 1957 as 4X-FDG-90

G-AOCN Mk.16, TA614, registered 5.56 to R. A. Short, Thruxton; to Hurn for overhaul 8.56; to the Israeli Air Force 1957 as 4X-FDL-92

G-AOCO Sea Mosquito Mk.33, TW246, registered 7.57 to R. A. Short; not converted; abandoned at Lossiemouth 1957

G-AOSS Mk.35, TK655, registered 7.56 to Derby Aviation Ltd., Burnaston; Miss R. E. M. Cowell, Burnaston 12.58; scrapped in 1960

G-ASKA Mk.35, RS709, 25.8.63, Mirisch Films Ltd., Bovingdon; P. F. M. Thomas (Skyfame Museum), Staverton 12.63; Grp. Capt. T. G. Mahaddie 8.64; to Col. E. A. Jurist, Harlinger, Texas ex Luton 10.12.71 as N9797

G-ASKB Mk.35, RS712, 30.8.63, Mirisch Films Ltd., Bovingdon; Grp. Capt. T. G. Mahaddie, Elstree 8.64; stored at West Malling in 1970

G-ASKC Mk.35, TA719, 19.8.63, P. F. M. Thomas, Staverton (Skyfame Museum); crash landed at Staverton 27.7.64; standing out minus engines in 1970

G-ASKH Mk.3, RR299, 10.9.65, Hawker Siddeley Aviation Ltd., Hawarden; airworthy in 1972, flown as RR299

G-AWJV Mk.35, TA634, registered 21.5.68 to Mayor, Aldermen and Citizens of the City of Liverpool; first flown at Speke 17.6.68; erected at London Colney/Salisbury Hall for permanent exhibition 7.10.70

de Havilland D.H.104 Dove Mks. 1 to 6

G-AGPJ (04000/P.1), 2.5.46, to the R.A.F. 2.52 as WJ310, rest. 3.54, to Cape Verde Islands 3.56 as CR-CAC; G-AGUC (04000/P.2), 17.6.46, crashed near Bournemouth 14.8.46; G-AHRA (04003), 23.9.46, crashed near New Milton, Hants. 13.3.47; G-AHRB (04005), 7.10.46, to Nigeria 5.51 as VR-NAJ, rest. 3.57, to Cape Verde Islands 10.57 as CR-CAD; G-AHRI (04008), 30.12.46, to Israel 8.57 as 4X-ARI, rest. 12.65, dismantled Little Staughton 1972; G-AHRJ (04004), 7.10.46, to the Sudan 8.57 as SN-AAA, rest. 6.55, to Iraq 7.55 as YI-ACT; G-AHYX (04018), 21.3.47, crashed at Isfahan, Persia 24.9.49; G-AICY (04019), 11.4.47, to Austria 7.57 as OE-FAB, rest. 6.64, stored at Stansted in 1970; G-AIIX (04010), 24.1.47, to the Sudan 8.47 as SN-AAB; G-AIIY (04016), 20.3.47, to the Sudan 8.47 as SN-AAC, rest. 4.67, to spares at Baginton 1968; G-AIWF (04023), 10.6.47, to South Africa 1.51 as ZS-DFA, rest. 5.53, to Iceland 7.64 as TF-BPD

G-AJAA (04031), 2.1.48, to Ethiopia 1.48 as ET-T-23; G-AJBI (04026), 23.4.47, to Burma 5.51 as XY-ACE, rest. 4.52, to Pakistan 6.52 as AP-AFT, rest. 4.53, to Burma 3.57 as XY-ACE, rest. 3.58, to Burma 4.60 as XY-ACE, rest. 1.61, w.f.u. at Gatwick 4.67, scrapped at Southend 4.70; G-AJDP (04028), 19.5.47, to Pakistan 3.49 as AP-AER, rest. 5.51, to Burma 5.52 as XY-ACW, rest. 3.53, to Burma 2.54 as XY-ACW, rest. 3.55, to Burma 4.59 as XY-ACW, rest. 5.60, to Nigeria 4.62 as 5N-ABU, rest. 6.65, w.f.u. 3.70; G-AJGT (04034), 7.7.47, converted to Dove 5X in 1952 and to Dove 7XC in 1961; G-AJHL (04043), 4.7.47, ditched in the Ionian Sea off Southern Italy 9.2.48; G-AJHX (04037), 9.7.47; G-AJJF (04041), 15.8.47; G-AJLV (04063), 20.2.48; G-AJLW (04033), 27.6.47, d.b.r. in forced landing 8 miles west of Droitwich 26.4.65

G-AJMA (04053), 12.1.48, to Ethiopia 1.48 as ET-T-24; G-AJNS (04057), to India 9.47 as VT-COV; G-AJOS (04036), 24.7.47, to the Sudan 8.47 as SN-AAD, later ST-AAD, rest. 6.67, to Senegal 11.71 as 6V-ACQ; G-AJOT (04051), 11.9.47, to Senegal 11.68 as 6V-ABL; G-AJOU (04058), 22.10.47, crashed on Mt. Coron, central France 13.5.48; G-AJPR (04029), 23.5.47, dismantled at Baginton in 1969; G-AJZT (04059), 29.9.47, crashed at Banstead, Surrey 9.6.51; G-AJZU (04054), to the Belgian Congo 8.47 as OO-CFC, later to military D 12

G-AKCF (04030), CF-DJI, 23.5.47, to Holland 3.60 as PH-MAD, rest. 11.66, to the Cameroons 12.67 as TJ-ACE; G-AKET (04056), 23.9.47, to Italy 8.54 as I-AKET, later

Royal Navy Mosquito P.R.Mk.16 NS742 at Thruxton in June 1956 with ferry marking G-AOCJ. (*M. J. Hooks*)

479

to Holland as PH-KLS, rest. 1.61, w.f.u. at Exeter 12.65, to Baginton as spares 2.68; G-AKJG (04071), 24.10.47, to Southern Rhodesia 8.51 as VP-YGP, rest. 10.51, d.b.r. in forced landing at Old, Northants. 20.1.65; G-AKJP (04064), 14.11.47; G-AKJR (04084), 7.11.47, to Pakistan 4.53 as AP-AGJ, rest. 6.65, w.f.u. at Gatwick 8.68; G-AKSK (04116), 25.2.48, crashed at Fritham, Hants. 23.7.55; G-AKSR (04121), to Pakistan 3.48 as AP-AKS, to Pakistan Air Force as P1301, rest. 3.62, to the Cameroons 10.65 as TJ-ACC; G-AKSS (04122), 8.4.48, to South Africa 2.51 as ZS-DFC, rest. 6.55; G-AKST (04125), 12.3.48, to Burma 4.52 as XY-ACV, rest. 7.51, to Pakistan 8.51 as AP-AFE, rest. 5.52, to Burma 7.53 as XY-ACV, rest. 3.54, wrecked in hangar collapse at Chittagong, East Bengal 31.10.60; G-AKSU (04126), 12.3.48, to Tanganyika 6.48 as VR-TBB, to Southern Rhodesia 6.64 as VP-YTF; G-AKSV (04161), 10.6.48, w.f.u. 8.66; G-AKSW (04166), 2.7.48, to Cape Verde Islands 8.68 as CR-CAR; G-AKYS (04135), 3.5.48, to Italy 2.63 as I-ORIF, rest. 1.64, to Senegal 5.65 as 6V-PRD

G-ALBF (04152), 19.7.48; G-ALBM (04170), G-5-1, 5.7.48; G-ALBY (04171), 5.7.48, to the Indian Air Force 12.48 as HW526; G-ALCU (04022), VT-CEH, 5.5.47; G-ALEC (04402), XB-SUU, G-APPD ntu, crashed in Cardiff 6.5.59; G-ALFM (04211), VP961, 25.11.48 (British Air Attaché, Pretoria), returned to the R.A.F. 11.49 as VP961; G-ALFT (04233), 2.2.49; G-ALFU (04234), 2.2.49; G-ALMR (04099), VT-CSO, 7.5.48, crashed in the River Ribble 12.4.60; G-ALTM (04236), 28.6.49, crash landed at Heathrow 22.6.55; G-ALTS (04260), VP977, civil only for one flight to Hatfield 14.10.49, repainted 16.10.49 as VP977; G-ALVD (04277), 11.1.50, to Pakistan 5.57 as AP-AJB; G-ALVF (04168), 8.9.50, to the Cameroons 5.65 as TJ-ACD; G-ALVS (04199), 24.1.50, airworthy in 1972; G-ALVT (04206), 2.2.50 (British Air Attaché, Buenos Aires), to Argentine Air Force 2.51 as T-90; G-ALYO (04261), VP978, 3.4.50, to the R.A.F. 1.53 as VP978; G-ALZB (04381), N1577V, 9.10.52, to Mexico 5.53 as XB-SUC; G-ALZC (04384), N1579V, 30.10.52, to U.S.A. 5.53 as N1579V; G-ALZD (04389), N1559V, 4.11.52, to U.S.A. 4.53 as N1559V

G-AMDD (04292), 4.9.50, to Swaziland 12.68 as VQ-ZJC; G-AMEI (04296), 2.10.50, to Switzerland 8.51 as HB-LAR; G-AMFU (04117), VP-KDE, 26.2.48, to Belgium 8.69 as OO-SCD; G-AMHM (04300), 4.4.51, to Katangan Air Force 10.63; G-AMJJ (04267), WB532, 2.8.51, returned to the R.A.F. 5.57 as WB532; G-AMJZ (04118), VP-KDF, 23.5.51, w.f.u. at Bahrein 9.60; G-AMKA (04328), to U.S.A. 8.51 as N4963N; G-AMKB (04329), to U.S.A. 8.51 as N4266C; G-AMKC (04331), to Mexico 11.51 as XB-REW; G-AMKD (04336), to U.S.A. 11.51 as N1515V; G-AMKS (04290), to South Africa 11.51 as ZS-DFJ, rest. 11.55; G-AMKT (04291), 29.11.51, crashed at Lahore, Pakistan 19.2.60; G-AMRN (04024), ZS-AVH, 7.3.52, to Iceland 10.64 as TF-EVM; G-AMUZ (04386), 6.1.53, w.f.u. 10.70; G-AMVR (04394), 28.11.52, to Japan 4.53 as JA-5005; G-AMVT (04375), 6.1.53, to Japan 3.53 as JA-5003; G-AMVV (04020), VP-YEU, 20.11.52, to Holland 6.58 as PH-MAC; G-AMWY (04407), 10.3.53, to Japan 5.53 as JA-5006; G-AMWZ (04388), N4282C, 1.12.52, to Canada 2.53 as CF-HGT

G-AMXN (04391), N4283C, 26.11.52, to Canada 2.53 as CF-HGQ; G-AMXO (04414), 5.3.53, to Canada 4.53 as CF-HGR; G-AMXP (04420), completed as Sea Devon for Royal Navy 5.55 as XJ319; G-AMXR (04379), N4280 C, 9.10.52, to Germany 8.55 as D-CFSB, later D-IFSB; G-AMXS (04382), N4281C, 14.10.52, to Venezuela 9.53 as YV-T-FTQ; G-AMXT (04392), N1561V, 21.11.52, to Royal Navy 10.54 as XJ347; G-AMXU (04393), N1562V, 9.12.52, to Angola 3.55 as CR-AHT; G-AMXV (04400), 10.2.53, to Australia 2.55 as VH-DHD; G-AMXW (04401), 10.2.53, to Royal Navy 10.54 as XJ349, rest. 5.61; G-AMXX (04406), 10.2.53, to Royal Navy 5.55 as XJ348; G-AMXY (04409), 12.2.53, to Royal Navy 10.54 as XJ323, rest. 1.62, to Zambia 1.69 as 9J-AAE; G-AMXZ (04410), 5.3.53, to Royal Navy 10.54 as XJ324; G-AMYM (04408),

The David Brown Corporation's unique Dove 8 first stage Riley conversion, G-ARDH, combined the standard tail unit with Lycoming engines.

24.4.53, to Japan 5.53 as JA-5007; G-AMYO (04086), VP-YEV, 23.3.53, sold in Senegal 7.69; G-AMYP (04421), completed as Sea Devon for Royal Navy 5.55 as XJ322; G-AMZJ (04429), 29.5.53, w.f.u. at Benina, Libya 4.65; G-AMZK (04430), 10.6.53, to Japan 8.53 as JA-5008; G-AMZN (04437), 3.11.53, to Sweden 5.72 as SE-GRA; G-AMZY (04431), 25.6.53, to Mk.8XC 4.63

G-ANAI (04422), 23.7.53, to Japan 8.53 as JA-5011; G-ANAN (04062), EP-ACH, 10.7.53, to Burma 3.55 as XY-ADE, rest. 3.56, to Senegal 6.69 as 6V-ABT; G-ANAP (04433), 24.8.53; G-ANBP (04438), 1.10.53, to U.S.A. 3.54 as N1584V; G-ANBR (04439), 1.10.53, to U.S.A. 10.53 as N1585V; G-ANCO (04440), to U.S.A. 5.54 as N1586V; G-ANDX (04435), 19.2.54, to R.A.F. 7.54 as XG496; G-ANDY (04441), completed as Sea Devon for Royal Navy 10.54 as XJ320, rest. 6.61, C. of A. 22.5.62, crashed at Turnhouse 29.5.62; G-ANFD (04444), 24.11.53, to U.S.A. 2.55 as N1588V; G-ANGE (04167), VT-CVA, 27.11.53, crash landed on desert strip in Libya 26.2.64; G-ANGU (04446), 26.2.54, to Ireland 8.70 as EI-AUK; G-ANJB (04448), to Venezuela 9.54 as YV-P-DPK; G-ANJC (04449), 20.1.54, to U.S.A. 2.54 as N1563V

G-ANMJ (04006), VP-YES, 8.3.54, w.f.u. 5.71; G-ANOV (04445), G-5-16, 1.4.54; G-ANPH (04450), 12.4.54; G-ANTO (04451), 24.8.54, to U.S.A. 8.54 as N1565V; G-ANUT (04454), 15.4.55; G-ANUU (04455), 10.5.55; G-ANUW (04458), 28.6.55; G-ANVC (04128), VR-NIT, 7.10.54, to Pakistan 1.55 as AP-AGT, rest. 4.55, to Burma 12.56 as XY-ADI, rest. 4.57, to Burma 4.58 as XY-ADI, rest. 4.59, to Burma 5.61 as XY-ADI, rest. 4.62, w.f.u. at Gatwick 2.66, scrapped at Southend 4.70; G-ANVU (04082), VR-NAP, 2.4.55

G-AOAG (04457), 24.5.55, to Australia 8.55 as VH-DHF; G-AOBZ (04127), VR-NIL, 27.5.55, scrapped at Southend 4.70; G-AOCE (04044), VR-NAB, 10.6.55, crash landed on beach, Dungeness 15.1.58; G-AODM (04460), 12.8.55, to U.S.A. 9.55 as N1509V; G-AODN (04338), F-OAKG, 25.8.55, to Switzerland 4.60 as HB-LAQ; G-AODV (04461), 23.11.55, to U.S.A. 1.56 as N50S; G-AOFI (04477), 15.11.56; G-AOIZ (04257), VP964, 18.6.56, to the R.A.F. 6.58 as VP964; G-AORM (04468), 24.5.56, to U.S.A. 6.56 as N70L; G-AOSE (04470), 2.9.59; G-AOTE (04471), 16.7.56, to Australia 10.56 as VH-DHE; G-AOUA (04475), to U.S.A. 9.56 as N435T; G-AOUF (04476), 4.10.56, to Germany 7.68 as D-IBYW; G-AOUG (04478), 22.11.56, re-registered in Kuwait 12.58 as 9K-AAB: G-AOUH (04479), 22.11.56, re-registered in Kuwait 12.58 as

Dove 6 G-AWFM equipped for geophysical survey work by Fairey Surveys Ltd. in 1969 using a proton magnetometer with the sensing head in a fibreglass 'stinger' tail.

9K-AAC; G-AOVY (04009), ZS-BCB, ZS-CAG, 15.6.60, reduced to spares 1.69; G-AOYC (04065), VT-COW, 17.4.57, to Indonesia 6.69 as PK-ICS; G-AOYD (04092), VT-CKE, 7.6.57, to U.S.A. 6.67 as N13114; G-AOZF (04482), 4.2.57, to Japan 2.57 as JA-5038; G-AOZW (04098), VR-NET, 3.4.57, w.f.u. at Biggin Hill 12.66

G-APAG (04114), VR-NIB, 17.4.57, w.f.u. at Benina, Libya 6.66; G-APBA (04487), 1.5.58, to the Argentine 8.58 as LV-PKY; G-APBB (04219), VT-DBG, remained in India, British registration ntu; G-APBG (04490), 6.6.57, to Japan 1.58 as JA-5046; G-APCZ (04313), F-BFVL, F-OANL, F-BFVL, 12.9.57, to Australia 9.67 as VH-MJD; G-APSK (04504), 6.3.59; G-APSO (04505), 23.3.59; G-APVX (04509), first flown 7.1.60, C. of A. 16.3.60, to Australia 5.72 as VH-WST; G-APZU (04511), 24.6.60

G-ARBH (04196), XY-ABS, 5.10.60; G-ARDE (04469), I-TONY, 29.11.60; G-ARDM (04175), XY-ABN, 22.4.61, to Senegal 2.64 as 6V-PRB; G-ARDN (04184), XY-ABQ, 22.11.60, to Holland 4.61 as PH-VLC, rest. 7.66, to Switzerland 2.67 as HB-LAX; G-AREG (04061), EP-ACG, OY-AAJ, 17.2.61, w.f.u. at Benina, Libya 3.66; G-ARGN (04001), CF-BNU, N7395, 6.12.67, w.f.u. at Cranfield 2.71; G-ARMT (04514), 5.7.61, to Australia 2.71 as VH-ADA; G-AROG (04207), VR-NOB, 14.7.62, w.f.u. at Baginton 10.65; G-AROH (04415), XB-TAN, XJ321, 19.3.64; G-AROI (04474), XK897, 18.11.63; G-ARTS (04369), N1572V, N20R, N6532D, to Holland 7.62 as PH-SAA, to Nigeria 2.66 as 5N-ACJ, rest. 6.68

G-ASDD (04452), OY-FAL, 13.8.64, to Italy 7.65 as I-ALGJ, rest. 1.66; G-ASMX (04486), PH-ION, 10.4.64, to Italy 7.65 as I-ALGO, rest. 1.66, to Australia 6.66 as VH-DHN; G-ASNG (04485), PH-IOM, to Switzerland 2.69 as HB-LFF, rest. 8.69; G-ASUV (04246), S.A.A.F. 105, Riley conversion, 6.9.65, to Nigeria 9.65 as 5N-AGF; G-ASUW (04256), S.A.A.F. 108, Riley conversion, 9.6.65, to Belgium 10.67 as OO-BPL; G-ASUX (04250), S.A.A.F. 107, Riley conversion, to the U.S.A. 1.66 as N668R; G-ATAP (04496), HB-LAP, 5.5.65, to Sweden 5.65 as SE-EUR; G-ATGI (04097), YI-ABK, TJ-ACA, Jordan Air Force D-100, 2.11.70, Riley conversion; G-ATGJ (04113), YI-ABL, TJ-ACB, Jordan Air Force D-101, 27.2.70, Riley conversion; G-ATGK (04288), TJ-ACC, Jordan Air Force D-102, Riley conversion, 7.8.66, to France 2.67 as F-BORJ; G-ATGL (04289), TJ-ACD, Jordan Air Force D-103, w.f.u. at Luton 9.71; G-AVHX (04132), VP-YHU, SN-AAE, ST-AAE, registered 9.3.67, w.f.u. 5.71; G-AWFM (04079), ZS-BCC, VP-RCL, VP-YLX, 9J-RHX, 24.4.68; G-AWRG (04073), VP954, conversion abandoned at Leavesden 12.69; G-AZPG (04462), HB-LAS, registered 13.3.72

de Havilland D.H.104 Dove Mk.8

G-APYE (04515), G-5-11, 20.5.60, to the U.S.A. 5.60 as N6533D; G-ARBD (04516), 12.5.61, to U.S.A. 5.61 as N6532D; G-ARBE (04517), 28.1.66; G-ARDH (04519), 1.9.60, Riley conversion 1966, to Denmark 9.71 as OY-DRP; G-AREA (04520), 25.4.61; G-ARFZ (04526), 6.10.61; G-ARHW (04512), 28.3.61; G-ARHX (04513), 28.3.61; G-ARJB (04518), 22.12.60; G-ARSI (04526), ntu, completed as G-ARFZ q.v.; G-ARSN (04525), to Ireland 10.67 as EI-ARV; G-ARUM (04528), 9.3.62; G-ARYM (04529), 25.5.62; G-ASHW (04532), 28.6.63; G-ASMG (04533), 18.11.63; G-ASPA (04536), 4.5.64; G-ASYR (04537), 5.1.65, to Ethiopian Air Force 1.65 as IEAF.803; G-ATAI (04538), 7.5.65; G-AVHV (04542), 22.5.67, crashed at Wolverhampton 9.4.70; G-AVVF (04541), 23.2.68

de Havilland D.H.106 Comet 1

G-ALVG (06001), G-5-1, f/f 27.7.49, C. of A. 21.4.50, Ministry of Supply; first flown with Sprite assisted take-off 7.5.51; scrapped at Farnborough 7.53

G-ALYP (06003), f/f 9.1.51, C. of A. 13.3.52, delivered to B.O.A.C. 13.3.52; crashed in the sea off Elba due to explosive decompression 10.1.54

G-ALYR (06004), f/f 28.7.51, C. of A. 16.10.51, B.O.A.C., Heathrow; withdrawn from use 4.54; used for fatigue tests at R.A.E., Farnborough 7.55

G-ALYS (06005), f/f 8.9.51, C. of A. 18.1.52, delivered to B.O.A.C. 4.2.52; w.f.u. 4.54; used for buffet fatigue tests at R.A.E., Farnborough 1955

G-ALYU (06007), f/f 31.12.51, C. of A. 29.2.52, delivered to B.O.A.C. 6.3.52; w.f.u. 4.54; used for passenger escape trials at Pengham Moors, Cardiff 1954

G-ALYV (06008), f/f 9.4.52, C. of A. 21.4.52, B.O.A.C., Heathrow; crashed near Calcutta and burned out 2.5.53

G-ALYW (06009), f/f 25.2.52, C. of A. 11.6.52, B.O.A.C., Heathrow; withdrawn from use 4.54; dismantled at Heathrow 6.55; components to Farnborough

G-ALYX (06010), f/f 9.7.52, C. of A. 22.7.52, B.O.A.C., Heathrow; withdrawn from use 4.54; engine test bed at Hatfield 1954; to Farnborough 1955

G-ALYY (06011), f/f 10.9.52, C. of A. 23.9.52, B.O.A.C., Heathrow; crashed in the Tyrrhenian Sea north of Stromboli, explosive decompression, 8.4.54

G-ALYZ (06012), f/f 23.9.52, C. of A. 30.5.52, delivered to B.O.A.C. 30.9.52; crashed on take-off from Ciampino, Rome 26.10.52

G-ALZK (06002), G-5-2, f/f 27.7.50, C. of A. 21.3.51, Ministry of Supply; loaned to B.O.A.C. 23.3.51–24.10.51; dismantled at Hatfield 3.57

de Havilland D.H.106 Comet 1A

G-ANAV (06013), f/f 18.1.52, CF-CUM, C. of A. 28.8.53, B.O.A.C., Heathrow; flight trials at Farnborough 1954; scrapped at Farnborough 1955

G-AOJT (06020), f/f 6.5.53, F-BGNX, C. of A. 15.5.53, registered 4.56 to de Havillands; flown Le Bourget–Farnborough 27.6.56; to R.A.E. fatigue tests 8.56

G-AOJU (06021), f/f 22.5.53, F-BGNY, C. of A. 18.10.57, Ministry of Supply; converted to Mk.IXB; to B.O.A.C. for crew training; to Boscombe Down 8.61 for Decca/Dectra trials as XM829

G-APAS (06022), f/f 16.3.53, F-BGNZ, C. of A. 10.1.58, Ministry of Supply; flown Le Bourget–Hatfield as G-5-23; to D.H. Propellers Ltd. (later H.S. Dynamics) for Firestreak tests as XM823

de Havilland D.H.106 Comet 2

G-ALYT   (06006), f/f 16.2.52, Comet 2X, C. of A. 10.6.52, Ministry of Supply; flown to
         No. 1 S. of T.T., Halton 28.5.59; to instructional airframe 7610M

G-AMXA   (06023), f/f 27.8.53, C. of A. 21.1.54, B.O.A.C., Heathrow; modified for radar
         trials; to No. 51 Sqn., Signals Command, R.A.F. 1963 as XK655

G-AMXB   (06024), f/f 3.11.53, C. of A. 18.2.54, B.O.A.C., Heathrow; modified to Comet
         T.Mk.2 for No. 216 Sqn., R.A.F., Lyneham 1955 as XK669 'Taurus'

G-AMXC   (06025), f/f 25.11.53, not certificated; converted for radar trials; to No.51
         Sqn., Signals Command, R.A.F. 1963 as XK659

G-AMXD   (06026), f/f 20.8.54, C. of A. 23.7.57, Comet 2E, Ministry of Supply; to
         R.A.E., Bedford 1959 for long range radio aid development as XN453

G-AMXE   (06027), f/f 18.7.55, not certificated; converted for radar trials; to No.51 Sqn.,
         Signals Command, R.A.F. as XK663

G-AMXF   (06028), f/f 12.3.56, not certificated; converted to Comet T.Mk.2 and later
         C.Mk.2 for No. 216 Sqn., R.A.F. Lyneham as XK670 'Corvus'

G-AMXG   (06029), f/f 16.7.56, not certificated; converted to Comet C.Mk.2 for No.216
         Sqn., R.A.F. Lyneham as XK671 'Aquila'

G-AMXH   (06030), f/f 21.8.56, not certificated; converted to Comet C.Mk.2 for No.216
         Sqn., R.A.F. Lyneham as XK695 'Perseus'

G-AMXI   (06031), f/f 29.9.56, not certificated; converted to Comet C.Mk.2 for No.216
         Sqn., R.A.F. Lyneham as XK696 'Orion'

G-AMXJ   (06032), f/f 17.11.56, not certificated; converted to Comet C.Mk.2 for No.216
         Sqn., Lyneham as XK697 'Cygnus'

G-AMXK   (06033), f/f 10.7.57, C. of A. 22.8.57, Comet 2E. delivered to B.O.A.C.
         26.8.57; d/d to Ministry of Aviation, R.A.E., Bedford 18.11.66 as XV144

G-AMXL   (06034), f/f 13.12.56, converted to Comet C.Mk.2 for No.216 Sqn., R.A.F.
         Lyneham as XK698 'Pegasus'; civil marks re-allocated to Chipmunk

de Havilland D.H.106 Comet 3

G-ANLO   (06100), f/f 19.7.54, C. of A. 31.11.55, Ministry of Supply; converted to
         Comet Mk.3B and f/f 21.8.58; d/d to R.A.E., Bedford 21.6.61 as XP915

de Havilland D.H.106 Comet 4 (*Hatfield or Chester* built)

G-APDA   (6401), f/f 27.4.58, C. of A. 30.9.58, d/d to B.O.A.C. 24.2.59; to Malaysian
         Airways 11.65 as 9M-AOA; to Malaysia-Singapore Airlines 3.66 as 9V-BAS;
         returned to Gatwick 11.69; to spares at Lasham 1972

G-APDB   (6403), f/f 27.8.58, C. of A. 29.9.58, d/d to B.O.A.C. 30.9.58, to Malaysian
         Airways 9.65 as 9M-AOB; rest. 6.70 to Dan-Air Services Ltd.

G-APDC   (6404), f/f 23.9.58, C. of A. 30.9.58, d/d to B.O.A.C. 30.9.58; to Malaysian
         Airways 11.65 as 9M-AOC; to Malaysia-Singapore Airlines 3.66 as 9V-BAT;
         rest. 10.70 to Dan-Air Services Ltd., Gatwick

G-APDD   (6405), f/f 5.11.58, C. of A. 13.11.58, d/d to B.O.A.C. 18.11.58; to Malaysian
         Airways 11.65 as 9M-AOD; rest. 11.55 to Dan-Air Services Ltd., Gatwick;
         leased to East African Airways Corp. 12.70 as 5Y-AMT

G-APDE   (6406)*, f/f 20.9.58, C. of A. 1.10.58, d/d to B.O.A.C. 2.10.58; to Malaysian
         Airways 11.65 as 9M-AOE; to Malaysia-Singapore Airlines 3.66 as 9V-BAU;
         rest. 11.69 to Dan-Air Services Ltd., Gatwick; leased to East African Airways
         Corp. 2.70 as 5Y-ALF

Comet 2E G-AMXD after transfer to the R.A.E., Bedford for radio development trials as XN453. (*Aviation Photo News*)

G-APDF (6407)*, f/f 11.12.58, C. of A. 23.12.58, d/d to B.O.A.C. 31.12.58; to the Ministry of Technology 1970 as XV814

G-APDG (6427)*, f/f 12.11.59, C. of A. 26.11.59, d/d to B.O.A.C. 7.12.59; to Kuwait Airways 12.66 as 9K-ACI; rest. 12.70 to Dan-Air Services Ltd.

G-APDH (6409)*, f/f 21.11.59, C. of A. 28.11.59, d/d to B.O.A.C. 6.12.59; crash landed at Singapore with faulty undercarriage 22.3.64

G-APDI (6428)*, f/f 7.12.59, C. of A. 19.12.59, d/d to B.O.A.C. 19.12.59; to Aerovias Ecuatorianas (AREA) 3.66 as HC-ALT

G-APDJ (6429)*, f/f 23.12.59, C. of A. 11.1.60, d/d to B.O.A.C. 11.1.60; leased to Dan-Air Services Ltd., Gatwick 10.67; sold to Dan-Air 6.72

G-APDK (6412)*, f/f 2.2.59, C. of A. 12.2.59, d/d to B.O.A.C. 12.2.59; Dan-Air Services Ltd., Gatwick 1966; leased to East African Airways 2.70 as 5Y-ALD; rest. 3.70

G-APDL (6413), f/f 27.4.59, C. of A. 4.5.59, d/d to B.O.A.C. 6.5.59; leased to East African Airways 10.65 to 3.67 as 5Y-ADD; Dan-Air Services Ltd., Gatwick 1.69; beyond repair in belly landing at Woolsington 7.10.70

G-APDM (6414)*, f/f 21.3.59, C. of A. 15.4.59, d/d to B.O.A.C. 16.4.59; to Middle East Airlines 3.67 as OD-AEV; leased to Malaysia-Singapore Airlines 1.68 as 9V-BBJ; rest. 3.69 to Dan-Air Services Ltd., Gatwick

G-APDN (6415), f/f 29.9.59, C. of A. 10.6.59, d/d to B.O.A.C. 11.6.59; Dan-Air Services Ltd., Gatwick 2.68; crashed north of Barcelona 3.7.70

G-APDO (6416)*, f/f 29.4.59, C. of A. 13.5.59, d/d to B.O.A.C. 14.5.59; Dan-Air Services Ltd., Gatwick 4.71

G-APDP (6417)*, f/f 29.4.59, C. of A. 9.6.59, d/d to B.O.A.C. 9.6.59; leased to Malaysia-Singapore Airlines 10.67 to 1.69 as 9V-BBH; rest. 2.69 and leased to Dan-Air Services Ltd., Gatwick; sold to Dan-Air Services Ltd. 3.72

G-APDR (6418)*, f/f 7.7.59, C. of A. 17.7.59, d/d to B.O.A.C. 20.7.59; to Cia Mexicana de Aviacion S.A. 1.65 as XA-NAZ

G-ARDS (6419)*, f/f 6.8.59, C. of A. 13.8.59, d/d to B.O.A.C. 18.8.59; to the R.A.F. 3.69 as XW626

G-APDT (6420)*, f/f 2.10.59, C. of A. 15.10.59, d/d to B.O.A.C. 19.10.59; leased to Mexicana 11.65–12.69 as XA-NAB; to cabin training unit, Heathrow 1.70

G-AZIY (6434)*, LV-PPA, LV-AHU, f/f 2.7.60, C. of A. 13.1.72, Dan-Air Services Ltd., Gatwick

G-AZLW (6432)*, LV-POZ, LV-AHS, f/f 18.2.60, registered 10.1.72 to Dan-Air Services Ltd., Gatwick; to spares at Lasham 1972

de Havilland D.H.106 Comet 4B (*Hatfield or Chester* built*)

G-APMA (6421), f/f 27.6.59, C. of A. 8.7.59, d/d to B.E.A. 20.12.59 as 'Sir Edmund Halley'; withdrawn from use 4.71

G-APMB (6422), f/f 17.8.59, C. of A. 3.9.59, d/d to B.E.A. 9.11.59 as 'Walter Gale'; Channel Airways Ltd., Stansted 7.70; Dan-Air Services Ltd. 5.72

G-APMC (6423), f/f 1.10.59, C. of A. 13.10.59, d/d to B.E.A. 16.11.59 as 'Andrew Grommelin'; B.E.A. Airtours Ltd., Gatwick 1.71

G-APMD (6435), f/f 16.3.60, C. of A. 28.3.60, d/d to B.E.A. 29.3.60 as 'William Denning'; B.E.A. Airtours Ltd., Gatwick 5.70

G-APME (6436), f/f 26.4.60, C. of A. 9.5.60, d/d to B.E.A. 10.5.60 as 'John Tebbutt'; Dan-Air Services Ltd., Gatwick 4.72

G-APMF (6426), f/f 5.1.60, C. of A. 26.1.60, d/d to B.E.A. 27.1.60 as 'William Finlay'; B.E.A. Airtours Ltd., Gatwick 5.70

G-APMG (6442), f/f 25.7.60, C. of A. 29.7.60, d/d to B.E.A. 31.7.60; B.E.A. Airtours Ltd., Gatwick 4.70

G-APYC (6437), f/f 8.4.60, C. of A. 25.4.60, B.E.A., Heathrow; d/d to Olympic Airways Ltd., Athens 26.4.60 as SX-DAK 'Queen Frederika'; rest. 12.69 to B.E.A.; Channel Airways Ltd., Stansted 2.70; Dan-Air Services Ltd. 6.72

G-APYD (6438), f/f 3.5.60, C. of A. 12.5.60, B.E.A., Heathrow; d/d to Olympic Airways Ltd., Athens 14.5.60 as SX-DAL 'Queen Olga'; rest. 12.69 to B.E.A.; Channel Airways Ltd., Stansted 3.70

G-APZM (6440), f/f 30.6.60, C. of A. 11.7.60, B.E.A., Heathrow; d/d to Olympic Airways Ltd., Athens 14.7.60 as SX-DAM 'Queen Sophia'; rest. 3.70 to B.E.A.; Channel Airways Ltd., Stansted 5.70

G-ARCO (6449), f/f 5.4.61, C. of A. 12.4.61, d/d to B.E.A., Heathrow 13.4.61; crashed in the Mediterranean, 170 miles west of Cyprus 12.10.67

G-ARCP (6451), f/f 12.4.61, C. of A. 18.4.61, d/d to B.E.A., Heathrow 19.4.61; B.E.A. Airtours Ltd., Gatwick 11.71

G-ARDI (6447), f/f 24.3.61, C. of A. 25.3.61, B.E.A.; d/d to Olympic Airways Ltd., Athens 25.3.61 as SX-DAO 'Princess Sophia'; rest. 12.69 to B.E.A.; Channel Airways Ltd., Stansted 4.70; scrapped at Southend 6.72

G-ARGM (6453), f/f 27.4.61, C. of A. 3.5.61, d/d to B.E.A., Heathrow 6.5.61; B.E.A. Airtours Ltd., Gatwick 5.70

G-ARJK (6452)*, f/f 4.5.61, C. of A. 10.5.61, d/d to B.E.A., Heathrow 15.5.61; B.E.A. Airtours Ltd., Gatwick 4.70

G-ARJL (6457), f/f 19.5.61, C. of A. 29.5.61, d/d to B.E.A., Heathrow 31.5.61; B.E.A. Airtours Ltd., Gatwick 4.70

G-ARJM (6456)*, f/f 8.6.61, C. of A. 22.5.61, d/d to B.E.A., Heathrow 26.6.61; destroyed in take-off disaster at Ankara airport, Turkey 21.12.61

G-ARJN (6459), f/f 21.7.61, C. of A. 2.8.61, d/d to B.E.A., Heathrow 4.8.61; B.E.A. Airtours Ltd., Gatwick 4.70

de Havilland D.H.106 Comet 4C (*Hatfield or Chester* built*)

G-AOVU (6424), f/f 31.10.59, C. of A. 2.3.60, de Havilland Aircraft Co. Ltd.; d/d to Cia Mexicana de Aviacion S.A. 8.6.60 as XA-NAR

G-AOVV (6425), f/f 3.12.59, C. of A. 8.12.59, de Havilland Aircraft Co. Ltd.; d/d to Cia Mexicana de Aviacion S.A. 13.12.59 as XA-NAS

G-ARBB (6443), f/f 7.10.60, C. of A. 10.10.60, de Havilland Aircraft Co. Ltd.; d/d to Cia Mexicana de Aviacion S.A. 29.11.60 as XA-NAT

G-AROV (6460)*, f/f 24.8.61, C. of A. 10.9.61, flown at S.B.A.C. Show 9.61; de Havilland Aircraft Co. Ltd.; d/d to Aerolineas Argentinas 26.4.62 as LV-PTS; re-registered on arrival as LV-AIB 'President Kennedy'; rest. 11.71 to Dan-Air Services Ltd., Gatwick

G-ASDZ (6457), f/f 5.11.62, C. of A. 13.11.62, de Havilland Aircraft Co. Ltd.; d/d to Sudan Airways Ltd., Khartoum 14.11.62 as ST-AAW

G-AYVS (6474)*, 9K-ACE, f/f 17.12.63, C. of A. 30.4.71, Dan-Air Services Ltd., Gatwick

G-AYWX (6465)*, 9K-ACA, f/f 14.12.62, C. of A. 28.5.71, Dan-Air Services Ltd., Gatwick

The oft-re-registered Heron 1 G-AOZM landing at Southend in Channel Airways livery 1969. (*John Goring*)

de Havilland D.H.114 Heron 1

G-ALZL (10903), 20.11.50, de Havilland Aircraft Co. Ltd.; temporarily LN-BDH 25.4.54–14.5.54; Airlines (Jersey) Ltd. 'Duchess of Paris' 8.55; Executive A/T Ltd., Baginton 11.62; to Cimber Air, Sønderborg 1.67 as OY-DGS

G-AMSP (14009), 2.4.53, de Havilland Aircraft Co. Ltd.; to de Havilland Aircraft of Canada Ltd. via Prestwick 3.4.53; re-registered CF-EYX

G-AMUK (14006), 23.9.52, Butler Air Transport Ltd., Sydney; re-reg'd. 10.52 as VH-AHB; rest. 5.56 to Gulf Aviation Ltd., Bahrein; Flying Facilities Ltd., Gatwick 8.67; Tradair Ltd. 11.69; scrapped at Southend 7.72

G-AMYU (14017), 30.4.53, Airlines (Jersey) Ltd. 'Duchess of Jersey'; crash landed at Guernsey 15.8.58; wreck airfreighted to Jersey as spares

G-ANAX (14024), 22.9.53, de Havilland Aircraft Co. Ltd.; flown to Tokyo for Japan Air Lines; re-registered JA-6151; All Nippon Airways 12.57

G-ANCI (14043), G-5-13, 22.6.55, Dragon Airways Ltd., Speke 'The Commander'; Overseas A/T Ltd. 4.57 (operated by Dan-Air 1957, Cambrian 1958, North-South Airlines 1959); Mercury A/L Ltd., Ringway 5.62; to Israel 3.66 as 4X-ARL; to Belgium 8.67 as OO-BIA; rest. 11.68 to Tradair Ltd.; scrapped at Southend 7.72

G-ANFE (14034), 10.11.53, Butler Air Transport Ltd., Sydney; re-reg'd. VH-ARB; rest. 5.56 to Gulf Aviation Ltd., Bahrein; sold in Liechtenstein 4.68

G-ANFF (14036), 12.1.54, de Havilland Aircraft Co. Ltd.; flown to Tokyo for Japan Air Lines; re-registered JA-6152; All Nippon Airways 12.57

G-ANFG (14037), 17.2.54, de Havilland Aircraft Co. Ltd.; flown to Tokyo for Japan Air Lines; re-registered JA-6153; to All Nippon Airways 12.57

G-ANLN (14035), 7.4.54, Airlines (Jersey) Ltd. 'Duchess of Guernsey'; Executive Air Transport Ltd., Baginton 10.62; to Jamaica 7.63 as 6Y-JCZ

G-ANNO (14049), 16.6.54, Vickers-Armstrongs Ltd.; B.A.C. (Holdings) Ltd., Weybridge 3.64; British Aircraft Corporation Ltd., Filton 1971; J.F. Airlines Ltd., Portsmouth 'Spirit of Enterprise' 5.72

G-ANSZ (14047), G-5-16, 28.7.54, Airlines (Jersey) Ltd. 'Duchess of Alderney'; Morton Air Services Ltd., Gatwick; temporarily 9L-LAI from 5.10.66 to 28.11.66; Executive Air Engineering Ltd., Baginton 9.70; Peters Aviation Ltd., Norwich 4.72

G-ANWZ (14081), 1.6.55, Airlines (Jersey) Ltd. 'Duchess of Sark'; Morton A/S Ltd., Gatwick 1.66; Executive A/S Ltd., Baginton 9.70; w.f.u. 5.71

G-ANXA (14044), G-5-11, 16.2.55, B.E.A. 'John Hunter', Renfrew (later Abbotsinch); renamed 'Sister Jean Kennedy' 5.60

G-ANXB (14048), G-5-14, 9.2.55, B.E.A. 'Sir James Young Simpson', Renfrew, later Abbotsinch

G-AOFY (14099), 11.4.56, B.E.A. 'Sir Charles Bell', Renfrew; fatal crash at night when landing at Port Ellen, Islay, Hebrides 28.9.57

G-AOXL (14015), PK-GHB, 29.5.57, Morton Air Services Ltd., Croydon, later Gatwick; J.F. Airlines Ltd., Portsmouth 11.71

G-AOXM (14016), PK-GHC, registered 10.56 to Field Aircraft Services Ltd.; not re-imported and registration not used; to Toa Airways as JA-6162

G-AOZM (14002), LN-PSG, 9.5.57, Manx Airlines Ltd., Speke 'City of Bradford'; to Itavia 1.60 as I-AOZM; rest. 11.62 to T. D. Keegan; Dan-Air Services Ltd., Gatwick 6.63; to Israel 2.66 as 4X-ARK; rest. 1.69 to Tradair Ltd.; scrapped at Southend 7.72

G-AOZN (14005), LN-SUD, 20.3.57, Manx Airlines Ltd., Speke; Mercury Airlines Ltd., Ringway 4.61; Executive Air Eng. Ltd., Baginton 6.67; to Sierra Leone Airways Ltd. 4.68 as 9L-LAL

G-APJS (14001), ZK-AYV, 31.12.57, Gulf Aviation Ltd., Bahrein; crashed on Mt. Saraceno, Southern Italy en route Athens–Leavesden 19.2.58

G-APKT (14019), CX-AOR, 30.6.53, registered 2.58 to Eagle Aircraft Services Ltd., Ringway; Morton Air Services Ltd., Croydon, later Gatwick 5.61; to Sierra Leone Airways Ltd. 1.65 as 9L-LAG

G-APKU (14025), CX-AOS, 15.9.53, registered 2.58 to Eagle Aircraft Services Ltd., Ringway; British United Airways Ltd., Gatwick 11.61; to Sierra Leone Airways Ltd. 8.62 as 9L-LAD

G-APKV (14045), CX-AOU, 10.2.55, registered 4.58 to Eagle Aircraft Services Ltd., Ringway; Gulf Aviation Ltd., Bahrein 10.58; Aerocontacts Ltd., Gatwick 3.67; Tradair Ltd., Southend 9.69; w.f.u. 9.70; scrapped at Southend 7.72

G-APKW (14046), CX-AOV, 17.2.55, registered 4.58 to Eagle Aircraft Services Ltd., Ringway; Gulf Aviation Ltd., Bahrein 9.59; Aerocontacts Ltd., Gatwick 3.67; to the Congo 2.69 as 9Q-CRL; rest. 6.69 to Tradair Ltd., Southend; Peters Aviation Ltd., Norwich 5.72

G-AXFH (14022), PK-GHG, JA-6161, 21.5.69, Tradair Ltd., Southend

de Havilland D.H.114 Heron 2

G-AMTS (14007), 3.9.53, de Havilland Aircraft Co. Ltd.; to Queen's Flight 7.56–9.56 as XL961; Humber Ltd., Baginton 10.60; crashed on take-off from Biggin Hill 16.7.61

G-ANCJ (14082), 22.2.56, de Havilland Aircraft Co. Ltd.; to Leeward Islands Air Transport 3.56 as VP-LIB; later to Jamaica Air Services as 6Y-JED

G-ANOL (14052), 27.8.54, de Havilland Aircraft Co. Ltd. 'Excalibur'; to Bahamas Airways Ltd. 7.55 as VP-BAO; crashed at St. Kitts 23.8.59

G-ANPA (14053), 28.6.54, de Havilland Aircraft Co. Ltd.; to the Canadian Comstock Co. Ltd. 6.54 as CF-HLI; later to Apache Airlines, Arizona as N1420Z

G-ANPV (14098), G-5-24, de Havilland Engine Co. Ltd., Leavesden; T.I. (Group Services) Ltd., Elmdon 12.59; C. of A. 18.1.60; to Connellan Airways Ltd., Alice Springs 12.70 as VH-CLX

G-ANUO (14062), 15.3.55, Shell Aviation Ltd., Heathrow; British Nuclear Design and Construction Ltd. and G.E.C. Ltd., Heathrow 4.71

G-ANVH (14074), 12.8.55, de Havilland Aircraft Co. Ltd.; to de Havilland Aircraft of Canada Ltd. 8.55 as CF-IJR; later to Puerto Rico as N570PR

G-ANYJ (14080), 5.5.55, Dragon Airways Ltd., Speke 'Conqueror'; to Norway 2.57 as LN-SUB; to U.S.A. 11.60 as N4789C after overhaul at Leavesden

G-AODY (14089), 1.12.55, Dragon Airways Ltd., Speke 'Centurion'; to Norway 9.57 as LN-SUA; to Denmark 4.58 as OY-ADU; rest. 10.70 to Progressive Airways Ltd., Norwich 'County of Norfolk'; to Puerto Rico 7.71 as N576PR

G-AOGC (14094), 11.5.56, Shell Refining and Marketing Co. Ltd., Heathrow; to Holland 11.60 as PH-ILO; rest. 3.67 to Executive Air Engineering Ltd., Baginton; to Puerto Rico International Airlines 4.67 as N17600

G-AOGO (14096), 23.3.56, Cambrian Airways Ltd., Rhoose; Morton Air Services Ltd., Croydon 12.58; E. S. & A. Robinson (Holdings) Ltd., Filton 6.69

G-AOGU (14097), 26.3.56, Cambrian Airways Ltd., Rhoose; Metropolitan Air Movements Ltd., Biggin Hill 1.61; to Germany 6.62 as D-CASI; to Denmark 3.64 as OY-DPO; rest. 6.67 to Executive Air Engineering Ltd., Baginton; to Germany 9.70 as D-CAHA

G-AOGW (14095), 25.5.56, Vickers-Armstrongs Ltd., Wisley; British Aircraft Corporation Ltd., Wisley 3.64

G-AOHB (14100), 30.10.56, Shell Refining and Marketing Co. Ltd., Heathrow; to Iceland 4.65 as TF-AIN; to Puerto Rico Intern. A/L 11.66 as N16729

The former Dragon Airways G-ANYJ reworked with Lycoming engines as N4789C for Puerto Rico International Airlines Inc. (*Aviation Photo News*)

G-AORG (14101), G-5-16, 3.5.56, Airlines (Jersey) Ltd. 'Duchess of Brittany'; to
         No.781 Sqn. Royal Navy, Lee-on-Solent 7.61 as XR441

G-AORH (14102), 14.5.56, Airlines (Jersey) Ltd. 'Duchess of Normandy'; to No.781
         Sqn. Royal Navy, Lee-on-Solent 7.61 as XR442

G-AORJ (14104), 29.6.56, Cambrian Airways Ltd., Rhoose; to N. V. Phillips,
         Eindhoven 1.59 as PH-ILA; to Puerto Rico 1.69 as N561PR

G-AOTI (14107), G-5-19, 30.8.56, Rolls-Royce Ltd., Hucknall; Rolls-Royce (1971)
         Ltd., Filton 5.71

G-AOXZ (14109), G-5-11, 19.12.56, Gulf Aviation Ltd., Bahrein; not delivered; sold to
         Bahamas Airways Ltd. 1.57 as VP-BAN; later to U.S.A. as N19D

G-AOZX (14112), G-5-15, 12.3.57, de Havilland Aircraft Co. Ltd.; to Sultan of
         Morocco, Rabat 3.57 as CN-MAA

G-APEV (14125), 31.8.57, de Havilland Aircraft Co. Ltd.; to Aerolinee Siciliane 9.61 as
         I-AOVE; to Cimber Air, Sønderborg 10.64 as OY-AFN

G-APHW (14118), 7.10.57, de Havilland Aircraft Co. Ltd.; to the Banco Nacional de
         Mexico 1.58 as XB-ZIP; later fitted with 340 h.p. Lycoming engines

G-APMV (14128), 27.6.58, Ferranti Ltd., Turnhouse; to Puerto Rico via Prestwick
         21.3.72 as N579PR

G-APPD (14127), 11.12.58, de Havilland Aircraft Co. Ltd.; to Jordan Air Force 1.59 as
         H-106; rest. 7.65 to Sir Robt. McAlpine & Sons Ltd., Luton; to Nor-Fly A/S,
         Eggemoen 2.66 as LN-NPH

G-APRI (14126), 2.1.59, de Havilland Aircraft Co. Ltd.; to Jordan Air Force 1.59 as
         H-105; rest. 7.65 to Sir Robt. McAlpine & Sons Ltd., Luton; to U.S.A. 12.65
         as N782R; fitted with Lycomings for Virgin Is. A/S

G-APRK (14050), SA-R5, 24.7.59, Balfour Marine Engineering Co. Ltd., Southend; to
         Holland 5.61 as PH-VLA; damaged at Frankfurt 1.5.63; repaired at Baginton;
         to Denmark 10.64 as OY-DPN; rest. 7.66 to Executive Air Eng. Ltd.; tem-
         porarily OY-DGK 1.67 to 3.67; leased to Bristow 7.67 to 10.67 as
         5N-AGM; to Cimber Air, Sønderborg 4.68 as OY-DGK

G-APSW (14132), 16.4.59, de Havilland Aircraft Co. Ltd.; to Portuguese Timor 8.59 as
         CR-TAI; lost at sea north of Port Darwin, Australia 26.1.60

G-APXG (14137), f/f 26.11.59, C. of A. 12.12.59, H.H. Shaikh Abdulla Mubarak Al
         Sabah C.I.E., Kuwait; to Kuwait 12.59 as K-ABAA, later 9K-BAA

G-AREC (14140), f/f 14.10.60, C. of A. 4.11.60, English Electric Co. Ltd., Warton;
         B.A.C. (Operating) Ltd., Warton 3.64; to Puerto Rico International Airlines
         11.68 as N562PR

G-ARKU (14072), VR-NAQ, 13.4.55, registered 3.61 to Overseas Aviation Ltd., Jersey;
         to the Royal Navy 7.61 as XR443

G-ARKV (14091), VR-NCE, 15.12.55, registered 3.61 to Overseas Aviation Ltd.,
         Jersey; to the Royal Navy 6.61 as XR444

G-ARKW (14092), VR-NCF, 5.1.56, registered 3.61 to Overseas Aviation Ltd., Jersey;
         to the Royal Navy 6.61 as XR445

G-AROS (14077), VR-NAW, I-AOGO, 26.5.55, registered 5.61 to Executive Air
         Transport Ltd., Baginton; to Germany 3.63 as D-CASA; rest. 6.63; to
         Israel 2.64 as 4X-ARJ; rest. 3.67; to Puerto Rico Intern. A/L 3.67 as
         N13663

G-ARTI (14143), 30.10.61, E. S. & A. Robinson (Holdings) Ltd., Filton 'Esandar'; to
         Air Paris, Le Bourget 12.69 as F-BRSK

G-ARUA (14114), I-BKET, 19.6.57, Humber Ltd., Baginton; Executive Air Eng. Ltd.,
         Baginton 7.65; to Cimber Air, Sønderborg 12.66 as OY-DGR

VR-NCE, one of several Heron 2s delivered to West African Airways 1955–56, was reimported in 1961 as G-ARKV.

G-ARVX   (14086), VR-NCC, I-AOBI, Handley Page Ltd., Radlett; Hants and Sussex Aviation Ltd., Portsmouth 3.62; to Denmark 10.62 as OY-ADF; to Puerto Rico Intern. A/L 11.67 as N551PR after overhaul at Baginton

G-ASCX   (14124), West German Air Force CA + 002, 1.9.62, Ferranti Ltd., Ringway; sold to Connellan Airways Ltd., Alice Springs, Australia 2.70 as VH-CLV and converted to Lycoming engines

G-ASFI   (14108), G-5-15, West German Air Force CA + 001, 28.5.63, Shackleton Aviation Ltd., Sywell; to Portuguese Guinea 9.64 as CR-GAT; sold to Connellan Airways Ltd., Alice Springs 5.70 as VH-CLW and converted to Lycomings

G-ASUU   (14087), S.A.A.F. 121, 2.5.65, registered 8.64 to Executive Air Transport Ltd., Baginton; sold in Canada 6.71

G-ASUY   (14085), S.A.A.F. 120, Keegan Aviation Ltd., Panshanger; to Denmark 6.65 as OY-DPR; rest. 2.68 to Executive Air Eng. Ltd., Baginton; to Puerto Rico International Airlines 5.68 as N554PR

G-ASUZ   (14116), EC-ANY, 20.10.65, Morton Air Services Ltd., Gatwick; to Puerto Rico International Airlines 11.68 as N565PR after overhaul at Baginton

G-ASVA   (14121), EC-AOB, 10.1.65, Morton Air Services Ltd., Gatwick; to Puerto Rico International Airlines 11.68 as N564PR after overhaul at Baginton

G-ASVB   (14122), EC-AOC, Morton Air Services Ltd., Gatwick; left Gatwick 16.11.64 on delivery to Fiji Airways Ltd. as VQ-FAE

G-ASVC   (14123), EC-AOF, Morton Air Services Ltd., Gatwick; left Gatwick 16.11.64 on delivery to Fiji Airways Ltd. as VQ-FAF

G-ASXA   (14065), VT-DHD, 8.10.64, Aerocontacts Ltd., Gatwick; Flying Facilities Ltd., Gatwick 12.65; sold in Hawaii 7.66 as N16720

G-ATCZ   (14076), VR-NAV, I-AOLO, OY-BAO, 26.8.65, British Westpoint Airlines Ltd., Exeter; to Apache Airlines 3.66 as N12333; Lycomings fitted later

G-ATFE   (14067), VT-DHE, Aerocontacts Ltd., Gatwick; sold to Connellan Airways Ltd., Alice Springs, Australia 6.65 as VH-CLS

G-ATRZ   (14069), VT-DHG, 16.7.66, Flying Facilities Ltd., Gatwick; to Hawaii 9.66 as N16721

G-ATSA   (14073), VT-DHK, 1.9.66, Flying Facilities Ltd., Gatwick; to Hawaii; delivered direct from India via Singapore 11.9.66; became N16722

G-AVCF (14110), VP-KVC, 5Y-KVC, registered 12.65 to Shackleton Aviation Ltd., Sywell; fitted with Lycoming engines at Baginton; to U.S.A. 9.67 as N54R

G-AVTU (14148), last Heron built and erected after two years in store at Hawarden, C. of A. 17.1.68, Hawker Siddeley Aviation Ltd., Hatfield

G-AWDT (14147), OY-AFO, 22.3.68, Nuclear Power Group Ltd., Ringway; to Puerto Rico 10.71 as N577PR

G-AYLH (14054), LN-NPI, LN-SUL, OY-ADV, 11.12.70, Progressive Airways Ltd., Norwich 'City of Norwich'; to Canada via Stornoway 10.11.71

G-AZSO (14051), ZS-DIG, 25.5.72 Fairflight Charters Ltd., Biggin Hill

de Havilland D.H.A.3 Drover 2

G-ALLK (5003), VH-EBQ, registered 31.3.49 to the de Havilland Aircraft Co. Ltd.; cancelled 5.51 as not imported; retained by Qantas Empire Airways Ltd. as VH-EBQ; crashed in the Huon Gulf off New Guinea 16.7.51

G-APPP (5002), VH-BMU, registered 3.59 to the Air Navigation & Trading Co., Ltd., Squires Gate; not imported; registration cancelled 9.59

G-APXX (5014), VH-EAZ, VH-EAS, registered 12.60 to the Air Navigation & Trading Co. Ltd.; d/d Liverpool Docks–Squires Gate by road 19.9.61; by road to Southend Historic Aircraft Museum 19.5.67

de Havilland D.H.C.1 Chipmunk (*Canadian-built*)

G-AJVD (10), 1.7.47, re-registered G-ARFW (owner's initials) 3.60, d.b.r. near Cherbourg 20.6.66; G-AKCS (18), 21.8.47, to Australia 6.50 as VH-AFR; G-AKDN (11), 15.3.48; G-AKEV (1), CF-DIO-X, 18.11.47, w.f.u. at Panshanger 1.51; G-ARFW, see G-AJVD above

de Havilland D.H.C.1. Chipmunk Mks.10, 21 and 22 (*British-built*)

G-ALWB (C1/0100), 2.5.50, to Austria 8.56 as OE-ABC, rest. 4.61, crated to Beirut for Lebanese Army 4.63, rest. 4.64; G-AMLC (0414), 11.10.51, to Australia 5.54 as VH-MLO; G-AMMA (0470), 2.4.52, to Denmark 7.69 as OY-DHJ; G-AMUC (0824), 30.10.52; G-AMUD (0825), 30.10.52, crashed at Porchfield, I.O.W. 22.3.53; G-AMUE (0831), 17.11.52, night air collision with R.A.F. Balliol near Middle Wallop 22.10.56; G-AMUF (0832), 18.11.52; G-AMUG (0833), 28.11.52; G-AMUH (0834), 3.12.52; G-AMXL (0242), WD301, OH-HCA, 11.11.60; G-AMZL (0004), WB552, returned to the R.A.F. 7.53 as WB552

G-ANAG (0944), 25.6.53, to Japan 2.54 as JA-3090; G-ANOW (0972), 2.4.54, to South America by sea 3.54, sold in Uruguay 9.68; G-ANWB (0987), 13.3.55

G-AOFE (0150), WB702, 15.3.57; G-AOFF (0196), WB749, to Finland 3.57 as OH-HCE, rest. 6.61, C. of A. 6.7.61; G-AOJM (0079), WB633, 15.8.56, to Germany 8.56 as D-ECEM; G-AOJN (0248), WD306, 15.10.56, to Germany 10.56 as D-EFOM; G-AOJO (0113), WB665, 25.5.56, to Germany 6.56 as D-EDUG, rest. 11.56, to Nigeria 1.60 as VR-NBH; G-AOJP (0199), WB751, 22.6.56, to Germany 6.56 as D-EFOL, rest. 2.57, to Germany 1.58 as D-EFOL; G-AOJR (0205), WB756, 6.6.56, to Germany 6.56 as D-EGIM, rest. 11.56, to Germany 1.58 as D-EGIM; G-AOJS (0192), WB745, 15.6.56, to Germany 6.56 as D-EHOF, rest. 2.57, to Nigeria 1.60 as VR-NBI; G-AOJV (0147), WB699, 14.8.56, to Germany 8.56 as D-EJAN; G-AOJW (0171), WB719, 7.9.56, to Germany 9.56 as D-EFUS; G-AOJY (0077), WB631, 11.12.57, d.b.r. on the ground at Lulsgate 24.6.66; G-AOJZ (0181), WB732, 17.5.57, crashed 7 miles S.W. of Perth 31.5.66; G-AOPZ (0161), WB713, 21.5.57, crashed at Netherthorpe 8.4.62

G-AORE (0206), WB757, 23.5.58, sold in the U.S.A. 8.71; G-AORF (0089), WB648,

The Airways Aero Club's Chipmunk 22 G-APOY after modernisation by Bristol Aircraft in 1959.

10.5.57, crashed at White Waltham 21.7.68; G-AORK (0238), WD298, 26.7.57, to the U.S.A. 1.69 as N8342; G-AORL (0131), WB683, 27.3.57, shipped to the U.S.A. 1.69; G-AORP (0134), WB686, 7.2.57, crashed near St. Abb's Head, Berwickshire 8.5.60; G-AORR (0018), WB566, 23.1.57, to Switzerland 1.57 as HB-TUB; G-AORS (0223), WD284, 9.11.56, to Germany 12.56 as D-EHUM; G-AORU (0170), WB718, 26.4.57, to Switzerland 8.57 as HB-TUD; G-AORV (0177), WB725, 20.6.57, crashed at Crowcombe, Somerset 9.11.60; G-AORW (0130), WB682, 22.5.58; G-AOSA (0285), WD348, 19.2.57, crashed at Coupar, Angus 4.12.66; G-AOSB (0287), WD349, to Australia 7.58 as VH-RSN; G-AOSC (0057), WB616, registered 7.57, not converted; G-AOSF (0023), WB571, 12.2.57, to Switzerland 2.57 as HB-TUA; G-AOSH (0022), WB570, 28.2.57, to Switzerland 3.57 as HB-TUC; G-AOSI (0054), WB613, 2.4.57, to Singapore 5.57 as VR-SDW; G-AOSJ (0071), WB628, 18.1.57, crashed near Kidlington 26.2.61; G-AOSK (0178), WB726, 17.10.58; G-AOSN (0026), WB574, 13.2.58; G-AOSO (0227), WD288, 7.11.57; G-AOSP (0174), WB722, registered 7.56, not converted; G-AOSR (0062), WB621, to Australia 1.61 as VH-BSV; G-AOST (0135), WB687, 25.2.57, sold in the U.S.A. 6.70; G-AOSU (0217), WB766, 26.3.57, Lycoming conversion abandoned at Staverton 9.70; G-AOSV (0016), WB564, to Finland 10.56 as OH-HCD; G-AOSW (0221), WD283, to New Zealand 12.59 as ZK-BSV; G-AOSX (0512), WG462, OH-HCC, 9.2.61, crashed at Walpole St. Peter, Norfolk 3.11.64; G-AOSY (0037), WB585, 16.10.56; G-AOSZ (0080), WB635, 15.3.57

G-AOTA (0127), WB679, registered 7.56, not converted; G-AOTB (0142), WB695, registered 7.56, not converted; G-AOTC (0158), WB712, 19.7.57, to spares at Burnaston after heavy landing at Perth 31.1.58; G-AOTD (0040), WB588, not converted, dismantled at Farnborough 1967; G-AOTG (0541), WG491, 18.3.57, shipped to the U.S.A. 12.68; G-AOTH (0052), WB611, 28.7.58, crated to Beirut for Lebanese Army 4.63, rest. 4.64, crashed near Henley 6.2.70; G-AOTL (0122), WB674, registered 7.56, not converted; G-AOTM (0862), WP988, 29.10.56; G-AOTN (0024), WB572, to Australia 9.57 as VH-BON; G-AOTO (0204), WB755, registered 7.56, not converted; G-AOTP (0034), WB582, 7.2.57, crashed at Bushey Heath, Herts. 11.6.59; G-AOTR (0045), WB604, 10.9.56, sold in Germany 9.56; G-AOTS (0046), WB605, 8.10.56, to Germany 10.56 as D-EMID; G-AOTT (0053), WB612, 31.12.56, to Germany 12.58 as D-EMUM;

G-AOTU (0219), WB768, 12.6.57, to Nigeria 11.62 as 5N-AGO; G-AOTV (0482), WG408, 12.4.57; G-AOTW (0208), WB759, 27.9.56, to Germany 10.56 as D-ELEF; G-AOTX (0005), WB553, 12.6.57, to Switzerland 6.69 as HB-TUL; G-AOTY (0522), WG472, 28.6.57; G-AOTZ (0475), WG401, 4.7.57, to Belgium 3.72 as OO-FFT

G-AOUB (0162), WB714, registered 7.56, not converted; G-AOUC (0486), WG412, registered 7.56, not converted; G-AOUM (0616), WK607, 18.4.57, to New Zealand 5.57 as ZK-BSS; G-AOUN (0137), WB689, 16.10.56, to Belgium 8.69 as OO-NCL; G-AOUO (0179), WB730, 25.10.56; G-AOUP (0180), WB731, 8.11.56; G-AOZJ (0256), WD319, EI-AHV, 31.10.57, to Switzerland 11.57 as HB-TUE; G-AOZP (0183), WB734, 5.4.57; G-AOZU (0164), WB728, EI-AHP, 20.9.57, to Nigeria 11.62 as 5N-AGP; G-AOZV (0230), WD290, EI-AHT, 23.12.57

G-APAB (0115), WB667, 27.1.58, to Malaya 1.58 as VR-RCF; G-APAC (0167), WB715, 21.3.58, crashed at Luton 8.5.62; G-APCV (0176), WB724, 8.11.57, to Australia 12.57 as VH-FBB; G-APLO (0144), WB696, EI-AHU, 10.3.59; G-APMW (0078), WB632, EI-AJA, 28.8.58, crashed at Stanley, Perthshire 27.6.62; G-APNC (0540), WG490, 14.8.58, to Germany 8.58 as D-EGAP; G-APOE (0685), WP793, 13.11.58, sold in the U.S.A. 1.70; G-APOY (0898), WZ867, 18.2.59; G-APPA (0792), WP917, 18.6.59; G-APPK (0214), WB764, EI-AJE, 20.3.59; G-APPM (0159), WB711, 8.12.59; G-APSB (0930), WZ883, 16.11.59, to Puerto Rico 4.71 as N111PR; G-APSC (0673), WP782, 21.9.59, sold in the U.S.A. 8.71; G-APTF (0392), WG320, 12.2.65, to the Irish Air Corps 3.65 as '199'; G-APTG (0440), WG353, 13.5.60, crashed landing at Elstree 3.10.66; G-APTS (0683), WP791, 5.10.59; G-APUS (0297), WD358, registered 6.59, conversion abandoned at Biggin Hill 1960; G-APYG (0060), WB619, OH-HCB, 24.4.61

G-ARCR (0277), WD336, EI-AJF, 26.8.60; G-ARDF (0314), WD375, 18.10.60, d.b.r. landing at Thruxton 11.7.71; G-ARDW (0848), WP982, 7.11.61, crashed at Netherthorpe 11.5.68; G-ARGG (0247), WD305, 15.2.62; G-ARGH (0185), WB736, 29.9.61, crashed at Skegness 18.7.66; G-ARMB (0099), WB660, 5.12.61; G-ARMC (0151), WB703, 15.12.61; G-ARMD (0237), WD297, 3.11.61; G-ARME (0320), WD381, 13.9.61, crashed near Sandown, I.O.W. 29.3.66; G-ARMF (0394), WG322, 20.11.61; G-ARMG (0575), WK558, 3.10.61; G-ARTP (0061), WB260, EI-AJC, 7.2.62, to Ireland 4.62 as EI-AMH, rest. 11.64, to the Irish Air Corps 3.65 as '200'; G-ARWB (0621), WK611, 15.3.63; G-ASFE (0875), WZ853, 6.12.63, ground collision with Chipmunk G-AOST at Tollerton 16.8.64

Chipmunk Mk.23 crop sprayer G-APOS landing at Farm Aviation Ltd.'s Rush Green airfield, Herts. in 1965. (*M. D. N. Fisher*)

G-ATDE (0182), WB733, 8.7.66, returned to the R.A.F. 12.67; G-ATDF (0735), WP850, 29.6.65, returned to the R.A.F. 12.67; G-ATDP (0527), WG477, 29.6.65, returned to the R.A.F. 12.67; G-ATDX (0513), WG463, 1.7.65, returned to the R.A.F. 12.67; G-ATDY (0492), WG418, 1.7.65, returned to the R.A.F. 12.67; G-ATEA (0514), WG464, 4.8.65, returned to the R.A.F. 12.67; G-ATEB (0896), WZ866, 20.7.65, returned to the R.A.F. 12.67; G-ATHC (0835), WP969, 8.10.65, returned to the R.A.F. 12.67; G-ATHD (0837), WP971, 19.10.65, returned to the R.A.F. 12.67; G-ATJI (0750), WP863, 12.11.65, returned to the R.A.F. 12.67; G-ATJJ (0797), WP921, 12.11.65, returned to the R.A.F. 12.67; G-ATJK (0805), WP927, 13.10.65, returned to the R.A.F. 12.67; G-ATTS (0765), WP895, 7650M, 19.10.66, Turbo-Chipmunk with Rover TP-90, to the U.S.A. 10.69 as N2247

de Havilland D.H.C.1 Chipmunk Mk.23

G-AOTF (C1/0015), WB563, registered 6.56 to the R.A.E. Aero Club, Farnborough; stored until d/d to Rush Green 20.11.63 for conversion to Mk.23; C. of A. 14.4.64, Farm Aviation Ltd., Rush Green; Air Tows Ltd., Lasham 11.68

G-APMN (C1/0128), WB680, 18.6.58, de Havilland Aircraft Co. Ltd., Leavesden; leased to Fison-Airwork Ltd., Bourn; crashed at Fox's Farm, Potter Hanworth Fen, near Lincoln 27.7.58; remains to Croydon 24.10.58 as spares

G-APOS (C1/0763), WP893, 29.8.58, de Havilland Aircraft Co. Ltd., Leavesden; Farm Aviation Ltd., Rush Green 11.62; to U.S.A. 12.68 as N8345

G-ASPW (C1/0602), WK580, 7155M, 6.7.64, Farm Aviation Ltd., Rush Green; crashed at Wheathampstead, Herts. while crop spraying 1.7.67

G-ATVF (C1/0265), WD327, 28.7.66, Farm Aviation Ltd., Rush Green; converted 1970 to two seat Mk.22 Mod.; R.A.F. Gliding Assoc., Bicester 4.70

de Havilland D.H.C.2 Beaver 1

G-ALOW (36), 11.7.49, to Southern Rhodesia 11.52 as VP-YKA; G-AMVU (190), CF-GCR, 23.12.52, temporarily to the R.A.F. 9.54 as XH455, to Sierra Leone 9.56 as VR-LAV; G-ARTR (25), ZS-DCG, 14.10.61, to New Zealand 8.64 as ZK-CKH; G-ASTK (1502), CF-OSQ, ST-ACA, VR-AAX, 6.7.64, sold in Iran 5.66; G-AZLU (1558), VH-IDS, first flown at Southend 2.3.72, C. of A. 28.3.72

Desoutter I (including Koolhoven F.K.41)

G-AAGC (4102), F.K.41, registered 16.4.29 to the Desoutter Aircraft Co. Ltd.; to J. Williamson, Cape Town 1930 as ZS-ADX; fitted with Hermes I; South African C. of A. 30.12.32; impressed by S.A.A.F. in 1939 as '1598'

G-AALI (4103), F.K.41, registered 28.8.29 to the Desoutter Aircraft Co. Ltd.; to Australia 10.29 as VH-ULX; crashed at Condobolin N.S.W. 10.11.37

G-AANA (D.14), 18.2.30, National Flying Services Ltd., Hanworth (N.F.S.); Aircraft Exchange & Mart Ltd. 11.34; crashed at Stansted, Essex 9.4.35

G-AANB (D.15), 18.2.30, N.F.S.; Rollason Aircraft Services Ltd., Croydon 7.33; E. P. Fairbairn, Castle Bromwich 7.35; impressed 12.41 as HM508

G-AANC (D.16), 29.3.30, N.F.S. Ltd., Hanworth; crashed at Leith Hill 12.9.31

G-AAND (D.20), 2.4.30, N.F.S. Ltd., Hanworth; withdrawn from use 12.33

G-AANE (D.24), 19.5.30, N.F.S. Ltd., Hanworth; crashed at Plaxton, Kent 4.7.30; rebuilt with major components of unreg'd. aircraft D.26; C. of A. with this c/n 26.10.31 to Rollason Aircraft Services Ltd., Croydon; J. Willson 1.34; crashed 12.35

Koolhoven F.K.41 VH-ULX which made a fleeting one-day visit to England as G-AALI 28–29 August 1929. (*H. G. Martin*)

G-AAPK   (D.1), 14.11.29, N.F.S. Ltd., Hanworth; F. P. Smith, Castle Bromwich 7.35; Aylesbury Airport Ltd. 8.36; C. T. Balme, Southend 7.37; D. E. Bianchi, Hanworth 9.38; Flg. Off. J. Newton, Watchfield 10.40; w.f.u.

G-AAPP   (D.2), 16.11.29, N.F.S. Ltd., Hanworth; E. D. Ayre, Hanworth 10.31; to South Africa with 'The Spartan Circus'; d.b.r. at Cape Town 21.11.31

G-AAPR   (D.3), 16.11.29, N.F.S. Ltd.; to AERA, Antwerp 6.30 as OO-ALF

G-AAPS   (D.4), 27.5.30, N.F.S. Ltd., Hanworth; W. S. Stephenson, Hanworth 12.32; R. O. Shuttleworth, Old Warden 4.34; impressed 7.41 as ES946

G-AAPT   (D.5), 7.12.29, N.F.S. Ltd., Hanworth; Gipsy II conversion by Rollasons 12.34; S. H. Holland, Gatwick 3.35; R. D. Gerrans, Broxbourne 9.37; registration cancelled as 'lapsed' 12.46

G-AAPU   (D.6), 14.12.49, N.F.S. Ltd., Hanworth; Gravesend Aviation Ltd. 9.32; Aero Research Ltd., Duxford 7.38; w.f.u. at Cambridge 8.39

G-AAPX   (D.8), 6.1.30, N.F.S. Ltd., Hanworth; w.f.u. at expiry 31.12.30

G-AAPY   (D.9), 30.1.30, N.F.S. Ltd., Hanworth; C. B. Wilson, Croydon 1.30; M. L. D. Scott, Skegness 'Avis' 10.34; registration cancelled 12.46

G-AAPZ   (D.25), 19.8.31, N.F.S. Ltd., Hanworth; W. S. Stephenson, Hanworth 12.32; R. O. Shuttleworth, Old Warden 2.35; preserved by the Shuttleworth Trust

G-AATF   (D.19), 28.1.30, W. L. Hope, Croydon; Southern Aircraft Ltd., Shoreham 10.30; Rollason Aircraft Services Ltd., Croydon 2.33; Lord Ronaldsway, Portsmouth 8.33; beyond repair in take-off accident at Hanworth 9.5.34

G-AATI   (D.10), 14.1.30, C. E. Kay and H. L. Piper (New Zealand Flight machine 'Aorangi'); to Waikato Aviation Co. 12.30 as ZK-ACJ; to Blackmore's Air Services with Gipsy III engine; crashed at Taneatua 8.11.50

G-AATJ   (D.11), 18.1.30, N.F.S. Ltd., Hanworth; Southern Aero Club, Shoreham 5.32; beyond repair in crash at Shoreham 2.9.34; cancelled 8.45

G-AATK   (D.12), 6.2.30, N.F.S. Ltd., Hanworth; Aircraft Exchange & Mart Ltd., Hanworth 6.35; Aero Engines Ltd., Bristol 9.35; Sqn. Ldr. A. H. Wheeler, Old Warden 7.36; impressed 8.41 as HH980 for Saunders-Roe Ltd.

G-AATW   (D.13), 6.2.30, N.F.S. Ltd.; to AERA, Antwerp 6.30 as OO-ALG

G-AATX   (D.18), 10.4.30, N.F.S. Ltd., Hanworth; Maidstone Flying Services Ltd., West
Malling 7.32; crashed at Edenbridge, Kent 1.10.32

G-AAVO   (D.22), 16.4.30, N.F.S. Ltd., Hanworth; Phillips & Powis Ltd., Woodley 6.30;
registration cancelled 12.36

G-AAWT   (D.23), 9.5.30, Cirrus Aero Engines Ltd. (Hermes IV engine); Southern
Aircraft Ltd., Shoreham 4.31; to Dutch East Indies 10.33 as PK-SAN

G-ABMW   (D.28), 6.6.31, British Red Cross Society, Croydon; A. E. Clouston, Northolt
7.35; R. Grubb, Peterborough 10.36; C. G. M. Alington, Gatwick 6.38; A. A.
Rice, Norwich 4.39; impressed 5.42 as HM560

G-ABRN   (D.29), 12.11.31, British Red Cross Society, Woodford; Light Planes (Lancs)
Ltd., Woodford 10.31; Wiltshire School of Flying Ltd., High Post 4.36; registration cancelled 12.46

Desoutter II

G-AAZI   (D.27), 26.6.30, Desoutter Aircraft Co. Ltd., Croydon; W. F. Rickard,
Croydon 12.30; Rollason Aircraft Services Ltd., Croydon 7.33; R. O.
Shuttleworth, Old Warden 1.35; impressed 11.41 as HM507; burned
12.45

G-ABCU   (D.32), 2.10.30, Miss W. E. Spooner, Heston; ditched in Mediterranean Sea off
Naples 3.12.30; wreck burned at Heston 5.31

G-ABCV   (D.33), 16.9.30, Aeronautical Corporation of Canada Ltd., Winnipeg;
Winnipeg Flying Club 11.30 as CF-CBZ; burned in hangar fire 21.3.38

G-ABDZ   (D.34), 26.8.30, University Motors Ltd., Croydon; delivered to Count J. de
Wenckheim via Cologne 29.8.30; re-registered 10.30 as H-MAAA, later
HA-AAA, scrapped 1937–38

G-ABFO   (D.38), 14.11.30, Personal Flying Services Ltd., Croydon; crashed on the coast
10 miles south of Stranraer, Wigtownshire in fog 22.5.32

G-ABIG   (D.39), 19.1.31, Northern Aviation Ltd., Northern Rhodesia; to the Belgian
Congo 6.33 as OO-CAB; to South Africa 11.36 as ZS-AHR

G-ABOM   (D.30), EI-AAD, 1.9.30, R. L. Baker, Dublin; flown to Australia 3.32, became
VH-UEE 'Miss Flinders'; re-reg'd. 8.51 as VH-BQE; withdrawn from use
9.61; permanent exhibit at Launceston Airport, Tasmania

Douglas DC-3

G-AGBB (1590), PH-ALI, 25.7.40, shot down by German fighter over the Bay of
Biscay 1.6.43; G-AGBC (1939), PH-ALR, 5.8.40, crashed at Heston Airport 21.9.40;
G-AGBD (1980), PH-ARB, 29.7.40, to Netherlands Govt. 1945 as NL202, to K.L.M. 2.46
as PH-TBD, rest. 8.46 as Skyways Ltd. 'Skyhawk', to Jugoslavia 5.53 as YU-ABM;
G-AGBE (2022), 25.9.40, to Netherlands Govt. 1945 as NL201, to K.L.M. 2.46 as PH-TBE,
rest. 8.46 as Skyways Ltd. 'Skyward', crashed at Lons le Saulnier, France 18.11.46;
G-AGBI (2019), PH-ARW, 17.8.40, burned out in German air raid on Whitchurch Airport,
Bristol 24.11.40; G-AGEN (4118), NC33655, 42-38251, reserved 7.42 for B.O.A.C.,
ntu, to R.A.F. in India 8.42 as MA943, to Indian Govt. 8.43 as VT-ARI; G-AICV (1943),
PH-ALV, D-ARPF, PH-TBF, 7.9.46, Skyways Ltd. 'Skyliner', to spares at Dunsfold
1950; G-AJDC (2205), NC25660, 42-65582, NC25660, ZS-BTO, 19.2.53, to Sweden
3.53 as SE-BWD; G-AJDG (2199), NC21794, ZS-BTN, 17.10.50, to U.S.A. 8.55 as
N90C; G-ATXS (4103), NC33612, PP-PCJ, PP-ASJ, registered 26.7.66, abandoned at
Fort Lauderdale, Florida in 1968

Douglas C-47A Dakota 3

These aircraft were Dakota 3s when first issued with a British C. of A. Many were built as earlier marks and had become Dakota 3s by modification, others were built as Dakota 4s but were re-engined for certification as Dakota 3s. A number were later re-engined and upgraded to Dakota 4s. Named B.E.A. aircraft were modernised by Scottish Aviation Ltd. in 1950 as the 'Pionair' class.

G-AGFX (6223), 42-5635, FD769, 3.3.43, to South Africa 6.49 as ZS-DCZ; G-AGFY (6224), 42-5636, FD770, 23.3.43, to South Africa 7.48 as ZS-DAH; G-AGFZ (6225), 42-5637, FD771, 3.4.43, beyond repair landing at Bromma 21.4.44; G-AGGA (6231), 42-5643, FD777, 8.4.43, temporarily VT-CPB and AP-AAB in 1947, to French Indo China 7.48 as F-OACA; G-AGGB (6227), 42-5639, FD773, 13.4.43, to South Africa 9.49 as ZS-DDJ; G-AGGI (9050), 42-32824, FD796, 6.5.43, to South Africa 5.49 as ZS-DCY

G-AGHE (9189), 42-23327, FD827, 19.5.43, to Malaya 8.48 as VR-SCR; G-AGHF (9186), 42-23324, FD824, 13.5.43, to U.S.A. 3.51 as N9994F; G-AGHH (9187), 42-23325, FD825, 20.6.44, to Greece 11.49 as SX-BAN; G-AGHJ (9413), 42-23551, FD867, 4.12.43, to Iraq 12.46 as YI-GHJ, rest. 5.47, B.E.A. 'Albert Ball', w.f.u. at Luton 8.65; G-AGHK (9406), 42-23544, FD860, 5.6.43, crashed at Oviedo, Spain 17.4.46; G-AGHL (9407), 42-23545, FD861, 6.7.43, B.E.A. 'Lanoe Hawker', to Ghana 4.60 as 9G-AAF; G-AGHM (9623), 42-23761, FD901, 25.8.43, to Kenya 12.48 as VP-KGI, rest. 3.51, B.E.A. 'Edward Maitland', to Cyprus 6.69 as 5B-CBD; G-AGHN (9414), 42-23552, FD868, 2.9.43, to New Guinea 11.49 as VH-BZB; G-AGHO (9862), 42-24000, FD941, 18.9.43, to U.S.A. 3.51 as N9993F; G-AGHP (9408), 42-23546, FD862, 17.9.43, B.E.A. 'Bert Hinkler', crashed near Nemours, France 16.5.58; G-AGHR (10097), 42-24235, FL514, 5.10.43, crashed at Luqa, Malta 24.10.45; G-AGHS (10099), 42-24237, FL516, 13.10.43, B.E.A. 'Horace Short', sold in Cyprus 7.69; G-AGHT (10103), 42-24241, FL520, 20.10.43, crashed at Luqa, Malta 14.8.46; G-AGHU (9863), 42-24001, FD942, 28.10.43, to Hong Kong 2.48 as VR-HDQ

G-AGIO (11907), 42-92140, FL548, 19.10.43, to Hong Kong 12.47 as VR-HDO; G-AGIP (11903), 42-92136, FL544, 21.1.44, B.E.A. 'Horatio Phillips', to Morocco 8.63 as CN-ALI; G-AGIR (11932), 42-92162, FL568, 14.1.44, crashed in Atlas Mts. 28.8.44; G-AGIS (12017), 42-92239, FL607, 29.1.44, B.E.A. 'Sir Ross Smith', to French Indo China 2.54 as F-OAOE; G-AGIT (11921), 42-92152, FL560, 24.3.44, to Hong Kong 10.47 as VR-HDP; G-AGIU (12096), 42-92310, FZ561, 9.2.44, B.E.A. 'Edward Busk', to Mali 3.61 as TZ-ABB; G-AGIW (12186), 42-92391, FZ630, 23.2.44, crashed at Mill Hill, Middlesex 17.10.50; G-AGIX (12053), 42-92271, FL628, 1.3.44, crashed at Sywell 31.7.48; G-AGIY (12102), 42-92315, FZ567, 15.4.44, crashed at El Adem 23.1.46; G-AGIZ (12075), 42-92291, FL647, 8.3.44, B.E.A. 'Sir Oliver Swann', to French Indo China 5.54 as F-OAQJ

G-AGJR (11995), 42-92219, FL589, 5.2.44, to Holland 2.46 as PH-TAY; G-AGJS (12173), 42-92379, FZ618, 1.3.44, to Royal Netherlands Air Force 2.46 as NL-204, later PH-TAZ; G-AGJT (12172), 42-92378, FZ617, 4.5.44, to Holland 1.46 as PH-TBA; G-AGJU (12169), 42-92375, FZ614, 24.7.44, crashed at Whitchurch, Bristol 3.1.47; G-AGJV (12195), 42-92399, FZ638, 3.8.44, B.E.A. 'John Porte'; G-AGJW (12199), 42-92402, FZ641, 23.8.44, B.E.A. 'Wilfred Parke', to Ghana 4.60 as 9G-AAD; G-AGJX (12014), 42-92236, FL604, 29.8.44, crashed at Stowting, Kent 11.1.47; G-AGJY (12019), 42-92240, FL608, 13.10.44, to Hong Kong 10.47 as VR-HDN; G-AGJZ (12054), 42-92272, FL629, 28.10.44, B.E.A. 'John Stringfellow', to Ghana 4.60 as 9G-AAE

First Dakota 3 operated by a private company was Scottish Airlines' G-AGWS, converted at Prestwick in 1946 from surplus U.S.A.F. stock.

G-AGWS (6208), 41-38749, 9.1.46, temporarily WZ984 in 1952, to Canada 5.52 as CF-FCQ; G-AGYX (12472), 42-92648, KG437, 23.3.46, B.E.A. 'George Holt Thomas', to Holland 8.65 as PH-MAG; G-AGYZ (12278), 42-108843, FZ681, 21.3.46, B.E.A. 'Sir Charles Kingsford Smith'; G-AGZA (12455), 42-92633, KG420, 10.3.46, crashed at South Ruislip, Middlesex 19.12.46; G-AGZB (12180), 42-92385, FZ624, 13.3.46, B.E.A. 'Robert Smith-Barry', crashed near Ventnor, I.O.W. 6.5.62; G-AGZC (12222), 42-92423, FZ662, 13.6.46, B.E.A. 'Samuel Cody', to Mali 3.61 as TZ-ABA; G-AGZD (12450), 42-92628, KG415, 3.6.46, B.E.A. 'Percy Pilcher', to Bahamas 7.63 as VP-BCC; G-AGZE (12416), 42-92598, KG386, 20.6.46, to France 4.49 as F-BEFS; G-AGZF (9174), 42-23312, 11.5.46, to the French Air Force 10.52; G-AGZG (9803), 42-23941, 16.5.46, temporarily WZ985 in 1952, to the French Air Force 11.52 as 223941

G-AHCS (12348), 42-108850, 12.7.46, crashed at Oslo 7.8.46; G-AHCT (12308), 42-108846, KG313, 12.7.46; G-AHCU (13381), 42-93466, KG621, 23.7.46, B.E.A. 'Charles Ulm', w.f.u. at Southend 10.66; G-AHCV (12443), 42-92622, KG408, 4.8.46, B.E.A. 'Sir George Cayley', w.f.u. at Southend 3.66; G-AHCW (13308), 42-108946, 23.8.46, crashed at Exhall, near Coventry 19.2.49; G-AHCX (13335), 42-93425, KG604, 5.9.46, B.E.A. 'Spenser Grey', to the Yemen 7.62 as YE-ABC; G-AHCY (12355), 42-92543, KG348, 12.9.46, crashed at Saddleworth, Yorks. 19.8.49; G-AHCZ (11924), 42-92155, FL563, 30.10.46, to Iraq 12.46 as YI-HCZ, rest. 4.47, B.E.A. 'Charles Sampson', to Cyprus 6.69 as 5B-CBC; G-AHDA (12177), 42-92383, FZ622, cannibalised at Speke 4.47; G-AHDB (12077), 42-92293, FL649, cannibalised at Speke 4.47; G-AHDC (13481), 42-93556, KG664, cannibalised at Speke 4.47; G-AHLX (14035), 43-48219, KG803, 21.6.46, to Jugoslavia 12.47 as YU-ABG; G-AHLY (13849), 43-48033, KG750, 4.7.46, to Jugoslavia 12.47 as YU-ABF; G-AHLZ (14008), 43-48192, KG776, 10.7.46, to Jugoslavia 12.47 as YU-ABI

G-AIAZ (13459), 42-93536, KG647, to Australia 10.46 as VH-SMI; G-AIBA (9860), 42-23998, FD939, to the R.A.F. 10.46, later re-registered G-AKSM q.v.; G-AIJD (9049), 42-32823, FD795, 2.1.47, to Venezuela 1.51 as YV-C-AVK; G-AIOD (25292), 43-48031, KG748, 12.12.46, to Luxembourg 1.48 as LX-LAB, rest. 7.48, to Belgium 11.48 as OO-APB; G-AIOE (12373), 42-92559, KG364, 31.12.46, to Greece 3.48 as SX-BBA;

G-AIOF (12332), 42-92522, KG333, 31.12.46, to Greece 3.48 as SX-BBB; G-AIOG
(12482), 42-92657, converted for Iceland 12.46 as TF-ISG; G-AIRG (25288), 43-48027,
KG744, 30.11.46, to Burma 3.48 as XY-ABF; G-AIRH (12445), 42-92624, KG410,
18.12.46, to South Africa 5.48 as ZS-DDC; G-AIWC (12474), 42-93550, KG658,
22.4.47, to Aden 6.55 as VR-AAK, rest. 4.58, to Belgium 2.62; G-AIWD (13475),
42-93551, KG659, 7.7.47, B.E.A. 'John Dunne', to Aden 6.67 as VR-ABF; G-AIWE
(13479), 42-93554, KG662, 20.1.47, to Spain 5.52 as EC-AGS; G-AIYT (12486),
42-92661, KG451, 6.1.47, to South Africa 3.47 as ZS-BCJ

G-AJAU (12433), 42-92613, KG398, 23.6.47, to Malaya 10.47 as VR-SCP; G-AJAV
(12386), 42-92571, KG377, 12.8.47, to U.S.A. 9.50 as N19D; G-AJAY (13375),
42-93461, KG616, 23.5.47, to Spain 6.50 as EC-AET; G-AJAZ (10100), 42-24238,
FL517, 28.4.47, to Spain 12.48 as EC-ADR; G-AJBB (12477), 42-92553, 10.3.47, to
India 6.47 as VT-CJH; G-AJBC (12304), 42-92497, FZ698, 25.6.47, to Greece 2.48 as
SX-BBC; G-AJBD (13012), 42-93134, KG529, 11.7.47, to Greece 2.48 as SX-BBD;
G-AJBG (14003), 43-48187, KG771, 27.3.47, crashed at Bovingdon 20.5.48; G-AJBH
(14015), 43-48199, KG783, 4.7.47, to the French Air Force 11.52

G-AJDE (13182), 42-93287, ZS-BCA, 27.9.48, to Kenya 5.49 as VP-KGL, to South
Africa 2.50 as ZS-DBV, rest. 5.50, B.E.A. 'Sir David Henderson', to Holland 2.61 as
PH-SSM; G-AJGX (12162), 42-92369, FZ607, 21.4.47, to Greece 11.47 as SX-BAI;
G-AJHY (13388), 42-108954, KG628, 22.8.47, B.E.A. 'William Henson', to the Congo
10.64 as TN-AAF; G-AJHZ (12421), 42-92602, KG391, 10.7.47, B.E.A. 'Bentfield
Hucks', to Spain 6.62 as EC-ASQ, rest. 3.64; G-AJIA (12208), U.S.N. 17126,
42-108836, FZ664, 25.6.47, B.E.A. 'Sir John Alcock', to Mali 3.61 as TZ-ABC;
G-AJIB (9624), 42-23762, FD902, 28.7.47, B.E.A. 'Griffith Brewer', w.f.u. at Southend
10.65; G-AJIC (9487), 42-23625, FD869, 23.5.47, B.E.A. 'Roy Chadwick', derelict at
Benina, Libya 8.66

G-AJLC (4930)*, 42-6478, TJ167, 6252M, NC74139, to Belgium 11.47 as OO-APC;
G-AJLX (14038), 43-48222, KG806, 28.7.49, to India 7.50 as VT-DDK; G-AJLY
(13452), 42-93530, 30.4.48, to Ceylon 5.48 as VP-CBA, later CY-ACE; G-AJLZ
(10101), 42-24239, FL518, 5.11.47, to Luxembourg 12.47 as LX-LAA; G-AJNR
(12095), 42-92309, FZ560, 30.7.47, to India 8.47 as VT-COK; G-AJPF (13456),
42-93534, KG644, 5.12.47, to Canada 1.51 as CF-IOC; G-AJRW (19569), 43-15103,
23.6.47, to Malaya 8.47 as VR-SCM; G-AJRX (12209), 42-92411, FZ650, 8.7.47, to
Malaya 8.47 as VR-SCN; G-AJRY (13331), 42-93421, KG607, 22.7.47, to Malaya 8.47
as VR-SCO, later VR-RCO, 9M-ALO, PK-AKR, N96U, CU-P-702, N702S, G-ASDX
ntu, rest. 11.62; G-AJTO (12647), 42-92806, registered 20.5.47, to Australia 3.48 as
VH-INF; G-AJVY (12358), 42-108851, KG351, 30.9.47, to Dakar 7.50 as F-OAGZ;
G-AJVZ (19361), 42-100898, TS432, 24.6.48, crashed at Ringway 27.3.51; G-AJXL
(9628), 42-23766, ZS-DDV, not converted, re-registered G-AMGD q.v.; G-AJZD
(12333), 42-92523, KG334, 25.7.47, to France 11.50 as F-BFGU; G-AJZX (9051),
42-32825, 3.4.48, to Indonesia 1.51 as PK-PAB

G-AKAY (12006), 42-92229, FL597, 26.8.47, to Malaya 5.51 as VR-SCG; G-AKGX
(9874), 42-24012, FD953, 10.9.47, to Nigeria 2.58 as VR-NCS; G-AKII (12299),
42-92492, FZ693, 22.11.47, to Bahamas 2.60 as VP-BBR; G-AKIJ (13304), 42-93397,
KG581, 5.1.48, to Nigeria 2.58 as VR-NCP; G-AKIK (13497), 42-93562, KG670,
12.12.47, to the French Air Force 3.57; G-AKIL (25282), 43-48021, KG738, 30.10.47,
to U.S.A. 11.51 as N9988F; G-AKJH (13164), 42-93271, KG572, 19.4.48, B.E.A.
'Edward Hillman', to Ireland 7.67 as EI-ARR, rest. 12.67, to Swaziland 10.68 as VQ-ZEB;

* Registered as a Douglas C-53/DC-3A

500

G-AKJN (12489), 42-92663, KG454, 29.11.47, to Tunisia 2.51 as F-OAIG; G-AKLL (14005), 43-48189, KG773, 28.1.48, to Spain 6.50 as EC-AEU; G-AKNB (9043), 42-32817, FD789, 5.12.47, to Burma 3.50 as XY-ACN, rest. 11.50, B.E.A. 'Sir Sefton Brancker'; G-AKPW (13729), 42-93779, KG728, 13.2.48, to Malaya 3.48 as VR-SCQ; G-AKSM (9860), 42-23998, FD939, G-AIBA, 24.4.48, to Iceland 3.51 as TF-ISB; G-AKVX (12587), 42-92752, registered 16.3.48, to South Africa 6.48 as ZS-BYX

G-ALBG (14014), 43-48198, KG782, 21.12.48, to the French Air Force 5.49, F-BNPT in 1966; G-ALCA (12159), 42-92366, FZ604, SAAF.6817, 21.9.48, to Pakistan 9.48 as AP-ABW; G-ALCB (11911), 42-92143, FL551, SAAF.6869, 15.10.48, to Pakistan 11.48 as AP-ADH, rest. 6.50, to spares at Tollerton 1.51; G-ALCC (10106), 42-24244, FL523, SAAF.6808, 12.4.49, B.E.A. 'Harry Hawker', to Cyprus 6.69 as 5B-CBE; G-ALEZ (12066), 42-92283, FL640, ZS-BVF, remained in South Africa 2.49 as ZS-DBP; G-ALFO (20401), 43-15935, VH-BHC, 31.12.48, to U.S.A. 12.50 as N94529; G-ALLI (19362), 42-100899, TS433, 17.5.49, B.E.A. 'Sir Samuel Instone', to Southern Rhodesia 3.60 as VP-YRK; G-ALPM (19566), 43-15100, TS435, not taken up, sold in South Africa 6.49 as ZS-BRX; G-ALPN (12218), 42-108837, ZS-DDZ, 8.11.50, B.E.A. 'Sir Godfrey Paine', w.f.u. 11.68; G-ALTT (12000), 42-92223, ZS-DBZ, 2.7.49, B.E.A. 'Charles Grey', to Iceland 8.63 as TF-FIS, rest. 1.64, to Ethiopia 4.64 as ET-ABI; G-ALVZ (16675), 44-77091, KP219, 6.3.50, to Malaya 5.51 as VR-SDD, rest. 5.61, to spares at Bahrein 1970

Dakota 3 G-AIWE 'Crewsendeavour', based at Southend for charter work in 1950 by Crewsair Ltd., was owned, as the name implied, by the company's aircrew. (A. J. Jackson)

G-ALWC (13590), 42-93654, KG723, 16.8.50; G-ALWD (12911), 42-93043, KG507, not flown as such, re-registered G-AMDZ q.v.; G-ALXK (16080), 44-76496, KN405, 1.6.50, B.E.A. 'Rex Pierson', w.f.u. at Lasham 11.69; G-ALXL (16487), 44-76903, 18.5.50, B.E.A. 'Charles Rolls', to Cyprus 7.69 as 5B-CBB; G-ALXM (16465), 44-76881, KN583, 25.4.50, B.E.A. 'William Rhodes-Moorhouse', to Holland 7.60 as PH-MAA; G-ALXN (14661), 43-48845, KJ934, 8.6.51, B.E.A. 'Sir Henry Royce', temporarily to Dart Dakota 1951, first as G-37-1, reverted to standard 1952, to spares at Southend 1964; G-ALXO (16699), 44-77115, converted for Aer Lingus 6.50 as EI-AFL; G-ALYF (19350), 42-100887, TS424, 30.4.50, B.E.A. 'Pionair', to spares at Prestwick 1967

G-AMBW (25275), 43-48014, KG731, HC-SBS, 30.5.51, temporarily XB246 in 1952, to Viet Nam 11.53 as F-VNAU; G-AMDB (14987), 43-49171, KJ993, 15.8.51, B.E.A. 'Claude Johnson', temporarily to Dart Dakota 1951, first as G-37-2, reverted to standard 1952, w.f.u. at Lympne 12.67; G-AMDZ (12911), 42-93043, KG507, G-ALWD, 21.12.50, B.E.A. 'Frank Barnwell', w.f.u. at Southend 3.70; G-AMFV (10105), 42-24243,

FL522, SAAF.6810, ZS-DEF, 11.12.50, B.E.A. 'Richard Howard-Flanders'; G-AMGD (9628), 42-23766, ZS-DDV, G-AJXL, 26.10.50, B.E.A. 'George Brackley', to Southern Rhodesia 12.61 as VP-YTT; G-AMHJ (13468), 42-108962, KG651, ZS-BRW, 22.6.51; G-AMJU (14489), 43-48673, KJ894, 10.2.52, temporarily XF757 in 1954; G-AMJX (15635), 43-49819, KN214, 5.11.51, B.E.A. 'Reginald Mitchell', to Morocco 8.63 as CN-ALJ; G-AMJY (16808), 44-77224, KP254, 27.12.51, B.E.A. 'James McCudden', to Ceylon 11.59 as 4R-ACI

G-AMKE (14483), 43-48667, KJ888, 23.11.51, B.E.A. 'Frederick Lanchester', to Southern Rhodesia 10.62 as VP-YUU; G-AMMJ (16770), 44-77186, KP233, VP-BAU, 13.3.52, to Canada 3.52 as CF-FAX; G-AMNV (16833), 44-77249, KP279, 6.10.52, B.E.A. 'Sir Eric Geddes', to Spain 12.62 as EC-ATM, rest. 11.63, to Sweden 5.65 as SE-EDI, to Senegal 7.65 as 6V-AAM, rest. 10.65, to Swaziland 12.65 as VQ-ZEA; G-AMNW (14177), 43-48361, KJ838, 12.9.52, B.E.A. 'Frank Searle', w.f.u. at Southend 2.66; G-AMPP (15272), 43-49456, KK135, 16.10.52, temporarily XF756 in 1954; G-AMVA (16415), 44-76831, KN552, 12.3.53, temporarily to Iran 11.59 as EP-ABE, w.f.u. 2.71; G-AMVK (15530), 43-49714, KK198, 3.2.53, to Aden 6.55 as VR-AAM; G-AMYV (16195), 44-76611, KN469, 22.5.53, temporarily XF623 in 1954, to South Arabian Air Force 10.67 as '204'; G-AMZZ (16592), 44-77008, KN648, 20.11.53, temporarily to Iran 11.59 as EP-ABD, w.f.u. 5.71

G-ANAS (16509), 44-76925, KN611, direct to South Africa 8.53 as ZS-DHY; G-ANLF (11979), 42-92204, ZS-DHO, 23.1.54, temporarily F-OAOR in 1954, to Belgium 9.61 as OO-SBH; G-ANYF (15555), 43-49739, ZS-DIY, 9.2.55, to Canada 2.55 as CF-HTH; G-ANZE (25309), 43-48048, KG765, 31.3.55, to Burmese Air Force 8.55 as UBT-714; G-ANZF (15125), 43-49309, Pakistan H704, 17.3.55, to Burmese Air Force 7.55 as UBT-713; G-ANZG (16498), 44-76914, Pakistan C407, AP-AFH, 3.3.55, to Swedish Air Force 4.55 as '79005'

G-AOAL (16426), 44-76842, KN559, AP-ADA, F-OAQA, 8.7.55, to Burmese Air Force 7.55 as UBT-712; G-AOBN (11711), 42-68784, SE-BAU, F-OAIF, 4.6.55; G-AOCT (12813), 42-92955, 22.8.56, to Madagascar 10.56 as F-OAYR; G-AODD (10239), 42-24377, NC36412, OD-AAO, 20.8.55, to Burmese Air Force 9.55; G-AOGX (20777), 43-16311, AP-AED, to Algeria 10.56 as F-OAYM; G-AOJI, KN550, 7.2.57, to Aden 3.57 as VR-AAO, rest. 10.58, to Bahamas 12.58 as VP-BAH; G-AOXI (14168), 43-48352, KJ829, G-37-2 (first Dart Dakota), 15.11.56, reverted to KJ829 in 1957, rest.

Dakota 3 G-AVNF ready to leave Luton for Jordan, 17 June 1967. It was the only one of five SADIA aircraft taken by Handley Page Ltd. in part exchange for Dart Heralds to reach England. (*Aviation Photo News*)

4.63, scrapped at Usworth 1964; G-AOYE (10028), 42-24166, FL510, 7.5.57, to French Air Force 5.57 as 24166

G-APBP (13173), 42-93279, F-BAXJ, D-CABA, to Trinidad 7.57 as VP-TBW; G-APNK (25623), 43-48362, KJ839, formerly Mamba Dakota testbed, to Bahamas 11.58 as VP-BAB, later VP-LIX; G-ATBE (9813), 42-23951, EI-ANK, 28.7.66, to Canada 4.70 as CF-CQT; G-ATXT (4306), U.S.N. 4699, N95481, PP-ANC, PP-ASP, registered 26.7.66, to Bolivia 7.68 as CP-820; G-ATXU (19176), 42-100713, N54325, PP-YPP, PT-BEJ, PP-ASR, registered 26.7.66, abandoned at Fort Lauderdale, Florida 1968; G-ATZF (12324), 42-92515, KG327, LN-NAB, SE-CFM, OE-LBC, registered 16.9.66, to Hong Kong 11.66

G-AVNF (9004), 42-5697, PP-BRA, PP-AND, registered 5.67, to Jordan 6.67 as JY-ADE; G-AVPW (12476), 42-92652, KG441, 29.12.67; G-AXJU (16175), 44-76591, KN452, 8.1.70, to Kenya 1.70 as 5Y-AKB

Douglas C-47B Dakota 4

These aircraft were Dakota 4s when first issued with British C. of A. Some were later re-engined to become Dakota 3s and others were modernised for airline operation as Dakota 6s.

G-AGKA (25586), 43-48325, KJ802, 22.1.45, to Aden 2.50 as VR-AAA; G-AGKB (25588), 43-48327, KJ804, 26.11.44, to Brazil 2.50 as PP-VBT; G-AGKC (25591), 43-48330, KJ807, 14.11.44, to Viet Nam 2.52 as F-VNAE; G-AGKD (25595), 43-48334, KJ811, 3.1.45, damaged beyond repair in Malta 23.12.46; G-AGKE (14361), 43-48545, KJ867, 14.11.44, to Aden 2.50 as VR-AAB, later to TJ-ABN, JY-ABN, VR-AAB, rest. 5.61, sold in the Lebanon 10.71; G-AGKF (25807), 43-48546, KJ868, 3.1.45, to France 6.49 as F-BEFQ; G-AGKG (25818), 43-48557, KJ879, 4.3.45, to Burma 3.50 as XY-ACL; G-AGKH (25810), 43-48549, KJ871, 21.2.45, to Iraq 5.47 as YI-GKH, rest. 11.47, to Aden 2.50 as VR-AAC; G-AGKI (26099), 43-48838, KJ928, 17.1.45, to Kenya 10.49 as VP-KHK; G-AGKJ (26105), 43-48844, KJ933, 3.2.45, to Aden 2.50 as VR-AAD; G-AGKK (26100), 43-48839, KJ929, 7.2.45, to Algeria 4.49 as F-OAFQ; G-AGKL (26107), 43-48846, KJ935, 7.2.45, to Ireland 5.48 as EI-ADW, rest. 10.48, to French Indo China 6.49 as F-OADA; G-AGKM (26431), 43-49107, KJ992, 20.2.45, beyond repair at El Adem, Libya 8.4.45; G-AGKN (26429), 43-49168, KJ990, 26.2.45, crashed near Toulon, France 14.7.48

G-AGMZ (14978), 43-49162, KJ985, 29.3.45, temporarily VT-CPA and AP-AAA in 1947, to Aden 3.50 as VR-AAE; G-AGNA (14967), 43-49151, KJ976, 11.4.45, crashed at Basra 1.5.45; G-AGNB (15274), 43-49458, KK137, 7.3.45, to Iraq 7.47 as YI-GNB, rest. 11.47, to Aden 2.50 as VR-AAF; G-AGNC (15283), 43-49467, KK145, 30.5.45, to Ireland 5.48 as EI-ADX, rest. 11.48, to Algeria 4.49 as F-OAFR; G-AGND (15280), 43-49464, KK142, 4.3.45, to Bahamas 8.61 as VP-BBT; G-AGNE (15276), 43-49460, KK139, 5.6.45, to Kenya 11.49 as VP-KHN; G-AGNF (15534), 43-49718, KK201, 16.3.45, to Burma 3.50 as XY-ACM; G-AGNG (15552), 43-49736, KK216, 15.3.45, to Ireland 5.48 as EI-ADY, rest. 10.48, to Canada 1.51 as CF-GVZ; G-AGNK (15539), 43-49723, KK206, 22.3.45, B.E.A. 'Edward Mannock' 4.51, to spares at Southend 1964

G-AKAR (15444), 43-49628, 31.10.47, to Brazil 12.50 as PP-VBV; G-AKDT (25606), 43-48345, KJ822, 11.5.48, to Kenya 6.50 as VP-KIF; G-AKNM (14354), 43-48538, KJ860, 20.5.48, temporarily CF-GON in 1951, to Belgium 2.53 as OO-CBU; G-AKOZ (15743), 43-49927, KN259, 3.12.48, to French Air Force 11.52 as 49927

G-AMCA (16218), 44-76634, KN489, 11.10.50; G-AMNL (16644), 44-77060, KN682, 8.2.52, to Italy 10.61 as I-TAVO; G-AMPO (16438), 44-76854, KN566, 26.7.52, to Norway 3.65 as LN-RTO, rest. 9.69; G-AMPS (15993), 44-76409, KN371,

Fairey Air Survey's Dakota 4 G-AMCA with ventral camera bulge. This aircraft flew all over the world for more than 20 years, photographing the terrain for mapping purposes. (*Aviation Photo News*)

11.9.52, to Southern Rhodesia 5.53 as VP-YKN; G-AMPT (16187), 44-76603, KN462, 31.8.52, to Southern Rhodesia 6.53 as VP-YKM; G-AMPY (15124), 43-49308, KK116, 3.8.54, to Jordan 12.57 as JY-AAE, rest. 4.58, to Iceland 8.64 as TF-FIO, rest. 7.65, to U.S.A. 12.68 as N15751, rest. 11.70; G-AMPZ (16124), 44-76540, KN442, 23.1.53, to Lebanon 4.65 as OD-AEQ, rest. 8.65, to Holland 3.66 as PH-RIC, rest. 6.66, to Iceland 7.66 as TF-AIV, rest. 9.69; G-AMRA (15290), 43-49474, KK151, 12.3.53, temporarily XE280 in 1953; G-AMRB (16670), 44-77086, KP214, 14.4.54, crashed at Largs, near Renfrew 28.3.56

G-AMSF (14380), 43-48564, KJ886, 13.6.52, temporarily XF646 in 1954, beyond repair at Elmdon 5.3.60; G-AMSH (16583), 44-76999, KN642, 25.7.52, temporarily XF648 and XF667 in 1954, to Aden 3.67 as VR-ABE; G-AMSI (14642), 43-48826, KJ919, 16.5.53, to South Africa 8.53 as ZS-DHW; G-AMSJ (16477), 44-76887, KN590, 6.5.53, to Italy 10.61 as I-TAVI; G-AMSK (16206), 44-76622, KN477, 6.6.53, to Southern Rhodesia 8.55 as VP-YNH; G-AMSL (14946), 43-49130, 18.5.53, destroyed in taxying accident at Dukhan Airport, Arabia 18.2.56; G-AMSM (15764), 43-49948, KN274, 20.5.53; G-AMSN (16631), 44-77047, KN673, 9.4.54, to Switzerland 2.68; G-AMSO (16820), 44-77236, KP266, to Kenya 11.52 as VP-KKH; G-AMSR (14799), 43-48983, KJ952, 8.7.52, to South Africa 8.54 as ZS-DJZ; G-AMSS (16092), 44-76508, KN415, 30.8.52, to Iran 11.68 as EP-AIQ; G-AMST (16207), 44-76623, KN478, to Kenya 10.52 as VP-KKI; G-AMSU (16800), 44-77211, KP246, 24.10.52; G-AMSV (16072), 44-76488, KN397, 24.10.52; G-AMSW (16171), 44-76587, KN449, 5.9.52, crashed in the Pyrenees 7.10.61; G-AMSX (16448), 44-76864, KN573, 27.11.52, to British Guiana 3.66 as VP-GCF

G-AMVB (14637), 43-48821, KJ915, 1.1.53, temporarily XF647 in 1954, burned out on ground at Masjid-I-Sulaiman, Iran 22.10.58; G-AMVC (16642), 44-77058, KN681, 9.3.53, temporarily XF645 in 1954, crashed on Croglin Fell, Cumberland 17.10.61; G-AMVL (16660), 44-77076, KN698, 6.2.53, temporarily XF746 in 1954, to South Africa 4.55 as ZS-DKR; G-AMWV (14155), 43-48339, KJ816, 23.4.53, to Ireland 6.66 as EI-APB, rest. 9.67, scrapped 5.69; G-AMWW (16262), 44-76678, KN492, 22.5.53, to Ireland 6.67 as EI-ARP, rest. 8.67; G-AMWX (15846), 44-76262, 11.6.53, destroyed by tide after forced landing on beach at Mers-les-Bains, N. France 17.12.65; G-AMYB (16598), 44-77014, 20.4.53, to Sudan 1.57 as SN-AAK rest. 8.71, temporarily 5N-AJE; G-AMYJ (15968), 44-76384, KN353, 20.5.53, temporarily XF747 in 1954; G-AMYS (15009), 43-49293, KK104, to Southern Rhodesia 6.53 as VP-YKO; G-AMYT (14360),

43-48544, KJ866, to Southern Rhodesia 8.53 as VP-YKL; G-AMYW (16272), 44-76688, 12.8.53, beyond repair in forced landing in the interior of Saudi Arabia 8.4.67; G-AMYX (16294), 44-76710, KN509, 1.7.53, temporarily XF619 in 1954, to Ireland 8.66 as EI-APJ; G-AMYY (14992), 43-49176, KJ998, to Southern Rhodesia 6.53 as VP-YKP; G-AMYZ (16823), 44-77239, KP269, not converted, scrapped at Croydon 7.53

G-AMZA (16821), 44-77237, KP267, not converted, scrapped at Croydon 7.53; G-AMZB (15535), 43-49719, KK202, 26.6.53, to Belgium 3.62; G-AMZC (16522), 44-76938, KN620, 23.5.53, crashed at Dusseldorf, Germany 22.12.55; G-AMZD (16112), 44-76528, 19.6.53, crashed in the Montseny Mts. north of Barcelona 19.8.59; G-AMZE (14368), 43-48552, KJ874, 2.11.53, to spares at Baginton 3.64; G-AMZF (15633), 43-49817, KN212, 11.7.53, temporarily XF748 in 1954, to Canada 6.66 as CF-RTY; G-AMZG (16668), 44-77084, KP212, 26.6.53, to Iceland 6.66 as TF-AIO; G-AMZH (15665), 43-49849, KN241, 18.9.53, to Australia 5.65 as VH-SBW; G-AMZR (16335), 44-76751, to the Sudan 5.54 as SN-AAJ; G-AMZS (15137), 43-49321, to the Sudan 5.54 as SN-AAI, rest. 8.71, temporarily 5N-AJF; G-AMZW (15654), 43-49838, to the Sudan 10.53 as SN-AAH; G-AMZX (15287), 43-49471, KK149, to the Sudan 9.53 as SN-AAG

G-ANAD (15770), 43-49954, KN279, to Aden 3.54 as VR-AAI; G-ANAE (14656), 43-48840, KJ930, 31.7.53, to Aden 4.68 as VR-ABH; G-ANAF (16688), 44-77104, KP220, 17.2.54; G-ANEG (16696), 44-77112, 29.4.54, to the Lebanon 4.65 as OD-AEP, rest. 8.66, returned to Lebanon 10.71; G-ANLI (16013), 44-76429, Pakistani H712, to French Indo China 2.54 as F-OAPB; G-ANLJ (12498), 42-108865, KG463, Pakistani H706, to French Indo China 5.54 as F-OAQE; G-ANLK (14357), 43-48541, KJ863, Pakistani H713, to U.S.A. 3.54 as N1592V, later N90M; G-ANLL (16816), 44-77232, KP262, Pakistani H716, to French Indo China 3.54 as F-OAPP; G-ANLM (15669), 43-49853, Pakistani H710, AP-ACD, to Algeria 5.54 as F-OAQD; G-ANLY (14644), 43-48828, Pakistani H701, to Burma 6.54 as XY-ADD; G-ANLZ (16769), 44-77185, Pakistani H714, to Burma 6.54 as XY-ADB

G-ANMA (16197), 44-76613, KN471, Pakistani H717, to Australia 3.54 as VH-MML; G-ANMB (15663), 43-49847, Pakistani H718, to France 5.54 as F-BGSM; G-ANMC (14348), 43-48532, Pakistani H719, to Burma 6.54 as XY-ADC; G-ANTB (15762), 43-49946, KN273, 23.12.54, crashed near Jersey Airport 14.4.65; G-ANTC (14666), 43-48850, KJ938, 10.6.55; G-ANTD (14969), 43-49153, 16.4.55, to the Cameroons 2.69 as TJ-ACF, rest. 9.70

G-AOFZ (9131), 42-32905, ZS-BJZ, XY-ACP, 19.7.56, to Southern Rhodesia 7.56 as VP-YON, rest. 2.60, crashed at Azaiba, Muscat 17.8.66; G-AOGZ (16534), 44-76950, KN628, 1.7.56, to U.S.A. 1.69 as N4849; G-AOUD (14128), 43-48312, I-TRES, 6.6.57, to U.S.A. 1.69 as N4848; G-AOZA (15800), 44-76216, KN297, 2.7.57, to the French Air Force 8.57; G-AOZI (16119), 44-76535, to U.S.A. 1958 as N9848F

G-APBC (15676), 43-49860, KN250, 1.5.58; G-APML (14175), 43-48359, KJ836, 6.6.58; G-APPJ (16861), 44-77277, to Ghana 1.59 as 9G-AAC; G-APPO (20453), 43-15987, OY-DDO, EI-AFB, VR-TBT, 9.6.59, w.f.u. at Luton 8.67; G-APUC (12893), 42-93027, EI-ACH, 6.7.59, to Nepal 4.64 as 9N-AAM

Douglas DC-4

G-AOXK (42931), OY-DFI, 4.11.56, Air Charter Ltd. 'Golden Fleece', to Tanzania 7.63 as 5H-AAH; G-APEZ (42921), NC33682, 24.1.58, w.f.u. at Baginton 7.66; G-APTT (42916), VH-ANE, N5518V, 17.5.59, to the Cameroons 11.61 as TJ-ABD; G-ARYY (42907), NC33679, N33679, 2.7.62, scrapped at Southend 1.70; G-AZSI (42987), OY-DFO, OO-SBL, Belgian Air Force KX-2, registered 11.4.72, to spares at Stansted 6.72

Douglas C-54A Skymaster

G-AJPL (7464), 42-107445, NL-309, PH-TAK, 8.9.47, Skyways Ltd. 'Sky Wisdom', crashed at Castel Benito, Libya 4.2.49; G-AJPM (10376), 42-72271, NL-314, PH-TBS, 30.9.48, Skyways Ltd. 'Sky Freedom', to France 5.50 as F-BELS; G-AJPN (10375), 42-72270, NL-310, PH-TAL, 29.12.47, Skyways Ltd. 'Sky Champion', to France 6.50 as F-BELR; G-AJPO (3094), 41-37303, NL-300, PH-TAB, 21.10.47, Skyways Ltd. 'Sky Alliance', to France 6.50 as F-BELQ; G-AOFW (10351), 42-72246, N88919, I-DALV, N1436V, 9.12.55, Air Charter Ltd. 'Jason', converted to Carvair 1964; G-APCW (10299), 42-72194, NC93266, 15.8.57, to Congo 9.62 as 9Q-PCW; G-APID (10408), 42-72303, N54305, YV-C-EVB, N75337, 24.11.57, sold in Spain 9.67; G-APYK (10279), 42-72174, N56006, 10.3.60, crashed on Mt. Canigou, Pyrenees, 3.6.67

G-AREK (10365), 42-72260, NC57777, VP-CBD, CY-ACA, VH-INY, N5520V, D-ADAL, 21.10.60, converted to Carvair LX-IOH in 1962; G-ARIC (10306), 42-72201, U.S.N. 39162, N53487, 21.7.61, Congo 4.62 as 9Q-RIC; G-ARIY (3116), 42-32941, N88747, 24.7.62, w.f.u. at Speke 7.64; G-ARJY (10288), 42-72183, N30068, d.b.r. landing at Dublin 19.6.61; G-ARLF (10278), 42-72173, N50787, TF-RVH, 1.6.61, d.b.f. at Malaga, Spain 8.10.61; G-ASEN (10412), 42-72307, N88936, CF-CPD, VR-HFF, 4.6.63, temporarily TF-FIM in 1964, to South Africa 2.71 as ZS-IJT; G-ASFY (10335), 42-72230, NC88922, HB-ILC, 25.4.63, to U.S.A. 11.68 as N3454; G-ASOG (10359), 42-72254, N75415, HB-ILB, N9760F, 25.3.64, crashed at Frankfurt 21.1.67

Douglas C-54B Skymaster

G-ALEP (18327), 43-17127, NC74628, ZS-BYO, 21.1.49, Mining & Exploration Ltd. 'Discoverer', to Australia 4.51 as VH-INX; G-ANYB (10528), 42-72423, NC88723, N59952, 24.1.55, Air Charter Ltd. 'Atalanta', converted to Carvair prototype 1961; G-APNH (18333), 43-17133, N37477, 18.6.58, converted to Carvair 1964–65; G-ARWI (18349), 43-17149, NC90450, 6.3.62, to Nigerian Air Force 1.69 as '401'; G-ARXJ (18370), 43-17170, N8344C, N4270, N100J, 2.11.62, to Panama 6.67 as HP-451

Douglas C-54D, C-54E and C-54G Skymaster

G-APIN (10736), C-54D, 42-72631, N2570A, 5.3.58, destroyed on ground by enemy air attack, Kamina, Congo 17.9.61; G-ARWK (35936), C-54G, 45-483, N904, 20.5.63, IPEC-Air Ltd. 'Spirit of Enterprise', to Germany 9.67 as D-ADAD; G-ASPM (10543), C-54E, 42-72438, N66644, HZ-AAI, 19.6.64, to Africair Ltd., Johannesburg ex Manston 5.9.72; G-ASPN (10337), C-54E, 42-72232, U.S.N. 39175, NC49288, AP-ADL,

Caledonian Airways' Douglas DC-7C G-ASID at Newcastle/Woolsington on 25 May 1963. (*I. Macfarlane*)

N49288, HZ-AAG, 25.5.64, to South Africa 4.72, as ZS-IRE; G-ASRS (27353), C-54E, 44-9127, N90901, SA-R4, HZ-AAW, 20.3.64, to Belgium 8.64 as OO-FAI; G-ASZT (10640), C-54D, 42-72535, U.S.N. 91997, N4043A, D-AMAX, VP-MAA, 8.8.65, to Southern Rhodesia 8.65 as VP-YYR, temporarily 9J-RBL 1.66, rest. 3.66, to the Congo 6.68 as TN-ABC

Douglas DC-6A

G-APNO (45531), 11.10.59, to Switzerland 12.68 as HB-IBS; G-APNP (45532), 18.10.59, to Switzerland 12.68 as HB-IBT; G-APOM (45519), N7821C, 7.10.59, crashed at Shannon 26.3.61; G-APON (45058), N6814C, 5.10.59, to U.S.A. 6.64 as N6814C; G-APSA (45497), CF-MCK, 19.3.59, to Saudi Arabia 2.64 as HZ-ADA; G-ARMY (45457), N7818C, N660NA, VR-BBP, 20.5.61, to Saudi Arabia 4.64 as HZ-ADB

Douglas DC-6B

G-APZT (43263), N90751, 28.4.60, to Kuwait 4.64 as 9K-ABB; G-AREP (43846), N90769, 23.9.60, to Kuwait 9.63 as 9K-ABC; G-ARTO (44083), N90962, 6.10.61, to Kuwait 4.64 as 9K-ABA; G-ARWJ (43844), CF-CUQ, VR-BBQ, 1.3.62, returned to Canada 12.62 as CF-CUQ; G-ARXZ (45326), CF-CZS, 19.3.62, returned to Canada 10.64 as CF-CZS; G-ARZO (45078), CF-CZQ, OD-ABP, 25.5.62, returned to Canada 12.62 as CF-CZQ; G-ASRZ (44176), OO-CTN, 24.4.64, returned to Belgium 11.64 as OO-CTN; G-ASTS (43831), OO-CTK, 18.6.64, Caledonian Airways Ltd. 'County of Midlothian', returned to Belgium 11.64 as OO-CTK; G-ASTW (43826), N91306, 18.6.64, to Belgium 3.66 as OO-GER

Douglas DC-7C (*B.O.A.C.*)

G-AOIA (45111), 23.10.56, to U.S.A. 5.64 as N90803; G-AOIB (45112), 17.11.56, to U.S.A. 3.64 as N90802; G-AOIC (45113), 27.11.56, to U.S.A. 2.64 as N90801; G-AOID (45114), 26.11.56, to U.S.A. 5.63 as N90778; G-AOIE (45115), 15.12.56, to Caledonian Airways Ltd. 4.64 as 'County of Perth', to Holland 6.67 as PH-SAK; G-AOIF (45116), 3.1.57, to U.S.A. 6.64 as N90804; G-AOIG (45117), 24.12.56, to U.S.A. 4.63 as N90773; G-AOIH (45118), 14.1.57, to U.S.A. 5.63 as N90774; G-AOII (45119), 29.1.57, converted to DC-7CF in 1960, to Denmark 6.65 as OY-KNE; G-AOIJ (45120), 19.4.57, converted to DC-7CF in 1960, to U.S.A. 6.65 as N16465

Douglas DC-7C (*Caledonian Airways Ltd.*)

G-ARUD (45160), OO-SFD, EP-ADU, 29.11.61, 'Star of Robbie Burns', crashed at Douala, Cameroons 4.3.62; G-ARYE (45308), OO-SFG, 5.4.62, 'Flagship Bonnie Scotland', to Germany 3.66 as D-ABAR; G-ASHL (45495), OO-SFK, 13.4.63, 'County of Ayr', returned to Belgium 10.65 as OO-SFK; G-ASID (45161), OO-SFE, 17.5.63, returned to Belgium 10.63 as OO-SFE, rest. 12.63 as 'County of Lanark', beyond repair landing at Istanbul 28.9.64; G-ASIV (45310), OO-SFJ, 30.5.63, returned to Belgium 3.64 as OO-CFJ, to U.S.A. 7.64 as N8299H, rest. 12.64, to Germany 3.66 as D-ABAK

Douglas DC-7CF (*Trans Meridian London Ltd.*)

G-ATAB (45361), N6348C, 19.3.65, Dan-Air Services Ltd., scrapped at Lasham 1972; G-ATMF (44873), N731PA, N7314, 5.1.66, 'Sir Benjamin', Trans Meridian Air Cargo Ltd., Stansted in 1971, to France 3.72, as F-BTDJ; G-ATOB (44875), N733PA, N7334, 11.2.66, 'Lady Thelma', to Bermuda 12.67 as VR-BCT; G-AVXH (44881), N739PA, N7398A, 21.1.68, to U.S.A. 4.69 as N7398A; G-AWBI (44884), N742PA, N7421, 1.2.68, 'African Trader' to U.S.A. 4.69 as N7421

Druine D.31 Turbulent (*Amateur-built aircraft. See also Volume 3, Rollason Turbulent, for factory-built machines*)

G-APCM (PFA.163), Ardem 4CO2, A. to F. 12.12.58, Rev. P. J. O'Kelly, Belfast; first flown at Ards 22.12.58; later fitted with cockpit canopy; wrecked at Aldergrove 29.11.64

G-APOL (PFA.439), D.36 with J.A.P. J-99, A. to F. 9.9.60, P. J. Houston, South Nutfield; 1,200 c.c. Volkswagen in 1962; Usworth Flying Group 12.63; Ardem 4CO2 in 1966; D. J. C. Robertson, Stirling 8.69

G-APST (PFA.472), 1,200 c.c. Volkswagen, A. to F. 18.12.62, T. G. Breakell, Squires Gate; W. D. Anderson, Turnhouse 12.66; W. H. Thorburn, Peebles 1.69; W. S. Shackleton Ltd., Sywell 5.69; Sherwood F/C, Tollerton 11.71

G-APUY (PFA.509), 1,200 c.c. Ardem 4CO2 Mk.1, A. to F. 29.8.63, K. F. W. Turner, Staverton; R. W. Hayne and K. F. Gardner, Staverton 2.71

G-APVN (PFA.511), 1,500 c.c. Volkswagen, A. to F. 16.2.66, J. P. Knight, Rochester; J. H. Pickering, Whatfield 5.67; R. Sherwin, Shoreham 11.71

G-APWP (PFA.497), 40 h.p. Pollman Hepu, A. to F. 22.8.61, C. F. Rogers, Great Gransden, Herts; first flown at Panshanger 19.7.61; w.f.u. 10.70

G-ARBL (PFA.533), construction commenced by D. G. Wiggins at Sidcup, Kent in 1960; transferred to J. D. Watt, Upminster, Essex 1961; not completed by 1972

G-ARIM (PFA.510), construction commenced by A. Schima at Durham 1960; not completed; components used in the construction of G-AWBM

G-ARRU (PFA.502), described as a 'Turbulent 2004C Class 1'; construction begun by J. O'Connor, Elstree 1960; later transferred to D. Westwood, South Norwood; construction not completed by 1972

G-ARTF (PFA.161), 1,200 c.c. Ardem 4CO2 Mk.1, A. to F. 2.2.62, D. G. Jones, Baginton

G-ASBW (PFA.404), 1,200 c.c. Ardem 4CO2 Mk.1, A. to F. 3.6.66, J. Smith, Scalloway, Shetland; J. S. Swanson, Fordoun 6.68

G-ASFX (PFA.513), 1,500 c.c. Ardem 4CO2 Mk.2, A. to F. 9.6.67, E. F. Clapham and W. B. Dobie, Staverton

G-ASPU (PFA.1623), 1,200 c.c. Volkswagen, A. to F. 24.3.66, A. S. Usherwood, Rochester; fitted 1,500 Volkswagen in 1968; P. O. Warren, Slinfold 7.72

G-ASSY (PFA.586), 1,100 c.c. Volkswagen, A. to F. 25.10.68, F. J. Parker, Fairoaks

G-ASTA (152), F-PJGH, built at St. Brieuc, France with 1,200 c.c. Volkswagen, A. to F. 2.5.66, J. Miller, St. Albans; E. R. Walters, Sherburn 5.66; E. A. Ireland, Sudbury, Suffolk 5.69; C. J. Richardson, Thruxton 1.71; J. Heaton, Thruxton 1.72

G-ATBS (PFA.1620), 36 h.p. J.A.P. J-99, A. to F. 8.3.67, C. R. Shilling, Rochester 'Miss Moon'; 1,200 c.c. Volkswagen in 1968; J. A. Thomas, Rochester 1.72

G-ATHP (PFA.432), VT-XAG, 1,500 c.c. Ardem 4CO2 Mk.2, A. to F. 20.5.66, D. J. Naismith, Booker, later Blackbushe; crashed at Membury 5.10.68

G-ATKR (PFA.1615), 1,200 c.c. Ardem 4CO2 Mk.1, A. to F. 2.11.66, M. G. Cove, Bristol, first flown at Lulsgate 10.8.66; A. R. Worters, Redhill 9.68; G. M. Jones, Redhill 2.72; P. Channon, Fairoaks 5.72

G-AVPC (PFA.544), under construction at Borgue Farm, Kirkcudbright in 1971

G-AWBM (PFA.1647), 1,200 c.c. Volkswagen, J. R. D. Bygraves 'Barn Stormer'; built at Old Warden 1968–70, A. to F. 8.5.70

G-AWDH (RH-01), under construction by R. E. L. Hewitt, Upper Hartfield, near Sherburn-in-Elmet in 1971; based at Sherburn 1972

G-AWDO (PFA.1649), 1,500 c.c. Volkswagen, A. to F. 9.9.69, R. Watling-Greenwood, Uckfield, Sussex

G-AWFR (SU.001), under construction by S. W. Usherwood at Rochester in 1972

G-AWLB (A.E.S.1), under construction by A. E. Shoulder at Lincoln in 1972

G-AWMR (43), 1,200 c.c. Volkswagen, first flown at Dunkeswell 1.8.70, A. to F. 11.12.70, S. J. Hargreaves

G-AWWT (PFA.1653), 1,500 c.c. Volkeswagen, built by D. A. Levermore at Kingsdown, Kent 1970–71, A. to F. 22.4.71, based at Rochester

Druine D.53 and D.54 Turbi

G-AOTK (PFA.230), D.53, 62 h.p. Walter Mikron II, A. to F. 13.8.59, T.K. Flying Group, Hatfield; fitted Mikron III in 12 in. longer nose 10.70

G-APBO (PFA.229), D.53, 62 h.p. Walter Mikron II, A. to F. 7.9.60, Rutherglen F/G, Strathaven; stored at Prestwick less engine 1966; under reconstruction at Abbotsinch 1972

G-APFA (PFA.232), D.54, 65 h.p. Coventry Victor, A. to F. 9.9.57, Britten-Norman Ltd., Bembridge; Ulair Ltd., Elstree 6.59; converted to 65 h.p. Continental engined cabin type; Wolverhampton Ultra Light Flying Group, Halfpenny Green 6.62; K. Sedgwick, Halfpenny Green 8.71

Lancashire Prospector E.P.9 G-APWX at Luluabourg, Belgian Congo while en route to Abercorn, Northern Rhodesia during the African sales tour, July 1960.

Edgar Percival E.P.9 (*Lancashire Prospector E.P.9s commence at c/n 41*)

G-AOFU (20), 30.10.56, Edgar Percival Aircraft Ltd., Stapleford; Air Ads Ltd., Stapleford 6.57; crashed while crop spraying at Maturabi, Sudan 3.11.62

G-AOZO (29), G-43-8, 6.3.57, Edgar Percival Aircraft Ltd.; Lancashire Aircraft Co. Ltd., Squires Gate 4.58; re-engined as Prospector 9.59; flown to Lympne 30.9.63; C. of A. renewed 20.1.71

G-AOZY (23), G-43-2, 14.2.57, Edgar Percival Aircraft Ltd.; to Ernst Lund KG. 4.57; destroyed in crop spraying accident at Wunsdorf, Germany 6.5.57

G-APAD (27), G-43-6, 23.4.57, Edgar Percival Aircraft Ltd.; shipped to Australia, arrived 17.5.57; sold to Super Spread Aviation Pty. as VH-SSX

G-APBF (26), G-43-5, 14.5.57, Edgar Percival Aircraft Ltd.; to Ernst Lund KG. 11.57 as D-EDUV; damaged in Germany 7.7.58; airfreighted back as spares

G-APBR (28), G-43-7, 29.5.57, Wright, Stephenson & Co. Ltd.; flown to Australia 9.57; d/d to Super Spread Aviation Pty. as VH-SSV; later to Airesearch Exploration Pty., Melbourne as VH-DAI

G-APCR (21), G-43-1, 9.9.57, Bahamas Helicopters (U.K.) Ltd., Tripoli, Libya; crashed on take-off in the Fezan, Libya 19.8.58

G-APCS (24), G-43-3, 26.7.57, Bahamas Helicopters (U.K.) Ltd., Tripoli, Libya; Fulair Ltd., Yeovil 8.62; crashed in Gibraltar Harbour 24.8.62

G-APCT (25), G-43-4, 26.7.57, Bahamas Helicopters (U.K.) Ltd., Tripoli, Libya; to Trabajos Fotográficos Aéreos S.A., Madrid 4.62 as EC-ASO

G-APFY (32), G-43-2, 17.9.57, Wright, Stephenson & Co. Ltd.; flown to Australia 9.57 on delivery to Super Spread Aviation Pty.; re-registered VH-SSW, crashed at Moorabbin 14.4.58

G-APIA (33), G-43-3, 15.10.57, B. J. Snook, Stapleford; flown to Australia 10.57 on delivery to Skyspread Ltd.; re-registered VH-FBY on arrival

G-APIB (34), G-43-1, 11.10.57, B. J. Snook, Stapleford; flown to Australia 10.57 on delivery to Skyspread Ltd.; re-registered VH-FBZ on arrival

G-APLP (35), G-43-8, first flown 19.3.58, C. of A. 31.3.58, Crop Culture (Aerial) Ltd., Bembridge; Lancashire Aircraft Co. Ltd., Squires Gate 7.59; overturned in forced landing on Blackpool beach and submerged 15.7.59

G-APWX (41), first flown at Squires Gate 9.10.59, C. of A. 22.10.59, Lancashire Aircraft Co. Ltd.; sold in the U.S.A. 11.68 as N8395

G-APWZ (42), first flown at Squires Gate 23.2.60, C. of A. 22.4.60, Lancashire Aircraft Co. Ltd., Lympne; d.b.r. in forced landing, Sevenoaks 27.9.70

G-APXW (43), 26.8.60, Lancashire Aircraft Co. Ltd., Samlesbury; based at Lympne from 7.61; dismantled at Ford 8.71

G-ARDG (47), Cheetah engined Prospector Series 2, Lancashire Aircraft Co. Ltd., Samlesbury; flown to Lympne 7.61; application for C. of A. cancelled

G-ARLE (44), G-47-1, 5.9.61, Lancashire Aircraft Co. Ltd.; A.D.S. (Aerial) Ltd., Stapleford 10.61; crashed while crop spraying in Sudan 10.64

G-ARTU (38), XM797, 30.11.62, Steels (Aviation) Ltd., Staverton; Flying Facilities Ltd., Lulsgate 5.63; G.R.M. Airwork Ltd., Staverton 1.66; Old Warden Flying & Parachute Group 2.69; repainted as XM797 at Elmdon 3.69; crashed at Old Warden Aerodrome, Biggleswade 6.9.69

G-ARTV (39), XM819, 15.2.62, Steels (Aviation) Ltd., Staverton; to Germany 2.62 as D-ELSA; rest. 8.68 to L. Hornett, Elstree; sold in Belgium 2.72

English Electric Canberra

G-ATZW (71018), B.Mk.2, WD937, f/f in civil markings 28.10.66, C. of A. 20.12.66, B.A.C. (Operating) Ltd., Warton; withdrawn from use and stored at Samlesbury 10.67

G-AYHO B.Mk.62, WJ613, G-27-111, registered 22.7.70 to the British Aircraft Corporation, Warton; reverted to Class B marks 10.70; left Warton 17.11.70 on delivery flight to the Argentine Air Force as B-101

G-AYHP B.Mk.62, WJ713, G-27-112, as G-AYHO above, delivered as B-102

Ercoupe 415

G-AKFC (4784), 415-CD, NC7465H, OO-ERU, 29.8.47, Ministry of Supply evaluation at Boscombe Down 1947–52 as VX147, rest. 2.52, crashed at Halfpenny Green 13.8.67; G-ASNF (4754), 415-CD, NC9464, PH-NCF, 20.3.65; G-ATFP (2168),

415-D, N99545, 12.7.66, burned out on ground at Southend 27.7.68; G-AVTT (4399), 415-D, NC3774H, SE-BFZ, 26.4.70; G-AXZW (2654), 415-C, N2031H, 22.6.70, K. Savage, Pittsburgh, U.S.A.

Fairchild 24W-41A Argus 2
G-AITG (356), 42-32151, FK347, registered 31.10.46, ditched off Silloth 11.11.46; G-AIXC (836), 43-14872, HB599, 1.4.47, sold abroad 3.48; G-AIXM (856), 43-14892, HB619, 18.12.46, to Australia 2.52 as VH-BLB; G-AIYO (850), 43-14886, HB613, 14.3.47, w.f.u. at White Waltham 2.58; G-AIZE (565), 43-14601, 6.6.47, to U.S. ownership at Heathrow 1949 as N9996F

G-AJAT (300), 41-38856, EV792, 8.5.47, to Germany 12.55 as D-EJES; G-AJBF (869), 43-14905, HB632, 4.9.47, to Finland ex Croydon 3.11.51 as OH-FCH; G-AJDO (284), 41-38840, EV776, 12.6.47, to Australia 5.50 as VH-AKY; G-AJDT (350), 42-32145, FK341, 30.4.47, to Finland ex Croydon 5.3.52 as OH-FCL; G-AJFY (368), 42-32163, FK359, 20.5.47, to Kenya 11.47 as VP-KES; G-AJGW (322), 42-32117, FK313, 2.7.47, to Belgium 8.53 as OO-ACF; G-AJLB (842), 43-14878, HB605, registered 2.4.47, not converted, registration cancelled 7.47; G-AJNN (325), 42-32120, FK316, 12.6.47, scrapped at Elstree 4.52; G-AJOW (298), 41-38854, EV790, 6.8.47, to Italy 11.53 as I-AJOW; G-AJOX (361), 42-32156, FK352, 10.9.47, to Finland 5.51 as OH-FCE; G-AJOY (367), 42-32162, FK358, 23.6.47, damaged beyond repair in forced landing at Colebrook, Devon 20.12.49; G-AJOZ (347), 42-32142, FK338, 15.9.47, w.f.u. at Elmdon 12.63, to Southend 6.67 for Historic Aircraft Museum, to Northern Aircraft Preservation Society 6.72

G-AJPA (352), 42-32147, FK343, 15.10.47, to New Zealand 7.50 as ZK-AUW; G-AJPB (290), 41-38846, EV782, 23.6.47, to Sweden 5.50 as SE-BRU; G-AJPC (324), 42-32119, FK315, 23.5.47, to Finland 1.52 as OH-FCJ; G-AJPD (366), 42-32161, FK357, 11.12.47, to Holland 4.50 as PH-NFW; G-AJPE (344), 42-32139, FK335, 28.7.47, w.f.u. 7.53; G-AJPI (851), 43-14887, HB614, 10.7.47; G-AJRZ (722), 43-14758, FZ782, 4.9.47, derelict at Southend 1959; G-AJSA (218), 41-38774, HM174, 6.8.47, crashed in 1949; G-AJSB (316), 42-13580, EV808, 23.7.47, crashed 20.3.48; G-AJSG (837), 43-14873, HB600, 25.9.47, to Australia 1.55 as VH-DDG; G-AJSH (845), 43-14881, HB608, 2.6.47, crashed at Fairoaks 30.3.58; G-AJSM (859), 43-14895, HB622, 25.9.47, to New Zealand 12.48 as ZK-ASZ; G-AJSN (849), 43-14885, HB612, 3.6.48, damaged beyond repair 5.70; G-AJSO (854), 43-14890, HB617, 10.11.47, to Australia 12.50 as VH-AKZ; G-AJSP (872), 43-14908, HB635, 20.9.48, to Holland 4.56, re-registered PH-NGY in 1958; G-AJSR (858), 43-14894, HB621, 24.3.48, to Finland 11.51 as OH-FCG; G-AJSS (870), 43-14906, HB633, 9.7.47, to Finland 2.52 as OH-VSE; G-AJST (342), 42-32137, FK333, registered 8.5.47, sold in Belgium 8.53; G-AJSU (229), 41-38785, HM185, 29.7.47, to the Belgian Congo 5.48 as OO-CDM; G-AJSV (306), 30.10.47, d.b.r. in forced landing at Montreuil, N. France 1.11.47; G-AJSW (280), 41-38836, EV772, 30.10.47, to Belgium 8.48 as OO-DER; G-AJSX (293), 41-38849, EV785, 14.8.47, derelict at Biggin Hill 5.63; G-AJSY (263), 41-38819, EV755, 29.7.47, crashed at Coquilhatville, Belgian Congo 25.9.47; G-AJTR (224), 41-38780, HM180, 19.9.47, to Finland 11.51 as OH-FCI; G-AJVI (208), 41-38764, HM164, 25.9.47, to France 10.53 as F-BBIO; G-AJVM (861), 43-14897, HB624, registered 3.6.47, not converted, to spares at Exeter 1953 to service G-AJOZ and G-AJPI; G-AJXA (360), 42-32155, FK351, 10.11.47, sold in Australia 11.51

G-AKCJ, 41-38862, EV798, 4.7.49, to Australia 9.51 as VH-AZL; G-AKFN (839), 43-14875, HB602, 3.2.49, to Australia 9.60 as VH-UEL; G-AKGW (343), 42-32138, FK334, 5.12.47, to Finland 8.51 as OH-VSD; G-AKIZ (287), 41-38843, EV779, 4.2.49, to Finland 1.52 as OH-FCK; G-AKJA (302), 41-38858, 1.6.48, to Finland 7.52 as OH-FCO; G-AKJB (285), 41-38841, EV777, 20.7.48, to South Africa 4.49 as ZS-DCX; G-AKJK (309), 42-13573, EV801, registered 8.10.47, to Malaya 2.48 as VR-RBE, to Australia 7.53 as VH-AIO; G-AKJL (339), 42-32134, FK330, 19.1.48, to Australia 12.50 as VH-ALF; G-AKJM (314), 42-13578, EV806, 28.2.48, to Australia 6.51 as VH-AVN; G-AMAZ (756), 43-14792, FZ816, N79922, registered 11.5.50, application for C. of A. withdrawn at Bahrein 5.52

Fairchild 24R Argus 3
G-AJDD (1130), 44-83169, KK512, registered 23.9.48 to F. Bosworth, not certificated, destroyed by fire on the ground at Bahrein 18.4.49; G-AKPX (960), 43-14996, HB722, registered 12.1.48 to R. L. Whyham, to Finland ex Squires Gate 1.6.50 as OH-FCA; G-AMBA (1146), 44-83185, KK528, N79925, registered 11.5.50 to Gulf Aviation Ltd., application for C. of A. withdrawn at Bahrein 5.52

Fairey III to IIIF
G-EAAJ   III, (F.127), N9, K-103, registered 1.5.19 to Fairey Aviation Co. Ltd.; to Norwegian Navy 5.20; civilianised 8.27 as N-20; crashed 12.6.28

G-EADZ   IIIA, (F.246), N2876, registered 6.6.19 to Navarro Aviation Co.; not converted; sold to Lt. Col. G. L. P. Henderson and converted as G-EAMY

G-EALQ   III, (F.128), N10, registered 28.8.19 to Fairey Aviation Co. Ltd.; Schneider Trophy 1919; Amphibian Competition 1920; scrapped in 1923

G-EAMY   IIIC, (F.246), N2876, G-EADZ, registered 18.9.19 to Lt. Col. G. L. P. Henderson; operated on skis in Sweden and crashed there 8.20

G-EAPV   IIIC, (F.302), N2255, registered 1.12.19 to Lt. Col. G. L. P. Henderson; shipped to Sweden with G-EAMY; sold locally 12.20

G-EARS   IIIC, (F.333), N9256, registered 17.3.20 to Fairey Aviation Co. Ltd.; shipped to Newfoundland; to Montreal 8.20 as G-CYCF; crashed at St. John, New Brunswick 7.10.20; repaired at Hamble and flown 6.21 as G-EARS

Fairey Fox I G-ACXX in which Flg. Off. H. D. Gilman and J. K. L. Baines were killed when it crashed in Italy on 22 October 1934, second day of the Australia Race. (*Flight Photo 10945S*)

G-EBDI   IIIC, (F.330), N9253, registered 12.6.22 to Maj. W. T. Blake; forced landed and sank in the Gulf of Assam 25.8.22

G-EBKE   IIID, (F.576), C. of A. 17.10.24, Real Daylight Balata Estates Ltd., British Guiana; shipped back to U.K. 3.28; scrapped at Hamble 1929

G-EBPZ   IIID, (F.814), S 1076, C. of A. 5.2.27, Air Council; loaned to North Sea Aerial & General Transport Co. Ltd.; sank after undercarriage collapsed taking-off from Lake Victoria, Kenya 13.3.27

G-AABY   IIIF Lion, (F.1129), f/f 17.7.29, C. of A. 27.7.29, The Fairey Aviation Co. Ltd.; flown to Australia by Flg. Off. C. G. Davies 10–11.34; flown to New Guinea by Ray Parer 4.35 as VH-UTT; scrapped near Wewak 8.36

G-AASK   IIIF Jaguar, (F.1272), C. of A. 20.12.29, Air Survey Co. Ltd.; withdrawn from use 12.34

G-AATT   IIIF Jaguar, (F.1315), 5.2.30, Air Survey Co. Ltd.; crashed 10.30

Fairey Fox I

G-ACAS   (FA.35756*), 23.3.33, Luxury Air Tours Ltd., Hanworth; caught fire in the air, burned out on landing at Littlehampton, Sussex 14.7.33

G-ACXO   (F.856), J 7950, 17.9.34, New Guinea Centenary Flight Syndicate; flown in the Australia Race 10.34; sold in New Guinea 3.35 as VH-UTR; scrapped 1936

G-ACXX   (F.876), J8424, 18.10.34, J. K. Campbell-Baines; crashed and burned near Foggia, Italy 22.10.34 while competing in the Australia Race

* As documented. Believed to be the fuselage part number.

Fairtravel Linnet (*including Garland-Bianchi Linnet*)

G-APNS   (001), first flown 1.9.58, C. of A. 8.10.58, P. A. T. Garland and D. E. Bianchi, White Waltham; P. A. T. Garland 1.60; stored at Rochester 1972

G-APRH   (002), 10.4.62, P. A. T. Garland and D. E. Bianchi, White Waltham; P. A. T. Garland 1.60; Fairtravel Ltd., Denham 5.62; Cardiff Ultra Light Aeroplane Club, Rhoose 10.63; W. Paterson, Squires Gate 6.65; E. R. Perry, Barton 10.66; damaged beyond repair landing at Jersey 5.5.67

G-APVO   (003), the third and last Garland-Bianchi Linnet, ordered by the Croydon Flying Club 8.59; not completed, registration cancelled 8.61

G-ASFW   (003), new airframe not derived from G-APVO, first flown at White Waltham 20.3.63, C. of A. 28.6.63, Fairtravel Ltd.; Blackbushe Aviation Ltd. 12.65; Kestrel F/G 10.69; crashed on take-off from Biggin Hill 25.10.69

G-ASMT   (004), first flown at Blackbushe 9.7.64, C. of A. 14.7.64, Fairtravel Ltd.; Glassridge Ltd., Bognor Regis 9.64; G. Thomas, Swansea 4.68; Dr. J. J. Bowen, Haverfordwest 12.68

G-ASZR   (005), 27.5.65, International Travel Ltd., Blackbushe; Dart Aircraft Ltd., Blackbushe 1.69; Blackbushe Aviation Ltd. 10.69

Felixstowe F.3

G-EAQT   (S.607), N4019, Short-built, registered to Short Bros. Ltd. 24.1.20; to Lebbaeus Hordern 3.20; first flown at Rochester after air yacht conversion 28.5.20, C. of A. 15.11.20, shipped to Australia but not erected; hull given to Botany Bay fishermen 1921 for use as a hut

G-EBDQ   N4177, Phoenix Dynamo-built, registered to the Aircraft Disposal Co. Ltd. 26.6.22 for delivery to Maj. W. T. Blake in Montreal; the aircraft was not required and was sold to a foreign purchaser 11.22

Fokker F.III

G-AALC (1558), delivered Amsterdam–Croydon 7.8.29 as T-DOFF, C. of A. 23.8.29, British Air Lines Ltd., Croydon, destroyed in collision with house on take-off from Croydon 11.9.29; G-AARG (1561), delivered Kastrup–Croydon 17.9.29 as T-DOFC, C. of A. 12.10.29, British Air Lines Ltd., Croydon, flown twice only (13.10.29 and 19.12.29) then stored at Heston until delivered to P/O G. G. Stead at Worthy Down 7.2.31, w.f.u. 12.31

The Fokker F.VIIA G-EBTQ 'St. Raphael', lost over the Atlantic after take-off from Upavon on 31 August 1927, was the last British civil aeroplane to include the letter Q in its registration.

Fokker F.VIIA

G-EBPL (4938), H-NADH, registered 30.10.26 to Rt. Hon. F. E. Guest, resold to Fokker, d.b.r. in forced landing at Estaires, France during delivery to Amsterdam 12.1.27; G-EBTQ (5023), H-NAEC, 24.8.27, H.S.H. Princess Alice of Lowenstein-Wertheim 'St. Raphael', left Upavon for transatlantic flight 31.8.27, lost at sea; G-EBTS (4953), H-NADK, 2.9.27, R. H. McIntosh 'Princess Xenia', Air Communications Ltd. 8.28, Duchess of Bedford 'The Spider' 9.29, C. D. Barnard 9.32, British Air Navigation Co. Ltd., Heston 10.34, Sir D. H. Bhuwandwalla, Bombay 5.35, scrapped 3.37; G-AEHE (4984), PH-ADN, registered 2.6.36 to Prof. Gilbert Murray on behalf of the League of Nations, returned to Holland 12.36 as PH-EHE; G-AEHF (c/n K.L.M.1, using parts of H-NADH and 'DJ), PH-ADX, registration details the same as for G-AEHE, to Sweden 8.37 as SE-AGH

Fokker F.VIIA/3m

G-EBPV (4982), first flown for Albert Lowenstein, Dübendorf as H-NADS, registered 1.12.36 to Rt. Hon. F. E. Guest, to Avio Linee Italiane 3.27 as I-BBEC; G-EBYI (5063), first flown as H-NAEK, 30.5.28, D. H. Drew on behalf of A. Lowenstein, Lt. Cdr. Glen Kidston 10.28, d.b.r. in forced landing near Mongalla, Sudan 7.29, sold back to Fokker 3.30; G-EBZJ (5087), H-NAEL, 7.7.28, Maj. A. P. Holt, sold abroad 10.30

Fokker F.XII

G-ADZH (5284), PH-AFV, 23.3.36, British Airways Ltd., Croydon, sold in Spain 8.36; G-ADZI (5285), PH-AFU, 31.1.36, British Airways Ltd., Croydon, burned out in crash landing at Biarritz 15.8.36 while on delivery to Spain; G-ADZJ (5292), PH-AIE, 8.1.36, British Airways Ltd., Croydon, sold in Spain 8.36; G-ADZK (5301), PH-AII, 7.2.36, British Airways Ltd., Croydon, d.b.r. landing at La Rochelle in fog 16.8.36 while on delivery to Spain; G-AEOS (5291), PH-AID, 3.11.36, British Airways Ltd., Croydon (later Gatwick), scrapped by B.O.A.C. 6.40; G-AEOT (5300), PH-AIH, 3.11.36, British Airways Ltd., destroyed in night crash near Gatwick 19.11.36

Fokker F.XXII

G-AFXR (5360), PH-AJR, 10.8.39, British American Air Services Ltd., Heston, Scottish Aviation Ltd., Prestwick 10.39, impressed 10.41 as HM159 'Brontosaurus', later 'Silvia Scarlet', crashed into Loch Tarbert and exploded 3.7.43; G-AFZP (5357), PH-AJP, 29.8.39, Scottish Aviation Ltd., Prestwick, impressed 10.41 as HM160, rest. 10.46 for Scottish Airlines, scrapped at Prestwick 7.52

Ford 4AT-E

G-ABEF (4AT-61), NC9678, 15.10.30, H. S. Cooper, Ford, to British Air Navigation Co. Ltd., Heston 7.34 as 'Vagabond', to Holdens Air Transport Ltd., New Guinea 6.35 as VH-UDY; G-ACAK (4AT-68), NC8406, EC-KKA, 8.4.33, H. S. Cooper, Ford, to Holdens Air Transport Ltd., New Guinea 12.34 as VH-USX

Ford 5AT-C and 5AT-D

G-ABFF (5AT-68), 5AT-C, NC409H, first flown 3.8.29, C. of A. 15.10.30, H. S. Cooper, Ford, re-registered 1.31 as G-ABHF, to Guinea Airways Ltd. 10.34 as VH-UTB; G-ABHO (5AT-60), 5AT-C, first flown 5.7.29, C. of A. 20.12.30, Lord Lovelace, Heston 'Tanganyika Star', to British Air Navigation Co. Ltd., Heston 1.34 as 'Voyager', to Guinea Airways Ltd. 6.35 as VH-UBI; G-ACAE (5AT-107), 5AT-D, NC440H, C. of A. 13.4.33, Hon. A. E. Guinness, Dublin and Heston, impressed 4.40 as X5000, beyond repair in forced landing on shore of Belfast Lough, Co. Down 19.9.40

Foster Wikner Wicko

G-AENU (1), F.W.1, 19.9.36, Foster Wikner Aircraft Co. Ltd.; converted to F.W.2 in 1937, stored at Birmingham 1939–46; rest. 9.46 to W. H. Leadbetter, Elmdon; Air Navigation & Trading Co. Ltd., Squires Gate 8.50; derelict at Plymouth in 1953

G-AEZZ (2), F.W.3, 8.9.37, Foster Wikner Aircraft Co. Ltd., Eastleigh; conv. to G.M.1 in 1938; Cardiff Aeroplane Club 8.38; impressed 7.41 as ES943

G-AFAZ (4), G.M.1, 19.9.38, Bristol and Wessex Aeroplane Club, Whitchurch; impressed 5.41 as ES924 for the A.T.A., White Waltham

G-AFJB (5), G.M.1, 1.11.38, Midland Aero Club, Castle Bromwich; Rolls-Royce Ltd., Hucknall 7.40; impressed 7.41 as DR613 for Cunliffe-Owen Aircraft Ltd., Eastleigh; rest. 10.45 to G. N. Wikner; Miss P. M. Bennett, Eastleigh 5.46; M. J. Dible, Denham 1.55; Southport Aero Club 10.56; withdrawn from use 7.63; preserved at Berkswell Forge, Warwickshire

G-AFKK (8), G.M.1, 3.7.39, Foster Wikner Aircraft Co. Ltd., Eastleigh; impressed 5.41 as ES913 for the A.T.A., White Waltham; to No.24 Sqn. in 1942

G-AFKS (6), G.M.1, 5.1.39, Foster Wikner Aircraft Co. Ltd., Eastleigh; Nash Aircraft Sales Ltd. 7.39; impressed 8.42 as HM574; scrapped at Eastleigh 1946

G-AFKU (7), G.M.1, 14.6.39, Foster Wikner Aircraft Co. Ltd.; F. L. Dean, Cardiff 7.39; impressed 8.41 as ES947; struck balloon cable and crashed in the sea off Cardiff 26.11.42 while in service with No.24 Sqn.

G-AFVK (9), G.M.1, not certificated, registered 13.6.39 to Foster Wikner Aircraft Co. Ltd., Eastleigh; impressed 10.41 as HM499; later 4962M

G-AGPE (11), G.M.1, HM497, 4.4.46, G. N. Wikner, Eastleigh; Miss P. M. Bennett, Eastleigh 4.46; w.f.u. 7.48; scrapped at Eastleigh 5.49

Forney F-1A (*c/n 5750 and above Carlsbad-built*)

G-ARHA (5725), N3030G, 22.12.60; G-ARHB (5733), 27.4.61; G-ARHC (5734), 26.5.61; G-ARHD (5735), 24.2.61; G-ARHE (5736), 28.2.61, crashed at Kelvedon Hatch, Essex 4.6.65; G-ARHF (5737), 26.1.62; G-ARHG (5738), 30.3.61, crash landed at Biggin Hill 3.6.64; G-AROO (5750), N25B, 10.11.61; G-AROP (5751), N25B, 25.7.61, destroyed in air collision with Auster J-1S G-AMVN over Fyfield, Essex 24.4.69; G-AROR (5752), N25B, 13.10.61; G-ARVO (5931), not taken up; G-ARXR (5762), N3059G, 2.7.62, crashed near Biggin Hill 29.4.67; G-ARXS (5731), N3037G, D-EBSA, 27.7.62, to Ireland 12.70 as EI-AUT; G-ASBC (5760), N3057G, 31.7.62, struck tree and burned landing at Stapleford 7.9.66; G-ASLN (5729), N3035G, 14.11.63

Fournier RF-3

G-ATBP (59), 28.8.66; G-ATFI (67), not imported; G-AYJD (11), F-BLXA, registered 8.9.70

Fournier RF-4D

G-AVHY (4009), 5.4.67; G-AVKD (4024), 12.6.67; G-AVLW (4025), 15.8.67; G-AVNX (4026), 11.9.67; G-AVNY (4029), 1.11.67; G-AVNZ (4030), 2.11.67; G-AVWY (4031), 13.1.68; G-AVWZ (4032), 20.1.68; G-AWBJ (4055), 12.2.69; G-AWEK (4071), 17.4.69; G-AWEL (4077), 23.4.69; G-AWEM (4078), 23.4.68; G-AWGN (4084), 12.6.68; G-AWGO (4085), 12.6.68, destroyed in air collision with Fournier RF-5 G-AYBS off the Needles, I.O.W. 24.6.72; G-AWLZ (4099), 30.10.68; G-AXJS (4148), 12.9.69; G-AYHY (4156), 3.9.70; G-AZIG (4033), OO-WAC, 22.12.71; G-AZUU (4095), F-BPLD, 16.6.72

Fournier RF-5

G-AYAI (5071), 22.5.70; G-AYBS (5074), 20.6.70, destroyed in air collision with RF-4D G-AWGO 24.6.72; G-AYME (5089), 9.12.70; G-AYZX (5100), 18.6.71; G-AZJC (5108), 23.2.72; G-AZPF (5001), D-KOLT, 12.4.72; G-AZRK (5112), 29.6.72; G-AZRM (5111), 21.4.72; G-AZZW (5113), registered 20.7.72

Gardan GY-20 Minicab (*French-built*)

G-ATPV (A.155), Barritault JB.01 built at Baugé, Marne-et-Loire 1956, F-PHUC, F-PJKA, A. to F. 20.4.66; G-AWUB (A.205), built at Béarn 1954, F-PERX, A. to F. 30.4.69; G-AWWM (A.195), GY-201, built at Béarn 1955, F-BFOQ, A. to F. 9.4.70

Gardan GY-20 Minicab (*British-built*)

G-AVRW (OH-1549/PFA.1800), built at Kidderminster 1967–68 by R. F. Hart, A. to F. 20.4.68, based at Halfpenny Green in 1972

G-AWEP (PFA.1801), built at Preston 1964–69 by F. S. Jackson, assembled at Samlesbury, first flown 21.6.69 by R. P. Beamont, C. of A. 18.7.69

G-AZJE (JBE.1/PFA.1806), registered 1.12.71 to J.B. Evans, Ventnor, Isle of Wight

Gardan GY-80 Horizon 150 (*one 150 h.p. Lycoming O-320-A*)

G-ATXF (40), F-BLOX, 19.8.68

Gardan GY-80 Horizon 160 (*one 160 h.p. Lycoming O-320-B3B*)

G-ASJY (13), 15.8.64; G-ASZS (70), 27.4.67; G-ATDG (101), 29.6.67; G-ATDH (105), 29.6.67; G-ATGY (121), 14.9.67; G-ATJT (108), 5.11.67; G-AZAW (104),

F-BMUL, 29.7.71; G-AZRX (14), F-BLIJ, 26.5.72; G-AZYA (57), F-BLPT, registered
7.7.72

Gardan GY-80 Horizon 180 (*one 180 h.p. Lycoming O-360-A1A*)
   G-AVMA (196), 10.7.68; G-AVRS (224), 23.9.68; G-AWAC (234), 21.2.69;
G-AYOL (176), F-BNQJ, N3788, 13.1.71

General Aircraft Monospar ST-3
G-AARP (S.S.1), 21.7.31, C. W. Hayward for the Monospar Wing Co. Ltd.,
           Brockworth; scrapped at Hanworth in 1932

General Aircraft Monospar ST-4 Mk.I
G-ABUZ (1), 27.7.32, General Aircraft Ltd., Croydon; P. Bailey, Croydon 4.34
           operated it privately until 1939; registration cancelled 12.46
G-ABVN (2), 19.8.32, Portsmouth, Southsea and I.O.W. Aviation Ltd.; B. Lewis and Co.
           Ltd., Heston 12.33; C. Kelman, Heston 12.36; shipped to Australia during
           1939–45 war; derelict at Bankstown, Sydney 1954
G-ABVO (3), 22.10.32, General Aircraft Ltd.; Hon. Brian Lewis, Heston 10.32; to H.H.
           Maharajah Shiraz of Patiala, India 11.34 as VT-ADT
G-ABVP (4), 12.8.32, A. C. M. Jackaman, Heston 'Peridot V'; Ace Air Services Ltd.,
           Speke 3.39; impressed 4.40 as X9434; scrapped 1.41
G-ABVR (5), 14.11.32, General Aircraft Ltd., Croydon; to W. Hocklin, Switzerland
           11.32 as CH-347; later to Alpar Berne as HB-ALU; later F-BDAZ
G-ABVS (6), 26.1.33, O. E. Armstrong; to Western Air Transport, Oranmore 2.33 as
           EI-AAQ; rest. 1.34; Flying Hire Ltd., Chilworth 8.35; C. G. M. Alington,
           Hatfield 8.36; S. A. Edwards, Lympne 11.36; registration canc. 7.39

Geoffrey Ambler's Monospar ST-6 G-ACCO during a visit to Brooklands in 1935, showing the retractable undercarriage conversion. (*via R. P. Howard*)

General Aircraft Monospar ST-4 Mk.II
G-ACCO (8), 2.3.33, G. H. Ambler, Yeadon; converted to Monospar ST-6 q.v.
G-ACCP (10), 17.3.33, Hon. A. E. Guinness, Heston; Cambridge Aero Club 7.34;
           Lundy & Atlantic Coast Air Lines, Barnstaple 11.38; w.f.u. 8.39
G-ACEW (11), 6.4.33, Highland Airways Ltd. 'Inverness'; C. H. Tutt, Gravesend 7.37;
           damaged beyond repair landing at Croydon 13.12.37

G-ACFR (12), 13.4.33, General Aircraft Ltd.; P. A. Wills, Croydon 1.34; Herts and Essex Aero Club, Broxbourne 6.36; w.f.u. 12.36

G-ACGM (17), 31.5.33, General Aircraft Ltd., Croydon; to Robert Germaine (Monospar agent in Morocco, Tripoli and Tunisia); sold abroad 10.33

G-ACHS (15), 12.5.33, Asiatic Petroleum Co. Ltd., Almaza, Cairo; crashed at Chahbar, Persia 10.11.33

G-ACHU (18), 13.6.33, Capt. R. G. Cazalet; converted to Monospar ST-6 q.v.

G-ACJE (21), 18.8.33, International Airlines Ltd., Croydon; to Italy 12.34 as I-AGAR

G-ACJF (19), 3.8.33, International Airlines Ltd., Croydon; G. S. Davison, Castle Bromwich 12.34; w.f.u. 3.39; scrapped at Heston in 1945

G-ACKT (29), 25.11.33, Duchess of Bedford, Woburn; crashed at Thrupp's Farm, Lidlington, Beds. 5.12.33

G-ADBY (26), 9.3.35, General Aircraft Ltd.; to South Africa 6.36 as ZS-AHE; impressed by S.A.A.F. in 1940 as '1507'

G-ADIK (27), 4.6.35, Commercial Air Hire Ltd., Croydon; used on Inner Circle air line; crashed 5.36

G-ADJP (28), 29.6.35, Commercial Air Hire Ltd., Croydon; R. K. Dundas Ltd., Hanworth 5.36; impressed 3.40 as X9367; d.b.r. at Congleton 21.6.40

G-ADLM (30), 22.7.35, Commercial Air Hire Ltd., Croydon; fatal take-off crash at Croydon 16.5.36

General Aircraft Monospar ST-6

G-ACCO (8), 2.3.33, converted ST-4 Mk.II, G. H. Ambler, Yeadon; impressed 3.40 as X9376; damaged in forced landing between Ringway and York 2.4.40; rebuilt by makers as DR849; d.b.r. landing at Kemble 22.4.42

G-ACGI (14), 1.7.33, prototype ST-6, General Aircraft Ltd., Croydon; Ipswich Airport Ltd. 11.36; Southern Airways Ltd. 4.38; impressed 5.40 as AV979

G-ACHU (18), converted from ST-4 Mk.II, C. of A. 28.5.37, R. G. Cazalet; L. W. Hamp, Wolverhampton 6.38; w.f.u. 5.39; rest. 3.41 to Murphy Bros., Wolverhampton; not flown

G-ACIC (20), 21.7.33, R. E. Gardner, Hamble; C. P. Dick, Hanworth 4.35; Romford Flying Club 8.38; burned in hangar fire at Maylands 6.2.40

General Aircraft Monospar ST-10

G-ACTS (32), T-5, 3.7.34, General Aircraft Ltd., Hanworth; H. M. Schofield, Hanworth 11.34; Portsmouth, Southsea & I.O.W. Aviation Ltd. 11.37; impressed 4.40 as X9453; used by the Royal Navy at Eastleigh in 1943

General Aircraft Monospar ST-12

G-ADBN (35), 1.3.35, General Aircraft Ltd.; to Robert Fretz 4.35 as HB-AIR; rest. 10.35 to P. Jensen, Stockholm; Air Dispatch Ltd., Cardiff 4.38; impressed 8.40 as BD150; struck off charge at Kemble 1942

G-ADDY (39), 8.4.35, Mrs. U. Lloyd, Hanworth; R. J. B. Seaman, Hanworth; sold abroad 12.36

G-ADDZ (40), 9.4.35, General Aircraft Ltd., Hanworth; sold abroad 6.37

G-ADLL (45), 19.7.35, O. G. E. Roberts, Hamble; G. W. Harben, Weston-super-Mare 5.39; impressed 3.40 as X9341; used by Station Flight, Honiley

General Aircraft Monospar ST-25 Jubilee

G-ADIV (46), 21.6.35, prototype; General Aircraft Ltd., Hanworth; Radio Transmission Equipment Ltd., Hanworth 12.35; crashed in Wigtown Bay 11.8.36

G-ADLT (50), 2.8.35, Air Commerce Ltd., Heston; Airwork Ltd., Heston 8.36; sold in France 5.37 as F-AQAC

G-ADMC (47), 23.7.35, Marshalls Flying School Ltd., Cambridge; to South Africa 10.38 as ZS-APC; S.A.A.F. impressment 1940 as '1426'

G-ADMD (49), 4.7.35, G. d'Erlanger, Hanworth; H. R. d'Erlanger, Gatwick 12.36; crashed near Trento, Italy 2.1.37

G-ADMZ (53), 17.9.35, Sir Michael Assheton-Smith, Heston; sold in Spain 6.36 as EC-AFF; re-registered 1943 as EC-CAR and postwar as EC-ABH

G-ADNM (51), 9.8.35, General Aircraft Ltd., Hanworth; to N. V. Van Melle 9.35 as PH-IPM 'Dubbele Arend'; Dutch registration cancelled 1.38

G-ADNN (52), 22.8.35, Aircraft Exchange and Mart Ltd., Hanworth; sold in Kenya 12.36 as VP-KCB; burned out 4.7.38

G-ADPI (54), 5.9.35, General Aircraft Ltd., Hanworth; Hubert Holliday (Mobiloil), Heston 12.35; sold in Spain 8.36

G-ADPK (55), 9.9.35, Crilly Airways Ltd., Braunstone; Portsmouth, Southsea and I.O.W. Aviation Ltd. 12.36; impressed 3.40 as X9348; rebuilt as DR848 after accident at Ringway 16.3.40; scrapped 8.42

G-ADPL (56), 19.9.35, Crilly Airways Ltd., Braunstone; Portsmouth, Southsea and I.O.W. Aviation Ltd. 12.36; impressed 3.40 as X9369

G-ADPM (57), 1.10.35, Crilly Airways Ltd., Braunstone; H. S. Ashworth, Stanley Park, Blackpool 12.36; destroyed in grandstand fire at Hooton 8.7.40

G-ADSN (58), 7.10.35, Aircraft Exchange and Mart Ltd., Hanworth; J. D. Kirwan, Hanworth 11.35; sold abroad 7.36

G-ADTE (59), 1.10.35, Mrs. Ursula E. Lloyd, Hanworth; crashed at Addis Alum, Ethiopia 26.12.35

G-ADVG (61), 16.10.35, Aircraft Exchange and Mart Ltd., Hanworth; sold in Spain 8.36

G-ADVH (62), 25.10.35, A. Batchelor, Ramsgate; Flt. Lt. G. Shaw, Thornaby 8.37; impressed 3.40 as X9365; crashed at Saighton Camp, Chester 4.4.40

G-ADWH (63), 6.11.35, General Aircraft Ltd.; to France 5.37 as F-AQAD

G-ADWI (64), 29.10.35, General Aircraft Ltd., Hanworth; temporarily G.A.L.26 with Cirrus Minors as T-6 and G-ADWI in 1936; to France 6.37 as F-AQCL

Monospar ST-25 Ambulance G-AEWN at Hanworth in 1937 showing the large stretcher loading hatch. (*via R. P. Howard*)

519

G-ADYN   (73), 4.2.36, Norman Holden, Selsey Bill; Williams and Co., Squires Gate 8.38; impressed 3.40 as X9373; scrapped 4.44

G-AEAT   (75), 21.4.36, Aerial Sites Ltd., Hanworth; crashed at Brasted, Kent 16.3.38

G-AEDY   (72), 12.3.36, General Aircraft Ltd.; converted via de Luxe to Universal 1936; Aircraft Facilities Ltd., Hooton 1.37; Utility Airways Ltd., Hooton 'Alcaeus' 6.39; crashed near Hanworth 10.1.40

G-AEGX   (80), 8.5.36, Ambulance; General Aircraft Ltd., Hanworth 'Florence Nightingale'; D. Corrigan 2.37; sold abroad 3.37

G-AHBK   (71), K8308, 6.6.46, Southern Aircraft (Gatwick) Ltd.; E. I. H. Ward, Gatwick 6.46; N. L. Hayman, Fairoaks 9.46; crashed at Barnsley Wold, near Cirencester 2.6.47

General Aircraft Monospar ST-25 Universal

G-AEDY   (72), conversion of ST-25 Jubilee via de Luxe model; see above

G-AEGY   (93), 15.5.36, General Aircraft Ltd., Hanworth; J. W. Adamson, York 11.38; impressed 4.40 as X9377; used by Rotol Ltd., scrapped 1944

G-AEJB   (82), 29.7.36, General Aircraft Ltd., Hanworth; Arabian Airways Ltd., Aden 5.37; A. Besse and Co. (Aden) Ltd. 12.42; reg'n. cancelled 1.46

G-AEJV   (83), 22.6.36, General Aircraft Ltd., Hanworth; W. E. Davies, Lympne 1.37; crashed at Lympne 12.3.38

G-AEJW   (84), 11.7.36, General Aircraft Ltd., Hanworth; to New Zealand Aerial Mapping Ltd., Hastings N.Z. 12.36 as ZK-AFF

G-AEMN   (88), 25.9.36, General Aircraft Ltd., Hanworth; sold abroad 11.36

G-AEPA   (94), 4.12.36, J. A. M. Henderson, Heston; H. S. Ashworth, Stanley Park, Blackpool 3.38; Blackpool F/S Ltd. 8.39; impressed 3.40 as X9372

G-AEPG   (87), 19.11.36, Lord Londonderry, Newtownards; to France 6.38 as F-AQOM; impressed 2.40 as W7977; returned to owner; re-impressed 4.40 as T9264

G-AESS   (79), 19.5.37, General Aircraft Ltd., Hanworth; reg'n. cancelled 1943

G-AEVN   (77), 15.3.37, Ambulance, D. Corrigan, Hanworth; N. Montefiore, Hanworth 5.37; registration cancelled 1.39

G-AEWN   (78), 28.4.37, Ambulance, R. B. Pickett, Hanworth; reg'n. canc. 12.37

G-AEYF   (95), 8.6.37, Ambulance, General Aircraft Ltd.; sold abroad 3.39

G-AEZU   (67), 16.5.38, British registration not used; to E. C. Lavanselle, France 5.38 as F-AQOL

G-AFBM   (96), 1.10.37, Freighter; General Aircraft Ltd.; to the Turkish Government for parachute training; left Hanworth on delivery 2.10.37

G-AFBN   (97), 1.10.37, Freighter: General Aircraft Ltd.; to the Turkish Government for parachute training; left Hanworth on delivery 2.10.37

G-AFDE   (98), 16.12.37, General Aircraft Ltd., Hanworth; sold abroad 1.38

G-AFIP   (99), 12.7.38, General Aircraft Ltd., Hanworth; impressed 3.40 as X9333; used by Boulton and Paul Aircraft Ltd., Wolverhampton

G-AFIV   (100), 31.3.39, General Aircraft Ltd., Hanworth; impressed 3.40 as X9334; beyond repair in forced landing near Pucklechurch, Glos. 4.12.43

G-AFSA   (101), 22.4.39, General Aircraft Ltd., Hanworth; impressed 3.40 as X9331; used by Vickers-Armstrongs Ltd.; scrapped 4.43

G-AFSB   (102), 22.4.39, General Aircraft Ltd., Hanworth; impressed 3.40 as X9330; used by No.7 A.A.C.U., Castle Bromwich; scrapped 3.41

G-AFWP   (103), 5.8.39, General Aircraft Ltd., Hanworth; impressed 3.40 as X9335; used by Vickers-Armstrongs Ltd.; scrapped 10.43
G-AGDN   (89), CF-BAH, 29.9.36, registered to General Aircraft Ltd. 11.41; C. G. M. Alington, Gatwick 5.45; scrapped 1.47

Cygnet II G-AGAL at Hanworth in 1941 after impressment as DG566. It was the only machine of the type not to survive the war.

General Aircraft G.A.L.42 Cygnet I
G-AEMA   (0001), 2.9.37, converted C.W. design; C. R. Chronander and J. L. Waddington, Hanworth; General Aircraft Ltd., Hanworth 4.39; w.f.u. 7.43

General Aircraft G.A.L.42 Cygnet II
G-AFVR   (109), 5.7.39, General Aircraft Ltd.; impressed 11.41 as HL539; used by No.530 Sqn., No.161 Sqn. and Vickers-Armstrongs Ltd.; rest. 2.46 to Newman Aircraft Ltd.; T. F. W. Gunton, Bircham Newton 4.49 (West Raynham from 1963); crashed at Woerth, Bas-Rhin, Northern France, 26.8.69
G-AGAL   (110), 17.2.41, General Aircraft Ltd.; impressed 3.41 as DG566 for No.24 Sqn., Hendon; to No.418 Sqn. 5.42; scrapped 7.43
G-AGAS   (117), 12.9.40, General Aircraft Ltd.; to T. L. Bridges, Argentina 8.41 as LV-FAH
G-AGAU   (118), General Aircraft Ltd.; impressed 7.41 as ES914; used by No.88 Sqn.; rest. 2.46 to Newman Aircraft Ltd.; C. of A. 24.9.46; Denham Air Services 'Dumbo' 7.48; crashed at Cowes/Somerton aerodrome 28.8.49
G-AGAW   (112), 28.9.40, General Aircraft Ltd.; to Werner J. Hein, Brazil 3.41 as PP-TDY; owned by Brasil Quartzo Ltda. in 1947; reg'n. cancelled 3.50
G-AGAX   (114), 7.11.44, General Aircraft Ltd.; R. C. Cox, Fairoaks 2.48; Sir Mark Norman, Fairoaks 2.49; L. V. D. Scorah, Staverton 6.49; D. Lamprell, Manchester/Wythenshawe 4.54; crashed near Barnsley, Yorks. 4.4.55
G-AGBA   (113), 13.6.41, General Aircraft Ltd.; impressed 6.41 as HM495; used by No.510 Sqn., Vickers-Armstrongs Ltd. and Portsmouth, Southsea and I.O.W. Aviation Ltd.; rest. 2.47 to R. L. Whyham; scrapped at Squires Gate 1.57
G-AGBN   (111), General Aircraft Ltd.; impressed 7.41 as ES915; rest. 2.46 to Newman Aircraft Ltd., C. of A. 28.8.46, airworthy at Biggin Hill in 1972

Gloster Meteor NF.Mk.14
G-ARCX   WM261, prototype first flown 23.10.53; to Ferranti Ltd., Turnhouse 9.60; first flown in civil markings 21.1.63, C. of A. 8.2.63; w.f.u. 2.69

G-ASLW (5814), WS829, delivered Lyneham-Hucknall for Rolls-Royce Ltd. 13.9.63, C. of A. 30.10.63; Target Towing Aircraft Ltd. 7.69; left Hurn 6.7.69 for Faro, Portugal; ditched in the Atlantic off Cape Verde Islands 6.11.69

G-AXNE WS804, delivered Bedford-Blackbushe for Target Towing Aircraft Ltd. 5.9.69; left for Bordeaux via Exeter 6.9.69 inscribed 'Enterprise Films'; abandoned after emergency landing at Bissau, Portuguese Guinea 1969

Glos-Airtourer 115 (*see also Victa Airtourer 100 and 115*)

G-AWDE (504), shipped on ss. *Rangitoto* 12.67; first flown at Staverton 7.5.68, C. of A. 2.7.68, Glos-Air Ltd.; Glamorgan Flying Club Ltd., Rhoose 10.70

G-AWMI (505), shipped with G-AWDE; C. of A. 4.10.68, Glos-Air Ltd., Staverton; Glamorgan Flying Club Ltd., Rhoose 10.70

G-AWOZ (507), shipped on ss. *Port Victor* 3.68; C. of A. 4.10.68, Glos-Air Ltd., Staverton; Biggin Hill Flying Club 2.69

G-AWRT (508), shipped with G-AWOZ; C. of A. 5.1.69; Glos-Air Ltd., Staverton

G-AWVG (513), shipped on ss. *City of Birkenhead* 6.68; first flown at Staverton 10.6.69, C. of A. 10.6.69, Glos-Air Ltd.; to Western Aviation Co., Kortrijk, Belgium 6.69 as OO-WIC

G-AWVH (512), shipped with G-AWVG; first flown at Staverton 3.9.70, C. of A. 7.9.70, Glos-Air Ltd.; Glasgow Flying Club, Abbotsinch 11.71

G-AYLA (524), shipped on ss. *Gothic* 2.69; first flown at Staverton 24.11.70, C. of A. 24.11.70, Glos-Air Ltd.

G-AZHT (525), T3 variant, shipped with G-AYLA; first flown at Staverton 24.1.72, C. of A. 27.1.72

G-AZOE (528), shipped on ss. *Irish Poplar* 4.69, first flown at Staverton 16.3.72, C. of A. 10.4.72, Glos-Air Ltd.

G-AZRP (529), shipped on ss. *Huntingdon* 5.69, 16.5.72, Glos-Air Ltd.

G-AZTM (530), shipped with G-AZRP, first flown at Staverton 4.5.72, C. of A. 30.6.72, Glos-Air Ltd.

G-AZTN (531), shipped on ss. *Delphic* 7.69, f/f at Staverton 12.6.72, C. of A. 13.6.72, Glos-Air Ltd.

Glos-Airtourer 150 and variants

G-AXAJ (A.522), T6 Super 150, first flown at Hamilton, N.Z. 12.68 as '522'; shipped on ss. *Sussex* 12.68; C. of A. 1.4.69, F. B. Miles, Staverton

G-AXIX (A.527), T4 Airtourer 150, shipped on ss. *Irish Poplar* 4.69; C. of A. 21.11.69, Glos-Air Ltd., Staverton; J. S. Coulson, Tollerton 2.72

G-AYMF (B.557), T6/24* Super 150, shipped on ss. *Cymric* 8.70; C. of A. 5.1.71, Glos-Air Ltd., Staverton; crashed at St. Just, Lands End 9.6.72

G-AYWM (A.534), T6 Super 150, shipped on ss. *Delphic* 7.69; first flown at Staverton 13.5.71, C. of A. 14.5.71, P. A. Dalton, Thruxton

G-AZBE (A.535), T6 Super 150, shipped with G-AYWM; first flown at Staverton 19.7.71, C. of A. 20.7.71, Glos-Air Ltd. (used by Lands End Aero Club)

G-AZDI (A.539), T6 Super 150, shipped on ss. *Port Nicholson* 10.69; first flown at Staverton 13.9.71, C. of A. 14.9.71, Glos-Air Ltd. (used by Glasgow Flying Club, Abbotsinch)

G-AZHI (A.540), T6 Super 150, shipped with G-AZDI, first flown at Staverton 4.11.71, C. of A. 1.12.71, Glos-Air Ltd. (used by Alouette Flying Club, Biggin Hill)

G-AZMN (A.550), T6 Super 150, shipped on ss. *Cumberland* 3.70; first flown at Staverton 8.2.72, C. of A. 9.3.72

G-AZOF (A.549), T6 Super 150, shipped with G-AZMN; first flown at Staverton 23.2.72, C. of A. 21.6.72, Glos-Air Ltd.

G-AZPD (B.569), T6/24* Super 150, first flown in N.Z. 4.10.71 as '569'; shipped on ss. *Adelaide Star* 11.71; 12.6.72, Glos-Air Ltd.; first flown at Staverton 9.5.72

G-AZZU (A.555), T6/24* Super 150, shipped with G-AYMF, registered 19.7.72 to Glos-Air Ltd., f/f at Staverton 23.8.72

* With electrically operated trimmer and flaps.

Handley Page H.P.12 (*O/400 civil conversion*)

G-EAAE (HP-16), D8350, 1.5.19, Handley Page Ltd., Cricklewood 'Vulture'; operated by Handley Page Transport Ltd., withdrawn from use 8.20

G-EAAF (HP-13), F5414, 1.5.19, Handley Page Ltd., crashed at Harker, near Carlisle 6.19; rebuilt as O/7, recertificated 14.8.19; w.f.u. 8.20

G-EAAG (HP-18), F5418, 1.5.19, Handley Page Ltd., Cricklewood 'Penguin'; operated by Handley Page Transport Ltd.; withdrawn from use 4.20

G-EAAW (HP-14), F5417, 1.5.19, Handley Page Ltd. 'Flamingo'; operated by Handley Page Transport Ltd., initially as G-5417; to Athens Exhibition 30.10.19, withdrawn from use at C. of A. expiry 4.20

G-EAKE (HP-22), J2252, 25.8.19, Handley Page Ltd.; flown to Stockholm by Tryggve Gran 8.19; crashed near Stockholm 30.6.20

G-EAKF (HP-19), J2249, 10.10.19, Handley Page Ltd., Cricklewood; operated by Handley Page Transport Ltd.; scrapped 10.20

G-EAKG (HP-20), J2250, 6.9.19, Handley Page Ltd., Cricklewood; operated by Handley Page Transport Ltd.; scrapped 8.20

G-EALX (HP-21), J2251, 30.10.19, Handley Page Ltd., Cricklewood; operated by Handley Page Transport Ltd.; withdrawn from use 10.20

G-EALY (HP-24), J2247, 17.10.19, Handley Page Ltd., Cricklewood; operated by Handley Page Transport Ltd.; withdrawn from use 10.20

G-EALZ (HP-23), J2243, 17.12.19, Handley Page Ltd., Cricklewood; operated by Handley Page Transport Ltd.; withdrawn from use 12.20

G-EAMA (HP-25), J2248, 7.11.19, Handley Page Ltd.; operated by Handley Page Transport Ltd.; crashed in fog at Golders Green 14.12.20

G-EAMB (HP-26), D4623, 23.12.19, Handley Page Ltd., Cricklewood; operated by Handley Page Transport Ltd.; withdrawn from use 12.20

G-EAMC (HP-27), D4624, 28.1.20, Handley Page Ltd.; used on *Daily Telegraph* Cairo-Cape flight; crashed 6 miles north of El Shereik, Sudan 25.2.20

G-EAMD (HP-28), D4633, 1.12.19, Handley Page Ltd., Cricklewood; flown to Warsaw for the Polish Government 12.19

G-EASO (HP-33), F5444, 15.4.20 (Lion engines), Handley Page Ltd., Cricklewood; 'Old Carthusian II' for abortive India flight; dismantled 4.21

Handley Page O/7

G-EAGN (HP-1), C9704, HP-1, K-162, 8.8.19, Handley Page Ltd., Cricklewood; civil registration not taken up; to the Chinese Government 8.19

G-EANV (HP-7), 2.10.19, Handley Page Ltd. 'Pioneer'; flown in South Africa for adver-
        tising purposes; crashed near Beaufort West, Cape Province 23.2.20
G-EAPA (HP-11), 9.12.19, Handley Page Ltd.; operated by Handley Page Transport
        Ltd.; to Handley Page Indo Burmese Transport Ltd. 1.21
G-EAPB (HP-12), J1934, 23.4.20, Handley Page Ltd.; operated by Handley Page Trans-
        port Ltd.; to Handley Page Indo Burmese Transport Ltd. 1.21
G-EAQZ (HP-10), 18.2.20, Handley Page Ltd.; operated by Handley Page Transport
        Ltd.; to Handley Page Indo Burmese Transport Ltd. 2.21

Handley Page O/10

G-EASX (HP-34), F308, 15.10.20, Handley Page Ltd.; operated by Handley Page
        Transport Ltd.; to H.H. Sir Wahjee Bahadur 4.21 as G-IAAC 'Pink
        Elephant'
G-EASY (HP-35), D4614, 23.6.20, Handley Page Ltd.; operated by Handley Page
        Transport Ltd.; to Handley Page Indo Burmese Transport Ltd. 4.21
G-EASZ (HP-36), F310, 25.6.20, Handley Page Ltd.; operated by Handley Page Trans-
        port Ltd.; to Handley Page Indo Burmese Transport Ltd. 4.21
G-EATG (HP-37), D4618, 23.6.20, Handley Page Ltd.; operated by Handley Page
        Transport Ltd.; withdrawn from use at Croydon 4.21
G-EATH (HP-38), D4631, 30.6.20, Handley Page Ltd.; operated by Handley Page
        Transport Ltd.; scrapped at Croydon in 1924
G-EATJ (HP-39), F307, 25.6.20, Handley Page Ltd.; operated by Handley Page Trans-
        port Ltd.; withdrawn from use at Croydon 4.21
G-EATK (HP-40), J2262, 15.7.20, Handley Page Ltd.; operated by Handley Page Trans-
        port Ltd.; tested with Jupiters 2.22 to 5.22; scrapped 8.22
G-EATL (HP-41), F312, 30.8.20, Handley Page Ltd.; operated by Handley Page
        Transport Ltd.; Swiss tour by W. L. Hope; withdrawn after accident 4.21
G-EATM (HP-42), D4609, 30.7.20, Handley Page Ltd.; operated by Handley Page
        Transport Ltd.; crash landed at Senlis, Northern France 30.12.21
G-EATN (HP-43), J2261, 13.7.20, Handley Page Ltd.; operated by Handley Page Trans-
        port Ltd.; crashed in France 14.1.22

Handley Page O/11

G-EASL (HP-30), C9699, 26.3.20, Handley Page Ltd.; operated by Handley Page
        Transport Ltd.; withdrawn from use and scrapped 4.21
G-EASM (HP-31), C9731, 26.3.20, Handley Page Ltd.; operated by Handley Page
        Transport Ltd.; withdrawn from use and scrapped 4.21
G-EASN (HP-32), D4611, 23.6.20, Handley Page Ltd.; operated by Handley Page
        Transport Ltd.; withdrawn from use and scrapped 4.21

Handley Page W8, W8a, W8b, W8f Hamilton and W9 Hampstead

G-EAPJ (W8-1), W8, first flown 4.12.19, C. of A. 7.8.20, Handley Page Ltd.; operated
        by Handley Page Transport Ltd as 'Newcastle', later 'Duchess of York'; crash
        landed at Poix, Northern France 10.7.23
G-EAVJ (W8a), W8a, not constructed, registration cancelled at census 10.1.23
G-EBBG (W8-2), W8b, 9.6.22, Air Council; operated by Handley Page Transport Ltd.
        as 'Bombay', later 'Princess Mary'; Imperial Airways Ltd., Croydon 3.24;
        crashed at Abbeville, Northern France 15.2.28

G-EBBH   (W8-3), W8b, 10.6.22, Air Council; operated by Handley Page Transport Ltd. as 'Melbourne', later 'Prince George'; Imperial Airways Ltd., Croydon; withdrawn from use at C. of A. expiry 4.29

G-EBBI   (W8-4), W8b, 30.6.22, Air Council, operated by Handley Page Transport Ltd. as 'Prince Henry'; Imperial Airways Ltd. 3.24; w.f.u. 3.24

G-EBIX   (W8-7), W8f, first flown 20.6.24, C. of A. 27.6.24, Air Council; operated by Imperial Airways Ltd., as 'City of Washington'; conv. to W8g; certificated as such 15.4.30; crashed at Neufchatel near Boulogne 30.10.30

G-EBLE   (W9-1), W9, 20.1.26, Imperial Airways Ltd. 'City of New York'; to New Guinea 1.29 as VH-ULK; crashed into mountainside near Salamaua 31.5.30

G-ACDO   (1), SABCA W8e, OO-AHJ, British Hospitals Air Pageants Ltd., Ford; aircraft not overhauled for British use; scrapped at Ford in 1934

The first SABCA-built Handley Page W8b, OO-AHJ, seen leaving Croydon on the SABENA service to Brussels in 1930, almost became G-ACDO in 1933.

Handley Page W10

G-EBMM   (W10-1), 5.3.26, Imperial Airways Ltd., Croydon 'City of Melbourne'; to National Aviation Day Displays Ltd., Ford 11.33 as 'Youth of New Zealand'; conv. to tanker; crashed at Aston Clinton, Bucks. 24.9.34

G-EBMR   (W10-2), 9.3.26, Imperial Airways Ltd. 'City of Pretoria'; to National Aviation Day Displays Ltd., Ford 11.33; conv. to tanker 1934; positioned in Malta to refuel Courier G-ABXN; not used; sold locally as scrap

G-EBMS   (W10-3), 9.3.26, Imperial Airways Ltd., Croydon 'City of London'; crashed in the English Channel 21.10.26

G-EBMT   (W10-4), 13.3.26, Imperial Airways Ltd., Croydon 'City of Ottawa'; crashed in the English Channel 17.6.29

Handley Page H.P.42E

G-AAGX   (42/1), 5.6.31, Imperial Airways Ltd., Cairo 'Hannibal'; lost at sea over the Gulf of Oman between Jask and Sharjah 1.3.40

G-AAUC   (42/4), 19.9.31, Imperial Airways Ltd., Cairo 'Horsa'; impressed 5.40 as AS981; burned out after forced landing near Whitehaven, Cumb. 7.8.40

G-AAUD   (42/3), 30.7.31, Imperial Airways Ltd., Cairo 'Hanno'; converted 1937 to H.P.42W; wrecked by gale at Whitchurch Airport, Bristol 19.3.40

G-AAUE   (42/2), 10.7.31, Imperial Airways Ltd., Cairo 'Hadrian'; impressed 5.40 as AS982; destroyed by gale at Doncaster 6.12.40

Handley Page H.P.42W

G-AAXC (42/5), 31.8.31, Imperial Airways Ltd., Croydon 'Heracles'; wrecked by gale at Whitchurch Airport, Bristol 19.3.40

G-AAXD (42/6), 13.11.31, Imperial Airways Ltd., Croydon 'Horatius'; wrecked in forced landing at Tiverton, Devon 7.11.39

G-AAXE (42/7), 10.12.31, Imperial Airways Ltd., Croydon 'Hengist'; converted to H.P.42E in 1935; burned out in hangar fire at Karachi 31.5.37

G-AAXF (42/8), 31.12.31, Imperial Airways Ltd., Croydon 'Helena'; impressed 5.40 as AS983; damaged beyond repair landing at Donibristle 1.8.40

Handley Page H.P.61 Halifax B.Mk.3

G-AGXA NR169, 16.5.46, G. N. Wikner 'Waltzing Matilda'; flown to Australia; to Aircarriers Ltd. 7.47 as VH-BDT; scrapped at Mascot, Sydney in 1948

G-AJPG NA684, not certificated, College of Aeronautics, Cranfield (instructional airframe); stood in the open for $2\frac{1}{2}$ years and scrapped 1948–49

Handley Page H.P.61 Halifax B.Mk.6 (*English Electric-built except G-AKNL*)

G-AIBG RG790, registered 17.11.47 to London Aero and Motor Services Ltd.; delivered to Stansted in R.A.F. markings 5.48 and used as spares

G-AJBE RG785, registered 17.11.47 to London Aero and Motor Services Ltd.; delivered to Stansted in R.A.F. markings 5.48; to Pakistan Air Force 10.49 (Note: Registration G-AJBE carried briefly 4.47 by Piper Cub q.v.)

G-AJSZ RG722, registered 14.5.47 to Lancashire Aircraft Corporation Ltd.; delivered to Bovingdon in R.A.F. markings 5.48 and used as spares

G-AJTX RG720, registered 27.5.47 to Lancashire Aircraft Corporation Ltd.; delivered to Bovingdon in R.A.F. markings and used as spares 5.48

G-AJTY RG756 ⎤
G-AJTZ RG757 ⎟ all other details identical with G-AJTX
G-AJUA RG824 ⎥
G-AJUB RG825 ⎦

G-ALOM, last Halifax B.Mk.6 to be registered, after delivery to Southend in June 1949.
(*A. J. Jackson*)

G-AKAP RG763, registered 1.7.47 to Airtech Ltd. and delivered to Thame in R.A.F. markings 8.47; broken up for spares and registration cancelled 3.48

G-AKAW RG784, registered 17.11.47 to London Aero and Motor Services Ltd.; delivered to Stansted in R.A.F. markings 5.48; to Pakistan Air Force 10.49

G-AKBI RG716, registered 4.10.48 to Lancashire Aircraft Corporation Ltd.; delivered to Bovingdon in R.A.F. markings and used as spares 5.48

G-AKJI RG695, registered 6.10.47 to Air Freight Ltd.; delivered to Doncaster with civil markings in whitewash; scrapped at Doncaster 1948

G-AKJJ RG698, all other details identical with G-AKJI

G-AKLI RG783, registered 17.11.47 to London Aero and Motor Services Ltd.; delivered to Stansted in R.A.F. markings 5.48; to Pakistan Air Force 10.49

G-AKLJ RG781 ⎱ all other details identical with G-AKLI
G-AKLK RG779 ⎰

G-AKNG RG658, registered 29.11.47 to Lancashire Aircraft Corporation Ltd.; delivered to Bovingdon in R.A.F. markings and used as spares 5.48

G-AKNH RG700 ⎫
G-AKNI RG717 ⎪ all other details identical with G-AKNG except G-AKNL (Handley
G-AKNJ RG759 ⎬ Page-built, c/n 1270)
G-AKNK RG712 ⎪
G-AKNL PP171 ⎭

G-AKUT RG736, registered 12.3.48 to London Aero and Motor Services Ltd.; delivered to Stansted with crude ferry marks; flown to Thame by Airtech Ltd. 7.6.49; repainted in Pakistan Air Force markings and delivered by air

G-AKUU RG813, flown to Thame by 8.9.48; all other details as G-AKUT

G-ALCD ST808, registered 2.5.49 to Lancashire Aircraft Corporation Ltd.; delivered to Bovingdon in R.A.F. markings and used as spares 7.49

G-ALCY RG719, registered 4.10.48 to Lancashire Aircraft Corporation Ltd.; delivered to Bovingdon in R.A.F. markings and used as spares 5.49

G-ALCZ RG774 ⎫
G-ALDZ RG822 ⎪ all other details identical with G-ALCY
G-ALEA RG826 ⎬
G-ALEB RG827 ⎭

G-ALEC RG847, all other details identical with G-ALCY. Note: Registration G-ALEC reallotted to de Havilland Dove, c/n 04402, ex G-APPD in 1959 q.v.

G-ALED RG853 ⎱ all other details identical with G-ALCY
G-ALEE RG877 ⎰

G-ALOM ST801, registered 27.4.49 to Aviation Traders Ltd., Southend; delivered in night camouflage with large red civil markings 6.49; to spares 11.49

Handley Page H.P.70 Halifax C.Mk.8

G-AGPC (1360), PP287, registered 25.10.47 to Anglo French Distributors Ltd., Gatwick; to Aero Cargo, Lyons 10.47 as F-BCJS; crashed at Lyons 1.12.48

G-AGTK (1347), PP274, 1.8.47, Anglo French Distributors Ltd.; to C.T.A.I., Le Bourget 8.47 as F-BCJX; d.b.r. Bovingdon 13.5.48

G-AHKK (1371), PP309, 21.7.47, Anglo French Distributors Ltd.; delivered to France by air 12.7.47 as F-BCJV

G-AHVT (1351), PP278, registered 25.6.47 to Anglo French Distributors Ltd.; delivered to Gatwick in R.A.F. markings by 15.8.47; delivered by air to France about 21.9.47 as F-BCJR; French C. of A. 29.12.47

G-AHWL (1393), PP331, registered 25.10.47 to Anglo French Distributors Ltd., Gatwick; to France 10.47 as F-BCJT

G-AHWM (1322), PP238, registered 21.6.46 to Handley Page Ltd., Radlett; to the R.A.F. 1.47 as PP238; restored 23.6.47 to Handley Page Ltd. as G-AJZY

G-AHWN (1314), PP230, registered 21.6.46 to Handley Page Ltd.; to the R.A.F. 1.47 as PP230; rest. 4.48 to Lancashire Aircraft Corporation Ltd., Bovingdon, C. of A. 1.10.48, named 'Air Viceroy'; withdrawn from use after undercarriage collapsed on landing at Schleswigland, Germany 6.7.49

G-AHYH (1334), PP261, registered 24.9.46 to B.O.A.C.; to R.A.F. 10.47 as PP261; rest. 9.48 to Lancashire Aircraft Corporation Ltd., Bovingdon as 'Air Merchant II', C. of A. 29.10.48; scrapped at Woolsington 28.10.49

G-AHYI (1373), PP311, registered 24.9.46 to B.O.A.C.; to R.A.F. 7.47 as PP311; rest. 1.48 to Anglo French Distributors Ltd.; delivered to Gatwick with daubed civil markings; Skyflight Ltd., Bovingdon 3.49; scrapped 1949

G-AHZJ (1331), PP247, 18.9.46, London Aero and Motor Services Ltd. (L.A.M.S.), Elstree 'Port of Marseilles'; d.b.r. 8.47

G-AHZK (1330), PP246, 15.11.46, L.A.M.S. 'Port of Naples'; Skyflight Ltd., Bovingdon 3.49; withdrawn from use in 1949

G-AHZL (1326), PP242, 26.10.46, L.A.M.S. 'Port of Oslo'; dismantled at Stansted 6.49

G-AHZM (1333), PP260, registered 17.7.46 to L.A.M.S., Elstree; cannibalised after undercarriage collapsed at Elstree 16.9.46

G-AHZN (1328), PP244, 28.8.46, L.A.M.S., Elstree; ditched off the seafront at Knocke, Belgium at 2.15 a.m. 26.9.46 while en route Bergamo–Heathrow

G-AHZO (1323), PP239, 24.12.46, L.A.M.S., Elstree 'Port of London'; Skyflight Ltd., Stansted 3.49; dismantled at Stansted 6.49

G-AIAN (1344), PP271, registered to B.O.A.C., Aldermaston 2.9.46; transferred to the R.A.F. 4.47 as PP271

G-AIAO (1345), PP272, registered to B.O.A.C., Aldermaston 2.9.46; transferred to the R.A.F. 4.47 as PP272

G-AIAP (1354), PP281, registered 2.9.46 to B.O.A.C., Aldermaston; transferred to the R.A.F. 4.47 as PP281; rest. 10.48 to Airtech Ltd., Thame; Eagle Aviation Ltd., Aldermaston 6.50; crashed on take-off at Calcutta 25.11.50

G-AIAR (1388), PP326, registered to B.O.A.C., Aldermaston 2.9.46; transferred to the R.A.F. 2.47 as PP326; rest. 10.48 to Airtech Ltd., Thame; Chartair Ltd., Thame 9.49; British American Air Services Ltd., Bovingdon 3.50; withdrawn from use at Thame 5.51

G-AIAS (1389), PP327, registered 2.9.46 to B.O.A.C., Aldermaston; scrapped 4.47

G-AIHU (1306), PP222, 25.9.47, Lancashire Aircraft Corporation Ltd., Bovingdon 'Air Adventurer'; flew into hill and burned near Rhyl 5.12.47

G-AIHV (1335), PP262, 10.4.47, Lancashire Aircraft Corporation Ltd., Bovingdon 'Air Trader'; withdrawn from use at Stansted 4.53

G-AIHW (1357), PP284, 29.4.47, Lancashire Aircraft Corporation Ltd.; wrecked in night landing at Heathrow 5.6.47 inbound from Spain with 6 tons of apricots

G-AIHX (1367), PP294, 7.6.47, Lancashire Aircraft Corporation Ltd., Bovingdon 'Air Merchant'; wrecked in night landing at Squires Gate 3.9.48

G-AIHY (1325), PP241, 19.6.47, Lancashire Aircraft Corporation Ltd. 'Air Explorer'; beyond repair in taxying accident at Le Bourget 28.12.49

G-AIID (1379), PP317, registered 24.9.46 to B.O.A.C., Aldermaston; transferred to the R.A.F. 4.47 as PP317; rest. 1.48 to Anglo French Distributors Ltd.;

delivered to Bovingdon with crude civil markings; Skyflight Ltd. 3.49; sold as scrap 10.49

G-AILO (1353), PP280, 27.10.47, College of Aeronautics, Cranfield; Lancashire Aircraft Corporation Ltd., Bovingdon 'Air Courier' 9.49; w.f.u. 9.51

G-AIOH (1324), PP240, 15.5.57, C.L. Air Surveys Ltd., Ringway; Bond Air Services Ltd., Gatwick 5.47; crash landed at Barcelona 30.5.47

G-AIOI (1327), PP243, 16.1.47, C.L. Air Surveys Ltd., Ringway; Bond Air Services Ltd., 3.48; written off after taxying accident at Tegel Aerodrome, Berlin 15.2.49

G-AITC (1382), PP320, 2.12.47, College of Aeronautics, Cranfield; World Air Freight Ltd., Bovingdon 3.49; beyond repair landing at Brindisi 20.1.50

G-AIWI (1302), PP218, 13.5.48, London Aero and Motor Services Ltd., Stansted; operated by Skyflight Ltd. on Berlin airlift; scrapped 1949

Halifax C.Mk.8 G-AJBK at Gatwick with Air Freight Ltd. titling on 20 September 1947.
(*E. J. Riding*)

G-AIWJ (1359), PP286, 15.5.47, London Aero and Motor Services Ltd., Stansted 'Port of Athens'; dismantled at Stansted 6.49; sold as scrap 3.50

G-AIWK (1368), PP295, 21.7.47, London Aero and Motor Services Ltd., Stansted 'Port of Sydney'; scrapped after vandalism at Mascot, Sydney 12.47

G-AIWL (1364), PP291, registered 18.11.46 to London Aero and Motor Services Ltd.; not converted; reduced to spares at Stansted 1949

G-AIWM (1339), PP266, 4.12.47, London Aero and Motor Services Ltd., Stansted 'Merchant Venturer'; scrapped at Stansted in 1949

G-AIWN (1319), PP235, 23.5.47, L.A.M.S., Stansted 'Port of Darwin'; Payloads Ltd. 10.47; Bond Air Services Ltd., Gatwick 5.49; w.f.u. 5.50

G-AIWO (1363), PP290, registered 18.11.46 to London Aero and Motor Services Ltd.; not certificated; reduced to spares at Stansted during 1947

G-AIWP (1361), PP288, 26.1.48, London Aero and Motor Services Ltd., Stansted; operated on Berlin airlift by Skyflight Ltd.; sold as scrap 3.50

G-AIWR (1329), PP245, London Aero and Motor Services Ltd., Stansted; to L.A.M.S. (South Africa) Ltd. 12.47 as ZS-BUL 'Port of Durban'; crash landed at Port Sudan 25.11.47

G-AIWT   (1338), PP265, 3.4.47, L.A.M.S. 'Port of Sydney'; Payloads Ltd., Bovingdon 10.47; withdrawn from use at C. of A. expiry 9.48

G-AIZO   (1366), PP293, 18.8.47, Union Air Services Ltd., Gatwick 'County of Surrey'; Bond Air Services Ltd., Gatwick 5.49; crashed at Berkhampstead 23.5.48

G-AJBK   (1337), PP264, 11.7.47, Air Freight Ltd., Gatwick; sold in France 10.47 as F-BCJZ; damaged beyond repair in France 12.47

G-AJBL   (1349), PP276, 15.9.47, Air Freight Ltd., Gatwick (moved to Bovingdon 5.48); scrapped at C. of A. expiry 6.7.49

G-AJCG   (1390), PP328, LN-OAS, 20.8.47, Peteair Ltd. 'Sky Tramp'; cancelled 6.49

G-AJNT   (1332), PP259, registered 14.4.47 to Payloads Ltd.; sold in France 6.47 and flown to Toussus le Noble as F-BCQY

G-AJNU   (1352), PP279, registered 14.4.47 to Payloads Ltd.; to Pakistan Airways 5.48 as AP-ACH

G-AJNV   (1365), PP292, registered 14.4.47 to Payloads Ltd.; to Air Globe, Geneva 8.47 as HB-AIF; to the Egyptian Air Force 12.48

G-AJNW   (1369), PP296, 27.4.49, Payloads Ltd., Thame; Westminster Airways Ltd., Thame 5.49; withdrawn from use at C. of A. expiry 4.50

G-AJNX   (1374), PP312, 30.1.48, Payloads Ltd.; Bond Air Services Ltd., Gatwick 2.48; to Pakistan Airways ex Bovingdon 8.5.48 as AP-ABZ

G-AJNY   (1384), PP322, 2.4.48, Payloads Ltd., Thame; Bowmaker Ltd., Bovingdon 4.48; to Pakistan Airways ex Bovingdon 8.5.48 as AP-ACG

G-AJNZ   (1385), PP323, 26.11.47, Payloads Ltd.; World Air Freight Ltd., Bovingdon 'Trade Wind' 11.47; crashed near Port St. Mary, Isle of Man 28.9.48

G-AJPJ   (1336), PP263, 15.10.47, Chartair Ltd., Thame; British American Air Services Ltd., Bovingdon 11.48; sold to Mayflower Air Services Ltd.; flown from White Waltham to Israel by unauthorised pilot 20.7.48

G-AJPK   (1375), PP313, 20.8.47, L.A.M.S., Stansted; Payloads Ltd. 8.47; R. M. Hoyes, Bovingdon (t/a VIP Services Ltd) 11.47; withdrawn from use 10.48

G-AJXD   (1392), PP330, 23.6.47, Anglo French Distributors Ltd., Gatwick; to S.A.N.A., Le Bourget 6.47 as F-BCJQ

G-AJZY   (1322), PP238, G-AHWM, 18.3.48, Lancashire Aircraft Corporation Ltd., Bovingdon 'Air Monarch' 4.48; crashed and burned near Great Missenden 8.3.51 inbound from Gothenburg to Bovingdon with a cargo of reindeer

G-AJZZ   (1396), PP334, 8.7.48, Lancashire Aircraft Corporation Ltd., Bovingdon; conv. to tanker for Berlin airlift; crashed in night landing at Schleswigland, Germany 21.3.49

G-AKAC   (1340), PP267, 2.11.48, Payloads Ltd.; World Air Freight Ltd., Bovingdon 11.48; crashed and burned between Fuhlsbüttel and Berlin 29.4.49

G-AKAD   (1356), PP283, 1.3.48, British American Air Services Ltd., Bovingdon; damaged beyond repair in belly landing at Rennes, France 17.5.48

G-AKBA   (1303), PP219, 8.3.48, Airtech Ltd., Thame; leased to Alpha Airways (Pty.) Ltd., Bovingdon; crashed on take-off from Albacete, Spain 25.5.48

G-AKBB   (1321), PP237, 16.4.48, Airtech Ltd., Thame; British American Air Services Ltd., Bovingdon 4.48; beyond repair landing at Schleswigland 11.2.49

G-AKBJ   (1317), PP233, 8.12.48, Lancashire Aircraft Corporation Ltd., Bovingdon 'Air Ambassador'; crash landed at Tegel, Berlin during airlift 1.6.49

G-AKBK   (1315), PP231, 11.1.49, Lancashire Aircraft Corporation Ltd., Bovingdon; scrapped at Bovingdon in 1950

G-AKBP   (1362), PP289, registered 16.7.47 to Payloads Ltd.; to Air Globe, Geneva 8.47 as HB-AIL; to the Egyptian Air Force 12.48

G-AKBR (1391), PP329, 9.9.48, Payloads Ltd., Stansted; Anglo French Distributors Ltd., Gatwick 9.48; operated by Skyflight Ltd. on Berlin airlift from 9.48; Eagle Aviation Ltd., Aldermaston 8.49; scrapped in 1950

G-AKCT (1346), PP273, registered 1.8.47 to Payloads Ltd.; to Air Globe, Geneva 9.47 as HB-AIK; to the Egyptian Air Force 12.48

G-AKEC (1355), PP282, 4.2.48, Lancashire Aircraft Corporation Ltd., Bovingdon 'Air Voyager'; damaged beyond repair when blown against Halton G-AHDV by gale at Squires Gate 17.12.52

G-AKGN (1395), PP333, 25.8.48, British American Air Services Ltd., Bovingdon; Chartair Ltd., Thame 8.49; scrapped after gale damage at Thame 17.12.49

G-AKGO (1386), PP324, registered 10.9.47 to Airtech Ltd. and delivered to Stansted in R.A.F. colours 5.48; not converted for civil use

G-AKGP (1307), PP223, registered 10.9.47 to Airtech Ltd., Thame; to Societé Anonyme de Navigation Aériennes 6.48 as F-BESE 'Ker Goaler'; C. of A. 17.8.48; scrapped at Blackbushe in 1950

World Air Freight Ltd.'s Halifax C.Mk.8 G-AKGZ at Thame on 11 June 1948. It crashed during the Berlin airlift four months later. (*E. J. Riding*)

G-AKGZ (1400), PP338, 28.1.48, World Air Freight Ltd., Bovingdon 'North Wind'; crashed on take-off from Gatow, Berlin during the airlift 8.10.48

G-AKIE (1391), PP329, registered 15.9.47 to London Aero and Motor Services Ltd., Stansted; registration cancelled; (the aircraft was flying as G-AKBR)

G-AKJF (1301), PP217, registered 26.9.47 to London Aero and Motor Services Ltd., Stansted; not converted; sold to Sky Taxis Ltd., Johannesburg

G-AKXT (1304), PP220, 29.12.48, Lancashire Aircraft Corporation Ltd., Bovingdon 'Air Rover'; scrapped at Bovingdon in 1950

G-ALBS (1313), PP229, registered 14.6.48 to Hyland Automobiles (England) Ltd., Wakefield, Yorks.; not converted; scrapped at Bovingdon 8.50

G-ALBT (1343), PP270⎫
G-ALBU (1381), PP319 ⎬ all other details identical with G-ALBS
G-ALBV (1383), PP321⎭

G-ALBZ (1348), PP275, 2.2.49, Lancashire Aircraft Corporation Ltd., Bovingdon (unnamed); written off in landing collision with Halifax G-AHWN at Schleswigland, Germany due to tyre burst 10.5.49 while on Berlin airlift

G-ALCX (1397), PP335, 18.11.48, Lancashire Aircraft Corporation Ltd., Bovingdon
'Air Regent'; scrapped at Bovingdon in 1952
G-ALEF (1399), PP327, LN-OAT (Vingtor Airways), 11.10.48, Eagle Aviation Ltd.,
Luton 'Red Eagle'; scrapped at Luton in 1950

Halifax C.Mk.8 G-AGZP reworked as a Halton for the Maharajah of Baroda in 1946.
(E. J. Riding)

Handley Page H.P.70 Halton (*with Short and Harland conversion number*)
G-AGZP (1398), PP336, 20.3.46, British American Air Services Ltd., Bovingdon; to
Alpha Airways (Pty.) Ltd. 4.47 as ZS-BTA; rest. 8.49 to Lancashire Aircraft
Corporation Ltd., Bovingdon; scrapped at Bovingdon in 1953
G-AHDL (1308/SH.23C), PP224, 18.9.46, B.O.A.C. 'Fitzroy'; Aviation Traders Ltd.,
Southend 7.48; Westminster A/W Ltd., Blackbushe 2.49; crashed at Gatow,
Berlin 1.4.49
G-AHDM (1312/SH.20C), PP228, 20.7.46, B.O.A.C. 'Falmouth'; Aviation Traders
Ltd. 7.48; Westminster Airways Ltd., Blackbushe; scrapped at Blackbushe
9.50
G-AHDN (1318/SH.24C), PP234, 24.3.47, B.O.A.C. 'Flamborough'; Aviation Traders
Ltd., Southend 7.48; scrapped at Southend 11.50
G-AHDO (1320/SH.29C), PP226, 13.8.47, B.O.A.C. 'Forfar'; Aviation Traders Ltd.
7.48; Bond Air Services Ltd., Southend 3.49; scrapped at Southend 11.50
G-AHDP (1341/SH.25C), PP268, 24.3.47, B.O.A.C. 'Fleetwood'; Aviation Traders
Ltd., Southend 7.48; w.f.u. after undercarriage collapsed at Schleswigland
9.4.49 during Berlin airlift; registration cancelled 3.51
G-AHDR (1342/SH.26C), PP269, 7.7.47, B.O.A.C. 'Foreland'; E. M. Sutton 6.48; sold
to the Louis Breguet company in France 6.48 as F-BECK
G-AHDS (1350/SH.22C), PP277, 24.8.46, B.O.A.C. 'Fremantle'; Aviation Traders
Ltd., 7.48 (operated by Bond Air Services Ltd.); w.f.u. 7.51
G-AHDT (1370/SH.27C), PP308, 4.6.47, B.O.A.C. 'Fife'; Aviation Traders Ltd.,
Southend 7.48 (operated by Bond Air Services Ltd.); scrapped in Germany
11.49
G-AHDU (1372/SH.18C), PP310, 10.7.46, B.O.A.C. 'Falkirk'; Aviation Traders Ltd.
7.48 (operated by Bond Air Services Ltd.); scrapped at Southend 7.50

G-AHDV (1376/SH.21C), PP314, 19.8.46, B.O.A.C. 'Finisterre'; Aviation Traders Ltd. 7.48; Westminster Airways Ltd., Blackbushe 3.49; Lancashire Aircraft Corporation Ltd., Bovingdon 2.51; blown against Halifax C.Mk.8 G-AKEC by gale and damaged beyond repair at Squires Gate 17.12.52

G-AHDW (1377/SH.19C), PP315, 29.7.46, B.O.A.C. 'Falaise'; Aviation Traders Ltd. 7.48; scrapped at Southend 11.50

G-AHDX (1378/SH.28C), PP316, 4.6.47, B.O.A.C. 'Folkestone'; Aviation Traders Ltd. 7.48; Worldair Carriers Ltd., Heathrow 3.50; crashed in the Swiss Alps 16.4.50

Handley Page H.P.71 Halifax A.Mk.9

G-AKKP (1548), RT885, registered 9.3.50 to Aviation Traders Ltd., Southend; not converted for civil use

G-AKKU (1555), RT892, registered 9.3.50 to Aviation Traders Ltd.; not converted

G-ALIR (1479), RT791, registered 9.3.50 to Aviation Traders Ltd. and delivered to Southend in night camouflage; not converted; scrapped at Southend 11.50

G-ALON (1451), RT763, 1.6.49, Aviation Traders Ltd., Southend; operated on Berlin airlift by Bond Air Services Ltd.; scrapped at Southend 6.50

G-ALOO (1475), RT787, registered 27.4.49 to Aviation Traders Ltd., Southend; delivered by air to the Egyptian Air Force 2.50 with Arabic serial 1158

G-ALOP (1520), RT846, registered 27.4.49 to Aviation Traders Ltd., Southend; delivered by air to the Egyptian Air Force 2.50 with Arabic serial 1155

G-ALOR (1551), RT888, registered 27.4.49 to Aviation Traders Ltd., Southend; delivered by air to the Egyptian Air Force 2.50 with Arabic serial 1157

G-ALOS (1589), RT937, 15.6.49, Aviation Traders Ltd., Southend; operated on Berlin airlift by Bond Air Services Ltd.; scrapped at Southend 7.49

G-ALSK (1506), RT832, registered 9.3.50 to Aviation Traders Ltd., Southend; delivered in night camouflage with crude lettering 4.50; not converted

G-ALSL (1542), RT879, registered 9.3.50 to Aviation Traders Ltd., Southend; not delivered; reduced to spares at Harwarden 11.50

G-ALUT (1576), RT924, registered 10.8.49 to Aviation Traders Ltd., Southend; delivered in night camouflage with white letters; scrapped at Southend 11.50

G-ALUU (1522), RT848, registered 10.8.49 to Aviation Traders Ltd., Southend; delivered in night camouflage with white letters; scrapped at Southend 11.50

G-ALUV (1536), RT873, registered 10.8.49 to Aviation Traders Ltd., Southend; delivered in night camouflage with white letters; scrapped at Southend 1.50

G-ALVH (1476), RT788, registered 12.9.49 to Aviation Traders Ltd., Southend; delivered by air to the Egyptian Air Force 5.50 with Arabic serial 1163

G-ALVI (1481), RT793, registered 12.9.49 to Aviation Traders Ltd., Southend; delivered by air to the Egyptian Air Force 1.50 with Arabic serial 1156

G-ALVJ (1526), RT852, registered 12.9.49 to Aviation Traders Ltd., Southend; delivered by air to the Egyptian Air Force 2.50 with Arabic serial 1159

G-ALVK (1564), RT901, registered 12.9.49 to Aviation Traders Ltd., Southend; delivered by air to the Egyptian Air Force 3.50 with Arabic serial 1160

G-ALVL (1570), RT907, registered 12.9.49 to Aviation Traders Ltd., Southend; delivered by air to the Egyptian Air Force 4.50 with Arabic serial 1162

G-ALVM (1590), RT938, registered 12.9.49 to Aviation Traders Ltd., Southend; delivered by air to the Egyptian Air Force 3.50 with Arabic serial 1161

G-ALYI (1547), RT884, registered 9.3.50 to Aviation Traders Ltd., Southend; delivered from Harwarden in night camouflage 12.5.50; scrapped at Southend 5.51

G-ALYJ   (1464), RT776

G-ALYK   (1473), RT785

G-ALYL   (1511), RT837   registered 9.3.50 to Aviation Traders Ltd. and delivered to

G-ALYM   (1460), RT772   Southend in night camouflage for reduction to spares

G-ALYN   (1450), RT762

G-AMBX   (1447), RT759, registered 23.5.50 to R. A. Short; scrapped at Broughton 2.51

G-AMCB   (1558), RT895

G-AMCC   (1510), RT836

G-AMCD   (1556), RT893   registered 7.6.50 to Aviation Traders Ltd. and delivered to

G-AMCE   (1553), RT890   Southend in night camouflage for reduction to spares

G-AMCF   (1587), RT935

G-AMCG   (1490), RT816

Handley Page H.P.68 Hermes 1

G-AGSS   (H.P.68/1), registered 20.8.45 to Handley Page Ltd., Radlett; crashed at Kendall's Hall, Radlett on first test flight 3.12.45

Handley Page H.P.74 Hermes 2

G-AGUB   (H.P.74/1), 2.9.48, Ministry of Supply, Radlett; transferred to military marks 10.53 as VX234; to R.R.E., Defford; scrapped at Pershore in 1969

Handley Page H.P.81 Hermes 4

G-AKFP   (H.P.81/1), 14.10.49, B.O.A.C. 'Hamilcar'; leased to Airwork Ltd., Blackbushe 1953, temporarily XD632 in 1953; sold to Airwork Ltd. 2.57; beyond repair in take-off collision with Dakota VT-AUA at Calcutta 1.9.57

G-ALDA   (H.P.81/2), 14.10.52, B.O.A.C. 'Hecuba'; leased to Airwork Ltd. 1952, temporarily WZ838; sold to Airwork Ltd. 1.57; Falcon Airways Ltd., Blackbushe 10.59; Air Safaris Ltd., Gatwick 12.60; Air Links Ltd., Gatwick 11.62; flown to Southend 22.12.64 and scrapped there in 1965

G-ALDB   (H.P.81/3), 30.11.49, B.O.A.C. 'Hebe'; leased to Airwork Ltd. 1952, temporarily WZ839; burned out in crash at Pithiviers, France 23.7.52

G-ALDC   (H.P.81/4), 14.12.49, B.O.A.C. 'Hermione'; leased to Airwork Ltd. 1952, temporarily WZ840; sold to Airwork Ltd. 1.57; Falcon Airways Ltd. 'James Robertson Justice' 6.59; crashed landing at Southend 9.10.60

G-ALDD   (H.P.81/5), 19.12.49, B.O.A.C. 'Horatius'; Skyways Ltd., Bovingdon 4.55; withdrawn from use at C. of A. expiry 17.7.59 and scrapped at Stansted

G-ALDE   (H.P.81/6), 7.2.50, B.O.A.C. 'Hanno'; Skyways Ltd., Bovingdon 1.55; to Bahamas Airways Ltd. 1.60 as VP-BBO; rest. 5.61 to Air Safaris Ltd., Gatwick; scrapped at Hurn 5.62

G-ALDF   (H.P.81/7), 27.2.50, B.O.A.C. 'Hadrian'; leased to Airwork Ltd. 1952, temporarily WZ841; lost at sea off Trapani, Sicily 25.8.52

G-ALDG   (H.P.81/8), 9.3.50, B.O.A.C. 'Horsa'; Airwork Ltd. 8.57; Falcon Airways Ltd. 10.59; Britavia/Silver City Airways Ltd., Manston 'City of Chester' 12.59; scrapped at Gatwick 10.62

G-ALDH   (H.P.81/9), 20.3.50, B.O.A.C. 'Heracles'; Skyways Ltd., Bovingdon 8.55; d.b.r. when undercarriage collapsed at Heathrow 8.3.60; scrapped at Stansted

G-ALDI   (H.P.81/10), 6.7.50, B.O.A.C. 'Hannibal'; Britavia Ltd., Blackbushe 7.54, temporarily XJ309; operated by Silver City Airways Ltd., Manston as 'City of Coventry'; flown to Stansted 10.10.62 and scrapped

Hermes 4 G-ALDA in service with Air Safaris Ltd. in 1961. (*Aviation Photo News*)

G-ALDJ   (H.P.81/11), 7.7.50, B.O.A.C. 'Hengist'; Britavia Ltd., Blackbushe 7.54; destroyed in night landing crash at Blackbushe 5–6.11.56

G-ALDK   (H.P.81/12), 12.7.50, B.O.A.C. 'Helena'; Britavia Ltd., Blackbushe 7.54, temporarily XJ281; d.b.r. in crash landing at Drigh Road, Karachi 5.8.56

G-ALDL   (H.P.81/13), 21.2.51, B.O.A.C. 'Hector'; Skyways Ltd., Bovingdon 6.55; to Bahamas Airways Ltd. 1.60 as VP-BBP; rest. 4.61 to Air Safaris Ltd., Gatwick; Skyways Ltd., Stansted 12.61; Air Links Ltd., Gatwick 8.62; flown to Southend 31.8.62 and reduced to spares for G-ALDA

G-ALDM   (H.P.81/14), 17.7.50, B.O.A.C. 'Hero'; Air Safaris Ltd., Gatwick 11.56, leased to Silver City Airways Ltd., Manston until 12.59; scrapped Hurn 5.68

G-ALDN   (H.P.81/15), 20.7.50, B.O.A.C. 'Horus'; forced landed in the Sahara Desert 150 miles south east of Port Etienne, French West Africa 26.5.52

G-ALDO   (H.P.81/16), 20.7.50, B.O.A.C. 'Heron'; leased to Airwork Ltd. 1952; scrapped at Blackbushe 3.59

G-ALDP   (H.P.81/17), 24.8.50, B.O.A.C. 'Homer'; Britavia Ltd., Blackbushe 7.54, temporarily XJ269, operated by Silver City Airways Ltd., Manston as 'City of Truro'; flown to Stansted 10.10.62 and scrapped

G-ALDR   (H.P.81/18), 29.8.50, B.O.A.C. 'Herodotus'; Skyways Ltd., Bovingdon 4.55; withdrawn from use at C. of A. expiry 8.59 and scrapped at Stansted

G-ALDS   (H.P.81/19), 6.9.50, B.O.A.C. 'Hesperides'; Skyways Ltd., Bovingdon 4.55; withdrawn from use at C. of A. expiry 1.60 and scrapped at Stansted

G-ALDT   (H.P.81/20), 13.9.50, B.O.A.C. 'Hestia'; Skyways Ltd., Bovingdon 4.55; to M.E.A. 6.55 as OD-ACB; rest. 10.55; to Bahamas Airways Ltd. 10.60 as VP-BBQ; rest. 6.61 to Air Safaris Ltd., Gatwick; Skyways Ltd., Stansted 12.61; withdrawn from use at C. of A. expiry 6.62 and scrapped at Stansted

G-ALDU   (H.P.81/21), 12.10.50, B.O.A.C. 'Halcyone'; Britavia Ltd., Blackbushe 7.54, temporarily XJ280; Kuwait Airways Ltd. 7.56–1.57; operated by Silver City Airways Ltd., Manston as 'City of Gloucester'; scrapped at Stansted 11.62

G-ALDV   (H.P.81/22), 29.9.50, B.O.A.C. 'Hera'; Skyways Ltd., Bovingdon 4.55; burned out in test flight crash at Meesden Green, Herts. 1.4.58

G-ALDW (H.P.81/23), 30.10.50, B.O.A.C. 'Helios'; Skyways Ltd., Bovingdon 4.55; blown up by saboteur at Nicosia, Cyprus 4.3.56

G-ALDX (H.P.81/24), 13.12.50, B.O.A.C. 'Hyperion'; Britavia Ltd., Blackbushe 7.54, temporarily XJ267; Kuwait Airways Ltd. 7.56–1.57; w.f.u. 1.60

G-ALDY (H.P.81/25), 16.1.51, B.O.A.C. 'Honor'; Skyways Ltd., Bovingdon 9.54; to M.E.A. 6.55 as OD-ACC; rest. 10.55; withdrawn from use at Stansted 12.58

Handley Page H.P.82 Hermes 5

G-ALEU (H.P.82/1), registered 14.10.48 to Handley Page Ltd., Radlett; d.b.r. in wheels-up landing at Chilbolton 10.4.51; to spares at Boscombe Down

G-ALEV (H.P.82/2), registered 14.10.48 to Handley Page Ltd., Radlett; dismantled at Farnborough 9.53; fuselage by road to Southend 1958 for use by Aviation Traders Ltd. for mock-up of freight door installation

The prototype Marathon G-AGPD flying in Miles Class B markings as U-10 in 1946.

Handley Page (Reading) H.P.R.1 Marathon (*Miles-built prototypes*)

G-AGPD (6265), 4.9.47, first flown 19.5.46 as U-10, Ministry of Supply; crashed near Amesbury, Wilts. 28.5.48

G-AHXU (6544), 19.4.50, Ministry of Supply, Woodley; transferred to military marks 1951 as VX231; dismantled at Bitteswell 10.59

G-AILH (6430), 28.10.49, Ministry of Supply, Woodley; converted to prototype Marathon T.Mk.11 in 1952 as VX229

Handley Page (Reading) H.P.R.1 Marathon (*production aircraft*)

G-ALUB (101), 13.1.50, Ministry of Supply, Woodley; painted up as B.E.A. 'Rob Roy'; converted to T.Mk.11 for the R.A.F. in 1952 as XA249

G-ALVW (102), 28.12.51, Ministry of Supply, Woodley; converted to T.Mk.11 in 1952 as XA250; to No.2 A.N.S., Thorney Island, coded B in 1954

G-ALVX (103), 15.1.51, Ministry of Supply, Woodley; converted to T.Mk.11 in 1952 as XA251

G-ALVY (104), 28.9.50, Ministry of Supply, Woodley; to T.Mk.11 in 1952 as XA252; No.2 A.N.S., Thorney Island, coded M; scrapped at Shoreham 2.62

G-ALXR   (105), 15.1.51, Ministry of Supply, Woodley; converted to T.Mk.11 in 1952 as XA253; to No.2 A.N.S., Thorney Island, coded A in 1954

G-AMAX   (106), 28.9.50, Ministry of Supply, Woodley; converted to T.Mk.11 in 1952 as XA254; to No.2 A.N.S., Thorney Island, coded L in 1954

G-AMAY   (107), 5.10.50, Ministry of Supply, Woodley; converted to T.Mk.11 in 1952 as XA255; to No.2 A.N.S. Thorney Island, coded M in 1954

G-AMDH   (108), 13.11.50, Ministry of Supply, Woodley; converted to T.Mk.11 in 1952 as XA256; to No.2 A.N.S. Thorney Island, coded D in 1954

G-AMEK   (109), 19.1.51, Ministry of Supply, Woodley; to T.Mk.11 in 1952 as XA257; to No.2 A.N.S., coded O; sold for scrap at Hullavington 10.58

G-AMEL   (110), 14.9.51, Ministry of Supply, Woodley; to T.Mk.11 in 1952 as XA258; to No.2 A.N.S., coded L; sold for scrap at Hullavington 10.58

G-AMEM   (111), 23.2.51, Ministry of Supply, Woodley; to T.Mk.11 in 1952 as XA259; to No.2 A.N.S., Thorney Island, coded K in 1954

G-AMEO   (112), 12.3.52, Handley Page (Reading) Ltd.; to West African Airways Corp. 7.51 as VR-NAI; rest. 9.51; to Germany 8.55 as D-CFSA

G-AMEP   (113), 23.2.51, Ministry of Supply, Woodley; to T.Mk.11 in 1952 as XA260; sold for scrap at Hullavington 10.58, virtually unused

G-AMER   (114), 23.2.51, Ministry of Supply, Woodley; to T.Mk.11 in 1952 as XA261; to No.2 A.N.S., coded B; scrapped by Miles at Shoreham 2.62

G-AMET   (115), 30.4.51, Ministry of Supply, Woodley; converted to T.Mk.11 in 1952 as XA262; sold to Derby Aviation Ltd. as spares 10.58

G-AMEU   (116), 30.4.51, Ministry of Supply, Woodley; converted to T.Mk.11 in 1952 as XA263; to East Anglian Flying Services Ltd. as spares 10.58

G-AMEV   (117), 6.6.51, Ministry of Supply, Woodley; converted to T.Mk.11 in 1952 as XA264; to East Anglian Flying Services Ltd. as spares 10.58

G-AMEW   (118), 29.6.51, Ministry of Supply, Woodley; to T.Mk.11 in 1952 as XA265; rest. 10.57 to Derby Aviation Ltd., w.f.u. at Burnaston 7.61

G-AMGN   (119), 29.6.51, Ministry of Supply, Woodley; to T.Mk.11 in 1952 as XA266; to No.2 A.N.S., coded J; sold for scrap at Hullavington 10.58

G-AMGO   (120), 9.7.51, Ministry of Supply, Woodley; to T.Mk.11 in 1952 as XA267; to No.2 A.N.S., coded Q; sold for scrap at Hullavington 10.58

G-AMGP   (121), 10.7.51, Ministry of Supply, Woodley; converted to T.Mk.11 in 1952 as XA268; to No.2 A.N.S., Thorney Island, coded G in 1954

G-AMGR   (122), 17.8.51, Ministry of Supply, Woodley; to T.Mk.11 in 1952 as XA269; to No.2 A.N.S., coded P; scrapped by Miles at Shoreham 2.62

G-AMGS   (123), 9.7.51, Ministry of Supply, Woodley; to T.Mk.11 in 1952 as XA270; to No.2 A.N.S., coded F, sold for scrap at Hullavington 10.58

G-AMGT   (124), 17.8.51, Ministry of Supply, Woodley; to T.Mk.11 in 1952 as XA271; to No.2 A.N.S., coded A; crashed at Calne, Wilts. 30.9.54

G-AMGU   (125), 17.8.51, Ministry of Supply, Woodley; converted to T.Mk.11 in 1952 as XA272; to No.2 A.N.S., Thorney Island, coded H in 1954

G-AMGV   (126), 17.8.51, Ministry of Supply, Woodley; converted to T.Mk.11 in 1952 as XA273; to No.2 A.N.S., Thorney Island, coded C in 1954

G-AMGW   (127), 10.9.51, Handley Page (Reading) Ltd.; to W.A.A.C., Lagos 7.52 as VR-NAN; rest. 10.55 to Derby Aviation Ltd. as 'Millersdale'; withdrawn from use at Burnaston 4.61

G-AMGX   (128), 21.9.51, Handley Page (Reading) Ltd.; to W.A.A.C., Lagos 9.52 as VR-NAO; rest. 5.55 to Balfour Marine Engineering Co. Ltd., Southend; withdrawn from use at C. of A. expiry 8.56; scrapped at Southend 1962

G-AMHR (129), 21.9.51, Handley Page (Reading) Ltd.; to W.A.A.C., Lagos 10.52 as VR-NAR; rest. 10.55 to Derby Aviation Ltd. as 'Monsaldale'; withdrawn from use at Burnaston 7.61

G-AMHS (130), 19.10.51, Handley Page (Reading) Ltd.; to W.A.A.C., Lagos 10.52 as VR-NAS; to R.A.E., Farnborough 3.55 as XJ830; rest. 9.58 to Air Navigation and Trading Co. Ltd.; scrapped at Hurn in 1959

G-AMHT (131), 30.11.51, Ministry of Supply, Woodley; to T.Mk.11 in 1952 as XA274; rest. 6.59 to F. G. Miles Ltd., Shoreham, flown 2.62 and scrapped

G-AMHU (132), 16.11.51, Ministry of Supply, Woodley; converted to T.Mk.11 in 1952 as XA275

G-AMHV (133), 19.10.51, Handley Page (Reading) Ltd.; to W.A.A.C., Lagos 7.52 as VR-NAT; to R.A.E., Farnborough 3.55 as XJ831; rest. 9.58 to Air Navigation and Trading Co. Ltd., Squires Gate; to Canada 3.61 as CF-NUH

G-AMHW (134), 3.10.51, Handley Page (Reading) Ltd.; to W.A.A.C., Lagos 7.52 as VR-NAU; to Royal Jordanian Air Force 9.54 as VK-501

G-AMHX (135), 16.11.51, Ministry of Supply, Woodley; converted to T.Mk.11 in 1952 as XA276

G-AMHY (136), 16.11.51, Ministry of Supply, Woodley; R.A.F. serial XA277 allotted; released to Far East Airlines, Japan 1954 as JA-6009

G-AMHZ (137), 16.11.51, Ministry of Supply, Woodley; R.A.F. serial XA278 allotted; released to Far East Airlines, Japan 1954 as JA-6010

G-AMIA (138), 18.1.52, Handley Page (Reading) Ltd.; to Union of Burma Airways by air 12.52; crashed at Myaungmya Airport 4.8.53 as XY-ACX

G-AMIB (139), 28.2.52, Handley Page (Reading) Ltd.; to Union of Burma Airways by air 12.52, became XY-ACY

G-AMIC (140), 28.2.52, Handley Page (Reading) Ltd.; to Union of Burma Airways by air 12.52, became XY-ACZ

Handley Page (Reading) Ltd. H.P.R.3 Herald

G-AODE (147), first flown 25.8.55, C. of A. 20.7.56, Handley Page Ltd.; first flown as Dart Herald 11.3.58; crashed at Milford, Surrey 30.8.58

G-AODF (148), first flown 3.8.56, C. of A. 27.8.56, Handley Page Ltd.; first flown as Dart Herald 17.12.58; first flown as Series 200 8.4.61; re-registered 8.61 as G-ARTC; w.f.u. at Radlett 5.62; derelict in 1970

Handley Page H.P.R.7 Dart Herald

G-APWA (149), Ser.100, first flown 30.10.59, C. of A. 25.11.59, Handley Page Ltd.; leased to SADIA, Brazil 3.64 as PP-ASV; rest. 3.65 for lease to British Midland Airways Ltd.; sold to SADIA 11.66 as PP-SDM

G-APWB (150), Ser.101, first flown 6.7.61, C. of A. 27.7.61, leased to Jersey Airlines Ltd.; Ministry of Aviation (for B.E.A.), Renfrew 3.62; Autair International Airways Ltd., Luton 11.66; to Lineas Aereas la Uracca 11.70 as HK-718

G-APWC (151), Ser.101, first flown 2.11.61, C. of A. 28.12.61, Ministry of Aviation (for B.E.A.), Renfrew; Autair International Airways Ltd., Luton 11.66; to Lineas Aereas la Uracca, Colombia 11.70 as HK-715

G-APWD (152), Ser.101, first flown 19.4.62, C. of A. 27.4.62, Ministry of Aviation (for B.E.A.), Renfrew; Autair International Airways Ltd., Luton 11.66; to Lineas Aereas la Uracca, Colombia 11.70 as HK-721

G-APWE (153), Ser.201, first flown 13.12.61, C. of A. 29.12.61, Airlines (Jersey) Ltd.; British United Airways (C.I.) Ltd. 3.67; British Island Airways Ltd., Jersey 5.70

G-APWF (154), Ser.201, first flown 29.3.62, C. of A. 6.4.62, then as G-APWE above

G-APWG (155), Ser.201, first flown 27.4.62, C. of A. 17.5.62, then as G-APWE above

G-APWH (156), Ser.201, first flown 23.5.62, C. of A. 6.6.62, then as G-APWE above

G-APWI (157), Ser.201, first flown 8.5.63, C. of A. 22.5.63, British United Airways Ltd.; to Far Eastern Air Transport, Formosa 11.68 as B-1009

G-APWJ (158), Ser.201, first flown 29.5.63, C. of A. 18.6.63, British United Airways Ltd., Gatwick; British Island Airways Ltd., Jersey 5.70

G-ARTC (148), see G-AODF above

G-ASBG (164), Ser.203, first flown 13.11.62, C. of A. 8.2.63, Handley Page Ltd., Radlett; to Itavia, Rome/Ciampino 4.63 as I-TIVA

G-ASBP (163), Ser.204, first flown 22.9.62, C. of A. 26.11.62, British United Airways Ltd., Southend and Gatwick; to Air Manila 10.66 as PI-C867

G-ASKK (161), Ser.211, first flown 5.7.62, CF-MCK, PI-C910, C. of A. 7.8.63, Handley Page Ltd.; leased to Autair International Airways Ltd., Luton 8.63; leased to SADIA 12.63 as PP-ASU; rest. 2.65 to British Midland Airways Ltd.; British United Airways (C.I.) Ltd. 12.66; British Island Airways Ltd., Jersey 8.70

G-ASPJ (173), Ser.210, first flown 18.2.64, C. of A. 12.3.64, Handley Page Ltd.; to Globe Air 3.64 as HB-AAK; to Europe Aero Service 7.68 as F-OCLY; re-registered 5.69 as F-BLOY

Dart Herald Ser.214 G-ASVO at the Farnborough S.B.A.C. Show, September 1964 before delivery to SADIA as PP-SDG. (*Richard Riding*)

G-ASVO (185), Ser.214, first flown 2.7.64 as G-8-3, C. of A. 3.9.64, Handley Page Ltd., Radlett; to SADIA, Brazil 10.64 as PP-SDG

G-ATDS (189), Ser.209, first flown 30.6.65, C. of A. 27.7.65, Handley Page Ltd., Radlett; to Arkia, Israel 7.65 as 4X-AHT

G-ATHB (162), Ser.210, first flown 8.8.62, CF-MCM, HB-AAG, registered 22.7.65 to Handley Page Ltd., C. of A. 15.2.66; to Far Eastern Air Transport, Formosa 2.66 as B-2001

G-ATHE (165), Ser.207, first flown 21.12.62 as Jordan Air Force 109, later Alia JY-ACR, registered 26.7.65 to Handley Page Ltd., C. of A. 17.8.65, to Bavaria Flug, Munich 4.66 as D-BOBO; rest. 10.68 to Handley Page Ltd.; to Far Eastern Air Transport, Formosa 4.69 as B-2011, out of service by 6.72

G-ATIG (177), Ser.214, first flown 9.9.65, C. of A. 16.9.65, Handley Page Ltd., Radlett; to SADIA, Brazil 9.65 as PP-SDI

G-AVEZ (169), Ser.210, HB-AAH, first flown 25.7.63, registered 31.1.67 to Airlines (Jersey) Ltd.; British United Airways (C.I.) Ltd. 3.67, C. of A. 7.3.67; leased to SADIA 1.68 as PP-ASW; rest. 4.68 to British United Airways (C.I.) Ltd.

G-AVPN (176), Ser.213, D-BIBI, first flown 2.4.64, registered 22.6.67 to Handley Page Ltd.; leased to Itavia, Rome/Ciampino 9.68 and sold 7.70 as I-TIVB

G-AYMG (179), Ser.213, D-BEBE, first flown 19.3.65, registered 13.11.70 to British Island Airways Ltd., Jersey; C. of A. 10.2.71

Jetstream 1 G-AXGM leaving Prestwick for Keflavik, 12 July 1969, on delivery to International Jetstream Corporation for re-registration as N12218. (*Aviation Photo News*)

Handley Page H.P.137 Jetstream 1

G-ATXH (198), first flown 18.8.67 with Astazou 12s, C. of A. 26.3.68, Handley Page Ltd.; fitted 7.69 with Astazou 14-CO1 engines as Jetstream 2; parked at Filton 3.72

G-ATXI (199), first flown 8.3.68, C. of A. 30.5.68, Handley Page Ltd.; first flown with Garrett TPE.331 engines 7.5.69; scrapped at Radlett in 1969

G-ATXJ (200), first flown 28.12.67, C. of A. 28.8.68, Handley Page Ltd., Radlett; first flown 18.9.69 as Series 2; engineless at Luton 1972

G-ATXK (201), first flown 8.4.68, C. of A. 26.4.68, Handley Page Ltd., Radlett; to the International Jetstream Corporation, U.S.A. 5.68

G-AWSE (202), first flown 6.12.68, C. of A. 17.1.69, Handley Page Ltd., Radlett; to Cal-State Air Lines, Long Beach, California 7.69 as N1039S

G-AWVI (204), first flown 22.1.69, C. of A. 31.1.69, Handley Page Ltd., Radlett; to Cal-State Air Lines, Long Beach, California 8.69 as N1040S

G-AWVJ (206), first flown 25.3.69, C. of A. 3.5.69, Handley Page Ltd., Radlett; to Cal-State Air Lines, Long Beach, California 5.69 as N1036S; returned to Prestwick 24.5.72

G-AWVK (208), first flown 17.4.69, C. of A. 8.5.69, Handley Page Ltd., Radlett; to Cal-State Air Lines, Long Beach, California 5.69 as N1035S; returned to Blackbushe 12.70 as demonstrator for Jetstream Aircraft Ltd.

G-AWYM (210), first flown 17.5.69, C. of A. 6.6.69, Handley Page Ltd., Radlett; to U.S.A. 6.69; sold to James R. Coson, Burbank, Los Angeles as N62BS

G-AWYN (212), first flown 29.5.69, C. of A. 9.6.69, Handley Page Ltd., Radlett; to U.S.A. 7.69; sold to the National Steel Corporation as N340

G-AWYP (213), first flown 14.6.69, C. of A. 20.6.69, Handley Page Ltd., Radlett; to International Jetstream Corp., St. Louis, Missouri 6.69 as N137HP

G-AXEK (203), G-8-4, first flown 2.1.69, C. of A. 31.5.69, Handley Page Ltd., Radlett; C.S.E. demonstrator; to South Central Air Transport, U.S.A. 6.72

G-AXEL (207), G-8-6, first flown 4.3.69, C.S.E. Aviation Ltd.; British Steel Corporation 9.69; crashed at Courtyard Farm, near Hunstanton 29.9.69

G-AXEM (205), G-8-5, first flown 10.2.69, Handley Page Ltd., Radlett; to Bavaria Flug, Munich 10.69 as D-INAH; crashed and burned at St. Moritz 6.3.70

G-AXEP (209), G-8-7, first flown 2.5.69, C. of A. 21.5.69, Handley Page Ltd., Radlett; to U.S.A. 5.69; sold to Hoover Corporation as N5V

G-AXFV (211), G-8-8, first flown 24.4.69, Handley Page Ltd., Radlett; conv. as Jetstream 2 prototype 11.69; Cranfield Institute of Technology 9.70, C. of A. 29.9.70; Jetstream Aircraft Ltd., Leavesden 6.71 as Series 200; Terravia Trading Services Ltd. 2.72

G-AXGK (215), first flown 16.6.69, C. of A. 8.7.69, Handley Page Ltd., Radlett; to U.S.A. 7.69; sold to Walter W. Selover, Burbank, Los Angeles as N200PA

G-AXGL (216), first flown 21.6.69, C. of A. 27.7.69, Handley Page Ltd., Radlett; to U.S.A. 6.69; sold to Cal-State Air Lines as N1037S; returned to Prestwick 24.5.72

G-AXGM (218), first flown 2.7.69, C. of A. 11.7.69, Handley Page Ltd., Radlett; to U.S.A. 7.69; to International Jetstream Corporation as N12218

G-AXGN (220), first flown 4.7.69, C. of A. 18.7.69, Handley Page Ltd., Radlett; to U.S.A. 7.69; sold to Cal-State Air Lines as N1038S

G-AXHB (214), first flown 12.6.69, C. of A. 18.6.69, Handley Page Ltd., Radlett; to Northwest Industries Ltd., Edmonton, Alberta 6.69 as CF-QJB

G-AXHJ (217), first flown 17.6.69, C. of A. 24.6.69, Handley Page Ltd., Radlett; to U.S.A. 7.69; to K. R. Craven Corporation as N12217

G-AXIK (221), first flown 10.7.69, C. of A. 17.7.69, Handley Page Ltd., Radlett; to U.S.A. 7.69; to International Jetstream Corporation as N12221

G-AXIL (223), first flown 25.7.69, C. of A. 19.8.69, Handley Page Ltd., Radlett; to U.S.A. 9.69; to International Jetstream Corporation as N12223

G-AXIM (224), first flown 31.7.69, C. of A. 18.8.69, Handley Page Ltd., Radlett; to U.S.A. 9.69; to International Jetstream Corporation as N12224

G-AXJZ (227), first flown 21.7.69, C. of A. 26.9.69, Handley Page Ltd.; to International Jetstream Corp. 9.69 as N12227; to G. C. Murphy & Co. as N510E

G-AXKG (229), first flown 28.7.69, C. of A. 14.11.69, Handley Page Ltd., Radlett; to U.S.A. 12.69; re-registered N10EA; stored by Airspur, Canada 1971

G-AXLO (231), 12.11.70, Handley Page Ltd., Radlett; to U.S.A. 11.69; to Di Georgio Corporation, Burbank, Los Angeles as N10DG

G-AXLP (233), 18.11.69, Handley Page Ltd., Radlett; to U.S.A. 11.69 as N8943; sold to the Standard Oil Corporation as N815M

G-AXON (225), 3.10.69, Handley Page Ltd., Radlett; to International Jetstream Corporation 11.69; sold to Buckner Industries as N10AB

G-AXRE (235), first flown 2.12.69, C. of A. 8.12.69, Handley Page Ltd., Radlett; to U.S.A. 12.69; re-registered N10GA; stored by Airspur, Canada 1971

G-AXRF (237), 23.12.69, Handley Page Ltd., Radlett; to Associated Aero Leasing 12.69 as N2527; re-registered N666WB; stored by Airspur, Canada 1971

G-AXRG (238), 16.1.70, Handley Page Ltd., Radlett; to U.S.A. 2.70 as N1136C; stored by Airspur at Edmonton, Canada in 1971 as N10360

G-AXRH (240), 27.1.70, Handley Page Ltd., Radlett; to U.S.A. 2.70 as N4770; stored by Airspur at Edmonton, Canada in 1971

G-AXRI (241), intended for German distributors, Jetsale Schwabe & Co., Munich but scrapped at Radlett before completion

G-AXUI (222), G-8-9, 1.1.70, Handley Page Aircraft Ltd., Radlett; Cranfield Institute of Technology 9.70; f/f 6.72 after refit as flying laboratory

G-AXUM (245), Handley Page Aircraft Ltd., Radlett; Cranfield Institute of Technology 9.70

G-AXUN (246), Handley Page Aircraft Ltd., Radlett; Terravia Trading Services Ltd., Sywell 9.70; Cranfield Institute of Technology 7.71

G-AXUO (248), 26.1.72, Handley Page Aircraft Ltd., Radlett; Terravia Trading Services Ltd., Sywell 9.70 (later Jetstream Aircraft Ltd.); to Air Wasteels, Metz, France, ex Leavesden 26.1.72; became F-BTMI

G-AXUP (251), Handley Page Aircraft Ltd., Radlett; to Jetstream Aircraft Ltd.

G-AXUR (259), Handley Page Aircraft Ltd., Radlett; to Jetstream Aircraft Ltd.

G-AXVF (230), 9.1.70, Handley Page Aircraft Ltd., Radlett; stored at Edmonton, Canada by Airspur in 1971

G-AXXS (249), G-8-14, Handley Page Aircraft Ltd., Radlett; Terravia Trading Co. Ltd., Sywell 9.70 (later Jetstream Aircraft Ltd.); Scottish Aviation Ltd. 7.72

G-AXXT (261), Handley Page Aircraft Ltd., Radlett; to Jetstream Aircraft Ltd.

G-AXXU (268), Handley Page Aircraft Ltd., Radlett; to Jetstream Aircraft Ltd.

G-AYWR (243), G-8-13, Terravia Ltd., Leavesden

Handley Page H.P.137 Jetstream 3M

G-AWBR (258), prototype, first flown 21.11.68, C. of A. 9.7.69, Handley Page Ltd., Radlett; scrapped at Radlett in 1970; nose to Stansted fire school

Hawker Tomtit (*civil construction*)

G-AALL (9), 11.6.30, H. G. Hawker Engineering Co. Ltd., Brooklands; Miss D. Guest, Brooklands 11.30; Hawker Aircraft Ltd. 5.33; scrapped in 1937

G-AASI (12), 30.9.30, H. G. Hawker Engineering Co. Ltd.; Reid & Sigrist Ltd., Brooklands 2.33; Wolseley Motors Ltd., Castle Bromwich 7.33; J. Hopcroft, Hatfield 4.36; W. Humble, Firbeck 3.39; scrapped during 1939–45 war

G-ABAX (27), 26.6.30, H. G. Hawker Engineering Co. Ltd.; Reid & Sigrist Ltd., Brooklands 2.33; Wolseley Motors Ltd., Castle Bromwich 7.33; sold to S.U. Carburettors Ltd., Tollerton 9.36; not flown again

G-ABII (54), 31.1.31, H. G. Hawker Engineering Co. Ltd.; Gloster Aircraft Ltd., Brockworth 3.43; R. C. Cox, Fairoaks 11.46; E. Williams, Fairoaks 8.47; damaged beyond repair at Somerton Aerodrome, Cowes, I.O.W. 10.4.48

G-ABOD (55), registered 9.7.31 to H. G. Hawker Engineering Co. Ltd., C. of A. 2.1.33; Wolseley Motors Ltd./Lord Nuffield 7.33, used by the Tollerton Aero Club; scrapped during the 1939–45 war

Hawker Tomtit (*civil conversions*)

G-AEES K1782, 11.5.36, L. J. Anderson, Hanworth; Southern Aircraft (Gatwick) Ltd., 2.39; destroyed in hangar fire at Maylands, Romford, Essex 6.2.40

G-AEVO K1451, 1.4.37, C. B. Field, Kingswood Knoll, Surrey; L. C. Stanynought, Gatwick 12.37; C. Plumridge, Redhill 10.38; scrapped at Redhill 1946–47

The famous Tomtit G-AFTA, with headrest removed, flying near Old Warden in its original R.A.F. colours, 1969. (*Miss D. E. Wright*)

G-AEVP   J9782, reserved 11.3.37 for C. B. Field; registration not taken up; aircraft civilianised as G-AFFL

G-AEXC   J9781, 5.4.38, L. J. Anderson, Hanworth; Herts and Essex Aero Club, Broxbourne 8.38; scrapped during 1939–45 war

G-AFFL   J9782, 11.3.38, C. B. Field, Kingswood Knoll, Surrey; H. D. Rankin, Southend 7.38; smashed up and deposited in a Southend garage 1939; dumped at Newmarket 1941–42

G-AFIB   K1781, 15.8.38, C. V. Tillett, Hanworth; Leicestershire Aero Club 5.39; A. Henshaw 2.41; Vickers-Armstrongs Ltd. 8.41; used as road block 10.43

G-AFKB   K1785, 2.11.38, Southern Motors & Aircraft Ltd., Gatwick; Leicestershire Aero Club, Braunstone 5.39; crashed at Braunstone 13.7.39

G-AFTA   K1786, 28.4.39, Leicestershire Aero Club; A. Henshaw 6.42; G. P. Shea-Simmonds 2.46; G. Goodhew, Kidlington 5.46; R. C. S. Allen, Chalgrove 11.47; N. Duke 4.49; Hawker Aircraft Ltd., Dunsfold 7.50; repainted as K1786 for the Shuttleworth Trust, Old Warden 1967

G-AFVV   K1784, 4.7.39, Leicestershire Aero Club, Braunstone; A. Henshaw, Castle Bromwich 2.41; registration cancelled 11.45

G-AGEF   K1783, 8.7.42, C. B. Field, Kingswood Knoll, Surrey; Vickers-Armstrongs Ltd. 12.42; written off in accident 18.10.43

Hawker Siddeley H.S.121 Trident 1C (*British European Airways fleet*)
Note: Dates given are first flight/C. of A. issued

G-ARPA (2101), 9.1.62/21.6.62; G-ARPB (2102), 20.5.62/21.6.62, retained by Hawker Siddeley Aviation Ltd. for Autoland trials 7.64 to 1.67; G-ARPC (2103), 25.8.62/7.9.62; G-ARPD (2104), 17.1.63/6.1.65; G-ARPE (2105), 3.6.63/4.6.63; G-ARPF (2106), 18.10.63/13.12.63; G-ARPG (2107), 9.1.64/20.1.64; G-ARPH (2108), 8.3.64/24.3.64; G-ARPI (2109), 14.4.64/1.5.64, crashed on take-off from London/Heathrow 18.6.72; G-ARPJ (2110), 1.5.64/22.5.64; G-ARPK (2111), 13.6.64/26.6.64; G-ARPL (2112), 27.7.64/6.8.64; G-ARPM (2113), 28.9.64/9.10.64; G-ARPN (2115), 24.11.64/4.12.64; G-ARPO (2116), 13.1.65/27.1.65; G-ARPP (2117), 12.2.65/24.2.65;

G-ARPR (2119), 1.4.65/9.4.65; G-ARPS (2120), 23.5.65/1.6.65, withdrawn from use after cabin fire at Heathrow 29.7.69; G-ARPT (2121), 30.6.65/7.7.65; G-ARPU (2122), 13.8.65/24.8.65, destroyed on the ground at Heathrow 3.7.68 by crashing Airspeed Ambassador 2 G-AMAD; G-ARPW (2123), 7.10.65/15.10.65; G-ARPX (2124), 13.5.66/23.5.66; G-ARPY (2126), first flown 3.6.66, total loss in crash at Felthorpe, Norfolk during maiden flight; G-ARPZ (2128), 22.6.66/30.6.66

Kuwait Airways' first Trident 1E, 9K-ACF, ready to leave Heathrow on delivery 19 March 1966. It had spent the first part of its test life as G-ASWU. (*Aviation Photo News*)

Hawker Siddeley H.S.121 Trident 1E

G-ASWU (2114), first flown as Trident 1 on 2.11.64, C. of A. 19.3.65, Hawker Siddeley Aviation Ltd., Hatfield; first flown as Trident 1E 5.3.66; to Kuwait Airways 3.66 as 9K-ACF; rest. 1.72 to B.E.A., Heathrow

G-ASWV (2118), first flown 9.6.65, C. of A. 30.6.65, Hawker Siddeley Aviation Ltd., Hatfield; to Kuwait Airways 5.66 as 9K-ACG; written off in forced landing near Kuwait Airport 30.6.66

G-ATNA (2130), first flown 23.11.65 as AP-ATK, C. of A. 17.1.66, Hawker Siddeley Aviation Ltd., Hatfield; to Pakistan International Airlines 3.66 as AP-ATK

G-AVYA (2135), first flown 28.5.69, Hawker Siddeley Aviation Ltd., Hatfield; to Air Ceylon 7.69 as 4R-ACN

G-AZND (2134), first flown 21.11.66 as 9K-ACH; delivered 30.1.72 to B.E.A., Heathrow

Hawker Siddeley H.S.121 Trident 2E (*British European Airways aircraft*)

Note: Dates given are first flight/C. of A. issued

G-AVFA (2140), 27.7.67/16.10.67; G-AVFB (2141), 2.11.67/6.6.68, to Cyprus Airways Ltd. 6.72 as 5B-DAC; G-AVFC (2142), 3.1.68/6.8.68; G-AVFD (2143), 15.3.68/10.4.68; G-AVFE (2144), 9.4.68/7.5.68; G-AVFF (2145), 14.5.68/29.5.68; G-AVFG (2146), 19.6.68/3.7.68; G-AVFH (2147), 17.7.68/31.7.68; G-AVFI (2148), 6.8.68/13.9.68; G-AVFJ (2149), 2.10.68/18.12.68; G-AVFK (2150), 2.11.68/16.1.69; G-AVFL (2151), 31.1.69/13.2.69; G-AVFM (2152), 25.3.69/24.4.69; G-AVFN (2153), 7.5.69/23.5.69; G-AVFO (2156), 22.6.70/22.6.70; G-AZXM (2154), 5B-DAA, registered 28.6.72

Registrations G-AZFT to 'FY reserved 29.9.71 for ferrying Trident 2Es c/n 2157–2162 ordered by the People's Republic of China; a further six, G-BABP to 'BV, c/n 2163–2168, reserved 21.8.72

Hawker Siddeley H.S.121 Trident 1E-140

G-AVYB (2136), first flown 13.2.68, C. of A. 19.3.68, Channel Airways Ltd., Stansted; Northeast Airlines Ltd., Woolsington 2.72

G-AVYC (2137), first flown 15.1.69, C. of A. 28.3.69, Hawker Siddeley Aviation Ltd.; leased until re-reg'd. to Northeast Airlines, Woolsington 1.72

G-AVYD (2138), first flown 17.2.69, C. of A. 28.2.69, Hawker Siddeley Aviation Ltd.; leased until re-reg'd. to Northeast Airlines, Woolsington 1.72

G-AVYE (2139), first flown 23.4.68, C. of A. 15.5.68, Channel Airways Ltd., Stansted; British European Airways Corporation, Heathrow 1.72

Hawker Siddeley H.S.121 Trident 3B (*British European Airways aircraft*)
Note: Dates given are first flight/C. of A. issued

G-AWYZ (2301), 11.12.69/11.3.70; G-AWZA (2302), 9.3.70/7.12.70; G-AWZB (2303), 18.8.70/28.8.70; G-AWZC (2304), 24.12.70/8.2.71; G-AWZD (2305), 5.3.71/23.3.71; G-AWZE (2306), 28.3.71/7.4.71; G-AWZF (2307), 30.4.71/10.5.71; G-AWZG (2308), 3.6.71/11.6.71; G-AWZH (2309), 7.7.71/14.7.71; G-AWZI (2310), 4.8.71/6.8.71; G-AWZJ (2311), 9.9.71/13.9.71; G-AWZK (2312), 8.10.71/15.10.71; G-AWZL (2313), 8.11.71/18.11.71; G-AWZM (2314), 8.12.71/14.12.71; G-AWZN (2315), 12.1.72/17.1.72; G-AWZO (2316), 9.2.72/14.2.72; G-AWZP (2317), 8.3.72/15.3.72; G-AWZR (2318), 5.4.72/10.4.72; G-AWZS (2319), 29.4.72/4.5.72; G-AWZT (2320), 26.5.72/5.6.72; G-AWZU (2321), 28.6.72/4.7.72; G-AWZV (2322), 2.8.72; G-AWZW (2323); G-AWZX (2324); G-AWZY (2325), re-registered G-AYVF; G-AWZZ (2326)

The short fuselage first prototype D.H.125, G-ARYA, ready for take-off at the Farnborough S.B.A.C. Show, September 1962. (*Aviation Photo News*)

Hawker Siddeley H.S.125 (*Prototypes*)

G-ARYA (25001), 30.8.63, Hawker Siddeley Aviation Ltd., Hatfield; to Apprentice Training School, Chester by road to become instructional airframe 22.4.68

G-ARYB (25002), Hawker Siddeley Aviation Ltd., Hatfield; to Apprentice Training School, Astwick Manor, Herts. by road 5.6.68

Hawker Siddeley H.S.125 Series 1

G-ARYC (25003), 19.8.63, Hawker Siddeley Aviation Ltd.; loaned to Bristol Siddeley Engines Ltd., Filton; transferred to Rolls-Royce Ltd., Hucknall 1968

G-ASEC (25004), 30.5.63, Hawker Siddeley Aviation Ltd.; loaned to Bristol Siddeley Engines Ltd., Filton; Hawker Siddeley communications, Hatfield 11.69

G-ASNU   (25005), 21.10.64, Hawker Siddeley Aviation Ltd.; to Krupps, Essen 10.64 as
          D-COMA; rest. 12.65 to Air Hanson Ltd. (Gregory Air Taxis Ltd.), Denham;
          Clarke, Chapman & Co. Ltd., Woolsington 4.69

G-ASSI   (25008), 28.7.64, Hawker Siddeley Aviation Ltd.; Reyrolle Parsons Ltd.,
          Woolsington 7.66

G-ASSM   (25010), 1.2.65, B.S.R. Ltd., Elmdon; Litchfield Co. Ltd., Hamilton, Bermuda
          6.70

G-ASTY   (25007), 19.6.64, Hawker Siddeley Aviation Ltd.; to Chartag, Zürich 2.65 as
          HB-VAH; to Air Affaires, Nice 6.65 as F-BKMF 'Orion III'; crashed in the
          Mediterranean off Nice 5.6.66

Hawker Siddeley H.S.125 Series 1A

G-ASSH (25017), to U.S.A. 10.64 as N3060 (later N3060F); G-ASSJ (25013),
10.9.64, to U.S.A. 9.64 as N125J (later N2426 and N7125J); G-ASSK (25014), 21.9.64,
to U.S.A. 9.64 as N125G (later N735AK and N621ST); G-ASSL (25016), to Canada
12.64 as CF-RWA (later CF-OPC); G-ASYX (25019), 8.2.65, to U.S.A. 2.65 as
N1135K; G-ASZM (25020), 22.2.65, to U.S.A. 2.65 as N167J (later N959KW);
G-ASZN (25021), 4.3.65, to U.S.A. 3.65 as N575DU (later N575D, N2504 and N228G);
G-ASZO (25022), reg'n. not taken up, to Canada 2.65 as CF-FDA (later CF-SDA);
G-ASZP (25023), 9.3.65, to U.S.A. 3.65 as N1125

G-ATAY (25026), 25.3.65, to U.S.A. 3.65 as N225KJ/N225K/N225LL; G-ATAZ
(25029), 13.5.65, to U.S.A. 5.65 as N10122; G-ATBA (25030), 19.5.65, to U.S.A. 5.65
as N413GH; G-ATBB (25031), 4.6.65, to U.S.A. 6.65 as N1923M; G-ATBC (25032),
1.6.65, to U.S.A. 6.65 as N65MK; G-ATBD (25033), 14.6.65, to U.S.A. 6.65 as N1125G
(later N125G, N1256 and N1125G again); G-ATCO (25035), 15.6.65, to U.S.A. 6.65 as
N1515P; G-ATCP (25038), 7.7.65, to U.S.A. 7.65 as N926G; G-ATGA (25043),
20.8.65, to U.S.A. 8.65 as N125J (later N1230V); G-ATGS (25046), 17.9.65, to U.S.A.
9.65 as N48UC; G-ATGT (25047), 24.9.65, to U.S.A. 9.65 as N778SM (later N580WS);
G-ATGU (25051), 18.10.65, to U.S.A. 10.65 as N9300; G-ATIK (25052), 8.11.65,
to U.S.A. 11.65 as N816M; G-ATIL (25057), 24.11.65, to U.S.A. 11.65 as N118K;
G-ATIM (25060), 7.12.65, to U.S.A. 12.65 as N2601 (later N2728 and N22DL); G-ATKK
(25064), 15.12.65, to U.S.A. 12.65 as N230H (later N125JG); G-ATKL (25065),
30.12.65, to U.S.A. 1.66 as N631SC; G-ATKM (25066), 15.4.66, to U.S.A. 4.66 as

Hawker Siddeley H.S.125 Ser.1A G-ATGT after sale to the American Signal Oil
Company, September 1965, as N778SM. (*Aviation Photo News*)

N925CT; G-ATKN (25070), 19.1.66, to U.S.A. 1.66 as N502M (later N214JR, N2148J and N84W); G-ATLI (25073), 2.2.66, to U.S.A. 2.66 as N372CM (later N372GM and N36MK)

G-ATNM (25082), 16.3.66, to U.S.A. 3.66 as N909B (later N2125B and N2125); G-ATNN (25084), 5.4.66, to U.S.A. 4.66 as N1125G (later N435CM and N154TR); G-ATNO (25088), 5.4.66, to U.S.A. 5.66 as N1230B; G-ATNP (25091), 13.5.66, to U.S.A. 5.66 as N1230G; G-ATNR (25096), 28.6.66, to U.S.A. 6.66 as N235KC; G-ATNS (25098), 12.7.66, to U.S.A. 7.66 as N10121 (later N666SC); G-ATNT (25100), 15.7.66, to U.S.A. 7.66 as N125J (later N952B); G-ATOV (25074), 22.2.66, to U.S.A. 2.66 as N400NW; G-ATOW (25083), 29.3.66, to U.S.A. 3.66 as N16777 (later N435T); G-ATOX (25087), reg'n. not taken up, to Canada 5.66 as CF-ALC; G-ATSN (25093), 24.5.66, to U.S.A. 5.66 as N77D; G-ATSO (25095), 8.6.66, to U.S.A. 6.66 as N125Y, to Canada 6.67 as CF-SHZ, later to U.S.A. as N1929G

G-ATUU (25102), 21.8.66, to U.S.A. 8.66 as N756; G-ATUV (25103), 2.9.66, to U.S.A. 9.66 as N553 (later N210M); G-ATUW (25104), 26.8.66, to U.S.A. 8.66 as N257H (later N140AK); G-ATUX (25107), 6.9.66, to U.S.A. 9.66 as N7125J (later N2426); G-ATUY (25108), 9.9.66, to U.S.A. 9.66 as N1025C (later N901TC); G-ATUZ (25109), 14.9.66, to U.S.A. 9.66 as N201H; G-ATXE (25101), G-5-11, 21.7.66, to U.S.A. 7.66 as N142B (later N2246); G-ATZE (25110), G-5-11, 22.9.66, to U.S.A. 9.66 as N3125B

Hawker Siddeley H.S.125 Series 1B

G-ATFO (25037), 18.8.65, to Grundig, Germany 12.66 as D-CAFI, later to U.S.A. as N787X (later N26T); G-ATPB (25089), 11.8.66, Rolls-Royce (1971) Ltd.; G-ATPC (25009), 29.6.66, to the R.A.E., Bedford 3.71 as XW930; G-ATPD (25085), 14.7.66, Shell Aircraft Ltd., Heathrow; G-ATPE (25092), 26.8.66, Shell Aircraft Ltd., Heathrow; G-ATSP (25097), 15.9.66, to Busy Bee Air Services, Oslo 1.68 as LN-NPE; G-ATWH (25094), 15.7.67, G.K.N. Group Services Ltd., Elmdon; G-AWUF (25106), HZ-BIN, 1.1.69, Lamport & Holt Line Ltd., Speke; G-AWYE (25090), HB-VAT, 4.2.69, Rolls-Royce (1971) Ltd., Filton; G-AYRY (25105), D-CKCF, 2.3.71, McAlpine Aviation Ltd., Luton

Hawker Siddeley H.S.125 Series 3A

G-ATLJ (25075), 10.2.66, to U.S.A. 2.66 as N666N (later CF-MDB); G-ATLK (25078), 2.3.66, to U.S.A. 3.66 as N40DC; G-ATLL (25079), 4.3.66, to U.S.A. 3.66 as N440DC; G-ATYH (25111), 3.10.66, to U.S.A. 10.66 as N1041B; G-ATYI (25112), 6.10.66, to U.S.A. 10.66 as N2525; G-ATYJ (25114), 14.10.66, to U.S.A. 10.66 as N425K (later N44K); G-ATYK (25115), to U.S.A. 11.66 as N229P; G-ATYL (25118), to U.S.A. 11.66 as N733UT

G-AVAD (25119), 31.10.66, to U.S.A. 11.66 as N213H; G-AVAE (25121), 16.11.66, to U.S.A. 11.66 as N795J; G-AVAF (25122), 29.11.66, to U.S.A. 3.67 as N12225; G-AVAG (25123), 9.12.66, to U.S.A. 2.67 as N700M; G-AVAH (25124), 18.1.67, to U.S.A. 4.67 as N1125J (later N552N); G-AVDL (25126), G-5-11, 23.1.67, to U.S.A. 2.67 as N510X; G-AVDM (25129), G-5-12, 24.1.67, to U.S.A. 2.67 as N521M

Hawker Siddeley H.S.125 Series 3A-RA

G-AVHA (25134/NA700), G-5-11, 16.3.67, to U.S.A. 4.68 as N514V; G-AVHB (25136/NA701), 11.4.67, to U.S.A. 5.68 as N506W (later N506N); G-AVJD (25137/NA702), 26.4.67, to Canada 5.67 as CF-AAG (later CF-KCI); G-AVOJ

(25139/NA703), 18.7.67, to U.S.A. 5.68 as N612G (later N2G); G-AVOK (25141/NA704), 31.8.67, to U.S.A. 6.68 as N75C; G-AVOL (25142/NA705), 18.7.67, to U.S.A. 8.68 as N7055 (later N9040); G-AVRH (25146/NA706), 18.7.68, to U.S.A. 7.68 as N77617 (later N214JR); G-AVRI (25148), 9.8.67, to U.S.A. 8.67 as N1125J (later N8125J and N450JD); G-AVRJ (25149), 10.8.67, to U.S.A. 8.67 as N1125E; G-AVTY (25151), 25.9.67, to U.S.A. 9.67 as N125F; G-AVTZ (25152), 31.10.67, to Canada 11.67 as CF-QNS; G-AVXM (25153), 12.1.68, to U.S.A. 1.68 as N30F; G-AVXN (25155), 23.1.68, to U.S.A. 1.68 as N32F; G-AVZJ (25156), 29.1.68, to U.S.A. 1.68 as N522M; G-AVZK (25158), 1.3.68, to Mexico 3.68 as XB-PUE; G-AVZL (25159), to Canada 3.68 as CF-WOS; G-AWKH (25160/NA707), 24.7.68, to U.S.A. 7.68 as N350NC (later N873D); G-AWKI (25161/NA708), 5.8.68, to U.S.A. 8.68 as N9149 (later N756N); G-AWMV (25163/NA709), G-5-16, 22.8.68, to U.S.A. 8.68 as N208H

Hawker Siddeley H.S.125 Series 3B

G-ATZN (25116), 30.12.66, The Rank Organisation Ltd., Heathrow; G-AVAI (25125), 23.5.67, to Busy Bee Air Services, Oslo 9.68 as LN-NPA; G-AVGW (25120), 28.4.67, crashed at Luton 23.12.67; G-AVOI (25128), 13.10.67, Fortes (Publicity Services) Ltd., Heathrow; G-AVPE (25127), 25.8.67, B.A.C. Ltd., Filton; G-AVRD (25130), to Switzerland 3.68 as HB-VAZ (later F-BSIM); G-AVRE (25131), G-5-11, to France 5.68 as F-BPMC; G-AVRF (25133), 16.9.68, B.A.C. Ltd., Filton; G-AVVA (25138), to Switzerland 4.68 as HB-VBN (later I-BOGI); G-AVXK (25143), 6.3.68, to Germany 7.68 as D-CHTH, rest. 3.72 to Ferranti Ltd., Turnhouse; G-AVXL (25145), G-5-20, 22.4.68, to Busy Bee Air Services, Oslo 12.69 as LN-NPC, rest. 2.72 to McAlpine Aviation Ltd., Luton; G-AWMS (25150), G-5-13, 28.8.68, R.T.Z. Services Ltd., Heathrow; G-AXPS (25135), HB-VAY, 1.12.69, crashed on take-off at Turnhouse 20.7.70; G-AZVS (25132), OY-DKP, 5.6.72, Imperial Tobacco Group Ltd., Filton

Hawker Siddeley H.S.125 Series 3B-RA

G-AVDX (25113), G-5-13, 10.7.70, C.A.A., Flying Unit, Stansted; G-AVRG (25144), 7.9.67, Court Line Aviation Ltd., Luton 'Halcyon Day'; G-AVVB (25140), G-5-17, 30.7.68, Beecham Group Ltd., Heathrow; G-AWWL (25169), to Bell Bros. Pty. Ltd., Perth, W.A. as VH-BBJ, (later N3L), rest. 7.72 to McAlpine Aviation Ltd., Luton; G-AXEG (25172), 13.3.70, to South Africa 2.71 as ZS-CAL; G-AXPU (25171), HB-VBT, 31.10.69, Imperial Chemical Industries Ltd., Luton; G-AZCH (25154), EP-AHK, 17.8.71, Shell Aircraft Ltd., Heathrow

Hawker Siddeley H.S.125 Series 400A

G-AWMW (25170/NA710), 13.9.68, to U.S.A. 10.68 as N1259K; G-AWMX (25173/NA711), 24.9.68, to U.S.A. 10.68 as N125J (later N3711L); G-AWMY (25174/NA712), 15.11.68, to U.S.A. 11.68 as N1199M; G-AWPC (25175/NA713), 20.11.68, to U.S.A. 11.68 as N217F; G-AWPD (25176/NA714), to Canada 11.68 as CF-NER; G-AWPE (25179/NA715), 19.12.68, to U.S.A. 12.68 as N778S (later N200CC); G-AWPF (25180/NA716), 21.1.69, to U.S.A. 1.69 as N196KC

G-AWXB (25183/NA717), 5.2.69, to U.S.A. 2.69 as N162A; G-AWXC (25187/NA718), 21.2.69, to U.S.A. 3.69 as N600L; G-AWXD (25188/NA719), 13.3.69, to U.S.A. 4.69 as N545S; G-AWXE (25185/NA720), 8.4.69, to U.S.A. 4.69 as

Hawker Siddeley H.S.125 Ser.400A G-AXPX in factory finish with the 'North American' production number NA735 on the nose, staging through Prestwick en route to Bermuda 16 November 1969. (*J. Guthrie*)

N140C; G-AWXF (25186/NA721), 21.4.69, to U.S.A. 5.69 as N125G; G-AXDO (25190/NA722), 8.5.69, to U.S.A. 5.69 as N2125B (later N1393); G-AXDP (25191/NA723), to U.S.A. 5.69 as N511YP; G-AXDR (25195/NA726), 15.7.69, to U.S.A. 7.69 as N111MB; G-AXDS (25196/NA727), 24.7.69, to U.S.A. 7.69 as N814M

G-AXJD (25198/NA728), 4.9.69, to U.S.A. 9.69 as N24CH; G-AXJE (25200/NA729), 11.9.69, to U.S.A. 9.69 as N702S; G-AXJF (25201/NA730), 24.9.69, to U.S.A. 9.69 as N220T; G-AXJG (25202/NA731), 4.10.69, to U.S.A. 10.69 as N65LT; G-AXOA (25203/NA732), 17.10.69, to U.S.A. 10.69 as N125F (later N500AG); G-AXOB (25204/NA733), 27.10.69, to U.S.A. 10.69 as N380X; G-AXOC (25205/NA734), 4.11.69, to U.S.A. 11.69 as N125J, later N111RB; G-AXOD (25207/NA736), 2.12.69, to U.S.A. 12.69 as N30PR; G-AXOE (25208/NA737), 12.12.69, to U.S.A. 12.69 as N2500W; G-AXOF (25210/NA738), 30.12.69, to U.S.A. 1.70 as N702D; G-AXPX (25206/NA735), 14.11.69, to Bahamas 11.69 as VP-BDH

G-AXTR (25211/NA739), 6.2.70, to U.S.A. 2.70 as N125DH; G-AXTS (25212/NA740), 11.4.69, to U.S.A. 2.70 as N702P; G-AXTT (25213/NA741), to Canada 2.70 as CF-CFL (replacing c/n 25193); G-AXTU (25214/NA742), 26.2.70, to U.S.A. 2.70 as N40PC; G-AXTV (25216/NA743), 13.3.70, to U.S.A. 3.70 as N9138 (later XC-GOB); G-AXTW (25218/NA744), 20.3.70, to U.S.A. 5.70 as N575DU; G-AXYE (25220/NA745), to U.S.A. 4.70 as N41BH (later N125AR); G-AXYF (25222/NA747), to U.S.A. 5.70 as N43BH (later N125EH); G-AXYG (25224/NA748), to U.S.A. 5.70 as N44BH (later N22DH); G-AXYH (25225/NA749), to U.S.A. 6.70 as N45BH (later N81T); G-AXYI (25226/NA750), to U.S.A. 7.70 as N46BH (later N300P)

Hawker Siddeley H.S.125 Series 400B

G-AWXN (25177), 24.3.70, to South African Air Force 7.70 as '01'; G-AWXO (25178), 29.4.69, Green Shield Stamp Co. Ltd., Leavesden; G-AXDM (25194), 24.10.69, Wavertree Ltd., Hamilton, Bermuda; G-AXFY (25189), G-5-20, 23.5.69, to Royal Malaysian Air Force 6.69 as FM1200; G-AXLU (25181), 13.3.70, to S.A.A.F. 3.70 as '02'; G-AXLV (25182), 9.12.69; to S.A.A.F. 4.70 as '03'; G-AXLW (25184), 5.5.70, to S.A.A.F. 5.70; G-AXLX (25199), 7.4.70, to Switzerland 4.70 as HB-VBW, rest. 4.70 to Turbo Union Ltd., Filton; G-AXYJ (25217), 16.6.70, Hawker Siddeley Aviation Ltd.

G-AYEP (25219), 7.7.70, British Steel Corporation; G-AYER (25238), 5.10.70, The Rank Organisation Ltd., Heathrow; G-AYFM (25227), 22.7.70, Ford Motor Co. Ltd., Stansted; G-AYIZ (25223), 8.9.70, to Netherlands Antilles 5.71 as PJ-SLB; G-AYLG (25254), 13.4.71, British Steel Corporation; G-AYLI (25240), 17.12.70, J. C. Bamford Excavators Ltd., Elmdon; G-AYNR (25235), HB-VCE, 1.1.71, Diamond Products (Sales) Ltd., Heathrow; G-AYOI (25243), sold in Brazil 4.71; G-AYOJ (25246), 2.9.71, Hawker Siddeley Aviation Ltd.; G-AYOK (25250), 15.2.71, sold in Gabon 8.72; G-AYRR (25247), 4.10.71, Hawker Siddeley Aviation Ltd.; G-AZAF (25249), 16.7.71, D. Robinson, Cambridge; G-AZEK (25259), 11.11.71, to the South African Air Force 2.72; G-AZEL (25260), 29.11.71, to S.A.A.F. 2.72; G-AZEM (25269), 14.12.71, to S.A.A.F. 2.72

G-AZUF, first production Beech Hawker B.H.125 Series 600A, in United States markings as N82BH.

Hawker Siddeley B.H.125 Series 600A
G-AZUF (6001), 16.5.72, Hawker Siddeley Aviation Ltd., Hawarden; to U.S.A. 5.72 as N82BH

Hawker Siddeley H.S.125 Series 600B
G-AYBH (25256), prototype, 4.8.71, Hawker Siddeley Aviation Ltd.; G-AZHS (25268), 31.12.71, Hawker Siddeley Aviation Ltd.

Hawker Siddeley H.S.650 Argosy Series 102
G-AOZZ (6651), first flown 8.1.59, C. of A. 19.12.61, B.E.A., Heathrow; Hawker Siddeley Aviation Ltd., Bitteswell 7.65; test flown 11.68 as G-11-1, to Universal Airlines, Willow Run, Michigan 12.68 as N896U

G-APRL (6652), first flown 14.3.59, C. of A. 26.8.59, Sir W. G. Armstrong Whitworth Aircraft Ltd., Bitteswell; to Riddle Airlines 8.61 as N6507R; to Capitol Airlines 7.62; to Zantop Air Transport 2.64 as N602Z; to Universal Airlines 1968 as N890U

G-APRM (6653), first flown 26.4.59, C. of A. 24.11.61, B.E.A., Heathrow; Hawker Siddeley Aviation Ltd., Bitteswell 3.65; replaced G-ASXL with B.E.A. 7.65 to 11.66; stored until delivered to Rolls-Royce Ltd., Filton 4.69

G-APRN   (6654), first flown 13.5.59, C. of A. 4.6.59, B.E.A., Heathrow; Hawker Siddeley Aviation Ltd., Bitteswell 5.65; test flown 1968 as G-11-2; to Universal Airlines 1.69 as N897U; rest. 5.71 to Sagittair Ltd.

G-APVH   (6655), first flown 20.7.59, C. of A. 17.6.60, Sir W. G. Armstrong Whitworth Aircraft Ltd., Bitteswell; to Riddle Airlines 6.61 as N6504R; to Capitol Airlines 6.62; to Zantop Air Transport 1966; to Universal Airlines 1968 as N891U

G-APWW (6656), first flown 23.9.59 as G-1-3, C. of A. 23.1.61, Sir W. G. Armstrong Whitworth Aircraft Ltd., Bitteswell; to Riddle Airlines 1.61 as N6503R; to Capitol Airlines 6.62; to Zantop Air Transport 1966; to Universal Airlines 1968 as N892U; rest. 3.72 to Sagittair Ltd., Heathrow

G-AZHN   (6657), G-1-4, N6505R, N600Z, N893U, 28.10.71, Sagittair Ltd., Heathrow

Hawker Siddeley H.S.650 Argosy Series 222

G-ASKZ   (6799), first flown 11.3.64, Hawker Siddeley Aviation Ltd., Bitteswell; stored at Bitteswell 1965; reduced to spares 9.67

G-ASXL   (6800), first flown 17.12.64, C. of A. 19.1.65, B.E.A., Heathrow; flew into high ground near Piacenza, Italy 4.7.65 on approach to Milan

G-ASXM   (6801), 24.2.65, B.E.A., Heathrow; to Midwest Airlines Ltd., Winnipeg ex Heathrow 15.6.70, became CF-TAG; to Aer Turas, Dublin 11.71 as EI-AVJ

G-ASXN   (6802), 26.3.65, B.E.A., Heathrow; left Heathrow 7.70 on delivery to Midwest Airlines Ltd., Winnipeg

G-ASXO   (6803), 27.4.65, B.E.A., Heathrow; to Midwest Airlines Ltd., Winnipeg 4.70 as CF-TAX

G-ASXP   (6804), 14.6.65, B.E.A., Heathrow; crashed on take-off from Stansted while crew training and burned out 4.12.67

G-ATTC   (6805), 11.11.66, B.E.A., Heathrow; left Heathrow 29.4.70 on delivery to Midwest Airlines Ltd., Winnipeg, re-registered CF-TAZ on arrival

The seldom photographed Argosy Series 200 prototype, G-ASKZ, at Bitteswell in March 1964.

Glider Registrations

Although a special sequence of glider registrations was instituted, and markings G-GAAA to 'AE issued, for a Slingsby T.5 Hjordis, three T.9 King Kites and a T.4 Falcon III respectively for participation in the International Soaring Competitions on the Wasserkuppe, Germany, 4–18 July 1937, no other such markings were issued. Normally British gliders are registered by the British Gliding Association which allots a number, prefixed by the letters BGA, to be painted on or near the tail but in April 1949, commencing G-ALJN, it became mandatory for gliders to be registered in the same sequence as powered aircraft.

After a year this scheme was dropped and thereafter gliders were only given lettered registrations if flown abroad, as in the case of G-AXZG to 'ZI, the Cirrus, Libelle and ASW-12 sailplanes flown by the British team at the World Gliding Championships at Marfa, Texas in 1970.

G-ALJN	Chilton Olympia	G-ALKW	Slingsby Cadet
G-ALJO	EoN Olympia	G-ALKX	Slingsby T.21B
G-ALJP	EoN Olympia	G-ALKY	Rhönbussard
G-ALJS	EoN Olympia	G-ALKZ	Baynes Scud II
G-ALJT	EoN Olympia	G-ALLA	EoN Olympia
G-ALJU	Slingsby T.21B	G-ALLB	EoN Olympia
G-ALJV	EoN Olympia	G-ALLC	Slingsby Gull 1
G-ALJW	DFS Weihe	G-ALLD	EoN Olympia
G-ALJX	EoN Olympia	G-ALLE	Slingsby Tutor
G-ALJY	EoN Olympia	G-ALLF	Slingsby Prefect
G-ALJZ	EoN Olympia	G-ALLG	Slingsby T.21B
G-ALKA	EoN Olympia	G-ALLH	Slingsby T.21B
G-ALKB	Slingsby Tutor	G-ALLL	Sproule-Ivanoff Camel
G-ALKC	Slingsby Tutor	G-ALLM	EoN Olympia
G-ALKD	Slingsby Cadet	G-ALLN	Slingsby Prefect
G-ALKE	Slingsby Cadet	G-ALLO	Slingsby Cadet
G-ALKF	Slingsby T.21B	G-ALLP	Slingsby Cadet
G-ALKG	DFS Weihe	G-ALLR	EoN Primary
G-ALKH	DFS Kranich 2	G-ALLS	EoN Olympia
G-ALKM	EoN Olympia	G-ALLT	Slingsby T.21B
G-ALKN	EoN Olympia	G-ALLU	EoN Baby
G-ALKO	EoN Olympia	G-ALLV	EoN Primary
G-ALKP	Slingsby Tutor	G-ALLW	EoN Primary
G-ALKR	DFS S.G.38	G-ALLX	EoN Primary
G-ALKS	Slingsby T.21B	G-ALLY	EoN Primary
G-ALKT	Slingsby Cadet	G-ALLZ	Go III Minimoa
G-ALKU	Grunau Baby 2	G-ALME	Rhönbussard
G-ALKV	EoN Primary	G-ALMF	Hawkridge Venture

G-ALMG	DFS Weihe	G-ALPX	Slingsby Cadet
G-ALMH	Slingsby Tutor	G-ALPY	Slingsby Cadet
G-ALMI	Slingsby Gull 1	G-ALPZ	Slingsby Cadet
G-ALMJ	EoN Olympia	G-ALRA	Grunau Baby
G-ALMK	Slingsby Cadet	G-ALRB	EoN Olympia
G-ALML	Slingsby Cadet	G-ALRC	Grunau Baby
G-ALMM	Grunau Baby 2B	G-ALRD	Scott Viking 1
G-ALMN	EoN Primary	G-ALRE	Slingsby Cadet
G-ALMO	EoN Primary	G-ALRF	Slingsby Cadet
G-ALMP	Zlin Krajanek	G-ALRG	Slingsby Tutor
G-ALMT	EoN Olympia	G-ALRH	EoN Baby
G-ALMW	EoN Olympia	G-ALRJ	Slingsby Tutor
G-ALMX	Slingsby Cadet	G-ALRK	Hutter Nimbus
G-ALMY	EoN Olympia	G-ALRL	EoN Olympia
G-ALMZ	EoN Primary	G-ALRM	Hutter Nimbus
G-ALNB	EoN Olympia	G-ALRN	Slingsby Cadet
G-ALNC	EoN Primary	G-ALRO	Grunau Baby
G-ALNE	EoN Olympia	G-ALRP	Grunau Baby
G-ALNF	EoN Olympia	G-ALRR	Grunau Baby
G-ALNG	EoN Olympia	G-ALRS	EoN Baby
G-ALNH	Slingsby Kite 1	G-ALRT	Hutter Nimbus
G-ALNI	Slingsby Kite 1	G-ALRU	EoN Baby
G-ALNJ	Slingsby T.21B	G-ALRV	EoN Baby
G-ALNK	Slingsby Tutor	G-ALRZ	Baynes Scud II
G-ALNL	EoN Olympia	G-ALSI	L-107 Lunak
G-ALNM	EoN Olympia	G-ALSN	Slingsby T.21P
G-ALNO	Slingsby Cadet	G-ALSO	Grunau Baby 2
G-ALNP	Slingsby Petrel	G-ALTH	Slingsby Gull 4
G-ALNR	Slingsby Falcon	G-ALTI	Slingsby Kite 2
G-ALOT	Baynes Scud II	G-ALTJ	Cambridge 1
G-ALOY	Slingsby Cadet	G-ALTK	Slingsby Cadet
G-ALOZ	RFD Dagling	G-ALTL	Slingsby Kite 1
G-ALPA	Slingsby Gull 1	G-ALTN	Grunau Baby 2
G-ALPB	Slingsby Gull 4	G-ALTU	Slingsby Cadet
G-ALPC	Slingsby Prefect	G-ALTV	EoN Olympia
G-ALPD	Slingsby Tutor	G-ALTY	Slingsby Cadet
G-ALPE	Slingsby Tutor	G-ALUD	Slingsby Kite 1
G-ALPG	Grunau Baby	G-AOGL	DFS Meise
G-ALPH	Slingsby Kite 1	G-APEW	EoN Olympia 403
G-ALPI	Slingsby Cadet	G-APLD	EoN Olympia 419
G-ALPJ	Slingsby Gull 1	G-APLS	EoN Olympia 415
G-ALPL	DFS Weihe	G-APLT	EoN Olympia 419X
G-ALPO	EoN Olympia	G-APSI	EoN Olympia 401
G-ALPP	Slingsby Petrel	G-APSX	EoN Olympia 419X
G-ALPR	Slingsby Kite 1	G-APUU	Breguet Fauvette
G-ALPS	EoN Primary	G-APWL	EoN Olympia 460
G-ALPT	Grunau Baby 2	G-APXC	EoN Olympia 2B
G-ALPU	Slingsby Tutor	G-ARBJ	Slingsby Skylark
G-ALPV	EoN Olympia	G-ARFU	EoN Olympia 460
G-ALPW	EoN Primary	G-ARTE	EoN Olympia 460

G-ARUB	EoN Olympia 460	G-ATPZ	L-13 Blanik
G-ASCV	DFS Weihe	G-ATRA	L-13 Blanik
G-ASHP	EoN Olympia 460	G-ATRB	L-13 Blanik
G-ASKX	L-13 Blanik	G-ATRF	L-13 Blanik
G-ASKY	L-13 Blanik	G-ATWW	L-13 Blanik
G-ASMP	EoN Olympia 460	G-ATWX	L-13 Blanik
G-ASPR	Standard Austria	G-ATWY	L-13 Blanik
G-ASVS	L-13 Blanik	G-AVIF	L-13 Blanik
G-ASXW	L-13 Blanik	G-AVUW	Schleicher Ka 6E
G-ASZK	L-13 Blanik	G-AWTP	Schleicher Ka 6E
G-ASZL	L-13 Blanik	G-AXZG	Standard Cirrus
G-ATCG	L-13 Blanik	G-AXZH	Libelle 15
G-ATCH	L-13 Blanik	G-AXZI	Schleicher ASW 12
G-ATEO	Slingsby Dart 1	G-AYCZ	Slingsby Kestrel
G-ATPX	L-13 Blanik	G-AZOY	Slingsby Kestrel
G-ATPY	L-13 Blanik		

In Volume 3 this Appendix lists the airships, free balloons and miscellaneous craft which were allotted British civil aircraft markings.

Index of Aeroplanes

AESL
  Airtourer, 314
Aeronca
  C-3, 36
Aerostructures
  Sundowner, 188
Airmaster
  H2-B1 Helicopter, 318
Airship
  R-33, 75
Airspeed
  A.S.5 Courier, 235, 523
  A.S.23, 360
  A.S.57 Ambassador, 272
Alon
  Aircoupe, 364
Armstrong Whitworth
  F.K.8, 397
  Argosy, 56
Auster
  J-1 Autocrat, 429
Avro
  504K, 13, 112
  504N, 14
  548, 55
  552, 14
  574, 575, 586 and 587, 13, 14
  594 Avian, 15, 16, 386
  621 Tutor, 136
  652A Anson, 143
  671 Rota, 22
  688 Tudor, 243
  696 Shackleton, 283, 285
  733, 283

B.A.C.-Aerospatiale
  Concorde, 287
Barritault
  JB.01, 377, 514
B.A.T.
  F.K.23 Bantam, 41
  F.K.26, 64

B.E.
  2c replica, 116
Beardmore
  Inflexible, 208
Beechcraft-Hawker
  B.H.125, 279, 550
Blériot
  monoplane, 226
Boulton and Paul
  P.9, 190
Bristol
  Type 84 Bloodhound, 233
Britten-Norman
  BN-2A Islander, 142

Canadair
  C-4, 243, 249
Carstedt
  CJ-600A Jet Liner, 167, 169
Chilton
  D.W.1, 7
Chrislea
  C.H.3 Ace and Super Ace, 7, 9, 385
  C.H.4 Skyjeep, 10, 386
  L.C.1 Airguard, 289
Cierva
  C.6, 13, 386
  C.8, 13, 14, 386
  C.9, 15, 16
  C.10, 15
  C.11, 15, 386
  C.12, 15, 16
  C.17, 15, 16, 386
  C.18, 15, 16, 386
  C.19, 16, 17, 18, 21, 386, 387, 388
  CL.20, 23, 24
  C.24, 19, 386
  C.25, 19, 386
  C.28, 24
  C.30 variants and Rota, 21, 22, 388, 390
  C.40, 25

Cierva—(contd.)
  W.11 Air Horse, 290
  W.14 Skeeter, 290, 291
  CR.LTH-1 Grasshopper 3, 291
Civilian
  C.A.C.I. Coupé, 27, 391
C.L.W.
  Curlew, 292
Clarke
  Cheetah, 76, 292, 293
Clutton
  FRED, 293
Coates
  Swalesong SA.1, 382
  Swalesong SA.2 and SA.3, 382
Comper
  C.L.A.7 Swift, 30, 391, 392
  C.25 Autogiro, 19, 386
  C.97 Trimster, 382
  Kite, 295
  Mouse, 294
  Streak, 294, 295
Consolidated
  28 Catalina, 352, 392, 393
    PBY, 352, 392
  32 Liberator, 353, 393, 394
    LB-30 and LB-30A, 353, 393
Convair
  240-5, 353
  340-D2, 354
Cranwell
  C.L.A.2, 295
  C.L.A.3, 30, 296
  C.L.A.4, 296
  C.L.A.4A, 296
Cunliffe-Owen
  Concordia, 297
Currie
  Wot, 36, 394, 395
  Wot/S.E.5A replica, 37, 38, 395
Curtiss
  T-32 Condor, 354, 395
  CW-20, 355
  C-46A, 355
C.W.
  Cygnet, 221, 382
  Swan, 221, 382

Darmstadt
  D-22, 356

Dart
  Flittermouse, 297
  Kitten, 298, 395
  Pup, 298
De Bolotoff
  SDEB.14, 299
De Bruyne
  Snark, 299
  -Maas Ladybird, 300
Deekay
  Knight, 300
de Havilland
  D.H.4, 4A and 4R, 40, 49, 52, 58, 62,
    72, 81, 395
  D.H.6, 45, 396, 397
  D.H.9, 49, 58, 62, 225, 398, 402
  D.H.9A, 58, 62, 72, 400
  D.H.9B, 50, 401
  D.H.9C, 50, 51, 54, 62, 70, 72, 402
  D.H.9J, 55, 56, 399, 401, 402
  D.H.9R, 58, 59
  D.H.10, 323
  D.H.14A, 324
  D.H.16, 62, 403
  D.H.18, 64, 67, 70, 97, 404
  D.H.23, 382
  D.H.29, 67, 301
  D.H.32, 67
  D.H.34, 65, 67, 404, 405
  D.H.37, 71, 98, 301
  D.H.50, 40, 52, 54, 70, 74, 97, 101,
    202, 233, 405
  D.H.51, 302, 405
  D.H.53 Humming Bird, 71, 74, 406
  D.H.54 Highclere, 302
  D.H.60 Moth, 78, 154, 406
  D.H.60G Gipsy Moth, 84, 211, 409
  D.H.60GIII Moth and Moth Major, 90,
    414, 415, 416
  D.H.60M Moth, 93, 413, 417
  D.H.60T Moth Trainer, 94, 112, 418
  D.H.60T Tiger Moth, 112, 113, 423
  D.H.60X Moth, 80, 81, 86, 407, 409
  D.H.61 Giant Moth, 97, 418
  D.H.65 Hound, 325
  D.H.66 Hercules, 100, 233, 419
  D.H.67, 314
  D.H.71 Tiger Moth, 84, 205, 303
  D.H.75 Hawk Moth, 103, 419
  D.H.80, 106, 107, 420

D.H.80A Puss Moth, 106, 127, 190, 420
D.H.81 Swallow Moth, 154
D.H.82 Tiger Moth, 112, 118, 186, 423
D.H.83 Fox Moth, 47, 118, 122, 445
D.H.84 Dragon, 119, 122, 131, 142, 447, 449
D.H.85 Leopard Moth, 127, 451
D.H.86, 130, 142, 180, 454
D.H.87 Hornet Moth, 135, 457
D.H.88 Comet, 139, 151, 154, 160, 384, 459
D.H.89 Rapide, 142, 148, 164, 459
D.H.89B Dominie, 144, 465
D.H.90 Dragonfly, 148, 470
D.H.91 Albatross, 151, 154, 160, 472
D.H.92 Dolphin, 382
D.H.94 Moth Minor, 154, 472, 476
D.H.95 Flamingo, 157, 476
D.H.98 Mosquito, 160, 186, 477
D.H.104 Dove, 164, 180, 356, 479, 483
D.H.106 Comet, 172, 479, 483
D.H.108, 172
D.H.114 Heron, 180, 487
D.H.115 Vampire T.Mk.55, 324
D.H.A.3 Drover 2, 356, 492
D.H.C.1 Chipmunk, 186, 492
D.H.C.2 Beaver, 357, 495
D.H.C.3 Otter, 358
Desoutter
    Mk.I Monoplane, 190, 192, 495
    Mk.II Monoplane, 191, 192, 193, 497
    Dolphin, 190
Dornier
    Do J Wal, 358
    Do 28, 359
Douglas
    Boston, 223
    DC-1, 359
    DC-2, 24, 140, 360
    DC-3, 360, 362, 497, 500
    C-47A Dakota 3, 361, 498
    C-47B Dakota 4, 361, 503
    C-54, 362, 506
    Dart Dakota, 361
    DC-4, 362, 505
    DC-6, 362, 507
    DC-7, 363, 507

Druine
    Turbulent, 303, 436, 508
    Turbi, 304, 509
Dudley Watt
    D.W.2, 305

E.A.A.
    Sport Biplane, 305
Edgar Percival
    E.P.9, 195, 509
Edwards
    Gyrocopter, 306
English Electric
    Canberra, 325, 510
    Wren, 306
Enstrom
    F-28, 363
Ercoupe
    415, 364, 510
Evans
    VP-1 Volksplane, 307

Fairchild
    24, 364, 365
    Argus, 365, 366, 509, 511
    -Hiller FH-1100, 366
Fairey
    III to IIIF, 199, 200, 201, 202, 203, 512
    Fantôme, 329
    Fremantle, 326
    Firefly, 328, 330, 331
    Fox, 326, 327, 329, 512, 513
    Fulmar, 331
    Gannet, 332
    Gyrodyne, 307
    Primer, 308
    Swordfish, 330
    Ultra Light Helicopter, 332
Fairtravel
    Linnet, 308, 513
Falconar
    F-9, 309
    F-11-3, 383
Fane
    F.1/40, 333
Farman
    Goliath, 65, 404
    S.11 Shorthorn, 383
F.E.2B (see Royal Aircraft Factory)

Felixstowe
  F.3, 334, 513
Fenton
  Cheel, 383
Fiat
  G.212, 367
Firth
  Helicopter, 309
Fleet
  F.7C-2, 367
Focke-Wulf
  Fw 190, 160
  Fw 200B Condor, 368
  C.30A Autogiro, 22
Fokker
  Dr. I Triplane, 368
  D.VII, 116, 383
  E.III, 369
  F.III, 369, 514
  F.VII, 101, 370, 371, 384, 514
  F.VIII, 371
  F.XI, 372
  F.XII, 372, 514
  F.XXII, 373, 515
  F.XXXVI, 373
  F.27 Friendship, 257, 374
  Universal, 373
Ford
  4AT, 374, 515
  5AT, 375, 515
Forney
  F-1A Aircoupe, 364, 516
Foster Wikner
  G.M.1 Wicko and Warferry, 205,
    515
Fournier
  RF-3, 4D and SF-531 Milan, 375, 376,
    516
  RF-5, 376, 516
Fuji
  FA-200-180, 376

Gadfly
  H.D.W.1, 310
Gardan
  GY-20 Minicab, 377, 516
  GY-80 Horizon, 377, 516, 517
  GY-201, 377
Garland-Bianchi
  Linnet, 308, 513

General Aircraft
  ST-1 and ST-2, 208
  ST-3, 208, 209, 517
  ST-4, 208, 209, 517
  ST-6, 210, 517, 518
  ST-10, ST-11 and ST-12, 211, 212, 215,
    216, 518
  ST-18 Croydon, 310
  ST-25 Jubilee and Universal, 25, 519
  G.A.L.26, 218, 519
  G.A.L.42 Cygnet, 221, 521
  G.A.L.45 Owlet, 223, 311
  G.A.L.47, 334
Globe
  GC-1B Swift, 378
Gloster
  I, 312
  II, 313
  III, 313
  A.S.31 Survey, 314
  Gamecock, 337, 338
  Gannet, 312
  Gladiator, 339
  Grebe, 336, 337
  Grouse I, 335
  Grouse II, 336
  Mars I Bamel, 311
  Mars III Sparrowhawk, 11, 332
  Meteor 4, 339
  Meteor T.Mk.7, 340
  Meteor P.V.7-8, 340
  Meteor Mk.8, 341
  Meteor N.F.Mk.14, 341, 521
Glos-Air
  Airtourer, 314, 522
  T2, T3, T4 and T6, 314, 522
Gnosspelius
  Gull, 315
Gordon
  Dove, 315
Gosport
  Flying Boat, 342
Gowland
  Jenny Wren, 316
Grahame-White
  G.W.E.4 Ganymede, 317
  G.W.E.6 Bantam, 316
  G.W.E.7, 317
  G.W.E.9 Ganymede, 317
  G.W.15, 383

Granger
  Archaeopteryx, 318
Griffiths
  G.H.4 Gyroplane, 383
Grumman
  G.21A Goose, 378
  G.21A Super Goose, 379
  G.21C Turbo Goose, 379
  G.73 Mallard, 380
  G.159 Gulfstream I, 380
  G.1159 Gulfstream II, 381
  G.164 Ag-Cat, 381
Gunton
  Special, 383

H2-B1
  Helicopter, 318
Hafner
  A.R.III Mk.2 Gyroplane, 319
Halton
  H.A.C.I Mayfly, 319
  H.A.C.II Minus, 320
Handley Page
  H.P.12 (O/400 variants), 41, 225, 226,
    227, 231, 523
  H.P.18 (W4, W8, W8a, W8b), 231, 232,
    236, 524
  H.P.26 (W8e, W8f Hamilton, W8g),
    232, 233, 235, 524
  H.P.27 (W9 Hampstead), 233, 524
  H.P.30 (W10), 234, 525
  H.P.32 Hamlet, 320, 321
  H.P.33 and H.P.35 Clive, 342
  H.P.34 Hare, 343
  H.P.39 Gugnunc, 321
  H.P.42 and H.P.45, 233, 235, 237, 249,
    525
  H.P.54 Harrow II, 343
  H.P.61, H.P.70 and H.P.71 Halifax,
    172, 241, 526, 527, 532, 533
  H.P.68, H.P.74, H.P.81 and H.P.82
    Hermes, 247, 534, 536
  H.P.137 Jetstream, 263, 540, 542
Handley Page (Reading) Ltd.
  H.P.R.1 Marathon, 252, 257, 536
  H.P.R.3 and 4 Herald, 257, 538
  H.P.R.5 Marathon, 257
  H.P.R.7 Dart Herald, 257, 258, 355,
    384, 538

Hanriot
  H.D.1, 344
Hants and Sussex
  Herald, 322
Hawker
  Cygnet, 322
  Fury I, 348
  Fury F.Mk.I, 350
  Hart, 346, 347, 417, 423
  Hawfinch, 345
  Hedgehog, 344
  Heron, 346
  Hunter T.Mk.66A, 350
  Hurricane, 348, 349
  Osprey, 347
  Tomtit, 268, 542, 543
  Woodcock II, 345
Hawker Siddeley
  H.S.121 Trident, 272, 543
  H.S.125, 277, 545
  H.S.650 Argosy, 7, 283, 550
  H.S.748, 284
  H.S.801 Nimrod, 178
  Harrier GR.Mk.1, 351
  Harrier T.Mk.52, 351

Koolhoven
  F.K.41, 190, 191, 495, 496

Lancashire
  Prospector, 197
Lockheed
  Lodestar, 160
Loiré et Olivier
  Le.O. C.301, 22

Miles
  M.57 Aerovan, 253
  M.60 and M.69 Marathon, 252
Millicer
  Airtourer, 314

Parnall
  Gyroplane, 14, 15
Percival
  Proctor, 10
Pfalz
  D.III replica, 116
Piel
  CP-301 Emeraude, 308

Pivot
    Monoplane, 383
Pobjoy
    Pirate, 28

R.A.E.
    Scarab, 76
Riley
    Dove, 167, 168, 482
    Heron, 183
Rollason
    Turbulent, 508
Royal Aircraft Factory
    F.E.2B, 333
    S.E.5A, 37, 38, 311
Rumpler
    C IV replica, 116, 433, 441
    C V replica, 116, 438, 439
Ryan
    B-1 Brougham, 104

Sasin
    SA.29 Spraymaster, 188
Saunders
    ST-27, 183, 184
S.E.5A (see Royal Aircraft Factory)
Short
    Solent, 248

Slingsby
    Type 56 S.E.5A replica, 37, 38, 395
    Type 58 Rumpler C IV replica, 116,
        433, 438, 439, 441
Supermarine
    Spitfire, 270

Thruxton
    Jackaroo, 116, 435, 437, 441, 442, 443,
        444
Tokyo Gasu Denki
    Chidorigo, 120
Twyford-Enstrom
    Solent, 363

Vickers
    Viscount, 161, 257, 361
Victa
    Airtourer, 314

Weir
    W-1 and W-4, 24
Westland
    -Lepère CL.20, 23, 24
Wicko
    Sports Monoplane, 205
    Wizard, 205